Special Edition

Using

Samba

Richard Sharpe

with

Tim Potter

Jim Morris

CONTENTS AT [

que®

A Division of Macmillan USA
201 W. 103rd Street
Indianapolis, Indiana 46290

Associate Publisher
Tracy Dunkelberger

Acquisitions Editor
Gretchen Ganser

Development Editor
Hugh Vandivier

Managing Editor
Thomas F. Hayes

Project Editor
Tonya Simpson

Copy Editor
Cynthia Fields

Indexer
Sandra Henselmeier

Proofreaders
Jeanne Clark
Bob LaRoche

Technical Editors
Craig Armour
Matthew Chapman
(Sambateam)
Michael Gueterman
Darren Hiebert
Luke Leighton (Sambateam)
Brian Roberson (Sambateam)
Michael Warfield
(Sambateam)

Team Coordinator
Cindy Teeters

Media Developer
Craig Atkins

Interior Designer
Ruth Lewis

Cover Designers
Dan Armstrong
Ruth Lewis

Copywriter
Eric Borgert

3B2 Production
Brad Lenser

CONTENTS

About the Authors

As well as being a member of the Samba team, **Richard Sharpe** is a Linux consultant and a courseware developer and trainer who lives in Adelaide, South Australia. Before writing *Special Edition Using Samba*, he contributed about a third of the material in *Sams Teach Yourself Samba in 24 Hours*, also published by Macmillan USA.

Jim Morris is an engineer-turned-programmer who has made the migration from hardware to software development since obtaining a Bachelor of Science degree in Electrical Engineering Technology in 1988. Jim first began using UNIX systems in 1984 while working at IBM and has been an avid Linux user since early 1993. From 1994 on, he has used Samba to provide file and print services for many small and large companies, typically to replace or supplement existing Windows NT or Novell NetWare servers. Jim is currently employed as a software engineer by Retail Technologies Corporation in Kennesaw, Georgia, telecommuting from his home in Huntsville, Alabama.

Tim Potter is currently working for Linuxcare as a software engineer writing and maintaining open-source software, including Samba. He is responsible for various new features that should appear in Samba 3.0. Tim has also worked as an embedded programmer on telecommunications software and as a system administrator for Windows and UNIX machines.

DEDICATIONS

To the women in my life: Nicole and Natalie, my daughters; Carole, my wife; and also to my mother, Audrey Davis, who never even got to see me go to high school, let alone grow up to write books.

—*Richard Sharpe*

To my wife, Anna, for being patient during the writing and editing process.

—*Tim Potter*

ACKNOWLEDGMENTS

A book is the result of the efforts of a lot of people, and so it is with this book. First and foremost, I want to thank my contributing authors, Tim Potter, and Jim Morris: Without you, the book would not have been finished.

I would like to thank all the people who have been involved in Samba in one way or another, but surely Andrew Tridgell, Jeremy Allison, and Luke Leighton should be at the top of the list. Andrew deserves a special vote of thanks, not only for starting Samba but also for reviewing parts of this book. I would like to thank all the members of the Samba team for their assistance from time to time, and especially Jerry Carter. In addition, I would like to thank Matt Chapman and Charlie Brady for their help, along with Eckart Meyer and Rob Adams for their assistance.

Next I would like to thank all the users of Samba for making it such a popular package. I would like to offer a special thank you to all those users who posted their problems to the `linux.samba` and `comp.protocols.smb` mailing lists. These questions have been very useful in compiling a list of common problems with Samba.

I would like to thank the team at Macmillan: Gretchen Ganser, my acquisitions editor, for pressing me to do the book and Hugh Vandivier, my development editor, for making sure we got it all done. Thanks also to everyone else at Macmillan who made this book a reality.

Finally, I would like to thank my daughters, Nicole and Natalie, and my wife, Carole, for putting up with my long hours in front of the computers while I was writing yet another book. My love to you all.

—*Richard Sharpe*

I would like to thank my wife, Yvonne, and my children, Shannon, Chase, and Cassidy, for putting up with all the late nights and weekends that I worked on this project. Without their support, I wouldn't have gotten through it. I'm just sorry it was during the Christmas holidays, guys! I would also like to thank my employer, Retail Technologies Corporation, for letting me replace that first NetWare server with a Linux system running Samba back in 1994. Without the experience I had administering that server, and the ones that have followed since, I would not have near the depth of knowledge I now have on Samba, or on Linux for that matter.

—*Jim Morris*

TELL US WHAT YOU THINK!

As the reader of this book, *you* are our most important critic and commentator. We value your opinion and want to know what we're doing right, what we could do better, what areas you'd like to see us publish in, and any other words of wisdom you're willing to pass our way.

As an associate publisher for Que, I welcome your comments. You can fax, email, or write me directly to let me know what you did or didn't like about this book—as well as what we can do to make our books stronger.

Please note that I cannot help you with technical problems related to the topic of this book, and that due to the high volume of mail I receive, I might not be able to reply to every message.

When you write, please be sure to include this book's title and author as well as your name and phone or fax number. I will carefully review your comments and share them with the authors and editors who worked on the book.

Fax: 317-581-4666

Email: quetechnical@macmillanusa.com

Mail: Associate Publisher
        Que
        201 West 103rd Street
        Indianapolis, IN 46290 USA

INTRODUCTION

Samba has proven itself as a production file and print server for many organizations already, but with the enormous interest in Linux over the last year or so, people want to use Samba in small networks. So, although Samba was in use in many organizations before Linux became so popular, its use has exploded along with that of Linux.

Some would say that this increase in the use of Samba is only right because it is a great file and print server and that, because users do not have to pay client licenses to Microsoft, it also saves organizations lots of money.

But what is Samba? Briefly, it is a freely available file and print server for Linux and UNIX, as well as several other operating systems, such as OpenVMS, MVS, and AmigaOS. This means that Samba provides many of the same features as the following:

- Windows NT
- Novell NetWare
- Lantastic
- Banyan VINES
- PATHWORKS

Moreover, you do not pay for Samba because it comes with every Linux distribution that ships and is freely available on the network for anyone who wants to download it.

In addition, because the source to Samba is freely available, just like Linux, many people all over the world are capable of finding any bugs in Samba and suggesting improvements to Samba. And they do!

So, with Samba, not only do you get a great product for the cost of the distribution in most cases, you also get a dedicated team of bug fixers and product improvement developers around the world. Perhaps this is why many Fortune 500 companies continue to use Samba to provide file and print services for Windows clients and to integrate Windows into UNIX environments and vice versa.

However, the Microsoft Windows Networking area is quite complex, and when you add the differences between the way in which Windows operates and the way in which Linux/UNIX operates, many Samba newcomers find their initial experiences with Samba frustrating. This book was written and structured with the goal of making you productive with Samba very quickly.

Although this book focuses on the use of Samba with Linux, people who run Samba on other UNIX operating systems and even on non-UNIX operating systems can equally use it. This is because we show you how Samba operates and use numerous examples and screen shots that are directly relevant to the use of Samba.

A guiding principle for all the authors of this book has been to refer to the Samba source code and to test all examples that we provide in the book. As a result, you will find that this book is an authoritative resource. Some other books on Samba are little more than rehashes of the Samba manual pages, but *Special Edition Using Samba* provides critical information on all aspects of using Samba. Indeed, during the writing of the book, the authors uncovered aspects of Samba that were either not documented correctly or were bugs in the source code. Needless to say, fixes for the documentation problems have been submitted back to Samba, as have fixes for the source problems.

The following are some of the areas where we have contributed:

- A detailed understanding of how Win9x clients access profiles and how the `logon home` and `logon path` parameters relate to Win9x clients.
- Fixes for Win9x logon requests and GETDC requests.
- Documentation updates.
- Contributions to the Samba 3.0.0 code base and ongoing support of the VFS code in Samba.
- Development of the SMB decoder in Ethereal. In many ways, development of the SMB decoder in Ethereal has paralleled the writing of this book; as new chapters were written and new features were needed in Ethereal, they were written.

Accompanying this book is a Web site that contains the latest versions of Samba, including Samba 2.0.7, Samba pre3.0.0, and Samba TNG. It also includes all shell and other scripts, as well as Ethereal and the entire packet traces that were used in the screen shots showing packet formats. The URL for the Web site is

```
http://www.mcp.com/catalog/corp_bud.cfm?isbn=0789723190
```

We think you will find this book an outstanding resource on using Samba.

WHO SHOULD USE THIS BOOK?

This book is for almost everyone who uses Samba, whether you have just started using Samba or have been using Samba for quite some time. We are sure that most Samba users will find something useful in this book.

In addition, because Samba is continually evolving, you will find this book especially useful if you are updating from an older version of Samba or an older distribution of Linux that uses an older version of Samba. In writing this book, we authors used the latest versions of Samba, including Samba 2.0.7, Samba pre3.0.0, and Samba TNG. However, we have tried where possible to point out areas in which defaults have changed. We have also tried to indicate where problems might have occurred with older versions of Samba.

In many cases, this book contains ready-to-use `smb.conf` file snippets and other examples that you can put to use immediately. It also contains troubleshooting information that relates directly to common problems that people experience with Samba. The authors spent hours trawling the `comp.protocols.smb` and `linux.samba` newsgroups answering questions and looking for common problems, as well as answering questions on the various Samba mailing lists.

WHO SHOULD *NOT* USE THIS BOOK?

If you are a Samba developer, if you do not use Samba at all, or if you do not plan to use Samba, you will probably find that this book is not for you. You can probably find all the information that you need simply by looking at the source code.

However, even if you have used Samba for some time, you will probably find that there is something in this book that you did not know, along with new insights into how Samba works. You might just find new ways to use Samba and new ideas on how to employ Samba in your environment.

On the other hand, if you have difficulties with bits and bytes, and if you don't know the difference between a user and a group or between a file and a directory, you would be well advised to read an introductory book on computers before tackling this book.

HARDWARE NEEDED TO USE THIS BOOK

You will get much more from this book if you have access to some hardware while reading it. We have written it so that you can try all the examples (perhaps substituting your IP addresses and machine and workgroup names) as you read each chapter.

You will need at least the following hardware:

- A Linux or UNIX machine. You can get by with an old 486 or Pentium machine with 16MB of memory and a 500MB disk drive if you need to, but a more modern machine is useful in many cases. However, Samba and Linux are very lean and mean on resources in many ways.

- A Windows client of some sort. The version of Windows you use—for example, Windows 9x versus Windows NT—depends on the environment in which you use Samba, but you really must have a Windows client with which to test Samba.

  If you have a sufficiently powerful Intel-based Linux system, you can use VMware (www.vmware.com) and run Windows under a virtual machine, but you'll run into some configurations where you will need additional machines.

- To test some configurations, you will need more systems so that you can set up additional subnets. Older Linux systems operating as routers can be used to increase the size of your network.

- A network using either 10Base2 cabling or 10BaseT with a hub.

At a minimum, we suggest two machines with a 10Base2 or 10Base2 (crossover cable) between them.

How to Use This Book

Some people may prefer to read this book from cover to cover, but we expect these people to be in the minority because the book is organized into sections and topics, allowing you to pick and choose what you want to read.

The book is organized into four parts, with each part more detailed than the previous one and requiring more attention on your part.

Part I, "Getting Started"

Part I, "Getting Started," provides a detailed introduction to Samba. Its main focus is on Samba on Linux, but much of the information provided is relevant to non-Linux users as well.

Part I is divided into the following four chapters:

- Chapter 1, "What Is Samba?" introduces Samba and provides information on what Samba can be used for, how it got started, who develops Samba, and what other packages provide similar functionality (and thus can be replaced by Samba).
- Chapter 2, "Obtaining and Installing Samba," provides detailed instructions on obtaining Samba for all operating systems and building it. However, its main focus is on the installation of Samba under different Linux distributions.
- Chapter 3, "An Introduction to Using Samba," gives detailed information on setting up and using Samba for first-time users. It covers all the files and programs you need to be aware of that relate to Samba, and provides a simple Samba configuration file.
- Chapter 4, "An Introduction to the SMB Protocol," provides crucial information on the SMB protocol that underlies Samba and Microsoft Windows Networking. Packet traces and diagrams are used to explain the concepts in detail.

Part II, "Configuring Samba"

Part II, "Configuring Samba," provides authoritative information on configuring all aspects of Samba. It provides the basic information that will be built on in Parts III and IV.

Part II is divided into the following five chapters:

- Chapter 5, "Configuring and Managing Samba," provides a detailed overview of configuring Samba, including motivating the security models that Samba uses, as well as the various sections that can appear in the Samba configuration file. It also provides information on some of the GUI-based configuration tools available for Samba.
- Chapter 6, "File Sharing Under Samba," shows how to set up file shares under Samba and explains what the file sharing–related parameters do.
- Chapter 7, "Printer Sharing Under Samba," details how to set up printer shares and lists and explains the printer-related parameters.

- Chapter 8, "Samba and Password Management," discusses the ways in which Samba handles passwords and how to manage passwords under Samba. It details how to integrate Samba into other authentication systems.

- Chapter 9, "Samba Automation," explores the facilities that Samba provides for simplifying your Samba configuration. It provides examples of how to use virtual servers and other configurations that might be of use.

PART III, "CLIENT CONFIGURATION AND USE"

Part III, "Client Configuration and Use," takes you through the process of configuring the various clients that can be used with Samba. It provides detailed how-to guides to configure these clients with Samba.

Part III is divided into the following eight chapters:

- Chapter 10, "An Introduction to Microsoft Windows Networking," gives an overview of Windows Networking and provides the information you need to know to understand how to configure Samba better.

- Chapter 11, "Samba as a Logon and Profiles Server," provides detailed information on setting up Samba to be a logon server for Windows clients and to provide roaming profile support for Windows clients.

- Chapter 12, "Accessing Samba from Windows for Workgroups and Windows 9x," shows how to configure Windows for Workgroups and Windows 9x clients to get the most from your Samba server.

- Chapter 13, "Accessing Samba from Windows NT," shows how to configure Windows NT as a Samba client and how to make the most of your Samba server from Windows NT.

- Chapter 14, "Accessing Samba from OS/2," details how to configure OS/2 as a Samba client and how to make the most of your Samba server from an OS/2 client.

- Chapter 15, "Accessing Samba from Windows 2000," provides details on how to access Samba from Microsoft's latest Windows client, Windows 2000 Professional.

- Chapter 16, "Accessing Windows from UNIX Using Samba," shows how to access resources provided by Windows clients and servers from Linux and UNIX systems. These resources include file shares and printers.

- Chapter 17, "Samba and Browsing," gives a thorough understanding of how the Windows browsing protocol works and how to configure Samba as a browse server, both in local area networks and wide area networks.

PART IV, "ADVANCED TOPICS"

Part IV, "Advanced Topics," takes you through a tour of some of the more advanced things that can be done with Samba. Here, you will perhaps reach the pinnacle of Samba use.

Part IV is divided into the following eight chapters:

- Chapter 18, "Samba and Other Operating Systems," provides information on how to obtain and configure Samba for operating systems such as OpenVMS and MVS.

- Chapter 19, "Samba and Windows NT Domains," details how to set up Samba as a primary domain controller, a backup domain controller, and a member of a domain.

- Chapter 20, "Samba and LDAP," shows how to integrate Samba into an LDAP environment so you can centralize all your passwords.

- Chapter 21, "Samba and Performance," details which parameters to modify so you can get the best performance out of Samba.

- Chapter 22, "Samba in the Enterprise," suggests ways in which you can set up Samba in large organizations, including setting up Samba in high-availability environments.

- Chapter 23, "Troubleshooting Samba," provides an approach to troubleshooting Samba along with specific advice on resolving many common problems that occur with Samba, especially for first-time users.

- Chapter 24, "A Tour Through the Samba Source Code," is an overview of the Samba source code in case you want to start debugging problems with Samba or want to contribute to Samba.

- Chapter 25, "The Future of Samba," provides authoritative information on where the Samba team is taking Samba in the short and medium term.

APPENDIX AND GLOSSARY

Appendix A, "All Samba Parameters and Their Meanings," lists all the Samba parameters that have been used since Samba 1.9.17, along with their meanings, and a list of the versions in which each parameter appeared. This appendix is designed for those who are using older versions of Samba or who have upgraded to a newer version and want to see what new features are supported or what features are not available in the older version they are currently using.

The glossary provides succinct explanations of many special terms that you will encounter throughout the book.

CONVENTIONS USED IN THIS BOOK

This book uses the following typographic conventions to make reading easier:

- New terms appear in *italic* (instead of double quotation marks). The *italic* attribute also is used for emphasis.

- All code listings and commands appear in a special `monospace` font.

- Replaceable elements and placeholders use *`italic monospace`*, as in `man` *`command`*.

- The `mono bold` attribute is used for the text you type at the command prompt.
- In those occasions when a line of code is too long to fit on one line of this book, it is broken at a convenient place and continued on the next line. A code continuation character (➥) precedes the continuation of a line of code. (At the command prompt, you should type a line of code with this character as one lone line, without breaking it.)

Note

Notes explain interesting or important points that can help you understand concepts and techniques.

Tip from
Author

Tips describe shortcuts and alternative approaches to gaining an objective. Tips often help you in real-world situations.

Caution

Cautions appear where an action might lead to an unexpected or unpredictable result, including possible loss of data or other serious consequence.

GETTING STARTED

WHAT IS SAMBA?

In this chapter

by Richard Sharpe

Like Linux, Samba is an international success story. It is a freely available (and Gnome Public Licensed) file and print server for many operating systems. It competes directly with Microsoft's Windows NT operating system and is better in so many ways.

However, Samba is not without its criticism. It has a steep learning curve, with many people saying that it is difficult to use and hard to manage. Despite all this, it is in use in large and small corporations, government organizations, nonprofit organizations, small businesses, and—thanks to the success of Linux—private homes as well.

In many ways, this book is designed to let you quickly assimilate the information you need to manage Samba and to provide a resource that lets you get the most out of Samba for a long time to come.

That a package with the humble beginnings of Samba could rise to become the success story it is today, despite oft-repeated difficulties, speaks volumes about the power of the Internet to provide access to useful software for everyone.

WHAT SAMBA DOES

Samba is an *open source software (OSS)* package that implements a (mostly) Windows NT-compatible file and print server for Windows and UNIX clients. Figure 1.1 shows an example of two different client computers using a Samba server for file and print serving.

Figure 1.1
A file server sharing files and printers.

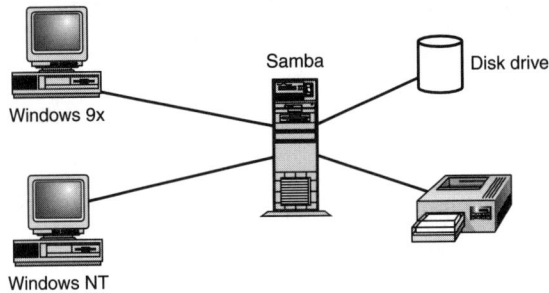

Windows 9x

Samba

Disk drive

Windows NT

More accurately, Samba is a file and print server that implements the *server message block (SMB)* protocol. SMB is the very same protocol that underlies Microsoft's Windows Networking protocols, which means that in most cases, Samba can be a low-cost and very effective replacement for Windows NT Server.

I talk more about the SMB protocol in Chapter 4, "An Introduction to the SMB Protocol."

Other types of clients can also access Samba when using SMB client software. For example, Thursby's Dave client for MacOS allows Macintosh computers to access SMB servers.

Since its inception in 1991, Samba has continued to improve in functionality. It now implements many of the same functions as Windows NT Server 4.0 and also has its own set of functions that Windows NT just does not have. In addition, the Samba team is very concerned with making Samba bug-for-bug compatible with NT Server, where Samba implements the functions that SMB server does.

Some of the functionality in Samba includes

- File and printer sharing—This is what Samba is all about for most people these days. Samba lets many different types of clients share files and printers from one or more servers.

- Windows Networking logon serving—This allows WIN9X client PCs to log on to a Samba server just as if it were an NT server and to have logon scripts run and profiles accessed. Figure 1.2 shows an example of a Windows 95 client logging on to a Samba server. As an aside, Figure 1.2 was captured by running Windows 95 in VMware under Linux.

Figure 1.2
Logging on to a Samba server from Windows 95.

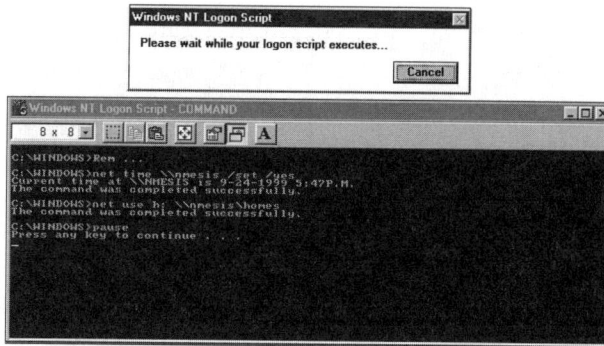

- Primary Domain Controller support—Samba can behave like a Primary Domain Controller.

- Domain member support—Samba can be a member of a domain and supports most of the Windows NT domain controller protocols (encrypted RPCs and so on).

- Support for Windows browsing—Samba supports browsing by Windows clients, as shown in Figure 1.3.

- WINS support—Samba can function as a Windows Internet name server for Windows clients.

- OpLock support—Samba provides OpLock support for clients, which allows them to cache files on clients.

- Experimental LDAP support—Samba has experimental LDAP support, which provides centralization of configuration information.

- NetBIOS aliasing—Samba provides NetBIOS aliasing, allowing a single Samba server to operate as several different servers.

- Automatic installation of printer drivers under Windows 9x—This lets users simply install printer drivers when they need access to new printers.

Figure 1.3
Browsing under Windows shows the Samba servers.

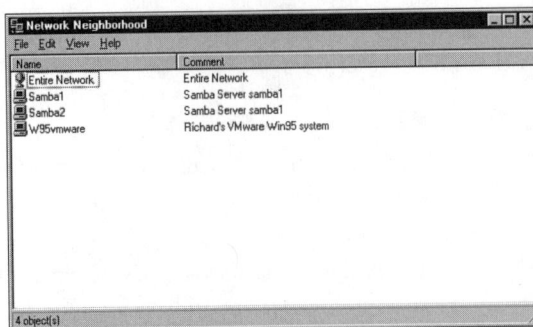

- Synchronization of passwords between Windows and UNIX systems—This allows users to maintain one password for both their UNIX and their Windows systems, considerably reducing their administrative burden.

- Support for SSL—With the use of SSL proxies, secure access to Samba servers can be provided over the Internet.

Samba includes many more examples of functionality than those listed here.

WHY SAMBA IS SO SUCCESSFUL

Samba is so successful for many reasons, including the following:

- Samba is free—Because users do not have to pay license fees to anyone, Samba provides a very cost-effective way to provide file and print services to large numbers of PCs.

- Samba is an open source software package—Anyone can provide fixes to Samba, which means that when bugs are found, they are quickly fixed.

- Samba is available for many platforms—Samba is available for a large range of platforms, from all kinds of UNIX (including Linux), to BeOS, OpenVMS, and even MVS. This means that you can integrate PCs into almost any computing environment.

- Samba has plenty of functionality—Samba makes it so easy to do neat things when providing file and print serving that system administrators find it very useful. Examples include the NetBIOS alias and virtual server functionality that Samba implements, which easily allow multiple servers to be combined into one.

- In addition to being available for many platforms, Samba provides support for a wide range of existing technologies. This allows PC serving to be easily integrated into existing environments. Examples include NIS and LDAP for authentication.

OPERATING SYSTEMS ON WHICH SAMBA RUNS

Although Samba initially ran only on UNIX—and a few versions of UNIX at that—it is now available for a truly enormous range of systems and operating systems. Samba comes standard with all Linux distributions these days, and is likely to be installed and running on Linux machines even if its owners don't know it.

Apart from Linux, Samba runs on all flavors of UNIX, including

- Solaris and SunOS from Sun Microsystems
- AIX from IBM
- HP-UX from Hewlett-Packard
- Tru64 UNIX from Compaq (formerly Digital UNIX from Digital)
- Irix from SGI
- ULTRIX from Digital (now Compaq)
- The various BSD variants, such as FreeBSD and OpenBSD

In addition, Samba runs on the following:

- OS/2
- BeOS
- OpenVMS
- AmigaOS
- Coherent
- MVS

This list must surely show that Samba is one of the most widely ported packages in the world. It definitely shows that Samba is the most widely ported file and print server available.

HISTORY OF SAMBA

Samba started as a simple hack to allow Andrew Tridgell to access files on his Sun machine from a PC running Digital's PATHWORKS for DOS product. In late 1991, Andrew, who was then a Ph.D. student at the Australian National University (my old university), acquired eXcursion, an X server for DOS. Because eXcursion required Digital's PATHWORKS for DOS product, Andrew could no longer use Sun's PCNFS product to access files on his Sun workstation.

To provide access to files on his Sun workstation, Andrew spent much time looking at packet traces to find out what the PATHWORKS package was doing on the wire, and then wrote a server for SunOS to handle the sorts of packets that the PATHWORKS client was sending.

Upon inquiring with Digital as to the legality of what he had done (implementing a protocol by staring at traces from the wire), Andrew was told "It is legal, but silly" because the protocol was all described in several specifications. As it turned out, these were specs such as RFC1001 and RFC1002, the NetBIOS over TCP/IP specs, as well as the various SMB specs, as PATHWORKS was an SMB client and server implementation.

Fortunately for the rest of us, Andrew was encouraged to release his program to the rest of the world, and he did. This brings us to why he called the package *Samba*. Initially, it was simply called *server*. Later, Andrew renamed it *SMBserver* when he found out that the protocol being implemented was the SMB protocol. However, in 1994, a company with a commercial SMB server informed Andrew that it had a trademark on the name *SMBserver*. Andrew was required to change the name of his package, and after searching the UNIX dictionary files for all words with the letters *s*, *m*, and *b* in them. Andrew says, "The name *Samba* looked like the best." It is certainly much better than SMBserver, and I am not sure I would want to be a member of the SMBserver team.

It is ironic to think that these days there are probably more implementations of Samba than that company currently has. That company was Syntax, Inc.

For a long time now, Samba has been developed by the Samba team, a group of people around the world who perform on-going development for Samba. Rather than forget anyone on the Samba team, I would suggest that you visit www.samba.org if you want to learn who the members are or if you want to join the Samba team.

OTHER SMB IMPLEMENTATIONS

Samba is but one of a large number of server implementations of the SMB protocol. To give you a feeling for how many other SMB server implementations there have been, I discuss several of them in the following sections. It is also useful to know which file sharing implementations implement one or another version of the SMB protocol so that you can understand which products and packages can operate with Samba.

IBM's PC NETWORK PROGRAM

The first SMB server implementation was IBM's PC Network Program. The earliest document I have on the SMB protocol is a copy of the IBM Personal Computer Seminar Proceedings from May 1985, which describes the SMB protocol.

IBM had implemented the PC Network Program for DOS 3.1 on the IBM PC Network, which was a broadband Ethernet-style network developed for IBM by Sytek. Many aspects of that early version of the SMB protocol are still in current versions.

IBM's LAN SERVER

Later, IBM developed the LAN Server series of SMB servers and provided them for members of its product range such as the AS400 series, the Risc Series 6000, and its mainframe products. LAN Server was also made available for OS/2 on Intel-based PCs.

MICROSOFT'S LAN MANAGER

Lan Manager was a Microsoft offering that implemented the SMB protocol. It ran on OS/2 and provided file and print sharing for DOS and Windows PCs.

MICROSOFT'S WINDOWS NT

Windows NT from Microsoft extended the SMB protocol to provide additional file and print services. It also introduced the concepts of domains into Microsoft Windows Networking and allowed networks to be constructed containing Primary Domain Controllers, Backup Domain Controllers, and Member Servers.

Windows NT was first introduced in 1993.

MICROSOFT'S WINDOWS FOR WORKGROUPS AND WINDOWS 9X

Microsoft's Windows for Workgroups products (especially WfWg 3.11) contained both SMB client and SMB server implementations. This allowed Windows for Workgroups machines to share files and printers with other Windows for Workgroups systems. Windows for Workgroups shipped in 1992.

When Windows 95 came out in 1995, it also had both client and server implementations of the SMB protocol. Windows 98 continued in the same fashion and provided both client and server versions of the SMB protocol.

COMPAQ'S (FORMERLY DIGITAL'S) PATHWORKS

Digital Equipment Corporation (DEC, now Compaq) implemented a series of SMB client and server products under the PATHWORKS trademark. It implemented the SMB protocol over DECnet as well as TCP/IP and allowed PC clients to access files and printers on OpenVMS (formerly VMS) servers as well as ULTRIX and Digital UNIX (currently Tru64 UNIX) servers. Many of Digital's later PATHWORKS servers were based on LAN Manager for UNIX or Advanced Server for UNIX (see the following sections on UNIX).

Samba can only provide services to PATHWORKS clients that use the TCP/IP protocols.

LAN MANAGER FOR UNIX

In the early 1990s, NCR ported the SMB server software from LAN Manager to UNIX and called it LAN Manager for UNIX, or LM/X. This package was adopted by many vendors as their product for providing file and print services to PCs.

ADVANCED SERVER FOR UNIX

When Windows NT became available, NCR (then a part of AT&T) ported the SMB server parts of NT to UNIX and called the resulting product Advanced Server for UNIX (or ASU). This product subsequently formed the basis of many vendors' commercial file and print server offerings for PCs. Because ASU was based on Windows NT's networking code, it provides native support for domains and can function as a Primary Domain Controller or a Backup Domain Controller.

SCO's VisionFS

SCO developed its own implementation of an SMB server and called it VisionFS.

Syntax's TotalNET Advanced Server

Syntax has provided an SMB server implementation for UNIX since 1987. Its product is called the Syntax TotalNET Advanced Server. The company originally had a product called SMBserver.

Sun's PC Netlink Server

Sun Microsystems has released its PC Netlink product, which was known as Cascade during development. It is based on AT&T's (or NCR's) Advanced Server for UNIX.

Other Approaches to File and Print Sharing

Several other approachesto file and print sharing have been used in the past and continue to be used today:

- NFS and PCNFS from Sun Microsystems
- Novell's NetWare file and print servers

Each of these approaches employs its own protocols, which are as proprietary as the SMB protocol is. Novell's solution has been in widespread use for some time, but it has never been very popular on other platforms (despite many vendors producing ports to their platforms). More recently, the MARS-NWE emulator for Linux has provided Netware emulation for Linux.

Samba Resources

Many Samba resources are available on the Internet, but the official Samba Web page is perhaps the most useful. This page is located at www.samba.org, and all new versions of Samba are posted there.

From Here...

Samba is a freely available file and print server. It has so much functionality it is almost impossible to describe. The following sections of this book will teach you more about Samba:

- In Chapter 2, "Obtaining and Installing Samba," you will see how to get Samba and install it if you don't already have it installed on your system.

- In Chapter 3, "An Introduction to Using Samba," you will learn how to start and stop Samba as well as the basics of the Samba configuration file.

- In Chapter 4, "An Introduction to the SMB Protocol," you will learn more about the SMB protocol.

- In Part II, "Configuring Samba," you will learn much more about the configuration and management of Samba.

- In Part III, "Client Configuration and Use," you will learn how to set up client PCs to access Samba.

## CHAPTER 2

OBTAINING AND INSTALLING SAMBA

In this chapter   *by Tim Potter*

Samba is readily and freely available as a piece of open source software. In fact, a precompiled version of Samba is probably available for your particular flavor of UNIX, especially if you are using Linux. You can also compile Samba from its source code if no prepackaged version is available or if you want to customize aspects of Samba to suit your particular circumstances.

At the time of writing, the latest version of Samba was version 2.0.6. You might want to upgrade your installation of Samba if it is not the most recent because important bugs and security problems are usually fixed in subsequent releases. Version 2.0.7 or higher is likely to have been released by the time this book goes to print.

OBTAINING SAMBA

There are two methods for installing or upgrading Samba on your UNIX system. If there is a prepackaged binary distribution for your operating system, it is usually quicker and easier to install this. Most versions of Linux come with a binary distribution of Samba, but if none is available, you must compile and install Samba from its source code.

> **Note**
>
> If Samba is already installed on your system, it might not be the latest version. This is especially true if the version of Samba was installed from a CD-ROM distribution of Linux. Check the version of Samba by using man samba. The version number should appear in each Samba manual page.

BINARY DISTRIBUTIONS

A binary distribution of Samba might be available for your particular operating system, especially if you are using Linux.

OBTAINING A BINARY DISTRIBUTION FOR LINUX

If your distribution of Linux is included in the following list, you can download a binary distribution or an update from the location shown:

Red Hat Linux	ftp://ftp.redhat.com/pub/redhat
SuSE Linux	ftp://ftp.suse.de/pub/suse
Debian	ftp://ftp.debian.org/debian/dists
TurboLinux	ftp://ftp.turbolinux.com/pub/TurboLinux
Caldera OpenLinux	ftp://ftp.calderasystems.com/pub/OpenLinux

Most Linux vendors provide a directory called updates where you can find updated versions of Samba.

Binary distributions of Samba for other flavors of UNIX are also available. The Samba FTP site maintains a collection of binary distributions. Packages are available for IRIX, Solaris, AIX, and VMS, among others. You can find these packages in ftp://ftp.samba.org/pub/mirrors/samba/ftp/bin-pkgs.

INSTALLING A BINARY DISTRIBUTION ON LINUX

Binary distributions of Samba should be installed using the package manager for your particular Linux distribution. If a previous version of Samba is already installed, you might need to use the upgrade option of your package manager.

SAMPLE INSTALLS

For Red Hat package-based Linux distributions such as Red Hat Linux, SuSE Linux, or Mandrake Linux, use the rpm program to install your binary Samba distribution. If the filename of your binary package is samba-2.0.6-1.i386.rpm, use this command to install it:

```
rpm -Uvh samba-2.0.5a-12.i386.rpm
```

The -Uvh options to rpm will also upgrade the existing version of Samba if one has already been installed. If you have installed Debian Linux, use the dpkg program to install or upgrade your binary version of Samba:

```
dpkg --install samba_2.0.6-1.deb
```

Substitute the actual filename of the Samba binary distributions in the preceding examples.

Many Linux distributions have a graphical install program that you can use instead of a command-line–based one. Figure 2.1 shows the Caldera OpenLinux installer, which can be invoked from the KDE desktop menu or by running /usr/local/bin/coastool. Samba can be installed or uninstalled by clicking the appropriate checkbox.

Figure 2.1
Caldera Open-
Linux graphical
installer.

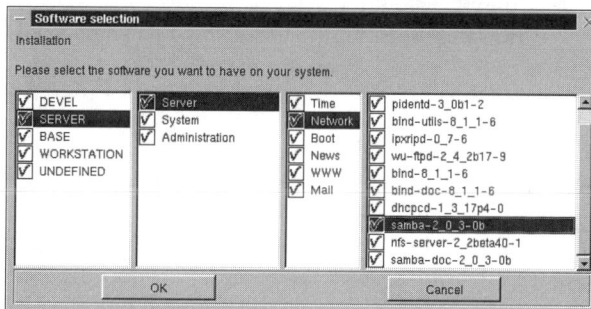

FILE LOCATIONS

An installation of Samba consists of several components. These are executable files such as the Samba server program itself, a configuration file called smb.conf, and a directory to write access log files. Don't worry too much about these files at the moment because I explain them later, but you should know where all the components of Samba are located on your file system.

In the various binary distributions of Samba, the location of configuration files, executable files, and log files can differ. Table 2.1 shows the locations for several binary versions of Samba. The default file locations are used if Samba is compiled from source.

TABLE 2.1   SAMBA CONFIGURATION FILE AND BINARY LOCATIONS

Operating System	smb.conf	Log Files	Binaries
Default	/usr/local/samba/ lib/smb.conf	/usr/local/samba/ var	/usr/local/ samba/bin
Red Hat Linux	/etc/smb.conf	/var/log/samba	/usr/bin, /usr/sbin
Debian	/etc/smb.conf	/var/log	/usr/{bin,sbin}
Caldera Open- Linux	/etc/samba.d/ smb.conf	/var/log/samba.d	/usr/bin, /usr/sbin

SOURCE DISTRIBUTIONS

If an appropriate binary distribution of Samba is not available or you want to compile Samba to use different directories than an existing binary distribution, you will be required to compile and install Samba from its source code.

OBTAINING A SOURCE DISTRIBUTION

You can freely obtain the full source code for Samba by using a WWW browser at http://www.samba.org/ or using an FTP program at ftp://ftp.samba.org/pub/mirrors/samba/ftp. Samba is distributed as a compressed tar archive named samba-x.y.z.tar.gz, where x.y.z is the version number. For the latest version of Samba, this filename would be samba-2.0.6.tar.gz.

Many mirrors of the Samba Web site are located around the world, so please use the mirror site closest to your physical location to minimize network traffic and load on the main Samba site. In fact, the main Samba Web and FTP sites at samba.org automatically direct you to a list of mirror sites, from which you can choose the closest.

UNPACKING THE ARCHIVE

After obtaining the source code for the latest version, you'll need to unpack, configure, and compile Samba before you can install it. If you have GNU tar installed on your system and the latest version of Samba, you can unpack the archive by running the following command at the command prompt:

```
tar xfvz samba-2.0.6.tar.gz
```

This command invokes the UNIX tar program to uncompress and extract the files contained in the samba-2.0.6.tar.gz archive file. If your version of tar, such as the one that comes with Solaris, does not support compression, a different set of commands is required:

```
gunzip samba-2.0.6.tar.gz
tar xfv samba-2.0.6.tar
```

You should unpack the Samba archive into a directory called samba-2.0.6.

Note

> Some operating systems, notably Solaris, do not ship with the GNU unzip program, gunzip, or the GNU tar program. You can download these programs from `ftp://ftp.gnu.org/gnu/gzip/gzip-1.2.4a.tar` and `ftp://ftp.gnu.org/gnu/tar/tar-1.13.tar`, respectively.

RUNNING THE CONFIGURE SCRIPT

Because Samba runs on many different flavors of UNIX, it must deal with the idiosyncrasies of each system. These include differently named header files and standard libraries, as well as bugs and nonstandard behavior in the operating system itself. All this information is encapsulated in the configure script in Samba's source directory.

To run the configure script for Samba, you must execute the following commands at a shell prompt. Be sure to change into the `samba-2.0.6` directory created by unpacking the source tar archive.

```
cd source
./configure
```

Running `configure` with no options installs Samba in a default location and default behavior. To get a list of options the configure script accepts, pass the `--help` option to the configure program like so:

```
cd source
./configure --help
```

A long list of options and information on their usage will be printed to the screen. The option list starts with the following text and continues for several pages:

```
Usage: configure [options] [host]
Options: [defaults in brackets after descriptions]
Configuration:
  --cache-file=FILE      cache test results in FILE
  --help                 print this message
  --no-create            do not create output files
  --quiet, --silent      do not print 'checking...' messages
  --version              print the version of autoconf that created configure

(remainder of output not shown)
```

By specifying arguments to the configure script, you can change the way Samba behaves or change the locations where Samba installs files.

Note

> Running the `configure` script before compiling Samba is different from configuring an already installed version of Samba.

After you have chosen the appropriate arguments to the configure script and invoked it, it can take several minutes to determine the internal information required to compile Samba on your system.

FILE LOCATION OPTIONS

Options to configure where Samba installs its files appear in Table 2.2. Each option takes an argument that is separated from the option name by an equals sign.

TABLE 2.2   CONFIGURE OPTIONS FOR FILE LOCATION

Configure Option	Description
--prefix	Specifies the top-level directory under which all Samba files are installed. For example, to install Samba under /opt/local, run configure with the argument --prefix=/opt/local. The default for this is /usr/local/samba.
--bindir	The executable part of Samba in installed in this directory. The default is *PREFIX*/bin, where *PREFIX* refers to the argument given to the --prefix option, or /usr/local/samba if the --prefix option has not been specified.
--localstatedir	Per-machine information about the currently running instance of Samba is stored here. This directory must be writable. The default is *PREFIX*/var.
--mandir	Manual pages for Samba are stored in *PREFIX*/man unless otherwise specified with this option.
--libdir	Auxiliary data required by Samba is stored in this directory. Presently, this consists only of code page information. The default is *PREFIX*/lib.
--with-swatdir	Files for the Samba Web Administration Tool (SWAT) are installed in this directory. The default is *PREFIX*/swat.
--with-lockdir	Samba's lock file information is stored here. This directory must be writable. The default for this option is *PREFIX*/locks.
--with-privatedir	Security information, such as user passwords, is stored in this directory. The default is *PREFIX*/private.

→   To learn more about the SWAT program, **see** Chapter 5, "Configuring and Managing Samba."

BEHAVIOR OPTIONS

Samba supports several different authentication, networking, and file system options, most of which are not enabled by default. To enable these options, you must run the configure script with an option of the form --with-foo to enable the imaginary foo option, or --without-foo to disable it. Table 2.3 shows the list of behavior options supported. All options are disabled by default.

Note

Not all operating systems support every one of the behavior options. You must examine your system to determine whether a particular behavior option is installed or supported.

TABLE 2.3 CONFIGURE OPTIONS FOR SAMBA BEHAVIOR

Configure Option	Description
--with-afs	The Andrew Filesystem (AFS) is a distributed file system originally developed at Carnegie-Mellon University. It is now supported commercially by the TransArc Corporation at http://www.transarc.com/Support/afs/. Samba AFS support enables users to be authenticated against the AFS password database so they can access resources exported by Samba. For more information about the Andrew Filesystem, visit http://www.cs.cmu.edu/afs/andrew.cmu.edu/usr/shadow/www/afs.html.
--with-dfs	Compiling with DFS support allows Samba to authenticate users against the Distributed Computing Environment/Distributed File Service (DCE/DCS). DCE is described more fully at http://www.opengroup.org/tech/DCE/.
--with-kerberos	Kerberos is a network authentication protocol developed at MIT. Samba can authenticate users using Kerberos only if it has been compiled with the --with-kerberos option. The Kerberos Web page at http://web.mit.edu/kerberos/ contains more information.
--with-smbwrapper	Smbwrapper is an experimental client program that runs under UNIX. It is distributed with Samba and can make SMB file systems appear to be locally mounted by intercepting file I/O operations and passing them to Samba if they refer to a file on an SMB server. It is available only for a small number of operating systems that support LD_PRELOAD functionality in their dynamic linker.
--with-automount	With automount support enabled, the location of a user's home directory is taken from a file in automounter map format.
--with-smbmount	The smbmount program supports native mounting of SMB file systems on machines running Linux.
--with-pam	Pluggable Authentication Modules (PAM) is a method of writing customized authentication methods under supported flavors of UNIX. You can find information on the Linux implementation of PAM and PAM in general at http://www.kernel.org/pub/linux/libs/pam/.

TABLE 2.3 CONTINUED

Configure Option	Description
--with-ldap	The Lightweight Directory Access Protocol (LDAP) is a directory service for storing, among other things, password information. Samba can authenticate users against an LDAP password database with this option. You can find information on LDAP at http://www.umich.edu/~dirsvcs/ldap/.
--with-nisplus, --with-nisplus-home	Enabling NIS+ (Network Information Services Plus) support allows a Samba server to authenticate users against NIS+ password maps. Enabling NIS+ home directories tells Samba to look up the location of user home directories in the NIS+ database. NIS+ is available only on some machines, including Solaris and some versions of Linux.
--with-ssl	The Secure Socket Layer (SSL) is a method for secure communications using public key cryptography. SSL support in Samba is enabled using this option.
--with-mmap	Samba can attempt to speed up access to shared files by mapping them to memory using the mmap() UNIX system call, but only if the --with-mmap option is specified at compile time. This configuration option is experimental and should not be used on production systems.
--with-syslog	The --with-syslog option tells Samba to write its log messages to the syslog facility. Writing Samba log messages to syslog can result in very large log files. This configuration option is also experimental.
--with-netatalk	Experimental support for the AppleTalk network protocol used by Macintoshes is enabled using this option. It is described more fully at http://www.umich.edu/~rsug/netatalk/.
--with-quotas	Disk quotas in Samba are supported using this option. Quota support is experimental because the programming interface to disk quotas is highly operating system-dependent.

Note   The smbwrapper program does not appear to work with systems based on version 2.1.x of glibc, the GNU C library.

→ To learn more about the smbwrapper program, **see** "smbsh," **p. 311**.

SAMPLE CUSTOMIZATION

As an illustration, at the Example Corporation the Samba administrator wants to install a customized version of Samba with NIS+ user authentication and NIS+ home directory support. The administrator also wants to have two Samba servers share executable files but have different configuration and log files. You can achieve this by running the `configure` script with these options:

```
./configure --nisplus --nisplus-homes
    ➥--libdir=/etc/samba
    ➥--localstatedir=/var/samba/logs
    ➥--lockdir=/var/samba/locks
    ➥--with-privatedir=/var/samba/private
```

This configuration allows the Samba executable files to be shared on multiple machines by having `/usr/local` mounted on the two Samba servers. Samba's configuration files are stored in the `/etc/samba` directory, and local machine information such as logs and lock files is stored in `/var/samba`. For most UNIX servers, the `/etc` and `/var` directories are unique to each machine.

COMPILING SAMBA

After Samba has been configured using the configure script, compiling Samba is very simple. Enter the following command at a shell prompt to compile Samba:

```
make
```

The compilation process can take 10 minutes or so because there are a large number of source files to process.

If compilation errors occur, you can use the following list to troubleshoot common problems:

- Check that a C compiler is installed correctly on your machine.
- Ensure you have sufficient free disk space. Approximately 20MB are required to unpack and compile Samba from source.
- If you are using Red Hat Linux, the `glibc-devel` package must also be installed.
- If you have specified any behavior options from Table 2.3, ensure that the appropriate software is actually installed. For example, if you specify Secure Sockets Layer support to be included in Samba, you must have installed the appropriate SSL libraries and header files for Samba to then compile correctly.

INSTALLING SAMBA

After the compilation process is complete, Samba should be installed into its final location. Type the following command as the root user:

```
make install
```

If Samba was not compiled using the process just outlined, or the compile process was interrupted, any uncompiled files are compiled before the install process starts.

The install process copies user and system executable files, man pages, code page information, and SWAT support files into the directories given by the file location options in Table 2.2 that were given to the configure script.

BUILDING BINARY DISTRIBUTIONS OF SAMBA

To prevent binary package maintainers from creating incorrectly installed versions of Samba, a set of template packaging scripts and configuration files has been created. You can use these to create your own binary distribution of Samba. These templates are available for many distributions of UNIX and Linux and can be found in the packaging subdirectory of the Samba source archive.

BUILDING NEW RPMs UNDER LINUX

The RPM Package Manager (RPM) creates packages from a set of source files, an optional set of patches, and a specifications (spec) file. A brief description of the spec file format and how it works is presented here, but for more information on creating RPM files, consult the RPM Web site at http://www.rpm.org/ and the RPM-HOWTO at http://www.linuxdoc.org/HOWTO/RPM-HOWTO.html. Quite a few Linux distributions are based on the Red Hat package format, including SuSE Linux, Caldera OpenLinux, and Mandrake Linux.

An RPM spec file defines how a Red Hat package is compiled and installed and specifies the location of files in the package. A spec file has the file extension .spec.

The easiest way to create your own RPM under Linux is to modify the template spec file in the packaging directory of the Samba distribution archive. If you have changed where Samba installs files using options to the configure script, a simple visual inspection of the template spec file should make obvious which portions to change.

SPEC FILE FORMAT

A spec file can be roughly divided into the following sections:

- A *preparatory section* describing where any source files are unpacked. This section begins with the text %prep.
- A *build section* describing where the software under consideration is compiled. This section begins with the text %build.
- An *install* section starting with the text %install that declares files and directories to be included in the RPM.
- A *postinstall section* that specifies any post-processing required to complete the installation. This section starts with %post and contains Bourne shell commands.

BUILDING THE RPM

To build a customized RPM file, you must copy the source files (the Samba archive and any files you want to add) into /usr/src/redhat/SOURCES, and you must copy the spec file into the /usr/src/redhat/SPECS directory. You can invoke the RPM program at the command line:

```
rpm -ba your_spec_file.spec
```

This attempts to build a binary and source RPM. The binary RPM is the one that the user will install, and the source RPM can be used to rebuild the binary RPM. If the RPM creation is successful, a binary RPM is created in the /usr/src/redhat/RPMS directory, and a source RPM is created in the /usr/src/redhat/SRPMS directory.

The RPM-HOWTO describes the build process in great detail, and this information is invaluable in troubleshooting problems in your spec file.

FROM HERE...

Now that Samba has been installed, you are ready to configure and start using it. The rest of Part I is an introduction to using Samba and a brief description of the SMB protocol.

CHAPTER **3**

AN INTRODUCTION TO USING SAMBA

In this chapter

by Glen Turner

Samba is a UNIX application that contains several components. It is configured through a configuration file, and commands are used to start and stop Samba.

This chapter covers

- The structure of Samba
- How to start and stop Samba
- How to start Samba at system startup time
- An initial Samba configuration
- How to test whether Samba is running

THE STRUCTURE OF SAMBA

Samba is structuredas several daemons, many programs, and a configuration file. Figure 3.1 shows the basic structure of Samba and broadly shows how clients interact with Samba.

Figure 3.1
Samba consists of several daemons that are accessed by clients using TCP and UDP.

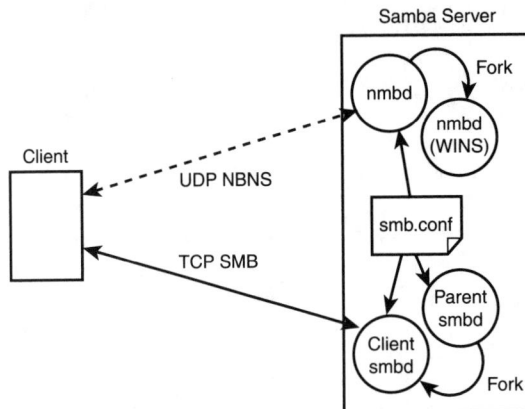

The following are some of the components of Samba:

- nmbd(8), the NetBIOS Name Service daemon—At least one nmbd(8) process is running in a properly configured Samba server, and if you have configured Samba to function as a WINS server (using wins server = yes), an additional copy of nmbd(8) will be created. A third copy of nmbd(8) can also run when Samba is using DNS to translate NetBIOS names.

  nmbd(8) handles NetBIOS name lookups as well as WINS requests. It also plays a big part in browsing, shown in Chapter 17, "Samba and Browsing."

- smbd(8), the Server Message Block daemon—At least one smbd(8) process is running in a properly configured Samba server. In addition, for every client connected to Samba, an additional smbd(8) is running. smbd(8) handles file and print access as well as LAN Manager API requests such as NetServerEnum, NetShareEnum, NetUserGetInfo, and so on.

- smb.conf, the Samba configuration file—This file lives in /etc under most Linux distributions and in /usr/local/samba/lib for standard UNIX installs. It contains all the configuration information for smbd(8) and nmbd(8).

- smbclient, the SMB client program—This program enables users to access other SMB servers, such as Windows NT and Windows 9x, from a UNIX system.

- nmblookup, the NMB lookup program—This program enables users to query servers for registered NetBIOS names.

- smbstatus, the SMB status command—Administrators use this command to learn information about who is accessing Samba and what shares they are using.

- smbprint—A shell script for printing to Windows systems from UNIX.

- smbtar—A shell script for backing up Windows systems from UNIX.

When clients access Samba, they use both TCP and UDP. Clients use TCP when they want to access file and print shares and log on to the network. To do this, they establish a TCP connection to smbd on port 139. Clients use UDP when they want to register or translate NetBIOS names, as well as when they are browsing the network. The UDP datagrams they send are sent to ports 137 and 138, depending on the function being used.

The nmbd(8) daemon is usually started at system startup time, but it can also be started manually. The smbd(8) daemon can be started in three different ways:

- At system startup time
- Manually, when the system administrator needs it
- Using inetd

The following section describes how to start smbd(2) and nmbd(2) manually or at system startup time.

How to Start and Stop Samba

Among the files that are installed under most versions of Linux when Samba is installed are two that are used to start and stop Samba:

- /usr/sbin/samba—Used by administrators to stop and start Samba if needed.

Note

If you have installed Samba from RPMs built by the Samba team for Red Hat Linux or TurboLinux, the /usr/sbin/samba command is installed for you. However, RPMs for other distributions, as well as the RPMs provided by Red Hat, do not contain this command.

- /etc/rc.d/init.d/smb—Used by the system to start Samba during system startup.

PART

I

CH

3

Both of these files are installed as executable files (with the X-bit set). Because the root account has /usr/sbin on its path, /usr/sbin/samba is available to root as a command. Each of these files takes exactly the same arguments, as shown in Table 3.1. In fact, the samba command is a copy of the script /etc/rc.d/init.d/smb.

TABLE 3.1 PARAMETERS ACCEPTED BY /etc/rc.d/init.d AND THE samba COMMAND

Parameter	Meaning
start	Start the Samba daemons (smbd and nmbd) if they are not already running.
stop	Stop the Samba daemons if they are running.
restart	Restart the Samba daemons. It just runs itself again twice with stop and start arguments.
status	Print status information about the Samba daemons.

You can start Samba with samba start, as shown in the following code:

```
samba start
Starting SMB services: smbd nmbd
```

You can stop Samba with samba stop, as shown in the following code:

```
samba stop
Shutting down SMB services: smbd nmbd
```

The following shows the results of querying the status of Samba and then restarting it:

```
[root@samba1 /root]# samba status
smbd (pid 11551 3818) is running...
nmbd (pid 3826) is running...
[root@samba1 /root]# samba restart
Restarting SMB services: Shutting down SMB services: smbd nmbd
Starting SMB services: smbd nmbd
done.
```

The results of the samba status command tell us that two smbd(8) processes are running, with process IDs of 11,551 and 3,818. The larger of these is probably the smbd(8) that handles my accesses to my home directories as I write this.

You can use the following methods to determine whether Samba is running:

- samba status—This command, as shown previously, tells you whether smbd and nmbd are running.
- ps -ax | grep mbd—This pipeline finds all the nmbd and smbd processes running.
- smbstatus—This command prints status information about Samba and the shares that users are accessing.

How to Start Samba at System Startup Time

Most Linux distributions use the System V init structure. Under these systems, you link the script /etc/rc.d/init.d into the directory /etc/rc.d/rc2.d using the following command:

```
ln -s /etc/rc.d/init.d/smb/etc/rc.d/rc3.d/S91smb
```

Samba starts automatically the next time you reboot your system.

You can also use the standard commands available under different distributions of Linux to manage run-level scripts to achieve the same as the above. These commands appear in Table 3.2.

TABLE 3.2   COMMANDS TO MANAGE RUN LEVELS UNDER VARIOUS VERSIONS OF LINUX

Operating System	Command to Use
Red Hat Linux	ntsysv
Linux Mandrake	ntsysv
TurboLinux	turboservice

Figure 3.2 is an example of using ntsysv under Red Hat Linux or Linux Mandrake to ensure that Samba starts at system startup. Simply use the down-arrow key to move to the smb entry, and then press the spacebar to enable Samba to start if it is not already selected.

Figure 3.2
Under Red Hat Linux and Linux Mandrake, you use ntsysv to manage which services start at system startup time.

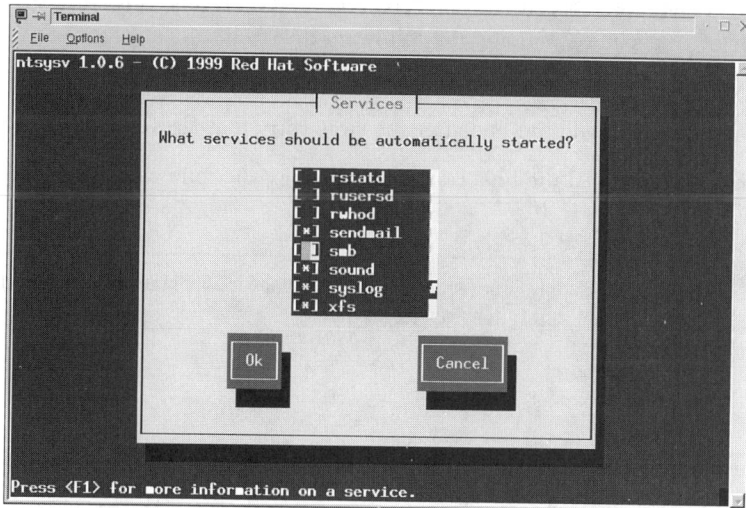

Figure 3.3 is an example of using TurboService under TurboLinux to ensure that Samba starts at system startup time. Again, simply use the down-arrow key to move to the smb entry and press the E key to enable Samba if it is not already enabled.

Figure 3.3
Under TurboLinux, you use TurboService to manage which services start at system startup time.

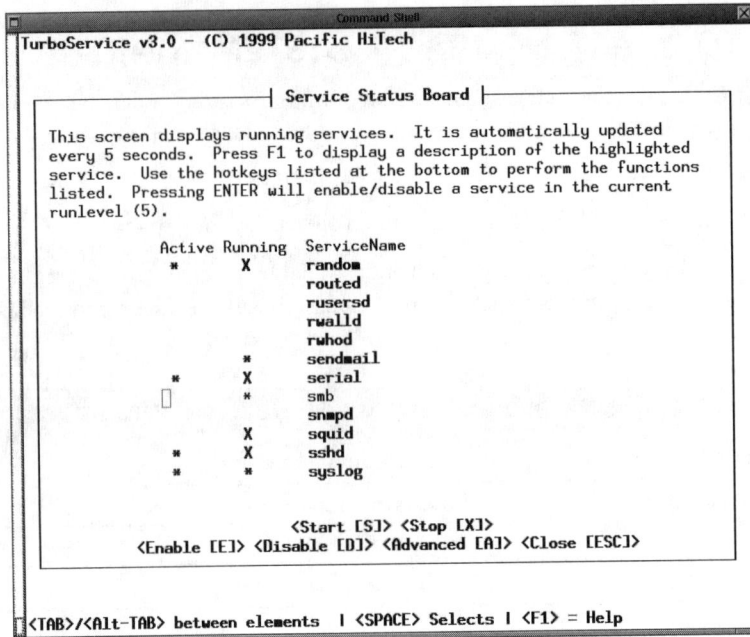

```
┌─                          Command Shell                          ─[X]─┐
│ TurboService v3.0 - (C) 1999 Pacific HiTech                          │
│ ┌──────────────────┤ Service Status Board ├──────────────────────┐  │
│ │                                                                  │  │
│ │ This screen displays running services.  It is automatically updated │
│ │ every 5 seconds.  Press F1 to display a description of the highlighted │
│ │ service.  Use the hotkeys listed at the bottom to perform the functions │
│ │ listed.  Pressing ENTER will enable/disable a service in the current │
│ │ runlevel (5).                                                    │  │
│ │                                                                  │  │
│ │          Active Running  ServiceName                             │  │
│ │             *      X     random                                  │  │
│ │                          routed                                  │  │
│ │                          rusersd                                 │  │
│ │                          rwalld                                  │  │
│ │                          rwhod                                   │  │
│ │                    *     sendmail                                │  │
│ │             *      X     serial                                  │  │
│ │          []        *     smb                                     │  │
│ │                          snmpd                                   │  │
│ │                    X     squid                                   │  │
│ │             *      X     sshd                                    │  │
│ │             *      *     syslog                                  │  │
│ │                                                                  │  │
│ │                                                                  │  │
│ │               <Start [S]> <Stop [X]>                             │  │
│ │       <Enable [E]> <Disable [D]> <Advanced [A]> <Close [ESC]>    │  │
│ └──────────────────────────────────────────────────────────────────┘  │
│ <TAB>/<Alt-TAB> between elements  | <SPACE> Selects | <F1> = Help     │
└──────────────────────────────────────────────────────────────────────┘
```

CONFIGURING smbd TO START FROM inetd

You can configure smbd(8) to start from inetd. To do this, edit /etc/inetd.conf using the editor of your choice, and add the following line to it:

```
netbios-ssn  stream tcp  nowait root /usr/sbin/smbd
```

You might like to add the line after the swat entry that already exists in /etc/inetd.conf.

After you have added the line, restart inetd using the following command:

```
killall -HUP inetd
```

Note

Starting smbd(8) from inetd is not the most efficient way of doing things. It is better to start it using run-level scripts.

CONSTRUCTING AN smb.conf FILE

When you install Samba on Linux systems, it places a default smb.conf file into /etc/smb.conf. This default smb.conf file contains many of the parameters you would use and is heavily commented to try to help new users come to grips with Samba. The following shows part of the default smb.conf file installed with Samba:

```
# This is the main Samba configuration file. You should read the
# smb.conf(5) manual page in order to understand the options listed
# here. Samba has a huge number of configurable options (perhaps too
```

```
# many!) most of which are not shown in this example
#
# Any line which starts with a ; (semicolon) or a # (hash)
# is a comment and is ignored. In this example we will use a #
# for commentary and a ; for parts of the config file that you
# may wish to enable
#
# NOTE: Whenever you modify this file you should run the command "testparm"
# to check that you have no basic syntactic errors.
#
#======================= Global Settings =====================================
[global]

# workgroup = NT-Domain-Name or Workgroup-Name
   workgroup = MYGROUP

# server string is the equivalent of the NT Description field
   server string = Samba Server

# This option is important for security. It allows you to restrict
# connections to machines which are on your local network. The
# following example restricts access to two C class networks and
# the "loopback" interface. For more examples of the syntax see
# the smb.conf man page
;   hosts allow = 192.168.1. 192.168.2. 127.
```

Unfortunately, as you can see, the file is simply too confusing for both new users and more experienced users, and I recommend deleting it and starting again. The following section provides a way to do this while keeping a backup in case you ever want to refer to the original smb.conf file.

In what follows, we will construct a basic smb.conf file that will be added to as we go along.

A SIMPLE smb.conf FILE

Save the current smb.conf file before creating a new one. Use the following command to create a backup copy:

```
su -
Password: *******
cp /etc/smb.conf /etc/smb.conf.bkp
cp /dev/null /etc/smb.conf
```

Do the Minimum as Root

The su command enables you to become the root superuser temporarily if you are a member of the wheel group. Rather than logging in as root, use su or sudo for those commands that must be run as root. Issue all other commands as a normal user. Sooner or later everyone makes typing mistakes or runs a program that goes horribly wrong. Not being the root user at this time is the difference between retyping a command and reconstructing your system.

After using su to become root, use the umask command to set the access permissions for newly created files. umask 022 gives root complete access but allows all other users to only read or run the file. umask 077 gives only root access to created files.

Listing 3.1 shows a simple smb.conf file that makes Samba visible to Windows 9x systems and provides access to home directories.

LISTING 3.1 A SIMPLE smb.conf FILE

```
[global]
    workgroup = sambanet
    server string = Samba Server
    guest account = pcguest
    log file = /var/log/samba/log.%m
    password level =

[homes]
    comment = Home Directories
    browseable = no
    writable = yes
```

If you enter the preceding as your smb.conf file (using your favorite editor; for example, vi /etc /smb.conf) and restart Samba (with samba restart), you should be able to see your new Samba server from Windows 9x or Windows NT when you browse the network. You should see a display similar to that shown in Figure 3.4. To see the comment field, click View, and select Details.

Note

To browse the network, you might need to use one of the Plain Password registry hacks provided with Samba. This will be the case for some versions of Windows 95, for Windows 98, for Windows NT SP3 and above, and for Windows 2000. An alternative is to use encrypted password support with Samba.

Figure 3.4
Browsing the network for your new Samba server.

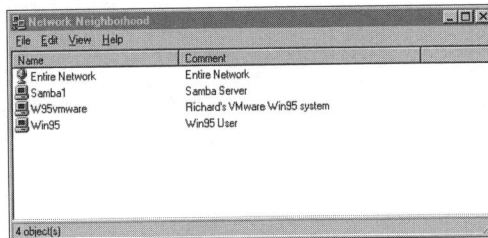

If you double-click on your Samba server, you should be able to see the shares that it supports. However, first-time Samba users might experience several problems. See the sections on common problems in Chapters 12–16. When everything is working, you should see a window similar to that shown in Figure 3.5.

You can check to see whether Samba is running with the following command:

```
ps ax | grep mbd
 9821 ?        S       0:00 smbd -D
 9829 ?        S       0:00 nmbd -D
 9831 ?        S       0:00 nmbd -D
 9836 ?        S       0:08 smbd -D
10164 ttyp2    S       0:00 grep mbd
```

Figure 3.5
Browsing your
server will
show you the
shares it
serves.

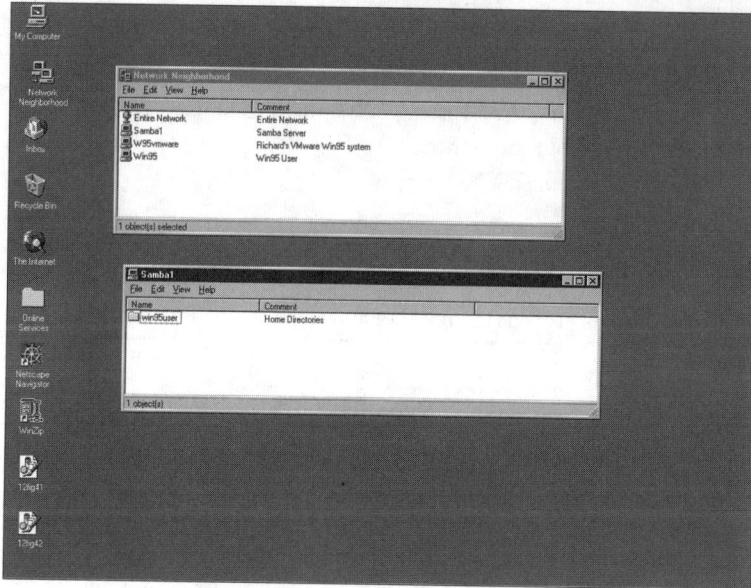

If you don't see at least one smbd(8) and one nmbd(8), Samba is not functioning correctly.
You should see Chapter 23, "Troubleshooting Samba," for more details on resolving
problems with Samba.

We discuss the structure of the smb.conf file in more detail in Chapter 5, "Configuring and
Managing Samba."

CHECKING WHO IS ACCESSING YOUR SAMBA SERVER

When you have Samba running correctly, you can check who is accessing Samba on your
server with the smbstatus command:

```
smbstatus

Samba version 2.0.6
Service     uid       gid       pid     machine
---------------------------------------------
rsharpe     rsharpe   rsharpe   9836    w95vmware (10.0.0.101)
  ➥Fri Mar 10 23:52:50 2000

Locked files:
Pid   DenyMode      R/W     Oplock       Name
---------------------------------------------------
9836  DENY_NONE    RDWR     NONE        /home/rsharpe/319003r.doc
                                         ➥Sat Mar 11 00:57:35 2000
9836  DENY_NONE    RDWR     NONE        /home/rsharpe/319005ar.doc
                                         ➥Sat Mar 11 00:05:39 2000

Share mode memory usage (bytes):
    1048256(99%) free + 232(0%) used + 88 (0%) overhead = 1048576(100%) total
```

The preceding code shows that the user rsharpe is accessing the service/share called rsharpe from a client that has a NetBIOS name of w95vmware.

Look in the files `log.nmb` (see Listing 3.2) and `log.smb` (see Listing 3.3) to ensure that the daemons started without any errors.

LISTING 3.2 `log.nmb` **AFTER SAMBA SUCCESSFULLY STARTS**

```
[1999/10/06 01:00:45, 1] nmbd/nmbd.c:main(684)
Netbios nameserver version 2.0.5a started.
Copyright Andrew Tridgell 1994-1998
```

LISTING 3.3 `log.smb` **AFTER SAMBA SUCCESSFULLY STARTS**

```
[1999/10/06 01:00:45, 1] smbd/server.c:main(628)
 smbd version 2.0.5a started.
 Copyright Andrew Tridgell 1992-1998
```

A common mistake is starting Samba a second time when the Samba daemons are already running. When this happens, the message shown in Listing 3.4 appears, marking the end of the attempt to start a second set of daemons.

LISTING 3.4 `log.smb` **RECORDS AN ERROR AFTER STARTING SAMBA WHEN IT IS ALREADY RUNNING**

```
[1999/10/06 01:00:45, 0] lib/pidfile.c:pidfile_create(86)
  ERROR: smbd is already running. File /usr/local/samba/var/locks/smbd.pid
         exists and process id 1165 is running.
```

FROM HERE...

In Chapter 7, "Printer Sharing Under Samba," we examine how to make the correct printer drivers automatically install on a client computer.

## CHAPTER 4

An Introduction to the SMB Protocol

In this chapter

by Richard Sharpe

Although it might not be generally known, anyone who uses Samba or the Microsoft Windows Networking protocols is using the SMB protocol. This protocol has been around in one form or another since 1984, and has been used in many different products and packages.

To understand some of the things that Samba does, you need to understand some aspects of the SMB protocol. In this chapter, we introduce you to the SMB protocol. The following sections present

- A simplified history of the SMB protocol.
- A discussion of where the SMB protocol fits from the perspective of the OSI model and the TCP/IP model as well as some common uses of the SMB protocol and the protocols that go around it.
- An explanation of NetBIOS. Is it an API, a protocol, or both?
- An overview of the SMB protocol, with displays of packet exchanges for important parts of the protocol.
- A list of further resources on the SMB protocol.

In subsequent chapters we will introduce more details of the SMB protocol as the need arises. We will illustrate them with displays of packet exchanges as appropriate.

HISTORY OF THE SMB PROTOCOL

The SMB protocol was designed by Dr. Barry Feigenbaum of IBM sometime in 1984. The earliest documentation on the SMB protocol that I am aware of is the IBM PC Network Technical Reference No. 6322916 First Edition. Because of its origins in the PC environment, and the existence of the NetBIOS API, the SMB protocol used NetBIOS from its inception.

The first product in which the SMB protocol was used was IBM's PC Network Program, which was developed in 1984. This product did not ship until 1985 because it was held up by DOS 3.1. By about 1986, IBM was working on its PC LAN Program and PCnet products and Microsoft was working on the MSnet series of products for DOS. In the same time frame, 3Com released its 3Com 3+Share products for PCs running DOS. In 1987, the NetBIOS over TCP/IP specifications were released in the form of RFC1001 and RFC1002. By 1990, versions of the SMB protocol for LAN Manager and LAN Server had been developed that contained more functionality than the original versions of the protocol.

In 1996, moved by Sun Microsystem's proposal of WebNFS as an Internet standard, Microsoft developed the Common Internet File System (CIFS) standard, which was little more than a document describing the SMB protocol as it had been implemented at that time.

The SMB protocol was extended on several occasions when vendors needed newer functionality. For example, when file servers were first implemented on DOS machines, there was little need for per-user protection on files, and as a result users did not authenticate to those early servers. However, when the SMB protocol was implemented on multiuser systems, methods were needed to allow clients to authenticate with a username and password. To accommodate these needs, the protocol was often extended.

> **Note**
>
> In what follows, the term *SMB* will be used to refer both to the protocol and the packets that are exchanged under the protocol. The context should make it clear what is being referred to.

WHERE DOES SMB FIT IN THE SCHEME OF THINGS?

As shown in Figure 4.1, the SMB Protocol is an Application layer protocol. It has been implemented over at least the following protocols:

- IPX—This implementation was done by Microsoft and allows clients to access SMB servers via Novell's IPX protocol. It uses NetBIOS over IPX. Please refer to the sidebar for more information on this combination.

- NetBEUI sometimes known as NetBIOS Frame Format, or NBF—This was developed by IBM and Microsoft and is used in LAN environments only. Because NetBEUI does not have network layer addresses, it cannot be routed; NetBEUI can only be bridged. NetBEUI is an implementation of NetBIOS over LLC (802.2).

- DECnet—This was developed by Digital for communication between PC clients and VAXen running DECnet.

- TCP/IP—This is the RFC standard NetBIOS over TCP/IP, often referred to as NetBT or NBT. NBT implements NetBIOS session services over TCP and NetBIOS datagram services over UDP.

IPX can be implemented over several variants of both Ethernet and Token Ring.

Over Ethernet, it can be implemented as Ethernet VII (with a type field of 0x8137, indicating that the payload is IPX); raw 802.3 (that is, with the first two bytes of the data field containing 0xFFFF—in other words, a DSAP and SSAP of all ones); 802.2 LLC with a DSAP, SSAP pair of 0x0,0x0; or as Ethernet SNAP, with a type field of 0x8137 in the SNAP header, indicating IPX.

Over Token Ring, IPX can be carried in LLC frames, with a DSAP, SSAP pair of 0xE0, 0xE0, or over LLC/SNAP with a type field of 0x8137.

Figure 4.1 tries to show how SMB has been implemented over other protocols in terms of the OSI model and the TCP/IP model; however, it is at best a conceptual view. NetBEUI, for example, is not a Network protocol, but SMB can be carried over NetBEUI.

In many respects, the NetBIOS layer, especially for NBT, performs no function, and Microsoft has made it possible to eliminate the NetBIOS layer in Windows 2000.

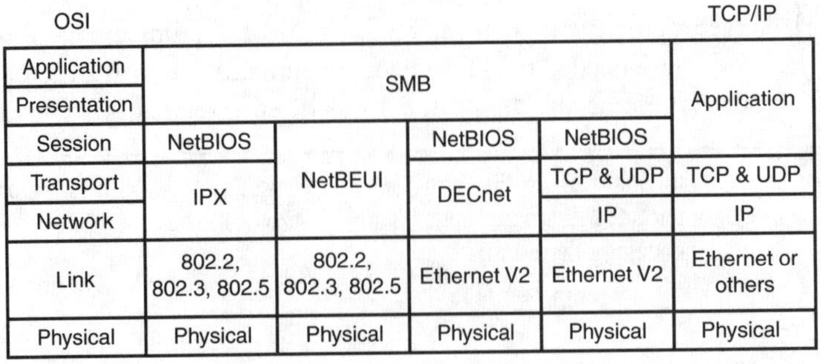

Figure 4.1
The SMB Protocol is an Application layer protocol that has been implemented over many other protocols.

OSI						TCP/IP
Application	SMB					Application
Presentation						
Session	NetBIOS			NetBIOS	NetBIOS	
Transport	IPX	NetBEUI	DECnet	TCP & UDP	TCP & UDP	
Network					IP	IP
Link	802.2, 802.3, 802.5	802.2, 802.3, 802.5	Ethernet V2	Ethernet V2	Ethernet V2	Ethernet or others
Physical	Physical	Physical	Physical	Physical	Physical	Physical

Whereas the SMB protocol has been implemented over so many protocols, Samba only implements SMB over TCP/IP, mainly for historical reasons. Because TCP/IP is the dominant protocol in use today, little effort has been put into extending Samba to use other protocols to carry SMB traffic, and the structure of Samba makes it troublesome to do so.

Because Samba implements the SMB protocol over TCP/IP, Samba must also implement NetBIOS over TCP/IP. We look briefly at this topic in the next section.

SAMBA AND NETBIOS

NetBIOS was developed by Sytek for IBM. It was originally an API designed to extend the PC BIOS and provided at least three sets of services:

- Name services—A means to allow computers to find each other by name. Under NetBIOS over TCP, name service requests are sent in UDP datagrams to port 137. Responses come from port 137.

- Session services—A means to allow computers to connect to each other and send streams of data to each other, for example, to read and write a file. Under NetBIOS over TCP, session service data is carried in TCP segments. Clients place connections to SMB servers on port 139. There is also a NetBIOS session establishment protocol that results in a 4-byte header for each SMB carried to and from the server.

- Datagram services—A means to send small amounts of data such as server announcements between clients and servers. Under NetBIOS over TCP, datagram service data is carried in UDP datagrams to and from port 138.

NETBIOS NAME SERVICES

Under NetBIOS, each system has one or more NetBIOS names. Samba can certainly have more than one NetBIOS name. A NetBIOS name service (NBNS) is used to manage NetBIOS names and IP addresses so servers can be accessed at the IP layer. Samba provides an NBNS function.

Samba provides WINS as well as an NBNS. WINS, or Windows Internet Name Service, allows name translations to work across subnets because it uses unicast datagrams rather than broadcast datagrams.

In addition, Windows hosts can use the nbhosts file to translate NetBIOS names. This is discussed further in Chapter 12, "Accessing Samba from Windows for Workgroups and Windows 9x," and Chapter 13, "Accessing Samba from Windows NT."

The NBNS allows nodes to register their NetBIOS names and to look up the translation from NetBIOS name to IP address. Before a connection is placed to a server, for example, as a result of a user performing a Map Network Drive function, the client would use the NBNS to retrieve the IP address of the selected server. Figure 4.2 provides an example of a user mapping a network drive. In this case, the client will request a translation of the NetBIOS name SAMBA1 to an IP address.

Figure 4.2
Mapping a network drive causes the client to translate the server's NetBIOS name to an IP address.

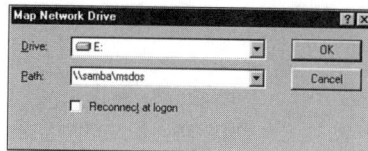

The different classes of NetBIOS names are

- Unique names—A unique name can have only one IP address associated with it. If a system attempts to register a name that is already registered, it gets an error response.

- Group names—A group name can have many IP addresses associated with it. When a system registers a group name, its IP address is added to the list of IP addresses maintained for that name. When a node translates a group name, the whole list of IP addresses associated with that name is returned.

- Internet group—These names are used in Windows NT to manage domains.

- Multihomed—These names are unique names where the system owning the name has multiple interfaces. Each of the IP addresses for the multihomed host is associated with the one name.

- Domain—These names are new to Windows NT 4.0 and are associated with NT domains.

As shown in Figure 4.3, NetBIOS names are 16 characters in length, with the last character indicating the type of name being used.

Figure 4.3
NetBIOS names are 16 characters in length, with the last character indicating the type of name.

NetBIOS Name Format

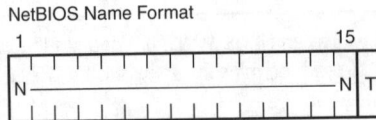

NetBIOS names are always converted to uppercase when sent to other systems, and can contain any characters except for the following:

- Any character less than a space, or 0x20 (that is, the control characters)
- " . / \ [ ] : | < > + = ; ,

NetBIOS names are padded to 15 characters with spaces, and the type character, or NetBIOS Suffix (as referred to in Microsoft literature) is placed in the 16th character position.

Some values for the NetBIOS suffix that we will be interested in are shown in Table 4.1. A more complete list can be found in Microsoft Knowledgebase article Q163409. NetBIOS name suffixes are also discussed in Chapter 17, "Samba and Browsing," and Chapter 19, "Samba and Windows NT Domains."

TABLE 4.1 SOME NETBIOS SUFFIXES USED IN WINDOWS NETWORKS

Suffix (0x)	Class	Meaning
00	Unique	Workstation name. Also known as the Workstation service by Microsoft.
00	Group	Domain/workgroup name. Registered by all members of the domain or workgroup.
03	Unique	Messenger name. Also known as the Messenger service by Microsoft.
20	Unique	Server name. Also known as the Server service by Microsoft.

SMB PROTOCOL OVERVIEW

The SMB Protocol is a client server protocol that allows clients to request access to resources on a server. A *client* is simply any system that requests resources from another system. The client sends requests and the server sends back responses. An example of this appears in Figure 4.4.

Figure 4.4
A client makes requests of a server and gets responses back.

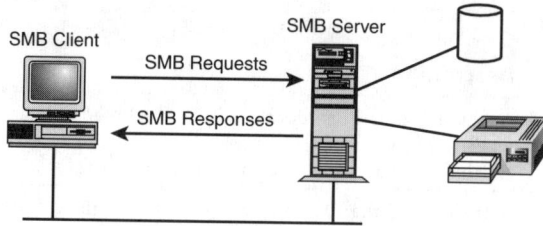

Clients access file and printer shares on servers. These shares are specified in the form of

`\\server\share`

where *server* is the NetBIOS name of the server the share is located on, and *share* is the name of the share.

An SMB is simply a block of data in a specific format sent on a TCP connection. As shown in Figure 4.5, an SMB has a header and possibly some data associated with it. The header has a fixed portion and a variable portion.

Figure 4.5
An SMB contains up to three sections: a fixed header portion, a variable header portion, and possibly a data portion.

SMB Format

Fixed header (33 bytes)	Variable header	Data (might not be present)

PART

I

CH

4

The fields in the SMB fixed header are listed in Table 4.2.

TABLE 4.2   THE FIELDS IN AN SMB HEADER

Field	Description
0xFFSMB	This is a literal that marks the beginning of the SMB.
Command	A one-byte field indicating the type of SMB being sent.
Error Class	A one-byte field indicating the error class in a response.
Error Code	A two-byte field indicating the type of error in a response.

TABLE 4.2   CONTINUED

Field	Description
Flags	An eight-bit field that contains in its top bit an indication of whether this SMB is a request or a response. The other bits are used to indicate capabilities that the client and server support.
Flags2	A 16-bit field that contains more flags that indicate capabilities supported by the client and server.
Reserved	A 12-byte field that is reserved.
Tree ID	A two-byte field that specifies the tree on the server to which this command or response relates.
Process ID	A 16-bit field that clients put in the SMB that can be used to indicate the process ID of the process sending the SMB.
User ID	A 16-bit field that indicates the validated User ID after a SessionSetup&X has been performed. The server generates this, and the client is responsible for using the correct value on subsequent requests.
Multiplex IS	A 16-bit field that clients use when they want to send multiple SMBs. This field allows the responses to be matched with the requests.

The variable portion of each SMB is determined by the SMB command and can contain usernames, passwords, and files to be accessed. Each command has a different format. There are some 78 SMB commands, but several of them have subcommands. In total, there are more than 100 different SMB commands and subcommands.

In addition to the simple case where one SMB request is sent from the client to the server and a single SMB is expected in reply, the SMB protocol allows multiple commands to be sent at a time. This is designed to reduce the round-trip times associated with sending multiple SMB requests.

Sending multiple requests at a time is accomplished with andX SMBs, and only some SMB commands can contain chained andX commands in them. Figure 4.6 shows what an SMB with an andX command would look like. It is possible to have many commands chained together; however, implementations rarely use more than two at a time.

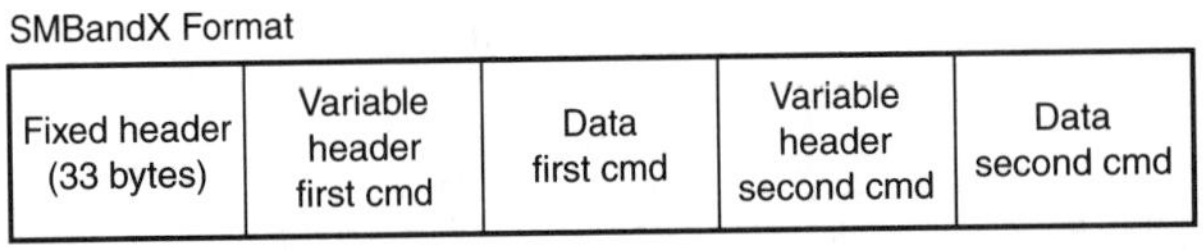

Figure 4.6
Multiple SMB
commands can
be sent to a
server at one
time as
SMBandX
commands.

SMBandX Format

Fixed header (33 bytes)	Variable header first cmd	Data first cmd	Variable header second cmd	Data second cmd

In the rest of this section we will follow along the packets exchanged as a client requests access to a resource and uses that resource. As shown in Figure 4.2, our client is attempting to access \\samba1\public.

Note

All packet traces were captured with Ethereal, an Open Source Software packet capture and decode utility. It is available at www.zing.org. In addition, all packets that are not essential to the discussion, such as acknowledgments, have been edited out of the captures.

Tip from
Richard Sharpe

Ethereal is a very powerful tool for debugging networking problems in general and Samba-related problems in particular. This is because Ethereal enables you to see the detail inside packets and understands much of the SMB protocol.

For example, you can use it to get a packet trace when Windows Networking is not working for you and to see exactly what went wrong. The error codes returned by a server are very helpful.

Before a connection can be made to SAMBA1, a NetBIOS name query is issued by the client (WIN95). This is shown in Figure 4.7 in frames one and two. The client WIN95 issues a name query in frame 1 looking for the name SAMBA1. The name query is sent to the WINS server because WIN95 is configured to use WINS. The middle pane in Figure 4.7 shows the name that was queried by WIN95. Frame 2 contains the response from the WINS server.

PART

I

CH

4

Figure 4.7
The client sends a Net-BIOS name query and gets a response.

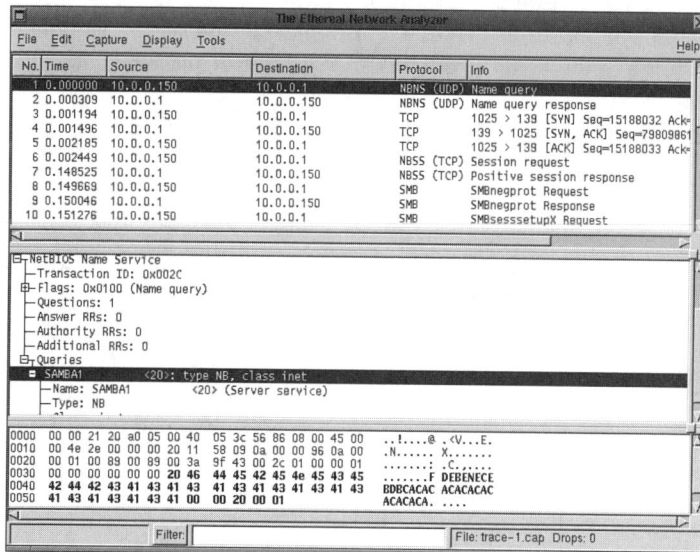

After WIN95 has the IP address of SAMBA1, it then establishes a TCP connection to SAMBA1. This is shown in Figure 4.8 in frames three, four, and five. These comprise the three-way handshake where a TCP connection is set up. Refer to a good reference text on TCP/IP if you need a better understanding of TCP/IP. One useful reference is *TCP/IP Illustrated, Volume 1*, ISBN 0-201-63346-9, by Richard Stevens.

Figure 4.8
The client establishes a TCP/IP connection.

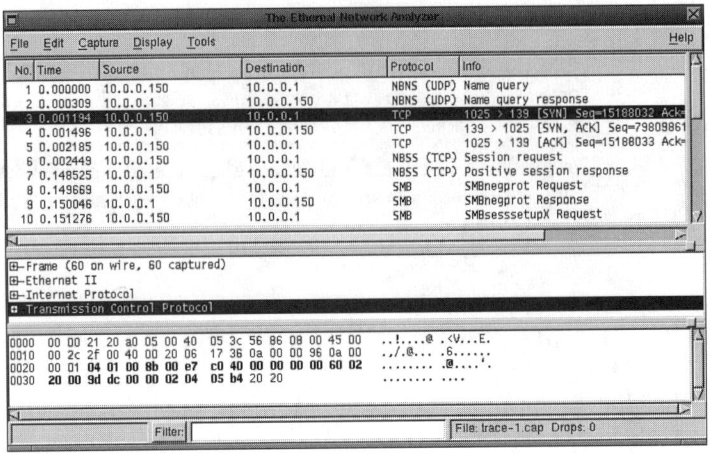

After the TCP connection is established, the client establishes a NetBIOS session with the server. This is shown in Figure 4.9 in frames six and seven. The middle pane in Figure 4.9 shows some of the fields in the NetBIOS session request message. Two fields of importance are

1. The Called Name—The NetBIOS name of the entity to which the session request is directed.

2. The Calling Name—The NetBIOS name of the entity that is making the request.

When a client accesses a share such as \\SAMBA1\PUBLIC, it places the name SAMBA1 in the Called Name field of the NetBIOS session request message.

Note

Windows servers require that the called name be the NetBIOS name of the server being connected to, except that Windows NT 4.0 and beyond also accept session requests for the called name *SMBSERVER. If you connect to a Windows server with the incorrect Called Name, you will get the infamous "Called name not present" error message.

Samba does not check the contents of the called name, so a Samba server can have multiple personalities and can maintain NetBIOS aliases. The actual NetBIOS name used in the NetBIOS session request is available, however. As we will see in Chapter 9, "Samba Automation," Samba uses the called NetBIOS name to implement virtual servers.

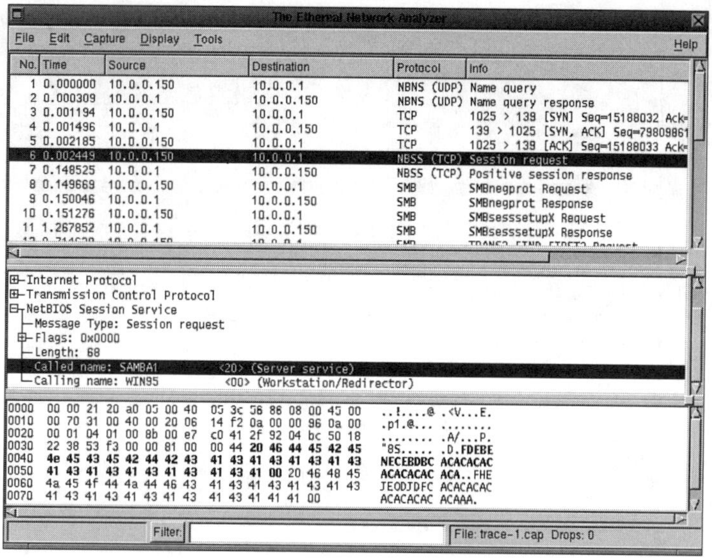

Figure 4.9.
The client establishes a NetBIOS session.

After the NetBIOS session is established, the SMB client and server can exchange SMBs, which means that the client can make requests for access to resources, and the server will respond appropriately.

The next step that the client takes is to negotiate a compatible SMB protocol variant with the server. From the beginning, the SMB protocol has allowed for protocol variants. These protocol variants allowed for changes in the protocol over time. We will look at some of those changes in a short while.

Figure 4.10 shows the client negotiating a protocol with the server. The client sends a Negotiate Protocol (negprot) request SMB containing a list of the protocols it understands to the server. If the server implements any of them, it chooses the best one and sends back a negprot response to the client specifying the protocol it has selected and, depending on the protocol variant selected, some other information for the client. These are shown in frames eight and nine in Figure 4.10. The middle pane shows some of the protocol variants that the client has supplied.

The server might choose from several SMB protocol variants. Some of those are listed in Table 4.3.

PART

I

CH

4

Figure 4.10
The client ne-
gotiates a pro-
tocol with the
server.

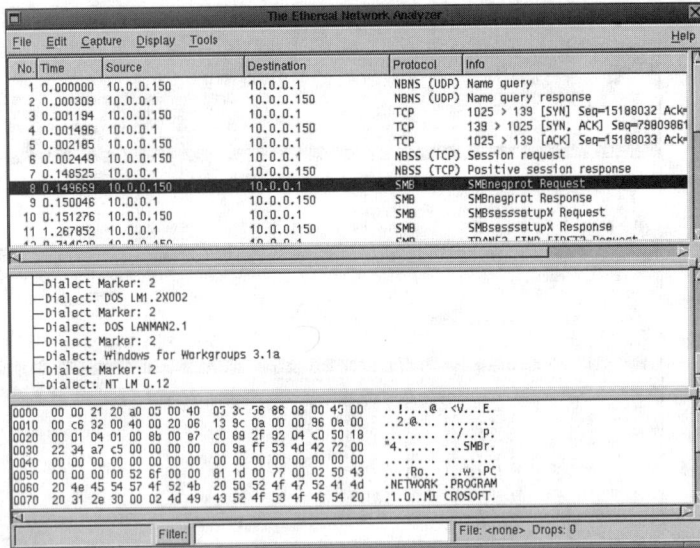

TABLE 4.3 SOME OF THE SMB PROTOCOL VARIANTS THAT HAVE BEEN DEVELOPED OVER TIME

Protocol	Description
PC Network Protocol	The original SMB Protocol as developed by IBM
LANMAN 1.0	The LAN Manager 1.0 protocol developed by Microsoft
Windows for Workgroups 3.1a	The variant developed for Windows for Workgroups
NT LM 0.12	The variant developed for Windows NT

The next step that the client takes is to authenticate to the server, or to log on. The client sends a Session Setup (sesssetupandX) SMB request. Among other things, this request contains the username and password that the client wants to use to authenticate with the server. If the server can validate the client's username and password, a response is sent back to that effect. This is shown in Figure 4.11 in frames 10 and 11. The middle pane shows the username and password sent by the client. As you can see, the password is sent as plain text in this example. The SMB protocol has the capability to send encrypted (or more accurately, hashed) passwords as well.

After the client has authenticated, it can start accessing resources on the server that it has access to, such as file and print shares. In fact, the client accomplishes two steps at this point. In Figure 4.11 you can see that the client has sent a sesssetupandX SMB request. This is one SMB that has a second request chained to it. In this case, the second request is a Tree Connect SMB (actually, it is a tconX request with no further requests), which requests access to the \\SAMBA1\PUBLIC share.

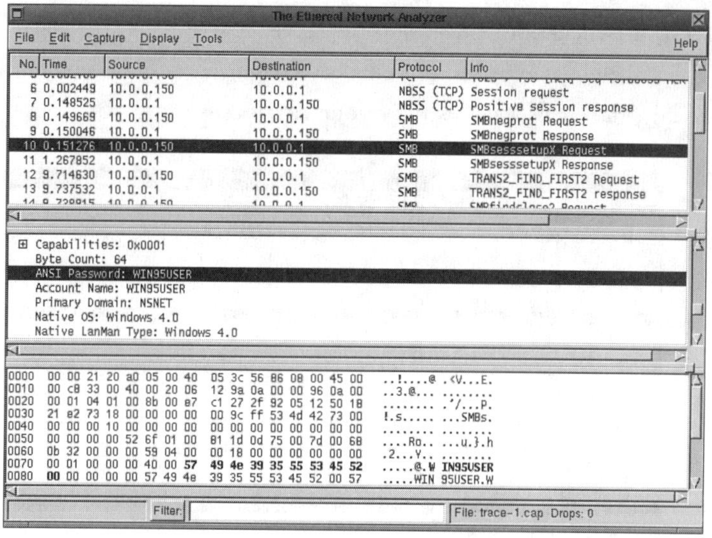

Figure 4.11
The client authenticates with the server.

The response in frame 11 indicates that the client is authenticated and gives the client access to the \\SAMBA1\PUBLIC share. At this point, the client is connected to the share.

The very first servers did not have a concept of users, so they made no provisions for user authentication. Shares were protected with a password, and when you knew the appropriate password, everything on the share was accessible. So, the original protocol variants did not have any authentication messages. They did not send Session Setup requests; they simply sent Tree Connect requests.

One of the reasons for the Negotiate Protocol step is to select a protocol that has authentication steps. The next step is for the client to request the resources it wants access to. Figure 4.12 shows the client sending an Open File (openandX) SMB request to the server to open a file. If the authenticated user is allowed to access the file in the manner requested, the request is granted and a file ID (FID) is returned for future access to the file. These requests are shown in frames 22 and 23 in Figure 4.12.

After the client has opened a file, the next steps are to read and write the file as needed and to close the file when the client is finished with the file.

In summary then, the following steps are involved in accessing a share on a server with the SMB protocol:

1. The client requests access to *server**share*.
2. The client translates the name *server* into an IP address.
3. The client establishes a TCP connection to the server on port 139.
4. When connected, the client establishes a NetBIOS session using <server> (in uppercase) as the called name.
5. When the NetBIOS session is established, the client negotiates a protocol.

PART

I

CH

4

6. Next, the client authenticates to the server.

7. Then, the client accesses, or connects to, the share that it is interested in.

8. Finally, the client accesses the resources it needs access to.

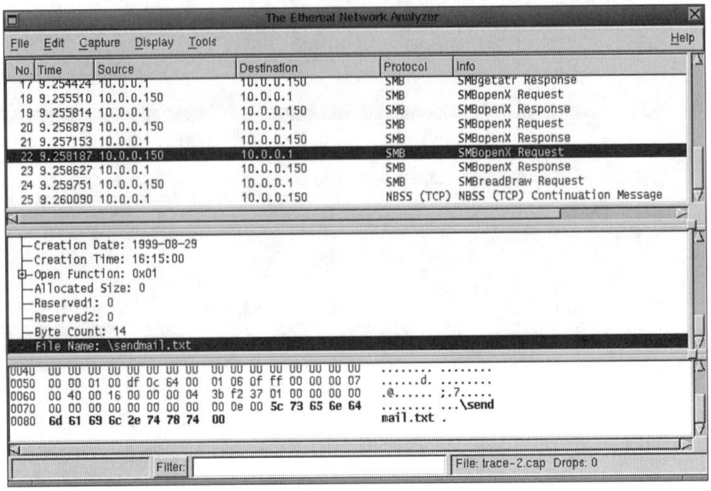

Figure 4.12
The client sends a request to open a file.

Things can go wrong in each of these steps. For example, name translation might fail or the server might be unreachable. To troubleshoot failures between SMB clients and servers, you must understand the steps performed.

One of the biggest challenges in debugging problems with Microsoft Windows networking and Samba is that SMB clients often provide cryptic error messages that do not give a good idea of which of the preceding steps have failed. Figure 4.13 shows an error message that is the result of a permissions problem on a Samba server. The cause of the error can be most obscure until you go digging in the source code. Windows NT also returns some equally obscure error results.

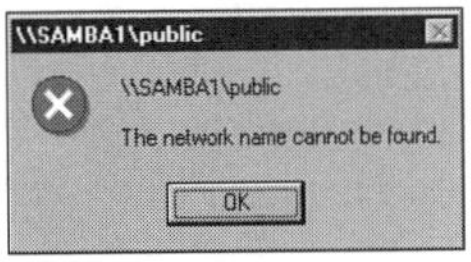

Figure 4.13
Windows can produce some obscure error messages. This one resulted from a protection problem on the Samba server.

In addition to this overview, subsequent chapters will build on this understanding of the basics of the SMB protocol.

Finally, if you look at frames 18 through 23 in Figure 4.14, you will see that the client sent an OpenX Request SMB to the server three times and received three replies. This is because on the first two attempts, the client chose access modes that were incompatible with the properties of the file that was being opened. Because this trace and Ethereal are on the CD-ROM that accompanies this book, you can explore the actual modes used yourself.

Figure 4.14
The client (Windows 95) actually sent three openX requests before it finally could get the file opened.

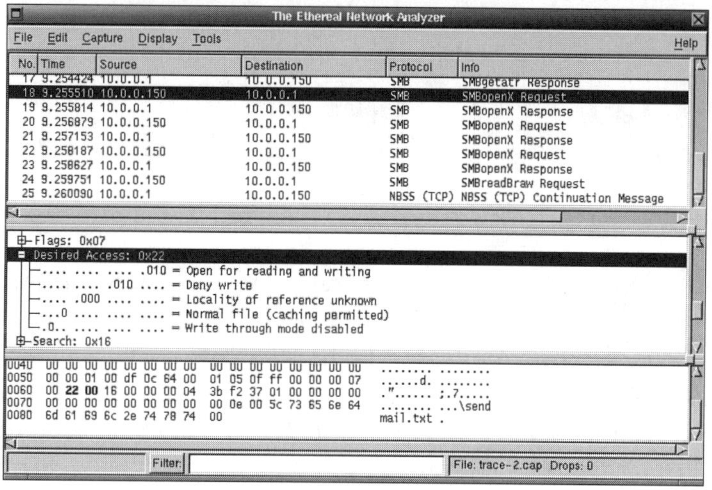

EXTENSIONS TO THE SMB PROTOCOL

The original SMB protocol was relatively simple and contained little more than these elements outlined previously. However, over time, Microsoft and others have found they needed to extend the SMB protocol to provide more functionality. All the advanced functions of Microsoft Windows Networking are implemented using SMB requests and responses. These include the following:

- The Browsing protocol, which uses mailslots, a unidirectional data transfer mechanism that is implemented using the SMB Transact requests.

- The Lan Manager Remote Administration Protocol, which allows API requests to be sent over the wire in an almost Remote Procedure Call fashion.

- The MS Remote Procedure Call protocol, which is an implementation of DCE/RPC over SMB. RPCs are packaged as SMB write and writeX requests and sent between the client and server.

Samba implements the important aspects of each of the preceding, which allows Samba to participate in browsing, as well as to join Windows NT domains. In addition, versions of Samba, such as Samba 2.0.4 and above, as well as Samba TNG, can function as primary domain controllers.

PART

I

CH

4

SMB PROTOCOL ERROR HANDLING

The SMB protocol has a reasonably structured approach to handling errors, but sometimes Windows (NT and 9x) does weird things with the returned errors.

Each response has an error field, with an error value of 0 indicating success. When the server determines that it cannot service a request made by the client, it returns an error from one of four classes of errors:

Error Class	Explanation
ERRDOS	DOS-style errors, such as file not found, no access, and so on.
ERRSRV	Server errors, such as bad password, invalid device, and so on.
ERRHRD	Hardware-style errors, such as not ready, write fault, and so on.
NT ERRORS	NT Error responses.

The client is responsible for translating the returned error into something to display to the client. The error message shown in Figure 4.13 is a result of the server returning an ERRSRV, invalid network name message (because the directory for the service was not accessible to the user the client logged in as).

FURTHER RESOURCES

Further material on the SMB protocol is available at the following locations:

`http://samba.anu.edu.au/cifs/docs/what-is-smb.html`

contains an overview of the SMB protocol.

`ftp://ftp.microsoft.com/developr/drg/CIFS/`

contains several SMB protocol documents as well as the CIFS draft specs.

`http://ourworld.compuserve.com/homepages/timothydevans/contents.htm`

contains information on NetBIOS and NetBEUI.

From Here...

You have now finished the first section of this book. You can read the following chapters to find out more about Samba:

- Chapter 5, "Configuring and Managing Samba," for help with configuring and managing Samba
- Chapter 6, "File Sharing Under Samba," for help with sharing files
- Chapter 7, "Printer Sharing Under Samba," for help with sharing printers

Part

I

Ch

4

CONFIGURING SAMBA

CHAPTER **5**

CONFIGURING AND MANAGING SAMBA

In this chapter

by Richard Sharpe

Samba can perform many functions, including the following:

- Provide file and print services
- Act as a logon server
- Function as a primary domain controller (PDC)
- Operate as a browse server or as a domain master browser

In addition, Samba gives you complete control over many of the things it does. For example, you can control who owns newly created files and what their permissions are set to. You can also run commands on the server every time a client connects to a particular share, or when a client disconnects from a particular share.

Many users will find their initial interest in Samba in its file and print serving capabilities. However, they will soon find themselves wanting to know more about how to manage Samba and how to get Samba to do more complex things.

In this chapter, you will learn how Samba is managed. First, we will look at the Samba security model and discuss how authentication is managed. Then, we will look at the following topics:

- How Samba is structured in terms of the processes that handle client requests, and so forth
- How the smb.conf file is structured and what each section does
- The log files created by Samba and how to use them for troubleshooting
- The GUI-based configuration tools available for Samba to make configuration easier

SECURITY MODELS

SMB servers such as Samba exist to share files between clients. How is access to those files controlled? We will answer this question after reviewing the way in which SMB clients connect to SMB servers.

When a client requests a connection to a share, it goes through the set of steps shown in Figure 5.1, as discussed in Chapter 4, "An Introduction to the SMB Protocol," in the "SMB Protocol Overview" section.

> **Note**
>
> Step 5 must be performed only if the server is in user-level security.

The very first SMB servers (like the IBM PC Network Program) had no concept of users because they were simply DOS 3.1 PCs running an SMB server. When a client was given access to a share, it could access any files on that share. However, subsequent servers, like LAN Manager and UNIX, did have a concept of users, so programmers had to find a way to allow clients to authenticate. They also had to find a way to allow a server to indicate that it wanted clients to authenticate. They achieved this by creating a new variant of the SMB protocol that supplied extra information in the response to a NEGPROT SMB request.

Samba is very security conscious. That is, all file accesses that Samba performs for a client are made in the context of a valid user of the server. This user determines which file accesses are allowed. You have control over which user is used to perform file accesses.

Figure 5.1
Accessing a
Samba server.

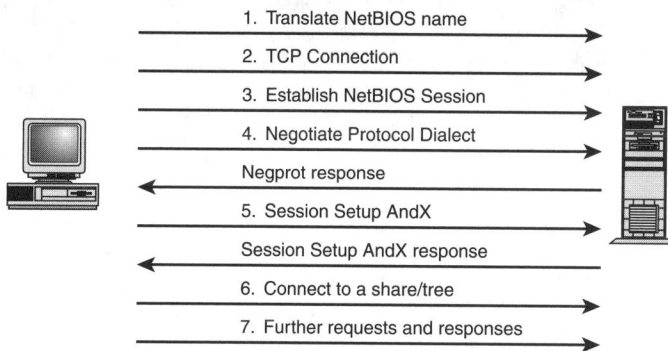

1. Translate NetBIOS name
2. TCP Connection
3. Establish NetBIOS Session
4. Negotiate Protocol Dialect
   Negprot response
5. Session Setup AndX
   Session Setup AndX response
6. Connect to a share/tree
7. Further requests and responses

Because of this history, there are two modes, or *security levels*, that a Samba server (and other SMB servers, like Win 9x) can be in:

- Share Level security—In this level, users do not have to authenticate with the server; however, they might need a per-share password before connecting to each share. Samba still requires a valid user (and possibly password) to perform file accesses. One way to handle this is by specifying a *guest account*.

- User Level security—In this level, the client must supply user information before it can access any shares. The client usually supplies this from the username and password used when logging on to Windows.

Figure 5.2 shows a Windows 95 system being set into Share Level security mode for sharing files and printers.

Figure 5.2
Win95 can op-
erate in either
Share level or
User level.

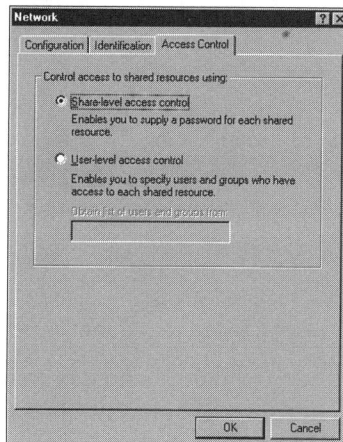

PART

II

CH

5

Note

The default security mode in which Samba operates changed when version 2.0.0 came out. Under versions prior to 2.0.0 (for example, 1.9.18p10), the default security mode in Samba was Share level security. However, for versions 2.0.0 and beyond, the default is User level.

This has become the largest source of problems for first-time Samba users because most recent Linux distributions are shipping with Samba 2.0.3 or better, and User level security requires that connecting clients submit a valid username and password when connecting to the server. In many cases people use different usernames on their Windows client to their Linux server. Windows 95 displays the dialog box shown in Figure 5.3 under these circumstances. Under earlier versions of Samba, it was possible to use a guest account.

Note

If you have checked the `smb.conf` manual pages (`man smb.conf`), you will have noticed that there are two other security modes that Samba can be in, `security = server` and `security = domain`.

Both of these modes are enhancements to user-level security and involve a Samba server using another SMB server to perform authentication. These modes are discussed in more detail in Chapter 8, "Samba and Password Management," as well as Chapter 19, "Samba and Windows NT Domains."

Figure 5.3
First-time
Samba users
often see this
password
dialog box.

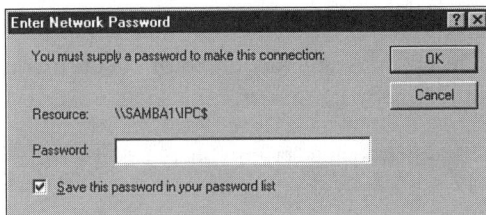

THE STRUCTURE OF SAMBA

As discussed in Chapter 3, "An Introduction to Using Samba," Samba consists of the two main components, nmbd and smbd, along with several subsidiary components for performing other tasks, such as smbclient, nmblookup, and smbstatus. The structure of Samba and its daemons is shown in Figure 5.4.

THE `smb.conf` FILE

Samba is controlled by the `smb.conf` file. Most current distributions of Linux install versions of Samba that place this file in `/etc`. However, the version of Samba that ships with Caldera OpenLinux places the `smb.conf` file in `/etc/samba.d`.

Figure 5.4
The structure
of Samba.

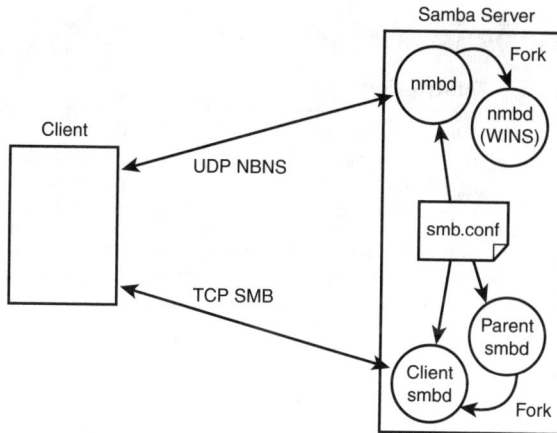

The smb.conf file consists of a series of sections, each containing a series of parameters that control the way Samba behaves. Except for the three special sections, global, homes, and printers (see Table 5.1), a section describes a single shared resource, which we will refer to as a *share*. Clients connect to shares and then access files within those shares.

Sections are marked with section names, which are simply names enclosed in square brackets. For example, the following marks the beginning of the homes section:

[homes]

The global section does not need to be marked with [global], but it is a good idea to get into the habit of doing so.

Parameters take the form of

name = value

where:

- ■ *name* is the name of the parameter, which can contain spaces. For example, os level is a valid parameter name.

> **Note**
>
> Samba ignores spaces in parameter names. Thus, oslevel is the same as os level, which is the same as osl evel. It is wise, however, to stick to the correct form of a parameter name (os level in this case).

- ■ *value* is the value assigned to the parameter and might be a string; a number; a name like True, False, Yes, No; a regular expression; and so on.

Table 5.1 details the sections that can occur in the smb.conf file.

TABLE 5.1 SECTIONS IN THE smb.conf FILE

Section	Description
[global]	This section is one of the three special sections and contains parameters that control the overall behavior of Samba. Examples include the security and netbios name parameters. The global section is the only section that does not specify a share.
[homes]	This is the second of the special sections. It is a compact way of specifying that the home directories for users on the Samba server are to be shared. It potentially specifies multiple shares.
[printers]	This is the third special section. It is a compact way of specifying that all the printers on the Samba server should be shared. It potentially specifies multiple shares.
[share name]	All other sections in the smb.conf file specify a single share of that name. Share names can include macros. For more information on this, please refer to the section titled "Extended Substitutions" in Chapter 9, "Samba Automation."

You can insert comments into the smb.conf file to help people understand what you are doing. There are two ways to insert comments. Simply place a semicolon (;) or a pound/hash character (#) as the first character of a line. In general, comments can only occur on lines by themselves.

You can also continue parameters across more than one line using the standard UNIX continuation character. That is, placing a back slash (\) on the end of a line forces Samba to treat the next line as a continuation of the current line.

You can insert spaces anywhere in a parameter's value that they are needed. You can also surround such strings with quotes if it makes you feel better, but Samba does not require that you do so.

Some parameters can appear only in the global section, whereas some parameters can appear in any section, including the global section. A share level parameter that appears in the global section provides a default value for those shares that do not specify the parameter.

One other very important facility resides in the smb.conf file: *variable substitutions*. These allow you to pick up values from variables built in to Samba or from information captured by Samba while it is running. Variable substitutions are one of the key components of Samba automation, and we show the meanings of some of these variables in Table 5.2.

→ To learn more about variable substitutions, **see** "The Samba Macros or Variable Substitutions," **p. 170.**

TABLE 5.2   SOME SAMBA VARIABLES

Variable	Meaning
%S	The name of the current service
%h	The hostname of the server: the first portion of the FQDN of the server
%m	The NetBIOS name of the client connected to this server instance
%L	The NetBIOS name of the server

When Samba is installed on your system, which can happen by default when you install Linux, it installs the manual pages for Samba as well as a default smb.conf file. To obtain information on a particular share or parameter, consult the smb.conf manual pages using

```
man smb.conf
```

A WORKING smb.conf FILE

In Chapter 3, we produced a simple smb.conf file. Here we will construct a slightly more complex smb.conf file and examine what it all means. Listing 5.1 shows that simple smb.conf file again.

LISTING 5.1   A SIMPLE smb.conf FILE

```
[global]
    workgroup = sambanet
    server string = Samba Server
    guest account = pcguest
    log file = /var/log/samba/log.%m
    password level = 8

[homes]
    comment = Home Directories
    browseable = no
    writable = yes
```

To this, we will add a simple share definition. You can do this by editing your smb.conf file with vi:

```
vi /etc/smb.conf
```

If your version of Linux is Caldera OpenLinux, you would use

```
vi /etc/samba.d/smb.conf
```

When you have the smb.conf file up in vi, add the following to the end of the file (after the line that says writable=yes):

```
[public]
    comment = Public share

    path = /home/samba
```

PART

II

CH

5

```
browsable = yes
writable= yes
```

If your version of Linux is Caldera OpenLinux, you will have to make the directory /home/ samba because the RPMs they use do not do this. You can create this directory using

```
mkdir /home/samba
```

When you exit from vi and you have restarted Samba, you should be able to browse your Samba server and see that there is a new share.

RESTARTING SAMBA

In Chapter 3, we talked about restarting Samba and introduced the samba command that you can use to restart Samba. In many cases you do not actually have to restart Samba when you make changes to the smb.conf file. It is often sufficient to send a HUP signal to all the smbd(8) daemons using the following command:

```
killall -HUP smbd
```

In this case, you should issue the preceding command to restart Samba.

> **Note**
>
> Using the command restart samba causes all current smbd(8) daemons to be terminated. Although all Microsoft clients implement reconnect, some applications, like Microsoft Word, get very upset if a share on which they have an open document gets disconnected.

WHAT DO THOSE PARAMETERS MEAN?

The smb.conf file shown in Listing 5.1 is simple enough, but what does each parameter do? The parameters are explained in Table 5.3.

TABLE 5.3 THE PARAMETERS IN OUR smb.conf FILE EXPLAINED

Parameter	Function
workgroup	This parameter specifies the workgroup or domain that your Samba server is in. Workgroups and domains are discussed in more detail in Chapter 10, "An Introduction to Microsoft Windows Networking."
server string	This parameter specifies a string that will show up against your Samba server when other users browse it.
guest account	This parameter specifies the name to use for the guest account when one is needed.
log file	This parameter specifies the location and name of log files for smbd. The last component of the log filename is log.%m, which means that each client will get a separate log file, with its name as part of the log file.

TABLE 5.3   CONTINUED

Parameter	Function
password level	This parameter specifies what Samba does if a username and password do not validate. Samba first tries the password as presented by the client. If that fails, Samba tries the password supplied, but converted to all lowercase. If that fails, Samba tries all combinations on n uppercase characters, where n is the value supplied for the password level.
comment	This parameter supplies a comment string for a share.
browseable	This parameter specifies whether a share is browseable. By default shares are, so you must specify this parameter only to hide a share from browsing.
path	This parameter specifies the location in the Linux file system from which files will be shared. The default value for this parameter is /tmp, so it is important to specify it.
public	This parameter specifies whether guest access to the share is allowed.
writable	This parameter specifies whether a share is writable. By default, shares are read-only.

You can find a complete description of all the smb.conf parameters in Appendix A, "All Samba Parameters and Their Meanings." In addition, parameters are described in more detail in each chapter as they are encountered.

→ For more details of setting up file shares, **see** Chapter 6, "File Sharing Under Samba."

→ For more details of setting up print shares, **see** Chapter 7, "Print Sharing Under Samba."

LOG FILES AND TROUBLESHOOTING

Samba writes error messages and some informational messages to its log files. Many Linux distributions, including Red Hat, Linux Mandrake, TurboLinux, and Yellow Dog Linux, create their log files in /var/log/samba. Table 5.4 shows the files that are created. Other versions of UNIX generally keep the log files in /usr/local/samba/var.

TABLE 5.4   LOG FILE CREATED BY SAMBA FOR MANY VERSIONS OF LINUX

File	Contents
log.smb	smbd writes its logging information in this file. When a client connects, if a log file parameter has been specified in the smb.conf file, the new smbd that is started writes to the logfile specified; otherwise, it writes to the file log.smb.
log.nmb	nmbd writes its logging information in this file.
log.name	If you have specified the log file parameter as shown in the simple smb.conf, when a user connects, smbd writes its logging information to the file log.name, where name is the NetBIOS name of the client.

However, under Caldera OpenLinux, Samba creates its log files in /var/log/samba.d. Table 5.5 shows the files that are created.

TABLE 5.5 LOG FILES CREATED UNDER CALDERA OPENLINUX

File	Contents
smbd	smbd writes its logging information in this file.
nmbd	nmbd writes its logging information in this file.
smb.*name*	Log files for each client, but you must configure it in the smb.conf file in /etc/samba.d.

Other distributions, like SuSE, keep their log files in /var/log but use the same log file structure as Red Hat-derived systems.

These log files are invaluable in troubleshooting problems with Samba. Samba can write a great deal of debugging information to the log files specified previously. The level of detail provided is controlled by the debug level parameter. The default value of this parameter is 0, which causes Samba to be very terse and print only errors that would prevent it from running. The following shows what you would expect to see in log.smb when Samba starts. The last message is a result of running Samba on a Linux system that can have only 1,024 open files per process.

```
[2000/02/08 14:42:16, 1] smbd/server.c:main(643)
  smbd version 2.0.6 started.
  Copyright Andrew Tridgell 1992-1998
[2000/02/08 14:42:16, 1] smbd/files.c:file_init(216)
  file_init: Information only: requested 10000 open files, 1014 are available.
```

If you want information about problems Samba encounters while trying to perform actions for clients, including errors like authentication failing, being unable to transmit packets, inability to open or create files, and so on, you must increase the debug level.

To obtain more information, add the following to the global section of your smb.conf file and restart Samba:

debug level = 6

A debug level of 6 is usually adequate. A debug level of 10 will supply even more information, including a hex dump of each packet as it is received.

Note
As already discussed previously in the section on the smb.conf file, Samba treats debug level and debuglevel as the same parameter. The documentation shows it as debuglevel, but I prefer to use debug level.

→ For more information on troubleshooting Samba, **see** Chapter 23, "Troubleshooting Samba."

COMMON PROBLEMS ACCESSING SAMBA

First-time Samba users often experience many problems that we will discuss here. Some of these problems are due to changes in the way that Samba operates since version 2.0.0, whereas others are due to changes in the way Windows 9x and NT operate. Others are simply the result of misconfiguration of TCP/IP, and so on.

→ For more information on resolving common problems, **see** Chapter 23, "Troubleshooting Samba." **See also** the "Common Problems" sections in Chapters 12, 14, and 15, **pages 241, 277,** and **295**.

ENTER NETWORK PASSWORD

Perhaps the biggest single problem first-time users experience is this one. You have set up Linux and installed Samba. Then you wade through the documentation and manage to create an `smb.conf` file (or modify the supplied one), so you start Samba. Having started Samba, you go to Windows 9x or Windows NT and browse the network and feel very happy because your Samba server shows up in Network Neighborhood. However, as soon as you click on the icon for your Samba server, you receive the display shown in Figure 5.5 asking for the network password for the `IPC$` share, a share you did not even know existed.

Figure 5.5
Windows wants your network password.

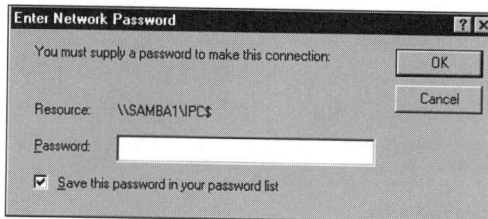

This problem occurs because browsing a machine accesses (performs a *treecon*, or tree connection request, on) the internal `IPC$` share. For more detail on *treecons*, refer to Chapter 4. It is caused by one of the following:

- You have logged on to Windows with a username and password that are not valid on your Linux server. You can test them out by trying to log in to Linux with them. You might need to add an account with `useradd` and set the correct password.

    This has become more of a problem since Samba 2.0.0 because the default security mode became `security=user` in that version. In prior versions the default was `security=share`, and you could rely on your guest account giving you access to the `IPC$` share.

- Your client is sending encrypted passwords to Samba, but Samba is not configured for encrypted passwords. Windows 98, Windows NT SP3 and above, and Windows 95 OSR2 and above encrypt passwords by default. One of the updates to earlier versions of Windows 95 also causes passwords to be encrypted.

    You can fix this either by disabling encrypted passwords on your client or by configuring encrypted passwords on your Samba server. We will look at enabling encrypted passwords in Chapter 8.

PART
II

CH
5

The directory /usr/doc/samba-$version/docs (where $version should be replaced with the version of Samba on your system) contains a series of files that will disable password encryption on Windows operating systems. These files are described in Table 5.6.

TABLE 5.6 FILES TO DISABLE ENCRYPTED PASSWORDS IN WINDOWS

File	Function
Win95_PlainPassword.reg	Disables encrypted passwords under Windows 95
Win98_PlainPassword.reg	Disables encrypted passwords under Windows 98
NT4_PlainPassword.reg	Disables encrypted passwords under NT4 SP3 and above
Win2000_PlainPassword.reg	Disables encrypted passwords under Windows 2000

You can simply copy the relevant file to your client and double-click on it to invoke it. You can use the mcopy command to copy these files to a floppy.

After you have identified which of the above caused your problem and rectified it, you should be able to browse your Samba server.

NETWORK NAME NOT FOUND

Perhaps the next most puzzling error is this one. You have created a share and are able to browse your Samba server, but when you try to access the new share, you receive the dialog box shown in Figure 5.6.

Figure 5.6
Samba reports
network name
not found.

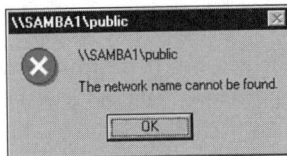

You do not get this message when you have mistyped a share name or for a share that does not exist. You only get this message from Samba for a share that does exist, but where the shared directory either does not exist or where you do not have access to the directory being shared.

To rectify this problem, simply create the shared directory if it does not exist, fix any mistyped directory names, or change the permissions on the directory so you can access it.

ACCESS IS DENIED

Another common problem is when you have created a share and made the share writable. You should be able to write to it. Unfortunately, you have forgotten about UNIX permission files and directories, while Samba does not forget UNIX permissions. The files you are trying to modify are simply inaccessible to the account you have logged on as.

If this happens, you might receive the dialog box shown in Figure 5.7.

Figure 5.7
Samba will not let you create the file or directory.

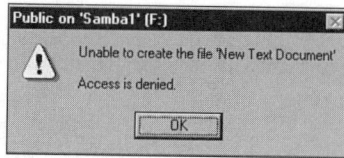

The solution to this problem is simple. Change the permissions on the UNIX file or directory that is the cause of the problems so that you do have access.

UNABLE TO GET MY HOSTNAME

This is one of those problems that prevents Samba from starting. Both nmbd and smbd look up the hostname of the system on which they are running and try to translate that into an IP address. You will see the following message in the log file `log.smb`:

```
[1999/10/19 23:15:22, 1] smbd/server.c:main(626)
  smbd version 2.0.6-pre1 started.
  Copyright Andrew Tridgell 1992-1998
[1999/10/19 23:15:22, 1] smbd/files.c:file_init(216)
  file_init: Information only: requested 10000 open files, 1014 are available.
[1999/10/19 23:15:22, 0] lib/util_sock.c:open_socket_in(854)
  Get_Hostbyname: Unknown host samba1.samba.com
```

The last line shows the problem. The `Get_Hostbyname` routine could not translate the server's hostname into an IP address. You would see a similar message in the `log.nmb` log file as well.

If the daemons cannot translate the hostname to an IP address, they will not start up. To fix this problem, ensure that your server's hostname can be translated, either in the `/etc/hosts` file or through DNS.

GENERAL CONNECTIVITY PROBLEMS

You might also experience general connectivity problems. These will often manifest themselves in a form of messages saying

```
The computer or sharename could not be found.
```

Figure 5.8 shows an example.

Figure 5.8
An error due to connectivity problems.

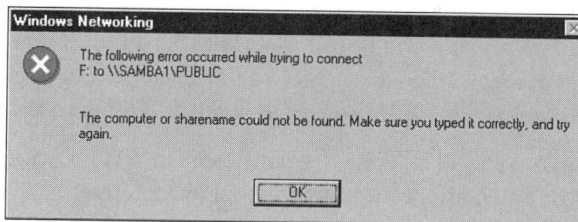

To solve these sorts of problems, you must use standard network troubleshooting techniques. Some approaches are outlined briefly here:

PART

II

CH

5

- Is TCP/IP installed and configured on your client? Because Samba only supports SMB over NetBIOS over TCP/IP, you must have TCP/IP installed and configured on your client. If it is not, fix this problem first.

- Can you ping your Samba server from the client using its IP address? If you can't, there are basic connectivity problems, such as cables not plugged in, incorrect subnet masks, or routing not working. Rectify the problem and try again.

- Are the Samba servers (smbd and nmbd) running? You can check this using one of the methods shown in Chapter 3. If they are not, try to start them as shown in Chapter 3, and if they still do not run, check their log files to find out why. Rectify the problem and try again.

GUI CONFIGURATION UTILITIES

For a long time the only way to configure Samba was manually. That is, you edited the smb.conf file and restarted Samba. Then a few Web-based and other approaches to configuring Samba started appearing. Finally, with Samba 2.0.0, the Samba team produced the Samba Web Administration Tool, or SWAT. This section introduces you to several of the GUI administration utilities available.

SWAT

The *Samba Web Administration Tool (SWAT)* is a new facility with Samba 2.0.0. It is a mini Web server and CGI scripting application designed to run from inetd that provides access to the smb.conf file on the system on which SWAT is running.

SWAT allows a suitably authorized person (with the root password) to configure all aspects of Samba via Web pages. SWAT also places help links to all configurable smb.conf options on every page, which allows administrators to easily understand the effect of any changes.

SWAT is installed by default, and all necessary configuration is performed when you install Samba from RPMs under all Linux distributions. To access SWAT, simply get your browser to connect to port 901 on your Samba server. For example, to use SWAT to configure samba1.samba.com, connect your browser to http://samba1.samba.com:901/. When your browser has contacted SWAT, you will be presented with an authorization dialog box asking for your username and password. You must enter a sufficiently privileged user here, like root. Figure 5.9 shows how you would use a browser to access SWAT on samba1.samba.com.

After you have logged in, you will be presented with the main SWAT page, shown in Figure 5.10, which enables you to choose from among the following areas:

- Home, which takes you back to the SWAT home page
- Globals, where you can manage the Samba [global] section of this Samba server
- Shares, where you can manage file shares for this Samba server
- Printers, where you can manage printer shares for this Samba server

- Status, where you can obtain status information about Samba on this server
- View, where you can view the current `smb.conf` file
- Password, where you can manage your password on your Samba server or on a remote machine

Figure 5.9
Accessing SWAT from a browser.

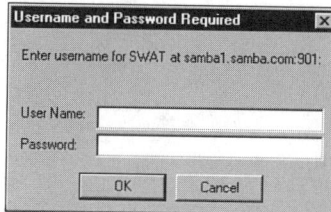

Figure 5.10
The SWAT home page.

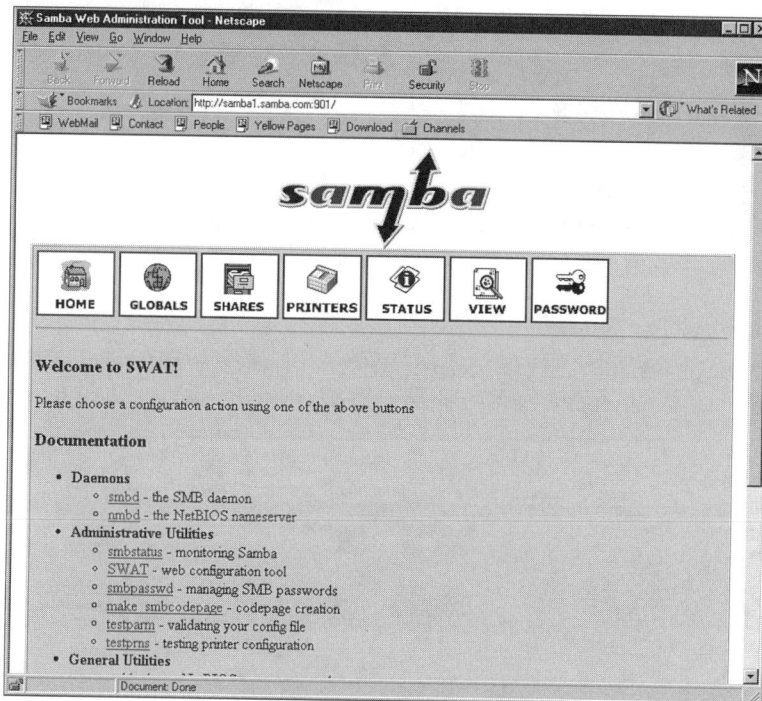

At any time you can return to the SWAT home page by clicking the HOME icon. The following sections discuss each of the configuration pages you can access.

MANAGING THE [global] SECTION

When you select the GLOBALS icon, SWAT returns with a Web page that allows you to modify many of the most relevant Samba global parameters. The Web page returned is shown in Figure 5.11. The Samba global variables are grouped into related options.

PART

II

CH

5

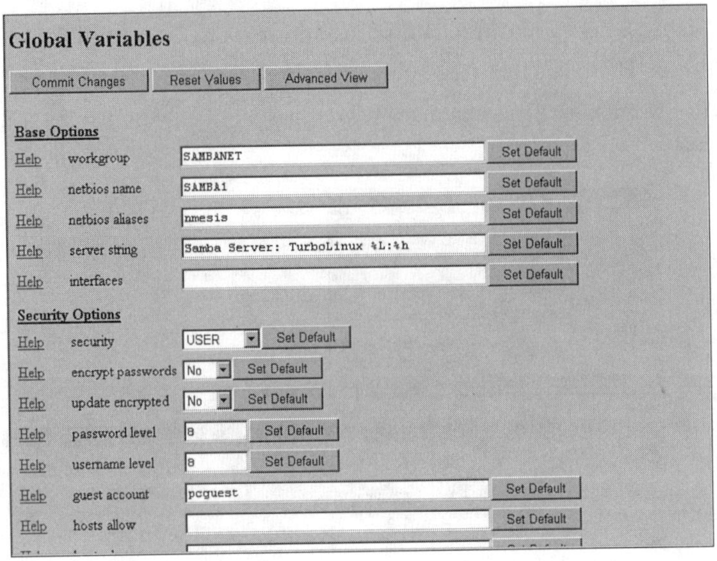

Figure 5.11
Modifying glo-
bal parameters
is easy with
SWAT.

Clicking the Advanced View button brings up the same set of groups of related options, but you can now edit all of them. To make a change, simply scroll down to the parameter you want to change, enter the new value, and then click on the Commit button.

MANAGING FILE SHARES

When you select the SHARES icon, SWAT returns a Web page that allows you to create new shares and modify existing shares. The page returned is shown in Figure 5.12.

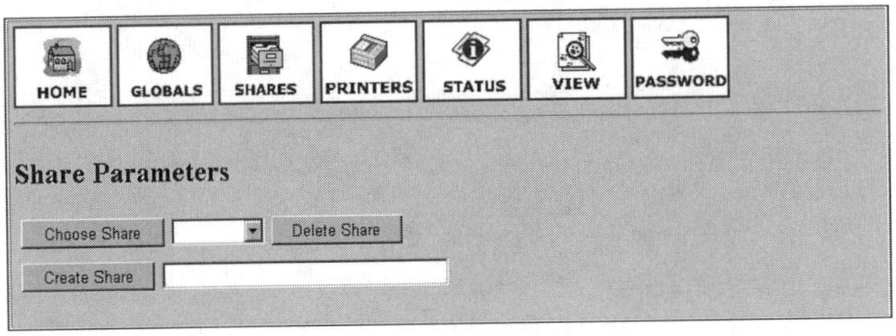

Figure 5.12
You can create
and modify
shares with
SWAT.

To modify any of the parameters of an existing share, select the share from the drop-down list box next to Choose Share, and click on Choose Share. You will then be presented with the page shown in Figure 5.13.

Similarly, to create a new share, enter the name of the share in the field next to Create Share, and then click on Create Share. You will also be presented with a page similar to that shown in Figure 5.13 with the name of your new share as the choice in the first field.

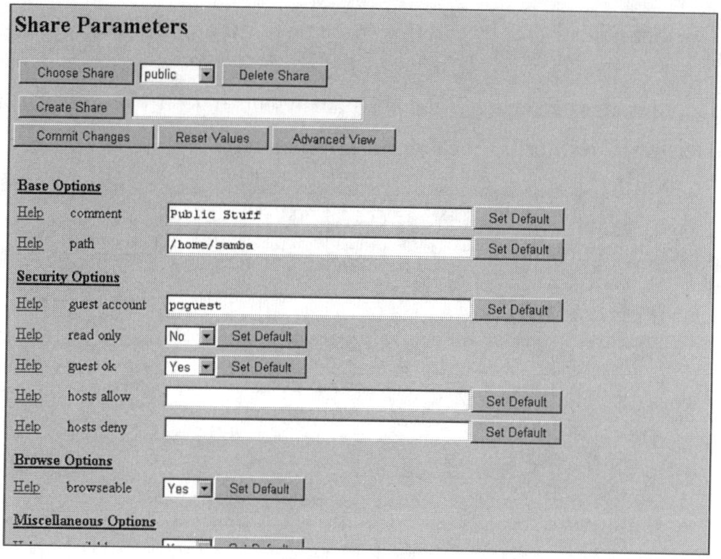

Figure 5.13
Modifying or
creating a
share with
SWAT.

From this page you can

- Choose another share by selecting it and clicking on Choose Share.
- Create a new share by entering its name in the appropriate field and clicking on New Share.
- Commit all your changes made so far by clicking on Commit Changes.
- Delete the share by clicking on Delete Share.

If you need to modify parameters not shown on this page, click on the Advanced View button and modify the appropriate parameters.

After you have made all the changes you need, click on Commit Changes and they will be made to the share. The changes you make are effected immediately by Samba.

MANAGING PRINTER SHARES

When you select the PRINTERS icon from any SWAT page, it returns a Web page that enables you to create new printers and modify existing printers. The page returned is shown in Figure 5.14.

To modify an existing printer, select it from the drop-down list box next to Choose Printer, and then click on Choose Printer. You will be presented with the page shown in Figure 5.15.

Similarly, to create a new printer, enter the name of the printer in the field next to Create Printer and click on Create Printer. You will also be presented with a page similar to that shown in Figure 5.15 with the name of your new printer in the first field.

From this page you can

- Choose another printer by selecting it and clicking on Choose Share.

PART

II

CH

5

■ Create a new printer by entering its name in the appropriate field and clicking on New Share.

■ Commit all your changes made so far by clicking on Commit Changes.

■ Delete the printer by clicking on Delete Share.

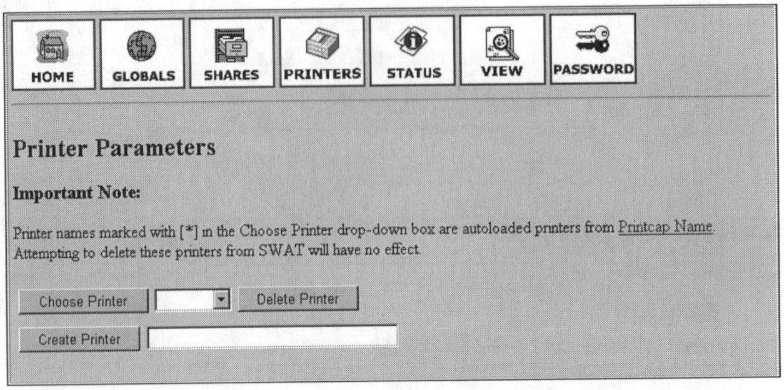

Figure 5.14
Creating and modifying printers with SWAT.

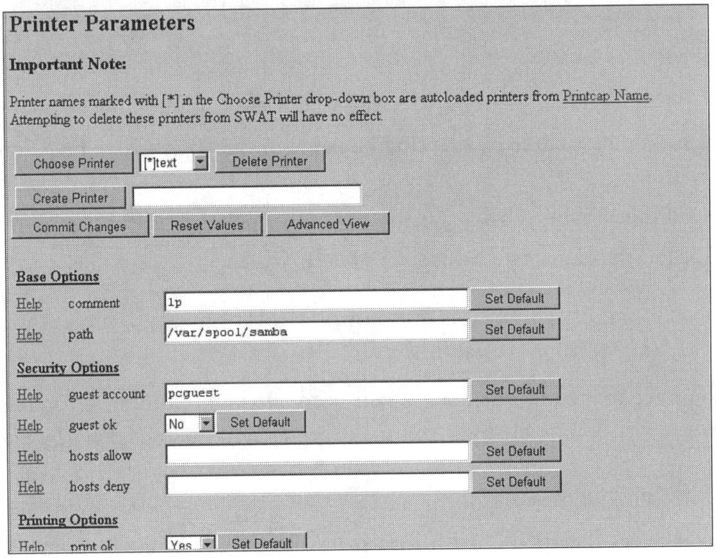

Figure 5.15
Modifying or creating a printer with SWAT.

If you need to modify parameters not shown on this page, click on the Advanced View button and modify the appropriate parameters.

After you have made all the changes you need, click on Commit Changes and they will be made to the share. The changes you make are effected immediately by Samba.

OBTAINING STATUS INFORMATION

When you select the STATUS icon from any page, it returns a Web page that provides status about Samba, as well as enabling you to stop and restart the Samba daemons. It also enables you to disconnect active users. The Web page SWAT returns appears in Figure 5.16.

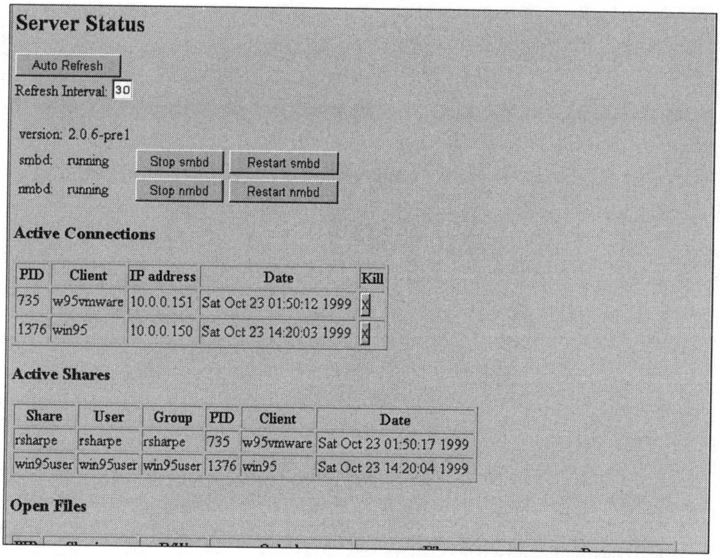

Figure 5.16
The SWAT
status page.

The status page also provides a means of having it refreshed on a continuous basis. Simply specify the refresh interval and click on Auto Refresh.

VIEWING THE COMPLETE smb.conf FILE

When you select the VIEW icon from any page, it returns a Web page that displays the whole smb.conf file. The page returned appears in Figure 5.17.

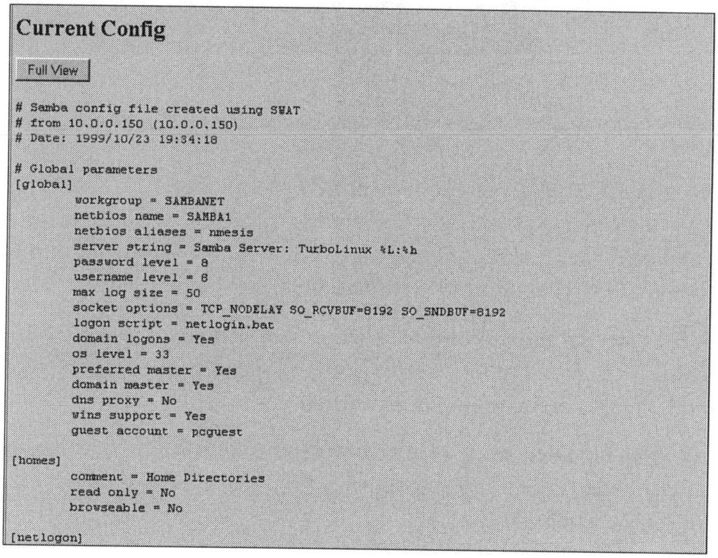

Figure 5.17
The smb.conf
file returned by
SWAT.

SWAT lists the Samba config as it appears in the smb.conf file. If you want a listing that includes the values of all the parameters that Samba maintains, simply click on the Full View button above.

CHANGING YOUR PASSWORD

If you select the PASSWORD icon from any page, it returns a Web page that enables you to modify your password on the Samba server SWAT is running from, or to change your password on another CIFS/SMB server elsewhere in your network. You can also add users, disable users, or enable users. The page returned appears in Figure 5.18.

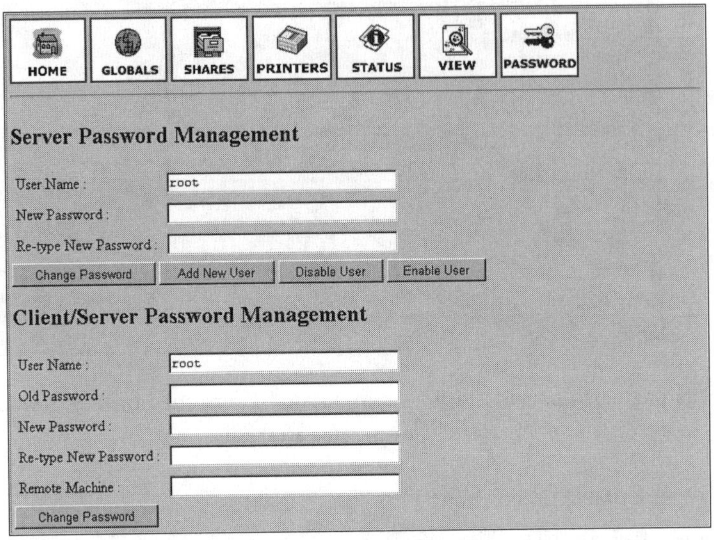

Figure 5.18
Changing your password with SWAT.

Note   SWAT operates only on your `smbpasswd` file, not on your normal UNIX password files.

WEBMIN

Webmin is a Web-based system administration package for UNIX systems. It provides facilities for managing Samba, as well as setting up accounts, configuring DNS, configuring Apache, and configuring sendmail and many other system administration tasks. Here we will concentrate on how Webmin helps with configuring Samba.

Webmin consists of a mini Web server written in Perl and a set of CGI programs that implement the functionality required to provide system configuration over the Web. To use Webmin you must obtain Webmin and install it.

Webmin can be obtained from `http://www.webmin.com/webmin/`. When you have retrieved Webmin, you must break out the gzipped tar file that it is distributed as. The following command sequence will do the job:

```
tar -zxvf webmin-${VERSION}_tar
```

On systems that do not use GNU Tar, you will need to unzip the file first. You can use `gzip -d webmin-${VERSION}_tar.gz` to do this (you can also use gunzip on some systems). In each command in the previous command sequence, `${VERSION}` should be replaced with the current version of Webmin. At the time of writing, the latest version of Webmin was 0.78.

After breaking the distribution out, simply change to the directory created in the preceding steps, usually webmin-*VER*, where *VER* is the version number of Webmin. You should then read the README for installation instructions. At the time of writing, this consisted of running the following command and answering the questions asked by the installation script:

```
./setup.sh
```

During installation, you will be asked for a password for the first Webmin user, admin. This password will be needed when you connect to the Webmin page.

At the time of writing, Webmin supports the following Linux distributions:

- Red Hat Linux 4.0 to 6.1
- Caldera OpenLinux 2.3 and 3.0 as well as OpenLinux Server 2.3e
- Slackware Linux 3.2 to 4.0 and 7.0
- Debian Linux 1.3 to 2.2
- Linux Mandrake 5.3, 6.0, 6.1 and 7.0
- SuSE Linux 5.1 to 6.3
- Colel Linux 1.0
- DELIX DLD 5.2 to 6.0
- MkLinux DR2.1 and 3.0
- TurboLinux 4.0

In addition, Webmin works on other distributions that are like Red Hat. For example, it works fine on TurboLinux 3.4.0 and above, including TurboLinux 6.0. It also supports several other UNIX operating systems, including FreeBSD, OpenBSD, Sun Solaris, BSDI, HP-UX, SGI Irix, Tru64 UNIX (formerly Digital UNIX), AIX, and SCO UNIXWARE.

For more complete details of the operating systems supported by Webmin, consult the Webmin Web page (www.webmin.com/webmin) and installation script.

After installing and starting Webmin, you can access it from your favorite browser, as shown in Figure 5.19, by accessing port 10,000 on the server on which you installed Webmin. If you changed the port number that Webmin sits behind from the default of 10,000, you should use your number rather than 10,000.

PART
II

CH
5

Figure 5.19
Connecting to
Webmin.

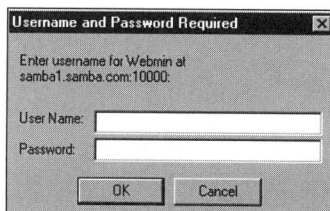

After you have entered the correct username and password, you are presented with the Webmin home page as shown in Figure 5.20. Webmin is capable of administering many aspects of UNIX systems, but we are only interested in its capabilities to administer Samba. To perform Samba-related configuration, select the Servers tab on the Webmin main page, which takes you to the Web page shown in Figure 5.21, where you should select Samba Windows File Sharing.

> **Note**
>
> Earlier versions of Webmin simply had all the administration icons located on the Webmin home page. If you are running a version prior to 0.78, or indeed after 0.78, you might need to adjust these instructions accordingly.

After selecting the Samba Windows File Sharing icon, Webmin presents the Samba Share Manager page, as shown in Figure 5.22. From this page, you can manage file and printer shares, as well as all aspects of the Samba global parameters. You can select global configuration sections by clicking on the icons shown at the bottom of Figure 5.22.

Figure 5.20
The Webmin main page. You should select Servers.

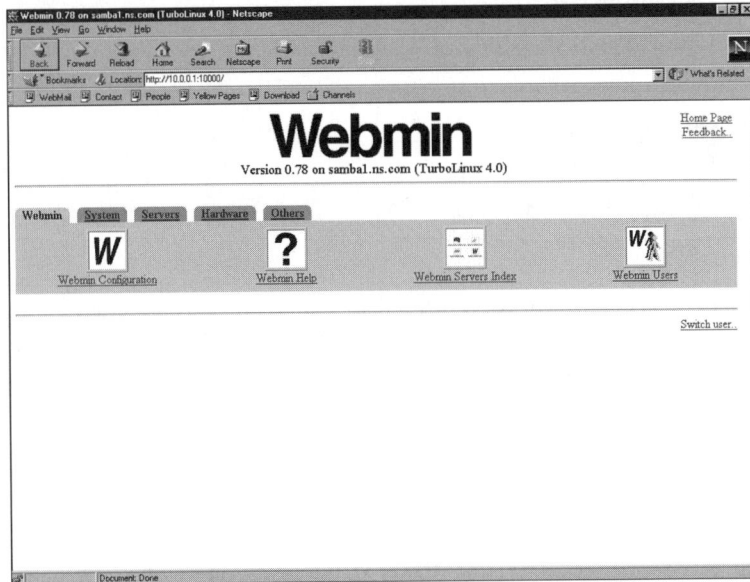

If you scroll down the page shown in Figure 5.22, you will see that it also supports management of encrypted passwords if you have enabled them and allows you to restart your Samba servers. Figure 5.23 shows you what the other half of the Webmin Samba management page looks like.

From these pages, you can perform the same set of functions you can with SWAT.

> **Note**
>
> Webmin does not create file shares with hyphens (-) in them and does not work with smb.conf files that use config or include parameters in them.

Figure 5.21
The Webmin servers page showing each of the servers supported.

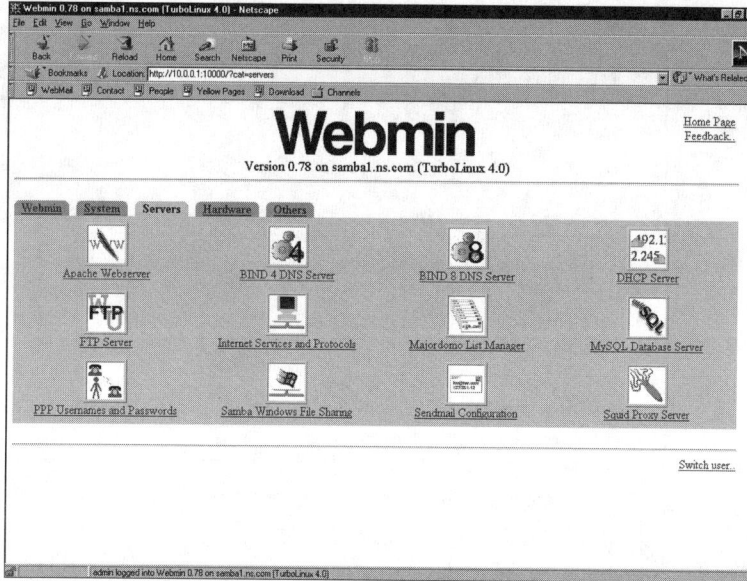

Figure 5.22
The Webmin Samba Share Manager page.

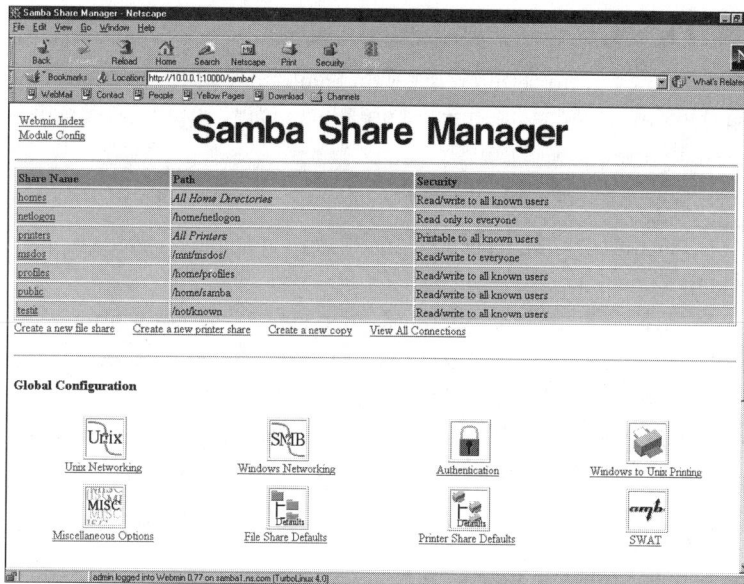

FURTHER RESOURCES

See the Samba DIAGNOSIS.txt file in docs/textdocs for more information in diagnosing problems in Samba.

See the smb.conf man pages for more information on all parameters. (Use man smb.conf on your Samba server.)

Figure 5.23
Webmin also allows you to restart Samba and manage encrypted passwords.

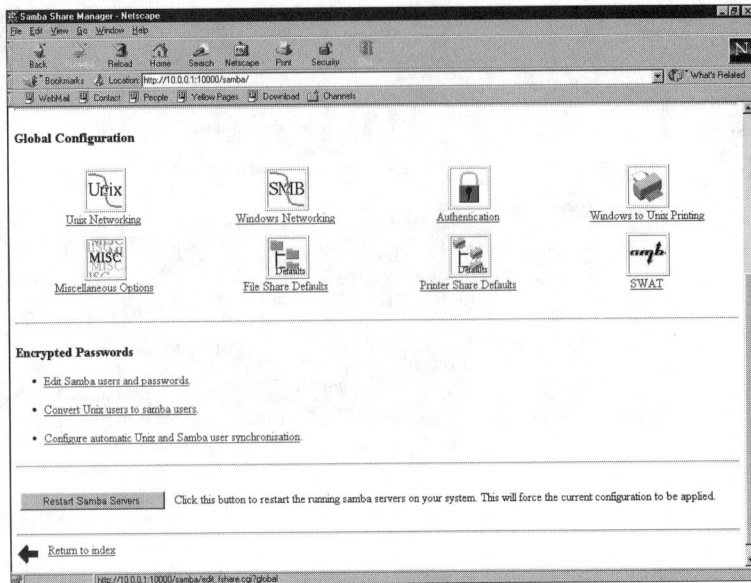

FROM HERE...

Now you know how to set up services on Samba and where to begin looking if things go wrong. However, Samba has much more functionality than we have covered so far in this chapter.

The next few chapters cover the basics of Samba in more detail:

- In Chapter 6, "File Sharing Under Samba," we look into managing file shares in much more detail.

- In Chapter 7, "Printer Sharing Under Samba," we cover printer shares in more detail.

- In Chapter 8, "Samba and Password Management," we examine password management under Samba.

- In Chapter 9, "Samba Automation," we look at the issues of server automation and how to do interesting things with the smb.conf file.

Subsequent chapters deal with more advanced issues, such as the following:

- Setting up Windows clients to access Samba
- Setting up Samba as a primary domain controller
- Using the LDAP functionality in Samba
- Getting the best performance out of your Samba server

CHAPTER **6**

FILE SHARING UNDER SAMBA

In this chapter

by Tim Potter

Sharing files is one of the main functions of Samba, and file shares can be configured at a detailed level. A Samba administrator can create guest shares that can be accessible to all users, or she can limit access to specific users or workstations.

In this chapter, you will first look at how Samba finds the shares users want to access. Then you will examine the parameters in smb.conf related to file sharing, starting with basic share properties and moving to more advanced topics such as opportunistic locks and internationalization.

FINDING AND ACCESSING SHARES

A user can request access to a share in several ways:

- By using the net use command from a DOS window:

  net use h: \\samba1\public

- By using the Map Network Drive dialog box from Windows. You can find this dialog box by right-clicking both Network Neighborhood or My Computer in most versions of Windows.

- By browsing the network and finding a server you are interested in, and then selecting one of the shares that it makes available.

To process a client's request to connect to a share, Samba first determines whether the requested share exists. The following simple approach determines whether it does:

1. Scan the smb.conf file looking for a section that matches the requested share name. If one is found, return it.

2. If the share is not found, check to see whether a [homes] section appears in the smb.conf file. If so, check the passwd file to see whether the share name matches a username. If it does, the [homes] share is cloned, and the new share is returned. For more information on the [homes] share, see the section titled "User Home Directories," later in this chapter.

3. If the share is still not found, check to see whether a [printers] section appears in the smb.conf file. If so, check to see whether the requested share matches a printer in the printcap file. If it does, clone the [printers] share, and return it. You will explore this subject in Chapter 7, "Printer Sharing Under Samba."

4. If you still can't find the share, check to see whether there is a default service, and if so, change its name to match the requested service and return it.

5. If you don't find a share, Samba returns an invalid network name error to the client.

If, in any of these steps, Samba cannot access the directory (path parameter) specified in the share, it returns an invalid network name error to the client. The following are some reasons why Samba might not be able to find the share:

- You have misspelled the name of the directory or forgotten to create it.
- The user requesting access to the share does not have permission to access the directory specified by the share.

Because of the order in which the checks discussed previously are performed, some share names will not be available:

- A sharename in the `smb.conf` file takes precedence over any entries in the `passwd` file or the `printcap` file, even if `[homes]` and `[printers]` sections are defined. Thus, the home share for the user `fred` will not be visible if a share called `fred` is defined in the `smb.conf` file.
- Home shares take precedence over printer shares. Thus, a printer called `fred` (in the `printcap` file) will not be visible if a user called `fred` is in the `passwd` file and the `[homes]` section has been defined, or if a share called `fred` is defined in the `smb.conf` file.

After Samba has determined that the share exists, it must check that the user has access to the share. This is done by determining who is accessing the share and whether that person is allowed to access the share (by use of the parameters discussed in the section titled "Restricting Access to Shares," later in this chapter).

Samba uses the following approach to determine who the user accessing the share is recorded as:

1. If the client has submitted a username/password pair previously (in an `SMBsesssetupX`) that validates, the validated user is recorded as the user seeking access. Some older clients can submit their username using the `\\server\service%username` syntax.
2. If the client has already submitted a valid username and now supplies a correct password (on the share request), the validated user is recorded as the user seeking access.
3. The client's NetBIOS name and any previously used usernames are validated using the operating system's standard mechanisms (or the `smbpassword` file) with the supplied password. If any validate successfully, the validated username is recorded as the user seeking access.
4. If the client has previously validated a username/password pair with the server (using an `SMBsesssetupX`) and the client passed the validation token in the share access request, the previously validated user is recorded as the user seeking access. This step is skipped if the share specifies revalidation (`revalidate = yes`).
5. If a `user =` field has been specified on the share, the client has supplied a password, and the combination of username specified in the share and the password validates, the validated user is recorded as the user seeking access.

However, if the service is a `guest-only` service, the `guest` account is recorded as the user seeking access without going through any of the preceding steps. Any supplied password is ignored.

PART

II

CH

6

After Samba determines which local user is regarded as accessing the share, it checks the various parameters (listed in the section "Restricting Access to Shares," later in this chapter) to determine whether that user can access the requested share. If that user is not allowed access to the share, Samba returns an Access Denied error.

However, even if Samba gives a user access to a share, two more sets of checks are still done before they can access files on the share:

1. To write to files in the share, the share must be writable. This is discussed further in the section titled "Basic Share Properties," which follows.

2. Normal Linux/UNIX file permissions must be satisfied. That is, the user must have access to the files in the share. See the section titled "UNIX Permission Mapping," later in this chapter, for more information on how to control the ownership and permissions on newly created files.

CONFIGURING FILE SHARES

You have already created a simple file share in Chapter 5, "Configuring and Managing Samba," and you should be familiar with the overall structure of the smb.conf file. This file share is reproduced in Listing 6.1.

LISTING 6.1 SIMPLE SHARE DEFINITION FROM CHAPTER 5

```
[public]
   comment = A public share
   path = /home/samba
   public = yes
   writable = yes
```

To create file shares, place a sharename in square brackets in the smb.conf file. Parameters applying to the share are inserted after this entry.

When describing smb.conf parameters, all parameters are share parameters, unless otherwise noted as being global. Global parameters can only appear in the [global] section of the smb.conf file. Share parameters can appear in the [global] section, in which case they are the default for all file shares unless overridden. If a parameter has an alternative name, or synonym, it is listed after the main parameter.

BASIC SHARE PROPERTIES

Samba allows several parameters to be specified in the smb.conf file that define the basic properties of a share (shown in Table 6.1). These include whether a share can be written to, whether it is visible to other workstations, and a text description of the share that appears in browse lists.

TABLE 6.1   BASIC SHARE PARAMETERS

Name	Type	Default	Description
`read only`	Boolean	`true`	Specifies that the share cannot be written to. Users specified in the `write list` parameter are given write access.
`writeable,` `writable, write ok`	Boolean	`false`	If the `writeable` parameter is true, files on the share can be changed. The user must have the correct UNIX permissions for writes to succeed. Permissions are dealt with later in this chapter. This parameter is the opposite of the read only parameter.
`Comment`	String	No comment string	The text of the comment parameter should describe the purpose of the share because a user browsing the share will see this string next to the sharename.
`Volume`	String	By default, the volume label is the name of the share	Allows the volume label of the share to be changed. The volume label appears when the file share is mapped as a network drive, and the properties of the share are shown as in Figure 6.1.
`browseable,` `browsable`	Boolean	`True`	If a share is marked as browseable, it appears in the list of shares visible when the Samba server is browsed. However, you can still access a non-browseable share by its sharename, so making a share not browseable does not increase security in any useful way.
`fstype`	String	The string `NTFS`	When the type of filesystem for the share is queried, the value of this parameter is returned. You should not need to change this parameter.
`available`	Boolean	`True`	If a share is available (that is, the value of this parameter is true), clients can connect to the share and access its resources. To disable a share temporarily to perform some administration on it, set available = `false` while you work on it. Remove the line to allow users to access the share again.

PART

II

CH

6

TABLE 6.1 CONTINUED

Name	Type	Default	Description
`path, directory`	String	`/tmp`	Specifies the UNIX path on the Samba server of the file share. Files and subdirectories under this path appear in the root directory of the share.
`time offset`	Integer	0, timestamps are not modified	The value of this parameter is the number of seconds Samba adds to the timestamp of each file on the share.

Figure 6.1
Changing the volume name of a share.

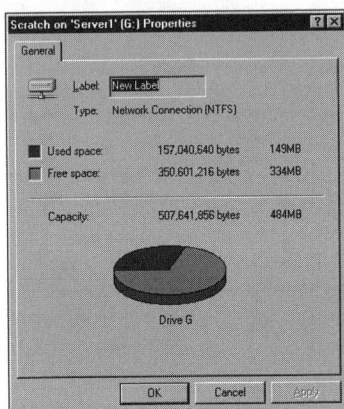

EXAMPLE

The share definition in Listing 6.2 creates a simple share called scratch. A Samba administrator can set up a share similar to this for users to store temporary files.

LISTING 6.2 A SIMPLE SHARE DEFINITION

```
[scratch]
     comment = Scratch space
     path = /scratch
     browseable = true
     writeable = true
```

FILE SELECTION

When creating a file share, it might be useful to allow only certain files or directories to be visible, as shown in Table 6.2. Samba allows files to be marked as inaccessible and hidden by using the DOS hidden attribute. Control over the use of symbolic links in file shares to enhance security is also available.

TABLE 6.2 FILE SELECTION PARAMETERS

Name	Type	Default	Description
`hide files`	String	No files are hidden by default	Allows a Samba administrator to specify a list of files that are hidden. Hidden files appear to clients to have the DOS hidden attribute set but can still be accessed if the user knows the filename, or his client program supports viewing hidden files.
`hide dot files`	Boolean	`True`	Specifies whether files starting with a dot appear with the DOS hidden attribute set. This is useful for UNIX home directories because they usually contain a large number of dot files that can result in visual clutter when browsing the share.
`veto files`	String	No files are vetoed	Contains a list of file and directory names that are marked by Samba as not visible and cannot be accessed by users. Entries in the list are separated by the / character, and the ? and * wildcard characters can be used. For example, to veto access to Windows executable files on a file share use `veto files = /*.exe/ *.com/*.bat/`. If the `case-sensitive` parameter is false, Samba will veto files without regard to case.
`delete veto files`	Boolean	`False`	If Samba is asked to delete a directory that contains files vetoed using the veto files parameter, the delete will not succeed unless the `delete veto files` parameter is true. Of course, the vetoed files are deleted only if the user has the correct UNIX permissions to do so.
`dont descend`	String	All directories are descended into	This parameter should contain a comma-separated list of directories that Samba should not attempt to enter. Directories in this list appear empty to a user attempting to access them. This parameter is useful to prevent inappropriate access to system directories such as `/proc` or `/dev`.
`follow symlinks`	Boolean	`True`	Samba will follow symbolic links in the file share if this parameter is `true`. Some Samba administrators disable `follow symlinks` for security reasons.

PART

II

CH

6

TABLE 6.2 CONTINUED

Name	Type	Default	Description
wide links	Boolean	True	Tells Samba whether to follow links that point outside the file share being accessed. For example, if wide links is true, a link in a user's home directory pointing somewhere else within his or her home directory will be allowed, whereas a link to /etc/passwd will not.

Note

The veto files parameter is really useful only for hiding certain types of files from users because it is impossible to specify complete pathnames. Use UNIX permissions or the dont descent parameter to restrict access to directories parameter should contain a instead of the veto files parameter.

Caution

Setting wide links to false has an adverse impact on performance because for every file opened, Samba must determine whether it lies inside the file share.

EXAMPLE

We extend our temporary storage space example to add a bit more security by disabling the wide links and follow symlinks parameters. The new share definition is given in Listing 6.3.

LISTING 6.3 ADDING SOME SECURITY PARAMETERS

```
[scratch]
    comment = Scratch space
    path = /scratch
    browseable = true
    writeable = true
    wide links = false
    follow symlinks = false
```

GUEST SHARES

If you have a share you want to give access to but do not want to manage usernames and accounts, you might want to set up a *guest share*. A guest share does not require a username or a password to access it. Anyone who can make a network connection to your Samba server will be able to access the share.

Note

Guest shares are also known as *anonymous shares*.

Table 6.3 shows `smb.conf` parameters that are used to set up guest access to a share.

TABLE 6.3   PARAMETERS CONTROLLING GUEST ACCESS

Name	Type	Default	Description
guest ok, public	Boolean	false	Specifies whether guest access to the share is allowed.
guest account	String	The default is set when Samba is compiled and is usually the UNIX user nobody. The UNIX group for this user will usually be the group named nogroup.	If guest access to the share is allowed, as specified by the guest ok parameter, the value of this parameter is the UNIX username that will be used by Samba for accessing the share.
guest only, only guest	Boolean	false	Only guest connections are allowed to this share if this parameter is true. The username used for access is specified in the guest account parameter.

Note

The guest only parameter is effective only if the share has been made a guest share by setting the guest ok parameter to true.

Note

Unless your Samba server is operating in security = share mode, you will probably want map to guest = bad user in the global section of your smb.conf file for guest shares to work properly. This is because Samba 2.0.0 and above operate in security = user mode by default, and guest ok has no effect.

PART

II

CH

6

EXAMPLE

Extending our scratch space file share example again, we can make the share completely anonymous by using some of the guest share parameters. This is shown in Listing 6.4.

LISTING 6.4   CREATING AN ANONYMOUS SHARE

```
[scratch]
    comment = Scratch space
    path = /scratch
    browseable = true
    writeable = true
    wide links = false
    follow symlinks = false
    guest account = nobody
    guest only = true
```

However, the disk containing the share can become full if too many people use it, so it might be prudent to restrict access to the share to people who actually need it.

RESTRICTING ACCESS TO SHARES

Creating a completely anonymous share using the guest only parameter might be useful in theory, but in practice a Samba administrator might want to limit users who can access a share. Samba supports access control to a share on a network level based on the Internet Protocol (IP) address of the connecting workstation, and also on the username of the user trying to connect to the share.

RESTRICTING ACCESS BY WORKSTATION

Access restriction based on workstation name is done using code from the TCP wrappers security package by Wietse Venema, which might be familiar to some UNIX administrators. The arguments to the hosts allow and hosts deny parameters are in a format similar to this package (see Table 6.4).

TABLE 6.4 HOST ACCESS RESTRICTION PARAMETERS

Name	Type	Default	Description
hosts allow, allow hosts	String	None, all hosts are permitted access to the share	A list of hosts that are permitted to access the share.
hosts deny, deny hosts	String	None, no hosts are denied access to the share	Takes a list of workstations that are denied access to the share unless the workstation is listed in the hosts allow parameter. The hosts deny list takes precedence over workstations listed in hosts allow.
use rhosts	Boolean	False	If this parameter is true, the .rhosts file in the user's home directory can be used to specify trusted hosts and users who can access the share without a password. This is considered a security risk because the connecting client is trusted to provide a correct username. The use rhosts parameter is a global parameter and must be specified in the global section of the smb.conf file.

TABLE 6.4 CONTINUED

Name	Type	Default	Description
hosts equiv	String	No hosts are trusted	The value of this parameter specifies a file containing a list of trusted users and hosts. Matching users and hosts will be allowed access to the share without specifying a password. Use of this parameter is considered a serious security risk because the client is trusted to provide a valid username. This parameter is a global parameter.

Hosts are specified using the following rules:

- Multiple hosts can be separated by either commas or whitespace.
- A host can be specified by its name or its IP address.
- IP address ranges can be specified either in network/netmask format, or by a partial IP address. For example, the following entries match all hosts in the 10.1.1.0 and 10.1.2.0 class C subnets:

  `hosts allow = 10.1.1.0/255.255.255.0 10.1.2.`

- If your system supports NIS netgroups then groups of hosts can be specified using the @ symbol.
- The ALL keyword matches all IP addresses.
- The EXCEPT keyword can be used to exclude addresses from a range.

For example, to allow access to all hosts in the workstations and servers netgroups, except for workstation3 and workstation4 and every host in the 10.1.2.0 subnet, use the following settings:

```
hosts allow = @workstations @servers
hosts deny = workstation3 workstation4 10.1.2.0/255.255.255.0
```

The format of the hosts equiv file is as follows:

- Hostnames are specified one per line. All users on the named host may log in without a password.
- An optional username may be given after the hostname separated by a space. This limits the trust to only the specified user.
- Netgroups may be specified with an @ symbol.
- Entries may be negated (that is, they are not trusted) by prefixing the hostname with a minus (–) sign.

EXAMPLE

Using the hosts allow and hosts deny parameters, it is possible to set up two types of access policy to file shares:

- A "mostly open" policy, which consists of setting hosts allow to ALL and explicitly denying workstations by adding them to the hosts deny list.

- A "mostly closed" policy, which consists of denying access to all workstations by setting hosts deny to ALL and explicitly enabling access by adding workstations to the hosts allow list.

The type of policy used, if any, depends on the conditions at your site. A mostly closed policy might be appropriate for a business network where confidential information is stored on Samba servers. The mostly open policy might work better within an educational environment.

We will restrict access to our scratch storage space share only to a handful of workstations by implementing the mostly closed policy. The new share definition appears in Listing 6.5.

LISTING 6.5 RESTRICTING SHARE ACCESS BY MACHINE

```
[scratch]
    comment = Scratch space
    path = /scratch
    browseable = true
    writeable = true
    wide links = false
    follow symlinks = false
    guest account = nobody
    guest only = true
    hosts deny = ALL
    hosts allow = workstation1, workstation2, workstation3
```

RESTRICTING ACCESS BY USER

It might be easier to restrict access to a share by specifying usernames instead of workstation names. This might be required especially if users do not use a single machine all the time but move around a lot. Samba enables you to configure a share to be readable by one group of users and writable by another, as well as allowing or denying access to the file share based on username. These parameters (shown in Table 6.5) can be combined with the host restriction parameters in the previous section to provide flexible access control to a share.

TABLE 6.5 USER ACCESS RESTRICTION PARAMETERS

Name	Type	Default	Description
read list	String	Empty	A list of usernames for which a given share is read-only. Groups of users can be specified by prefixing a UNIX group name on the Samba server with an @ symbol.
write list	String	Empty, write status is determined by the read only and writeable parameters	A list of users who are allowed to write to a file share. This is independent of the settings of the read only and read list parameters, so a user who appears in the read list and the write list will be able to write to files in the share. Groups of users can be specified using an @ symbol.
valid users	String	Empty, all users may access the service	A list of users who are allowed access to the share. Users who are not in this list are denied access when trying to connect to the share. Groups of users can be specified with the @ symbol.
invalid users	String	Empty, all users may access the service	A list of users who are denied access to the share. Users who are not in the list are allowed access. Groups of users in UNIX groups can be specified with the @ symbol. If a user is in both valid users and invalid users, the invalid users takes precedence and the user is denied access.

UNIX Permission Mapping

Because files on a Samba file share are stored on an underlying UNIX file system, file permissions must be managed. Samba contains several parameters to give the Samba administrator complete control over the permissions of files stored on Samba shares (see Table 6.6).

TABLE 6.6   UNIX PERMISSION PARAMETERS

Name	Type	Default	Description
create mask, create mode	String	0744	When a user creates a file on a share, the octal value of this parameter is used to mask the UNIX permissions on the file. Any permission bit not set in the create mask will be cleared on the newly created file. The default removes group and other write and execute permissions from new files.
directory mask, directory mode	String	0755	Used in a similar manner to the create mask parameter but is applied to directories. Any permission bits not set in the directory mask will be cleared in the newly created directory. The default removes group and other write permissions from new directories.
force create mode	String	000	Files created on the share will have set the octal permission bits specified in this parameter. This parameter is useful for allowing users of the share to access files created by others.
force directory mode	String	000	Directories created on the share have the permission bits specified in this parameter set. This parameter is useful in conjunction with force create mode for creating group-accessible files on a share.
force user	String	None	Forces all file operations performed on the share to be done as the specified UNIX user. This occurs only after a connection to a share. The connecting user must still provide a valid username and password to access the share.
force group, group	String	None	Forces all file operations on the share to be performed as the specified UNIX group in a similar manner to the force user parameter.
username map	String	Empty, no username mapping is performed	Allows a Samba server to perform transitions between Windows usernames and UNIX usernames. This is useful if a user wants to access her home directory and has a Windows username that is different from her UNIX username.

To enable username mapping, create a file containing username information and set the username map parameter to point to this file with the following line:

```
username map = /etc/username.map
```

Note

Under non-Linux versions of Samba, this file should go in `/usr/local/samba/lib`.

The format of the username information is one UNIX username followed by an equals sign and then a list of Windows or UNIX usernames. Only one entry is permitted per line. Some points to note about username mapping include the following:

- Lines starting with a # or a ; character are ignored.
- A * character can be used on the right side and will match any username.
- The username map file is processed line by line. If the connecting username matches any of the names on the right side, the username is replaced with the left side. Processing continues until the end of the file is reached or until a matching line starts with the ! character.
- UNIX groups can be specified on the right side by using the @ character. NIS netgroups, if supported, can also be used. A UNIX or NIS netgroup matches if the user is a member of that group.
- Windows usernames containing spaces can be specified by surrounding the username with double quotes. For example, "Alice Smith" can be mapped to the UNIX username "alice" by adding the following line to the username map file:

  ```
  alice = "Alice Smith"
  ```

- An unlimited number of username mappings is supported.

One use of username mapping is to map a group of users onto a single username so files can be shared on a Samba file share more easily.

```
!project = alice bob
guest = *
```

For this username map file, the users alice and bob are mapped to the username project. If the ! character were not present on the first line, every user connecting to the share would be mapped to the guest user.

EXAMPLE

Consider a Web site administered by several Webmasters all responsible for maintaining and adding content to the site. All Webmasters are in the UNIX group wwwgrp, and there is a shared UNIX user named wwwuser who should own all files on the Web site.

A Samba share for the Web site might look something like Listing 6.6.

LISTING 6.6 CREATING A SHARE FOR A WEB SITE

```
[wwwsite]
    comment = Web site
    path = /opt/servers/www
    browseable = true
```

LISTING 6.6   CONTINUED

```
writeable = true
force user = wwwuser
force group = wwwgrp
valid users = @wwwgrp
```

This share definition allows access to files on the UNIX directory /opt/servers/www where the Web site content is contained. All users in the UNIX group wwwgrp are allowed to access and write to the share using their own username and password. To prevent files created by one user not being writable by another (a common problem when using UNIX groups to share a common set of files), the force user and force group parameters ensure that all files and directories created are owned by the Web user account.

USER HOME DIRECTORIES

If a user connecting to a file share has a UNIX account of the same name on the Samba server, his home directory can be automatically made accessible. The [homes] section in the smb.conf file implements user home directories.

All smb.conf parameters applicable to normal file shares can be used in the [homes] section, although not all of them make sense.

If the username map parameter is used to map usernames, the home directory is the one for the UNIX user the Windows user has been mapped to.

> **Note**
> Making the [homes] section browseable by using the browseable parameter results in two browse entries appearing for the user's home directory. One is named homes and the other is the user's name.

HOME DIRECTORIES AND NIS

In some UNIX environments, UNIX user home directories can be spread across disks on many different machines. When a UNIX user logs in, his home directory is automatically mounted from the appropriate machine over the network.

Samba supports NIS home directories by telling the client to connect directly to the user home directory on the machine containing the home directory. Samba servers must be running on all machines containing NIS home directories.

> **Note**
> Samba must be compiled with the --with-nisplus-homes option for NIS home directories to work.

To retrieve the location of user home directories from the NIS home directory map, Samba requires one global parameter, nis homedir. It's a Boolean type and defaults to false.

EXAMPLE

The smb.conf fragment in Listing 6.7 is a sample configuration for user home directories. No guest access is allowed, files and directories created on the share are writable only by the user, and they are readable only by the user and the users group. No path is needed because Samba finds this information in the passwd entry for the user.

LISTING 6.7 HOME DIRECTORY CONFIGURATION

```
[homes]
browseable = false
public = false
read only = false
create mask = 0750
directory mask = 0750
```

When Alice browses the Samba server, she will see a share that corresponds to her UNIX home directory. It might look something like Figure 6.2.

Figure 6.2
Browsing a home directory share.

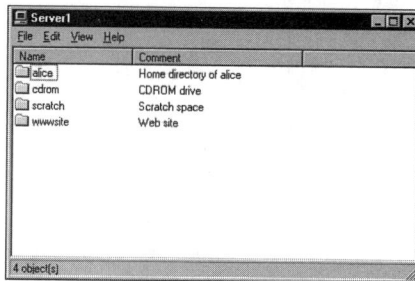

NT PERMISSION MAPPING

For Samba version 2.0.4 and greater, Windows NT 4.0 users can change NTFS permissions on files and directories through the Security tab of the Properties dialog box for a file or directory. To access the file properties dialog box, right-click on any file or directory on a Samba file share and select the Properties menu item. The NTFS file properties dialog box appears in Figure 6.3.

Currently, only the permissions and ownership security properties are handled by Samba. Any attempt to change the auditing information on a file or directory results in an access denied message if done by an NT administrator user, or a nonfunctional dialog box otherwise.

FILE PERMISSIONS

If the Permissions button on the file properties dialog box is selected, an administrator should be able to view and change three sets of permissions. These permissions correspond to the UNIX user, group, and other permissions on a file or directory. The File Permissions dialog box appears in Figure 6.4.

PART

II

CH

6

Figure 6.3
The NTFS file
properties
dialog box.

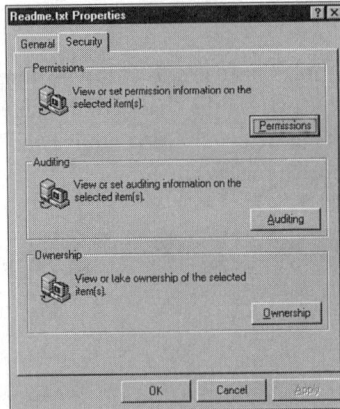

Figure 6.4
The NTFS File
Permissions
dialog box.

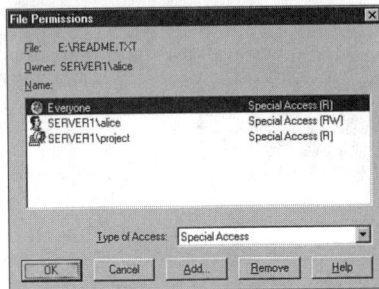

User permissions are represented by the permission name starting with the NT user icon. In Figure 6.4, the file is owned by Alice, and she has read and write access to the file. Group permissions are represented by the permission starting with the NT group icon. Group ownership of the file belongs to the UNIX group named "project." Other permissions are contained in the EVERYONE permission.

You can change file permissions by double-clicking the appropriate permission name. Only read, write, and execute permissions are supported by Samba. The NT Special Access or "O" permission is used to indicate that neither the read, write, nor execute UNIX permissions are set on the file.

Whether file permissions can actually be modified depends on the values of various `smb.conf` configuration parameters.

OWNERSHIP

By selecting the Ownership button of the File Properties dialog box, you can change ownership of a file. This is implemented by the Samba server changing the owner of the file to the UNIX user performing the take ownership operation.

Note

Only users with administrator access to a file share can take ownership of files. Administrator access can be granted to users with the `admin users` parameter.

The ownership dialog box appears in Figure 6.5. The owner of the file in question is the NetBIOS name of the Samba server, followed by a backslash, and then the UNIX username of the actual owner of the file.

Figure 6.5
The NTFS file properties ownership dialog box.

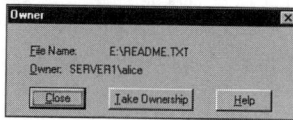

The `smb.conf` parameters that are relevant to NT file permissions are shown in Table 6.7.

TABLE 6.7   NT FILE PERMISSION PARAMETERS

Name	Type	Default	Description
nt acl support	Boolean	True for Samba version 2.0.4 and above; false for other versions	Tells Samba whether to convert Windows NT Access Control Lists (ACLs) into UNIX file permissions and allow these to be viewed or changed.
security mask	String	The value of the create mask parameter	Specifies which UNIX permissions a Windows NT user is able to change on a file using the Security tab of the Properties dialog box for that file. For example, setting this parameter to 0777 would allow the user to change all UNIX permission bits.
directory security mask	String	The value of the directory mask parameter	Specifies which UNIX permissions a Windows NT user is able to change on a directory using the Security tab of the Properties dialog box for that directory.
force security mode	String	Value of the force create mode parameter	The value of force security mode is the permission bits that are always set when a Windows NT user changes file security permissions.

PART
II

CH
6

TABLE 6.7 CONTINUED

Name	Type	Default	Description
force directory security mode	String	Value of the force directory mode parameter	The value of force directory mode is the permission bits that are always set when a Windows NT user changes directory security permissions.

ADVANCED smb.conf PARAMETERS

In this section, we look at several advanced Samba configuration parameters and what can be achieved with them.

SECURITY

As well as the parameters for restricting share access based on username and workstation name, Samba contains several other parameters to enhance the security of a Samba share. Table 6.8 lists a group of parameters relevant to security.

TABLE 6.8 ADVANCED smb.conf PARAMETERS

Name	Type	Default	Description
admin users	String	No admin users	Can contain a list of users who, when connected to the file share, have their file operations performed as the root user.
default service	String	No default service	If a user attempts to connect to a share that does not exist and a value for the default service parameter is set, the user is connected to the share of that name. Any underscore (_) characters in the service name are changed to the UNIX directory separation character (/).

TABLE 6.8 CONTINUED

Name	Type	Default	Description
map to guest	Boolean	Never, invalid users and bad passwords do not connect to the share	The value of this parameter specifies the behavior of Samba when a user attempting to connect to a file share gives an incorrect password or the username provided is not valid. This parameter is effective only if the security mode is set to user, server, or domain.
restrict anonymous	Boolean	False	Setting this parameter to true denies anonymous connections to shares. This means that every user connecting to a share on the Samba server must provide a valid username and password. This is a global parameter.
null passwords	Boolean	False	If this parameter is true, users connecting to accounts that have null (empty) passwords are allowed to succeed. This is considered a security risk. This is a global parameter.
root directory, root, root dir	String	The root directory of the Samba server, /	The root directory parameter can provide a secure environment, sometimes called a "padded cell," for Samba to operate in. This is achieved using the UNIX chroot() system call. When a user connects to the share, the Samba server sets the root directory of the process running smbd to be the directory specified. The operating system ensures that absolutely no access to files outside the directory specified will occur. A disadvantage of this is that some parts of Samba and the underlying operating system, such as dynamically linked libraries and password files, must be replicated under the root directory.

PART

II

CH

6

> **Note**
>
> Be very careful with the `admin users` parameter because any user in the admin users list can perform any operation on the file share regardless of the actual UNIX permissions on files.
>
> The name of the share will appear to be the one actually requested by the user, not the name of the share given in `default service`.

The `map to guest` parameter can have three settings. The case of these settings is not significant.

- If set to `Never`, an invalid login produces an error message and the connection attempt does not succeed.

- If the username specified does not exist and `map to guest` is set to `Bad User`, the connection attempt succeeds but as the UNIX user specified in the `guest account` parameter.

- If the specified username exists but the password given is incorrect, and `map to guest` is set to `Bad Password`, the connection will succeed but as the UNIX user given in `guest account`. This setting has the unfortunate side effect of silently mapping password typos to the guest account, which can be confusing for the user.

> **Note**
>
> Setting the `restrict anonymous` parameter to `true` might affect the performance of Samba as a primary domain controller (PDC) and is recommended only for networks consisting entirely of Windows NT machines.

→ To learn more about Samba as a PDC, **see** "Implementing a PDC with Samba," **p. 372**.

OPLOCKS

The SMB protocol used by Samba and clients connecting to it contains a method of file locking called *opportunistic locks*, or *oplocks*. This is a client-side locking protocol that basically allows SMB clients to cache file data instead of rereading it from the server. This can result in significant performance improvement. Oplocks may also cache open and close operations on a file but currently this is not supported by Samba.

Unfortunately, for oplocks to work correctly, all users accessing files on a Samba share must do so through the SMB protocol, or caching problems and data corruption can occur. A Samba user may change the contents of a file, but when the file is accessed locally on the Samba server, the changes do not appear. This problem can occur if a file share refers to a directory that is accessible through the Network File System (NFS) as well as from a Samba share. This can be true of UNIX user home directories.

For more information on oplocks, please consult the CIFS protocol specifications at `ftp://ftp.microsoft.com/developr/drg/CIFS/`.

Parameters that can be set in the `smb.conf` file relating to oplocks appear in Table 6.9.

TABLE 6.9   OPLOCK-RELATED PARAMETERS

Name	Type	Default	Description
oplocks	Boolean	True	Specifies whether Samba should allow oplocks on open files for the file share. In general, this parameter should be set to false if the file share can be written to by non-SMB client processes.
blocking locks	Boolean	True	If this parameter is true and an attempt is made by a client to lock a file and the lock cannot be obtained, Samba waits until the request can be satisfied or a timeout specified in the lock request occurs. If set to false, the lock request fails immediately if it cannot be obtained.
fake oplocks	Boolean	False	Tells Samba to grant all requests for oplocks on files that enable clients to cache file data. This parameter can be set to true for CD-ROMs to enhance performance because the underlying files are guaranteed not to change.
level2 oplocks	Boolean	False	Level 2 oplocks are a new type of oplock supported by Windows NT clients only. Setting this parameter to true enables these oplocks and can increase performance for Windows NT clients. This parameter is a global parameter.
ole locking compatibility	Boolean	True	Windows applications using Object Linking and Embedding (OLE) can use oplocks to communicate with other applications by locking large, nonexistent parts of files. This can produce problems in some versions of UNIX. This parameter is a global parameter.

PART

II

CH

6

TABLE 6.9 CONTINUED

Name	Type	Default	Description
veto oplock files	String	No files are vetoed	If the oplocks parameter is true, this parameter can tell Samba not to grant oplocks for specified files. Files are specified in a list format similar to the veto files parameter where list items are separated by / characters and wildcards can be used. This parameter should be used for files that are under contention by many clients to improve performance. To veto oplocks on semaphore files created by the NetBench benchmarking program, use the setting veto oplock files = /*.SEM/.
kernel oplocks	Boolean	True if your version of UNIX supports kernel oplocks; false otherwise	If your version of UNIX supports kernel oplocks, setting this parameter to false disables their use. Kernel oplocks prevent data corruption between SMB, NFS, and local file accesses where it would normally be necessary to disable oplocks. Currently, IRIX is the only operating system that supports kernel oplocks.
strict locking	Boolean	False	Well-written client programs check the status of locks they have made before attempting to read or write locked portions of files. If the strict locking parameter is true, Samba performs a lock check on every read and write to the share. This might have a performance penalty but might be necessary for buggy Windows applications. It should not be necessary to change this parameter unless locking problems are occurring.

Note

If your UNIX operating system supports kernel oplocks, the oplocks parameter can be set to true for shared filesystems because the operating system will ensure file consistency. Currently, only IRIX supports kernel-level oplocks.

Note

Enabling the fake oplocks parameter for shares where multiple clients might be writing files can cause data corruption.

NAME MANGLING

Long filenames or filenames that do not conform to the DOS eight-character filename with a three-character extension format (otherwise known as the "8.3 format") were first introduced in Windows 95. To Windows for Workgroups and DOS clients, these long filenames appear as a filename based somewhat on the original filename with a ~ (tilde) character, a number, and a shortened extension. Converting long filenames to 8.3 format is called *name mangling* and is performed by Samba automatically.

SAMBA'S NAME MANGLING ALGORITHM

The algorithm for converting long filenames to the 8.3 format is

1. Up to the first five alphanumeric characters of the mangled filename are copied from the long filename and converted to uppercase. These characters are taken before the rightmost dot character in the long filename.

2. The tilde character (~) is appended to the mangled filename followed by a sequence of two characters that are unique for all mangled files whose first five characters are identical.

3. The mangled filename extension is taken from the first three characters after the rightmost dot character in the long filename. The extension characters are converted to uppercase.

Some examples that clarify how the algorithm works appear in Table 6.10. All configuration parameters are set to their defaults.

TABLE 6.10   LONG FILENAMES WITH THEIR MANGLED EQUIVALENTS

Long Name	Mangled Name
Long Filename.txt	LONGF~II.TXT
Long Long Filename.txt	LONGL~BN.TXT
My.Document	MY~WG.DOC
My.Document.bak	MYDOC~WG.BAK

The mangled names look similar to their long equivalents, but similarly named files are difficult to distinguish simply by looking at their mangled names.

Some other properties of the name mangling algorithm are worth noting:

- UNIX files that start with a dot will be processed as if the leading dot were removed and an extension of three underscores appended (that is, "___"). They also have the DOS hidden attribute set.

- The name mangling algorithm might cause collisions if many files share the same first five characters. This can result in some files being inaccessible by clients that do not support long filenames.
- Mangled filenames remain the same across Samba sessions.

PARAMETERS IN smb.conf FOR NAME MANGLING

You can use several smb.conf parameters to customize the type of name mangling performed for these clients (see Table 6.11). The default settings are usually sufficient for most applications. The default settings are the same as a Windows NT server. Filenames are not case-sensitive, but filename case is preserved.

TABLE 6.11   NAME MANGLING PARAMETERS

Name	Type	Default	Description
mangled names	Boolean	True	Determines whether long file-names should be mangled to fit into 8.3 format filenames, or simply ignored. If mangled names is false, files with long file-names are not visible to DOS or Windows for Workgroups clients.
mangling char	String	The tilde (~) character	Specifies the character used in name mangling.
case sensitive, casesignames	Boolean	False	Defines whether filenames are case-sensitive. If this parameter is false, Samba must look for filenames with differing case until it finds one that matches.
mangled map	String	Empty, no files are mangled	Allows Samba to perform dynamic translation of filenames that cannot be represented under DOS without name mangling. The format of the string is a series of white space separated pair of filename specifications surrounded by parentheses. If a filename matches the first filename in the pair, it is replaced with the second filename. The * wildcard character may be used to represent zero or more characters. To map all files ending in the .text extension to the .txt extension, the following setting of mangled map can be used: mangled map = (*.text *.txt).

TABLE 6.11 CONTINUED

Name	Type	Default	Description
default case	String	Lower	Specifies the default case for new filenames. May be either the string "upper" or "lower". These values are not case-sensitive.
preserve case	Boolean	True	Determines whether new files are created with the filename case provided by the client or adjusted to comply with the case given by the default case parameter.
mangle case	Boolean	False	If files exist that are not the default case, they are mangled if this parameter is true.
mangled stack	String	50	Specifies how much internal space Samba should use to keep track of mangled filenames. More memory is consumed if this value is increased, but the chance of long filenames being successfully mangled also increases. Each unit occupies 256 bytes for name mangling on the Samba server. This is a global parameter.
short preserve case	String	True	New files that are created in the 8.3 format and are uppercase are converted to the default case if this parameter is true. If this parameter is true and the preserve case parameter is also true, new long filenames are not changed, while new short filenames are created with lowercase.

Note

The case sensitive parameter is a local parameter, but the documentation for Samba versions older than 2.0.6 mistakenly mark it as a global parameter.

The short preserve case parameter is also a local parameter, but the documentation for Samba versions older than 2.0.6 mistakenly mark it as a global parameter.

MAGIC SCRIPTS

Samba allows shell scripts and other commands to execute when certain events occur. This functionality allows for handling unusual situations such as mounting CD-ROM devices or performing post-processing of files copied to Samba file shares. The parameters in Table 6.12 are used to implement magic scripts on a Samba server.

TABLE 6.12 MAGIC SCRIPT PARAMETERS

Name	Type	Default	Description
preexec, exec	String	None	Specifies a command that executes on the Samba server whenever a user connects to a share. The command executes as the UNIX user connecting to the share.
postexec	String	None	Specifies a command that executes on the Samba server whenever a share is disconnected. The command executes as the UNIX user who is disconnecting from the share.
root preexec	String	None	Operates in the same manner as the prexec parameter, but the command executes on the Samba server as the root user.
root postexec	String	None	Identical to the postexec parameter, but the command executes on the Samba server as the root user.
magic script	String	None, magic scripts are disabled	The value of the magic script parameter is a file that exists on the file share being accessed. When this file is closed, the server executes its contents. Any output generated by the script is placed in the filename specified by the magic output parameter. The script file is deleted after it has completed execution.
magic output	String	magic script.out	Specifies the filename output the magic script appears in. If two copies of the script execute in the same directory, the results can be unpredictable.

> **Note**
>
> The magic script parameter is an experimental part of Samba and might be removed in subsequent releases.

> **Note**
>
> The magic output parameter is experimental and might be removed in subsequent releases of Samba.

EXAMPLE

Listing 6.8 uses the `root prexec` and `root postexec` parameters to mount a CD-ROM dynamically when a user connects to the share and unmount it when disconnecting from the share.

LISTING 6.8 AUTOMATICALLY MOUNTING A CD-ROM DRIVE

```
[cdrom]
        path = /mnt/cdrom
        writable = false
        root preexec = mount /mnt/cdrom
        root postexec = umount /mnt/cdrom
```

This configuration works for a single user setup but might unmount the CD-ROM at an inopportune time when multiple users access the share at once. More sophisticated locking is required to cope with a multiple-user situation.

DOS COMPATIBILITY

Some of the parameters given in Table 6.13 might be required to support legacy DOS applications and some Windows applications with Samba servers.

TABLE 6.13 PARAMETERS FOR DOS COMPATIBILITY

Name	Type	Default	Description
dos filetimes	String	False	Under UNIX, only the owner of a file may change the file's timestamp. Under DOS and Windows, any user with write access to a file can change the timestamp for that file. To tell Samba to implement the DOS/Windows semantics, this parameter must be set to true.
dos filetime resolution	String	False	If this parameter is true, Samba rounds down the reported timestamp of a file to the closest two seconds when a client requests a timestamp with one-second resolution. This parameter must be true if using Visual C++ on a Samba file share with oplocks. Otherwise, Visual C++ incorrectly reports files as having changed.
delete readonly	Boolean	False	Samba allows files and directories that have the DOS readonly attribute set to be deleted if this parameter is true. DOS does not allow a read-only file to be deleted, but under UNIX, the write permissions do not affect whether a user can delete a file.

PART

II

CH

6

TABLE 6.13 CONTINUED

Name	Type	Default	Description
map archive	Boolean	True	If this parameter is true, Samba maps the DOS archive attribute to the UNIX owner execute bit. Many backup programs use the archive bit to indicate whether a file has changed since it was last backed up because the archive attribute is set whenever a file is modified.
map hidden	Boolean	False	Samba can use the UNIX world execute bit to implement the DOS hidden attribute if this parameter is true.
map system	Boolean	False	The UNIX group execute bit can be used to implement the DOS system attribute if this parameter is true.
fake directory create times	Boolean	False	UNIX does not record the timestamp when a directory is created. Samba can either return the UNIX ctime (last change time) or the epoch when required to return a directory create time. If this parameter is true, all directories appear to have a create time of 1-1-1980.
change notify timeout	String	60 seconds	The SMB protocol defines a request that the SMB server notify a client when files in a particular directory have changed. This is called a *change notify* request. The change notify timeout parameter specifies the length of time in seconds between scans to determine whether changes have occurred in a directory. Repeated scans of directories can place a load on the Samba server, especially if the directory contains a large number of files.

Note

The value of the create mask must not mask out the UNIX owner execute bit for this parameter to operate correctly. Set the create mask value to include the octal value 100.

Note

Again, the value of the create mask parameter must not mask out the UNIX world execute bit. It must include the octal value 001 for the map hidden parameter to operate correctly.

Make sure the `create mask` includes the octal value 010 if you are using the `map system` parameter.

Note

The `fake directory create times` parameter is required for compatibility with Visual C++ makefiles, which use directory names as dependencies.

INTERNATIONALIZATION

Samba supports the use of non-English characters in filenames through its internationalization features. Several of the international character sets defined by the ISO (International Organization for Standardization) Standard 8859 are supported. This covers most Western and Eastern European languages, as well as Russian Cyrillic. Support is also present in Samba for the Japanese language through Shift-JFS.

ABOUT CHARACTER SETS AND CODE PAGES

The ISO 8859 standard defines a set of character sets in which the English alphabet characters and all other ASCII characters are mapped in the range 0x20 to 0x7f. Character values in the range 0xa0 to 0xff represent accented and other national characters. The *de facto* standard character set for use on the Internet is ISO-8859-1, which corresponds to all major Western European languages. A description of each character set defined in ISO 8859 can be found at `http://cyzborra.com/charsets/iso8859.html`.

Code pages are a collection of graphics characters that DOS and Windows clients use to represent international characters. They are given numbers such as 437 or 850. Table 6.14 shows the `smb.conf` parameters related to internationalization.

TABLE 6.14   PARAMETERS FOR INTERNATIONALIZATION

Name	Type	Default	Description
character set	String	None, no filename translation occurs	Defines the character set used by clients and maps incoming filenames from a DOS code page to a UNIX character set. This is a global parameter.

TABLE 6.14   CONTINUED

Name	Type	Default	Description
client code page	String	850, the MS-DOS Latin-1 code page	Describes which DOS code page a client is using. Many code pages are supplied with Samba and can be found in the lib/codepages directory of your Samba installation. A typical PC in use in an English-speaking country will have either code page 437 (U.S. ASCII) or code page 850 (Latin-1) active. This is a global parameter.
codingsystem	String	No mapping is performed	Specifies how to map Shift-JIS Japanese characters from the client code page into UNIX filenames.
valid chars	String	All U.S. ASCII characters are valid by default	Allows a Samba administrator to specify additional characters that can be used in filenames. This is a global parameter, although it appears as a share parameter in the Samba documentation. The character set parameter can have several values. All values are not case-sensitive.

- The string ISO8859-1 corresponds to the Western European character set. The client code page parameter must be set to code page 850 for filename translation to operate correctly.

- The string ISO8859-2 is for Eastern European languages. The client code page parameter must be set to code page 852 for filename translation to operate correctly.

- The string ISO8859-5 is appropriate for Cyrillic languages. Code page 866 is required by clients for filename translation to operate correctly.

- The string KOI8-R is for an alternative mapping of Cyrillic characters. Again, code page 866 is required.

Note

For the valid chars parameter, it might be useful to add accented characters to the filename set because by default they are not allowed in filenames. Characters can be specified individually or as an octal value. An uppercase and lowercase pair of characters is specified by separating the start and end character with a colon.

Character values can be written in decimal, octal, or hexadecimal format. Octal values are preceded with a leading zero character, and hexadecimal characters start with the prefix "0x."

FROM HERE...

We have presented a large number of smb.conf parameters that you can use to configure a file share under Samba. We now move on to describing parameters used to configure a printer share.

## CHAPTER 7

PRINTER SHARING UNDER SAMBA

In this chapter

by Tim Potter

One main duty of Samba, other than file sharing, is printer sharing. Printer sharing under Samba allows users of Microsoft Windows-based machines to print and manipulate printers installed on UNIX servers. Samba also allows UNIX users to access printers installed on Microsoft Windows servers. This process is covered in Chapter 16, "Accessing Windows from UNIX Using Samba."

This chapter deals with the following topics related to printer sharing under Samba:

- A brief introduction to installing and accessing printer shares from Windows 95/98 and Windows NT clients
- A discussion of how Samba finds printer shares
- A discussion of the various printing styles supported by Samba
- Configuration of printer shares under Samba and how to customize printer behavior
- Troubleshooting printer shares using the testprns and smbclient programs that come with Samba
- Some advanced topics such as automatic printer driver installation for Windows 95 and 98 clients, and a recipe for creating a "virtual" printer

ACCESSING PRINTER SHARES FROM WINDOWS

Printer shares are accessed from Microsoft Windows clients as if they were standard Windows network printers. But before a printer can be accessed, it must be installed on the Windows client machine. The following is a brief description of how to access Samba printers for Windows 95/98 and Windows NT clients. More detailed information on client access to Samba is given in Chapter 12, "Accessing Samba from Windows for Workgroups and Windows 9x," and Chapter 13, "Accessing Samba from Windows NT."

INSTALLING PRINTERS USING THE ADD PRINTER WIZARD

One method of installing a Samba network printer is to use the Add Printer Wizard. This can be performed on Windows 95/98 and Windows NT client machines. Perform the following steps to install a Samba network printer using the Add Printer Wizard:

1. Start the Add Printer Wizard by selecting Settings, Printers from the Windows Start menu.
2. Double-click the Add Printer icon to start the Add Printer Wizard.
3. Click the Next button to pass through an introductory dialog box, select the Network Printer radio button, and then click the Next button again.
4. You will now be asked to enter the network path of the Samba share. This dialog box appears in Figure 7.1. The can be used to browse the network to find appropriate printer shares to install. Click the Next button to accept the name you have entered. The Do You Print from MS-DOS Based Programs radio button can be set to Yes to redirect an unused parallel port to the printer, but we will not consider this here.

Figure 7.1
Installing a
network printer
using the Add
Printer Wizard.

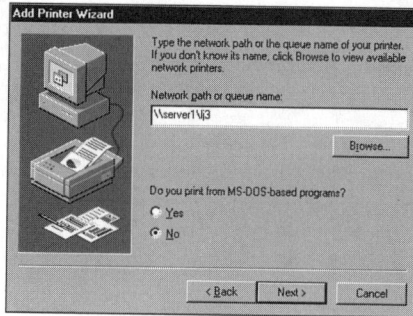

Note

If an invalid printer name is entered here, the Add Printer Wizard displays a message saying that the network printer is currently offline and asking whether to install the printer anyway.

5. Select the manufacturer and type of the network printer being installed, and click the Next button. You might be prompted to insert installation media if drivers for this printer are already installed, or asked whether the existing drivers should be replaced. It is often safer to retain the existing driver files if they already exist.

6. Enter the name the Samba network printer will be installed as, and click the Next button.

7. If you want to print a test page on the Samba network printer, select the appropriate setting and click the Finish button to exit the Add Printer Wizard and complete the installation of the printer.

After the last step has been completed, Windows will attempt to install the appropriate printer drivers for the Samba network printer. Normally, a Windows installation CD or a network share containing a copy of the required Windows CD is needed to install the printer drivers. Windows will ask for the correct CD to be inserted or the location of a network share can be entered.

If the client machine is running Windows 95 or Windows 98, it is possible to store the printer driver files on the Samba server. Doing this avoids having to use an installation CD-ROM or have a copy of the CD-ROM on a network share. This process is explained later in this chapter.

INSTALLING PRINTERS FROM NETWORK NEIGHBORHOOD

The other method for installing a Samba network printer is to browse for the printer, either using Windows Explorer or the Network Neighborhood, and select Install from the File menu for the printer. To do this, perform the following steps:

1. Use the Network Neighborhood or Windows Explorer to browse for the Samba server hosting the printer you want to install.

PART

II

CH

7

2. Select the printer by single-clicking it in Windows Explorer or Network Neighbor-hood. Printers available on a remote machine are in a folder called Printers, browsable under the name of the machine.

3. To install the printer, either right-click the selected printer and select Install from the menu, or open the File menu and select Install. An example appears in Figure 7.2.

Note

Some installations of Windows might display the printers in Windows Explorer or the Network Neighborhood slightly differently from that previously described.

Figure 7.2
Installing a network printer from Network Neighborhood.

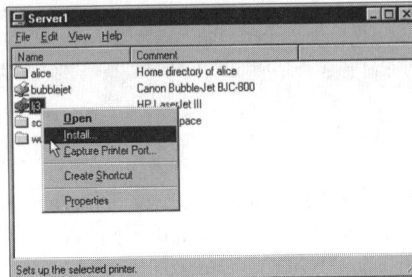

4. Provide answers to questions asked in dialog boxes. This process should be similar to installing a printer using the Add Printer Wizard.

PRINTING AND MANAGING SAMBA PRINTER SHARES UNDER WINDOWS

From the client's point of view, printing to and managing a Samba printer installed on a UNIX server is identical to printing and managing one installed on a Microsoft Windows server. This is usually achieved by using the printer queue applet. The printer queue for the printer installed in the previous section appears in Figure 7.3.

Clients can pause and resume the printer, as well as pause and cancel individual print jobs by using the Printer menu of the print queue menu, or by selecting printer jobs and using the Document menu.

Note

Depending on the printing style supported by the UNIX server running Samba, not all printer management functions normally available in Windows might be supported by Samba. For example, some Samba printers might not be paused or resumed but individual documents can still be cancelled or paused. The "Printing Styles Supported by Samba" section contains more information on which particular printer functions are supported.

Figure 7.3
The printer queue window for a Samba network printer.

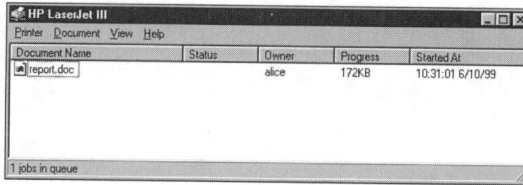

REMOVING SAMBA PRINTER SHARES UNDER WINDOWS

A Windows user can remove a Samba network printer the same way a network printer is installed on a Windows server. One method is to select the printer in the Printers applet from the Control Panel, and select the Delete option from the File menu.

HOW SAMBA FINDS PRINTER SHARES

As discussed in the section on "Finding and Accessing Shares" in Chapter 6, "File Sharing Under Samba," Samba uses the same process to find printer shares. It also respects all accessibility parameters, such as hosts allow, hosts deny, valid users, invalid users, and so on.

The main point to notice here is that an explicit share name, such as [fred], overrides any printer in the printcap file. In addition, any name pulled in as a result of the [homes] section overrides any name pulled in as a result of the [printers] section.

CONFIGURING PRINTERS UNDER SAMBA

Samba has been written to simplify access to printers already installed on a UNIX server. If one or more printers are installed and work correctly under UNIX, it is a simple matter to tell Samba to make these printers available. This is achieved using the [printers] section in the smb.conf file.

THE [printers] SECTION

The [printers] section defines a special share name that, if it appears in the smb.conf file, enables Windows users to connect to any printer installed on the Samba server. By default, the list of printers to export is taken from the /etc/printcap file. Modifying the setting of the printcap name parameter, as discussed in the following text, can change the location of this file.

Another property of the [printers] section is that all parameters set in it are applied to all printers exported by Samba. This allows a Samba administrator to set security and other parameters globally across all printer shares. A sample [printers] section appears in Listing 7.1.

Note

The [printers] share must have the printable parameter set to true; otherwise, Samba will not load the configuration file.

LISTING 7.1 A SAMPLE [printers] SHARE DEFINITION

```
[printers]
    comment = UNIX printer %p
    path = /var/spool/samba
    printable = yes
```

All macro substitutions mentioned in Chapter 9, "Samba Automation," can be used, as well as a few extra ones related to printing. The following explains these additional macros:

- %s and %f are replaced with the name of the file being printed. This is not necessarily the same as the name of the document being printed from the user's point of view.

> **Note**
>
> Earlier versions of the smb.conf man page suggested that the %f and %s macros were different, with %s providing the full pathname of the spool file if it was not preceded by a slash (/). The %f macro supposedly provided the spool filename.
>
> With at least Samba 2.0.5 and above, these two macros provide the spool filename only.

- %p is replaced by the name of the printer.
- %j is the job number as generated by the UNIX printing system when the print job is submitted. This number is parsed from the output of the print command and lpq command parameters.

Table 7.1 shows two smb.conf parameters that are useful in both the [printers] and [global] sections.

TABLE 7.1 GLOBAL PRINTER CONFIGURATION

Name	Type	Default
printcap name, printcap	String	The default is the string /etc/printcap except for AIX machines where /etc/qconfig is used. System V-based machines use the output of the lpstat -v command to determine available printers. This parameter is a global parameter.
printer name, printer	String	None, but might be the string 'lp' on some systems.

The first parameter enables a Samba administrator to override the location of the printcap file where UNIX printer definitions are stored. When the [printers] section in the smb.conf file is used, this option can be used to limit the number of printers actually made available or to provide aliases to printers. This parameter is a global parameter.

The format of a `printcap` file used to specify aliases is one entry per line, with aliases specified by pipe (|) characters. For example:

```
lj3|HP LaserJet III
bj|Canon BubbleJet
```

The `printer name` parameter specifies the name of the UNIX printer to send print jobs to. If specified in the global section of the `smb.conf` file, its value is the UNIX printer used when no printer name is given for the print share. This parameter allows a different name to be given to the Samba printer. For example, to share the UNIX printer called lj3 as a Samba printer called laserjet, use the following `smb.conf` fragment:

```
[laserjet]
    printer name = lj3
```

CUSTOMIZING INDIVIDUAL PRINTERS

A Samba administrator can use the `[printers]` share to set printer share properties for all printers, but it is sometimes necessary to modify parameters for an individual printer. For example, the use of a color laser printer might have to be restricted to a certain set of users to avoid excessive or unauthorized use.

To specify additional parameters for a printer, create a section in the `smb.conf` file using the name of the printer you want to modify. Listing 7.2 shows an example of adding some settings to an HP LaserJet III named lj3. For this printer, only the users alice and bob can send jobs to the printer.

LISTING 7.2 CUSTOMIZING PRINTER SHARE SETTINGS

```
[lj3]
     comment = HP LaserJet III in mail room
     valid users = alice bob
```

BASIC PRINTER SHARE PROPERTIES

In a similar manner to file shares, several `smb.conf` parameters (listed in Table 7.2) can control the basic properties of a printer share. These parameters can be used in either the `[printers]` section or a section referring to an individual Samba printer.

TABLE 7.2 BASIC PROPERTIES FOR PRINTER SHARES

Name	Type	Default	Description
comment	String	No comment string	The text should describe the purpose or location of the printer share because a user browsing it will see this string next to the printer share name.

TABLE 7.2 CONTINUED

Name	Type	Default	Description
printable, print ok	Boolean	False	If this parameter is true, the share specifies a printer share. Because the default for printable is false, every printer share must explicitly set it to true.
path	String	/tmp	Specifies the location where files spooled for printing are stored. Ensure there is sufficient disk space available to store as many spooled documents as you think could be printed at once.
min print space	String	0, so print jobs can always be spooled	Contains the minimum amount of free disk space in kilobytes required before a user can spool a print job for the specified printer. This amount of space must be present in the directory specified by the path parameter.

Note

For the path parameter, this directory should not be the same as the spool directory for the UNIX printer. After a file has been spooled by Samba into the directory specified by the path parameter, it is spooled again into the actual spool directory for the UNIX printer by the printing system.

PRINTING STYLES SUPPORTED BY SAMBA

Printing under UNIX is done slightly differently for each flavor of UNIX. For example, System V-based versions of UNIX use the lp and lpstat commands to manage the print queue, but HPUX uses the lpr and lpq commands to achieve the same result. These differences in command names and arguments would normally make printing on different flavors of UNIX difficult. Fortunately, Samba is capable of detecting the type of operating system and the commands required to control printers. This information is called a *printer style*.

The style of printing is determined by thesetting of the printing parameter in the smb.conf file. The printing style includes default values for several smb.conf parameters.

The printing style defines how to perform the following actions:

- Spooling a job to the printer—Samba executes the command in the print command parameter.
- Removing a spooled job from the printer queue—This is achieved using the lprm command parameter.

- Retrieving the status of any documents in the printer queue and printing their progress—The `lpq command` is used to obtain this information.

- Pausing and resuming print jobs using the `lppause command` and `lpresume command`—Some printing styles do not support pausing and resuming print jobs.

- Pausing and resuming the printer queue (as opposed to individual printer jobs) using the `queuepause command` and `queueresume command`—Some printing styles do not support pausing and resuming of printer queues.

When Samba is compiled, the printing style is automatically determined. It should not be necessary to change it unless you are not using the default printing software that comes with your flavor of UNIX.

THE `printing` PARAMETER   The value of the `printing` parameter affects the defaults for the commands used to access and control behavior of Samba printers. The `printing` parameter (a string type) can be one of the following values, depending on the flavor of UNIX on which the Samba server is running:

- The string `BSD` for BSD-based UNIX machines such as Linux, FreeBSD, and OpenBSD.

- The string `SYSV` for System V-based machines such as Solaris and Digital UNIX.

- The strings `HPUX`, `QNX`, or `AIX` for supporting printing under these particular UNIX operating systems.

- LPRng (Line Printer Next Generation) is a reimplementation of the BSD printing services with many improvements. LPRng support is enabled by setting `printing` to the string `LPRNG`. More information on LPRng can be found at `http://www.astart.com/LPRng.html`.

- The Common UNIX Printing System, or CUPS, is a new implementation of printing services under UNIX. Set the `printing` parameter to the string `CUPS` to enable support for it. The CUPS Web page is at `http://www.cups.org/`.

Note

CUPS support is new for Samba 2.0.6.

- PLP (Public Line Printer) is a predecessor to LPRng, and Samba support for it is enabled by setting `printing = plp`.

- SoftQ is another printing style supported by Samba, which is not very common.

The setting of the `printing` parameter is not case sensitive.

The default value is determined by Samba at compile time. Samba can automatically detect operating systems based on BSD and System V, as well as HPUX, QNX, and AIX.

PART

II

CH

7

> **Note**
>
> You should not normally need to change the setting of the `printing` parameter because Samba usually does a good job of detecting it at compile time. The exception is the LPRng and CUPS printing styles, which must be explicitly specified.

The settings for the various printing parameters for `printing = sysv` are

```
lpq command = lpstat -o%p
lprm command = cancel %p-%j
print command = lp -c -d%p %s; rm %s
lppause command = lp -I %p-%j -H hold
lpresume command = lp -I %p-%j -H
queuepause command = lpc stop %p
queueresume command = lpc start %p
```

The values for `printing = hpux` are

```
lpq command = lpstat -o%p
lprm command = cancel %p-%j
print command = lp -c -d%p %s; rm %s
queuepause command = disable %p
queueresume command = enable %p
```

Pausing and resuming print jobs are not supported under the HPUX printing style.

For `printing = qnx`:

```
lpq command = lpq -P%p
lprm command = lprm -P%p %j
print command = lp -r -P%p %s
```

Pausing and resuming print jobs and printer queues are not supported under the QNX printing style.

For `printing = softq`:

```
lpq command = qstat -l -d%p
lprm command = qstat -s -j%j -c
print command = lp -d%p -s %s; rm %s
lppause command = qstat -s -j%j -h
lpresume command = qstat -s -j%j -r
```

For `printing = bsd, printing = aix, printing = lprng, and printing = plp`:

```
lpq command = lpq -P%p
lprm command = lprm -P%p %j
print command = lpr -r -P%p %s
```

Pausing and resuming print jobs and printer queues are not supported under the BSD, AIX, LPRng, and PLP printing styles.

For printing = cups:

```
lpq command = /usr/bin/lpstat -o%p
lprm command = /usr/bin/cancel %p-%j
print command = /usr/bin/lp -d%p -oraw %s; rm %s
queuepause command = /usr/bin/disable %p
queueresume command = /usr/bin/enable %p
```

Pausing and resuming print jobs are not supported by Samba under CUPS.

MANAGING PRINT JOBS

Print job management includes tasks such as pausing, resuming, and removing jobs from the print queue. Table 7.3 shows the smb.conf parameters used to implement this functionality in Samba.

TABLE 7.3   PRINT JOB MANAGEMENT PARAMETERS

Name	Type	Default	Description
Lppause command	String	None, unless the value of printing is either the string SYSV or the string softq[1]	Specifies the command executed by the Samba server to stop printing or spooling the current print job.
Lpresume command	String	None, unless the value of printing is either the string SYSV or the string softq[2]	Executed on the Samba server to continue printing a print job paused by the lppause command.
lprm command	String	Depends on the setting of the printing parameter	States the command executed on the Samba server to remove a print job from the specified printer.
Postscript	Boolean	False	Setting this parameter to true tells Samba to add a PostScript header to the start of every print job. This is useful for clients that do not generate output in the correct PostScript format.

TABLE 7.3   CONTINUED

Name	Type	Default	Description
print command	String	Depends on the value of printing[3]	The Samba server executes this command when a client has finished spooling a file. The command should send the spooled file to the required UNIX printer or other device for processing. Can be specified in the global section of the smb.conf file where it is used as a default for every printable share that does not supply its own print command.

[1] *If* printing *is the string* SYSV, *the default* lppause command *is* lp -I %p-%j -H hold. *If it is the string* softq, *the* lppause command *is* qstat -s -j %j -h.

[2] *If the value of* printing *is the string* SYSV, *the* lpresume command *defaults to* lp -I %p-%j -H resume. *If* printing *is the string* softq, *the default is* qstat -s -j %j -r.

[3] *If* printing *is* BSD, AIX, QNX, LPRNG, *or* PLP, *the default* print command *is* lpr -r -P%p %s. *For* printing *being equal to the strings* SYS *or* HPUX, *the default is* lp -c -d%p %s; rm %s. *For* printing *being* SOFTQ, *the default is* lp -d%p -s%s ; rm %s.

> **Note**
>
> Samba does not remove spooled files after they have been processed, so the print command parameter should remove the spool file in addition to sending it to the printer.

> **Note**
>
> It should be possible to use the various printing parameters shown in Table 7.3 in the global section of your smb.conf file. These parameters would then specify defaults that override the settings provided by the printing parameter. However, bugs in Samba 2.0.6 prevented this from occurring. This has been fixed in Samba 2.0.7 and above.

PRINTER QUEUE MANAGEMENT

Samba contains several configuration parameters to allow management of printer queues. Again, the setting of the printing parameter should set the printer queue management parameters to working defaults.

The smb.conf parameters in Table 7.4 modify the behavior of printer queues.

TABLE 7.4 PRINTER QUEUE MANAGEMENT PARAMETERS

Name	Type	Default	Description
`lpq command`	String	Depends on the setting of the `printing` parameter	Specifies which command executes on the Samba server to obtain printer queue information for the specified printer.
`lpq cache time`	String	10 seconds	Samba keeps a cache of the printer queue information as returned by the `lpq command` to avoid executing it too often. The `lpq cache time` specifies the time in seconds before the cached printer queue information is renewed. Cached information is kept for each different `lpq command` specified in `smb.conf`.
`queuepause command`	String	Depends on the setting of the `printing` parameter	Executed by the Samba server to pause the print queue for the specified printer. No further jobs should be able to be submitted to the printer after the `queuepause command` has been executed.
`queueresume command`	String	Depends on the setting of the `printing` parameter	Should undo the effects of the `queuepause command` and allow print jobs to be submitted to the specified printer.

EXAMPLE

In most situations, simply setting the value of the `printing` parameter for your flavor of UNIX will be enough to get printing working under Samba. However, if your printer requires some special options to work correctly, you might need to explicitly modify some of the printing style parameters.

Some UNIX printers support special printing options such as printing on both sides of the paper or automatic conversion to other printer languages, such as PostScript. This is usually achieved by passing special options to the `lp` command. This usually occurs when spooling printer jobs by executing the value of the `print command` parameter.

The particular UNIX software that comes with the HP LaserJet III supports printing on both sides of the paper (duplexing) by passing `-o vd` to the `lp` command when spooling a document to be printed. The printer is installed on a UNIX server running the Solaris operating system. To enable duplexing on this printer for all jobs spooled, the value of the `print command`

PART

II

CH

7

parameter should be changed as shown in Listing 7.3. The original value of `print command` was taken from its default value when the printing style was set to SYSV.

LISTING 7.3   ADDING OPTIONS TO THE print command PARAMETER

```
[lj3]
      comment = HP LaserJet III in mail room
      print command = lp -o vd -c -d%p %s; rm %s
```

ADVANCED TOPICS

Having described how printing works under Samba and most of the printing-related configuration parameters, we now look at some more advanced usage of the printing system.

AUTOMATIC PRINTER DRIVER INSTALLATION

When installing a printer shared from a Windows NT server, you can also install printer drivers over the network. This can be useful for large numbers of client machines, when visiting each machine and installing printer drivers from installation media can be time consuming or inconvenient. Samba supports automatic printer driver installation for Windows 95 and Windows 98 clients. In the current version of Samba, automatic driver installation for Windows NT clients is not supported.

> **Note**
>
> Experimental support for Windows NT client automatic printer driver installation is now supported in the development version of Samba. This must be obtained from the Samba CVS repository. Retrieving and compiling a development version of Samba is mentioned in Chapter 24, "A Tour Through the Samba Source Code."

Automatic printer driver installation under Windows 95/98 is implemented by creating a special file share called PRINTER$ and copying the appropriate printer driver files to it. The driver files associated with a particular printer can be found by using the `make_printerdef` program.

USING make_printerdef

To install printer drivers automatically, the following information is needed:

- The brand name of the printer as it is known by Windows.
- Files from the Windows machine on which the printer in question has already been installed. The files are called MSPRINT.INF or MSPRINTx.INF, where *x* is a number, usually between 2 and 4. These are usually found in the C:\WINDOWS\INF directory of the Windows machine.

- A list of printer driver files. This information is generated by the `make_printerdef` program and must be copied to the `PRINTER$` share.

- A printer definition entry. This is also generated by `make_printerdef`.

The `make_printerdef` program is needed to generate the last two items in the list by using the first two items. It is called in the following manner:

```
make_printerdef inffile printername > /tmp/printers.def
```

The `inffile` parameter is one of the `MSPRINT.INF` or `MSPRINTx.INF`. If the required information cannot be found in the `MSPRINT.INF` file, call `make_printerdef` again but substitute the one of the `MSPRINTx.INF` files.

The `printername` parameter refers to the brand name of the printer as known by Windows. The exact spelling of this name is important because it must match the name of the printer as it appears in any of the `MSPRINT.INF` or `MSPRINTx.INF` files. To determine the printer name, try to install the printer using the Add Printer Wizard as a local printer. The printer name is given in the right-hand scrolling list, adjacent to the list of printer manufacturers. This appears in Figure 7.4.

> **Note**
>
> If the printer name contains space characters, it must be surrounded with double quotes when invoking the `make_printerdef` program.

Figure 7.4
Determining printer names for automatic printer driver installation.

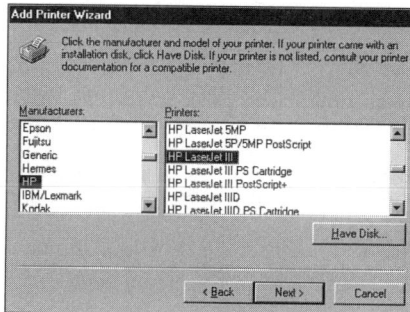

For our HP LaserJet, the exact spelling of the printer name is HP LaserJet III. This is the name that should be used as the *printername* parameter.

The output of `make_printerdef` is captured and stored in the file `/tmp/printers.def`. This file contains the printer definition information and will be required later to complete the setup of Samba for automatic printer driver installation.

EXAMPLE

We illustrate the process of setting up automatic printer driver installation for our HP LaserJet III printer by going through the process outlined earlier. We assume that Samba has been installed in the default location in the /usr/local/samba directory. If your installation directory is different from this, substitute it in the following examples.

Using a floppy disk, copy the MSPRINT.INF and MSPRINT2.INF files from a Windows 95 machine to the /tmp directory on the UNIX machine. By using the Add Printer Wizard, determine that the name of the printer as it is known by Windows is HP LaserJet III. The make_printerdef program is invoked like this:

```
make_printerdef /tmp/MSPRINT.INF "HP LaserJet III" > /tmp/printers.def
```

After some introductory debugging information, the make_printerdef program lists the files required to install the printer driver. This output appears in Listing 7.4.

LISTING 7.4 LIST OF PRINTER DRIVER FILES TO INSTALL IN THE PRINTER$ SHARE

```
Copy the following files to your printer$ share location:
HPPCL5MS.DRV
UNIDRV.DLL
UNIDRV.HLP
ICONLIB.DLL
FINSTALL.DLL
FINSTALL.HLP
```

These files can usually be found in the SYSTEM directory of the Windows installation, usually C:\WINDOWS\SYSTEM. Copy these files from the Windows 95 machine into a directory called /usr/local/samba/lib/drivers. This directory is the path of the PRINTER$ share. You might need to be the root user to do this.

The file /tmp/printers.def created on the UNIX machine contains printer definition information needed by Samba for the automatic install process. The following are the contents of the file for the HP LaserJet III:

```
HP LaserJet III:HPPCL5MS.DRV:HPPCL5MS.DRV:UNIDRV.HLP::EMF:HPPCL5MS.DRV,
UNIDRV.DLL,UNIDRV.HLP,ICONLIB.DLL,FINSTALL.DLL,FINSTALL.HLP
```

Copy this file to the Samba install directory using the following command. This also might need to be done as the root user. Ensure that the text occupies only one line in the file.

```
cp /tmp/printers.def /usr/local/samba/lib
```

Note

If support for installation of printer drivers for multiple printers is required, printer definition information for all printers is required. In this case, run the make_printerdef program for the second printer as previously, but use two greater-than signs, >>, to append the printer information to the /tmp/printers.def file.

Now that you have created printer definition information and made a list of files required to install the driver, you are ready to configure Samba itself for driver installation.

CREATING THE PRINTER$ SHARE

Add the following lines to your smb.conf file to set up the PRINTER$ share. Substitute the actual directory where your printer drivers have been copied in the path parameter.

```
[printer$]
     comment = Printer drivers
        path = /usr/local/samba/lib/drivers
        public = yes
        writeable = no
```

Samba also needs to know the location of the printer definition file. Add the following configuration parameters to the global section of the smb.conf file to tell Samba where this file is located:

```
[global]
          printer driver file = /usr/local/samba/lib/printers.def
```

SHARING THE PRINTER

Finally, you must create a printer share that can be installed by Windows 95/98 client machines. The printer is shared using the following printer share. Note that the value of the printer driver parameter must correspond exactly to the printer name used when calling the make_printerdef program. If the printer driver name contains spaces, double quotes are not required.

```
[lj3]
          comment = HP LaserJet III
          browseable = yes
          printable = yes
          public = yes
          printer driver = HP LaserJet III
```

TESTING

We can test our automatic printer installation by configuring Samba as shown earlier and by attempting to install the printer by performing the following steps on a Windows 95 or Windows 98 client machine:

1. Browse the Samba server using the Network Neighborhood. A shared printer named lj3 should be visible. If this is not the case, check that you have added the printer correctly in the previous section.

2. Move the cursor over the shared printer, right-click the lj3 icon, and select Install from the menu.

The printer should be installed on the Windows machine, and the printer driver files should be automatically downloaded and installed from the Samba server. Depending on your version of Windows, several dialog boxes might be displayed asking about printing from MS-DOS, whether the printer is to be the default printer, and printing a test page on the newly installed printer. Answer these appropriately for your system.

If, during the printer installation process, Windows asks for a particular file to be copied from the installation media, there is a problem with either the PRINTER$ share or the printer definition file. Check that the user can connect to the PRINTER$ share and that the file requested by Windows is actually present in the share. Also check that the value of the printer driver parameter is the same value used when make_printerdef was invoked. The PRINTER$ share is the default value for the printer driver location parameter. This parameter is explained in Table 7.5.

Configuration Parameters

Table 7.5 is a summary of all smb.conf parameters that apply to configuring automatic printer driver installation.

Table 7.5   Parameters for Automatic Printer Driver Installation

Name	Type	Default	Description
printer driver	String	None	Specifies the string returned by the Samba server when clients request the printer driver for a particular printer. If no printer driver string is specified, the client machine presents the user with a list of drivers to select from. The correct value for the printer driver string can be chosen from this list for the driver files to be automatically installed.
printer driver file	String	The directory PREFIX/ lib/printers.def, where PREFIX is the directory in which Samba is installed (usually the directory /usr/local/samba).	Points to the location of the printers.def file, which contains the information required to automatically install printer drivers for Windows 95 clients.

TABLE 7.5   CONTINUED

Name	Type	Default	Description
printer driver location	String	None; however, Windows 95/98 clients default to use a share named PRINTER$ on the server where the printer share is located.	Specifies the name of the share from which printer driver files can be loaded. For transparent printer driver installation, this share should ideally be a guest share. For security reasons this share should not be writeable. This share can point to another SMB server. For example, printer driver location = \\server2\printer$ tells clients to install printer driver files from the PRINTER$ share on the SMB server named SERVER2.

CREATING A VIRTUAL PRINTER

In this section, we will create a virtual printer that can be printed to by Windows clients, but with output handled by Samba and not actually sent to a real printer. The output will be sent to a shell script, and any operation can be performed on the data. As an example, we will be mailing all output sent to the printer to Alice's email address at the Example Corporation.

CONFIGURING A VIRTUAL PRINTER UNDER SAMBA

To create the virtual printer, we must first have a printer share that can be accessed by client machines. Add the printer definition contained in Listing 7.5 to the smb.conf file.

LISTING 7.5   VIRTUAL PRINTER ENTRY IN smb.conf

```
[virtual]
        path = /tmp
        printable = yes
        public = yes
        browseable = yes
        printer driver = Generic / Text Only
        print command = /usr/local/bin/vlpr %s
```

The share given in Listing 7.5 defines a printer, but there is no actual hardware that the share is connected to. In fact, the standard UNIX printer system is bypassed. Output sent to the virtual printer share is processed by the command specified in the print command. This is a shell script named /usr/local/bin/vlpr, which we must create before the virtual printer can be used.

PART

II

CH

7

Listing 7.6 shows a sample UNIX shell script that will mail anything sent to the printer to Alice, whose email address is alice@example.com. The %s macro argument in print command is expanded to the name of the file to which the document has been spooled.

LISTING 7.6 VIRTUAL PRINTER PROCESSING SCRIPT /usr/local/bin/vlpr

```
#!/bin/sh
FILE=$1
cat $FILE | mail alice@example.com
```

Note
By setting the printer driver type to Generic / Text Only, print jobs sent to the virtual printer will be converted to text format before being emailed to Alice. If the virtual printer were installed as a PostScript or other type of printer, Alice might receive an unreadable message consisting of printer control codes.

Don't forget to make /usr/local/bin/vlpr executable so Samba can run it when a job is sent to the virtual printer. Enter the following at a command prompt to achieve this:

```
chmod a+x /usr/local/bin/vlpr
```

INSTALLING THE VIRTUAL PRINTER

To install the virtual printer on client machines, follow the instructions for installing a normal network printer at the beginning of this chapter. The virtual printer must be installed as type Generic / Text Only because it does not understand any printer formatting codes. This can be found under the manufacturer name of Generic.

TESTING THE VIRTUAL PRINTER

You test the virtual printer in a similar way to a normal printer: by sending it a test page. Do this either from the Network Neighborhood or from the Printers link within the Control Panel applet. Right-click the printer icon and select the Properties item from the menu. At the properties dialog box click the Print Test Page button. If the virtual printer has been installed correctly, Alice should be mailed a text version of the standard Windows printer test page.

Note
Don't forget to change the email address in the /usr/local/bin/vlpr script to one that actually exists to view output sent to the virtual printer.

TROUBLESHOOTING

Several basic techniques specific to printer shares can be used to troubleshoot printing problems. Here we suggest a few and how to use them to determine the source of a problem:

- Check that the printer is installed correctly on the UNIX server by attempting to print to it using your UNIX printing software. If the printer in question does not work under UNIX, it is unlikely to work under Samba. Fix any problems under UNIX before performing any more troubleshooting with Samba.

- Use the `testparm` and `testprns` programs to verify the syntax of the configuration parameters in the `smb.conf` file. Typos in configuration parameters or values are easy to make when doing a quick edit of Samba's configuration files, and these can invalidate a printer share or cause it not to work as expected.

- Attempt to print to the printer using the `smbclient` program as detailed further in this section. The `smbclient` program is useful for troubleshooting because it provides more debugging information than using a Windows client.

- Try specifying the full path to the UNIX printing software used by Samba, because commands invoked might not be in the current path when Samba tries to execute them. For example, the command to list queued jobs for Linux, using the BSD printing style, should be changed from

  `lpq command = lpq -P%p`

  to point to the full path of the `lpq command`:

  `lpq command = /usr/bin/lpq -P%p`

- Check Samba's log files for any relevant error messages regarding printing. It might be useful to set the `log level` parameter to increase the level of debug messages produced. A useful but not too verbose log level is log level three. Add this line to the global section in the `smb.conf` file:

  `log level = 3`

THE `testprns` PROGRAM

Samba comes with a test program called `testprns` designed to verify the syntax of printer shares. This program is designed to perform several simple checks to determine the validity of a specific printer share.

The `testprns` program is invoked as

`testprns printername [printcapfile]`

where the `printername` specifies the name of the printer share to test, and the optional `printcapfile` argument refers to the printer capabilities file where UNIX printers are located. This is, by default, the file `/etc/printcap` or `/etc/qconfig` under the AIX operating system. If you have used the `printcap file` parameter to specify an alternative printer capabilities file, this file should be used instead.

Unfortunately, the `testprns` program does not check much more than the existence of the printer in the printer capabilities files. A more useful troubleshooting resource is the `testparm` program.

THE testparm PROGRAM

The testparm program is useful for troubleshooting printer share problems. Because it shows the default values for all of Samba's configuration parameters, testparm can check the actual values of parameters against the values intended by the Samba administrator. This technique applies to printer shares as well as file shares.

TROUBLESHOOTING USING smbclient

An excellent method of troubleshooting most Samba problems, including printer problems, is to use smbclient, which is a command-line program that runs under UNIX and can connect to SMB shares. It is described in full in Chapter 16 (with other UNIX client programs), but a brief overview is given here.

To use smbclient to test printer shares, it must be invoked with the name of the service to connect to and the -P option to connect as a printer. Invoking smbclient from the command line should be done like this:

```
smbclient '\\servername\sharename' -P
```

The service name consists of two parts: the NetBIOS name of the server, followed by the name of the printer share to connect to. The service name starts with two backslashes, and the server name is separated from the share name by another backslash. This format is also known as the *Universal Naming Convention*, or simply as a *UNC name*. For example, the UNC name of the HP LaserJet III printer share called lj3 on the UNIX machine run by Samba called server1 is '\\server1\lj3'.

> **Note**
>
> When specifying service names to smbclient on the UNIX command line, it is important to enclose the name in single quotes to avoid the UNIX shell interpreting the backslash characters as escapes.

To connect to the HP LaserJet III printer share, invoke smbclient as shown in Listing 7.7. The initial output produced by smbclient also appears.

LISTING 7.7 TESTING A PRINTER SHARE USING smbclient

```
$ smbclient '\\server1\lj3' -P
Added interface ip=10.1.1.3 bcast=10.1.1.255 nmask=255.255.255.0
Got a positive name query response from 10.1.1.2 ( 10.1.1.2 )
Password:
Domain=[NTDOM] OS=[Unix] Server=[Samba 2.0.5a]
smb: \>
```

By default, smbclient requests a password to connect to the specified share. For a public or guest share, no password is required and the user can press Enter at the password prompt. The -N option can be given on the command line to tell smbclient not to ask for a password.

If smbclient can successfully connect to the share, it indicates that a Windows client can also connect to the share. The next stage is testing whether a document can be spooled to the printer.

To test document spooling to the printer share, use the put command of smbclient. For example, we can create a dummy file called README.TXT and send it to the printer by entering put README.TXT at the smbclient prompt. The output of smbclient should look something like this:

```
smb: \> put README.TXT
putting file README.TXT as \README.TXT (2.34006 kb/s) (average 1.11733 kb/s)
smb: \>
```

This output from smbclient tells us that the README.TXT file has been successfully sent to the UNIX printer. At this point, the contents of the dummy file should appear on the printer. If not, then there is most likely a problem with the UNIX printing system that is causing the document not to be printed.

TESTING AS DIFFERENT USERS

One of the more useful features of smbclient is the capability to specify a workgroup and username on the command line that is used to connect to the share. This is extremely useful for testing because it does not require logging out and logging back in, which are usually required to perform the same task under Microsoft Windows. The command-line options used to perform this are

- -U *user*[%*password*]—The username and password can be specified with this option. For example, to tell smbclient to connect as the user alice with password secret, the argument to the username option would be alice%secret. The *password* parameter is optional. If the username argument is not specified, smbclient looks in the USER environment variable.

- -W *workgroup*—Use the workgroup name *workgroup* to connect to the printer share. If the -W option is not specified, the workgroup specified in the *workgroup* configuration parameter is used.

For example, to test that Alice, a member of the NTDOM workgroup, can access the lj3 printer share, use the following smbclient command:

```
smbclient '\\server1\lj3' -P -U alice -W NTDOM
```

Alice will usually need to enter her password to complete the connection process. Any errors produced by smbclient can be used to further troubleshoot any problems with the printer share.

ERROR MESSAGES

smbclient produces error messages for the following situations. These messages can be useful for determining the reason behind a particular problem occurring with Samba printing shares.

PART

II

CH

7

- `Invalid network name in tree connect`—The server or share name given to `smbclient` is not correct. Check that the server specified is running Samba and that the given share name exists in the `smb.conf` file.

- `Bad password - name/password pair in a Tree Connect or Session Setup are invalid` —The user and workgroup name specified in a call to `smbclient` is not allowed to access the printer share, or the password given is not correct.

- `Connection to servername failed`—The server name specified cannot be found on the network. It might not be present if it is a Windows server, or it might not be running Samba if it is a UNIX server.

FROM HERE...

We have looked at the configuration of two important parts of Samba: file sharing and printer sharing. The remaining chapters in this section of the book concentrate on two other topics concerning the configuration of Samba:

- Managing passwords using Samba
- Automating commonly performed tasks with Samba

## CHAPTER 8

Samba and Password Management

In this chapter

by Richard Sharpe

Because Samba is used in environments with many different password management facilities, it can manage passwords in many different ways. You will find this flexibility very useful because Samba can grow with you as your use of Samba grows.

In this chapter we will

- Explore the ways in which the SMB protocol handles passwords
- Look at how Samba can use the standard Linux/UNIX authentication system
- Discuss the use of encrypted passwords with Samba
- Explain how to configure Samba to authenticate against other SMB servers
- Examine how to configure Samba to authenticate in an NIS/NIS+ environment
- Look at the issues of password synchronization between Samba and the other password systems in use
- Present information on some other authentication mechanisms that can be used with Samba

THE SMB PROTOCOL AND PASSWORDS

As discussed in Chapter 4, "An Introduction to the SMB Protocol," the SMB protocol provides for authentication of clients when accessing a server. To authenticate, the client sends an SMBsesssetupX request to the server. This SMB carries the client's username and password. Figure 8.1 shows an example of a client authenticating with a server. The middle pane in Figure 8.1 shows the username and password that the client used. You should notice that the password is in plain text.

> **Note**
>
> The password appears to have been duplicated in the password display. What actually happened is that some Win9x clients place the username in the password field area for some weird reason, and our username is the same as our password.

Sending passwords over the network in plain-text form is very insecure because, as you can see, anyone equipped with a sniffer can capture passwords. Many tools are available that can capture passwords without requiring you to capture packets and sift through them for passwords.

ENCRYPTED PASSWORDS AND THE SMB PROTOCOL

Because plain-text passwords are vulnerable to capture, the SMB protocol supports the use of encrypted passwords. We use the term *encrypted* but the passwords are not really encrypted; instead, a challenge response technique is used that is based on an irreversible hash of the user's password. SMB clients and servers actually employ several approaches to encrypted passwords.

Figure 8.1
A client
authenticates
by sending a
username and
password in an
SMBsesssetupX
request.

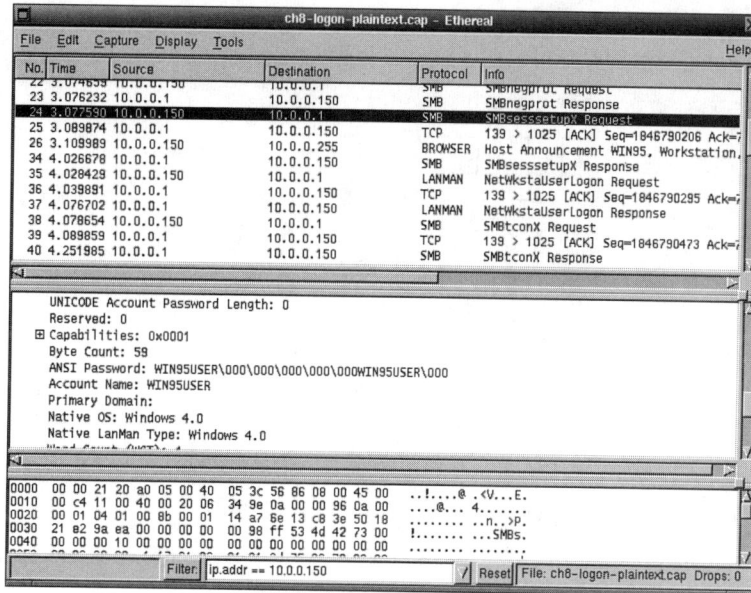

Because the SMB protocol's password encryption scheme uses the password hashes that the server OS uses, we begin our discussion there. Like all good password management techniques, Windows NT—and LAN Manager before it—do not keep users' passwords in their password databases (stored in the Registry by the Security Account Manager [SAM] under Windows NT) in plain text. Instead, they both apply an irreversible hashing function to the user's plain-text password and store the result of that hash. The LAN Manager hash is referred to as the *LM Hash*, whereas the newer, NT hash is referred to as the *NT Hash*.

The NT Hash is computed as MD4(Unicode(Pass)). The password is converted to Unicode, and the MD4 hash of it is computed, which results in a 16-byte hash.

The LM Hash is computed in the following manner:

1. The user's password is converted to uppercase and padded to 14 characters with nulls, if needed.

2. The result is converted into two 7-byte keys. Each 7-byte key (56 bits) is converted to a 64-bit DES key by adding a 0 after each seventh bit.

Note

A DES contains only 56 bits of information. However, it is passed to the routines performing the DES function as 64 bits, or 8 bytes. Each byte has a parity bit that is ignored by the DES function but can be used to detect some errors in the key.

3. Each key is used to encrypt the string KGS!@#$% using DES.

4. The results of each DES encryption are concatenated into a 16-byte hash.

That is, the following computation is performed to produce LMHASH[0..15]:

```
LMHASH[0..7]  = DES(Pass[0..6], "KGS!@#$%")
LMHASH[8..15] = DES(Pass[7..13], "KGS!@#$%")
```

This procedure is shown graphically in Figure 8.2.

Figure 8.2
The LM Hash concatenates the result of two encryptions.

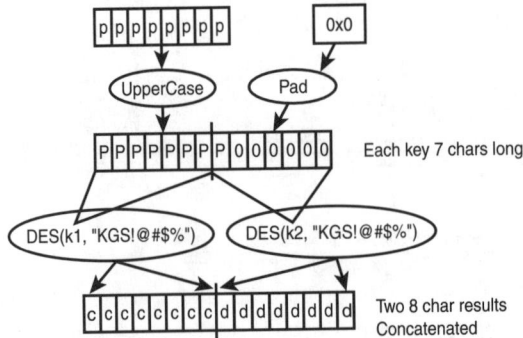

The NT Hash is computed in the following way:

1. The user's password is padded to 129 characters with nulls, if needed.

2. The resulting string is then converted to Unicode.

3. The resulting string password is then hashed with MD4, producing a 16-byte value.

That is, the following computation is performed to produce NTHASH[0..15]:

```
NTHASH[0..15] = MD4(Unicode(Pass))
```

Although plain-text passwords with the SMB protocol are handled by simply including the plain-text password in the SMBsesssetup, encrypted passwords use a more complicated challenge/response procedure as shown in Figure 8.3.

Figure 8.3
The SMB protocol uses a challenge/response method to authenticate users when using encrypted passwords.

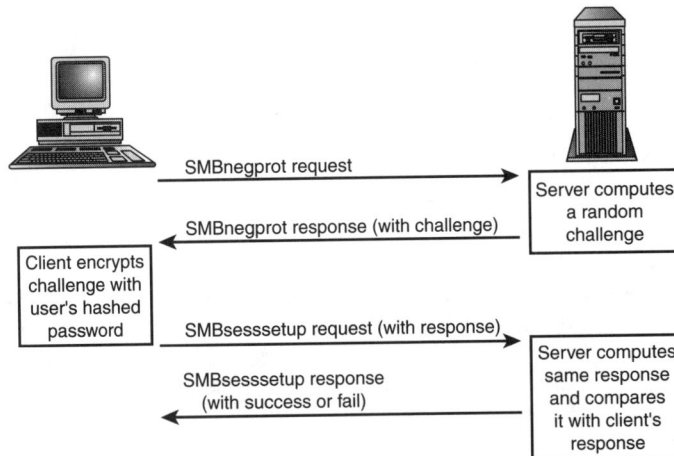

The procedure commences when the client sends an SMBnegprot request to the server. The SMBnegprot response returned by the server contains an 8-byte challenge that the client must respond to correctly. This challenge is different for each login request. (Samba actually computes a random 8-byte string each time an SMBnegprot is received.) Figure 8.4 shows the challenge sent by the server. However, this challenge/response procedure is attempted only if the server is prepared to accept encrypted passwords.

Figure 8.4
The server sends an 8-byte challenge for use when the client wants to authenticate.

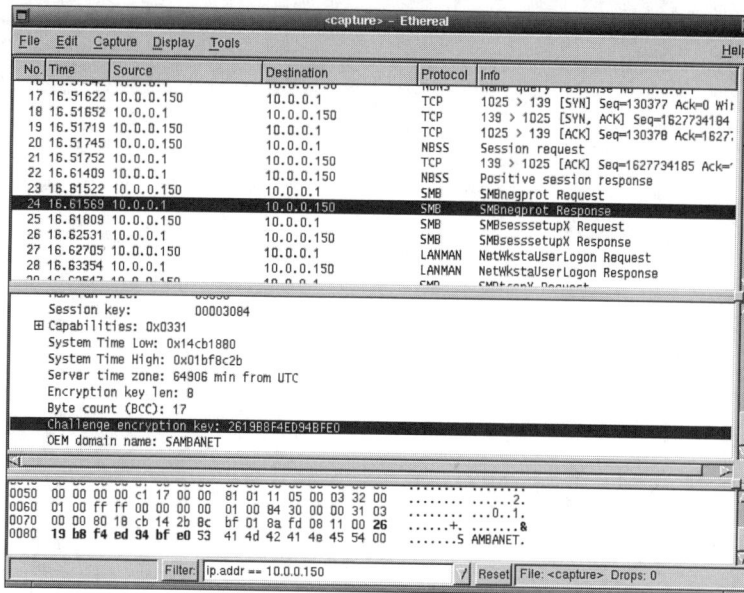

When the client sends the SMBsesssetupX request to authenticate with the server, it returns in the password field, a 24-byte value that has been computed in the following way:

1. The user's 16-byte password hash is extended to 21 bytes by appending five null bytes.

2. This 21-byte value is used as three 56-bit DES keys to encrypt the challenge sent by the client. Each encryption results in an 8-byte value.

3. These 8-byte values are concatenated to form a 24-byte value, which is returned to the server in the SMBsesssetupX request.

This avoids sending the password in any form that can be recovered and relies on the fact that the client and server share a secret. Figure 8.5 shows the password value sent back from a Windows 95 client when encrypted passwords are used.

Because neither the user's password nor his password hash is sent over the network during this process, this authentication process is theoretically very secure. However, there are problems with the actual implementation that we discuss in the next section.

Why worry about sending the password hash over the wire? The password hash is a password equivalent. If attackers were to capture a user's password hash, they could not use it with any standard client (for example, Microsoft Windows). However, they could modify a client such as smbclient, or write their own client, and then gain access to the server as the user whose password hash they have captured.

Figure 8.5
Windows 95 sends back the challenge encrypted with the user's password hash.

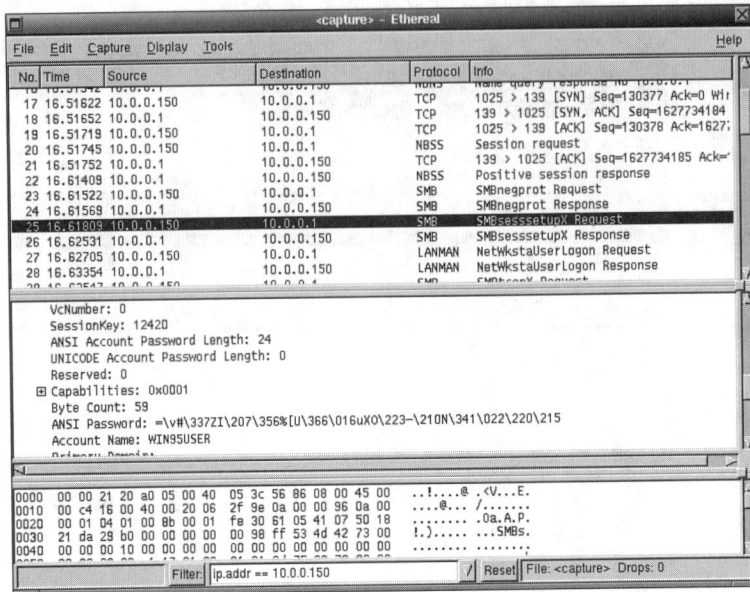

Unfortunately, as discussed later in this section, some clients use the LM Hash, whereas other clients use the NT Hash in generating the response used in an SMBsesssetupX request. Windows NT clients use the NT Hash, whereas others use the LM Hash or plain-text passwords.

> **Note**
>
> Because a user's hashed password is a password equivalent, hashed passwords must be protected from unauthorized viewing! Anyone who can read the file containing hashed passwords can take control of an NT-based network.

Microsoft changed the authentication mechanism with Windows NT4 SP5 and above to make it more secure. This new approach is referred to as *NTLMv2* and is used by Windows NT systems. The response sent back by authenticating clients is constructed in the following way:

1. The client's username is converted to uppercase as a Unicode string.

2. The resulting Unicode string is concatenated with the user's domain name as a Unicode string (workstation domain name is used if the user is not logging on to the domain of the server).

3. The whole lot is hashed with HMAC_MD4 using the NT Hash of the user's password as the key. The key is truncated to 64 bytes if it exceeds 64 bytes. This then forms the key Kr for the next step.

4. The challenge sent by the server is then hashed using HMAC_MD4 with Kr from the previous step as the key and returned in the SMBsesssetupX. Again, the key, Kr, is truncated to 64 bytes if it exceeds 64 bytes.

Table 8.1 summarizes the various authentication methods used with the SMB Protocol.

TABLE 8.1 AUTHENTICATION METHODS USED IN THE SMB PROTOCOL

Password Method	Description
Plain-text Password	The client sends plain-text passwords
LM Hash	The client computes the LAN Manager Hash of the user's password and encrypts the challenge with that when sending an SMBsesssetupX request.
NTLM, NTLMv1	The client computes the NT Hash of the user's password and encrypts the challenge with that when sending an SMBsesssetupX request.
NTLMv2	The client computes the HMAC_MD4 Hash of the user's username and domain name using the NT Hash of the user's password, and then hashes (using HMAC_MD4) the challenge with that when sending an SMBsesssetupX request.

Unfortunately, different clients use different mechanisms to send passwords. Table 8.2 is a summary of the various methods used by clients.

TABLE 8.2 PASSWORD METHOD USED BY DIFFERENT WINDOWS CLIENTS

Client	Password Method
Windows for Workgroups	Plain-text passwords
Windows 9x(*)	Plain-text and LM Hash
Windows NT to SP4(*)	Plain-text and NTLM
Windows NT SP5 and above	Plain-text and NTLMv2
Windows 2000	Plain-text and NTLMv2

Note

You can control whether Windows NT SP4 and above use NTLMv2 by modifying the LMCompatibility registry entry. For more information, see the following Web site:

http://support.microsoft.com/support/kb/articles/Q147/7/06.asp

> **Note**
>
> The only version of Samba that understands NTLMv2 is Samba TNG. The other versions currently understand only NTLM. The default value of `LMCompatibility` for Windows NT 4.0 SP4 and above allows interoperability with servers that only understand NTLM.

> **Note**
>
> Windows 2000, Windows NT SP3 and above, as well as Windows 95 with the VREDIR update and Windows 98 will send encrypted passwords by default.
>
> Defining a particular registry entry can turn these encrypted passwords off. Samba comes with `.reg` files to achieve this.

> **Note**
>
> Windows NT up to SP3 actually included two responses in the `SMBsesssetupX` request. One was encrypted with the LM Hash of the user's password; the other was encrypted with the NT Hash of the user's password.

PASSWORD VULNERABILITIES WITH THE SMB PROTOCOL

Sending plain-text passwords exposes a very large vulnerability. Anyone sniffing the wire will retrieve the user's username and password. Game over!

However, you should be aware of problems with some of the hashing approaches used in the SMB protocol. The key problem is that, although the length of the response might suggest strength, at 24 bytes long, it is calculated by appending three smaller encryptions of the same value (the 8-byte challenge), with five bytes of the last key being zero.

These problems make it possible to attack the password hash in a piecemeal fashion if an attacker has captured the challenge sent by the server. In addition, because of the way the LM Hash is calculated, it becomes very easy to check whether the user's password is less than eight characters in length. As it turns out, a program called L0PHTCRACK (see www.l0pht.com) was constructed to crack passwords used in this way. It was also effective against some versions of NT as well because both the LM Hash and NT Hash versions of the response were sent over the wire.

Because Win 9x clients only use the LM Hash to encrypt the response when logging on, they are vulnerable to attacks like L0PHTCRACK.

> **Note**
>
> Microsoft Knowledge Base Article Q239869 provides information on how to upgrade Win 9x clients to use the NTLMv2 challenge/response authentication approach.
>
> This information is available at
>
> http://support.microsoft.com/support/kb/articles/Q239/8/69.ASP

Note

Microsoft Knowledge Base Article Q147706 contains information on how to disable LM Authentication under Windows NT.

This information is available at

`http://support.microsoft.com/support/kb/articles/Q147/7/06.ASP`

AUTHENTICATING AGAINST THE passwd FILE

The default password mechanism supported by Samba is plain-text passwords, with Samba authenticating all usernames and passwords against the standard Linux/UNIX authentication system, /etc/passwd. By using this mode, you ensure that password changes from both Linux and Windows clients operate on the one set of passwords, those in /etc/passwd.

Note

The material in this chapter assumes that your Samba server is in user-level security. Your smb.conf file should have security = user, security = server, or security = domain. For a discussion of these last two, see the section "Authenticating Against Another SMB Server," later in this chapter.

Each user who will access resources on a Samba server from a Windows client must have an account on the Samba server. If you need to add an account for the client, you can do this with the useradd command under most versions of Linux:

useradd newuser

You can obtain more information about the useradd command with man useradd.

Note

The useradd command is part of the shadow-utils RPM. You might need to install this RPM to use the command.

Note

Other versions of UNIX have their own commands for adding users. Consult your System Administration documentation for more information.

Note, however, that Microsoft has made changes to most of its clients, such that they will not work with plain-text passwords. These clients will either

■ Refuse to talk to servers that do not support encrypted passwords. NT 4.0 SP3 and above do this, as well as Windows 2000. As soon as such a client receives an SMBnegprot response indicating that the server does not support encrypted passwords, the client disconnects.

■ Insist on sending an encrypted password regardless of what mode the server has indicated it is in. Windows 95 with the VREDIR update, as well as Windows 98 and Windows Millenium, behave this way.

However, all newer Microsoft clients that insist on using encrypted passwords also check a registry entry to see whether they should use plain-text passwords. To simplify the process of setting this registry entry, Samba provides a series of reg files that can simply be double-clicked from within the Windows Explorer. Table 8.3 gives a summary of the available registry setting files.

Note

Using plain-text passwords on your network creates a big security problem. Password sniffers can get lots of passwords from your network. You are strongly advised not to use plain-text passwords!

TABLE 8.3   THE PLAIN-TEXT PASSWORD REGISTRY SETTING FILES AVAILABLE WITH SAMBA

File	Purpose
Win95_PlainPassword.reg	This file sets the plain password registry entry for Windows 95 systems that have had the VREDIRE update applied and for OSR2 and above.
Win98_PlainPassword.reg	This file sets the plain password registry entry for Windows 98.
NT4_PlainPassword.reg	This file sets the plain password registry entry for Windows NT 4.0 SP3 and above.
Win2000_PlainPassword.reg	This file sets the plain password registry entry for Windows 2000.

You can easily copy these files to a floppy if you have the mtools RPM installed on your version of Linux. For example, the following command copies the reg file for Windows 95 (you must replace $version with the version of Samba you are using):

mcopy /usr/doc/samba-$version/docs/Win95_PlainPassword.reg A:

If you don't have the mtools RPM, you can mount the floppy and copy the file using the following commands (again, you must replace $version with your version of Samba):

```
su -
password: ******
mount -t vfat /dev/fd0 /mnt/floppy
copy /usr/doc/samba-$version/docs/Win95_PlainPassword.reg /mnt/floppy
```

Another password issue to be aware of with Samba is that some clients, particularly Windows for Workgroups and early versions of Windows 95, convert both the username and password to uppercase before sending them to the server. Samba has two parameters to handle this behavior: `password level` and `username level`.

Before discussing these parameters, however, we should look at the way Samba handles authentication failures when not using encrypted passwords (that is, in plain-text password mode). Samba performs the following steps to authenticate a user:

1. Samba tries to retrieve the user's entry from the authentication system in use (which could be the `passwd` file, NIS, and so on).

   If this step fails, Samba converts the user's name to all lowercase and tries to retrieve the information again.

   If it still fails, Samba tries first with the username in all uppercase, and then the first letter uppercase, then last letter uppercase, then all combinations of uppercase letters up to the count provided by the `username level` parameter.

   If no user can be found, authentication fails at this point.

2. If a user was found in the previous step, Samba checks the password supplied by the client. If it matches (after hashing), authentication succeeds.

   If authentication fails with the supplied password, Samba then converts the password to all lowercase and checks the password again. If it matches, authentication succeeds.

   However, if authentication still fails, Samba tries to authenticate with all combinations of uppercase characters up to the number specified in the `password level` parameter.

The `password level` parameter, then, should be set to the expected number of uppercase characters in a user's password if they use mixed-case passwords. You need this parameter only if you have any Windows for Workgroups clients or Windows 95 clients before OSR2 because only these clients convert passwords to uppercase before sending them.

The `username level` parameter is generally not required unless you use mixed-case usernames.

A suggested setting of the `password level` parameter, which must be placed in the global section of your `smb.conf` file, is

```
password level =
```

SAMBA AND ENCRYPTED PASSWORDS

Although Samba supports the default password mode of plain-text passwords, it is easy to configure Samba to use encrypted passwords. To do this, do the following:

1. Add the following parameters to the global section of your `smb.conf` file:
   ```
   encrypt passwords = yes
   smb password file = /etc/smbpasswd
   ```

2. Create the file /etc/smbpasswd. You can use the mksmbpasswd.sh script to create this
    file from your /etc/passwd file in the following way:

```
mksmbpasswd.sh < /etc/passwd > /etc/smbpasswd
```

Because the password hashes in your /etc/passwd file are also one-way functions (which
might be in your /etc/shadow file, and not even in /etc/passwd), all users in your /etc/
passwd file that are migrated to your /etc/smbpasswd file will have empty passwords. That is,
they can log on to the network without a password.

> **Caution**
>
> Using mksmbpasswd to convert your /etc/passwd file without setting passwords for
> all the entries in the smbpasswd file creates a large security hole!

> **Note**
>
> You will probably want to remove accounts that should not be accessible from
> Windows clients. The example given previously in step 2 will migrate all accounts,
> including bin, daemon, sync, shutdown, and so on. You should not enable network
> clients to gain access to these accounts.

It might not be appropriate to migrate all your users from the /etc/passwd file and reset their
passwords in one day. Just imagine the calls you will get if you have hundreds of users in your
/etc/passwd file.

To help migrate from plain-text password to encrypted passwords, Samba provides the
update encrypted parameter. This parameter enables you to build an encrypted password file
over a period of time as Windows users change their passwords, and then convert to using
encrypted passwords when you think you have enough users in your /etc/smbpasswd file.

To use this feature, you must have the encrypt passwords parameter set to no. You would set
the following three parameters in the global section:

```
encrypt passwords = no
update encrypted = yes
smb password file = /etc/smbpasswd
```

However, an even better way to build an smbpasswd file is to take it from an NT server. We
will explore this option next.

EXTRACTING HASHED PASSWORDS FROM NT

It is possible to extract the NT and LM password hashes that Windows NT keeps in the
SAM. Jeremey Allison of the Samba team first released a tool to do this called pwdump. Tod
Sabin of Bindview has released an improved tool called pwdump2. This new tool is available at
http://razor.bindview.com/tools/index.shtml.

After you download `pwdump2.zip` and extract the file `pwdump2.exe`, you run it in the following way, where `$pid` is replaced with the process ID of `lsass.exe` on your system:

pwdump2 $pid

You can find the process ID of `lsass.exe` using the task manager.

Because `pwdump2` dumps the NT and LM hashes in the `smbpasswd` format that Samba uses, you might want to redirect the output of `pwdump2` to a file in the following way:

pwdump2 $pid > smbpasswd

After you have extracted the current users and their password hashes from NT, you can transfer the file to your Samba server, and your users will not have lost their passwords.

For more information on `pwdump2`, see the Web page `http://razor.bindview.com/tools/desc/pwdump2_readme.html`.

CHANGING PASSWORDS FROM WINDOWS CLIENTS

Samba fully supports changing passwords from Windows clients. You can change passwords from Windows 9x clients while using either plain-text passwords or encrypted passwords. Figure 8.6 shows an example of a user on a Windows 9x client attempting to change his password. This window can be reached from the Passwords icon in the Windows 9x Control Panel.

Figure 8.6
Windows users can change passwords on Samba.

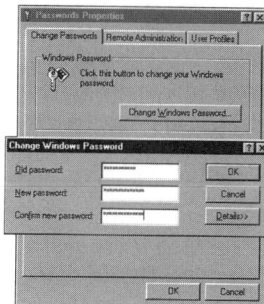

Windows NT users can change their password by pressing Ctrl+Alt+Delete while logged on and selecting the Change Password button on the Windows NT Security dialog box that comes up.

→ For information on synchronizing passwords between Samba's smb passwd file and your UNIX authentication systems, **see** "Password Synchronization," **p. 162**.

AUTHENTICATING AGAINST ANOTHER SMB SERVER

Although much of the focus of this chapter is about using Samba to maintain and manage passwords for your Windows users, Samba can be integrated into an NT-based network as well.

Samba can be integrated into NT-based networks in two different ways:

- As an SMB server doing passthrough authentication.

- As a member of a domain, with all authentication done by a PDC or BDC.

Figure 8.7 shows an example of a Samba server operating in either of these modes.

Figure 8.7
Samba can
pass authenti-
cation requests
through to
another SMB
server.

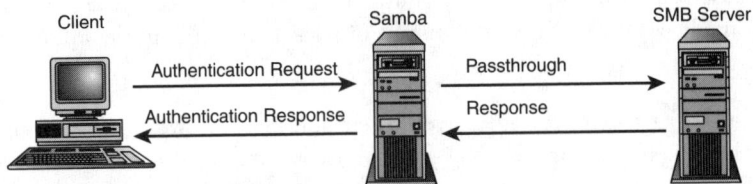

To set up Samba to authenticate against another SMB server in either of these ways, your Samba server must be configured for encrypted passwords. To configure this, simply include the following parameter in the global section of your smb.conf file:

```
encrypt passwords = yes
```

In addition, if you are using security=domain, you must also ensure that your Samba server is in the same domain or workgroup as the server you are authenticating against. Simply include the appropriate workgroup parameter in the global section of your smb.conf file:

```
workgroup = <workgroup of server authenticating against>
```

However, if you are using security=server, the server you are authenticating against need not be in the same domain or workgroup as your Samba server.

The next parameter that must be set up in either case is to specify the password server parameter. This parameter specifies the NetBIOS names of the one or more password servers your Samba server will authenticate. For example:

```
password server = server1 server2
```

After these parameters have been configured, the remaining steps depend on which method you want to use.

Note

Because the names in the password server parameter are NetBIOS names, you might want to specify the methods and order that Samba uses to resolve NetBIOS names. You can use the name resolve order parameter to control this.

To configure Samba to perform passthrough authentication to another SMB server, you must use security = server in the global section of your smb.conf file. Listing 8.1 shows the relevant parameters from the global section set to enable a Samba server to authenticate against another SMB server.

PART
II

CH
8

LISTING 8.1 THE GLOBAL SECTION PARAMETERS REQUIRED TO AUTHENTICATE AGAINST ANOTHER SMB SERVER

```
[global]
   workgroup = myworkgroup
   security = server
   encrypt passwords = yes
   password server = server1 server
```

To configure Samba to authenticate against domain controllers, your Samba server must be a member of the domain in which the domain controllers exist. First, you must include `security = domain` in the global section of your `smb.conf` file. Second, you must join the domain in which the domain controllers exist. Listing 8.2 shows the relevant parameters from the global section set to allow a Samba server to authenticate against the domain controllers of a domain.

LISTING 8.2 THE GLOBAL SECTION PARAMETERS REQUIRED TO AUTHENTICATE AGAINST DOMAIN CONTROLLERS

```
[global]
   workgroup = mydomain
   security = domain
   encrypt passwords = yes
   password server = my-pdc, my-bdc
```

Note

Samba 2.0.6 enables you to specify an asterisk (*) in the password server parameter. When this is done, Samba attempts to automatically locate the domain controllers in the domain in which your server exists.

After you have configured your `smb.conf` file correctly, you must join the domain against which your Samba server will authenticate. You can do this with the `smbpasswd` command in the following way:

```
smbpasswd -j mydomain
```

In addition, you must have added your Samba server as a member of the domain, by using either user manager for domains if your domain controllers are Windows NT servers, or the following commands if your domain controller is a Samba server:

```
useradd machine$
smbpasswd -a -m machine
```

Of course, you will need to change `machine` to the name of your server. In addition, the machine name given on the `useradd` command has a dollar sign ($) on the end.

→ For more information on setting up Samba as a member of a domain, **see** Chapter 19, "Samba and Windows NT Domains."

Each of these methods has its advantages and disadvantages.

Setting up a Samba server to authenticate against another SMB server is very simple. However, if the SMB servers you are authenticating against are domain controllers, you must ensure that all users who use your Samba server can actually log on to the domain controllers from the Samba server because that is where their logons will appear to originate.

On the other hand, setting up a Samba server to authenticate as a member of a domain is more complicated and requires more steps.

AUTHENTICATING AGAINST NIS/NIS+

Samba supports authenticating by using the popular Network Information Services (formerly Yellow Pages) (NIS) and Network Information Services Plus (NIS+). Support for authentication through NIS is built into your operating system in most cases and is handled by using nsswitch. To enable support for NIS+, Samba must be built with the appropriate options. Each of these is discussed here.

> **Note**
>
> If you use NIS or NIS+, you must use plain-text passwords from your Windows clients to your Samba server. This is because there is no way to extract the user's plain-text password from the LM Hash or NT Hash and then convert it to a UNIX password hash.

To enable NIS support, you must set up NIS in your Linux/UNIX environment. Setting up NIS and NIS+ is beyond the scope of this book, but more information can be found in the NIS HOWTO, often kept in /usr/doc/HOWTO on a Linux system. You can also find this document on the Web at http://metalab.unc.edu/mdw/HOWTO/NIS-HOWTO.html. You can find more information on configuring NIS for non-Linux systems in the system administration documentation for your version of UNIX.

NIS and NIS+ are implemented as client/server systems. There is a master NIS server, perhaps with some slave servers. These servers keep information such as user information (including hashed passwords), host information, group information, aliases, and so on. Clients are other Linux and UNIX systems that require access to this information. Figure 8.8 shows this in more detail. The main difference between NIS and NIS+ is that NIS+ uses encrypted RPCs to improve security (with NIS, password hashes are sent over the network in the clear).

The main configuration to perform to enable your Samba server to access password and other information on a NIS server is through the file /etc/nsswitch.conf. This file specifies what information will be looked up on the NIS server. Listing 8.3 shows an example of the entries needed in the nsswitch file to enable password checking against the NIS server.

Figure 8.8
NIS and NIS+ centralize the normal Linux/UNIX system management databases.

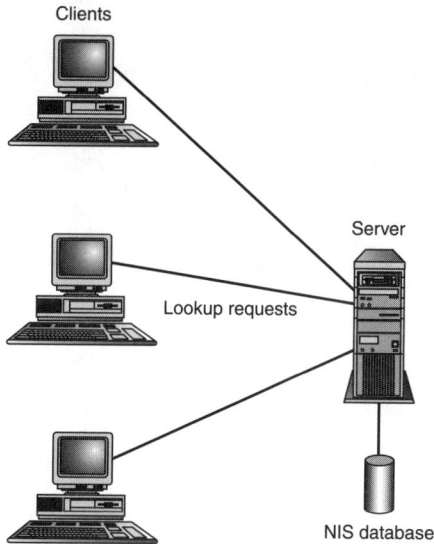

LISTING 8.3 ENTRIES REQUIRED IN THE FILE /etc/nsswitch.conf TO ALLOW AUTHENTICATION AGAINST AN NIS SERVER

```
#
# /etc/nsswitch.conf
#
# An example Name Service Switch config file. This file should be
# sorted with the most-used services at the beginning.
#
# The entry '[NOTFOUND=return]' means that the search for an
# entry should stop if the search in the previous entry turned
# up nothing. Note that if the search failed due to some other reason
# (like no NIS server responding) then the search continues with the
# next entry.
#
# Legal entries are:
#
#       nisplus              Use NIS+ (NIS version 3)
#       nis                  Use NIS (NIS version 2), also called YP
#       dns                  Use DNS (Domain Name Service)
#       files                Use the local files
#       db                   Use the /var/db databases
#       [NOTFOUND=return]    Stop searching if not found so far
#

passwd:     compat
group:      compat
```

To ensure that your Linux Samba server actually takes part in NIS, you must provide NIS configuration in the file /etc/yp.conf and ensure that /etc/rc.d/init.c/ypbind runs at system startup time.

SAMBA AND NIS+

To use Samba in an NIS+ environment, you must rebuild Samba to include NIS+ support. The following steps are involved:

1. Obtain the Samba source from `www.samba.org` and select your closest mirror.

2. Break out the source and run the configure script with the `-with-nisplus` parameter:

   `./configure -with-nisplus`

3. Build Samba and install it.

4. Configure your client to access the NIS+ server.

→ For more information on obtaining and building Samba, **see** Chapter 2, "Obtaining and Installing Samba."

→ For more information on configuring your Linux-based Samba server as a NIS+ client, **see** the NIS-HOWTO either in the `/usr/doc/HOWTO` directory on your Linux system or at `http://metalab.unc.edu/mdw/HOWTO/NIS-HOWTO.html`.

PASSWORD SYNCHRONIZATION

One of the biggest problems with using the more secure encrypted password approach with Samba is that your Samba server keeps password hashes in two places:

- `/etc/passwd`, or wherever you keep your UNIX password hashes

- `/etc/smbpasswd`, or wherever you keep your SMB password hashes

This eventually results in password synchronization problems because users will change their passwords from Windows or Linux/UNIX without realizing that their password in the other environment remains unchanged. Figure 8.9 shows this in diagram form.

> **Note**
>
> Password synchronization problems do not occur when plain-text passwords are in use because there is only one place where authentication information is stored.

Figure 8.9
Password synchronization problems result from having two places where authentication information is kept.

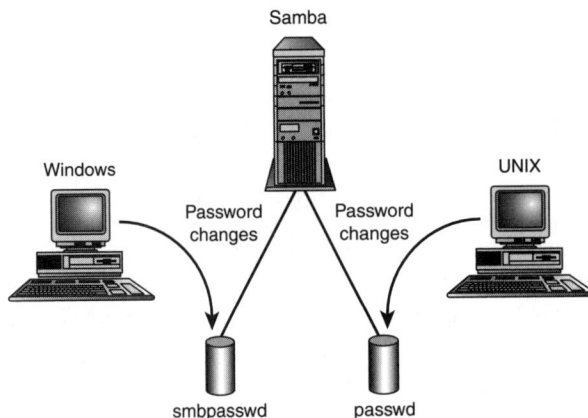

Samba enables you to synchronize passwords between the SMB and UNIX environments on your server. This is managed with the parameters listed in Table 8.4.

TABLE 8.4 PARAMETERS PROVIDING FOR PASSWORD SYNCHRONIZATION

Parameter	Function
unix password sync	This parameter specifies whether encrypted passwords are synchronized with Linux/UNIX passwords when clients change their passwords. This synchronization is performed with the commands specified in the passwd program parameter. This can be done because Samba has access to the plain-text version of the new password, but it does not have access to the plain-text version of the old password.
passwd program	This parameter specifies the commands or scripts to be used by Samba to change a user's password under UNIX. Any occurrence of %u in the string is replaced with the username of the user changing the password.
passwd chat	This parameter specifies a series of expect/send sequences that help manage the process of changing passwords. Samba fires up a separate process to change a user's password and runs the programs specified in the passwd program parameter. The expect/send sequences will generally be specific to the programs specified in that parameter.
passwd chat debug	This parameter specifies that Samba should log all strings sent to and received from the passwd program at a debug level of 100. This is generally to be avoided because it means that the log file will contain users' passwords in clear-text form.

Listing 8.4 shows an example of the parameters you need to set in the global section of your smb.conf file to ensure that passwords are synchronized between Samba and UNIX.

LISTING 8.4 PARAMETERS REQUIRED FOR PASSWORD SYNCHRONIZATION

```
[global]
  ...
  unix password sync = yes
  passwd program = /bin/passwd %u
passwd chat = *New*password* %n\n *new*password* %n\n *updated successfully*
```

Note

The passwd chat sequence shown in Listing 8.4 is relevant to a Linux machine using PAM. A different sequence might be applicable if you are on a different system or if you are not using PAM.

> **Note**
>
> By choosing the appropriate `passwd program`, you can have Samba synchronize passwords with whatever password mechanism you are using. For example, using `/usr/bin/yppasswd` you can update passwords under NIS.

If your `passwd chat` script does not work, the user's UNIX password will not be changed, and as a result, Samba will not change the user's encrypted password either. You can use a couple of techniques to determine what is going on with password changing:

- Carefully check out the prompts your `passwd program` issues.
- Set the `passwd chat debug` parameter to `true`. This causes `smbd(8)` to log all text sent between `smbd(8)` and the `passwd program`.

> **Note**
>
> Setting the `passwd chat debug` parameter to `true` poses a large security problem. This is because any users who change passwords while this parameter is set will have their passwords written in clear text to the log file.

There is no mechanism for ensuring that password changes made from Linux are injected into the `smb passwd` file. We discuss solutions to this problem in the next section.

USING THE `smbpasswd` FILE FOR ALL AUTHENTICATION

As discussed in the previous section, it is possible to synchronize passwords between the `smb passwd` file and whatever password mechanism you are using on all your Linux/UNIX systems. However, the biggest problem is that password synchronization does not work from Linux/UNIX to Samba.

There are several solutions to this problem, all of which revolve around making the `smb passwd` file the central repository of authentication information. They all use the Pluggable Authentication Modules (PAM) support that is available in Linux, Solaris, and many other versions of UNIX to enable the standard system authentication routines to be replaced with code that authenticates against an `smb passwd` file, and thus uses encrypted password.

The following are the solutions:

- `pam_smb`—David Airlie's package to enable a PAM-aware operating system to authenticate against an SMB server. It enables authentication against Windows NT as well as Samba. It does not allow passwords to be changed from Linux/UNIX, however.

- pam_ntdom—Luke Leighton's improvement of the preceding idea to use the NT Domain protocols for authentication. It does not allow passwords to be changed from Linux/UNIX, however.
- pam_smblib—Steve Langasek's module that enables a PAM-aware operating system to authenticate against a Samba smb passwd file. It also allows passwords to be modified from Linux/UNIX, but only on the system that the user is logged on to.

Each of these is discussed briefly in the following sections.

pam_smb

The latest stable version of pam_smb is 1.1.5. It can be obtained in source form from the download area of your local mirror through www.samba.org.

After you have downloaded the source you must build it, install it, and then create the appropriate configuration files.

The following steps are involved:

1. Break out the tar file you have downloaded:

   ```
   tar zxvf pam_smb-1.1.5-tar.gz
   ```

> **Note**
>
> On systems that do not use GNU tar, you might want to use something like the following command:
>
> ```
> gunzip -dc pamsmb-1.1.5-tar.gz | tar xvf -
> ```

2. Change to the directory broken out and run configure to configure the source:

   ```
   cd pam_smb.1.1.5
   ./configure
   ```

3. Make the software:

   ```
   make
   ```

4. Copy the file pam_smb_auth.so to /lib/security under Linux:

   ```
   cp pam_smb_auth.so /lib/security
   ```

5. Change /etc/pam.d/login so that it has the following in it:

   ```
   #%PAM-1.0
   auth    required    /lib/security/pam_securetty.so
   auth    required    /lib/security/pam_smb_auth.so
   auth    required    /lib/security/pam_nologin.so
   ```

   That is, the line with pam_pwdb.so in the group of auth lines should be changed to the one with pam_smb_auth.so shown previously.

> **Note**
>
> Because all authentication on a Linux system is managed using PAM, you will most likely want to modify the PAM configuration files for types of access, including ftp,

sshd, rlogin, and so on. Indeed, any file in the directory /etc/pam.d that contains
auth required /lib/security/pam_pwdb.so will need to be modified.

6. Create the file /etc/pam_smb.conf with the three lines in it

```
DOMAIN-NAME
AUTH-SERVER-1
AUTH-SERVER-2
```

where *DOMAIN-NAME* is the domain name or workgroup name in which your
authentication server is located, and *AUTH-SERVER-1* and *AUTH-SERVER-2* are the DNS
or hosts filenames of two SMB servers in the domain that can authenticate users.

For more information on pam_smb, see David Airlie's Web page on the subject at http://
www.csn.ul.ie/~airlied/pam_smb/.

pam_ntdom

The latest version of pam_ntdom is 0.23. It is available from the download area of your local
Samba mirror through www.samba.org.

Download the source file, pam_ntdom-0.23.tgz, and break the source out with the following
command:

```
tar zxvf pam_ntdom-0.23.tgz
```

After you do that, follow the README file for instructions on building and configuring
pam_ntdom.

pam_smbpasswd

The latest version of pam_smbpass is 0.73, but that version is for Samba-TNG. Earlier
versions work with Samba 2.0.7 and earlier.

You can obtain the source for pam_smbpass from ftp://ftp.netexpress.net/pub/pam/.

After you have the source, you will need to break it out, configure it, make it, install the
resultant shared libraries in /lib/security, and then configure PAM to use the new shared
libraries.

OTHER SOURCES OF AUTHENTICATION

Samba has the capability to use other sources of authentication, including

■ Kerberos 4—For Kerberos 4 support, Samba must be configured and compiled with
the --with-krb4 option. For more information about Kerberos 4, see http://
web.mit.edu/kerberos/www/.

- Kerberos 5—For Kerberos 5 support, Samba must be configured and compiled with the `--with-krb5` option. For more information about Kerberos 5, see `http://web.mit.edu/kerberos/www/`.

- LDAP, although the LDAP support is currently in a state of flux—For more information on LDAP support, see Chapter 20, "Samba and LDAP."

- Pluggable Authentication Modules, or PAM—PAM is the primary authentication mechanism for Linux and some versions of Solaris. Samba supports PAM as an authentication mechanism, which means that Samba can use any authentication mechanism PAM makes available.

PARAMETERS AFFECTING AUTHENTICATION

The following parameters all relate to password management and authentication of clients:

```
add user script
allow trusted domains
delete user script
encrypt passwords
map to guest
min password length
null passwords
passwd chat debug
passwd chat
passwd program
password level
password server
restrict anonymous
security
smb passwd file
unix password sync
update encrypted
use rhosts
username level
username map
```

FROM HERE...

The next chapter in this book, "Samba Automation," deals with Samba automation and brings you to the end of this part. In it you will learn how to run shell scripts when users map network drives and how to set up Samba virtual servers.

You can read about the following in subsequent sections:

- Using Samba from various Windows and non-Windows clients
- Many advanced topics on Samba

CHAPTER **9**

SAMBA AUTOMATION

In this chapter

by Richard Sharpe

In Chapter 6, "File Sharing Under Samba," and Chapter 7, "Printer Sharing Under Samba," you learned how to set up file and printer shares. In Chapter 8, "Samba and Password Management," you learned about password management, and in Part III, "Client Configuration and Use," you will learn more about how to configure clients to access Samba. In this chapter you learn how to make the most of your `smb.conf` file.

Samba has a very powerful set of features that helps to make the `smb.conf` file more compact and provides great flexibility in configuring it:

- `smb.conf` macros or variable substitutions
- Include files
- Config file parameter

Combined with the `preexec` and `postexec` parameters, these features allow you to automate many operations that would otherwise require manual control and other programs to implement. See Chapter 6 and Appendix A, "All Samba Parameters and Their Meanings," for more information on these commands.

THE SAMBA MACROS OR VARIABLE SUBSTITUTIONS

The first feature that assists with automation is macros or variable substitutions. Samba maintains many variables internally relating to connections, services, users, and so on. Many of these are available for substitution into parameters in the `smb.conf` file.

> **Note**
>
> Parameters can only be substituted into string parameters, which are parameters that define strings, such as the `path` parameter.

Variable substitution is performed by Samba when one or more macros appear in the string value of a parameter. A macro is introduced with the percent (%) character and consists of a single character name. For example, the following parameter might be used to define the path for some share:

```
path = /home/%u/public
```

It uses the `%u` macro, which will substitute the user's name into the string, and will result in the path being `/home/win95user/public` if the current user is `win95user`.

Three general classes of variable substitutions in Samba are

- Basic substitutions—A set of substitutions performed on all string variables, both global and local (per share).
- Extended substitutions—A set of substitutions that are applied for some parameters and include both the basic substitutions as well as a few more.
- Ad-hoc substitutions—Additional parameter-specific substitutions performed on some parameters.

The reason for the difference between basic substitutions and extended substitutions is that there are times when Samba does not have the information required by extended substitutions. For example, %u (the username used for file accesses) is not available until a TreeCon is performed by the client.

> **Note**
>
> A *TreeCon* is a request in the SMB protocol and occurs when a client does the equivalent of net use d: \\server\share. For more information, please refer to Chapter 4, "An Introduction to the SMB Protocol."

We will explore each of these in the following sections and point out when each substitution is relevant as well.

BASIC SUBSTITUTIONS

These substitutions are performed on all string parameters in the smb.conf file. They are performed regardless of whether the value of the parameter is set in the smb.conf file or by a default in the source code. The basic substitutions performed appear in Table 9.1.

TABLE 9.1   BASIC VARIABLE SUBSTITUTIONS

Macro	Meaning
%a	Returns the remote architecture, where it can be determined. It will be one of OS2, WfWg, Samba, WinNT, Win95, WIN2K, or UNKNOWN. This value becomes available after the client has performed a NetProt SMB request. It is not relevant in nmbd.
%d	Returns the process ID of the current process. This value is available from the time smbd or nmbd starts.
%h	Returns the first component of Hostname of the machine on which Samba is running. This value is available from the time smbd or nmbd starts.
%m	Returns the NetBIOS name of the client. This value is available only after the client has established a NetBIOS session. It is not available in nmbd and is not available when non-NetBIOS SMB is being used.
%v	Returns the version number (string) of Samba. This value is available from the time that smbd or nmbd starts.
%G	Group name of the primary group of the user specified in %U. This value is only available in smbd from the time that the client does a logon (sends a SessSetupAndX SMB).
%I	Returns the client's IP address. This value is available from the time that smbd or nmbd starts.
%L	Returns the server's NetBIOS name. This value is available from the time that smbd or nmbd starts.
%M	Returns the client's DNS name. This value is available from the time that smbd starts. It is not available in nmbd.

TABLE 9.1 CONTINUED

Macro	Meaning
%N	Returns the NIS home directory server for the current user. It is obtained from the user's NIS auto.map entry. The default is %L if Samba was not compiled with --with-automount, but most Samba RPMs under Linux are compiled with --with-automount. It only available in smbd from the time the client does a logon. It is not relevant in nmbd.
%R	Returns the remote protocol, which is the short name of the protocol selected during the NegProt (see Chapter 4). This is available in smbd from the time the client sends its NegProt SMB request.
%T	Returns the current time on the server. This value is available from the time that smbd or nmbd starts.
%U	Returns the username for the current session. This is the username that the user wanted, not necessarily what he or she got (see map user in Chapter 8). This information is taken from the SessSetupAndX that is performed by the client, so it will not be available before that time, that is, during smbd initialization and in nmbd.
%$	Expands and returns the environment variable following %$. The syntax is %$(env-var). This value is available from the time that smbd or nmbd starts.

Note that circumstances will arise under which some macros will not be defined. In those cases, the macro name itself will be printed. One case is when a macro is used in a string that nmbd will print. For example, the following global parameter tries to create a server string that includes both types of group name along with the translation of the environment variable MACHTYPE:

```
server string = Samba Server: %g %G:%$(MACHTYPE)
```

However, the result in Figure 9.1 shows that %g and %G are not translated. This is because these macros simply do not have a value under nmbd, and it is nmbd that generates the server announcement messages from which the Network Neighborhood display is built.

Figure 9.1
Some variables are not translated in Network Neighborhood.

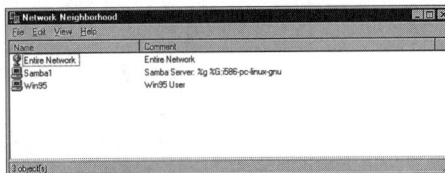

However, using the same macros in a string that smbd is going to use, as in the following share-level parameter creates the share comment as shown in Figure 9.2:

```
Comment = Public Stuff: %g : %G : %$(MACHTYPE)
```

EXTENDED SUBSTITUTIONS

Over and above the basic substitutions, Samba applies the extended substitutions as shown in Table 9.2 on some occasions.

Figure 9.2
The macros
show up in the
share com-
ment.

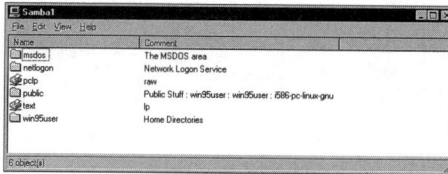

TABLE 9.2   EXTENDED SUBSTITUTIONS

Macro	Meaning
%g	Returns the group name of the connection or service. This value is available in smbd after the client has done a TreeCon request.
%u	Returns the username of the connection or service. This value is available within a service context. Unlike %U, which is the name the client logged on with, %u is the account name used to access a particular service, and parameters like force user will affect the value of %u.
%H	Returns the home directory of the current user. This value is available within a service context.
%P	Returns the path for the current service. This value is available within a service context.
%S	Returns the current service name. This value is available within a service context.

Samba applies the standard substitutions after applying the extended substitutions shown in Table 9.2. This means that if an extended substitution should contain a macro, the standard substitutions process it.

Extended substitutions are applied in several places in Samba, including in the printing code, where the command to be executed to print a job (print command) has the following substitutions applied:

1. Basic substitutions are applied on the print command string.
2. Ad-hoc substitutions, as listed following, for the print filename and print queue name.
3. Extended substitutions are applied on the result.

This means that if the substitutions in steps 1 and 2 result in further macros, they are substituted in step 3. For example, a %$ environment variable macro could result in further macros being substituted.

The following parameters have extended substitutions applied to them:

- comment
- print command
- logon script
- lpq command
- lprm command

- `lppause command`
- `lpresume command`
- `path`
- `preexec`
- `postexec`
- `root preexec`
- `root postexec`
- The service name, for example, `[spec-%L]`

> **Note**
>
> Substitutions work even in service names.

This last substitution is significant because it is not a parameter at all, but a service name. Using something like the following, you can construct a service (share) whose name is determined at runtime by Samba:

```
[spec-%L]
    comment = A special share for the NetBIOS name %L
    path = ...
```

Figure 9.3 shows what such a share would look like from Windows 95's Network Neighborhood. There are many interesting uses for substitutions such as this.

Figure 9.3
A share with a macro in its name.

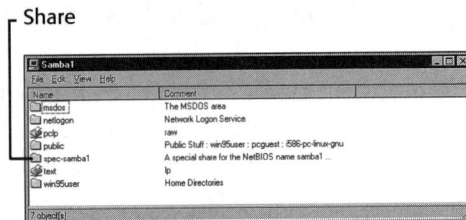

On the other hand, using a macro where it does not have a value leads to that macro remaining in the text. For example, the following share specification in your `smb.conf` file leads to a surprising share name (one that you probably cannot access under Windows):

```
[spec-%u]
    comment = Another special share
    path = ...
```

Figure 9.4 shows what such a share looks like from Windows 95's Network Neighborhood. However, when you click on the share, you get a dialog box from Windows saying "The network name cannot be found."

AD-HOC SUBSTITUTIONS

Samba also does several ad-hoc substitutions that are performed as needed to support specific features in some parameters.

Figure 9.4
A share with a
%u macro in its
name.

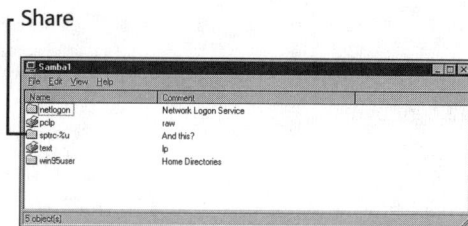

For example, in handling the `print command` parameter, Samba applies the following ad-hoc substitutions:

- `%s`, which is replaced with the print filename
- `%f`, which is replaced with the print filename
- `%p`, which is replaced with the printer name (or the print service name if no printer name is defined)

Although the Samba documentation, particularly the `smb.conf` manual page, implies there is a difference between the `%s` and `%f` macros, there appears to be no difference in current versions of Samba.

Note

This is likely to be fixed in the `smb.conf` manual pages by the time you read this book because I submitted an update to the documentation.

The following parameters have ad-hoc substitutions applied to them:

- `add user script`
- `comment`
- `delete user script`
- `ldap filter`
- `force group`
- `force user`
- `lpq command`
- `lprm command`
- `lppause command`
- `lpresume command`
- `message command`
- `passwd program`
- `passwd chat`
- `print command`
- `read list`

PART

II

CH

9

- `valid users`
- `invalid users`
- `user, users, username` (all synonyms)
- `write list`

Because each command is described fully in Appendix A and in the chapters dealing with them, we will not look at them further here.

INCLUDE FILES

The second feature that assists with automation is include files. Samba's `smb.conf` file can include other files, and because the names of these included files can contain macros, the behavior of Samba can be modified at runtime.

The `include` file parameter is

`include = file-name`

where `file-name` is the name of any file in the file system. Because `file-name` can contain macros, such as `%m`, you can have different behavior for different clients.

> **Note**
>
> Samba silently ignores include files that do not exist. This allows you to use an `include` parameter that works in some situations and not others, without crashing Samba, simply due to the presence or absence of the appropriate files.

One use of the `include` parameter is as an aid in troubleshooting. By adding the following to the `[global]` section of your `smb.conf` file you can affect the behavior of Samba for individual clients because the `%m` in the `include` file parameter is replaced with the NetBIOS name of the client:

`include = /var/log/samba/conf.%m`

Next, by creating files in `/var/log/samba` for clients with a `debug level = 6` parameter as appropriate, as shown next, you can increase the debug level for individual clients without affecting all clients:

`echo " debug level = 6" > /var/log/samba/conf.win95`

Another use is to have different include files for different client architectures or users. The following allows you to include additional parameters for some client architectures:

`include = /etc/smb.conf.%a`

Then, by simply creating the file `/etc/smb.conf.WinNT`, you can include parameters that are included only for Windows NT systems.

We will explore more of the potential of include files in the "Examples" section that follows.

CONFIG FILES

The third feature that assists with automation is the `config file` parameter. This parameter allows you to replace the entire config file another config file.

The syntax of this parameter is as follows:

```
config file = <file-name>
```

Because the `config file` parameter can take any of the basic substitutions, you can set up different config files for each client. However, using the `config file` parameter is not as flexible as using the `include` parameter shown previously, because the whole configuration file is replaced when you use the `config file` parameter.

EXAMPLES

We will explore some ways in which Samba's automation features can be used. We will look at the following:

- Virtual servers
- Running shell scripts when a client accesses a share

In the sections on the various Windows clients we will also look at other automation examples.

SAMBA VIRTUAL SERVERS

Samba provides support for virtual servers. This support uses the `config file` parameters `netbios aliases` and `include`. We will run one Samba server that supports one or more NetBIOS aliases, and we will associate different parameters with each NetBIOS name the server is known as.

First, the main part of the `smb.conf` file will look like this:

```
[global]
   workgroup = sambanet
   server string = Samba Server %L
   netbios name = Samba1
   netbios aliases = Samba2
   guest account = pcguest
   log file = /var/log/samba/log.%L.%m
   password level = 8
   username level = 8
   include = /etc/smb.conf.%L
```

Then, the file `/etc/smb.conf.samba1` will contain the following:

```
   security = user
   os level = 33
   domain logons = yes
   logon script = netlogon.bat
   domain master = yes
```

```
    preferred master = yes
    wins support = yes
    load printers = yes
[homes]
    Comment = Homes area
    browsable = no
    writable = yes
[netlogon]
    comment = Network Logon Service
    path = /home/netlogon
    guest ok = yes
[printers]
    comment = All Printers
    path = /var/spool/samba
    browsable = no
    guest ok = no
    writable = no
    printable = yes
```

Finally, the file /etc/smb.conf.samba2 will contain the following:

```
    security = share
[shared]
    comment = More Public Stuff : %G : %g : %$(MACHTYPE)
    path = /tmp
    public = yes
    writable = yes
    printable = no
```

When you browse the network, you will see the two servers, Samba1 and Samba2, as shown in Figure 9.5.

Figure 9.5
Network Neighborhood shows both Samba1 and Samba2.

Comment strings

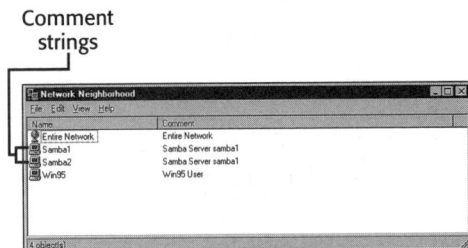

Figure 9.5 shows the comment containing the name Samba server samba1 for both Samba1 and Samba2, despite the two having different NetBIOS names. This is because nmbd generates this information, and it only knows about the name Samba1 when it evaluates the server string.

If you double-click the server Samba1, you should see the window shown in Figure 9.6, whereas double-clicking on Samba2 produces the window shown in Figure 9.7. Thus, the one server produces two different results through the use of include files.

Figure 9.6
Samba1 has
several shares.

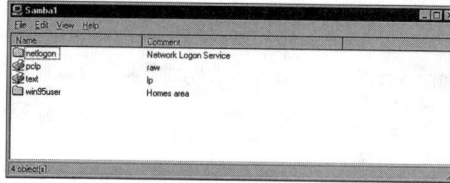

Figure 9.7
Samba2 has
only one share.

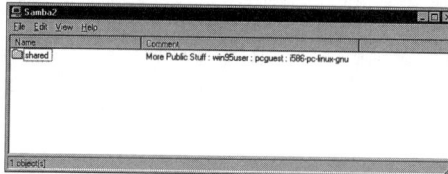

HOW DOES IT WORK?

The use of include files as shown works for the following reasons:

- nmbd reads the files /etc/smb.conf and /etc/smb.conf.samba1 because the %L macro only has the value samba1 from nmbd's point of view. This is fine, because everything nmbd needs is in /etc/smb.conf, in any case. Because we have provided a NetBIOS alias, nmbd advertises both Samba1 and Samba2 as servers. The only minor problem is that the comment field shows samba1 in both cases.

- smbd reads /etc/smb.conf and then /etc/smb.conf.samba1 if smbd was accessed as Samba1 or /etc/smb.conf.samba2 if smbd was accessed as Samba2.

Note

We put several parameters in /etc/smb.conf.samba1, such as wins support = yes and os level = 33, that could just as easily have been put in smb.conf because these parameters are only interpreted by nmbd. However, I thought it was cleaner to put them in /etc/smb.conf.samba1.

It is important to understand what is going on with virtual servers so you can best use them and can resolve problems when they occur.

Figure 9.8 shows a client accessing two virtual servers on one Samba server. When a client accesses a server with a different NetBIOS name than the one it is currently accessing, it places a new connection to the server. This happens even though the new NetBIOS name might resolve to an IP address that the client already has a connection with. In the figure, when the client accesses a resource via NetBIOS Name 1, a TCP connection is placed to the server, which starts up an smbd to process the client's requests. Then, when the client accesses a resource via NetBIOS Name 2, a new TCP connection is placed to the server, which starts up another smbd to process the client's requests. Each of these smbd processes has a different context and looks like a different server to the client. Because they can include files based on several different macros, they can behave in very different ways, as discussed previously.

Figure 9.8
Samba virtual servers are implemented by separate smbd processes.

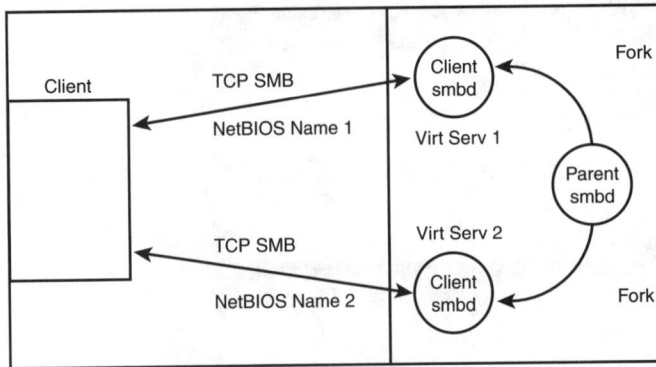

RUNNING SHELL SCRIPTS ON THE SERVER

By combining preexec (or root preexec) parameters with variable substitutions, you can run shell scripts on the Samba server when a client accesses a share. For example, some users delete important files from their [homes] share (such as .bashrc). You would like to ensure that they always have all the correct files when they connect to a share.

You can do this by adding the following to the [homes] share, and then creating the shell script /usr/local/sbin/copyuserfiles to copy all files from /etc/skel that the user currently does not have:

```
root preexec = /usr/local/sbin/copyuserfiles %U
```

> **Note**
>
> We use %U in the root preexec parameter because it provides the name that the client logged on with. Using %u would lead to interesting surprises when shares also have the force user parameter specified.

The shell script, copyuserfiles, would look something like the following:

```
#!/bin/sh
cp -r /etc/skel/* /home/$1
```

> **Note**
>
> The macro %U in the root prexec shown previously is passed in as the first parameter of the shell script copyuserfiles. It is accessed as $1 in the shell script.

FURTHER INFORMATION

For further information on automation, please see the smb.conf man pages and the Samba technical archive. You can access the smb.conf man pages at any time by using the following command:

```
man smb.conf
```

FROM HERE...

You have now finished reading Part II, "Configuring Samba." The next steps are to

1. Read one of the chapters from Part III, "Client Configuration and Use."
2. Move to Part IV, "Advanced Topics," and explore such topics as using Samba as a Primary Domain Controller or using Samba with LDAP.

PART

II

CH

9

PART III

CLIENT ACCESS TO SAMBA

## CHAPTER 10

AN INTRODUCTION TO MICROSOFT WINDOWS NETWORKING

In this chapter

by Richard Sharpe

This book is about Samba, which was developed by Andrew Tridgell in the early 1990s to allow PCs to access files on a Sun workstation. Since that time, Samba has been extended to provide many of the same functions as Microsoft's Windows NT operating system. In that sense, this book is as much about Microsoft Windows Networking as it is about Samba.

In Part III, "Client Configuration and Use," we delve into the details of accessing Samba servers from different Windows clients, as well as other clients. To help in understanding the remaining chapters in this part, we provide an overview of Microsoft Windows Networking.

In this chapter, we discuss the following:

- What Microsoft Windows Networking is
- The SMB protocol and its relevance to Microsoft Windows Networking
- NetBIOS names and how they relate to Microsoft Windows Networking
- The ways in which passwords are handled under Microsoft Windows Networking
- What workgroups and domains are and their differences
- The use of workgroups and domains by Windows NT
- Browsing under Microsoft Windows Networking

WHAT IS MICROSOFT WINDOWS NETWORKING?

Although Microsoft Windows Networking includes a lot of functionality, fundamentally it can be viewed as a set of programs, libraries (DLLs), and protocols that allow operating systems from Microsoft and others to share resources between systems through one or more networking technologies.

The resources that can be shared include

- Files
- Printers
- Other objects by way of MSRPC and DCOM

Microsoft Windows Networking achieves this sharing in a simple, uniform manner, at the file system level, by shipping operations on remote files over the network transparently. Whenever a reference is made to a file in the form of a UNC (`\\ server\share\file-path`) or a virtual drive (`H:\file-path`), the Win32 APIs pass the call to the Installable File System Manager (IFSMGR). This then passes the request to a redirector to turn the request into network operations, as shown in Figure 10.1.

The redirector is a software component (`vredir.vxd` in Win9x, `rdr.sys` in Windows NT and Windows 2000) that converts file and other operations into a series of SMB and other requests sent across the network to an SMB server.

Figure 10.1
An overview of the relation-ship between the Win32 API and `vredir.vxd` in Windows 9x and other Windows operating systems.

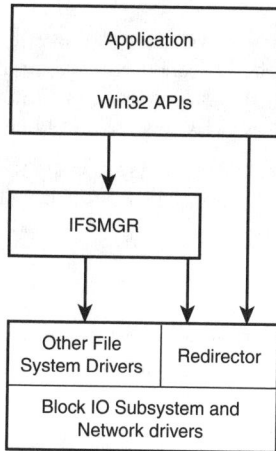

```
┌─────────────────────────────────┐
│           Application           │
│                                 │
│           Win32 APIs            │
└─────────────────────────────────┘
              │   │
              ▼   │
┌─────────────────┐
│     IFSMGR      │
└─────────────────┘
    │    │    │
    ▼    ▼    ▼
┌───────────────┬─────────────────┐
│ Other File    │                 │
│ System Drivers│   Redirector    │
├───────────────┴─────────────────┤
│   Block IO Subsystem and        │
│      Network drivers            │
└─────────────────────────────────┘
```

> **Note**
>
> The redirector is responsible for sending authentication information to the remote SMB server. The original versions of the redirector under Windows 95 and Windows NT sent plaintext passwords unless the remote SMB server required encrypted passwords.
>
> Since the vredir update for Windows 95, SP3 for Windows NT, and with Windows 98 from the original version and now with Windows NT, the default behavior of the redirector is always to send encrypted passwords unless a registry parameter has been set to allow plaintext passwords. More information on this topic is available in Chapter 12, "Accessing Samba from Windows for Workgroups and Windows 9x," Chapter 13, "Accessing Samba from Windows NT," and Chapter 15, "Accessing Samba from Windows 2000."

These SMBs and other requests can be communicated with other systems that understand Microsoft Windows networking using any one of the following protocols as transports:

- NetBEUI (often referred to as NBF in Microsoft literature)
- TCP/IP
- IPX

However, we will only discuss the use of TCP/IP by Microsoft Windows Networking because it is the only protocol that Samba can use to provide file and print sharing for Microsoft Windows systems.

> **Note**
>
> Microsoft literature refers to NetBEUI and IPX as *transports*, possibly to indicate that they are not transport protocols. IPX is a network layer protocol. NetBEUI is essentially NetBIOS implemented on top of 802.2 LLC, which is a link layer protocol.

> Transport protocols are generally connection-oriented and provide end-to-end error control and sequenced delivery of data. They are usually very reliable. Network protocols simply deal with getting packets from one system in the network to another. They usually make no guarantees about delivery of the data being carried.
>
> By using a transport protocol, such as TCP, higher layers of the software spend less time worrying about whether requests reached the server and more time dealing with application requests.

In addition to supporting the redirecting of file operations across the network, the redirector supports other Microsoft Windows Networking functions such as network logons and network browsing.

Microsoft Windows Networking uses the concept of *shares* to support the sharing of file and printer resources. To access a share, you can use one of the following techniques:

- Specify a UNC as a file or pathname, for example, *server\share\file-path*.
- Use the Map Network Drive dialog box (right-click on Network Neighborhood, then Map Network Drive) to access a share on another system and map it to a local drive number.
- Use the net use command from within a command prompt window. For example:

  net use h:\\server1\my-home

When accessing shares, be aware of the security model being used by the server offering the share as well as the way in which authentication occurs. We will look at both of these in subsequent sections.

SECURITY MODELS

Because of the legacy of the SMB protocol on which Microsoft Windows Networking is based, servers support two security models when providing access to shares:

- Share-level security, where the server does not control access to files in the share by user. If any authentication is required, it is only a share password, perhaps with different passwords for read and write access to the files on the share.
- User-level security, where the server wants a valid username and password pair before access will be allowed to any shares the server offers.

In general terms, one can say the following:

- Microsoft operating systems such as Windows for Workgroups and Windows 9x default to share-level security. However, as shown in Figure 10.2, Win9x can specify user-level security, but it must be given the name of a domain controller to authenticate users against.

- Windows NT cannot be placed into share-level security. All accesses must be made using a valid account on the server. However, Windows NT does allow you to give everyone all access to files on a share if you desire.

Figure 10.2
Windows 9x can operate in either share-level or user-level security.

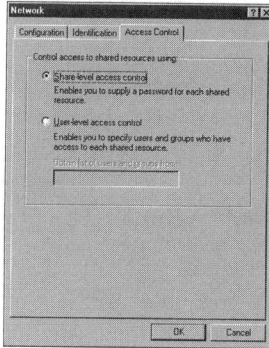

Because operating systems such as Windows for Workgroups, Windows 9x, and Windows NT using the FAT file system do not have per-file protection capabilities, they cannot make access decisions about individual files even if they are using user-level security. However, Windows NT, when using NTFS, can control file access at the file level and provides Access Control Lists for controlling who has access to files. This is because Windows NT performs all file accesses in the security context of a valid account on the server.

Samba can operate either in share-level or user-level security, but it uses whatever file-level access controls are available in the operating system on which it runs. This means, as discussed in Chapter 6, "File Sharing Under Samba," that all file accesses are performed in the security context of a valid account on the server. In share-level security, this account is often the guest account.

Workgroups and Domains

Microsoft Windows networking distinguishes two different ways of managing user accounts and password files:

- A *workgroup* is a collection of systems that shares resources among each other, but each manages its own set of users and passwords.

- A *domain* is a collection of systems that shares resources among each other, but all user account information is centrally managed by one or more domain controllers. It's usual to have a primary domain controller and one or more backup domain controllers, especially in larger networks.

It is important to note that from the perspective of the SMB protocol, there is no difference between a workgroup and a domain. The same sort of SMBs gain access to servers. However, from an administrative point of view, there are differences that mainly relate to the amount of administration to be done.

One important difference relates to user accounts and passwords. Under a workgroup, all Windows NT servers and Samba servers maintain their own user and password information, and these local sources of authentication information are used for all authentication decisions. This means that administrators need to ensure that the correct accounts are available on all servers in the workgroup and be aware that password synchronization problems can arise.

However, in a domain, a domain controller is used for all authentication. Thus, only one source of authentication information exists (backup domain controllers get their authentication information from the primary domain controller), so administration of a domain is easier, and password synchronization problems do not exist.

Under Windows NT, the Security Accounts Manager (SAM) is the repository of authentication information. On most Samba servers, it is the /etc/passwd and other files because Samba mostly runs on UNIX systems. However, Samba can also implement a SAM-like database, called the smbpasswd file.

→ For more information on password management, **see** Chapter 8, "Samba and Password Management."

When it comes to accessing resources in workgroups and domains, however, there are many similarities. The following sections discuss each of these.

ACCESS TO RESOURCES IN A DOMAIN

To access resources in a domain, a client must first log on to the domain by entering a username, a password, and a domain into a logon information dialog box as shown in Figure 10.3.

Figure 10.3
Logging on to the domain from a Win9x client.

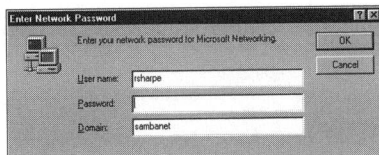

When you fill in the information required in Figure 10.3 and log on to the domain, your client performs the following steps, as shown in Figure 10.4:

1. Finds a logon server for the domain. This appears in frames 1 and 2 in Figure 10.4.

2. Registers the logon user's name as a NetBIOS name. This appears in frames 3 and 4 in Figure 10.4. This allows WinPopup messages to be sent to the logged-on user.

3. Translates the NetBIOS name of the logon server, in this case Samba1. This appears in frames 5 and 6 in Figure 10.4.

4. Connects to the logon server, sets up a session, negotiates a protocol, and sends a SessSetupAndX SMB, with the username and password specified. These appear in frames 7 through 15 in Figure 10.4. It also caches this username and password information for later use. If the user's credentials are incorrect at this point, the logon fails.

5. Sends a NetWkstaUserLogon LanMan request to the server with the user's details. The response to this request contains information such as whether the user can log on to that client and at that time. It also contains the name of the user's logon script. This appears in frames 16 and 17 in Figure 10.4.

6. Connects to the \\logon-server\netlogon share and opens and executes the logon script specified in the response to the NetWkstaUserLogon request discussed previously. Connecting to the netlogon share is shown in frames 18 and 19 in Figure 10.4, while opening the user's logon script is shown in frames 20 and 21. The rest is not shown.

7. The client then connects to the user's home share to retrieve any profile information. The client sends a NetUserGetInfo LanMan request to obtain the user's home share name. Profiles allow each user to have a customized setup for the Windows client he or she logs on to and allow people to move around from client to client and have their environment follow them around (also called *roaming profiles*).

Your client uses normal SMB requests to access logon scripts and profiles. For example, it will issue an SMBopen to open your logon script and then an SMBreadDraw request to read the logon script.

Accessing resources from a Windows NT client in a domain is even more complex because NT clients must have joined the domain, and they log on using Microsoft's Remote Procedure Call (MSRPC) facility. Although the steps are analogous to those just described, they are much more complex, and no tools are available as yet that can view the protocol messages sent back and forth.

To access resources on any server in the domain, you must still authenticate with that server unless you already have a connection with that server. That is, your client must still present your username and password to access the new server, even if it is a domain controller or member of the domain. If the server you are accessing is a member of the domain, it forwards the authentication request to a domain controller.

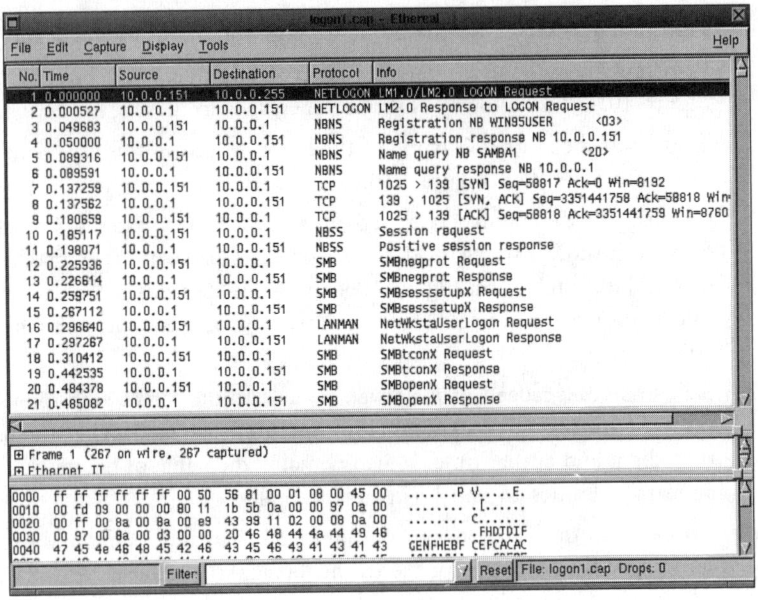

Figure 10.4
Logging on to the network from a Win9x client requires that many SMB requests be sent to the server.

> **Note**
>
> This means that your client sends a `SessionSetupAndX` to each server in the network that you connect to, with your username and password contained in it. The server then authenticates you, perhaps using passthrough authentication (sending authentication to a domain controller or other SMB server).

When you access resources from a Windows 9x client, you can access them only as the user who logged on to the client; however, Windows NT enables you to access resources on the server as a different user from the one you logged on to the client as.

More information on using Samba as a Logon and Profiles server is provided in Chapter 11, "Samba as a Logon and Profiles Server," while Chapter 12 provides more details on accessing Samba from Windows 9x.

ACCESS TO RESOURCES IN A WORKGROUP

To access resources in a workgroup, you must log on to the client. This caches your username and password information (unless you tell Windows not to cache that information). This logon results in little network traffic being sent, with only the logon user's name being registered as a NetBIOS name.

> **Note**
>
> It is possible to switch off this password caching. You can use the policy editor to do this, or you can add the following registry key and give it a value of 1:
>
> `HKEY_LOCAL_MACHINE\Software\Microsoft\Windows\CurrentVersion\`
> `Policies\Network\DisablePwdCaching`

To access resources on any server in the workgroup your client must connect to the server and authenticate with that server, unless it already has a connection open with the server. This is really no different from what happens when a client accesses a server in a domain, as discussed previously. The difference here is that there is no separate logon phase, and there is no support for running logon scripts or roaming profiles.

Because each server has a separate authentication database, you might need different passwords for each server. If you are using a Windows NT client, you can use different usernames on each server because Windows NT enables you to connect as a different user. If you are using a Windows 9x client, you must have the same account configured on each server.

However, there is a problem with each server maintaining its own authentication database. They might not contain the same usernames, and passwords can get out of sync on each database. This can lead to large amounts of user frustration as users try to access servers but no longer have the required authentication information.

→ For more information on password maintenance, **see** Chapter 8, "Samba and Password Management."

PART
III

CH
10

BROWSING

Microsoft Windows Networking provides a means of finding other servers in the network. The process of doing this is referred to as *browsing*, and it is supported by a part of the SMB protocol and the following servers:

- Server and workgroup/domain announcements—All servers send these announcements when they start up, as well as periodically. They are sent as mail slot messages to \MAILSLOT\BROWSE, and they contain information about the server or workgroup or domain that the announcement relates to.

- Browse masters—This is a server that accumulates the announcements it sees and builds a list of all the servers and domains or workgroups seen on the network.

- Backup browse servers—These are servers that copy the browsing information from the browse master periodically. They are also prepared to become the browse master if it fails.

- A browse master election protocol/process—This elects the browse master if one does not exist.

When a user wants to browse the servers on the network, his system sends a QueryBrowseServers request to the network. The browse master should return a list of backup browse servers. The user's system then selects a server at random from the returned list and sends a NetServerEnum or NetServerEnum2 to it to retrieve the list of servers and domains/workgroups in the network.

However, the list of servers and domains/workgroups returned is simply a list of the NetBIOS names of the servers and domains/workgroups that the backup browse server knows about. The client system still must translate these names into IP addresses if it wants to access any servers in the list. It must use the standard NetBIOS Name Service facilities to perform this translation, which might require access to a WINS server.

→ To learn more about browsing, **see** Chapter 17, "Samba and Browsing."

NetBIOS Names

Whenever Microsoft Windows Networking clients access servers or services, they do so using NetBIOS names. As discussed in Chapter 4, "An Introduction to the SMB Protocol," NetBIOS names are 15 characters in length and are padded with spaces if they are shorter than 15 characters.

When you access a resource on a server, using the following command, for example

```
net use h: \\samba1\homes
```

the server name, samba1, is used as a NetBIOS name, and a NetBIOS Name Server is used to translate this name into an IP address. A WINS server can also be used to translate these names.

Additionally, when a Windows client starts up, it registers a multitude of NetBIOS names:

- ClientName<00> as a unique name, indicating that it is registering as a workstation
- ClientName<03> as a unique name, for the messenger service
- ClientName<20> as a unique name if the client is configured to share files or printers
- Workgroup<1E> as a group name, indicating that the client can take part in elections
- Workgroup<00> as a group name, indicating its membership in that workgroup

An example of a client called Win95 starting up appears in Figure 10.5.

NetBIOS names are used throughout Microsoft Windows Networking, and it is important that you be aware of them.

Note

Windows 2000 implements a NetBIOS-less version of the SMB protocol. This means that server names are not required to be NetBIOS names and the NetBIOS session setup portion of any connection to a server is not performed. This has the unfortunate consequence that virtual servers become impossible.

However, Windows 2000 tries a NetBIOS-less connection on port 445, and if that fails, it then tries to connect on the standard NetBIOS port of 139. See Chapter 15 for more information on this.

Figure 10.5
Windows registers several NetBIOS names on startup.

THE SMB PROTOCOL

To log on to the network, or indeed access any services on a server in a Microsoft Windows Network, clients use the SMB protocol. As described in Chapter 4, the following general steps are taken at a protocol level:

1. A TCP connection is placed to the server after the server's IP address is translated from its NetBIOS name (or its DNS name, under some circumstances).

2. The client negotiates an appropriate protocol variant to use between the client and the server.

3. The client logs on to the server by sending a `SessSetupAndX` request if the protocol variant supports this SMB.

4. The client then connects to one or more shares using the TreeCon SMB request.

5. The client then opens files or performs other actions as necessary.

These steps are illustrated in Figure 10.6.

Figure 10.6
The steps involved in accessing resources on an SMB server.

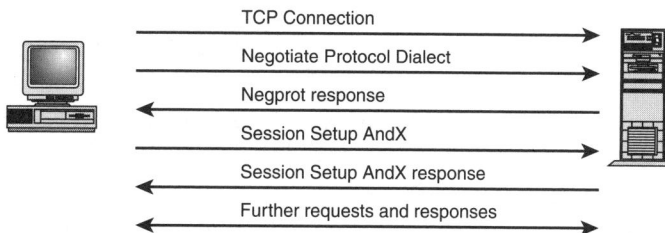

PASSWORDS

Microsoft Windows clients and servers deal with passwords in two different formats:

- Plaintext passwords—This used to be the default, but since Windows NT Service Pack 3 and the vredir update for Windows 95, plaintext passwords are disabled. They can be reenabled by setting a registry setting. Samba comes with sample `regedit` files to do this for Windows 9x, Windows NT, and Windows 2000. Instructions to enable plaintext passwords are contained in the chapters on those operating systems.

- Encrypted passwords—There are two different ways to encrypt passwords. Windows 9x uses the older LAN Manager encryption, but it is relatively easy to break. Windows NT has its own form of password encryption, which is much stronger.

Samba can understand both password types, but, as mentioned in Chapter 8, "Samba and Password Management," you cannot convert hashed passwords that are already stored on your server from one type to the other.

FURTHER RESOURCES

The following provide more information about the topics discussed in this section:

- *The Windows NT Networking Guide* from the Microsoft Windows NT Resource Kit, by Microsoft Press.

- *The Microsoft Windows 98 Resource Kit*, by Microsoft Press.

- The file `/usr/docs/samba-$version/docs/textdocs/DOMAIN.txt` on your Linux system after you have installed Samba.

- The Web site `http://burks.bton.ac.uk/burks/pcinfo/osdocs/win95l/95nworkm.htm#e27` provides more information on caching passwords under Windows 9x.

- The Web site `http://support.microsoft.com/support/kb/articles/q137/8/26.asp` provides information on password caching.

FROM HERE...

The remainder of Part III shows how to configure various client operating systems to access Samba.

- Chapter 11, "Samba as a Logon and Profiles Server," looks at how to set up Samba to support network logons and profile serving.

- Chapter 12, "Accessing Samba from Windows for Workgroups and Windows 9x," shows how to configure Windows for Workgroups and Windows 9x to access a Samba server.

- Chapter 13, "Accessing Samba from Windows NT," details how to configure NT Workstation and Server to access a Samba server. It does not deal with Samba as a PDC because this is dealt with in Part IV, "Advanced Topics."

- Chapter 14, "Accessing Samba from OS/2," explores the topic of accessing Samba from OS/2.

- Chapter 15, "Accessing Samba from Windows 2000," discusses how to configure Windows 2000 to access a Samba server.

- Chapter 16, "Accessing Windows from UNIX Using Samba," looks at how Samba can be used to access Windows systems from UNIX systems.

- Chapter 17, "Samba and Browsing," discusses Windows network browsing and how to configure Samba to provide browsing support.

PART

III

CH

10

## CHAPTER 11

SAMBA AS A LOGON AND PROFILES SERVER

In this chapter

by Jim Morris

Most network operating systems provide a facility to process user logons at the network level as opposed to logging in to a local workstation. A logon server handles this process. Although the primary purpose of a network logon is to perform user authentication, the SMB networking protocol as implemented by Microsoft Windows extends the logon process in several areas. These extensions include the capability to execute network *logon scripts*, to access network-wide *system policy files*, and to utilize *roving profiles*. These concepts are explained in more detail over the next several pages.

In this chapter we will examine in detail

- General information about what a logon server does
- How Samba works as a logon server, including support for logon scripts and system policies
- How Samba supports roaming profiles

If you are already familiar with logon servers and want to know the specifics of how Samba deals with this subject, feel free to skip the rest of this introduction. If the logon and profile servers are new to you, read on!

WHAT A LOGON SERVER DOES

A logon server should be considered a crucial part of all but the smallest of networks. By centralizing user authentication to a logon server, the burden of maintaining user accounts and passwords on every workstation on a network is eliminated. If the logon server is used to provide logon script processing and roving profile storage, users can have their own customized drive mappings and Windows desktop settings available, regardless of the specific PC they log on from. All these features can work together to dramatically improve the "network experience" of your users.

USER AUTHENTICATION

The primary purpose of a logon server is to authenticate users of the network. Authentication typically consists of verifying that the user exists in a particular network domain and that the user entered the correct network password. If authentication fails, the network logon fails, and access to network resources is denied. Depending on the client system and configuration, it might be possible to log on and use the client PC without performing a valid network logon first.

After a client PC has performed a successful network logon to a domain logon server, the client uses the same authentication information (username and password) for all other network resources that are accessed during that network session. Hence, the use of the network logon server enables a single logon to the network, regardless of whether network resources are being accessed on the logon server itself or on other servers within the network domain.

On most Samba and Windows-based networks, the logon server is typically the same system as the primary domain controller (PDC). However, Samba has the capability to service Windows 95 and Windows 98 domain logons without necessarily being configured as a true domain controller. This is not true of Windows NT domain logons, which require certain functionality of a PDC to be present on the logon server. This means that if a Samba server is to handle Windows NT network logons, it must be configured as a PDC as well.

→   For information on configuring Samba to act as a PDC, **see** Chapter 19, "Samba and Windows NT Domains."

LOGON SCRIPTS

Another important function of the logon server is to provide network logon scripts, which a network client executes immediately after a successful logon. For Windows clients, these scripts consist of DOS-style batch files, which can be used to perform a variety of tasks. The following are some typical uses of a logon script:

- Setting up network drive and printer connections
- Synchronizing the client PC's time to a server
- Displaying important messages (Message of the Day, for example)

For logon script processing to occur, both the client PC and the Samba server must be configured to support domain logons. If the client PC is not configured to log on to a network domain, the logon script is never processed. Likewise, if the Samba server is not properly configured to supply a logon script, no logon script processing occurs.

SYSTEM POLICIES

When accessing a logon server, Windows 95 and Windows 98 systems can load system policies from a CONFIG.POL file stored on the Samba server. The policy file enables you to define the features that are available to specific machines or specific users on the network. Policy files essentially contain information that is loaded into the Windows registry on the client PC upon each network logon. The information in the policy file replaces any settings that might have been modified locally on each client PC. Therefore, through the use of policies, you can force all workstations to be configured a certain way. Policy files are created by the network administrator using a special tool called the *System Policy Editor*.

→   For more detail about system policy files and the System Policy Editor, **see** "System Policies," **p. 210**.

ROAMING PROFILES

Windows 95, Windows 98, and Windows NT systems support the use of a roaming profile server, which stores specific user configuration settings for a desktop PC. These settings are then available to users when they log in to other desktop PCs on the network.

PART

III

CH

11

HOW WIN9X CLIENTS ACCESS A LOGON SERVER

To understand how Win9x logons work, and some of the problems that can occur, you must know the sequence of steps that a Win9x client uses in logging on to the network.

Figure 11.1 shows a network trace of a Win9x client logging on to the network using a Samba server. The following steps are taken when a Win9x client logs on:

1. The Win9x client issues a NetLogon request. This request is sent to the broadcast address of the subnet in which the client resides, and is sent on the NetBIOS name of the workgroup/domain that it wants to log on to. This appears in frame 1 in Figure 11.1.

Figure 11.1
A Win9x client logs on to the network.

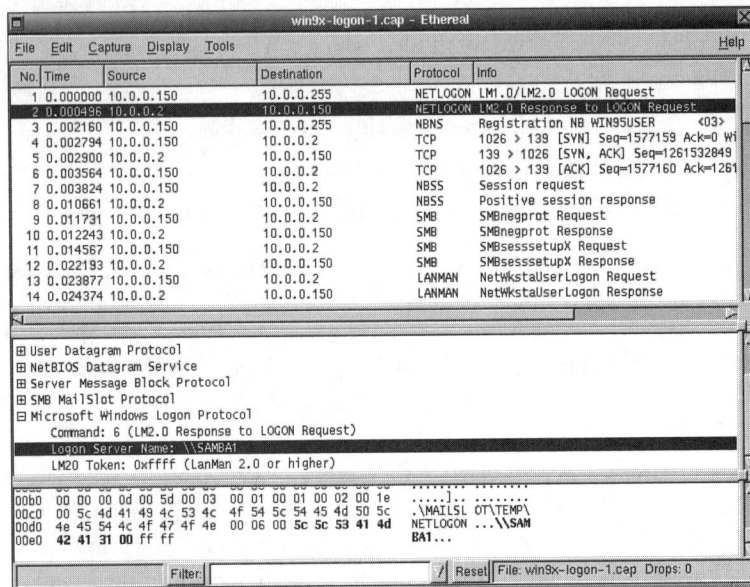

2. The Samba server in the domain in which the client wants to log on to responds with a NetLogon response that indicates the name of the server to log on to. This appears in frame 2 of Figure 11.1. The middle pane shows the response.

3. The Win9x client then registers the NetBIOS name of the logging-on user. This appears in frame three of Figure 11.1.

4. The Win9x client then connects to the nominated logon server, authenticates, and then connects to the IPC$ share. This appears in frames 4–12 in Figure 11.1.

   When authenticating the Win9x client, Samba uses the mechanism specified in the smb.conf file. For more information on authentication, see Chapter 8, "Samba and Password Management."

5. The Win9x client issues a `NetWkstaUserLogon` request to the logon server. The response contains the name of the server on which the user's logon script is located and the name of the logon script. This appears in frames 13 and 14 in Figure 11.1.

6. The Win9x client then connects to the server specified on the NetLogon share and reads and executes the user's logon script. This is partially shown in frames 15–18 in Figure 11.1.

7. Next, the Win9x client issues a `NetUserGetInfo` request to the logon server to retrieve information about the logging-on user, including their home share (which is also used as their roaming profiles share). The Win9x client looks for profile information in this location, as discussed in the "Windows 95 and Windows 98 Roaming Profiles" section later in this chapter. If profiles information is found, it is read and implemented at this point.

8. Next, the Win9x client reconnects to the NetLogon share on the logon server and looks for the `CONFIG.POL` file. If it is found, the policy file is put into effect. For more information on policies, see the "System Policies" section later in this chapter.

You can prevent a Win9x client from looking for the `CONFIG.POL` file by changing the registry entry `HKLM, System\CurrentControlSet\control\Update\UpdateMode` to 0.

> **Note**
>
> A Win9x network logon results in two connections to the NetLogon share.

HOW SAMBA WORKS AS A LOGON SERVER

Samba has supported network domain logons for Windows 95 and Windows 98 clients for many years. Domain logon processing for Windows NT clients has been available only since the release of Samba 2.0.0 in January 1999, which is the first Samba release that included enough of the undocumented Windows NT PDC functionality to permit Windows NT clients to work properly.

When configured as a logon server, Samba supports not only user authentication, but also the use of network logon scripts and roaming profiles.

NETWORK LOGON SUPPORT

For your Samba server to process network domain logons, you must configure your Samba server to process domain logons. In addition, if your logon server is in another subnet, you must ensure that

■   Your clients use WINS and you have a WINS server running in your network.

■   Your clients have an `lmhosts` file that enables them to resolve the NetBIOS name of the logon server to an IP address.

Note

Note that if multiple logon servers are configured in a domain, the network client uses the first server that answers its network logon broadcast request. In normal network configurations, you configure only a single server to handle network logons for a specific domain.

CONFIGURING A WINS SERVER

Network clients use a WINS server to resolve the NETBIOS network names used by the SMB network protocol to actual IP addresses. For Samba to work properly as a logon server, I recommend that you configure a WINS server and set all network clients to utilize the same WINS server. This WINS server need not be the same as your Samba server. Configure your Samba server using the appropriate instructions that follow.

SAMBA LOGON SERVER AS A WINS SERVER If you want the Samba server that is handling network logon requests to also be the WINS server, add the following options to the [global] section of your server's smb.conf file:

wins support = yes

Note

You should *never* configure more than one WINS server on a network.

If you configure Samba to act as a WINS server using the preceding option, omit all other options related to WINS server usage from your smb.conf file. Specifically, do not set other WINS-related Samba options such as wins server when you have enabled the wins support option.

SAMBA LOGON SERVER AS A WINS CLIENT If your Samba server will be utilizing another system as the WINS server, place the following entry in the [global] section of your smb.conf file:

wins server = x.x.x.x

Set this parameter to the IP address of a valid WINS server on your network.

USING AN lmhosts FILE ON CLIENTS

An alternative to using WINS is to use an lmhosts file on each client. The use of an lmhosts file protects you from problems when the WINS server is inaccessible, but causes problems in other areas. Because they require a file on each client, you must keep lmhosts files up-to-date, which can represent a large administrative load.

To use an lmhosts file, simply create one. Windows usually already contains a sample lmhosts file, lmhosts.sam. The sample lmhosts file contains much information on creating entries in the lmhosts file. All you must do is populate this file and rename it to simply lmhosts.

To add NetBIOS names to the `lmhosts` file, simply add lines in the following format:

```
Samba1 #PRE
```

Of course, you should add the IP addresses and names of your hosts.

> **Note**
>
> The #PRE suffix tells Windows to preload this entry into the name cache. This means that in trying to resolve this name, Windows will not cause any network traffic because it can get the information from the name cache.

ENABLING LOGON SUPPORT

For Samba to support network domain logons, you must add the following parameter to the `[global]` section of your Samba server's `smb.conf` file:

```
logon server = yes
```

This causes the Samba server to answer network logon broadcast requests for the network workgroup on which the Samba server is configured to be a member. For example, if the `[global]` section of the `smb.conf` contains

```
workgroup = development
```

then the Samba server services logon requests for the domain named `development`. Logon requests are not handled for other network domains.

LOGON SCRIPTS

For a Samba server to provide logon scripts for network clients, you must first enable the proper support in the `smb.conf` file. Then you must provide the logon scripts themselves using a special share on the Samba logon server.

> **Note**
>
> If you edit logon scripts under Linux or UNIX, ensure that the files contain DOS-style line endings (CR+LF) rather than UNIX-style line endings (LF).
>
> The command `todos` can be used to convert a Linux text file to a DOS-style text file.

CONFIGURING LOGON SCRIPT SUPPORT

To provide network logon scripts for execution by network clients, the Samba server must provide a special network share. This share must be named `[netlogon]` and should be readable to all users. For security reasons, you probably do not want this share writeable to the average user. Configure the share as shown in Listing 11.1.

LISTING 11.1 DEFINITION OF THE netlogon **SHARE**

```
[netlogon]
  comment = Netlogon share
  path = /shared/netlogon
  writeable = no
  guest ok = no
  browseable = no
```

In the [global] section of your smb.conf file, enter the following:

```
logon script = logon.bat
```

This causes each user to execute a login script named logon.bat. A DOS batch file like the one shown in Listing 11.2 should go into the appropriate location on the server (/shared/netlogon/logon.bat in the sample smb.conf entry above). The batch file in Listing 11.2 synchronizes a client PC's clock to that of a server named DARKSTAR, and then connects several file and printer shares to the same drive letter mappings for all clients.

LISTING 11.2 A SIMPLE NETWORK LOGON SCRIPT

```
@ECHO OFF
REM * Synchronize client's time to server *
NET TIME \\DARKSTAR /SET /YES
REM * Setup common shares that everyone uses *
NET USE X: \\DARKSTAR\XFER
NET USE I: \\DARKSTAR\APPS
REM * Connect some printer shares *
NET USE LPT1:   \\DARKSTAR\LJET3
```

If you have configured everything properly, Windows clients open a command prompt window to run the logon script, as shown in Figure 11.2. This happens immediately after closing the domain logon dialog box. If the logon script completes normally, this window should close automatically.

Figure 11.2
The logon script executes during Windows 98 logon.

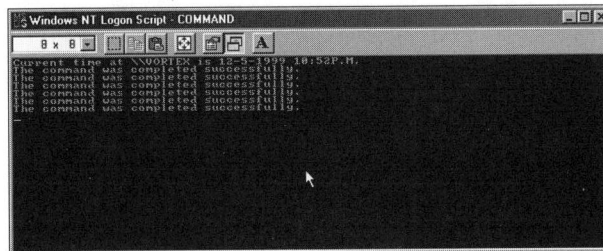

While a client PC is executing the logon script, the [netlogon] share is mapped to the Z: drive letter on the client. Therefore, it is perfectly acceptable for you to put any special utility programs that are needed during the logon process on the [netlogon] share and execute them from there by prefixing a Z:\ path to the command line in the logon script.

Tip from
Jim Morris

> During testing of your logon script, you might find it useful to insert the DOS `pause` command at the end of the script. This will enable you to see whether any errors occurred during script execution. Be sure to remember to remove the `pause` command after your script is working properly.

ADVANCED LOGON SCRIPT OPTIONS

Samba provides several mechanisms for use in the `smb.conf` configuration to provide advanced logon script functionality. All the `%` macros documented in the Samba manual are allowed in the naming convention used for the logon script. You can also use them as command-line parameters for the logon script. For example, by putting the following into the `[global]` section of your `smb.conf`, you can have separate logon scripts for each user:

```
logon script = %U.bat
```

Table 11.1 shows other useful substitution macros for use in logon scripts.

TABLE 11.1 USEFUL SUBSTITUTION MACROS FOR LOGON SCRIPTS

Macro	Replaced By	Possible Uses
%m	Client Machine NetBIOS Name	Useful if you want one logon script per client machine rather than per user.
%U	User Name	One logon script per user or dependencies in the logon script based on the username.
%G	User Group	Useful if you want the logon script to have different processing based on the user's default UNIX group.
%P	Negotiated Protocol	Useful if the logon script must be different based on the client protocol (NT1, LAN-MAN1, LANMAN2, CORE, and so on). This could be useful if the logon script that is processed must be different based on the client system in use (OS/2, LAN Manager for DOS, and so on).
%L	Server Name	Allows a logon script to be portable to different servers or if you change your server's name. Also useful if you have multiple virtual Samba servers on the same host.

Creative use of substitution macros, either as part of the script name or as command-line options to the script (with appropriate logic inside the script), allows for great flexibility in your logon script processing.

It is perfectly acceptable to include a path in the name of the logon script if you want the logon scripts to reside in a subdirectory on the `[netlogon]` share.

AUTOMATICALLY GENERATED LOGON SCRIPTS

On most networks with more than a handful of users, it is very limiting to have a single logon script for all users. It will quickly become a maintenance headache to have separate logon scripts for each user on your network. Using certain Samba options in the smb.conf file enables you to run a Linux or UNIX program, such as a Perl script, that generates a user logon script dynamically for each logon. Using a Perl script to generate logon scripts on-the-fly has the added benefit of giving you just one file to maintain rather than many. To do this, use the [netlogon] share settings shown in Listing 11.3.

LISTING 11.3 NETLOGON SHARE DEFINITION FOR AUTO-GENERATED LOGON SCRIPTS

```
[netlogon]
comment = Network Logon Scripts
path = /shared/netlogon
writeable = no
guest ok = no
root preexec = /shared/netlogon/genlogon.pl %U %G %L
root postexec = rm /shared/netlogon/%U.bat
```

The changes made to the [netlogon] share in Listing 11.3 involve the added directives for root preexec and root postexec. The reason for using root preexec and not simply the preexec option is that we have declared this share to be read-only to normal users. Therefore, unless we run the preexec command as root, it is unable to generate a logon script on the share.

The preexec command executes each time a service is connected to, and the postexec command executes each time a service is disconnected. In the example in Listing 11.3, a Perl script called genlogon.pl executes each time a user connects to the [netlogon] share, taking the username, user's primary UNIX group, and the NetBIOS name used for the server as parameters. After the logon process is complete, the postexec command deletes the generated file.

Listing 11.4 shows a real-world example of a genlogon.pl script.

LISTING 11.4 PERL SCRIPT TO GENERATE SAMBA LOGON SCRIPTS

```
#!/usr/bin/perl
#
# genlogon.pl
#
# Perl script to generate user logon scripts on the fly, when users
# connect from a Windows client.  This script should be called from smb.conf
# with the %U, %G and %L parameters. I.e:
#
#      root preexec = genlogon.pl %U %G %L
#
# The script generated will perform
# the following:
#
# 1. Log the user connection to /var/log/samba/netlogon.log
```

Listing 11.4   Continued

```
# 2. Set the PC's time to the Linux server time (which is maintained
#      daily to the National Institute of Standard's Atomic clock on the
#      internet.
# 3. Connect the user's home drive to H: (H for Home).
# 4. Connect common drives that everyone uses.
# 5. Connect group-specific drives for certain user groups.
# 6. Connect user-specific shares for certain users.
# 7. Connect network printers.

# Log client connection
($sec,$min,$hour,$mday,$mon,$year,$wday,$yday,$isdst) = localtime(time);
open LOG, ">>/var/log/samba/netlogon.log";
print LOG
➥"$mon/$mday/$year $hour:$min:$sec - User $ARGV[0] logged into $ARGV[1]\n";
close LOG;

# Start generating logon script
open LOGON, ">/shared/netlogon/$ARGV[0].bat";
print LOGON "\@echo off\r\n";

# These commands are common to all users
print LOGON "NET TIME \\\\$ARGV[2] /SET /YES\r\n";
print LOGON "NET USE H: \\\\$ARGV[2]\\$ARGV[0]\r\n";
print LOGON "NET USE I: \\\\$ARGV[2]\\APPS\r\n";
print LOGON "NET USE X: \\\\$ARGV[2]\\XFER\r\n";

# Connect shares just use by Software Development group
if ($ARGV[1] eq "SOFTDEV" || $ARGV[0] eq "softdev")
{
        print LOGON "NET USE M: \\\\$ARGV[2]\\SOURCE\r\n";
}

# Connect shares just use by Technical Support staff
if ($ARGV[1] eq "SUPPORT" || $ARGV[0] eq "support")
{
        print LOGON "NET USE S: \\\\$ARGV[2]\\SUPPORT\r\n";
}

# Connect shares just used by Administration staff
if ($ARGV[1] eq "ADMIN" || $ARGV[0] eq "admin")
{
        print LOGON "NET USE L: \\\\$ARGV[2]\\ADMIN\r\n";
        print LOGON "NET USE K: \\\\$ARGV[2]\\MKTING\r\n";
}

# Now connect Printers.  We handle just two or three users a little
# differently, because they are the exceptions that have desktop
# printers on LPT1: - all other users go to the LaserJet on the
# server.
if ($ARGV[0] eq "jim"
    || $ARGV[0] eq "yvonne")
{
print LOGON "NET USE LPT2: \\\\$ARGV[2]\\LJET3\r\n";
print LOGON "NET USE LPT3: \\\\$ARGV[2]\\FAXQ\r\n";
}
```

LISTING 11.4   CONTINUED

```
else
{
print LOGON "NET USE LPT1: \\\\$ARGV[2]\\LJET3\r\n";
print LOGON "NET USE LPT3: \\\\$ARGV[2]\\FAXQ\r\n";
}

# All done! Close the output file.
close LOGON;
```

The author of this text is not proficient in the art of Perl programming by any means. Listing 11.4 is just an example of what you can do to generate logon scripts on-the-fly. However, a little explanation of the Perl script is warranted.

The first thing you might notice is that nowhere is the server name used when creating the NET USE statements in the output file. Instead, the command-line argument that was supplied using %L is used to determine the server name. That way, this script can be fairly portable to multiple Samba servers, assuming the share names are the same, of course. Notice also how the user's login name and primary UNIX group are used through command-line arguments to the Perl script. If you use different UNIX groups for different classes of users when creating your Samba user accounts, this is a good way to map specific network shares for only certain classes of users. Finally, you can see how to set up specific resources for only certain users, based on the passed username.

> **Note**
>
> Your root preexec script will be executed twice by most clients because, as discussed previously in the section "How Win9x Clients Access a Logon Server," a Win9x client connects to the NetLogon share twice during the logon process.
>
> To avoid any adverse consequences of this, you must ensure that your script can be run twice without problems. If all you are doing is generating a login script, this should not be a problem. However, it will slow the logon process down slightly.

SYSTEM POLICIES

To support the Windows 95 and Windows 98 capability to load system policy files from the network logon server, you must first create and properly configure Samba to handle domain logon requests. You must also properly configure a [netlogon] share, although the use of logon scripts is not required to utilize system policies.

→ For more information about Samba and domain logon requests, **see** "How Samba Works as a Logon Server" and "Network Logon Support," **p. 203**.

Create a CONFIG.POL file using the Windows 95 or Windows 98 System Policy Editor, which is part of the resource kit for the respective operating systems. Figure 11.3 shows some of the settings configurable using the Windows 98 System Policy Editor.

Figure 11.3
You can use the System Policy Editor to configure settings for all Windows PCs.

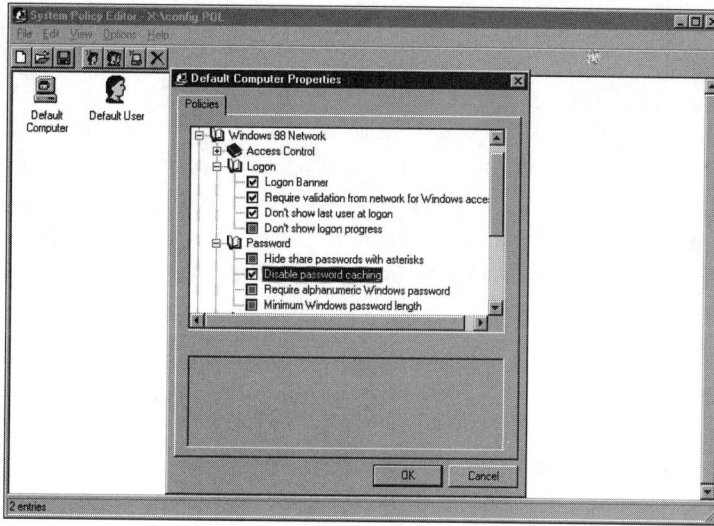

The system policy file is a powerful tool if you are administering a network with a large number of Windows 95 or Windows 98 client machines. It enables you to configure many of the network and other settings on the client systems without physically going to each system on the network and editing those settings using the Windows Control Panel.

After you finish editing the system policy file, place it on the [netlogon] share and give it the name CONFIG.POL.

Detailed information about creating system policies and using the System Policy Editor is contained in the "User Profiles and System Policies" chapter of the *Windows 95 Resource Kit* or the *Windows 98 Resource Kit*.

In addition, you should be aware that it is possible to switch off the loading of policies and to specify where they should be loaded from. Policies can be switched off by setting the registry key HLM\System\CurrentControlSet\Control\Update\UpdateMode to 0.

For more information on how to manage policies, please see the Microsoft Knowledge Base article at http://support.microsoft.com/support/kb/articles/Q185/5/89.ASP.

How Samba Supports Profiles

Windows 95, Windows 98, and Windows NT all support the use of a roaming profile server for storing user-specific configuration information. Some differences exist in how Windows 95 and Windows 98 handle profiles compared to Windows NT, and the way in which you configure Samba for roaming profiles for these operating systems differs as well.

Configuring Samba to Support Profiles

Windows 9x and Windows NT clients ask the logon server where their profiles are stored, but they use different mechanisms to get this information:

- Windows 9x clients send a NetUserGetInfo request to their logon server to obtain the information. The NetUserGetInfo response only contains the user's home directory location. This means that you have very little control over where Windows 9x clients get their profiles. However, because of bugs in the Windows 9x code dealing with the home share, you can place them in a subdirectory of the home share.

- Windows NT clients make a NetSamLogon RPC call to retrieve the appropriate information. The response contains a separate field for the profile location. You would use the logon home parameter to control where Windows NT clients keep their profiles.

Thus, Win9x clients are restricted to keeping their profiles in their home directory location, while Windows NT clients can have their profiles placed in any location they have access to.

PROFILES STORED IN USER'S HOME DIRECTORY

As already discussed, Windows 9x clients look for their profiles in their home directory. You would use the logon home parameter to control where a client's home directory is, and it turns out that Windows clients will accept a path in this parameter.

The following causes clients to store profiles in a subdirectory called profile beneath the users' home directory on the Samba server:

```
logon home = \\%L\%U\profile
```

This still enables the DOS command net use /home to work, because it seems that when this command is given, Windows strips any directory path off the end of the home share location.

If you want to ensure that profile information is accessed as a hidden file when users access their home directories using a mapped Samba share, you could name the logon home like this:

```
logon home = \\%L\%U\.roamingprofile
```

Because Samba's default operation is to map dot (.) prefixed directory and filenames on the server's UNIX-style file system to the DOS hidden attribute on the client, this would effectively hide the profile directory from casual examination or accidental deletion.

You would use the logon path parameter to specify the location of Windows NT clients' profiles. Use the following to place profiles for Windows NT clients in a hidden directory in their home share location:

```
logon path = \\%L\%U\.roamingprofile
```

You can configure profiles for both Windows 9x clients and Windows NT clients to the same location by placing the following parameters in the global section of your smb.conf file:

```
logon path = \\%L\%U\.roamingprofile
logon home = \\%L\%U\.roamingprofile
```

> **Note**
>
> There are known problems with Windows NT clients keeping their profiles in the home share. On occasion when logging out, NT clients will keep a connection open to the home share. The net result is that the next user gets the last user's profiles.
>
> It can be better to keep profiles outside the home share for NT clients.

PROFILES STORED ON A SHARE

Often, you might want to store profiles in a directory other than the user's home directory. You might do this because your users do not have valid login accounts, and therefore do not have home directories. Or you might simply want to store all profiles in a common location. To do this, set the logon path in the `[global]` section of your `smb.conf` to

```
logon path = \\%L\profiles\%U
```

> **Note**
>
> As discussed previously, you cannot locate the profiles for Windows 9x clients outside the home share location.

Next, create a `[profiles]` share on your Samba server. Note that this share must be browsable and writable by all users. Do this by adding the entries in Listing 11.5 to your `smb.conf`.

PART III

CH 11

LISTING 11.5 DEFINITION OF PROFILES SHARE

```
[profiles]
    description = Roving Profiles share
    path = /shared/profiles
    writeable = yes
    browseable = yes
    root preexec = /usr/local/sbin/mkprofiledir.sh %U %G
```

The last part of the share definition invokes a `preexec` script each time the share is connected. The script appears in Listing 11.6.

LISTING 11.6 SHELL SCRIPT TO CREATE USER PROFILE DIRECTORIES

```
#!/bin/sh
#
# mkprofiledir.sh
#
# Shell script to make sure a profile directory exists for each network user.
# If it doesn't exist, it will be created.
#
```

LISTING 11.6 CONTINUED

```
if [! -x /shared/profiles/"$1"]; then
    /bin/mkdir /shared/profiles/"$1"
    /bin/chown "$1" /shared/profiles/"$1"
    /bin/chgrp "$2" /shared/profiles/"$1"
    /bin/chmod 700 /shared/profiles/"$1"
fi
```

This script ensures that the [profiles] share contains a subdirectory for each user and that the subdirectory is accessible only by that user. If you elect not to use a script such as this, you must create the profiles subdirectories by hand and set the permissions appropriately for each user.

> **Note**
>
> The share name of *profiles* used in the previous section is arbitrary. If you want to use something else, substitute that in both the share definition and in the logon path option.

WINDOWS 95 AND WINDOWS 98 ROAMING PROFILES

For Windows 95 and Windows 98, a roaming profile enables each network user to store the contents of his desktop (including the My Documents folder) and Start menu in the logon path defined by the Samba server. Several subdirectories representing the desktop as well as a USER.DAT file containing configuration settings, are stored there. This enables the user to log on to different PCs with the same desktop shortcuts and Start menu programs available. Of course, for a program or shortcut to actually work on a PC, the appropriate program must be installed locally on that PC.

The User Profiles settings in the Passwords section of the Windows 95 or Windows 98 Control Panel controls the capability to utilize a roaming profile server. To enable roaming profiles, you must select the option to enable users to customize their own settings, as shown in Figure 11.4. You can also specify whether each user can customize the Start menu, the Desktop, or both.

Figure 11.4
Enable Profile support in the Passwords control panel in Windows 95/98.

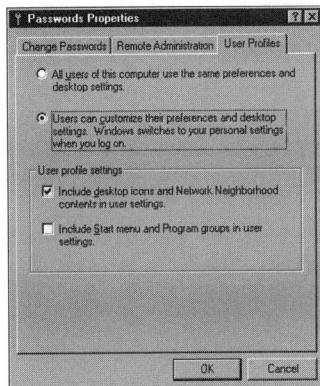

PART
III

CH
11

> **Note**
>
> Windows 95 and Windows 98 will load and save the user profile on the Samba server only if the primary logon is configured to be Client for Microsoft Networks in the Network settings of the Control Panel.

WINDOWS NT ROAMING PROFILES

Windows NT handles user profiles a bit differently from Windows 95 or Windows 98. The User Manager for Domains administration tool under Windows NT controls user profiles. The User Manager tool enables you to manually specify a network server and path for the profile. You must do this for each user on the Windows NT system for which you want to provide a network-based profile.

For the most part, after specifying the location with the User Manager for Domains tool, Windows NT automatically handles using the profile information on the Samba server in the same way as Windows 95 and Windows 98. However, in some circumstances you might need to use certain advanced configuration options on the Samba server to handle Windows NT roving profiles properly. These options are `logon drive` and `logon home`. If you need them, configure them as follows in the `[global]` section of your `smb.conf` file:

```
logon drive = h:
logon home = \\%N\%U
```

Set the `logon drive` option to any valid drive letter. The Windows NT system uses it during the logon process to map the home directory.

The `logon home` directory should preferably be in the same location that the user profiles are stored.

Once again, just as in the case of logon script processing, for roving profiles to work you must properly configure both the Windows client and the Samba server.

DETAILS OF THE smb.conf PARAMETERS REQUIRED

The `smb.conf` parameters discussed in this chapter are listed in Table 11.2. For more information on these settings, refer to the Samba documentation, and especially the `smb.conf` manual page, accessible from the server's command prompt by typing `man smb.conf`.

TABLE 11.2   smb.conf PARAMETERS USED IN THIS CHAPTER

Parameter	File Section	Meaning
wins support	global	Enables WINS server support in Samba.
wins server	global	Configures Samba to utilize another WINS server to resolve NetBIOS names to IP addresses.
logon server	global	Configures Samba to support domain logon requests from clients.

TABLE 11.2 CONTINUED

Parameter	File Section	Meaning
workgroup	global	Sets the workgroup and network domain in which the Samba server will participate.
comment	share	Sets the comment seen for a share when browsing the network.
path	share	Sets the UNIX directory path that is the top-level directory for a share.
writeable	share	Sets the default read/write status of a share.
guest ok	share	Determines whether guest user connections are allowed to a share.
browseable	share	Determines whether a share shows up in the browse list of a server.
logon script	global	Configures the path and filename for the logon script for domain logon script processing.
root preexec	share	Configures a command that runs on the Samba server when a client first connects to a share.
root postexec	share	Configures a command that runs on the Samba server when a client disconnects from a share.
logon path	global	Enables roving profile support and configures the path used to store user profiles.
logon drive	global	Sets the drive letter to which Windows NT clients will map the user home directory during the Windows NT logon process.
logon home	global	Sets the home directory for the logon process. Also enables the NET USE x: /HOME command to be used on clients to connect to the home directory specified. It can also be used to specify where profiles are kept for Win 9x clients.

COMMON PROBLEMS

People encounter several problems with network logons; some common ones are addressed in the following sections.

LOGON SCRIPT DOESN'T RUN ON CLIENT PC

If the logon script does not run on the client, check the following:

■ Make sure the client PC is configured to do a domain logon. See the appropriate chapter in this book for the client in question.

- Make sure that the [netlogon] share is configured properly and that everything points to a valid path on the Samba server.
- Check the permissions on the files in the [netlogon] directory. Make sure the user attempting to log on can read the logon script.

CLIENT PCs DO NOT FIND A VALID DOMAIN CONTROLLER

An error message of this sort occurs on a client PC when it is configured to log on to a domain but cannot find a domain controller. Check the following:

- Make sure that the client PC and the Samba server are configured to be in the same domain.
- Use smbclient to see the status of your Samba server. Type

  smbclient -N -L servername

- You should see a browse list for your Samba server, which should include things such as the [netlogon] share.
- Make sure that the netmask and broadcast address for both your Samba server and your Windows clients are correct. This is because the NetLogon request is broadcast, and if your netmask and broadcast address are incorrect, the Samba server will not see the NetLogon request.

CLIENT ERRORS ON LOGON/LOGOUT WHEN USING ROAMING PROFILES

This occurs if you have enabled roaming profile support but the directory on the server is not writeable to the user having the error. Make sure the user can write the share used by the logon path (or logon home) option and that the UNIX permissions for the directory permit the user to write to it.

MORE INFORMATION

For more information on the topics discussed in this chapter, refer to the following resources:

- The smb.conf manual page on your Samba server. Access this by typing man smb.conf.
- The files DOMAIN.txt, NTDOMAIN.txt, and PROFILES.txt in the /usr/docs/ samba-$version/docs/textdocs directory on your Linux or UNIX system after you have installed Samba.

PART

III

CH

11

ACCESSING SAMBA FROM WINDOWS FOR WORKGROUPS AND WINDOWS 9X

In this chapter

by Richard Sharpe

Windows 98 is the successor to Windows 95, and Windows 95 is the successor to Windows for Workgroups. Windows for Workgroups was the first successful Microsoft Windows Networking operating system. It was capable of accessing SMB servers of many types and was networked to SMB server products such as PATHWORKS from Digital Equipment Corporation and LAN Manager from Microsoft.

In this chapter, we examine how to configure Windows for Workgroups 3.11, Windows 95, and Windows 98 to access Samba. We will discuss the following:

- The general configuration of these operating systems to use Samba
- Using plain-text passwords
- Configuring plain-text passwords to use Samba as a logon server
- Automatically generating logon scripts
- Accessing Samba from DOS

For some of you, much of the material in this chapter will be well known; however, we focus now on how to integrate Windows for Workgroups and Windows 9x into a Samba server environment. For others, the material will be completely new.

ACCESSING SAMBA FROM WINDOWS FOR WORKGROUPS

In this section, we explore how to access Samba from Windows for Workgroups 3.11.

TCP/IP INSTALLATION AND CONFIGURATION

Windows for Workgroups 3.11 does not come with a TCP/IP protocol stack, so you must install one before you can access Samba servers from Windows for Workgroups. Microsoft provides one as a freely available add-on to Windows for Workgroups. It is available in the clients (\clients\tcp32wfw) area of its Windows NT Server CD and as a download from ftp://ftp.microsoft.com/peropsys/windows/public/tcpip/wfwt32.exe.

To install TCP/IP under Windows for Workgroups 3.11, perform the following steps:

1. Install Windows for Workgroups Networking.
2. Obtain the TCP/IP kit as discussed earlier, and if needed, extract it into a directory. If you have a Windows NT Server kit, you should have the following files:

```
Directory of D:\CLIENTS\TCP32WFW\DISKS\DISK1

    .           <DIR>      08-09-96 12:00a .
    ..          <DIR>      08-09-96 12:00a ..
    ARP    EXE    60,551 08-09-96 12:00a ARP.EXE
    FTP    EXE    81,968 08-09-96 12:00a FTP.EXE
    HOSTS  SAM       755 08-09-96 12:00a HOSTS.SAM
    IPCONFIG EXE   42,195 08-09-96 12:00a IPCONFIG.EXE
    LICENSE TXT    2,765 08-09-96 12:00a LICENSE.TXT
    LMHOSTS SAM    3,066 08-09-96 12:00a LMHOSTS.SAM
    MSTCP32 DEF      632 08-09-96 12:00a MSTCP32.DEF
```

```
MTCPIP32 HLP     228,780  08-09-96 12:00a MTCPIP32.HLP
NBTSTAT  EXE      33,227  08-09-96 12:00a NBTSTAT.EXE
NETSTAT  EXE      69,465  08-09-96 12:00a NETSTAT.EXE
NETWORKS            402  08-09-96 12:00a NETWORKS
OEMSETUP INF      1,091  08-09-96 12:00a OEMSETUP.INF
PING     EXE     58,307  08-09-96 12:00a PING.EXE
PROTOCOL           794  08-09-96 12:00a PROTOCOL
README   TXT     15,440  08-09-96 12:00a README.TXT
ROUTE    EXE     57,703  08-09-96 12:00a ROUTE.EXE
SERVICES         6,003  08-09-96 12:00a SERVICES
TCP32UI  DLL     63,904  08-09-96 12:00a TCP32UI.DLL
TELNET   EXE     57,216  08-09-96 12:00a TELNET.EXE
TELNET   HLP     21,778  08-09-96 12:00a TELNET.HLP
TRACERT  EXE     55,277  08-09-96 12:00a TRACERT.EXE
VDHCP    386     20,689  08-09-96 12:00a VDHCP.386
VIP      386     60,729  08-09-96 12:00a VIP.386
VNBT     386     89,545  08-09-96 12:00a VNBT.386
VTCP     386     46,802  08-09-96 12:00a VTCP.386
VTDI     386      5,323  08-09-96 12:00a VTDI.386
VUDP     386     15,850  08-09-96 12:00a VUDP.386
WINSOCK  DLL     41,440  08-09-96 12:00a WINSOCK.DLL
WSASRV   EXE      6,960  08-09-96 12:00a WSASRV.EXE
WSOCK    386     10,612  08-09-96 12:00a WSOCK.386
WSTCP    386     19,719  08-09-96 12:00a WSTCP.386
       31 file(s)    1,178,988 bytes
        2 dir(s)           0 bytes free
```

The same files are in the kit from the Microsoft FTP site.

3. In the Network group, double-click on Network Setup. This opens a window similar to that shown in Figure 12.1.

Figure 12.1
Network Setup enables you to add the TCP/IP software.

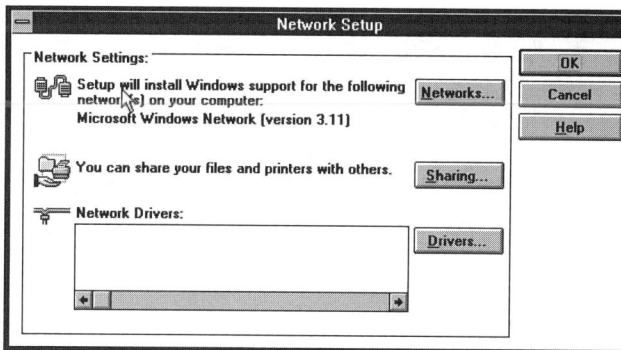

4. Click on Drivers to add a device driver if you do not already have one installed. This opens a window similar to that shown in Figure 12.2.

5. Click on Add Adapter to add your adapter. You will see a window similar to that shown in Figure 12.3.

Figure 12.2
Adding a driver so you can install TCP/IP.

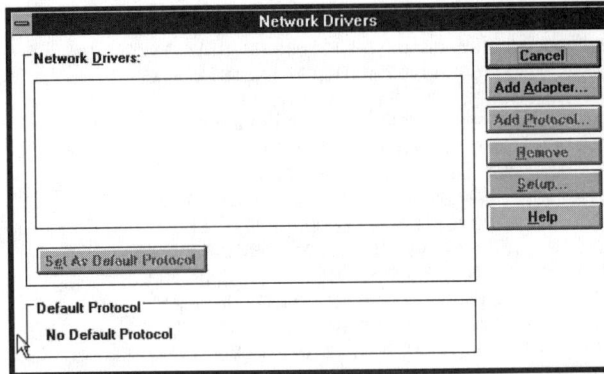

6. Select your adapter from the list and click OK. You might need to scroll the list to see your adapter, or you might need a vendor floppy. This opens a window similar to that shown in Figure 12.4.

Figure 12.3
You should select your network adapter.

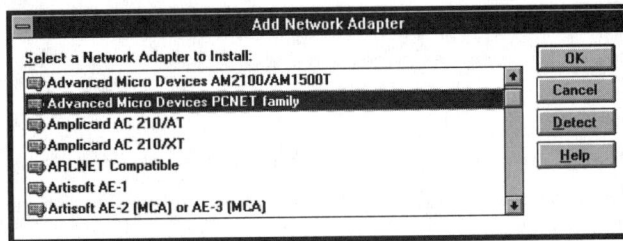

Figure 12.4
You now have two unnecessary protocols installed.

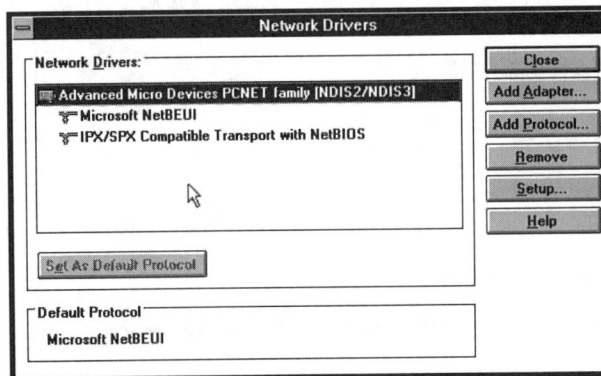

7. At this point you have the NetBEUI and IPX/SPX protocols installed, both of which are not needed for Samba access. Delete them if you do not need them, but only after you install the TCP/IP protocol.

Next, click on Add Protocol, which opens a window similar to that shown in Figure 12.5.

Figure 12.5
You must now install an unlisted or updated protocol.

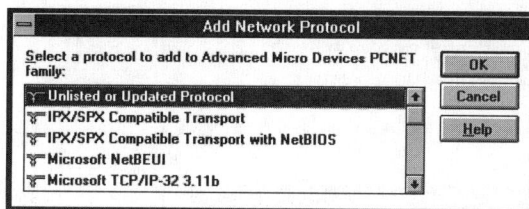

8. Select Unlisted or Updated Protocol and click OK, which opens a window similar to that shown in Figure 12.6.

Figure 12.6
You must specify the location of the protocol files.

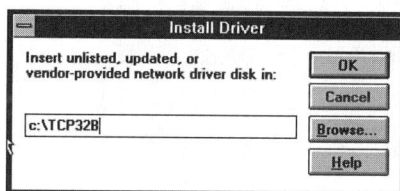

9. Next, enter the location of your files, which in this case is C:\TCP32B, but in your case might be A:\ or somewhere on the NT Server CD. After you click OK, you will see a window similar to the one shown in Figure 12.7.

Figure 12.7
You should select the TCP/IP-32 3.11b protocol.

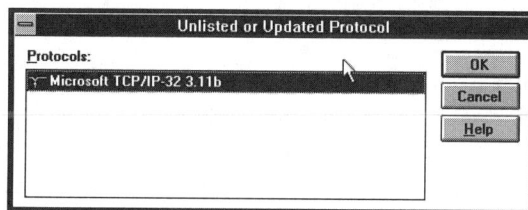

10. Click OK on the Unlisted or Updated Protocol window, click OK in the Add Network Protocol window, and finally click Close in the Network Drivers window. You will see a window similar to that shown in Figure 12.8.

11. Click OK, which should open the TCP/IP configuration dialog box similar to that shown in Figure 12.9.

12. Select Enable Automatic DHCP Configuration if you have a DHCP server on your network (such as the Internet Software Consortium's DHCP server), or enter your TCP/IP configuration details.

13. If you select DHCP, you might be presented with a dialog box warning you that any static IP addresses configured will be overwritten by DHCP. Simply click OK.

Figure 12.8
After deleting the unwanted protocols, your Network Setup display should look like this.

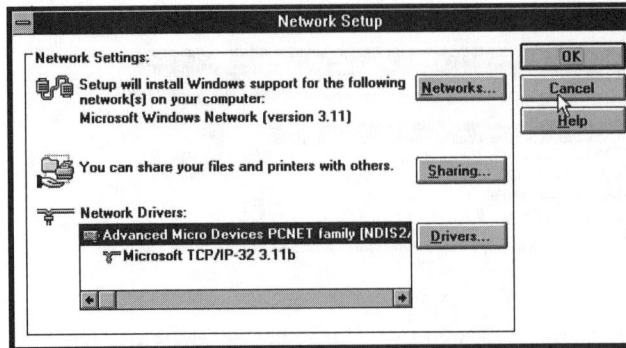

Figure 12.9
Configure TCP/IP on your system.

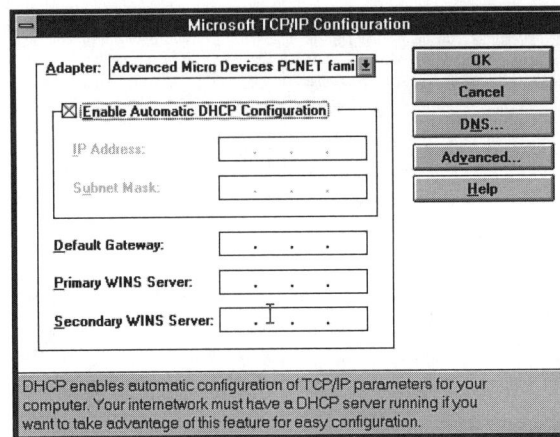

14. Click OK to complete the task required in Figure 12.9, and click OK on the Network Setup windows as well. After issuing some informative messages, you should be prompted to restart Windows.

At this point you might see Windows for Workgroups copying the files needed for TCP/IP as well as updating your CONFIG.SYS and AUTOEXEC.BAT files. You must restart Windows for Workgroups before the TCP/IP protocol can be used.

ACCESSING FILE SHARES ON SAMBA

After you have configured and installed TCP/IP for Windows for Workgroups, you can start accessing Samba. When Windows is restarted, you will be presented with a login dialog box similar to the one shown in Figure 12.10.

Figure 12.10
You must log in to Windows first.

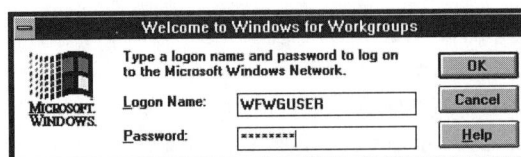

Enter the password for your account on the Samba server; use the correct case.

Although Windows for Workgroups converts passwords to uppercase before sending them to Samba, Samba knows how to handle this situation.

After you have logged on to Windows for Workgroups, you can access file shares on a Samba server in one of two ways:

- From a DOS prompt, issue a `net use` command such as the following:

  ```
  net use h: \\samba1\homes
  ```

  You can use any free drive letter instead of h (for example, d through z). See the following text for more information on accessing Samba from DOS.

- Use the Connect Network Drive menu item from File Manager to connect a share to a drive letter.

After you have connected a share on a Samba server to a drive letter, applications can access files on the share as if it were a local drive. Specifying the drive letter as part of the file specification does this. For example:

```
H:\myfile.txt
```

The redirector (see Chapter 10, "An Introduction to Microsoft Windows Networking") is the component that enables remote files to be accessed transparently in this way.

In the rest of this section we will concentrate on using the File Manager to access Samba.

The File Manager is in the Main group on your desktop. After you have started the File Manager (sometimes referred to as the *File Mangler*), select the Disk menu item, and then select Connect Network Drive. This will open the Connect Network Drive window similar to that shown in Figure 12.11.

When the dialog box shown in Figure 12.11 opens, it shows the servers that are known in your current workgroup/domain and shows you any other workgroups and domains of which the browse servers are aware. You can click on one of these to see what shares are available, as shown in Figure 12.11.

To connect a share to a drive letter, perform the following actions:

1. Select the drive to which you want to connect the share. In Figure 12.11 it has defaulted to E:, which is the next available drive.

2. Enter the name of the server and share in the path field. You can do this by typing the value into the path field or by clicking on the server you want in the Show Shared Directories On: combo box, and then selecting the share in the lower combo box. You can also use any combination of these two actions.

3. Select or deselect Reconnect at Startup. This field defaults to on, so you might want to deselect it.

PART

III

CH

12

Figure 12.11
You must connect to a network drive to access shares on a Samba server.

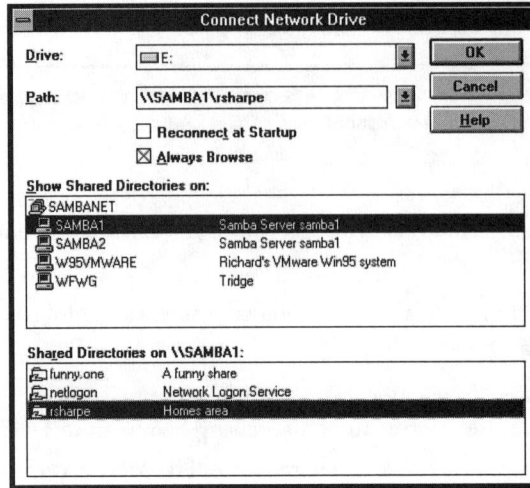

4. Click OK when you have finished.

When you have entered the appropriate information and clicked OK in the dialog box shown in Figure 12.11, Windows for Workgroups sends the appropriate SMBs to the server to connect your selected drive letter (E: in Figure 12.11) to the share you have chosen.

You can then browse the directory by selecting the appropriate drive letter in the icon bar in File Manager. Figure 12.12 shows the results of browsing a network drive.

Figure 12.12
You can browse network drives in File Manager.

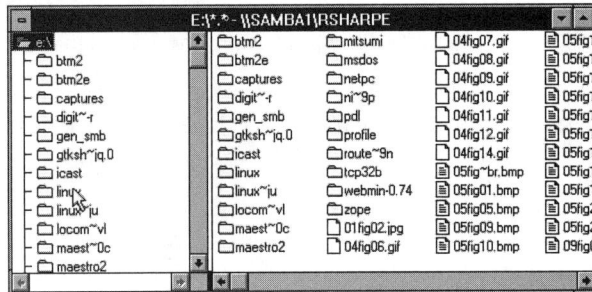

Under normal circumstances you would not manually connect drives to network shares each time. You would either

- Select Reconnect at Startup for all drives you connect to, so the next time you log on to Windows for Workgroups your network drives would be reconnected.

- Use logon scripts and log on to the network as discussed in the following text.

→ To learn more about setting up logon scripts, **see** "Logon Scripts for Windows for Workgroups," **p. 230**.

→ To learn how to set up any file shares under Samba, **see** Chapter 6, "File Sharing Under Samba."

On the Samba server you can see who is accessing file shares with the smbstatus command. The following shows what smbstatus might display if you are accessing a file share as the user WFWGUSER:

```
Samba version 2.0.6-pre1
Service       uid      gid       pid      machine
-----------------------------------------------
wfwguser      wfwguser wfwguser 9608     wfwg
➥(10.0.0.157) Fri Nov  5 17:11:30 199

No locked files

Share mode memory usage (bytes):
    1048464(99%) free + 56(0%) used + 56(0%) overhead = 1048576(100%) total
```

ACCESSING PRINTER SHARES ON SAMBA

To access printer shares on a Samba server, you must use Print Manager to connect a printer device (for example, LPT1 or COM1) to a printer share.

Use the following steps to achieve this:

1. Double-click Print Manager in the Main program group on your desktop.

2. Select the Printer menu item and click Connect NetworkPrinter. This opens the Connect Network Printer dialog box as shown in Figure 12.13.

3. Enter the appropriate information, including the Device Name and the Path. In Figure 12.13, we have selected LPT1: and \\samba1\pclp.

Figure 12.13
You connect the device to a network path.

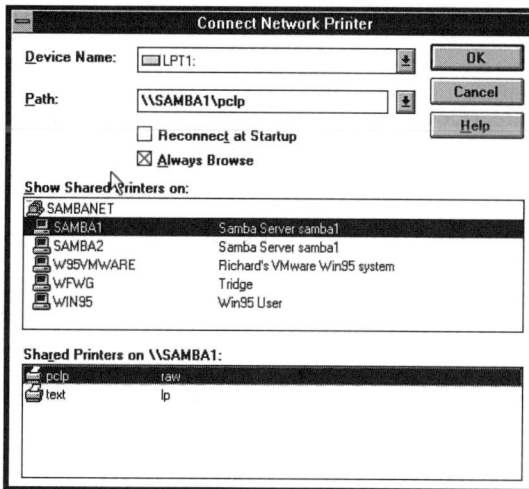

When setting up a network printer, choose a driver that is appropriate for the printer (for example, HP LaserJet 4) and send the print job to a raw queue on the Samba server. Windows formats the print job correctly, and by sending print jobs to a raw queue, the server will leave them alone.

You can check the status of print queues from Print Manager. Start Print Manager and it will show the status of all existing printers. Figure 12.14 shows an example of this.

Figure 12.14
Print Manager displays the status of print queues.

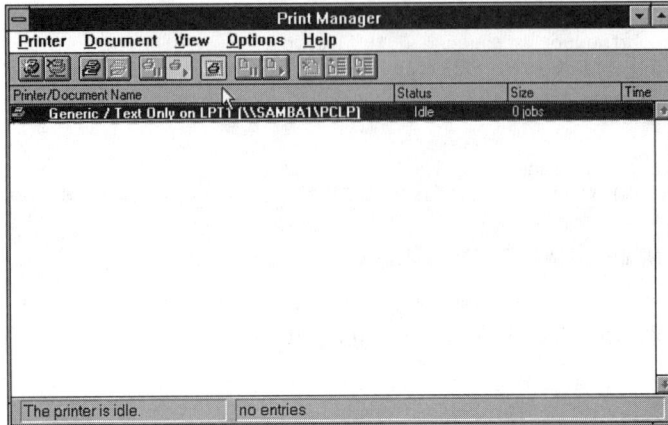

→ To learn more about setting up printer shares under Samba, **see** Chapter 7, "Printer Sharing Under Samba."

LOGGING ON TO THE NETWORK

Logging on to Windows for Workgroups as shown in the previous section does not verify your username and password pair against any Samba servers until you actually try to access a file or printer share.

You can configure Windows for Workgroups so that it logs on to a Samba server when you log on. By doing this, you are informed immediately if something is wrong with your username or password. You can run a logon script to set up shares and perform other tasks when you log on.

Use the Control Panel to configure network logons with the following procedure:

1. Open the Control Panel by double-clicking it. You will find it in the Main program group on your desktop.

2. Double-click the Network icon. This opens the dialog box shown in Figure 12.15.

3. Click the Startup icon to change the startup settings. This will open the dialog box shown in Figure 12.16.

4. In the Startup Settings dialog box, select Log On at Startup, and under Options for Enterprise Networking, select Log On to Windows NT or LAN Manager Domain. Enter the domain/workgroup name of your Samba server.

5. Finally, click OK and then click OK on the Microsoft Windows Network dialog box.

The next time you start up Windows for Workgroups, it will log you on to the network.

Figure 12.15
The Microsoft Windows Network dialog box enables you to configure network logons.

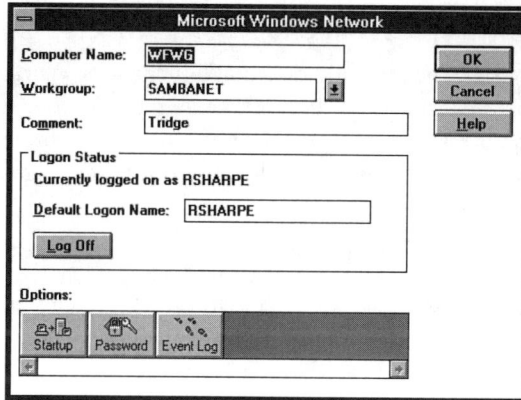

Figure 12.16
Ensuring you log on to the network.

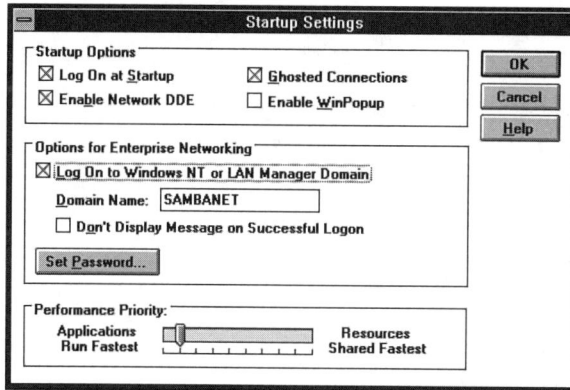

> **Note**
>
> You can log on (or log off) immediately by using the Log On/Off Application in the Network program group.

However, to enable Samba to support network logons, you must add the following parameter to the [global] section of your Samba server. You must not do this if there is an existing NT primary domain controller in that domain.

```
domain logons = yes
```

After you have restarted Samba, the next time you log on you will be presented with the message shown in Figure 12.17.

Figure 12.17
Windows for Workgroups tells you that you are logged on.

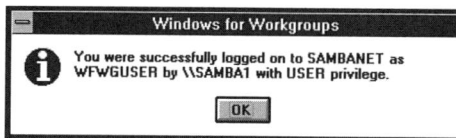

LOGON SCRIPTS FOR WINDOWS FOR WORKGROUPS

You can also run a logon script when you log on from Windows for Workgroups. As long as Windows for Workgroups is configured to log on to a workgroup/domain as discussed previously, all you must do is set up the appropriate parameters on your Samba server and Windows for Workgroups will run the specified logon script upon logging on to the workgroup/domain.

→   To learn how to set up Samba correctly as a logon server, **see** "Logon Scripts," **p. 201**.

After you have configured your Samba server as a logon server, construct the logon script. Here is a sample script:

```
net time \\samba1 /set /yes
net use h: \\samba1\homes
pause
```

This does the following:

- Synchronizes the time on your workstation to that on the server
- Sets the H: drive pointing at your home area on the Samba server
- Pauses the logon script so you can check whether any errors have occurred. When you are happy that the logon script is working, you can remove the `pause` statement.

> **Note**
> You will want to replace *samba1* in the previous script with the name of your server, or the logon script will not work. Also make sure that the file is in DOS format (each line ends with CR/LF rather than just LF); the simplest way to do this is to always edit it from the client.

> **Note**
> You must place the logon script in the `netlogon share` area on your Samba server for it to be used.

The next time you log on to the network, you will see a window similar to the one shown in Figure 12.18. Windows for Workgroups runs the logon script in a command window.

When users are running logon scripts during network logons, you will see a listing such as the following if you run `smbstatus` on your Samba server:

```
Samba version 2.0.6-pre1
Service     uid       gid       pid      machine
-----------------------------------------------
netlogon    wfwguser  wfwguser  9789     wfwg
➥(10.0.0.157) Fri Nov  5 20:01:28 1999
wfwguser    wfwguser  wfwguser  9789     wfwg
➥(10.0.0.157) Fri Nov  5 20:01:32 1999
```

```
Locked files:
Pid     DenyMode    R/W         Oplock          Name
----------------------------------------------------
9789    DENY_DOS    RDONLY      EXCLUSIVE+BATCH  /home/netlogon/netlogin.bat
➡Fri Nov  5 20:01:30 1999

Share mode memory usage (bytes):
    1048256(99%) free + 232(0%) used + 88(0%) overhead = 1048576(100%) total
```

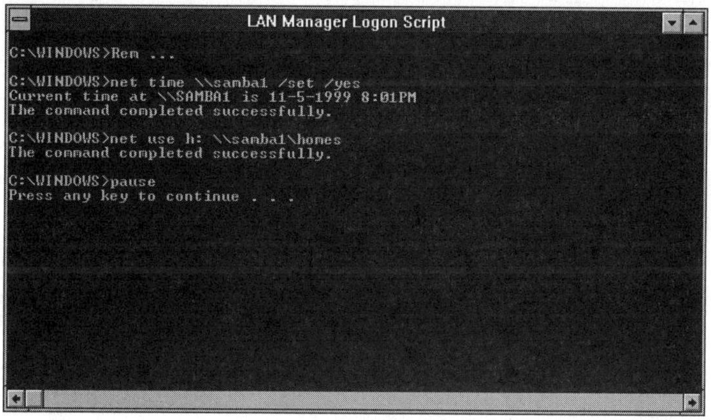

Figure 12.18
Windows runs
your logon
script in a
window.

WINDOWS FOR WORKGROUPS PASSWORD HANDLING UNDER SAMBA

How Samba handles passwords is explained in some detail in Chapter 8, "Samba and Password Management"; however, Windows for Workgroups does one thing to passwords that requires mention here.

Before Windows for Workgroups sends any passwords over the network, it converts them to uppercase. The uppercase version of the password the user typed is then sent as plain text over the network.

To ensure that Samba can actually authenticate your Windows for Workgroups users, and that your users do not need to set their UNIX passwords to uppercase, add the following parameter to the [global] section of your smb.conf file:

password level = 8

→ To learn more about this parameter in more detail, **see** Chapter 8, "Samba and Password Management."

ACCESSING SAMBA FROM WINDOWS 9X

In this section we explore how to configure Windows 9x to access Samba.

PART
III

CH
12

CONFIGURING WINDOWS 9X TO ACCESS SAMBA

Windows 9x has a built-in TCP/IP stack, so you do not need to install any additional software to use Windows 95 with Samba. However, you do need to configure it correctly.

To configure Windows 9x to access Samba, follow these steps:

1. Ensure that Microsoft Windows Networking is installed and that you have the Network Neighborhood icon on your Windows 9x desktop. If this is not the case, consult a book about Windows 95 or Windows 98 to learn how to install Microsoft Windows Networking.

2. Right-click on Network Neighborhood, which brings up a menu with several items. Select the last one, Properties. This opens the Network dialog box shown in Figure 12.19.

Figure 12.19
Use the Network dialog box to configure Windows 9x to access a Samba server.

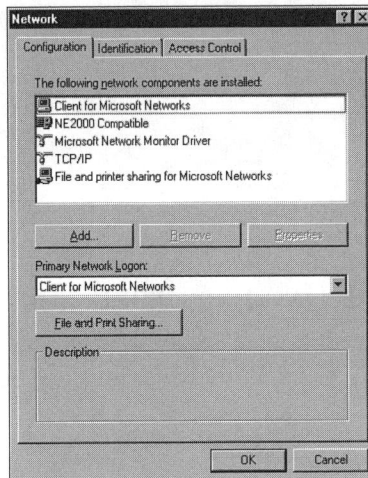

3. Select the Identification tab on the Network dialog box, and fill in the Workgroup field with the workgroup in which your Samba server is located. Figure 12.20 shows an example of this with the Workgroup field filled in with sambanet. You can fill in almost any other information you want for the other two fields.

4. Next, click OK on the Network dialog box. Windows 95 asks you to reboot Windows, which you should do. After you have rebooted and logged in, you are ready to access your Samba server.

If all has gone well, you should be able to access your Samba server.

If problems occur, see the following section titled "Common Problems."

Figure 12.20
Replace the default with your work-group.

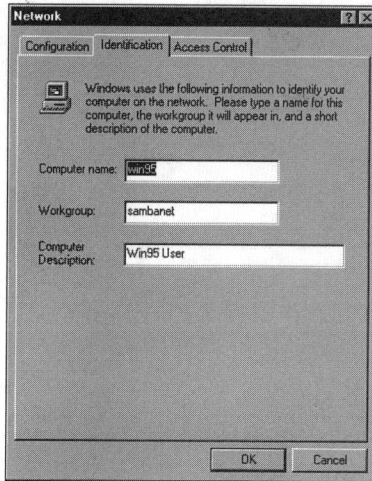

BROWSING THE NETWORK

After you have configured your Windows 9x system to access Samba, you should be able to browse the network. To do this, simply double-click on Network Neighborhood. This should bring up a window similar to that shown in Figure 12.21.

Figure 12.21
Network Neighborhood shows you the servers on the network.

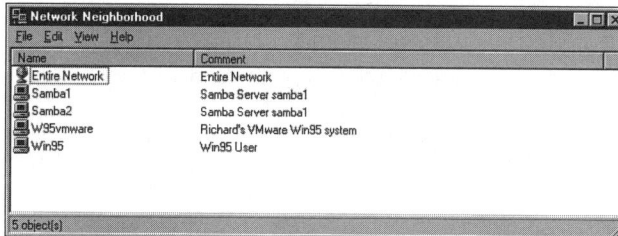

> **Note**
>
> If you are running a version of Samba prior to 2.0.6, you might get a message indicating that you cannot browse the network. This occurs because the default setup of Samba for those versions prevented browsing from occurring under most circumstances.
>
> → For more information on configuring Samba for browsing, **see** Chapter 17, "Samba and Browsing."

You can then double-click any of the computers in the Network Neighborhood window to list the shares that server provides. For example, clicking Samba1 in Figure 12.21 produces the display shown in Figure 12.22, which shows each share.

The information displayed in many of the screen shots in this chapter result from Samba 2.0.6 with the `smb.conf` file shown in Listing 12.1.

Figure 12.22
The shares
offered by
Samba1.

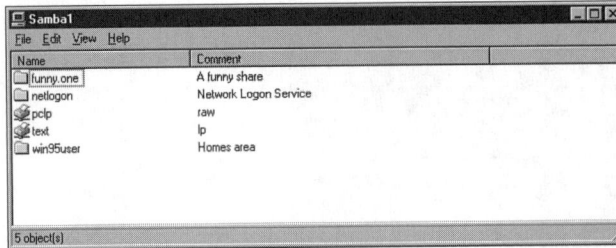

LISTING 12.1 THE MAIN PART OF OUR smb.conf FILE

```
[global]
    workgroup = sambanet
    server string = Samba Server %L
    netbios name = Samba1
    netbios aliases = Samba2
    load printers = yes
    guest account = pcguest
    log file = /var/log/samba/log.%L.%m
    password level = 8
    username level = 8

    include = /etc/smb.conf.%L
```

This smb.conf file includes another smb.conf file based on the NetBIOS name that the client has connected to (%L), and because we define two NetBIOS names (Samba1 and Samba2), there should be two other configuration files. Listing 12.2 and Listing 12.3 show these.

LISTING 12.2 THE include FILE FOR SAMBA1

```
    security = user
    os level = 33
    domain logons = yes
    logon script = %u.bat
    domain master = yes
    preferred master = yes
    wins support = yes
    debug level = 10

[homes]
    Comment = Homes area
    browsable = no
    writable = yes

[netlogon]
    comment = Network Logon Service
    path = /home/netlogon
    root preexec = /usr/local/sbin/mklogonscript %u %L %m > %P/%u.bat
    guest ok = yes

[printers]
    comment = All Printers
    path = /var/spool/samba
    browsable = no
```

LISTING 12.2   CONTINUED

```
    guest ok = no
    writable = no
    printable = yes

[funny.one]
    Comment = A funny share
    path = /tmp
```

LISTING 12.3   THE include FILE FOR SAMBA2

```
security= share

[shared]
    Comment = More Public Stuff
    path = /tmp
    public = yes
    writable = yes
    printable = no
```

→ For more detail on Samba virtual servers, such as those set up in Listings 12.1, 12.2, and 12.3, **see** Chapter 9, "Samba Automation."

ACCESSING FILE SHARES ON SAMBA

Windows 9x enables you to access files by browsing servers on the network, and most applications enable this as well. However, you can also map network drives to local drive letters. To do this, right-click on either the My Computer or Network Neighborhood icons on your desktop. If you select Map Network Drive from the menu that arises, you see the window shown in Figure 12.23.

Figure 12.23
You can map network drives on a Samba server.

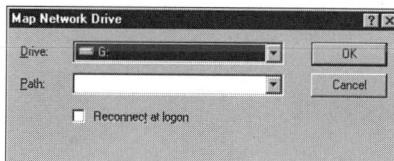

You can change the drive letter that is used, or you can leave it at the default. You must enter a value for the Path, but if you have ever mapped network drives before, Windows 9x remembers them, and you can select from among them in the drop-down list.

Note

People adopt some common standards in drive letter naming. For example, people often choose H for the home drive (alternatively, U can be used for the user's drive), while S is often used for the shared area. By using a logon script, as discussed later, you can ensure that all users use the same drive letters.

After you click OK in Figure 12.23, if all is correct, Windows 9x will map the drive and will open up the share in a window similar to that shown in Figure 12.24.

PART
III

CH
12

Figure 12.24
The homes share after you have mapped it.

Notice the files beginning with a dot (.), for example:

```
.bash_logout
.bash_profile
.bashrc
.inputrc
.rhosts
.Xdefaults
.xinitrc
.xsession
```

These are all UNIX dot files that you normally don't see when you use the ls command to list files. They are visible here because we have told the Windows Explorer to list all files. If you select one and, by using the right mouse button, select the properties of the file, a window similar to the one shown in Figure 12.25 appears.

Note

To configure the Windows Explorer to list all files, select View, Options. Then, from the tabbed window that is displayed, select View again, and then select Show All Files.

Figure 12.25
The properties of a file can be listed.

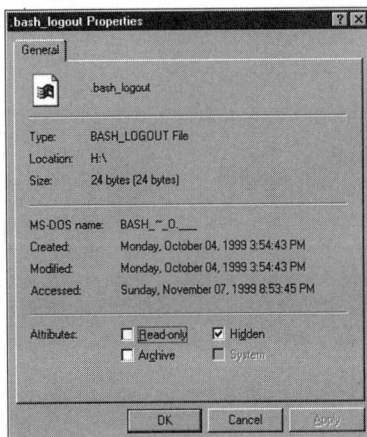

As you can see, these dot files have the Hidden attribute set. This is because Samba sets the `hide dot files` parameter to `yes` by default for all shares. If you do not want dot files treated as hidden files, simply add

`hide dot files = no`

After you have mapped a network drive, you can access the files on the Samba server as if they were local files.

ACCESSING PRINTER SHARES ON SAMBA

Windows 9x does not use a Print Manager application to provide access to printers on Samba servers. Instead, you set up remote printers using the Printers folder. You can access the Printers folder from either the My Computer icon or with Start, Settings, Printers. When you have opened the Printers folder, you will see a window similar to the one shown in Figure 12.26.

Figure 12.26
The shares offered by Samba1.

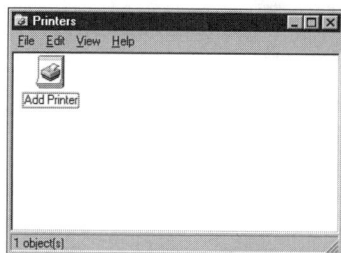

To install a new network printer, double-click the Add Printer icon. This opens the Add Printer Wizard window similar to the one shown in Figure 12.27.

Figure 12.27
The Add Printer Wizard helps you add a printer.

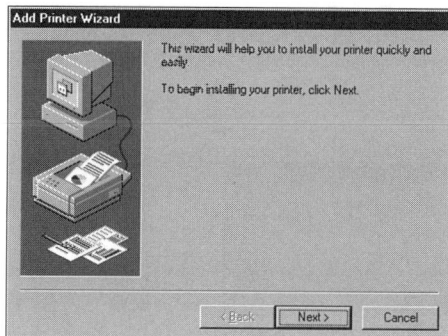

PART

III

CH

12

Because the first window in the Add Printer Wizard does not require any input from you, simply click Next to get to the window shown in Figure 12.28.

When you get to the window shown in Figure 12.28, select Network Printer and click Next to go to the window shown in Figure 12.29.

Figure 12.28
Create a net-
work printer.

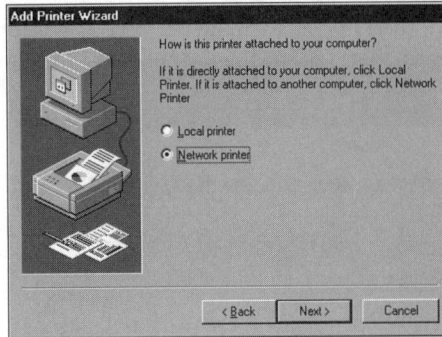

Figure 12.29
Select the
location of
your printer.

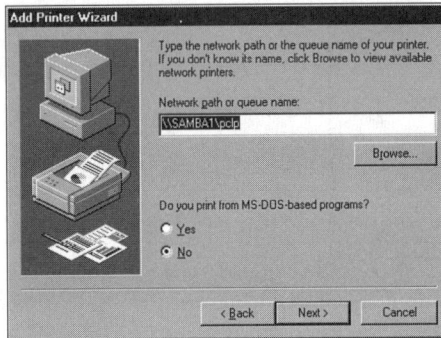

Enter the location of the printer in the Network path field of the window shown in Figure
12.29. You can use the Browse button to search the network, or you can simply type in the
name, such as \\SAMBA1\pclp, and then click Next to open the window shown in Figure
12.30.

Figure 12.30
Select the type
of printer you
are connec-
ting to.

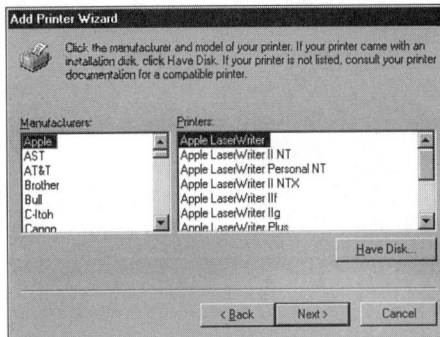

The window shown in Figure 12.30 enables you to choose the printer type and thus the driver
associated with the printer. You should select a printer type that matches the printer you are
connecting to. This ensures that the correct type of print files is sent to the printer.

After you have selected the printer type, you have a few more windows to deal with, most of which are self-explanatory. You will then have a network printer to which you can print.

To change an existing printer to print to a network printer, open the Printers folder, right-click on the printer you want to change, and select Properties. This opens the window shown in Figure 12.31.

Figure 12.31
The printer properties display enables you to change parameters.

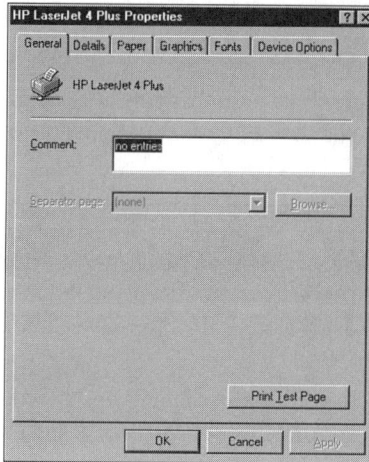

Select the Details tab, and change the Print To the Following Port field as necessary. An example appears in Figure 12.32.

Figure 12.32
Change the port you want to print to.

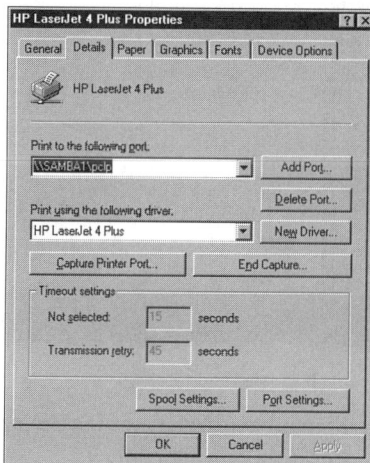

PART

III

CH

12

You can always check the status of a queue as well. Double-click on the printer you want to check in the Printers folder, and you see a display of all the print jobs in the queue. Figure 12.33 is an example.

Figure 12.33
You can display all print jobs in a queue.

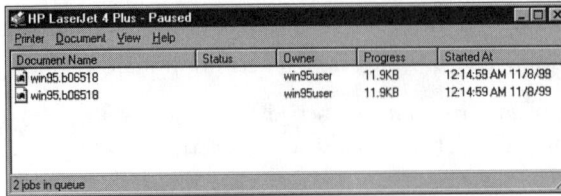

LOGGING ON TO THE NETWORK

Although the previous sections on Windows 9x assume that your username and password are correct with respect to the Samba server you are accessing, it is possible to log on to the network, just as it is with Windows for Workgroups.

> **Note**
>
> If you do not log on to the network, the username and password you use to log on to Windows are passed to your Samba server whenever you connect to it (actually, they are used in the SMBsessionsetupX request). This means that they must be correct.

To do this, bring up the Network dialog box by right-clicking on Network Neighborhood and selecting Properties. Then, select Client for Microsoft Networks and click on Properties. This opens the dialog box shown in Figure 12.34.

Figure 12.34
Configuring Windows 9x to log on to a domain.

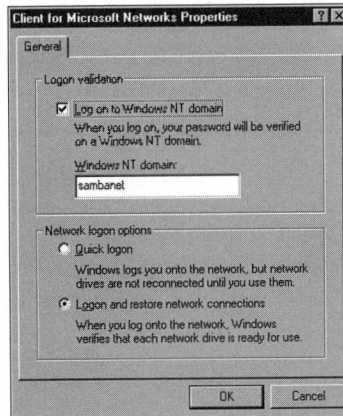

Select Log On to Windows NT Domain and specify the name of your Samba or Windows NT domain. If you have a Windows NT domain controller, setting domain logons = yes in your smb.conf file enables Samba to provide this logon functionality.

→ For more detail on configuring Samba as a logon server, see "Enabling Logon Support," **p. 205**.

When you click OK, Windows 9x asks whether you want to reboot the machine. After you have rebooted your Windows 9x system, the next time you log on to it you will be logging on to the network.

LOGON SCRIPTS

Windows 9x can use exactly the same logon scripts as Windows for Workgroups. Because the details of setting up logon scripts are Samba-specific, the instructions in the section of Windows for Workgroups applies here as well.

After you have set up the Samba support for logon scripts, the next time you log on to the network, you will see a window like that shown in Figure 12.35.

Figure 12.35
Your logon script executes in a DOS command box.

COMMON PROBLEMS

The first time you configure Samba and try to access your Samba server from Windows for Workgroups or Windows 9x can be a frustrating time. You might be unaware of many problems that can prevent you from accessing the Samba server.

Some common problems you might encounter and solutions to them are given in the following sections.

→ For more information on troubleshooting Samba, **see** Chapter 23, "Troubleshooting Samba."

PART
III

CH
12

NO DOMAIN SERVER WAS AVAILABLE TO VALIDATE YOUR PASSWORD

You have just entered your username and password along with your domain in the logon dialog box under Windows 9x. Your machine pauses for awhile as if going away to find the logon server. After a long while, you see the message box shown in Figure 12.36.

Figure 12.36
No domain server was available.

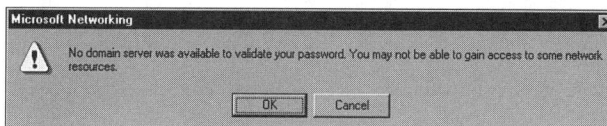

If this happens, one of the following is likely to be the cause:

- The logon server is down or unreachable. That is, your client cannot communicate with the logon server to validate your username and password.

  If the logon server is running, it can be a connectivity problem, and you should try the troubleshooting techniques discussed in Chapter 23, "Troubleshooting Samba." (For example, ping the logon server.)

■ You have not configured any of your Samba servers to be a logon server. That is, you have not added the parameter domain logons = yes in the global section of your smb.conf file.

Add the required parameter(s), restart Samba, and try to log on again.

CANNOT LOG ON TO THE NETWORK

You have entered your username and password and pressed Enter. Your workstation pauses for a long time and eventually, you see the message shown in Figure 12.37.

Figure 12.37
You can't log on to the Windows Network.

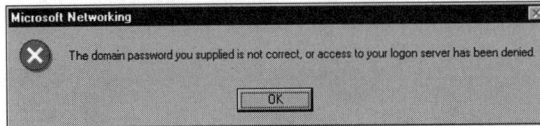

The reasons for this error are a bit more obvious:

■ You have submitted the wrong username or password—Ensure that the username and password you supplied are correct.

■ You have supplied the correct username and password, but your client sends encrypted passwords and your Samba server does not understand password encryption—If this is the case, either change your client so that encrypted passwords are not sent (see the following discussion on password encryption) or implement password encryption on your Samba server.

You can use a packet-sniffing program such as NetMon or Ethereal to determine whether encrypted passwords are being sent.

TEXT FILES LOOK FUNNY

You have opened up a text file (for example, one with a .txt extension) and the file looks funny. In particular, it looks like what is shown in Figure 12.38.

Figure 12.38
The text appears funny when viewed by Notepad.

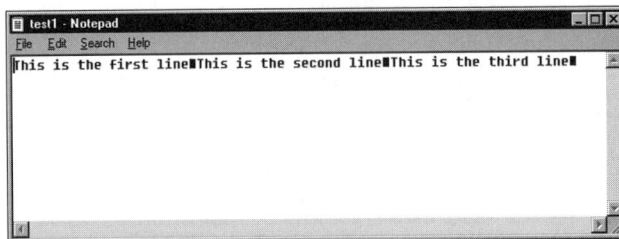

The files you see were probably generated under Linux/UNIX and not converted to MS-DOS/Windows format files. Windows and MS-DOS expect lines to have the two characters CR/LF (hexadecimal 0D/0A) on the end of each line, while Linux/UNIX only requires an LF character (hexadecimal 0A).

You can convert Linux/UNIX text files to MS-DOS format using the `todos` command that comes from the `tofrodos` package. This package also contains the `fromdos` command, which converts in the other direction.

After you have converted text files to MS-DOS format, they should appear correctly in Notepad.

Alternatively, you can use a better text editor that understands UNIX files; two examples are UltraEdit or Programmers' File Editor.

YOU HAVE CHANGED A FILE ON LINUX BUT IT IS UNCHANGED UNDER WINDOWS 9X

You have a package that generates reports under Linux and you want to view them under Windows. This works fine because you are using the `todos` command to ensure that text files appear correctly for Windows users.

However, one day, someone notices a problem in a file, so you fix the problem and regenerate the text files. Unfortunately, your users continue to complain that nothing has changed. You carefully check the files on the Samba server, and the files have definitely changed.

Your problem is because of *opportunistic locks (oplocks)*, which enable clients to cache files and control when files can be cached. (See Chapter 6, "File Sharing Under Samba," for more information about oplocks.) If a client has an oplock on a file, it does not expect that file to change on the server.

To prevent this problem, add the following to each share where you expect to change files on the Samba server while clients have files open:

```
oplocks = no
```

This parameter turns off oplocks for all files in the share. Note that this will have a performance impact.

You can also use the `veto oplock files` parameter, which turns off oplocks for the specified files only.

CANNOT BROWSE THE SERVER

You have logged on to your Windows client and Network Neighborhood seems to work because you can see all the servers on the network. However, when you try to see a list of shares, you are asked to provide a password for the IPC$ share on the server, as shown in Figure 12.39.

Figure 12.39
The server requires a password to access the IPC$ share.

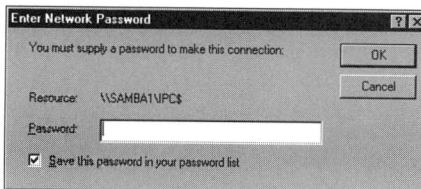

PART
III
CH
12

This happens for one of two reasons:

- Your client is using encrypted passwords but the Samba server is not configured for encrypted passwords. You should rectify this and try again.

- Your username and password are not valid on the Samba server. This can be because you are not using a valid username/password pair for the network or because your password on the Samba server is different from your password on your workstation. That is, you have a password synchronization problem.

CANNOT CREATE FILES IN A DIRECTORY

You can see a share and open files in that share, but you cannot create new files or directories in that share. This problem most likely results from one of three causes:

- The share is not writeable, so you cannot write to it.
- The share has a `write list` associated with it, and you are not in the write list.

    You can rectify both of these problems by adding or changing parameters in the `smb.conf` file.

- Although you can write to the share, its underlying UNIX permissions do not enable you to add files or directories to it. You can rectify this problem by changing the UNIX permissions on the directory that is being shared so you have the ability to create files in it.

PASSWORD CONVERTED TO UPPERCASE

Windows for Workgroups and some versions of Windows 95 convert passwords to uppercase before sending them to a Samba server. In these cases you would not be able to access a share because your username/password pair would be invalid. Samba solves this problem in the following way:

1. It tries the username/password pair as supplied by the client.
2. If this fails, it converts the password to all lowercase and then tries that combination.

However, a mixed-case password on the Samba server will not work. Samba provides the password level parameter, which causes Samba to uppercase the now lowercase password, one character at a time, and to attempt to authenticate the resulting combination.

For example, adding the following parameter to the [global] section of the `smb.conf` file tells Samba to try all combinations of up to eight characters in the password converted to uppercase:

```
password level = 8
```

As you can appreciate, this can be quite time consuming.

NETWORK NAME NOT FOUND

Sometimes when you try to map a network drive, either through the various Windows GUI tools or through the DOS net use command, you see the message Network name not found. If this occurs for a server that you know exists (perhaps because you have already mapped a share from that server), the reason for the error is one of the following:

- The directory specified in the share does not exist, perhaps because of a misspelling or because you have forgotten to create it.

- The directory specified in the share exists, but you do not have access to it as a result of the directory's permissions under Linux.

LOGON SCRIPT FAILS

You have configured logon scripts according to the previous discussion, or perhaps you are automatically generating logon scripts, as discussed in the section "Automatically Generated Logon Scripts" in Chapter 11, "Samba as a Logon and Profiles Server." However, your logon scripts are simply not working. There are two problems that you might encounter.

First, while you are being logged on to the network, the logon script is not being run. This is most likely because you have a problem in one of the following areas:

- You do not have a logon script parameter entry in the global section of your smb.conf file.

- You do not have a netlogon share defined in your smb.conf file.

- You do not have a script file in the netlogon share.

- The script file exists and is in the netlogon share, but the share is not accessible to users or the script file is not accessible to users.

The second problem that can occur is that the script file starts to run but it flashes past you quickly and none of its actions seems to do anything. This is most likely caused by the file being prepared under Linux/UNIX and not having properly terminated MS-DOS lines (it needs CR/LF and not only LF). It can also be caused by errors in the script file.

A simple way to debug the second of these problems is to include a DOS pause command as the last command of the script. After you are happy the script is working, simply delete the pause command.

PLAIN-TEXT PASSWORDS

As explained in Chapter 4, "An Introduction to the SMB Protocol," an SMB server can specify whether it handles encrypted passwords. It does this in its response to the NetProt SMB the client sends upon first connecting to the server.

By default, Samba expects plain-text passwords from clients because it authenticates against the UNIX /etc/passwd file. Windows for Workgroups and initial versions of Windows 95 and Windows NT prior to SP3 all handle this correctly and send plain-text passwords. However, at some point, Microsoft changed Windows 95 to send only encrypted passwords, which Windows 98 only sends. This can cause problems with clients unable to log on to a Samba server, unable to browse a Samba server, and unable to access shares on the Samba server.

Current versions of Samba ship with regedit files that can enable plain-text passwords on Windows 95 and Windows 98. No such file is needed for Windows for Workgroups because it was never modified to not send plain-text passwords.

These regedit files are usually kept in /usr/doc/samba-$version/docs, and also come in the docs directory in the distribution. They are called Win95_PlainPassword.reg and Win98_PlainPassword.reg. Copy these files to a floppy disk, and then double-click on them under Windows 9x to enable plain-text passwords. To copy these regedit files to a floppy, follow these steps:

1. Place a floppy disk in the floppy drive.

2. Mount the floppy with

   mount -t vfat /dev/fd0 /mnt/floppy

   Depending on your distribution, the mount point, /mnt/floppy, might be different.

3. Copy the files with

   cp /usr/doc/samba-$version/docs/Win95_PlainPassword.reg /mnt/floppy

   where $version is the version number of your Samba installation (and might be 2.0.6).

4. Unmount your floppy to use it in your Windows PC. You can unmount the floppy with

   umount /mnt/floppy

Under Windows 9x, double-click the registry file on the floppy to enable plain-text passwords.

For details on how to set up Samba to use encrypted passwords, refer to Chapter 8.

Accessing Samba from DOS

This section provides information on the net command, a very useful DOS command for accessing Samba, and a reference to information on how to create DOS boot floppies to start up and access a Samba server.

DOS Commands for Accessing Samba

Be aware of the syntax of the net command because it can be used to perform many of the actions that are otherwise performed with dialog boxes. The following explains some of the available net commands:

Command	Meaning
net help	This command lists help information about the net command.
net password	This command enables you to change your password on a Samba server.
net time	This command enables you to check the time on a Samba server and to set your local workstation's time from a Samba server.
net use	This command has many forms, one of which is to map drive letters to shares on Samba servers.
net view	This command enables you to see all the Samba and other SMB servers on the network.

Further information can be obtained from a DOS prompt by typing net help.

The following is an example of using the net use command by itself to list all currently mapped drives:

```
net use
Status          Local name      Remote name
_____
OK              H:              \\SAMBA1\HOMES
The command was completed successfully.
```

The following shows an example of mapping a drive to a share with the net use command:

```
net use s: \\samba2\shared
The command was completed successfully
net use
Status          Local name      Remote name
_____
OK              H:              \\SAMBA1\HOMES
OK              S:              \\SAMBA2\SHARED
The command was completed successfully.
```

DOS Boot Floppies for Accessing Samba

Occasionally, people want to construct boot floppies that can bring up a TCP/IP stack and access a Samba server. This can be done with a bit of effort. Charlie Brady has developed an approach to doing this that is described at http://www.nlc.net.au/~charlieb/0248.html.

FURTHER RESOURCES

The following references provide more information about the topics discussed in this chapter:

- *The Microsoft Windows for Workgroups Resource Kit*, by Microsoft (Part Number 3559B).

PART

III

CH

12

- *The Microsoft Windows 98 Resource Kit*, by Microsoft Press (ISBN: 1572316446).
- The file `/usr/docs/samba-$version/docs/textdocs/DOMAIN.txt` on your Linux system after you have installed Samba, or the file `docs/textdocs/DOMAIN.txt` in the Samba distribution.

FROM HERE...

If Windows for Workgroups or Windows 9x are the only clients you need to learn about, you might want to skip the rest of this part and move to Part IV, "Advanced Topics."

Other chapters in the rest of Part III are

- Chapter 13, "Accessing Samba from Windows NT"
- Chapter 14, "Accessing Samba from OS/2"
- Chapter 15, "Accessing Samba from Windows 2000"
- Chapter 16, "Accessing Windows from UNIX Using Samba"
- Chapter 17, "Samba and Browsing"

CHAPTER **13**

ACCESSING SAMBA FROM WINDOWS NT

In this chapter

by Tim Potter

One main reason to use Samba is to enable Windows clients to access resources on a UNIX server. In this chapter we will look at how Windows NT machines, both workstations and servers, can access Samba. This will consist of the following topics:

- Accessing file and print shares from Windows NT Server and Windows NT Workstation machines
- Accessing Samba when it is part of a Windows NT domain
- File permission manipulation on Samba file shares
- Miscellaneous issues, such as encrypted passwords, logon directories, and roaming profiles and how they relate to Windows NT

In each section we describe how to access a particular resource from a Windows NT client machine and briefly mention the relevant smb.conf parameters. A more complete description of these parameters is found in Chapters 6, "File Sharing Under Samba," and 7, "Printer Sharing Under Samba."

ACCESSING SHARES FROM WINDOWS NT MACHINES

Samba is designed to appear as a native Windows machine operating on an SMB network. As such, accessing a Samba server from a Windows NT machine is transparent, whether it is from a Windows NT Server or a Windows NT Workstation. Most of the time, users will not realize that the server they are accessing is a UNIX server running Samba.

ACCESSING FILE SHARES

File shares can be accessed using Windows Explorer, the MS-DOS command prompt, or from any Windows application. Figure 13.1 shows the Network Neighborhood for a small domain called SAMBADOM.

Figure 13.1
Spot the
Samba server.

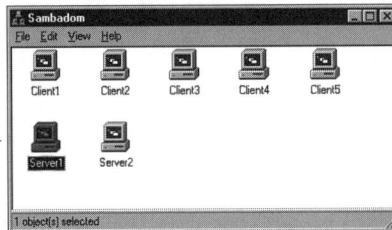

All file shares that are marked browseable in the smb.conf file show up when browsing a Samba server in the Network Neighborhood, as shown in Figure 13.2.

One caveat with using Samba to serve files to Windows NT clients is that file permissions might not behave in a way familiar to Windows NT users. File permission manipulation, if enabled on the Samba server, does not behave exactly the same way as if the file were stored on a Windows NT server. This is because of the way Samba maps NT permissions onto UNIX permissions. This behavior is explained in more detail later in this chapter.

Figure 13.2
Yes, it was
Server1.

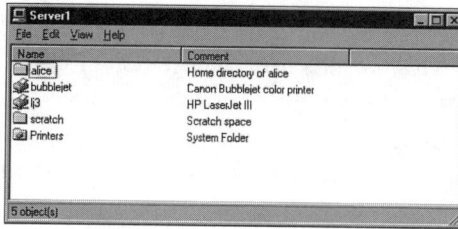

ACCESSING PRINTER SHARES

In the same way as file shares, printer shares on a Samba server can be accessed and installed on a Windows NT machine using the standard Windows programs and tools. A printer installed under Samba will appear as a standard network printer to Windows client machines.

As mentioned in Chapter 7, the capability to automatically install printer drivers by downloading the printer driver files over the network from another server is not currently implemented for Windows NT machines. Support for this feature will appear in version 3.0 of Samba.

One difference between printing to a Samba server from a Windows NT machine is that each Windows NT client machine must have printer drivers installed on it. This is because of the way Samba handles printer spooling.

Windows NT workstations can send a file to a printer on a Windows NT server, have the server process that file and perform any printer-specific transformations on it, and then send it to the printer. Under Samba, the workstation must perform the print processing itself then send the result to the printer. For this print processing to occur, the printer driver must be installed on the client.

Print processing performed on the Windows NT server machine takes some of the load from the Windows NT workstations and transfers it to the server. There are also administrative advantages to having print processing performed on a Windows NT server because default page and printer settings can be modified in one place and thosedefaults are then used by all client machines.

SAMBA AND WINDOWS NT DOMAINS

You should watch out for a few things when accessing Samba servers within the Microsoft Windows NT domain model. Domains and Samba are discussed in Chapter 19, "Samba and Windows NT Domains."

Samba can be accessed in one of two ways within the Windows NT domain model:

- The Samba server is part of a Windows NT domain.
- The Samba server is a standalone server.

Both ways of accessing Samba provide users with the same set of resources. A Samba server that is part of a Windows NT domain has the following properties:

PART

III

CH

13

- Usernames and passwords are validated against the same password database as other members of the domain. This provides better integration of UNIX and Windows because usernames and passwords are stored in only one space.

- The primary domain controller for the domain must be operating for users to be validated; otherwise, the resources available to domain users will not be accessible.

- After the user has logged in, he does not need to enter a password when accessing resources on the Samba server. The Samba server appears to be seamlessly integrated as part of the Windows NT domain.

When accessing Samba when it is configured as a standalone server:

- Usernames and passwords are validated against the local password file on the Samba server. Usernames and passwords cannot be the same as ones on the primary domain controller because this can confuse users.

- If the primary domain controller is not operating, users can still access the Samba server because usernames and passwords are validated against the local password file. In this case, the primary domain controller is no longer a single point of failure.

- A password is required to be entered when accessing the Samba server for the first time when the user has logged in. This can be annoying when Windows automatically reconnects a file share on the Samba server when a user logs in.

→ For more details on Samba and Windows NT domains, **see** Chapter 19, "Samba and Windows NT Domains."

NTFS AND FAT FILE PERMISSIONS

Under Windows NT, hard disk drives can be formatted with one of two file system types:

- The FAT (File Allocation Table) file system
- NTFS (NT File System)

The NT administrator chooses which file system to use when the disk is formatted. After it is formatted, the file system type cannot be changed, although a FAT file system can be converted to an NTFS file system using the CONVERT.EXE utility.

The NTFS file system has several advantages over FAT. These differences mainly stem from the design criteria used by Microsoft when creating each file system. The NTFS file system was designed as a high-performance, fault-tolerant, and secure system for storing files on server machines. The FAT file system is really a throwback from MS-DOS, which was originally designed for storing files on floppy disks and small hard drives.

Most serious NT installations use the NTFS file system in preference to FAT for several reasons. The following are a few of these reasons:

- Fault tolerance—A much-touted feature of NTFS is its capability to recover from a system crash without data loss by keeping track of uncompleted writes. When Windows NT is restarted, any disk writes that did not complete are finished, and the integrity of the disk is maintained. Thus, NTFS is what is known as a *journaling file system*.

- Large disk size—Due to its design, the FAT file system cannot be used on a disk partition larger than 4GB under Windows NT and starts to become inefficient with respect to space for partitions larger then 500MB. This is due to the large cluster size required by the FAT file system when formatting large disks. NTFS, however, theoretically allows for a disk to be as large as 2TB (2048GB) and does not suffer from the same inefficiencies as FAT for large disk sizes.

- Multiuser security permissions—NTFS incorporates the idea of users and groups owning particular files or directories as well as restricting particular types of access to files from other users of the system.

Samba emulates the behavior of both FAT and NTFS file systems through the use of the UNIX permission bits and owner and group settings for files and directories. Although this technique is adequate for emulating FAT file system permissions, it supports only a small subset of the available NTFS file system permissions. NTFS file system permissions are generally known as *Access Control Lists* or *ACLs*.

USING FAT FILE PERMISSIONS

The available FAT file permissions for a file or directory are the standard DOS file attributes:

- Read-only—Read-only files cannot be casually overwritten. Most DOS and Windows applications will ask the user for confirmation before modifying or deleting files or directories that are marked read-only.

- Hidden—Files that have the hidden attribute set cannot appear in directory listings or in Windows Explorer, although it is usually quite easy to circumvent this. For example, you can make hidden files visible in Windows Explorer by selecting the Show All Files radio button in the Options dialog box.

- Archive—The archive attribute typically determines whether a file has been changed since it was last backed up. Whenever a file is changed, its archive bit is set by the operating system to indicate that change. Backup programs read this attribute to determine whether a file should be backed up and clear it after backing up the file.

- System—The system attribute is reserved for operating system files to mark them as such and to ensure they are not accidentally overwritten. System files are usually not visible in directory listings in the same manner as hidden files.

These four attributes are a subset of the NTFS file permissions, so all files can have these permissions modified, whether they are on a drive formatted with NTFS or FAT.

PART

III

CH

13

CHANGING FAT PERMISSIONS USING WINDOWS EXPLORER

FAT file permissions can be quite easily modified. Select Properties from the File menu. The tab that is initially selected contains the FAT file permissions as shown in Figure 13.3.

Figure 13.3
FAT file per-
missions dialog
box.

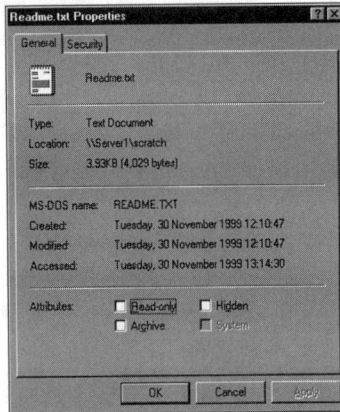

> **Note**
>
> It is not possible to set the system attribute using the file properties dialog box in Microsoft Windows NT 4.0 because it is permanently grayed out. Use the Windows 3.1 file manager application (WINFILE.EXE) or the command-line tool for changing FAT attributes (ATTRIB.EXE) described later in this chapter.

You can modify the four FAT file permissions by selecting or deselecting the appropriate check boxes in the Properties dialog box. Click the OK button after changing the permissions to apply the modifications to the file.

CHANGING FAT PERMISSIONS USING ATTRIB.EXE

If it is not appropriate to use Windows Explorer to modify FAT file permissions, you can use a command-line program from the MS-DOS command prompt. The attrib command is called in the following manner:

```
attrib [+R | -R] [+A | -A] [+S | -S] [+H | -H] filespec [/S]
```

You set or clear individual attributes by specifying a + or a - sign followed by the letter corresponding to the desired attribute. The letters R, A, S, and H correspond to Read-only, Attribute, System, and Hidden, respectively.

For example, in the README.TXT file, you can set the read-only attribute and clear the hidden attribute by calling attrib at the MS-DOS command prompt:

```
attrib +R -H README.TXT
```

A single file can be named in the filespec argument, or a group of files can be specified by using the * or? wildcard characters. If the /S option is used, all files matching filespec are processed in the current directory followed by matching files in all subdirectories.

SPECIFYING FAT FILE PERMISSIONS WITH smb.conf PARAMETERS

Chapter 6 deals with configuring Samba to emulate FAT file permissions. Table 13.1 summarizes the relevant smb.conf parameters required for this.

TABLE 13.1   THE smb.conf PARAMETERS USED FOR FAT FILE PERMISSION MAPPING

Parameter	Description	Default
create mask	Default permissions on new files	0744
directory mask	Default permissions on new directories	0755
map archive	Use UNIX owner execute bit for DOS archive attribute	true
map hidden	Use UNIX world execute bit for DOS hidden attribute	false
map system	Use UNIX group execute bit for DOS system attribute	false

As described in Chapter 6, Samba implements FAT file permissions using the three UNIX execute bits. The default settings for the smb.conf parameters in Table 13.1 do not fully enable all FAT file permissions under Samba. To do this, the Samba administrator must modify the values of the create mask, map hidden, and map system parameters as shown here:

```
create mask = 0755
map hidden = true
map system = true
```

This can be done either on a per-share basis or in the [global] section of the smb.conf file.

Windows always allows these file permissions to be changed, either through Windows Explorer or the ATTRIB.EXE program. However, the permission bits will only actually be changed if the map hidden and map system parameters are set as above. Otherwise, Samba will silently accept and not apply any changes to these permission bits.

USING NTFS FILE PERMISSIONS

NTFS file permissions are slightly more complicated than FAT file permissions because of the different design objectives of the NT file system. An NTFS file or directory can have five basic types of permissions applied to it:

- No Access—Files with the No Access permission cannot be read, written, or executed. Directories with the No Access permission cannot be read, written to, or have their contents read, written, or executed.

- Read—Files with the Read permission can be read or executed. Directories with the Read permission can have their contents listed and executed.

- Change—Files with the Change permission can be accessed like the Read permission and also have their contents or attributes changed. Directories with the Change permission can have their contents read, written, deleted, or attributes changed.

- Full Control—The Full Control permission allows all attributes of a file to be changed or deleted. This permission, applied to a directory, allows files within the directory to be modified or deleted.

- Special Access—The Special Access permission enables different properties of the preceding individual permissions to be combined.

Directories can have an additional three permission types that are not applicable to files:

- List—The List permission is the same as the Read permission.

- Add—The Add permission allows the contents of directories to be executed and written to, and new files created but not read. This permission is useful for write-only situations such as securing directories containing log files.

- Add and Read—A directory with Add and Read permission has the same attributes as the Add permission, but files in the directory can be read.

These permissions can be granted or denied to any number of individual users or groups of users. This is why the NTFS permission system is often referred to as an *Access Control List (ACL)*-based system. A file or directory can have associated with it a list of permissions that specify the particular access rights different NT users and groups have to that file or directory.

Unfortunately, current versions of Samba use only the UNIX owner and group attributes to implement NTFS ACL support. As a result, only these properties are available to be changed for files appearing on a file share exported by a Samba server.

Note

Many discussions have arisen about complete ACL support for Samba, but no agreement has been reached on the exact method for implementing it. Complete ACL support in Samba will probably not be implemented in the near future.

The capability to change NT security permissions is available only in Samba version 2.0.4 or greater.

The NTFS access controls implemented by Samba consist of three sets of permissions:

- An access control for the UNIX owner of the file or directory—This appears as a permission for the equivalent Windows NT user. Changing this permission enables the UNIX's owner read, write, and execute bits to be modified.

- An access control for the UNIX group of the file or directory—In a similar way to the owner permission, this appears as a permission for the equivalent Windows NT group. This permission can be changed to modify the UNIX group permission bits.

- An access control for the NT group named Everyone—This corresponds to the UNIX other read, write, and execute bits.

Under NTFS, you can directly specify the permissions of files created under a directory as a property of that directory. These permissions are called *inherited permissions*. If the permissions of a directory are being viewed under Samba, the inherited permissions are appended in parentheses to the actual permissions of the directory. These inherited permissions have no meaning under UNIX, and no attempt is made to emulate them.

CHANGING NTFS PERMISSIONS USING WINDOWS EXPLORER

Under Windows NT you can modify the NTFS permissions on a file by selecting that file from within Windows Explorer and selecting Properties from the File menu. NTFS permissions are available under the Security tab of this dialog box. Figure 13.4 shows the Properties dialog box with the Security tab selected for a sample file.

> **Note**
>
> NTFS file permissions can be manipulated only using machines running Microsoft Windows NT operating systems. Windows 95 clients have no access to NTFS file permissions.

Figure 13.4
NTFS security settings dialog box.

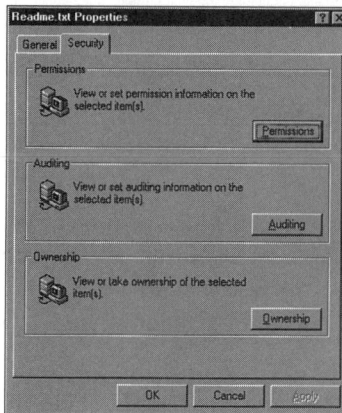

PART
III

CH
13

Three options for changing NTFS permissions correspond to the three buttons in the security settings dialog box. These options are Permissions, Auditing, and Ownership.

The NTFS permissions under Samba described previously consist of access controls that represent the UNIX owner, group, and other permissions for the file or directory. To change these permissions, first select the Permissions button in the Properties dialog box for the file or directory in question. A dialog box similar to Figure 13.5 should appear.

Figure 13.5
NTFS file per-
missions dialog
box.

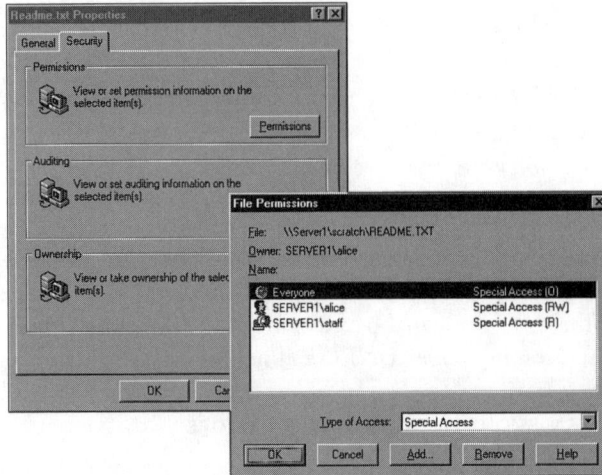

All file permissions appear as Special Access permissions, and it is only possible to change the Read, Write, and Execute permissions for each access control. The Delete and Change Permissions options can be checked but have no effect when they are modified. If a file or directory has no permissions at all, it will have the Take Ownership permission set only.

Note

> The NT users and groups appearing in NTFS access control dialog boxes are not NT domain users or groups. They are translations of the UNIX owners and groups that exist on the Samba server.

To modify permissions for the file, double-click the permission. This opens a Permissions dialog box that permits changes to the Read, Write, or Execute check boxes as appropriate. Click the OK button for the Permissions dialog box, and then click the OK button for the file permissions to apply the change.

The NTFS auditing functions are currently not implemented in both the release and development versions of Samba. Clicking the Auditing button in the Security settings dialog box gives an error if the user does not have administrator privileges, or gives an empty auditing dialog box that does not perform any useful function when the user does have administrator privileges.

Changing the ownership of a file under UNIX is not an operation a normal user can perform. The Owner dialog box in Figure 13.6, produced by selecting the Ownership button in the Properties dialog, does not work under Samba at the present time and is unlikely to be implemented in the near future.

Figure 13.6
NTFS owner-
ship dialog
box.

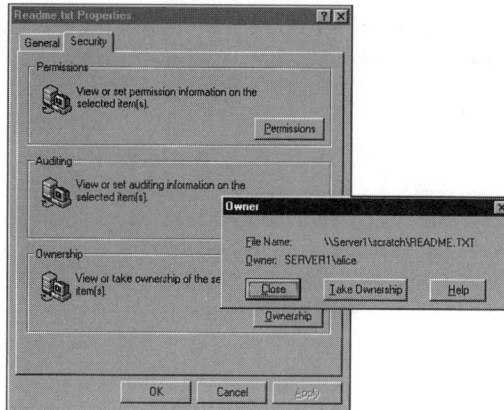

CHANGING NTFS PERMISSIONS USING CACLS.EXE

As with FAT file permissions, you can invoke a command-line program from the MS-DOS command prompt to change NTFS file and directory permissions. The `cacls` program can be used to add access permissions, revoke permissions for a specified user, or grant extra rights to an existing permission. The `cacls` program is invoked as follows:

```
cacls filespec [/E] [/C] [/T] [/R user] [/D user] [/G user:perm] [/P user:perm]
```

Table 13.2 explains the options.

TABLE 13.2 COMMAND-LINE OPTIONS FOR CACLS.EXE

Option	Description
/E	Edit the ACL instead of replacing it.
/C	When modifying permissions for multiple files, continue if an access denied error occurs.
/T	Change permissions for all matching files in the current directory as well as matching files in all subdirectories.
/R user	When using the /E option, revoke all access rights for the user given by *user*.
/D user	Deny the specified user access to the file or directory.
/G user:perm	Grant the user given by *user* the specified permission given by *perm*. The permission can be one of R for read access, C for change or write access, or F for full control.
/P user:perm	Replace the permission for *user* with the specified permission given by *perm*. The permission can be one of N for No Access, R for Read access, C for Change or Write access, or F for Full Control.

Multiple files can be specified in *filespec* by using the * and ? wildcard characters. If no options other than a file specification are given, the `cacls` program lists the access permissions for those files.

PART

III

CH

13

For example, to add Read access to the NT Everyone group on the file README.TXT, execute the following command at the MS-DOS command prompt:

```
cacls README.TXT /g everyone:R
```

This will set the UNIX other read bit on the file on the Samba drive.

Note

> Running cacls with only one argument, the *filespec*, should print a list of access controls for the file. This does not work with the current version of Samba. A list of access controls with an error regarding inability to resolve domain users is printed.

The command-line options to the cacls program are not easy to understand. It is usually easier to modify NTFS file permissions using Windows Explorer unless attributes must be changed from within a batch file.

CONFIGURING NTFS FILE PERMISSIONS WITH smb.conf PARAMETERS

Configuring Samba to enable the use of NTFS file permissions is described in the section "NT Permission Mapping" in Chapter 6. Table 13.3 gives an overview of the smb.conf parameters used for this.

TABLE 13.3   THE smb.conf PARAMETERS USED FOR NTFS FILE PERMISSION MAPPING

Parameter	Description	Default
nt acl support	Enable NT file permissions (ACLs)	True
security mask	Specify which NTFS permissions to map on files	0744
directory security mask	Specify which NTFS permissions to map on directories	0755
force security mode	NTFS permissions to always set on files	0
force directory security mode	NTFS permissions to always set on directories	0

If the nt acl support parameter is false, every file and directory will appear to have exactly one file permission. This permission will be of type Full Control by all users.

Note also, that like the parameters relating to FAT file permissions, the default values do not permit the full range of NTFS permissions to be modified by users. Specifically, the user is not allowed to change the Write and Execute status for the UNIX group and other permissions. To enable full user control over NTFS permissions, add the following smb.conf parameters either to the [global] section or on a per-share basis:

```
security mask = 0777
directory security mask = 0777
```

MISCELLANEOUS

In the last part of this chapter, we look at a couple of features of Samba that are peculiar to Windows NT. These features are the use of encrypted passwords, login directories, and roaming profiles.

ENCRYPTED PASSWORDS

Windows NT has two methods of sending password information over the network when verifying user logins:

- Encrypted passwords—A hashed version of the user's password is sent from a client machine to a server

- Plain-text, or non-encrypted passwords—The characters of the password are sent in the clear over the network

→ For more information on these two password modes, **see** Chapter 8, "Samba and Password Management."

Obvious advantages exist to using encrypted passwords in preference to plain-text passwords. For example, an intruder who is snooping packets from the network can capture plain-text passwords and use them to impersonate users on the network. There are, however, disadvantages because encrypted passwords cannot be decrypted and compared against passwords in the UNIX password database. A separate password file, called smbpasswd, is necessary in Samba's private directory to manage encrypted passwords. This directory is usually /usr/local/samba/private if Samba has been installed in the default location. The binary distributions of Samba for some Linux distributions look for the smbpasswd file in /etc or /etc/samba.

Windows NT machines that have Service Pack 3 or higher installed use encrypted passwords by default. The default for Samba is not to use encrypted passwords, so freshly installed Windows NT machines with Service Pack 3 or higher will not be able to access Samba shares. One of three solutions can be applied to this situation:

- Enable encrypted passwords in Samba—This might not be such a good idea because Samba will then not be able to authenticate network connections against the UNIX password database and will require an smbpasswd file to be constructed.

- Make the Samba server a member of a Windows NT domain—If domains are being used, the Samba server can be made a domain member and will then authenticate user connections against a primary domain controller. This is somewhat similar to enabling encrypted passwords in Samba because the UNIX password database is not being used. See Chapter 19 for details on making Samba servers domain members.

- Disable encrypted passwords on the Windows NT client machines—To disable encrypted passwords for Windows NT machines, a change to the Windows registry is required. This can either be done using a registry addition file that comes with the Samba source or by using the REGEDT32.EXE Windows application.

The easiest way is to obtain a copy of the `NT4_PlainPassword.reg` file that is distributed as part of the Samba source code. You can find it under the `docs/textdocs` directory. Copy this file to the Windows NT machine and, as a user with Administrator privileges, double-click on it to install it.

The other method is to use `REGEDT32` to add a key to the following hive:

`HKEY_LOCAL_MACHINE\system\CurrentControlSet\Services\Rdr\Parameters\`

Add a key of type `REG_DWORD` called `EnablePlainTextPassword`. Set this key to the value 1 to enable plain-text passwords.

When using Samba as a primary domain controller for a Windows NT network, you must use encrypted passwords. See Chapter 19 for information on using Samba as a PDC. Also, Chapter 8, "Samba and Password Management," gives a more thorough overview of password management under Samba than is given here.

RELEVANT smb.conf PARAMETERS

The `encrypt passwords` smb.conf parameter is used to specify whether Samba should use encrypted or plain-text passwords. This parameter is a Boolean parameter. The default is not to use encrypted passwords.

ACCESSING LOGIN DIRECTORIES

When users of a Windows NT domain log on to a machine, they can be given a directory of their own in which they can store their files. This directory is typically a network drive on a Windows NT server. Having a login directory on a per-user basis is useful because a Windows NT administrator can keep these directories all in one place for easy administration and backup.

For a Windows NT Server acting as a primary domain controller, the login directory for a user can be set by modifying the user in the User Manager for Domains administration application. When Samba acts as a primary domain controller for a domain, the login directories for users are specified by parameters in the smb.conf file.

RELEVANT smb.conf PARAMETERS

Two smb.conf parameters are relevant to user login directories:

- The `logon home` parameter specifies the location of user home directories in the form `\\servername\sharename`. The `logon home` directory can be accessed by using the `/HOME` option when mapping a network drive. For example, to map the H: drive to the user `logon home` directory, execute the following command at an MS-DOS command prompt:
  `net use h: /HOME`

- To map the `logon home` directory to a network drive automatically, the `logon drive` smb.conf parameter can be used. The drive letter specified is mapped as a network drive when the user logs in to the machine.

The chapter on using Samba as a primary domain controller, Chapter 19, gives more information on logon drives and user home directories.

ACCESSING ROAMING PROFILES

A *profile* under Windows NT is a set of user preferences and desktop settings that is associated with a particular user. Any files dragged and dropped onto the desktop are also part of a user profile. These settings and files are usually saved when the user logs out and restored when the user logs in again. This way, each user can customize the look and feel of his own desktop without affecting the settings of other users.

A *roaming profile* is stored on a server machine, typically the primary domain controller, and copied to the client when the user logs in to any workstation in the domain. Any changes made to the profile are made to this copy. When the user logs out, the profile is copied back to the server. The profile is roaming in the sense that it follows the user around no matter which workstation he logs in to. If roaming profiles are not enabled, changes made to desktop settings are relevant only to the workstation they were made on.

RELEVANT smb.conf PARAMETERS

Under Samba, roaming profiles are implemented using the logon path parameter. This can be configured to point to a file share on a Samba or Windows NT server. Samba must be operating as the primary domain controller for the domain in order for it to set the value of roaming profiles.

→ Roaming profiles are really only relevant if an NT workstation is logging on to a domain. For a more detailed discussion on this, **see** Chapter 19, "Samba and Windows NT Domains."

FROM HERE...

We have looked at how Samba appears when it is being accessed from Windows NT machines and have discovered that it behaves in a similar fashion to a native machine running Windows. We have also mentioned Samba as part of a Windows NT domain. This topic is discussed in detail in Chapter 19; refer to this chapter if you are interested in Samba and Windows NT domains.

The remainder of this section of the book considers accessing Samba as a client from other operating systems. We look at

- IBM's OS/2 operating system
- Windows 2000—Microsoft's most recent addition to the Windows range of operating systems
- Accessing file and print shares from UNIX using Samba
- Samba's support for other operating systems, such as VMS and BeOS

PART

III

CH

13

## CHAPTER 14

ACCESSING SAMBA FROM OS/2

In this chapter

by Tim Potter

OS/2 is an operating system initially developed by IBM in collaboration with Microsoft, but then later developed solely by IBM. Political considerations aside, OS/2 is still used in both desktop and server roles by many businesses and home users. OS/2 supports the LAN Manager and SMB protocols and can share and access resources with other machines running Samba and Microsoft Windows.

This chapter concentrates on issues using OS/2 with Samba. We look at

- Versions of OS/2 that can access Samba
- Configuring OS/2 to access Samba
- Using OS/2 to access Samba file and print shares
- Using Samba to access OS/2 file and print shares

We mainly concentrate on using OS/2 Warp 4 but other versions of OS/2 are also considered.

SUPPORTED VERSIONS

OS/2 comes in several different versions, all of which can theoretically be used as clients to access Samba. They are listed here in order of release:

- OS/2 Warp 3 and below—These versions of OS/2 cannot normally access a network using an Ethernet network card. TCP/IP networking is supported only through a dial-up modem. However, it is possible to install and configure a network card using a process detailed in the section "OS/2 Warp 3 and Below," later in this chapter.
- OS/2 Warp Connect—This version of OS/2 has operating system support for network cards and TCP/IP built in and will work with Samba.
- OS/2 Warp 4—Warp version 4 is the very latest version of OS/2 released by IBM. Like OS/2 Warp Connect, it supports TCP/IP networking natively and will work with Samba.

The screenshots and information in this chapter apply specifically to OS/2 Warp version 4 but can generally be adapted to OS/2 Warp Connect. However, network configuration might have to be performed with the MPTS (Multiprotocol Transport Services) application rather than with the OS/2 Selective Install for Networking applet.

CONFIGURING OS/2 TO ACCESS SAMBA

This section looks at configuring OS/2 networking to use Samba. Unfortunately, the network protocol required for communication with Samba is not installed by default.

OS/2 WARP 3 AND BELOW

As mentioned, OS/2 Warp 3 and all previous versions do not have native operating system support for network cards. However, it is possible to install a network card and access a

Samba server using it. This process is detailed in full at http://carol.wins.uva.nl/~leeuw/ lanman.html and does actually work. It requires a fair amount of work to implement, so it is not recommended for large numbers of OS/2 client machines.

This process is not covered in full here because of its complexity and the fact that the particular versions of OS/2 that don't support networking are not very common. An overview follows:

1. Install the Internet Access Kit and LAN Manager Client from the BonusPak CD-ROM that comes with OS/2.

2. Install the FreeTCP package. FreeTCP is a freely available TCP/IP protocol stack built to enable TCP/IP communications under OS/2 Warp version 3 and below.

3. Install and configure NDIS drivers for the network card installed. NDIS stands for Network Driver Interface Specifications and is a commonly used interface for writing network card drivers.

4. Install the Microsoft LAN Manager client for OS/2.

This process involves installing components of software packages from both IBM and Microsoft, as well as hand editing OS/2 configuration files. As such, neither IBM nor Microsoft officially support it.

OS/2 WARP CONNECT

Warp Connect is the first version of OS/2 to officially support TCP/IP networking over an Ethernet network card. To configure Warp Connect to access a Samba server, follow the instructions for OS/2 Warp 4 given next. The procedure is similar, except that the MPTS application should be used instead of the Selective Install for Networking setup option.

OS/2 WARP 4

The latest version of OS/2, Warp 4, can be configured to access a Samba server without too much difficulty. It is assumed that the NetBIOS and TCP/IP protocols are already installed on the workstation. Consult the OS/2 Warp documentation for information on installing and configuring the TCP/IP and NetBIOS services.

> **Note**
>
> Some users have reported the driver present on the OS/2 installation media for a popular brand of network card, the NE2000, as being unreliable. I recommend that you use the OS/2 driver distributed with your network card, or use the one from ftp://ftp.cdrom.com/pub/os2/network/ndis/ instead.

PART
III

CH
14

ADDING NETBIOS OVER TCP/IP PROTOCOL

Samba communicates over the network by encapsulating SMB packets using the TCP/IP protocol. As such, it cannot communicate with machines that use other network protocols to talk SMB, like NetBEUI and IPX. An OS/2 client must be configured to talk SMB over

TCP/IP. You do this by installing the NetBIOS over TCP/IP protocol on the OS/2 client workstation.

To install the IBM OS/2 NetBIOS over TCP/IP protocol, you must bind it to the network adapter installed in the OS/2 machine. This is done using the Selective Install for Networking application. Follow these steps:

1. Run the Selective Install for Networking application from the Install/Remove folder or menu. This can be reached either from the OS/2 WarpCenter toolbar at the top of the desktop or by selecting the System Setup icon from the OS/2 System folder.

2. Select the Advanced Installation option from the initial dialog screen and click the Next button.

3. From the OS/2 Warp Setup and Installation dialog box, select the File and Print Client check box and click the Next button. The File and Print Client service is also known as IBM Peer.

4. A dialog box labeled Configuration, containing a tree of items selected in the previous step, should appear. To begin adding a protocol to a network adapter, select the Network Adapters and Protocol Services item from the tree view. Information about the current configuration of network adapters and protocols should appear in the right pane of the configuration dialog box. It should look like Figure 14.1.

Figure 14.1
Configuring network adapters and protocol services.

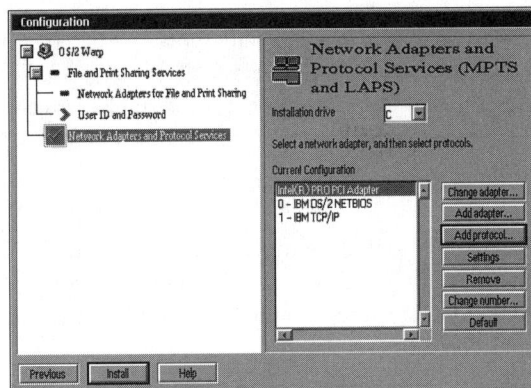

5. To actually add a new protocol, click the Add Protocol button from the right pane, and a dialog box should appear. From this dialog box, select the IBM OS/2 NetBIOS Over TCP/IP entry and click the OK button.

6. When installing additional protocols for network adapters, for some reason the logical adapter number is not updated correctly. The NetBIOS over TCP/IP protocol added in the previous section probably will have the same logical adapter number as a protocol that is already installed. To remedy this, click the NetBIOS Over TCP/IP

Protocol entry and click the Change Number button. Use the Change Logical Adapter Number dialog box to give the NetBIOS over TCP/IP protocol a unique logical adapter number.

The logical adapter number is used to prioritize access to a network card when different protocols are bound to it. This enables multiple network protocols to run over a single network card. I recommend that the most commonly used protocols be assigned a lower number to improve network performance.

> **Note**
>
> The MPTS application, available from the System Setup folder, can also be used to install the NetBIOS over TCP/IP protocol. The procedure required is similar to the one outlined previously, including reassigning logical adapter numbers.

Before the new protocol can be installed, a local administrator user ID and password must be specified.

CONFIGURING USER ID AND PASSWORD

The install program will not successfully complete without a local administrator username and password for the OS/2 client machine. Select the User ID and Password entry from the tree view in the Configuration dialog box. Figure 14.2 shows this dialog box with this item selected.

Figure 14.2
Entering a user ID and password for file and print client setup.

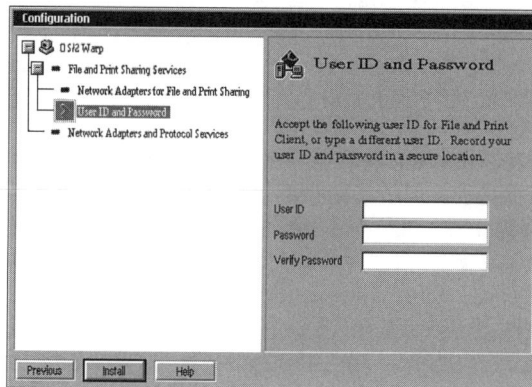

To configure an administrator user, enter a user ID and a password, with confirmation, in the right pane of the Configuration dialog box. The user ID and password used are subject to several constraints. The following usernames cannot be used:

- USERS
- LOCAL
- GUESTS
- ADMINS

PART

III

CH

14

- PUBLIC
- RPLGROUP
- SYSASID

Usernames cannot begin with IBM, SYS, or SQL. Passwords cannot contain any of the following characters:

"	/	\
[	]	;
|	<	>
+	=	,
?	*	

If you forget the administrator password, you can remove and reinstall the File and Print Client service. You can then specify another password.

FINISHING THE INSTALLATION

After installing the NetBIOS over TCP/IP protocol and configuring an administrator user, click the Install button to complete the process. OS/2 will reboot the workstation to apply the changes and copy files from the OS/2 installation media.

> **Note**
>
> Don't forget to apply any appropriate fixpaks after installing new operating system components. Fixpaks are operating system upgrades provided by IBM. The latest ones can be obtained from the download section of the IBM OS/2 Web site, `http://www.ibm.com/os2/`.

If problems occur after rebooting the workstation, try uninstalling TCP/IP networking and reinstalling TCP/IP and File and Print Client services all at once. Perform the following steps to do this:

1. Uninstall the File and Print Client service by selecting the File and Print Client Install/Remove option from the Install/Remove menu.
2. Uninstall TCP/IP by selecting the TCP/IP Services Remove option from the Install/Remove menu.
3. Reboot the workstation.
4. Reinstall the TCP/IP and File and Print Client services and the NetBIOS over TCP/IP protocol all at once.
5. Reboot the machine to apply the changes.

The workstation should now be ready to communicate with Samba.

ACCESSING SAMBA FROM OS/2

After the NetBIOS over TCP/IP protocol has been installed, an OS/2 machine is capable of communicating with a Samba server. This part of the chapter looks at the following topics concerning accessing Samba from OS/2:

- How authentication works between Samba and OS/2
- Browsing information and tips
- Accessing file and printer shares

AUTHENTICATION

Access to shared resources on an OS/2 machine is authenticated against local users stored on the machine. Local users can be added and removed through the local administrator account defined when the File and Print Client service is installed.

OS/2 supports both encrypted and plain-text passwords when being accessed from Samba. Passwords are also not case sensitive and are subject to the restrictions on characters mentioned previously.

By default, anonymous or guest access to an OS/2 machine is enabled. This means that anyone can connect to the machine over the network and browse available shares simply by specifying a username of GUEST when connecting. Some system administrators consider this a security risk. OS/2 also defaults to guest access when a user enters an empty password when connecting to the machine.

To disable guest access to an OS/2 machine, deny logon access to the GUEST user through the Users tab on the Shared Resource and Network Connections folder. This can be accessed from the Network Services entry in the Connections desktop folder. Select the GUEST user from the user list, and click the Update button. The dialog box that appears is shown in Figure 14.3.

Figure 14.3
Denying guest access to an OS/2 machine.

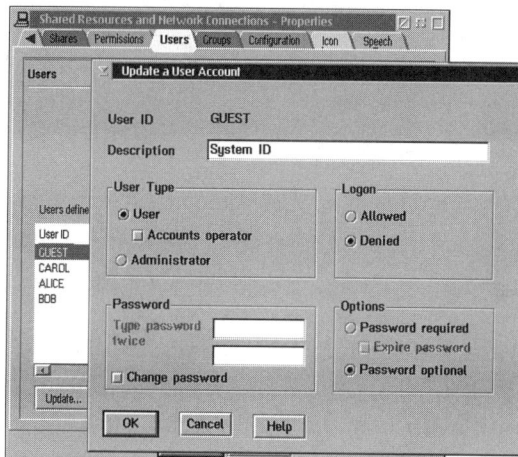

To deny logon access to the GUEST user, click the Denied radio button in the Logon control. Click the OK button to apply the change.

BROWSING

You can browse shares under OS/2 using the File and Print Client Resource Browser. This is in the Connections folder under the Network subfolder. Figure 14.4 is the window displayed when browsing the network. Note that only the server string of the Samba machine, which actually has a NetBIOS name of SERVER1, appears in the browse list.

Figure 14.4
Browsing the network from OS/2.

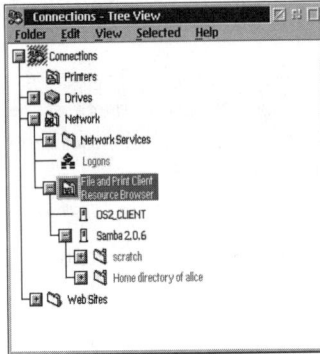

Remarkably few entries appear in the browse list, though, because of some interesting defaults for the configuration of Microsoft Windows machines.

The LAN Manager protocol defines a parameter that determines how announcements to LAN Manager version 2 browser broadcasts are handled. This parameter is called LM Announce. OS/2 machines use this parameter to ask for a list of NetBIOS machines on the network. Unfortunately, all Microsoft Windows operating systems ignore these browser broadcast requests by default. This results in OS/2 machines being unable to browse file and print client resources exported by Microsoft Windows machines. The shares, however, are still available and can be accessed using the NET.EXE program.

> **Note**
>
> UNIX servers running Samba require no modifications to appear in the browse lists of OS/2 workstations.

The procedure for modifying the value of the LM Announce parameter is different for each version of Windows:

- Windows for Workgroups—A change to the SYSTEM.INI file is required to enable LM Announce. In the [network] section of SYSTEM.INI, add a line of the form lmannounce=yes. SYSTEM.INI is usually located in the C:\WINDOWS\SYSTEM directory.

- Windows 95 and Windows 98—You can enable LM Announce on these machines by selecting the Network applet from the Control Panel and viewing the properties of File and Printer Sharing for Microsoft Networks in the Configuration tab. To enable

LM Announce, set the LM Announce property to have the value Yes as shown in Figure 14.5.

Figure 14.5
Setting LM Announce for Windows 95/98.

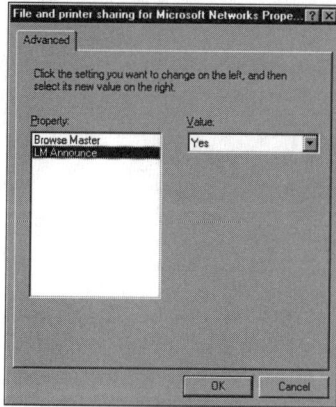

- Windows NT Server—From the Network Settings control panel applet select the properties of Server item under the Services tab. Click the Make Browser Broadcasts to LAN Manager 2.x Clients check box to enable LM Announce. Reboot the server for the changes to take effect.

- Windows NT Workstation—A registry key controlling LM Announce behavior must be changed. Change the registry entry Lmannounce from the default value 0 to the value 1 under the following key:

```
\HKEY_LOCAL_MACHINE\System\CurrentControlSet\Services\
➥LanmanServer\Parameters\
```

Because every Windows machine on the network requires a configuration change to enable LM Announce functionality, it is often easier just to enable LM Announce only on Windows servers and workstations for which OS/2 browsing support is required.

A limitation of OS/2 is that the name of a file share must be eight characters or less in length. If this is not so, OS/2 will display an error message saying More Data Available, and the share will not be browsable. The share, however, will still be accessible using the command-line NET.EXE program.

ACCESSING FILE AND PRINTER SHARES

Samba file and print shares can be accessed from either the graphical user interface provided by OS/2's Workplace Shell or from the command line using the NET.EXE program.

FILE SHARES

By browsing the network using the File and Print Client Resource Browser in the Connections folder, Samba file shares can be accessed just like other network shares. Figure 14.6 shows Alice browsing her home directory, which is stored on a Samba server.

PART
III

CH
14

Figure 14.6
Browsing a
Samba share
from OS/2.

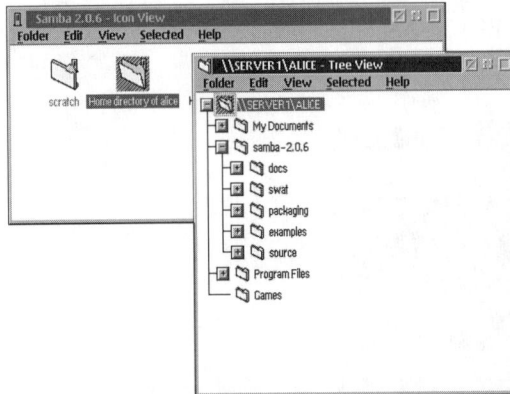

It is possible to open, read, write, and execute files on Samba shares using the Workplace Shell. Files and folders can be dragged and dropped between OS/2 drives and Samba shares as well as using the standard command-line tools.

When accessing Samba network shares, a local OS/2 logon must be used instead of a network logon. An OS/2 network logon is usually done using the Logon entry under the UPM services menu and is normally used to log on to a machine running OS/2 Warp Server. If the File and Print Client Resource Browser is used before a user has logged on locally, an OS/2 network logon screen appears. Do not use this screen, but rather log on locally using the Login entry under the UPM services menu. Domain logons using OS/2 network logons and Samba servers do not seem to be fully operational in the latest version of Samba at the time of writing.

EXTENDED ATTRIBUTES ON FILES

OS/2 enables metadata to be stored as part of a file. This metadata is called *extended attributes*, sometimes referred to as *EAs*. Some of the information that can be stored in the extended attributes of an OS/2 file includes

- Revision information such as comment and history fields
- Subject and keywords
- Application-specific data and an icon displayed by the OS/2 Workplace Shell

Extended attributes normally stay with the file when it is moved or copied between OS/2 machines. However, Samba does not support extended attributes, so any information stored in them is lost when a file is copied to a Samba file share.

PRINTER SHARES

Printer shares can be browsed in a similar manner to file shares; however, printer shares do not appear in the Connections tree view window. Figure 14.7 shows an empty printer queue displayed for the shared HP LaserJet III printer.

Figure 14.7
Browsing
Samba printer
shares from
OS/2.

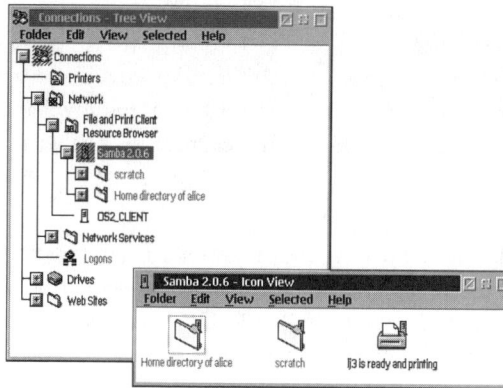

Unfortunately, the printer queue support in the current version of Samba for OS/2 clients does not work correctly. When viewing the status of the printer queue under the Workplace Shell, a stream of error messages saying More Data is Available will appear. Viewing jobs spooled in the printer queue does work using the command-line tools. Dragging and dropping files to the folder for a Samba shared printer also does not work.

The NET.EXE program can be used to overcome these limitations in Samba's OS/2 support. Because native printing is not supported through the OS/2 Workplace Shell, printer access can be implemented by redirecting an unused parallel port to the Samba printer. Table 14.1 shows the invocations of the NET.EXE program that you can use to perform common printing tasks.

TABLE 14.1 COMMAND-LINE INVOCATIONS FOR COMMON PRINTING TASKS

Command	Function
NET PRINT \\SERVER1\LJ3	Displays the printer queue for the LJ3 printer share on the Samba server SERVER1.
NET USE LPT1: \\SERVER1\LJ3	Maps the first parallel port, LPT1, to point to the LJ3 printer on SERVER1. Use another printer device, such as LPT2, if a peripheral is already attached to the first parallel port.
COPY README.TXT LPT1 :	Sends the README.TXT file to the Samba printer previously mapped to the LPT1: device.

ACCESSING OS/2 FROM UNIX USING SAMBA

A machine with OS/2 installed can share file and print resources just like any other machine that is part of an SMB network. OS/2 can share serial ports over the network using the SMB protocol, but this is not supported by Samba or any version of Microsoft Windows.

PART

III

CH

14

ACCESSING OS/2 USING smbclient

The smbclient program is required to access OS/2 file and printer shares from Samba. Some brief examples are given here, but the program is described in full in Chapter 16, "Accessing Windows from UNIX Using Samba." Refer to that chapter for further information.

BROWSING

You can browse the available shares by using the -L option to smbclient. We also use the -N option to tell smbclient not to ask for a password. Listing 14.1 shows the output of this. The OS/2 workstation is currently sharing two file shares. One share is for the operating system hard disk, and another is for the CD-ROM drive attached to the machine. A local printer, OS2_PRINTER, is also being shared.

LISTING 14.1 BROWSING SHARES EXPORTED BY AN OS/2 CLIENT MACHINE

```
client1$ smbclient -L '\\os2_client' -N
added interface ip=10.1.1.2 bcast=10.1.1.255 nmask=255.255.255.0
Got a positive name query response from 10.1.1.4 ( 10.1.1.4 )

        Sharename      Type       Comment
        ---------      ----       -------
        IPC$           IPC        Remote IPC
        ADMIN$         Disk       Remote Admin
        C              Disk       Hard disk
        CDROM          Disk       CD-ROM drive
        OS2_PRINTER    Print      Printer on LPT1

        Server                  Comment
        --------                -------
        OS2_CLIENT

        Workgroup               Master
        ---------               ------
```

ACCESSING FILE AND PRINTER SHARES

File and printer shares on an OS/2 machine can be accessed successfully using the smbclient program as described in Chapter 16. In lieu of a detailed description of smbclient, a short recipe for accessing file and printer shares is given next for the local OS/2 user alice.

To access the file share named C on the OS/2 machine, use the following command-line invocation of smbclient. Alice is required to enter her password when prompted.

```
smbclient '\\os2_client\c' -U alice
```

To access the OS2_PRINTER print share, use the following smbclient command line. Again, Alice is required to enter her password to successfully access the share.

```
smbclient '\\os2_client\os2_printer' -P -U alice
```

Documents can be spooled to the shared printer by using the appropriate smbclient commands.

OTHER ACCESS METHODS

The smbclient program is not the only way to access an OS/2 client machine on an SMB network. The smbmount and smbsh client programs distributed with Samba can also be used to access OS/2 file and print shares. Refer to Chapter 16 for a detailed description of using these access methods. The smbmount program is currently available only under Linux.

COMMON PROBLEMS

When diagnosing problems with OS/2 and Samba, it is prudent to apply the latest fixpaks for the appropriate version of OS/2 you are using. Fixpaks provide important bug fixes to the operating system that might affect the operation of Samba.

Some features that OS/2 users might be used to are not supported by Samba servers. For example, the extended attributes on files are not implemented by Samba. Another OS/2-specific feature not implemented by Samba is COM port sharing where serial ports on one machine can be shared with another machine in a similar manner to file shares.

Many people have reported success using OS/2 with Samba versions predating version 2.0. However, since then, quite a few improvements have been made to the OS/2 support. In fact, after Samba 2.0.6 was released, several patches and bug fixes have been added including fixes for smbclient access to OS/2 servers and better handling of large directory listings. These fixes will be available in Samba 2.0.7 when it is released.

FROM HERE...

The rest of this part of the book is devoted to describing the remaining client operating systems supported by Samba. We will look at

- Accessing Windows 2000 with Samba
- Accessing Windows from UNIX
- Examining other miscellaneous operating systems supported by Samba

Part IV, "Advanced Topics," is devoted to advanced topics with Samba.

CHAPTER **15**

ACCESSING SAMBA FROM WINDOWS 2000

by Richard Sharpe

In this chapter

Windows 2000 is the latest member of the Windows stable of operating systems, and it builds very much on the Windows NT 4.0 base. For that reason it is very different from Windows 9x.

At the time of writing, only Windows 2000 RC2 was available, but Windows 2000 is expected to ship by the time this book is in print.

We explore the following areas in this chapter:

- How to browse the network and find out what is available on servers in the network
- How to access Samba file shares from Windows 2000
- How to access Samba printer shares from Windows 2000
- How to join a domain so you can log on to the network
- How to use logon scripts
- How to use profiles
- Common problems in using Samba from Windows 2000

WINDOWS 2000

Windows 2000 comes in three different versions:

- Windows 2000 Professional—Microsoft has slated this to be a replacement for Windows 9x and Windows NT Workstation in corporate environments.
- Windows 2000 Server—This is a replacement for Windows NT Server.
- Windows 2000 Advanced Server—This contains many features over and above Windows 2000 Server.

In this chapter, we focus on using Windows 2000 Professional with Samba. Many of the concepts also apply to Windows 2000 Server and Windows 2000 Advanced Server.

BROWSING THE NETWORK

When you first install Windows 2000, you will not be able to browse any of your Samba servers. Windows 2000, like Windows NT SP3 and above and Windows 98, expects a Samba server to operate using encrypted passwords. We will set up Samba to use encrypted passwords when we add Windows 2000 to our Samba domain, but for the moment we want to operate Windows 2000 in plain-text mode.

Before you can browse your Samba servers, you might need to apply the plain-text password registry hack to your Windows 2000 system. You will need to apply this hack if your Samba server is not set up for encrypted passwords. For more information on setting up Samba to use encrypted passwords, see Chapter 8, "Samba and Password Management."

This file is located in `/usr/doc/samba-$version/docs` on many Linux systems and is called `Win2000_PlainPassword.reg`. Simply pop this file onto a floppy and invoke it on your Windows 2000 system. (You can double-click this file, which will apply the registry change.)

Note

If you have installed Samba from sources, either on a Linux system or another UNIX system, you will find the plain-text password registry hack files in your source tree in the docs directory. For example, `./samba-2.0.7/docs`.

Note

You must reboot your Windows 2000 system before the registry change takes effect.

When your Windows 2000 system is back up again, you should be able to browse the network. Simply double-click the My Network Places icon on the desktop. This will open the window shown in Figure 15.1.

Figure 15.1
My Network Places under Windows 2000.

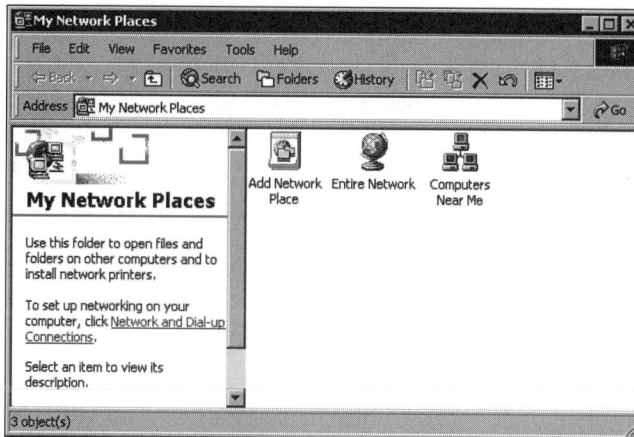

Next, double-click the Computers Near Me icon. This will take you to the window shown in Figure 15.2. You can also double-click on the Entire Network icon shown in Figure 15.1.

Figure 15.2
Computers Near Me under Windows 2000.

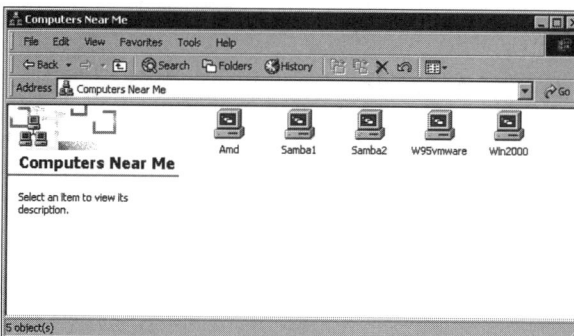

Figure 15.2 shows several systems in the Sambanet workgroup. By clicking View in the menu bar of the Computers Near Me window and selecting Details, you can obtain the view shown in Figure 15.3. This view shows the comments associated with each server.

Figure 15.3
Getting more detail from Computers Near Me under Windows 2000.

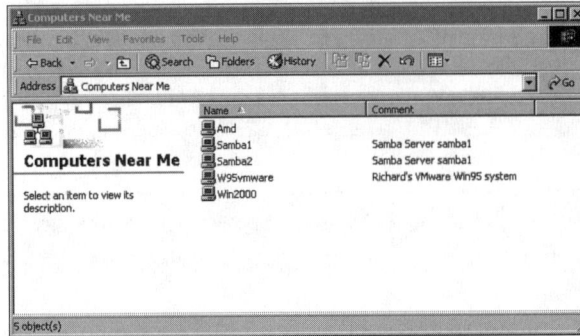

Two of the servers shown in Figures 15.2 and 15.3 are Samba virtual servers. The common `smb.conf` file for these servers appears in Listing 15.1.

LISTING 15.1 THE MAIN PART OF OUR `smb.conf` FILE

```
[global]
    workgroup = sambanet
    server string = Samba Server %L
    netbios name = Samba1
    netbios aliases = Samba2
    load printers = yes
    guest account = pcguest
    log file = /var/log/samba/log.%L.%m
    password level =
    username level =

    include = /etc/smb.conf.%L
```

The `smb.conf` file in Listing 15.1 pulls in the rest of the configuration file through an `include` parameter. Because the `include` parameter uses the `%L` macro, different configuration files can be pulled in for each NetBIOS name served by Samba. Listings 15.2 and 15.3 show the files included for Samba1 and Samba2, respectively.

LISTING 15.2 THE `include` FILE FOR SAMBA1

```
security = user
    os level =
    domain logons = yes
    logon script = %u.bat
    domain master = yes
    preferred master = yes
    wins support = yes
    debug level =

[homes]
```

LISTING 15.2 CONTINUED

```
    Comment = Homes area
    browsable = no
    writable = yes

[netlogon]
    comment = Network Logon Service
    path = /home/netlogon
    root preexec = /usr/local/sbin/mklogonscript %u %L %m > %P/%u.bat
    guest ok = yes

[printers]
    comment = All Printers
    path = /var/spool/samba
    browsable = no
    guest ok = no
    writable = no
    printable = yes

[funny.one]
    Comment = A funny share
    path = /tmp
```

LISTING 15.3 THE include FILE FOR SAMBA2

```
security = share

[shared]
    Comment = More Public Stuff
    path = /tmp
    public = yes
    writable = yes
    printable = no
```

These are reasonably standard configurations that provide for the following:

- Samba1—A user-level server with several shares
- Samba2—A share-level server with only the share shared

By clicking on either Samba1 or Samba2 you can browse the shares provided by either of them. Figures 15.4 and 15.5 show views of both Samba1 and Samba2 obtained by clicking on each icon in Figure 15.3.

In the next section we will explore how to access file shares from Samba under Windows 2000.

Figure 15.4
Viewing the shares available under Samba1.

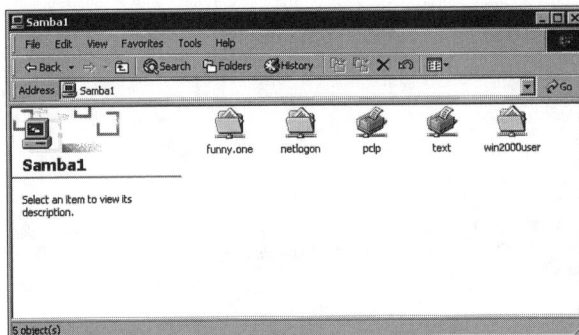

Figure 15.5
Viewing the shares available under Samba2.

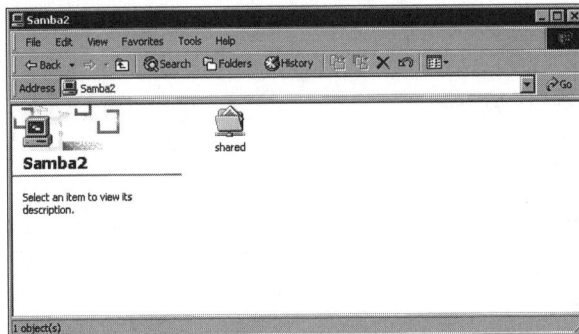

ACCESSING FILE SHARES

Windows 2000 provides the standard ways that we are accustomed to for accessing shares on Samba servers:

- Browse a share by double-clicking it from an Explorer window, as shown in Figures 15.4 and 15.5.

- Use the Map Network Drive dialog box, as shown in Figure 15.6.

- Use the Windows 2000 Command Prompt window to issue a net use command to map a network drive.

- Click Start, Run, enter \\server\share into the dialog box, and press Enter or click OK.

The first time you use any of these approaches to accessing file shares from Windows 2000, you will need to enter a valid username and password for the Samba server you are accessing. This is required because Windows 2000 Professional does not send a password when it tries to access the remote resource when using plain-text passwords.

Actually, here Windows requires the password so it can send a Sessionsetup&X to Samba. If you remove all drive mappings, Windows drops the connection to the Samba server as well.

This means you will need to provide the password again the next time you access that server. However, if you have logged on to the domain as described in the following text, this will not be required.

To access the Map Network Drive dialog box, right-click either My Computer or My Network Places and select Map Network Drive. This will open the window shown in Figure 15.6. In this dialog box you can select the drive to map to and the network path you want to map.

Figure 15.6
Mapping net-
work drives
under Win-
dows 2000.

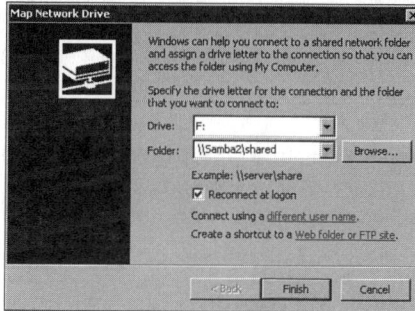

To map a network drive from a command prompt, open a command prompt window using Start, Programs, Accessories, Command Prompt. You can then use standard DOS net use commands. Figure 15.7 shows an example of a few net use commands.

Figure 15.7
Using the com-
mand prompt
to map net-
work drives.

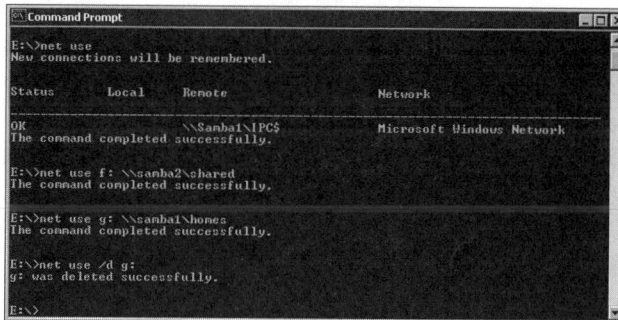

Table 15.1 shows the commands that can be used at a command prompt.

TABLE 15.1 NETWORK COMMANDS THAT CAN BE USED FROM A DOS BOX

Command	Description
net use	The net use command by itself will list all current drive mappings. Notice in Figure 15.7 that the only share listed is \\samba1\IPC$.
net use f: \\server\share	This command maps a share to a drive letter. The drive letter can be any unused drive letter.

TABLE 15.1 CONTINUED

Command	Description
net use \\server\share	This command connects to a share without mapping it to a drive.
net use /d \\server\share or net use /d d:	These commands enable you to remove access to a shared resource. The first allows you to simply refer to the shared resource, while the second allows you to refer to the drive letter it is mapped to.

When you have mapped a network drive, you can access files and folders on Samba servers as if they were local. Many applications also enable you to access remote resources without mapping the remote drives.

To remove access to a file share, simply use the Disconnect Network Drive dialog box, shown in Figure 15.8. Click on My Computer or My Network Places and select Disconnect Network Drive to open this dialog box.

Figure 15.8
Disconnecting network drives under Windows 2000.

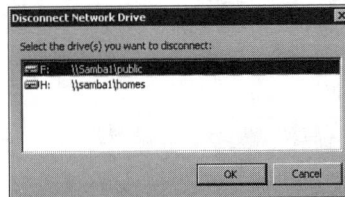

In the Disconnect Network Drive dialog box, select the drive you want to disconnect and click OK. You can also disconnect network drives using a command prompt as discussed previously.

ACCESSING PRINTER SHARES

To access printer shares under Windows 2000, you must add them to Windows 2000 as network printers. To do this, you can use one of the following two methods:

■ Use the Add Printer Wizard from the Printers folder (located through Start, Settings, Printers).

■ Double-click the correct printer icon in a window that is browsing the server where the printer resides (most likely reached from My Network Places).

Note

If you use the Add Printer Wizard, the account under which you add the new printer must be valid on your Samba server, and the password you logged in with must be valid.

If you use the Add Printer Wizard, you will see the window shown in Figure 15.9. Simply follow the instructions and click Next.

Figure 15.9
Adding a printer using the Add Printer Wizard under Windows 2000.

The dialog box shown in Figure 15.10 then opens, asking if your printer is a local or network printer. In this case it is a network printer, so select the Network Printer radio button.

Figure 15.10
The printer can be either local or on a Samba server.

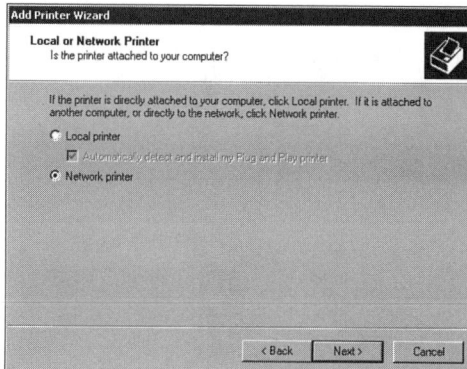

The next step is to provide the location of your printer as shown in Figure 15.11. Enter the name for the printer (using the format \\server\printer) in the Name field, and click Next to continue. If you do not know the name of your printer, you can click Next and browse your network. Windows 2000 might take a while to find the workgroups or domain in your network.

In the window shown in Figure 15.12, double-click the domain or workgroup that contains the printer you want to access, and then double-click the server that contains the printer you want to access. Finally, select the printer you want from the list shown, and click Next to open the window shown in Figure 15.13.

Figure 15.11
Enter the name of your printer, or click Next to browse.

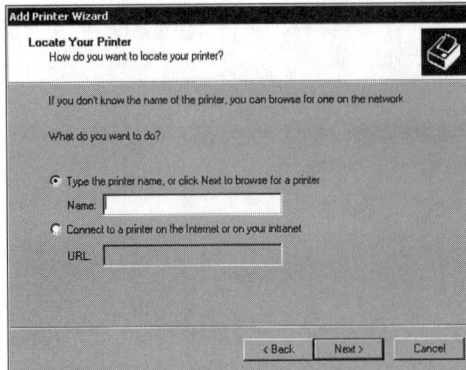

Figure 15.12
Browse the network to find your printer.

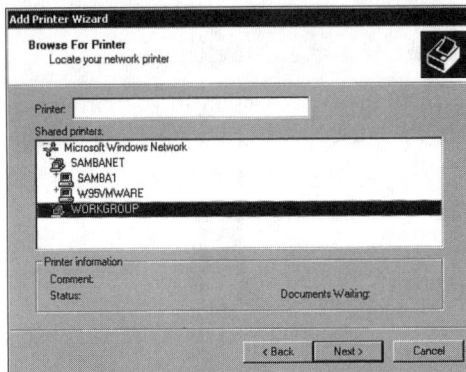

Figure 15.13
Specify whether your network printer should be the default printer.

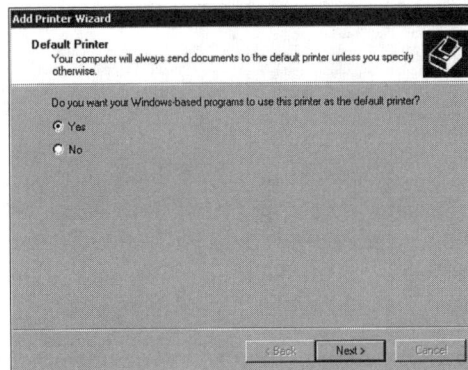

Next, specify whether your new printer should be made the default by clicking the appropriate radio button. Then, click Next to advance to the window shown in Figure 15.14. Finally, click the Finish button shown in Figure 15.14 to complete the process of specifying your new printer.

Figure 15.14
Finish the process of defining your network printer.

JOINING A DOMAIN

You can use Samba from a Windows 2000 system as if the Samba server were simply a member of a workgroup, but you will get more out of your Samba server if you set it up as a primary domain controller. Your Windows 2000 system will then become a member of the domain that your Samba server controls.

Because Samba TNG is the only version of Samba that currently supports Windows 2000 clients joining the domain, we provide details here on

- How to obtain a version of Samba TNG that will work.

- How to build Samba TNG.

- How to install and configure Samba TNG so that Windows 2000 clients can join your domain.

- How to add users to Samba TNG.

- The daemons that make up Samba TNG.

Note

It is possible to have some members of the Samba 2.0.x stream operate as primary domain controllers, but Windows 2000 requires functionality that is not in the Samba 2.0.x stream. At the time of writing, Samba TNG is the only version that supported this functionality. It is anticipated that Samba 3.0.x will also support this functionality in the second half of 2000.

OBTAINING THE CORRECT VERSION OF SAMBA TNG

You get Samba TNG from the following:

1. From the Samba TNG CVS tree. See Chapter 24, "A Tour Through the Samba Source Code," for more details on this approach.

2. From the Samba download area as one of the Alpha kits available. You can get it from the /samba/ftp/alpha/ directory on any of the Samba mirror sites. You need one of the Samba TNG Alpha versions. At the time of writing, Samba TNG 2.5 Alpha was available.

Note

At the time of writing, Samba TNG 2.5 Alpha has a bug in printing, which prevents at least Win9x clients from printing. You should get at least Samba TNG 2.6 Alpha.

The Samba TNG code is not intended as production software.

We will concentrate here on the second approach because these kits are all relatively stable releases, whereas the CVS tree is highly volatile and might not even compile at times when the developers are adding code.

Download Samba TNG from your favorite mirror site and unpack it using the following command:

```
tar zxvf samba-tng-alpha_2_5_tar.gz
```

Note

If you have downloaded the bzip2 archive of Samba TNG, you will need to uncompress it first with the following command:

```
bzip2 -d samba-tng-alpha_2_5_tar.bz2
```

Then you can unpack it using

```
tar xvf samba-tng-alpha_2_5_tar
```

How to Build Samba TNG

After you have unpacked the source archive, building Samba TNG is much the same as building one of the 2.0.x versions of Samba. First, change the directory to the Samba TNG source, and use the following steps:

```
cd source
./configure
make
```

If the build process worked correctly, you can install Samba into its correct locations using the following command:

```
make install
```

Note

There are no Linux RPMs for Samba TNG at this stage, so you will have to build and install the source if you need the functionality provided by Samba TNG.

To have your newly built version of Samba TNG start up automatically at boot time, copy the `samba-init.d` script from the `scripts` directory to the appropriate place on your system, and then create links in the appropriate run-level directory. Use the following commands on most Linux systems:

```
cp scripts/samba-init.d /etc/rc.d/init.d
ln -s /etc/rc.d/init.d/samba-init.d /etc/rc.d/rc3.d/S98samba
```

Of course, rather than calling your startup script `S98samba`, you can call the startup script whatever you want.

The previous instructions will install Samba TNG in the directories shown in Table 15.2.

TABLE 15.2   THE FILES INSTALLED FOR SAMBA TNG

Directory	Purpose
/usr/local/samba	The base directory for Samba. All binaries, configuration, log, and other Samba-related files go here.
/usr/local/samba/bin	This directory contains all the non-system binaries for Samba TNG, such as smbclient, smbstatusm, and so on.
/usr/local/samba/lib	This directory contains all the Samba TNG shared libraries along with the all-important smb.conf files.
/usr/local/samba/man	This directory contains the Samba TNG manual pages.
/usr/local/samba/private	This directory contains all the Samba private files, including the SID files for the domain and the smbpasswd file.
/usr/local/samba/sbin	This directory contains all the system binaries, such as smbd, nmbd, and the other Samba TNG daemons.
/usr/local/samba/var	This directory contains log files that are created by the Samba TNG daemons.

Note

The files in the Samba TNG private directory are very important. The smbpasswd file, in particular, will contain users' password hashes and should never be made world readable.

CONFIGURING SAMBA TNG SO WINDOWS 2000 CLIENTS CAN JOIN A DOMAIN

Samba TNG must be configured correctly to allow Windows 2000 clients to join the domain. You will need at least the following in the `smb.conf` file:

```
[global]
   workgroup = sambanet
   server string = Samba TNG Server %L
   netbios name = samba1
   security = user
```

```
domain master = yes
domain logons = yes
encrypt passwords = yes
smb passwd file = /usr/local/samba/private/smbpasswd
```

Of course, you will most likely want to add some shares, and you can configure Samba TNG to provide profiles and logon scripts. Please see Chapter 11, "Samba as a Logon and Profiles Server," for more information on this topic. However, the following additions will provide most of what is needed:

```
logon script = netlogin.bat
logon home = \\%L\%U\.profiles
logon path = \\%L\profiles\%U

[homes]
   Comment = Homes area
   browsable = no
   writable = yes

[netlogon]
   Comment = Network Logon Service
   path = /home/netlogon
```

You will have to create an appropriate `netlogin.bat` file.

> **Note**
>
> Samba TNG Alpha 2.5 and above can support network logons from Win9x clients as well as Windows NT and Windows 2000 clients.

How to Add Users to Samba TNG

With Samba TNG you must use the `samedit` utility to create new users. The first time you invoke `samedit`, you must use the following command:

`/usr/local/samba/bin/samedit -S . -U root% -l log`

This is needed because the Samba TNG `smbpasswd` file does not have any users in it. On the next and subsequent times that you invoke `samedit`, you can use the following command:

`/usr/local/samba/bin/samedit -S . -U root -l log`

You can add users with the following command, once in `samedit`:

`createuser fred -p password`

This command creates a user called `fred` with a password of `password`.

There is no need to create workstation trust accounts for Windows 2000 workstations because they do it for you when they join the domain.

The Samba TNG Daemons

The number of daemons with Samba TNG has grown. As well as the usual `smbd` and `nmbd`, Samba TNG contains the following additional daemons:

- `browserd`—Implements the browser API.

- `lsarpcd`—Implements the local security authority API.

- `netlogond`—Implements the network logon API.

- `samrd`—Implements the Security Access Manager API.

- `spoolssd`—Implements the SPOOLSS API.

- `srvsvcd`—Implements the net server API.

- `svcctld`—Implements the service control API.

- `winregd`—Implements the registry API.

- `wkssvcd`—Implements the netwksta API.

The Samba startup script, `samba-init.d`, knows how to start all these daemons at system startup time.

JOINING THE DOMAIN FROM WINDOWS 2000

To join a domain from Windows 2000, you must log on to your Windows 2000 system as a user that can perform these actions. You should use the administrator account or an account in the admin group.

First, right-click on My Computer, and select Properties. This will open the System Properties window as shown in Figure 15.15.

Figure 15.15
You can join a domain from the System Properties window.

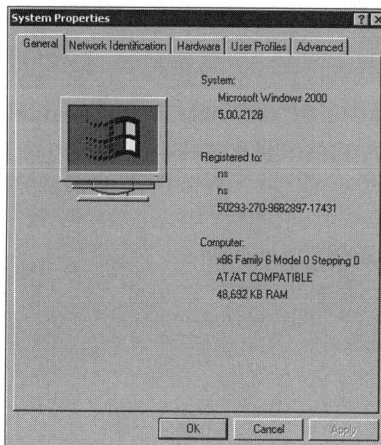

From the System Properties window, select the Network Identification tab, which will open the window shown in Figure 15.16.

When you reach the window shown in Figure 15.16, select the Properties button. This opens the Identification Changes window as shown in Figure 15.17. Click the Domain radio button, fill in the domain that you want to be a member of (in this case sambanet), and click OK.

Figure 15.16
You must select the Network Identification tab to join a domain.

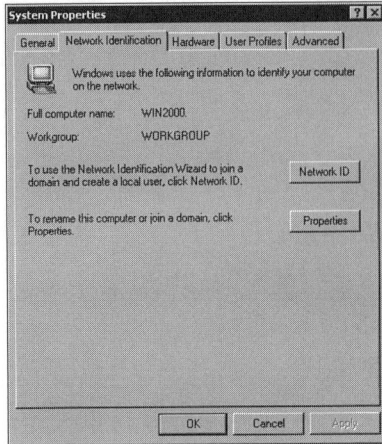

Figure 15.17
You must specify the domain that you are joining.

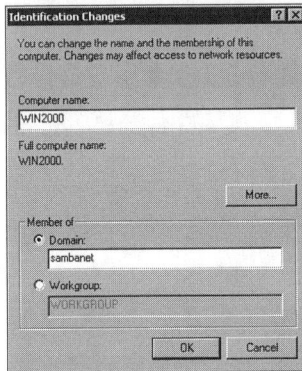

At this point, Windows 2000 attempts to join the domain. It will then open the window shown in Figure 15.18, asking for an account and password on the primary domain controller that has admin privileges. You should enter such an account. The root account is often a good choice. This step creates a workstation trust account for your Windows 2000 workstation.

Figure 15.18
Enter the username and password of a user who can join the domain.

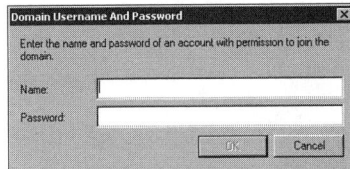

When Windows 2000 has finished joining the domain, it opens a dialog box saying Welcome to the Sambanet Domain. You must reboot your Windows 2000 system before you can log on to the domain.

LOGON SCRIPTS AND PROFILES

Support for Windows 2000 logon scripts and profiles is provided in the same way as it is for Windows NT4. You must set the parameters `logon path`, `logon drive`, and `logon script`. These might be configured in the following way in the global section of your `smb.conf` file:

```
logon script = %U.bat
logon path = \\%L\%U\profile
logon drive = h:
```

For more details on setting up logon scripts and profiles, see Chapter 11.

If your logon scripts want to set the local time, you must set up a domain group map. This is required because you must specify on your Windows 2000 client the name of a domain group that can set the time.

There are two general steps to achieving this:

1. Create a group on the domain, such as `Domain Users`. To do this, add the `domain group map` parameter to the `[global]` section of your `smb.conf` file:

   ```
   domain group map = /etc/domain.group.map
   ```

   This file should contain a line for each UNIX group that maps to a Windows group. For example:

   ```
   domainusers="Domain Users"
   ```

   Then you should create the UNIX group domainusers and the appropriate users to it.

2. Run the Windows 2000 Local Security Policy tool to add the group `Domain Users` to the list of users and groups who can change the system time in the User Rights Assignment area of the Local Policies area.

COMMON PROBLEMS

You might encounter several problems with Windows 2000 when accessing Samba. Some are listed in the next sections along with suggested solutions.

INABILITY TO SEE SAMBA SERVERS

Suppose you have just installed Windows 2000 on a client PC, and you go to browse the network but cannot see any of your Samba servers. This can be a frustrating problem. This problem occurs because your Samba servers are not using encrypted passwords and you have not applied the plain-text password registry hack.

To fix the problem, simply take the file that is in `/usr/doc/samba-$version/docs/Win2000_PlainPassword.reg` and apply under Windows 2000, as discussed previously in "Browsing the Network."

INABILITY TO BROWSE SOME SAMBA SERVERS

To browse Samba servers from Windows 2000, check the following:

1. Ensure that you have a valid guest account on the server.
2. Check that you are using encrypted passwords or that you have applied the plain-text password hack.

For more information on browsing, see Chapter 17, "Samba and Browsing."

CHANGING YOUR SID

On some occasions the SID file on your Samba server will be removed or replaced. If this occurs, your clients will not be able to log on to the domain. They will receive a message similar to the following:

```
The system cannot log you on due to the following error:
The name or security ID (SID) of the domain specified is inconsistent with
the trust information for that domain.
```

If this happens, each client will have to rejoin the domain.

FURTHER INFORMATION

For more information on setting up Samba as a primary domain controller, see the Samba NT DOM FAQ. This FAQ can be accessed at `/samba/docs/ntdom_faq/` `samba_ntdom_faq.html` on one of the `samba.org` mirrors.

FROM HERE...

Remaining chapters in this part are

- Chapter 16, "Accessing Windows from UNIX Using Samba"
- Chapter 17, "Samba and Browsing"

Part IV, "Advanced Topics," deals with topics such as using Samba with LDAP, Samba in the enterprise, and Samba performance tuning.

CHAPTER 16

ACCESSING WINDOWS FROM UNIX USING SAMBA

In this chapter

by Tim Potter

Although Samba is often used to allow users of Microsoft Windows-based computers to access resources on UNIX servers, it can work the other way around. Samba comes with several client programs that UNIX users can use to access Microsoft Windows servers.

This chapter looks at the following UNIX programs used to access Microsoft Windows or Samba servers:

- smbclient—A command-line client similar to the UNIX ftp program.
- smbprint—A print filter that enables UNIX systems to print to printers connected to Windows systems.
- smbtar—A shell script that enables UNIX administrators to back up Windows systems.
- smbmount—A program that can be used to natively mount SMB file systems onto a Linux file system. This uses the Linux smbfs kernel module.
- smbsh—A program that can be used to emulate mounting an SMB file system. This can be used with systems that do not support smbmount.
- rpcclient—A command-line–based Samba client program that can be used to invoke services based on Microsoft Remote Procedure Call (RPC).
- SMB integration into other application programs, such as Midnight Commander and Gnomba.

THE smbclient PROGRAM

Perhaps the easiest client program to use that comes with Samba is called smbclient . This program is a command-line–based program that is similar in operation to a command-line file transfer protocol (FTP) client.

BASIC USE

The basic use of the smbclient command is

```
smbclient '\\hostname\sharename'
```

where *hostname* is the NetBIOS name of the SMB server and *sharename* is the name of the share to connect to. This combination of hostname and sharename is called the *service name*.

> **Note**
>
> The single quotes surrounding the service name are necessary around the sharename because most UNIX shells interpret backslash characters in a special way. smbclient also accepts forward slashes instead of backslashes even though Windows does not. This feature can be used to avoid messy shell quoting.
>
> For example, the following are equivalent:
>
> ```
> smbclient '\\hostname\sharename'
> smbclient //hostname/sharename
> smbclient \\\\hostname\\sharename
> ```

The smbclient program will ask for a password and, if the user is allowed to connect to the service specified, a prompt will be presented. The output of a successful invocation of smbclient looks something like that shown in Listing 16.1.

LISTING 16.1 CONNECTING TO A FILE SHARE USING smbclient

```
$ smbclient '\\server1\scratch'
Added interface ip=10.1.1.1 bcast=10.0.0.255 nmask=255.255.255.0
Got a positive name query response from 10.1.1.2 ( 10.1.1.2 )
Password:
Domain=[NTDOM] OS=[Unix] Server=[Samba 2.0.6]
smb: \>
```

Several commands can be typed at the smb:\> prompt to perform basic file manipulation on the server. Some basic operations are presented next. Optional arguments to commands are given in square brackets with arguments given in italics.

dir [*mask*]

The dir command prints a list of files in the current directory of the file share. If a *mask* argument is specified, only files or directories matching that mask are displayed. The * and ? wildcard characters can be used to match one or more characters or just one character, respectively. For example, executing dir *.c will list all files on the server with the .c extension.

Listing 16.2 shows a directory listing for the root directory of a sample share containing the top level of a Web site as displayed by smbclient.

LISTING 16.2 SAMPLE DIRECTORY LISTING IN smbclient

```
smb: \> dir
  .                            D        0  Tue May 11 20:00:00 1999
  ..                           D        0  Tue May 11 20:00:00 1999
  News                         D        0  Wed Apr 21 14:10:22 1999
  Research                     D        0  Wed Apr 21 17:21:52 1999
  mailing-lists                D        0  Thu Mar 18 15:17:31 1999
  index.html                   A     2851  Wed May 12 20:41:16 1999
  Products                     D        0  Wed Apr 21 17:21:52 1999
            61968 blocks of size 8192. 39162 blocks available
```

A directory listing consists of several fields. The first field is the name of the file or directory. The second shows the DOS attributes of a file or directory. Attributes are taken from the following list:

D	The filename refers to a directory.
A	The DOS archive attribute is set on the file.
H	The DOS hidden attribute is set on the file.
S	The DOS system attribute is set on the file.
R	The DOS read-only attribute is set on the file.

The third field of a directory listing is the size, in bytes, occupied by the file or directory. Directories always appear to be zero bytes in size. The remaining text is a time stamp that is the time the file or directory was last changed.

A synonym for this command is `ls`.

cd [*directory*]

This command changes the current directory on the SMB server to the one specified in the argument. If no argument is given, the current directory is displayed.

If the change directory command completed successfully, the prompt displayed by `smbclient` should be updated appropriately. If the *directory* argument begins with a / character, the remainder of the argument refers to a directory structure starting from the root directory of the file share instead of the current directory.

> **Note**
>
> The `smbclient` program does not mind whether the DOS directory separator \ or the UNIX directory separator / is used.

lcd [*directory*]

This command changes the current directory on the local machine to the one specified in *directory*. If no argument is given, the local current directory is displayed. Files stored or fetched from the remote machine are stored or fetched from the current directory on the local machine.

get *remote-filename* [*local-filename*]

The `get` command fetches the file given by *remote-filename* from the SMB server and saves it in the current directory of the local machine. Normally the filename remains the same, but the file is saved as *local-filename* if this argument is specified.

> **Note**
>
> Wildcard characters in either the remote or local filename can be used, but they will not have the desired effect. The wildcards will be interpreted literally. For example, the command `get *.doc` will attempt to fetch the literal file named `*.doc`, not all files that have a `.doc` extension. Use the `mget` or `mput` commands to process groups of files.

put *local-filename* [*remote-filename*]

The `put` command is the opposite of the `get` command in that it attempts to store the file given by *local-filename* in the current directory of the SMB server. If a *remote-filename* is specified, the file is saved under this name rather than its local name.

del *remote-filename*

The file given by *remote-filename* is deleted from the SMB server. You must have the correct permissions to actually remove the file. A synonym for this command is rm.

!*shell-command*

Using the exclamation mark followed by a UNIX shell command causes smbclient to execute that command on the local machine. For example, typing !ls /tmp at the smbclient prompt will list all files in the /tmp directory.

COMMONLY USED OPTIONS

Several useful command-line options can be passed to smbclient.

-h

This command prints the list of options taken by the smbclient program and a short description of each one.

-U *username*[*%password*]

If the -U option is used, smbclient attempts to connect to the SMB server as the specified user. When no username is specified, the uppercase value of the USER or LOGNAME environment variables are used with USER being checked first. If no username is given, it defaults to the username GUEST. Passwords can be given as part of the username by separating them with a percent character (%).

-W *workgroup*

The -W option can be used to specify the workgroup or domain name of the server to connect to. By default, the workgroup name is the one specified in the workgroup parameter in the smb.conf file.

-I *hostname*

If, for some reason, the NetBIOS name of the service specified does not resolve properly, the IP address of the SMB server can be forced using the -I option. The hostname can be either an IP address or a string that can be resolved into an IP address.

-N

The smbclient program will not ask for a password to connect to the share if this option is given. If the share does actually require a password, the connection will not succeed.

-P

Connect to the service as a printer. Files written to the share using the put command will be sent to the printer associated with the share. The -P option is useful for debugging printer share problems and is discussed in Chapter 7, "Printer Sharing Under Samba."

-L

The -L option queries the specified SMB server for a list of available file and printer shares. For this option, only the NetBIOS name of the SMB server is required. The output of smbclient might look something like Listing 16.3.

> **Note**　Shares that are marked as non-browsable do appear in the output of smbclient -L.

LISTING 16.3 SAMPLE OUTPUT FROM smbclient -L

```
$ smbclient -L '\\server1' -N
Added interface ip=10.1.1.1 bcast=10.1.1.255 nmask=255.255.255.0
Got a positive name query response from 10.1.1.2 ( 10.1.1.2 )
Domain=[NTDOM] OS=[Unix] Server=[Samba 2.0.6]

        Sharename      Type         Comment
        ---------      ----         -------
        wwwsite        Disk         Web site
        cdrom          Disk         CDROM drive
        scratch        Disk         Scratch space
        printer$       Disk         Printer drivers
        IPC$           IPC           IPC Service (Samba 2.0.6)

        Server                      Comment
        ---------                   -------
        SERVER1                     Samba 2.0.6
        CLIENT1

        Workgroup                   Master
        ---------                   ------
        NTDOM                       SERVER1
```

The -L option is often extremely useful for debugging and testing Samba configurations.

ADVANCED OPTIONS

The following options are not commonly used but might be necessary in special situations.

-R order

The order parameter is a list of comma-separated values taken from the following list. NetBIOS names are resolved in the order specified of the following values:

lmhosts	Use the lmhosts file stored in the same directory as the smb.conf file.
host	Look up the NetBIOS name as an Internet hostname using /etc/hosts or the DNS.
wins	The name is looked up in the WINS server specified in the wins server configuration parameter.
bcast	Broadcast a name request on each network interface in an attempt to resolve it.

The order specified by the name resolve order parameter in the smb.conf file will be used if this option is not given.

-M netbiosname

The -M option allows the transmission of WinPopup messages to the Windows machine specified by netbiosname. This can be useful for notifying users or groups of users of system downtime or other events. Windows NT machines receive and display the message in a dialog box, but Windows 95, Windows 98, and Windows for Workgroups machines must run WINPOPUP.EXE to receive messages. If a WinPopup client is not running on a Windows 95/98/WfWG machine, the message will not be received. Listing 16.4 shows an example.

LISTING 16.4 SENDING A POP-UP MESSAGE

```
smbclient -M amd
added interface ip=10.0.0.2 bcast=10.0.0.255 nmask=255.255.255.0
nmask=255.255.255.0
Got a positive name query response from 10.0.0.156 ( 10.0.0.156 )
Connected. Type your message, ending it with a Control-D
This is a message ...
^D
sent 23 bytes
```

A Linux program to receive WinPopup messages, LinPopup, is available at http://www.littleigloo.org/software_002.php3.

-n netbiosname

This options allows the NetBIOS name of the machine on which smbclient is invoked to be set. By default, the hostname of the machine is used as the NetBIOS name.

-p portnum

Specifies the port number to make the connection to. Under Windows this number may not be changed, but it is possible to run Samba on a different port number under UNIX. The default is port 139.

PRINTING TO SMB PRINTER SHARES FROM UNIX

In previous chapters, we looked at using Windows clients to print to UNIX printers through Samba. It is also possible to use UNIX client machines to access printer shares installed on Windows servers. This is achieved by adding a printer definition to the /etc/printcap file and configuring it to send all output through the smbclient program. All this work is done through a shell script that comes with Samba called smbprint.

INSTALLING smbprint

If you have installed a prepackaged binary version of Samba, the smbprint program might already be installed. If you have compiled Samba from source, you might need to copy the smbprint program from the Samba source archive from the examples/printing directory. To do this, run the following commands from the directory in which the Samba archive was unpacked:

```
cd samba-2.0.6
cp examples/printing/smbprint /usr/local/bin
```

The smbprint script is used for BSD-based systems such as FreeBSD and Linux. Copy the examples/printing/smbprint.sysv file instead if you are using a System V-based UNIX such as Solaris.

MODIFYING /etc/printcap

To add the printer definition to the printing system on the UNIX machine, add the contents of Listing 16.5 to the /etc/printcap file. Modify the first line, containing the printer name, and all other occurrences of lj3 to your intended printer name.

LISTING 16.5 SAMPLE /etc/printcap ENTRY FOR PRINTING TO AN SMB PRINTER

```
lj3:\
     :lp=/dev/null:\
     :sd=/var/spool/lj3:\
     :mx#0:\
     :sh:\
     :af=/var/spool/lj3/acct:\
     :if=/usr/local/bin/smbprint:
```

Each line in the printer definition in Listing 16.5 has the following meaning:

- Normally, a device file for the printer must be specified, but because we are sending the printer output to a remote SMB server, this device is set to /dev/null with the lp= parameter.

- The spool directory for the printer is located at /var/spool/lj3 and is set with the sd= option. This directory is where printer output is spooled before being sent to the remote SMB server.

■ The maximum size of the print job is set to zero, which means that files of unlimited size can be printed. The `mx` parameter is used to do this.

■ No title page is printed for the print job by specifying the `sh` parameter.

■ Accounting file information is written into the `/var/spool/lj3/acct` directory with the `af=` parameter. The `smbprint` script uses the accounting directory to determine the location of the configuration file, described further on.

■ After the document has been spooled, it is sent through the `smbprint` shell script by specifying its name with the `if=` parameter.

Ensure that the spool directory specified (in Listing 16.5 it is `/var/spool/lj3`) exists and is writeable. Also, check that the location of the `smbprint` shell script is the same as the location mentioned.

CONFIGURING DOCUMENT DESTINATION

The printer requires one more element of configuration before it can be used. Create a file named `.config` in the `/var/spool/lj3` directory. This file must contain the name of the SMB server and the printer sharename to send the printed documents to. If a password is required to access the share, it must be specified as well. The format of the `.config` file should be in this format:

```
server='server1'
service='lj3'
password=''
```

Test the printer by sending a test document to it. If you are using a System V-based UNIX, use the `lp` command:

```
echo test | lp -P lj3
```

If you are using a BSD-based UNIX, use the `lpr` command:

```
echo test | lpr -P lj3
```

BACKING UP SMB SHARES FROM UNIX

Another utility that comes with Samba is `smbtar`. This shell script enables UNIX administrators to back up Windows-based systems to disk or tape on UNIX systems. Take the following steps to back up a directory on a Windows system:

1. Share the directory that you want to back up on the Windows system, if it is not already shared.

2. Run `smbtar` on the command line or in a script using the following command:
   ```
   smbtar -t server -x share -t tape-or-file
   ```
   server is the server where the share resides, *share* is the share to be backed up, and *tape-or-file* is the tape device file or file where you want to put the backup.

Table 16.1 shows the command-line parameters that the `smbtar` command accepts.

TABLE 16.1 THE COMMAND-LINE PARAMETERS FOR smbtar

Option	Description
-r	Restore to an SMB share rather than save from an SMB share. The default is to save to tapefile.
-i	Incremental backup. Back up files that have the Archive bit set. The default is to do a full backup.
-a	Reset the Archive bit on files that have been backed up. The default is to leave the Archive bit alone.
-v	Verbose mode. Print out verbose information about what smbtar is doing. The default is to be quiet during the backup.
-s server	The server to back up. There is no default server.
-p password	The password to use for the server. The default is that no password is used.
-x share/service	The share from which to back up. The default is to back up from the share called BACKUP.
-X	Exclude mode. The default is include mode.
-N file	Back up files that are newer than file. The default is to back up all files.
-b blocksize	Specifies the block size to use on the tar file. The default is to use the standard block size for tar: 20 blocks.
-d dir	Specify the directory to back up from the share. The default is \, or the top of that share.
-l log-level	Specify a Samba log level to use. The default is 2.
-u user	Specify the user to log in as on the server. The default is to use $LOGNAME, the user's login name.
-t file	The file to back up to. This can be a device-special file if backing up to tape. The default is to use $TAPE, and if that does not exist, use tar.out.

Listing 16.6 shows an example of using smbtar to back up a Windows share. The listing was truncated after a few files were saved.

LISTING 16.6 BACKING UP A WINDOWS SHARE USING smbtar

```
smbtar -s w95vmware -x c -v
server    is w95vmware
share     is c\\
tar args  is
tape      is tar.out
blocksize is
added  interface ip=10.0.0.2 bcast=10.0.0.255 nmask=255.255.255.0
nmask=255.255.255.0
Got a  positive name query response from 10.0.0.151 ( 10.0.0.151 )
      447 (   13.6 kb/s) \SCANDISK.LOG
    24854 (  433.4 kb/s) \BOOTLOG.TXT
```

LISTING 16.6	CONTINUED

```
93812 (   732.9 kb/s) \COMMAND.COM
 5166 (   420.4 kb/s) \SUHDLOG.DAT
 1641 (   133.5 kb/s) \MSDOS.SYS
   22 (     3.1 kb/s) \MSDOS.---
53236 (   775.9 kb/s) \SETUPLOG.TXT
    0 (     0.0 kb/s) \CONFIG.SYS
48659 (   609.2 kb/s) \BOOTLOG.PRV
28143 (   518.6 kb/s) \DETLOG.TXT
  489 (    19.9 kb/s) \NETLOG.TXT
             directory \WINDOWS\
```

MOUNTING LINUX FILE SYSTEMS WITH smbmount

The smbclient program is useful but limited in its capability to process files using other UNIX programs. Another Linux client program that comes with Samba allows easier access to files on an SMB server. smbmount enables users to mount file systems on SMB servers on the local machine. This enables the access and manipulation of files by other Linux programs, as the files appear as part of the UNIX file system. This is far superior to having to use the smbclient program.

> **Note**
>
> The remote SMB server can be either a Microsoft Windows server or a UNIX machine running Samba. The smbmount program, and indeed all the UNIX client programs, do not care which operating system is running on the SMB server.

However, the smbmount program contains a few limitations:

- At present, the smbmount program is available only for the Linux operating system because it relies on a kernel file system facility called smbfs. No other versions of UNIX can support smbfs at this time.

- All files mounted can be owned by only a single user and group. A side effect of this is that UNIX commands such as chown and chgrp might not operate as expected.

INSTALLING smbmount

Support for smbmount is enabled in Samba at compile time. This is done by passing the --with-smbmount to the configure script when compiling Samba. When Samba is compiled and installed, the following additional executables will be present in the bin directory:

- The smbmount program, which allows the mounting of remote SMB file systems. Various options describing how to mount the SMB share must be passed to smbmount for the mount to succeed. These are described later.

- smbumount performs the opposite operation to smbmount. It unmounts a previously mounted SMB file system.

- The smbmnt program is a helper program used by smbmount during the mounting process.

A symbolic link is also made from /bin/mount.smb on the machine Samba is installed on pointing at the /usr/local/samba/bin/smbmount executable, if Samba has been installed in the default location. This link allows the normal UNIX mount and umount commands to be used to mount SMB file systems as well as the smbmount and smbumount commands provided with Samba.

Note

If you are using a prepackaged binary distribution of Samba, smbmount support is probably already present and working as part of your package.

Normally, only the root user performs the mounting and unmounting of remote file systems. To enable mounting of SMB file systems by users, the smbmnt and smbumount programs must be made setuid. If Samba has been installed in the default location, /usr/local/samba, then you must perform the following command to enable users to mount SMB file systems:

```
chmod 4755 /usr/local/samba/bin/smbmnt /usr/local/samba/bin/smbumount
```

Note

Samba does not install the setuid of the smbmnt and smbumount programs for security reasons.

MOUNTING FILE SYSTEMS

The format of the smbmount command is

```
smbmount //servername/sharename mountpoint options
```

Table 16.2 shows the options available.

TABLE 16.2 AVAILABLE OPTIONS FOR smbmount

Option	Description
username=username [[/workgroup] %password]	The username, workgroup, and password can be specified using this option. For example, to perform the mount as user alice in the workgroup ntdom with password secret, the argument to the username option would be alice/ntdom%secret. If the username argument is not specified, smbmount looks in the USER environment variable.
password=password	An alternative method of specifying which password to use is to use the password option.

TABLE 16.2   CONTINUED

Option	Description
netbiosname=*servername*	The source NetBIOS name to connect as can be given using this option. The default is the local hostname.
uid=*arg*	All files mounted will be owned by this user ID, which can be either a username or a numeric value. The default is the user ID of the user calling the smbmount program.
gid=*arg*	All files mounted will have group ownership set to this group ID. It can be either a username or numeric value. The default is the group ID of the user calling the smbmount program.
port=*portnum*	Specifies the port number to connect to. This is equivalent to using the -p option in smbclient.
fmask=*mask*	This option is used to limit the permissions of files appearing under the mounted file system. Any permission bits not set in the fmask option will be cleared on the actual file permissions. For example, if the fmask option is set to 750, only user and group permission bits can be set on any file. This option behaves similarly to the create mask parameter in the smb.conf file.
dmask=*mask*	The permissions of directories under the mounted file system can be limited using this option in a similar manner to the fmask option and the directory mask smb.conf parameter.
debug=*level*	This option sets the debug level for smbmount, which can be useful for debugging connection or other problems. Debug messages are sent to standard output.
ip=*ipaddr*	The IP address of the remote host can be given with this option. This is useful if the NetBIOS server name cannot be resolved. This option is the same as the -I option in smbclient.
workgroup=*name*	The workgroup or domain name can be given with this option. The default is taken from the workgroup parameter in the smb.conf file. This option is the same as the -W option in smbclient.

PART

III

CH

16

TABLE 16.2   CONTINUED

Option	Description
sockopt=*arg*	TCP/IP socket options when making the connection to the remote machine can be specified using this option. They can also be set using the socket options parameter in the smb.conf file. More information about the use of socket options appears in Chapter 21, "Samba and Performance."
guest	If this option is given, smbmount tries to connect to the share without using a password.
ro	The file share is mounted read-only on the Linux machine.
rw	The file share is mounted with read/write permissions. By default, file shares are mounted read/write unless the read-only option is given.

To mount Alice's home directory at /home/alice/windows, use the following smbmount command as root:

```
smbmount -o username=alice //server1/alice /home/alice/windows
```

With Samba 2.0.6, it is possible to use the normal mount command to mount file systems. When using mount, the format is

```
mount -t smbfs -o options //servername/sharename mountpoint
```

> **Note**
>
> It is not possible to enter a password interactively when using mount. The password must either be given using the USER environment variable or with the username and password options.

ADDING ENTRIES TO /etc/fstab

If you want to have an SMB share mounted on your Linux machine regularly, it might be useful to add an entry for it in the file system table file /etc/fstab. This allows the SMB file system to be automatically mounted at boot, as well as mounted and unmounted from the command line easily.

For example, suppose Alice wants to mount the scratch space share set up in Chapter 5, "Configuring and Managing Samba," directly onto her Linux machine. Alice adds, or has her system administrator add the following line to the /etc/fstab file on her Linux machine:

```
//server1/scratch    /scratch    default,uid=alice    0 0
```

> **Note**
>
> Because we know the scratch space share is actually on another UNIX machine, it might be more useful to mount the share through NFS. This will avoid some of the limitations of smbmount mentioned earlier.

The scratch share will be mounted when Alice's machine is next rebooted, or the system administrator can mount it by hand.

UNMOUNTING FILE SYSTEMS

Unmounting an SMB file system mounted with Samba requires the smbumount program. If Alice's home directory on the *server1* machine has been mounted on /home/alice/windows, it can be unmounted using

```
smbumount /home/alice/windows
```

If an entry for the file system exists in the /etc/fstab file, the file share can be unmounted either by referring to its sharename or by the mount point.

USING AUTOMOUNT

If the automount package is installed, it is possible to have smbmount automatically mount SMB file systems when a user first accesses them. To do this, add the following line to the /etc/auto.misc file:

```
scratch   -fstype=smb,username=user,password=password   ://server1/scratch
```

Accessing files under the /misc/scratch directory will then be automatically mounted when first accessed by a user.

Unfortunately, the username and password are required to be stored in the automount map file, which limits the effectiveness of automounting SMB file systems.

smbsh

The smbsh program is an alternative method of accessing SMB file systems from UNIX. It is similar to the smbmount program in that it allows access to SMB file systems as part of the UNIX directory tree. This is achieved by intercepting all file input and output operations and redirecting them through Samba if they refer to a file on an SMB file system. Operations on normal files and directories fall through this filter and are unaffected.

smbsh support in Samba must be enabled at compile time by specifying the --with-smbwrapper option to the configure script. When Samba has finished compiling, the bin directory will contain the following two extra files:

■ The executable smbsh, used to integrate files from SMB file systems into the UNIX directory structure.

■ A dynamically linked library file called smbwrapper.so, used to override the normal UNIX system calls and replace them with calls to Samba. The smbsh program loads this library when it runs.

smbsh LIMITATIONS

A few types of operations are not supported by the smbwrapper program due to the way it operates:

■ Attempting to execute files under the /smb directory will not work. This includes shell scripts.

■ Statically linked executables will not be aware of the /smb directory because their file operations will not pass through smbsh.

■ Shell redirection to files located under the /smb directory will not work.

■ Using the mmap() system call on any file under the /smb directory is not possible.

■ UNIX systems based on GNU libc (glibc) version 2.1 will not be able to run smbsh due to changes in the way the library works. Unfortunately, this includes Red Hat Linux 6.0 and other recent Linux distributions. It is recommended that the smbmount program be used instead.

Despite its limitations, smbsh is still a useful program for browsing or quickly copying files to and from file shares on remote SMB servers.

USING smbsh

smbsh operates by running a login shell of the user invoking it. Any programs started under this shell will be able to access files on remote SMB servers by reading and writing to locations under the /smb directory. This directory acts as a mount point for remote SMB file systems, although no mounting actually takes place. It has the following properties:

■ Listing the /smb directory using the ls command will show all SMB servers available on the network, much like the Network Neighborhood applet under Windows.

■ Listing the /smb/servername directory will show all shares available on the SMB server given by servername. Non-browsable shares will not appear in the directory listing but can still be accessed normally.

■ All operations on files and directories below the /smb/servername directory will operate on the corresponding files on the SMB server given by servername.

When smbsh is invoked, it asks for a username and a password to be entered. This is used when making SMB connections to remote machines. The following are some of the command-line arguments taken by the smbsh program:

-U *user[%password]*	The username and password with which to connect can be specified using the -U option.
-W *workgroup*	The workgroup of the username with which to connect is given in the *workgroup* argument to the -W option.
-P *prefix*	The default directory prefix is /smb, but this can be changed by specifying an argument with the -P option.

Alice can run smbsh from her Linux machine and browse the network and the shares available on an SMB server. The output of Alice's activities in smbsh appears in Listing 16.7.

LISTING 16.7 A SAMPLE SESSION WITH smbsh

```
$ smbsh
Username: alice
Password:
smbsh$ ls /smb
total 0
   0 ./                0 ../              0 SERVER1/      0 SERVER2/
smbsh$ ls /smb/server1
total 0
   0 ./             0 alice/         0 scratch/
   0 ../            0 lj3/           0 wwwsite/
smbsh$
```

The username and password entered when smbsh initially runs are not verified against an SMB server until files in the /smb directory are accessed. If the password or username are incorrect, the user will not be aware of it until she attempts to access files or directories on SMB servers.

FILE PERMISSIONS

The permissions on files and directories created by smbsh are generated from the DOS permissions on the files obtained from the SMB server. The user, group, and other execute bits are set on the UNIX file if the DOS archive, system, and hidden attributes are set on file on the SMB server, respectively.

Other properties of the file created by smbsh worth noting include the following:

- Files that are writeable have the user write permission bit set. This bit is cleared for read-only files.

- All files and directories appear to be owned by the UNIX user that invoked the smbsh program.

- All directories appear to have a zero file size.

THE `rpcclient` PROGRAM

Machines running Microsoft Windows NT operating systems use a method of network communications called *Remote Procedure Call* (RPC). This method is often used to implement client/server operations between two machines. An RPC is simply a request sent by a client machine to a server machine to perform a particular operation, as illustrated in Figure 16.1. The server machine usually returns a result or status code.

Figure 16.1
Remote Procedure Call (RPC) diagram.

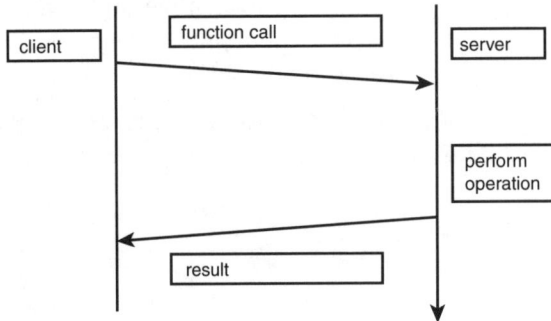

Several services, including remote administration, are implemented using RPC under Windows NT. These include the following:

- Functionality implemented by the Windows NT Server Manager applet. The Server Manager, among other things, allows an administrator to start and stop services on a remote Windows NT machine.

- Printing functionality, such as print job spooling and print queue management between Windows NT machines. Windows 95/98, Windows for Workgroups machines, and Samba machines implement printing using a different technique.

- User login authentication.

Samba comes with a program called rpcclient that can be used to make remote procedure calls to Windows NT machines. With this program it is possible to issue commands to the various Windows NT subsystems given earlier. rpcclient does not work with Windows 95/ 98 or Windows for Workgroups.

> **Note**
>
> The rpcclient program is extremely experimental and very much a work in progress. Many commands might not work properly or might cause rpcclient or the Windows server to crash. Applying the latest service packs to Windows servers can reduce the possibility of crashes.

Development is occurring on rpcclient at a rapid pace. It is recommended that, if some of the functionality of rpcclient is required, Samba be compiled from the HEAD branch of Samba.

→ For information on compiling Samba from CVS, **see** Chapter 24, "A Tour Through the Samba Source Code."

INVOKING rpcclient

It might be necessary to use the -U option to specify an appropriate username and -W to specify an NT domain name. Also, some rpcclient commands require administrator access to operate correctly. That is, the username given must be a local or domain administrator for the machine given.

To connect as administrator to the Windows NT machine called server2, use the following command line:

```
rpcclient -S '\\server2' -U administrator -W NTDOM
```

The administrator password for the Windows machine is required to complete the connection.

rpcclient COMMANDS

The rpcclient program has several commands that can be divided into sections. These sections are discussed, but each command is not mentioned individually.

> **Note**
>
> Typing help at the command prompt provides a current list of commands understood by rpcclient. Later versions have a reasonably up-to-date manual page. Unfortunately, it is largely up to the user to experiment with the various rpcclient commands because documentation is quite sparse.

The sections of commands are as follows:

- General workstation/server status and query commands—Several commands exist to query the current status of a remote machine. These include a list of open files, current connections, and general workstation information. These commands generally start with the prefix wks or svr.

- Registry manipulation commands—The remote getting and setting of registry commands is possible using rpcclient, although this functionality does not appear to work very well in Samba 2.0.6 version of Samba. The HEAD version from CVS does work a little better. The registry manipulation commands are prefixed with reg.

- Security access manager commands—Several commands to manipulate user accounts and security descriptors are present. These commands start with the prefix sam.

- Service manipulation commands—The CVS version of rpcclient contains some new commands that allow the starting and stopping of services on Windows NT machines. Other information on services is also available. The service command starts with an svc prefix.

Although rpcclient is not yet a stable program, the type and number of commands it can perform is wide. In the future, it should be possible to emulate almost every administration task possible under Windows NT using rpcclient.

SAMBA INTEGRATION IN OTHER PROGRAMS

A few other ways to access Samba from UNIX exist apart from the various UNIX clients bundled with Samba. These come in the form of Samba integration in other programs. In this section, we look at two such UNIX programs:

- The Midnight Commander—A program similar to Windows Explorer, Midnight Commander has a text-based interface and a graphical interface known as *GMC (GNOME Midnight Commander)*.

- Gnomba—A program meant to be a replacement for the Network Neighborhood applet under Microsoft Windows.

MIDNIGHT COMMANDER

The Midnight Commander is one of the many file manager programs available for UNIX. Midnight Commander has both a text-based interface and a graphical interface. It also has integrated Samba support for accessing file shares on SMB servers.

Midnight Commander has been chosen as the primary file manager for the GNOME project.

> **Note**
>
> The Midnight Commander is undergoing constant development and as such, certain functions such as the Samba integration might not be completely working. At the time of writing, the Samba integration for the Midnight Commander was not compiled by default.

OBTAINING AND INSTALLING MIDNIGHT COMMANDER

To obtain midnight commander, download it from the GNOME Web site at `http://www.gnome.org/mc` or one of the many GNOME mirrors around the world. Binary and source packages are available for most UNIX operating systems, although some binary packages might not have Samba support compiled in.

To compile Midnight Commander with Samba support, obtain a source package with version number 4.5.37 or higher. The latest version at the time of writing was version 4.5.41. Unpack it in a temporary directory and configure it using the following commands:

```
tar xfvz mc-4.5.41.tar.gz
cd mc-4.5.41
./configure --with-samba
make
```

To enable the graphical user interface, use the additional `--with-gnome` option when invoking the configure script. When Midnight Commander has compiled, install it as root with the command

```
make install
```

> **Note**
>
> On some versions of UNIX, the `tar` command might not accept the z option. You might need to use
>
> ```
> gzip -d mc-4.5.41.tar.gz; tar xfv mc-4.5.1.tar
> ```

> **Note**
>
> To compile the GNOME graphical user interface, the GNOME libraries and development packages must be installed.

USING THE MIDNIGHT COMMANDER

Midnight Commander implements Samba support through a *Virtual File System* (VFS) extension. The VFS in Midnight Commander is also used to implement an FTP file system, as well as transparent access to files in various compressed file formats and archives, such as .tar, .zip, .rpm, and .deb files.

To access Samba through the VFS extensions, the following format is required:

```
/#smb:servername/sharename
```

The /#smb: prefix in the location tells Midnight Commander to use the SMB virtual file system. The SMB server is given in the *servername* and the file share to connect to is specified by *sharename*. If the sharename is not given, Midnight Commander will browse the list of shares available on that server.

In Figure 16.2, Alice is using the Midnight Commander to browse the shares available from the SMB machine named *server1*.

Figure 16.2
The text-based interface for Midnight Commander.

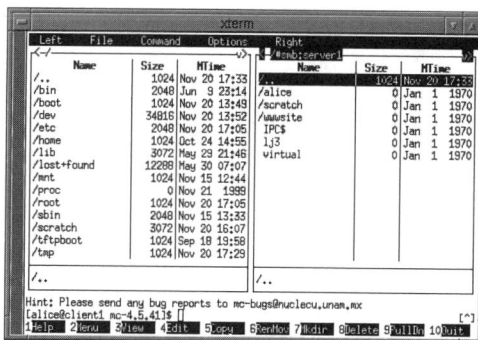

USING THE GNOME MIDNIGHT COMMANDER

Accessing SMB file shares under the GNOME Midnight Commander is similar to using the text-based version. Enter the name of the server to browse using the format described earlier in the *Location* entry field. Figure 16.3 shows what Alice sees when using the Midnight Commander to browse an SMB server.

Figure 16.3
GNOME
Midnight
Commander.

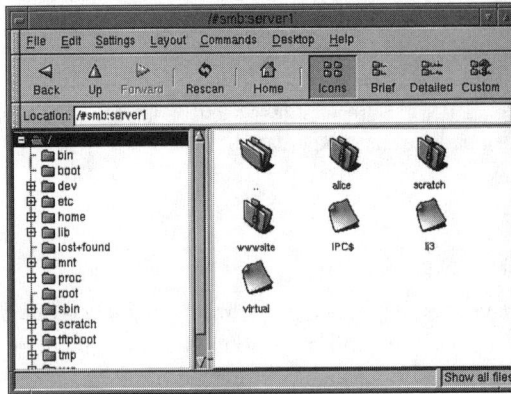

GNOMBA

The Gnomba program is a GUI front end for Samba implemented using the GNOME toolkit. Gnomba is intended to be a UNIX replacement for the Network Neighborhood applet found in Microsoft Windows. At the time of writing, the current version of Gnomba is version 0.5.1.

Currently, Gnomba supports browsing file and printer shares connected to Microsoft Windows and Samba servers as well as mounting file shares onto the local file system. This functionality is implemented by calling the `smbclient` and `smbmount` programs directly. Figure 16.4 shows Gnomba browsing a small section of the Example Corporation network.

Figure 16.4
Network
browsing with
Gnomba.

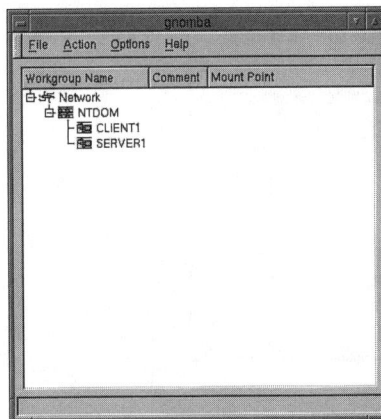

Gnomba is written for Linux, but you should be able to compile it under other UNIX operating systems. The `smbmount` program is available only for Linux, however, so only the browsing functions of Gnomba would be available.

OBTAINING AND INSTALLING GNOMBA

Binary packages for the Red Hat and Debian distributions of Linux, as well as the source code, are available from the Gnomba Web site at `http://gnomba.darkcorner.net/download.html`. However, compiling Gnomba from source requires that the GNOME development packages be installed, so it is probably easier to install a binary package.

To install the Intel i386 binary RPM package for Red Hat Linux, type as root:

```
rpm -i gnomba-0.5.1-1.i386.rpm
```

Under Debian Linux use the Debian package installer program `dpkg` as root:

```
dpkg -i gnomba-0.5.1-1_i386.deb
```

CONFIGURING GNOMBA

For Gnomba to discover SMB servers on the network, it must be given a range of IP addresses to scan. This method is used, rather than querying the NetBIOS master browser, because the process is many times quicker. Figure 16.5 shows the Gnomba Preferences dialog box configured to scan the 10.1.1.0 subnet of the Example Corporation.

Figure 16.5
Configuring the scan range for Gnomba.

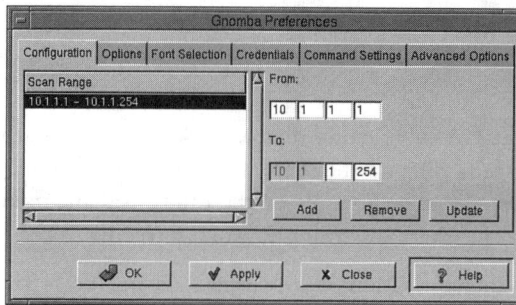

To add a range of IP addresses to scan for, follow these steps:

1. Enter the start IP address of the range to scan in the From fields.
2. Enter the ending IP address of the range to scan for, taking care not to use the broadcast IP address for the subnet in question. For the Example Corporation subnet used in Figure 16.5, the broadcast address is 10.1.1.255.
3. Click the Add button and then OK to close the dialog box.

When Gnomba is next started up, it will scan the range of IP addresses entered for SMB servers. A rescan of the network can be done by selecting Rescan from the File menu in the main Gnomba window.

BROWSING THE NETWORK

When Gnomba has detected Microsoft Windows or Samba servers on the network, it is possible to browse the list of file and printer shares exported by those machines. To do this, click on the server machine entries in the main Gnomba window. If the server allows guest connections, the list of file and printer shares for the server will appear; otherwise, a username and password dialog box will be presented. Enter a valid username and password to access the browse list on the server.

Figure 16.6 shows what Alice would see browsing the SERVER1 machine on the Example Corporation network using Gnomba. The various file and printer shares exported by the machines are shown as well as a file share for Alice's home directory.

Figure 16.6
Browsing an
SMB server
using Gnomba.

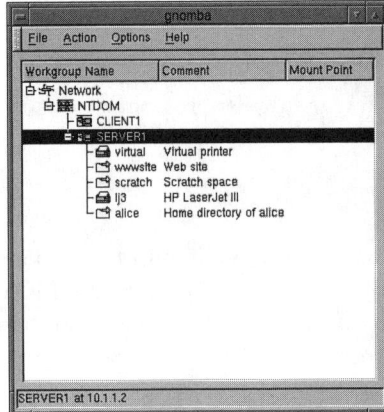

MOUNTING FILE SHARES

To mount a file share under Gnomba, either double-click on the share name entry in the tree-browsing window, or right-click on the share and select the Mount option from the menu. The smbmount program must be installed on the Linux machine running Gnomba and must be in the current path for share mounting to work correctly.

If the file share cannot be mounted, Gnomba will display a dialog box saying that the mount failed.

FROM HERE...

We have looked at several ways to access Samba from various flavors of Microsoft Windows and OS/2 as well as from UNIX-based machines. The rest of this part looks at accessing Samba from less commonly used operating systems such as OpenVMS, OS/390, and AmigaOS machines.

Part IV of this book looks at some advanced topics, including

- Optimizing Samba for performance improvements
- Samba and high availability
- Using the Secure Socket Layers (SSL) with Samba
- A tour of the Samba source code

CHAPTER 17

SAMBA AND BROWSING

In this chapter

by Richard Sharpe

Users in a Windows network must be able to find resources such as the following:

- Servers
- Shares
- Domains and Workgroups

Windows provides a protocol and programs and icons that make this process relatively easy and intuitive for users. The whole process is referred to as *browsing*.

Samba provides support for browsing, and a Samba-based network looks just like a Windows NT server from many perspectives.

However, many things can go wrong with browsing, and browsing has always been problematic in Microsoft Windows Networks.

In this chapter, we explore the following topics:

- The browsing protocols, so that you are better able to diagnose browsing problems
- How to configure Samba to support browsing in a local area network
- How to configure Samba to support browsing in a routed network
- Common problems with browsing

THE WINDOWS BROWSING PROTOCOLS

The Microsoft Windows browsing protocols have evolved over a long period of time. They involve a number of functions and protocols to achieve the end result of providing browse lists for users.

Two types of hosts take part in the browsing function:

- Clients are workstations and servers that access browse servers to obtain the browse list. The browse list is the list of workgroups or domains and the servers within each of those workgroups or domains.
- Servers are the systems in the network that collate the browse list. At times, servers act as clients and fetch the browse list from other servers. A browse server is simply referred to as a *browser*.

Browsing involves the following broad functions:

- A protocol to allow clients to obtain the browse list
- A group of servers on the network to maintain the browse list and a list of all the servers and domains
- A protocol to allow servers to announce their presence, and thus keep the browse list up-to-date
- Operational rules that allow browsers to remove systems from the browse list when they have not been heard from for a while

When users click on Network Neighborhood, if all goes well, they see a window like the one shown in Figure 17.1. However, a number of steps are taken in order to get the information presented. The list of servers shown in Figure 17.1 is the result of browsing a network containing one Samba server and a Windows 95 system. The Samba server used the global configuration shown in Listing 17.1.

Figure 17.1
Network Neighborhood shows the servers and workgroups you can access.

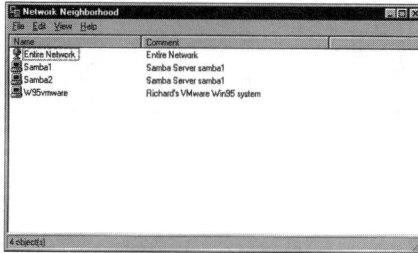

LISTING 17.1 THE GLOBAL CONFIGURATION FOR OUR SAMBA SERVER

```
[global]
    workgroup = sambanet
    server string = Samba Server %L
    netbios name = Samba1
    netbios aliases = Samba2
    load printers = yes
    guest account = pcguest
    log file = /var/log/samba/log.%L.%m
    password level =
    username level =
    security = user
    os level =
```

Figure 17.1 shows the following entries:

- Entire Network—Allows you to list all the workgroups or domains in the network.

- Samba1—The Samba server that allows you to list all the shares on it.

- Samba2—The NetBIOS alias for Samba1. It shows up as a separate server.

- W95vmware—The Windows 95 system which is running on VMware.

The actual over-the-wire steps required to obtain the above Network Neighborhood list are shown in Figure 17.2. The following is an explanation of the steps involved and the frames relating to each step:

1. The client sends a GetBackupList request on the subnet broadcast address (10.0.0.255 in this case) to the NetBIOS name *Domain*<1d> (Local Master Browser), where *Domain* is your domain or workgroup. This appears in frame 1 in Figure 17.2.

2. The client sends a NetBIOS name query for the name *Domain*<1b>. This appears in frames two and three of Figure 17.2. Frame three is the Samba server's response. This step is taken only if clients are configured to use WINS.

Figure 17.2
Only one back-up server, Samba1, is in the network.

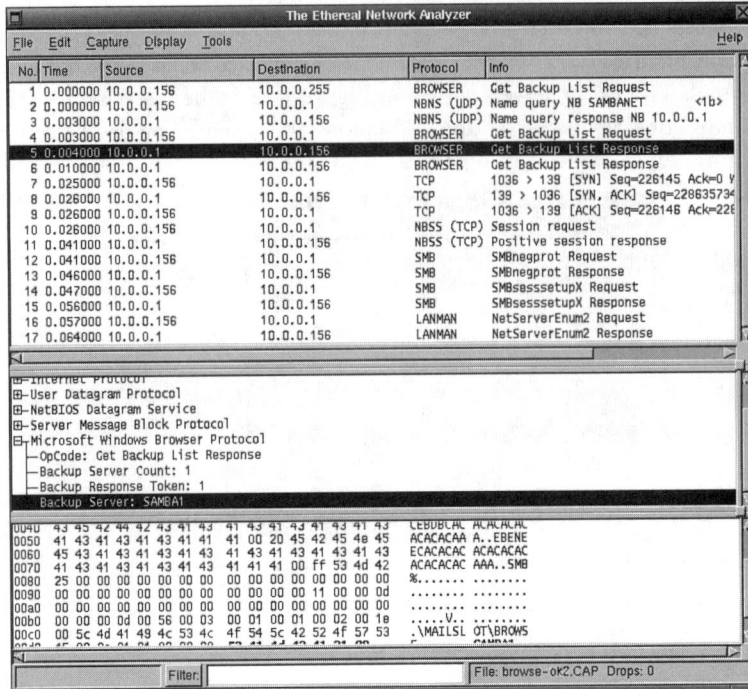

The Ethereal Network Analyzer

No.	Time	Source	Destination	Protocol	Info
1	0.000000	10.0.0.156	10.0.0.255	BROWSER	Get Backup List Request
2	0.000000	10.0.0.156	10.0.0.1	NBNS (UDP)	Name query NB SAMBANET <1b>
3	0.003000	10.0.0.1	10.0.0.156	NBNS (UDP)	Name query response NB 10.0.0.1
4	0.003000	10.0.0.156	10.0.0.1	BROWSER	Get Backup List Request
5	0.004000	10.0.0.1	10.0.0.156	BROWSER	Get Backup List Response
6	0.010000	10.0.0.1	10.0.0.156	BROWSER	Get Backup List Response
7	0.025000	10.0.0.156	10.0.0.1	TCP	1036 > 139 [SYN] Seq=226145 Ack=0 W
8	0.026000	10.0.0.1	10.0.0.156	TCP	139 > 1036 [SYN, ACK] Seq=228635734
9	0.026000	10.0.0.156	10.0.0.1	TCP	1036 > 139 [ACK] Seq=226146 Ack=228
10	0.026000	10.0.0.156	10.0.0.1	NBSS (TCP)	Session request
11	0.041000	10.0.0.1	10.0.0.156	NBSS (TCP)	Positive session response
12	0.041000	10.0.0.156	10.0.0.1	SMB	SMBnegprot Request
13	0.046000	10.0.0.1	10.0.0.156	SMB	SMBnegprot Response
14	0.047000	10.0.0.156	10.0.0.1	SMB	SMBsesssetupX Request
15	0.050000	10.0.0.1	10.0.0.156	SMB	SMBsesssetupX Response
16	0.057000	10.0.0.156	10.0.0.1	LANMAN	NetServerEnum2 Request
17	0.064000	10.0.0.1	10.0.0.156	LANMAN	NetServerEnum2 Response

```
⊞-Internet Protocol
⊞-User Datagram Protocol
⊞-NetBIOS Datagram Service
⊞-Server Message Block Protocol
⊟-Microsoft Windows Browser Protocol
  -OpCode: Get Backup List Response
  -Backup Server Count: 1
  -Backup Response Token: 1
  Backup Server: SAMBA1
```

```
0040  43 45 42 44 42 43 41 43   41 43 41 43 41 43 41 43   CEBDBCAC ACACACAC
0050  41 43 41 43 41 43 41 41   41 00 20 45 42 45 4e 45   ACACACAA A..EBENE
0060  45 43 41 43 41 43 41 43   41 43 41 43 41 43 41 43   ECACACAC ACACACAC
0070  41 43 41 43 41 43 41 43   41 41 41 00 ff 53 4d 42   ACACACAC AAA..SMB
0080  25 00 00 00 00 00 00 00   00 00 00 00 00 00 00 00   %....... ........
0090  00 00 00 00 00 00 00 00   00 00 00 00 11 00 00 0d   ........ ........
00a0  00 00 00 00 00 00 00 00   00 00 00 00 00 00 00 00   ........ ........
00b0  00 00 00 0d 00 56 00 03   00 01 00 01 00 02 00 1e   .....V.. ........
00c0  00 5c 4d 41 49 4c 53 4c   4f 54 5c 42 52 4f 57 53   .\MAILSL OT\BROWS
```

Filter: File: browse-ok2.CAP Drops: 0

Note

The first step requires a broadcast be sent. Browsing will fail if broadcasts fail. In addition, browsing across subnets will not work using broadcasts because the broadcast is a subnet-directed broadcast.

3. The client sends a GetBackupList Request to the NetBIOS name *Domain*<1b> via the IP address returned in step 2. This retrieves the list of Backup Browse servers from the Local Master Browser or the Domain Master Browser. This appears in frame 4 in Figure 17.2.

   Frames 5 and 6 contain the Samba server's response to the GetBackupList requests sent in frames 1 and 4. In the network the capture was taken from, there is only one server. The response is shown in more detail in Figure 17.2. Samba1 is the only backup server.

4. The client then chooses one of the servers in the list retrieved in steps 1 and 3 and issues a NetBIOS name query for that machine to find its IP address. This step is not needed if the client already has the server's IP address in its NetBIOS name cache, and therefore it does not appear in the trace shown in Figure 17.2.

5. The client then connects to the server selected and does a SMBsessionsetupX to log on to the backup browse server and connect to the IPC$ share. It may log on using the domain name as an account name or with an empty account name, and with no password in either case.

This is shown in frames 7–15 in Figure 17.2. Frames 7, 8, and 9 are the three-way handshake for the TCP connection, while frames 10 and 11 establish a NetBIOS session between the client and the server, and frames 12 and 13 are the NetProt request and response. Finally, frames 14 and 15 are the SMBsesssetupX request and response where the client logs on and connects to the IPC$ share. Figure 17.3 shows the account and password used to log on with, which are both null in this case.

Figure 17.3
The client submits a null account name and password to log on to the server before submitting a NetServerEnum2 request.

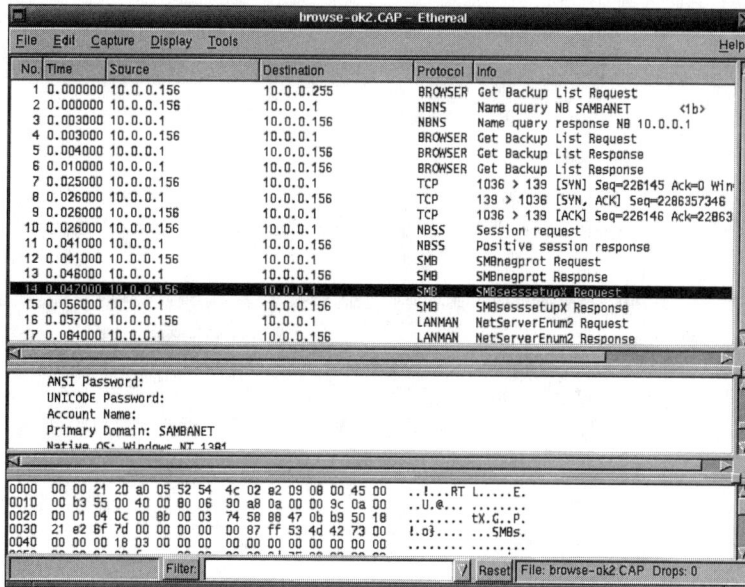

6. The client then issues a NetServerEnum2 request to retrieve the list of servers in the workgroup/domain from the backup server. These are shown in frames 16 and 17 in Figures 17.2, 17.3, and 17.4.

One field in the NetServerEnum2 request specifies the type of server that the client is interested in. This type field is a bit field, where each bit has a particular meaning. The meanings of the bits in this field are shown in Table 17.1. In a normal NetServerEnum2 request, a Windows 9X client asks for

- Server
- Print Queue Server
- Windows for Workgroups

Windows NT asks for

- Workstation, Server
- SQL Server
- Domain Controller

- Backup Domain Controller
- Time Source
- Apple Server
- Novell Server
- Domain Member Server
- Print Queue Server
- Dialin Server Xenix Server
- NT Workstation
- Windows for Workgroups
- NT Server

The detail from frame 17 appears in Figure 17.4. It lists the five servers in the workgroup. Notice that only the servers' names are shown, and not the IP addresses.

Figure 17.4
The `NetServerEnum2` response contains the browse list.

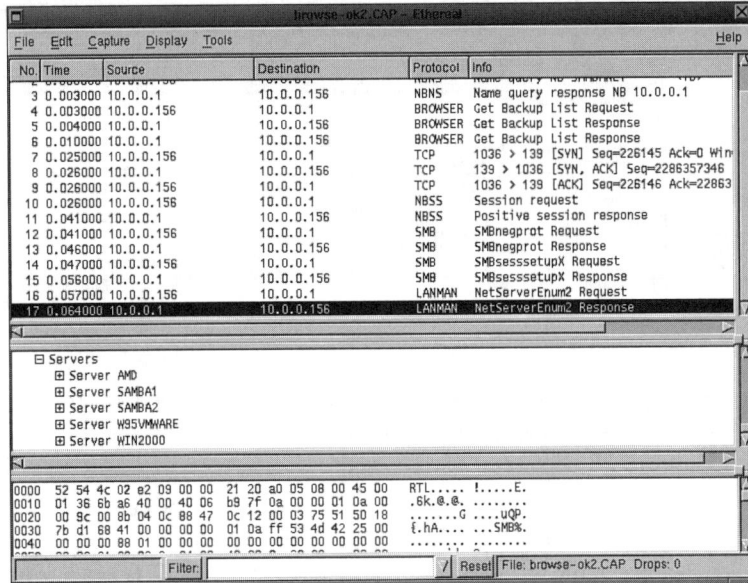

TABLE 17.1 SERVER TYPES

Server Type Mnemonic	Bit Value	Meaning
SV_TYPE_WORKSTATION	0x00000001	All workstations
SV_TYPE_SERVER	0x00000002	All servers
SV_TYPE_SQLSERVER	0x00000004	SQL Server server

TABLE 17.1   CONTINUED

Server Type Mnemonic	Bit Value	Meaning
SV_TYPE_DOMAIN_CTRL	0x00000008	Primary domain controller
SV_TYPE_DOMAIN_BAKCTRL	0x00000010	Backup domain controller
SV_TYPE_TIME_SOURCE	0x00000020	Timesource service
SV_TYPE_AFP	0x00000040	Apple File Protocol servers
SV_TYPE_NOVELL	0x00000080	Novell servers
SV_TYPE_DOMAIN_MEMBER	0x00000100	Domain Member
SV_TYPE_PRINTQ_SERVER	0x00000200	Server sharing print queue
SV_TYPE_DIALIN_SERVER	0x00000400	Server running dialin service
SV_TYPE_XENIX_SERVER	0x00000800	Xenix server
SV_TYPE_NT	0x00001000	NT server
SV_TYPE_WFW	0x00002000	Windows for Workgroups
SV_TYPE_SERVER_NT	0x00008000	Windows NT non-DC server
SV_TYPE_POTENTIAL_BROWSER	0x00010000	Potential browser server
SV_TYPE_BACKUP_BROWSER	0x00020000	Backup browser server
SV_TYPE_MASTER_BROWSER	0x00040000	Master browser server
SV_TYPE_DOMAIN_MASTER	0x00080000	Domain Master Browser
SV_TYPE_OSF	0x00100000	DEC OSF Server(1)
SV_TYPE_VMS	0x00200000	DEV VMS Server(1)
SV_TYPE_WIN9X	0x00400000	Windows 95 or above(1)
SV_TYPE_LOCAL_LIST_ONLY	0x40000000	Enumerate entries marked "local"
SV_TYPE_DOMAIN_ENUM	0x80000000	Enumerate Domains

PART

III

CH

17

Note

These definitions have been taken from the Microsoft document *CIFS/E Browser Protocol Preliminary Draft* by Paul Leach and Dilip Naik–browdif.txt. I could not find the values marked (1) anywhere; they have only been observed in NetMon traces.

Steps 1–3 are skipped if the client already has the backup browse server list. In addition, if the client already has a connection to the chosen backup browse server, the client performs the following steps (as shown in Figure 17.5):

1. Issues a tconX request to connect to the IPC$ share. An empty password is used. These appear in frames 7 and 8 in Figure 17.5. The middle pane shows that the null password was used.

2. Issues a NetServerEnum2 RAP request to retrieve the list of servers in the workgroup/domain. This appears in frames 9 and 10 in Figure 17.5.

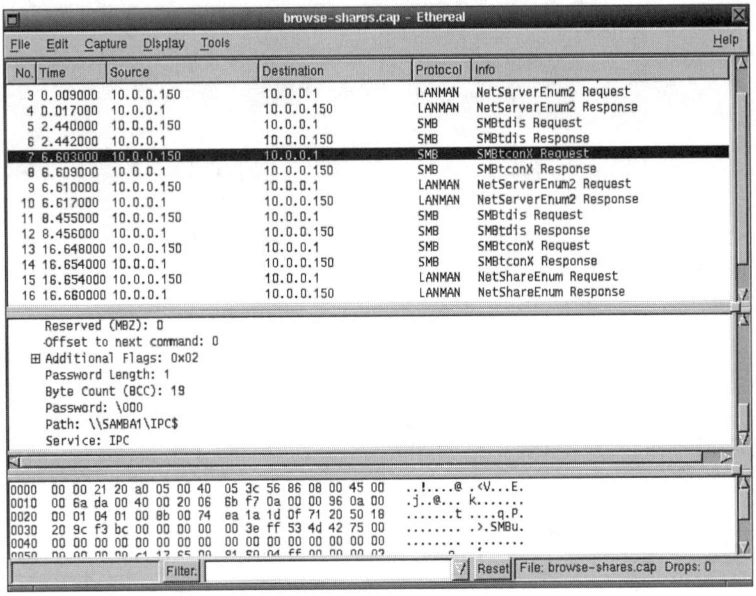

Figure 17.5
The client reconnects to the IPC$ share and issues a NetServerEnum2 request.

After the client has the browse list, you can browse individual servers by clicking on their icons. This causes the following steps to be performed (as shown in Figure 17.6):

1. The client issues a NetBIOS name lookup request for the name of the server the user chose. In this case there is a name lookup request for Samba1. These appear in frames 1 and 2 of Figure 17.6. If your client already has the server's NetBIOS name in its cache, this step will be omitted.

2. The client then connects to the Samba1 server, if not already connected, logs in, and connects to the IPC$ share, using a SMBsesssetupX request. This is shown in frames 3–11 in Figure 17.6. If your client already has a connection to the server, this step will be omitted, and a TCONX request to connect to the IPC$ share will be sent instead.

3. The client then issues a `NetShareEnum` request which elicits a `NetShareEnum` response from the server, as shown in frames 12 and 13 in Figure 17.6. The `NetShareEnum` response lists all the shares available on the server.

Figure 17.6
Your client sends these messages when browsing a server.

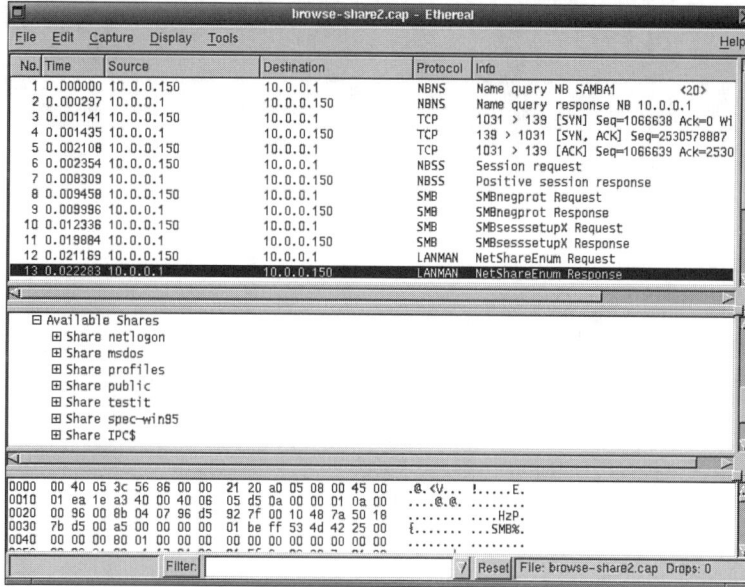

The following are points to note in the preceding:

- If any server returned in a browse list is not on the same subnet as the client, the client must be configured to use a WINS server.

- Because the client uses either a null account name and password or an account name that is likely to be invalid on the server, the Samba server must have a correctly configured guest account (the guest account must exist).

Failure to observe either of these can lead to browsing problems.

HOW BROWSE LISTS ARE COLLATED

How are the browse lists requested by clients built up over time? When a server starts, and periodically after that, it broadcasts a server announcement message. That is, these messages are sent to the broadcast address for the network. The server announcement message provides the name of the server and its type. Figure 17.7 shows an example of such broadcasts. Announcements are initially sent every minute, but this rate reduces over a period of time until it reaches a value of one every 12 minutes. Announcements are sent as NetBIOS broadcast datagrams to the workgroup name.

For example, the announcement shown in Figure 17.7 was sent to the NetBIOS name SAMBANET<1d>. This is the way the browse servers know what workgroup or domain each server is in.

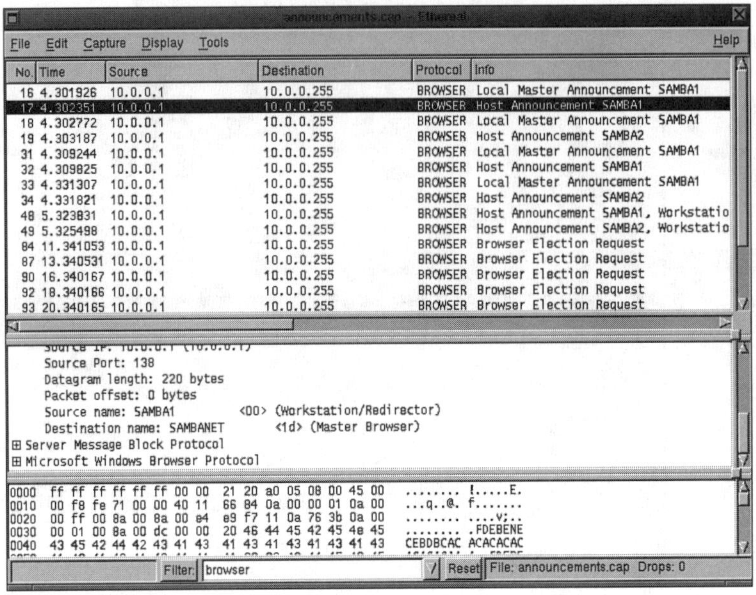

Figure 17.7
A server announces itself with an announcement message.

A server sends its announcements to the NetBIOS name of Domain<1d> (that is, Sambanet<1d>) and provides the following information:

- Server name—This name goes in the browse list and is what clients see when they retrieve the browse list.

- Update frequency—This is the time, in milliseconds, between announcements from the server.

- Major and minor version numbers—This is the version number of the browsing software on the server.

- Server type—This is a 32-bit field that provides information about the characteristics of the server. Table 17.1 lists the meanings of these bits.

- The election version of the server—This will be discussed later in relation to browser elections.

The master browser in each network collects these announcements and makes them available using backup browsers in each network. Several different types of browsers are in a network:

- Potential Browsers—A potential master browser is a server that can act as either a master browser or as a backup browser, but is not currently acting as either.

A potential browser must be prepared to become a backup browser if it receives a `BecomeBackup` request from the Master Browser (see Backup Browsers, following). It sets the `SV_TYPE_POTENTIAL_BROWSER` bit in all host announcements. It must also take part in elections for the master browser.

- Backup Browsers—Backup browsers are a subset of the potential browsers in a network. The master browser chooses them, and they periodically obtain the browse list from the master browser by sending a `NetServerEnum2` request to the master. A backup browser must answer `NetServerEnum2` queries from clients by providing them with the browse list.

    Backup browsers set the `SV_TYPE_BACKUP_BROWSER` bit in their host announcements, and listen to `LocalMasterAnnouncements` to determine the browser they should get the browse list from on their subnet.

    Backup browsers must take part in elections for the master browser and should initiate an election if they do not receive a response to their `NetServerEnum2` requests to the master browser.

- Master Browsers—There can be only one master browser in a subnet, unless the workgroup or domain spans multiple subnets, in which case there can be both a local master browser and a domain master browser. The master browser collates the browse list for the whole workgroup or domain by listening to `HostAnnouncements` and `DomainAnnouncements`, and responds to `NetServerEnum2` requests from backup browsers.

    The master browser sets the `SV_TYPE_MASTER_BROWSER` in its host announcements and chooses the set of backup browsers from the potential browsers. It sends a `BecomeBackup` request to each potential browser chosen to become a backup browser. It sends `LocalMasterAnnouncement` messages as well to ensure all browsers on the subnet know who the master browser is.

    If the workgroup or domain spans multiple subnets, the master browser also sends `MasterAnnouncement` messages to the Domain Master Browser (DMB), if it is not the DMB.

- Preferred Master Browsers—A preferred master browser is a potential browser with the following characteristics:
    - It must force an election upon startup.
    - It must participate in elections.
    - It must set the `PreferredMaster` bit in elections.
    - It should become a backup browser if it loses an election.

- Local Master Browsers—A local master browser is the master browser in each subnet. It is responsible for sending `DomainAnnouncements` for its domain. These announcements are sent to the NetBIOS name `<01><02>__MSBROWSE__<02><01>` and serve to let all other master browsers on the network know about the other domains and workgroups on the network.

PART
III

CH
17

- Domain Master Browser—If a workgroup or domain spans more than one subnet, a domain master browser is required to collate the browse lists from all the subnets.

  When a Windows NT domain controller is used, the PDC becomes the Domain Master Browser. It is also the Local Master Browser. However, under Samba, the LMB and DMB can be separate, as they are two separate pieces of functionality.

> **Note**
>
> You should avoid setting up a Samba server as a domain master browser if the domain already contains an NT PDC. An NT PDC must be the domain master browser, so if it finds another domain master browser in its domain, it demotes itself.

The DMB must set the `SV_TYPE_DOMAIN_MASTER` bit in its host announcements and must retrieve the browse lists from each subnet by periodically sending a `NetServerEnum2` request to the LMB on each subnet.

This complicated approach to collating browse lists is designed to prevent the browse server from being overwhelmed by browse requests (`NetServerEnum2` messages).

Clients do not send such messages to the LMB. Rather, they send `GetBackupList` requests to the LMB, and then they cache this information and send their requests for the browse list to backup servers chosen randomly from the backup list retrieved from the LMB.

Entries in the browse list are purged when the LMB does not receive a host announcement from that server after three times the announcement period in the last received host announcement. Because servers send host announcements once every 12 minutes (after they have been running for awhile), it may take up to 36 minutes before a server that is no longer operating is removed from the browse list.

BROWSER ELECTIONS

For browsing to operate correctly, a master browser (either Local Master Browser or Domain Master Browser) must be on a network. This is ensured by the Election protocol that browsers use.

Elections are initiated under a number of different circumstances:

- If a client does not receive a response to its `GetBackupList` requests, it initiates an election.
- If the master browser receives a `HostAnnouncement`, `LocalMasterAnnouncement`, or `DomainAnnouncement` from a server that claims to be the master browser for the workgroup they are both in, the master browser should demote itself and request an election.

- If a backup browser does not get a response to its periodic `NetServerEnum2` request, it should force an election.

- When a preferred master browser is started, it initiates an election. Thus, setting `preferred master = yes` in your `smb.conf` file will cause Samba to call an election when it starts up.

An election is initiated when a browser or a client sends an `ElectionRequest`. When a browser or potential browser receives an `ElectionRequest`, it checks to see whether it has won or lost this election in the following ways:

- If it has lost an election in the last few seconds, it loses this election.

- If its Election Version is greater than that in the `ElectionRequest`, it wins the election.

- If its Election Criteria are equal to that of the server or client requesting the election but it has been up longer, it wins the election.

- If its Election Criteria are equal to that of the requesting server, and it has been up the same amount of time, but its name is lexicographically lower, it wins the election. For example, Samba1 is lexicographically lower than Samba2.

- Otherwise, it loses the election and drops out of the process.

When a server wins an election, it issues another election request after a delay based on the following rules:

- The DMB and LMB delay for 100ms before sending an `ElectionRequest`.

- Backup browsers delay for a randomly chosen period between 200–600 ms.

- All other browsers delay for a randomly chosen period between 800–3,000 ms.

PART
III

CH
17

> **Note**
>
> Different sources of information from Microsoft give different values for the above delays. The draft Browser Protocol document referenced earlier provides the numbers I have given, while the Microsoft Windows NT Networking Guide from the Windows NT Resource Kit provides different numbers.

This causes a series of elections to occur, and any browser or potential browser that wins four elections in a row becomes the Master Browser and issues a `LocalMasterAnnouncement`. Potential and backup browsers use the `LocalMasterAnnouncement` to indicate who the local master browser is so they can keep their browse lists up-to-date using `NetServerEnum2` requests.

After the new `MasterBrowser` is elected, it sends out a `RequestAnnouncement` request to ensure it knows about all the servers in the network. Any server that receives a `RequestAnnouncement` request must respond with a `HostAnnouncement` within the next thirty seconds.

Figure 17.8 shows a trace of an election proceeding. The detail panel shows the Election Criteria for the system requesting the election.

The Election Criteria field in an `ElectionRequest` plays an important part in the election process. It is a 32-bit field and is made up of the following subfields:

- The first eight bits are the Election Desire Summary. It is a bit field that lists properties of the sending server. The possible values are shown in Table 17.2.

- The next 16 bits are the Election Revision. Samba sets this to 0x10F, as does Windows 2000 and Windows NT, while Windows 95 uses 0x415.

- The next eight bits are the Election OS Summary. This is also a bit field that lists the operating system types. The possible values are shown in Table 17.3. Table 17.4 shows the value used by various operating systems.

Figure 17.8
An election proceeds when a `RequestElection` request is sent.

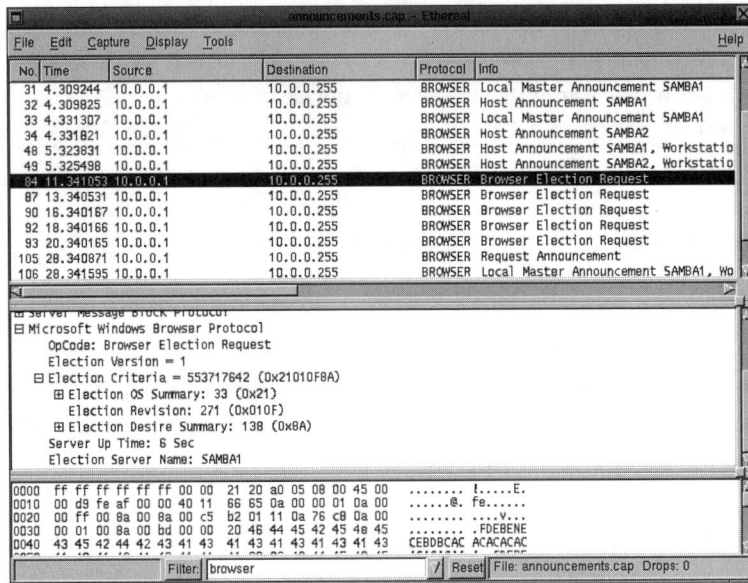

When an election occurs, the sender's election criteria are compared, as a 32-bit unsigned integer with the current server's election criteria. Figure 17.9 shows how the comparison is made. This means that the Election OS Summary is the most important part of the election criteria, and Samba gives you a direct way to control the OS Summary using its *os level* parameter.

TABLE 17.2 ELECTION DESIRE SUMMARY BITS

Bit Position	Meaning
0x01	Backup Browse Server
0x02	Potential Browse Server [This may be wrong]
0x04	Master Browse Server
0x08	Preferred Master Browse Server
0x10	Not Used

TABLE 17.2   CONTINUED

Bit Position	Meaning
0x20	WINS Client
0x40	Not Used
0x80	Primary Domain Controller/Windows NT Advanced Server

Figure 17.9
Samba compares the received election criteria with its own election criteria as an integer.

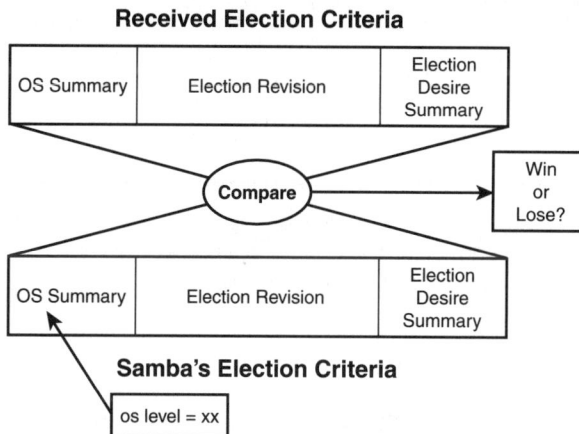

> **Note**
>
> The WINS Client bit is not documented in any of the documentation available on browsing, but NetMon reports it, as does Ethereal. I have verified that Windows NT Servers that are WINS clients set this bit, as well.

TABLE 17.3   ELECTION OS SUMMARY BITS

Bit Position	Meaning
0x01	Windows for Workgroups or Windows 9x
0x02	Not Used
0x04	Not Used
0x08	Not Used
0x10	Windows NT Workstation
0x20	Windows NT Server
0x40	Not Used

TABLE 17.4 ELECTION OS SUMMARY VALUES USED BY VARIOUS OPERATING SYSTEMS

OS	Value
Windows NT Server 3.51	32 (0x20)
Windows NT Server 4.0	32 (0x20)
Windows 2000 Server	32 (0x20)
Windows NT Workstation 3.51	16 (0x10)
Windows NT Workstation 4.0	16 (0x10)
Windows 2000 Professional	16 (0x10)
Windows 95 & Windows 98	1 (0x01)
Windows for Workgroups	1 (0x01)

Note

Some books on Samba erroneously claim that Windows NT Server 4.0 uses an Election OS Summary of 33. This is wrong.

SAMBA AND BROWSING THE LOCAL NETWORK

This section explores the Samba parameters that affect browsing in the local network. We build on the previous discussion about browsing in Microsoft Windows Networks.

Samba can function as

- A potential browser
- A backup browser
- A master browser
- A preferred master browser
- A local master browser
- A domain master browser

We will discuss setting up Samba as a Domain Master Browser further later.

If Samba is your only Windows file and print server, you will want to configure Samba to be a browse server. Enter the following set of entries in the global section of your `smb.conf` file:

```
os level =
local master = yes
preferred master = yes
```

The meaning of these parameters and all the other parameters that can affect browsing in the local network appears in the following section.

The following parameters affect browsing in the local network, and you can find them in Appendix A, "All Samba Parameters and Their Meanings":

```
announce as

announce version

auto services

browsable

browse list

comment

guest account

interfaces

lm announce

lm interval

load printers

local master

netbios alias

netbios name

os level

preferred master

server string

workgroup
```

SAMBA AND BROWSING THE WIDE AREA NETWORK

Browsing in wide area networks presents problems because many of the messages involved in browsing are sent to the broadcast address of a subnet. Routers generally do not route packets sent to broadcast addresses, and even if they did, the packets would be addressed to the wrong network. To overcome this problem, Samba can function as a Domain Master Browser (DMB), in the same way that Windows NT Server does. It also has several additional parameters that provide browsing support in wide area networks.

Figure 17.10 shows a network containing three subnets (Subnet 1, Subnet 2, and Subnet 3), each with its own Samba server (Samba1, Samba2, and Samba3). Each Samba server is the Local Master Browser in its subnet, but in each case, even if they are all in the same workgroup, users in each subnet cannot browse any of the servers in other subnets.

This is because the announcement messages sent by each Samba server cannot be seen in any other subnets. Thus, the browse lists collated by each Samba server will only contain the names of local servers.

Figure 17.10
Samba in a wide area network.

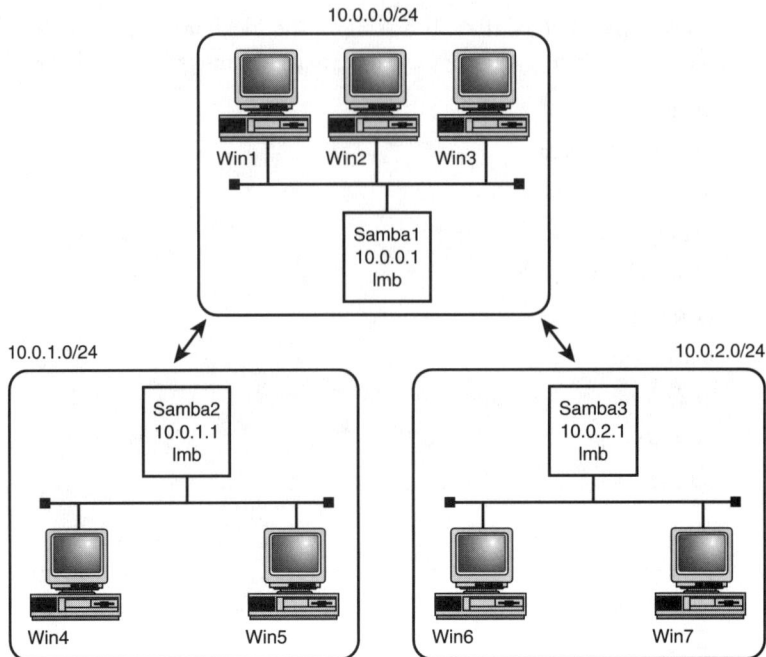

However, users can still access services on servers in other subnets, provided one of the following is true:

- The clients can translate server names for remote servers into IP addresses using DNS.
- The clients are configured to use a central WINS server, and all Samba servers are configured to register with this WINS server (which could be one of the Samba servers).
- The clients have the IP addresses for the remote servers in their LMHOSTS file.

Users could access services using the Map Network Drive dialog box or by using a DOS *net use* command. Unfortunately, these procedures do not allow clients to browse other subnets.

The solution to this problem is two-fold:

- Designate one of the Samba servers as a Domain Master Browser (DMB) by placing `domain master = yes` in the `[global]` section of the `smb.conf` file on that server. Only one Samba server in each domain or workgroup in your network should be configured as a DMB.

Note

Never configure a Samba server as the DMB in a domain if there is already a Windows NT PDC in that domain. The Windows NT PDC will refuse to function correctly, and your clients might be unable to log on to the domain.

This happens because a Windows NT PDC must be the domain master browser in its domain. If Samba registers the *DOMAIN*<1b> NetBIOS name associated with the domain master browser function, Windows NT is unable to do so, and it will not function as a PDC.

■ Make sure that all clients and servers use WINS. This ensures that all clients can actually translate the NetBIOS names returned in a browse list into IP addresses and that all local master browsers can find the domain master browser.

Of course, there must be a WINS server in the network. You can configure one of your Samba servers as the WINS server, but Samba can also use an NT server as a WINS server.

You can configure a Samba server as a WINS server by adding the following to the `[global]` section in its `smb.conf` file:

```
wins support = yes
```

You can configure a Samba server to use a WINS server by adding the following to the `[global]` section in its `smb.conf` file:

```
wins server = <IP of WINS server>
```

You should not use both the `wins support` and `wins server` parameters in your `smb.conf` file.

When a Samba server is configured as a domain master browser, it registers the NetBIOS unique name *DOMAIN*<1B>. When a local master browser detects that a domain master browser exists (by querying via WINS the NetBIOS name *DOMAIN*<1B>), it does two things:

1. Sends a `MasterAnnouncement` to the domain master browser. This informs the domain master browser of the presence of the local master browser.

2. Retrieves the domain master browser's browse list by sending it a `NetServerEnum2` request.

The `MasterAnnouncements` are sent once a minute initially, but after each announcement, this period is increased by one minute, until the announcement period is 12 minutes. When this value is reached, no further increases in the announcement period occur.

After a local master browser announces itself to a domain master browser, the domain master browser periodically retrieves the local master browser's browse list to keep its browse list up-to-date. With the domain master browser and the local master browsers operating in this way, the browse list is maintained across a wide area network.

In Figure 17.9, all Windows clients in each of the three subnets will be able to browse the three Samba servers: Samba1, Samba2, and Samba3. This happens because Samba1, configured as a domain master browser, registers the NetBIOS name *DOMAIN*<1B>, so Samba2 and Samba3 announce as local master browsers to Samba1. They also request Samba1's browse list. As a result of the `MasterAnnouncements` sent by Samba2 and Samba3, Samba1 also asks Samba2 and Samba3 for their browse lists.

Note

If any of the subnets in Figure 17.9 become unreachable from the others, users will see servers in the browse list that cannot be contacted. If the WINS server becomes unreachable from any subnet, browsing will fail in that subnet.

In addition, parameters like `remote announce` and `remote browse sync` enable users in remote subnets to become aware of more of the servers in each network. For these methods to work, your Windows client must be configured to use a single WINS server across the whole wide area network.

The parameters important to browsing in wide area networks are described in turn next.

Note

Only one Samba server in your network should be configured as a WINS server. All others should be configured as WINS clients. You can do this using the `wins server` parameter. If you already have an NT-based WINS server, do not configure any Samba servers as WINS servers.

The `remote announce` parameter is designed to be used in workgroups that are spread across subnets. It causes Samba to send host announcements to the remote server or network named in the parameter. The following shows an example of using this parameter:

`remote announce = 10.0.1.2`

This should result in the server at 10.0.1.2 adding the sending Samba server to its browse list.

The `remote browse sync` parameter is also designed to allow browsing to occur in a workgroup that is split across subnets. It sends a `MasterAnnouncement` to the servers specified, which causes them to retrieve the local Samba server's browse list. A Samba server will honor the `remote browse sync` parameter only if it is the local master browser on a network. The following shows an example of using this parameter:

`remote browse sync = 10.0.1.2`

The following parameters are important to browsing in a WAN, and you can find their full descriptions in Appendix A:

```
domain master

remote announce

remote browse sync

wins server

wins support

workgroup
```

BROWSING EXAMPLES

This section explores some browsing examples, both in local networks and wide area networks.

LOCAL SUBNET BROWSING

In a local area network, you can use the following global parameters:

```
workgroup = sambanet
```

This specifies the workgroup that the Samba server is in. All the clients need to be configured in the same workgroup.

```
netbios name = samba1
```

This specifies the NetBIOS name that the server advertises as. You only need this if you want your server to have a NetBIOS name different from the first component of its DNS name.

```
os level =
```

This specifies that your Samba server will win browser elections against all Windows-based browse servers. However, any Samba servers that are similarly configured will compete with this Samba server to be the local master browser.

PART

III

CH

17

> **Note**
>
> From Samba 2.0.6 and beyond, the default value for the `os level` parameter is 20. This means that Samba will take part in browsing, and unless there is an NT Server in the domain or workgroup, Samba will become the local master browser.

```
local master = yes
```

This parameter specifies that your Samba server should attempt to become the local master browser. This parameter is not strictly needed, as it is the default.

```
preferred master = yes
```

This parameter specifies that your Samba server should force an election when it starts up to ensure that it becomes the browse master.

I should note that the default values of some browser-related parameters changed in subtle ways in Samba 2.0.6 to allow browsing to work out-of-the-box. Versions prior to Samba 2.0.6 had default values that required modification for browsing to work. We will discuss the required changes here. Under Samba 2.0.5a and before, the default values for the parameters `os level`, `local master`, and `preferred master` were

```
os level =
local master = no
preferred master = no
```

These values ensure that Samba with an out-of-the-box configuration will not function as a local master browser. This means that a default configuration of a Samba 2.0.5a or earlier server does not support browsing. Clients who try to browse the network will get the message shown in Figure 17.11.

Figure 17.11
Unable to browse the network error message.

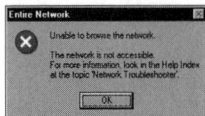

To configure a Samba 2.0.5a or earlier server for browsing, set these parameters as follows, and restart Samba:

```
os level =
local master = no
preferred master = yes
```

PREVENTING SAMBA FROM BECOMING INVOLVED IN BROWSING

In versions of Samba prior to 2.0.6, the default values of os level and preferred master were such that Samba would never win an election.

However, since Samba 2.0.6, os level defaults to a value of 20, while preferred master defaults to no. This means that Samba will not force an election on startup. It does mean that if an election is held, your Samba server will win over Windows NT Workstation and Windows 2000 Professional.

If you want to ensure that Samba does not take part in any elections, set the following parameters in the global section.

```
[global]
   ...
   os level =
   local master = no
   preferred master = no
```

Note These are the default values for versions of Samba prior to Samba 2.0.6.

WIDE AREA NETWORK BROWSING

There are three ways in which Samba can be configured for browsing in a wide area network, as discussed previously in the section "Samba and Browsing the Wide Area Network." In each case, your Samba servers must be configured to use WINS, as previously discussed.

In workgroups that span multiple subnets, you can use remote announce and remote browse sync parameters. For example, adding the following to the [global] section of your smb.conf file will cause your Samba server to announce itself to the server at 10.0.1.2:

```
remote announce = 10.0.1.2
```

As a result, your Samba server will appear on the browse list retrieved by clients in the 10.0.1.0/24 network.

Similarly, you can cause another Samba server to retrieve your Samba server's browse list. You do this by adding the `remote browse sync` parameter to the `[global]` section of your `smb.conf` file as shown the following:

```
remote browse sync = 10.0.1.2
```

Finally, you can configure one Samba server in your wide area network as a domain master browser. This will cause all your Samba servers to synchronize their browse lists as discussed previously in "Samba and Browsing the Wide Area Network." To configure a Samba server as a domain master browser, add the following to the `[global]` section of your `smb.conf` file:

```
domain master = yes
```

TOOLS FOR CHECKING BROWSING AND NETBIOS NAMES

You can use several simple tools to check browsing and to verify that browsing works. These are

- `nbtstat` under DOS—This command allows you to check out what NetBIOS names are registered using DOS.

  Use `nbtstat -a` *nbname* to check the NetBIOS names registered by *nbname*. An example appears in Figure 17.12.

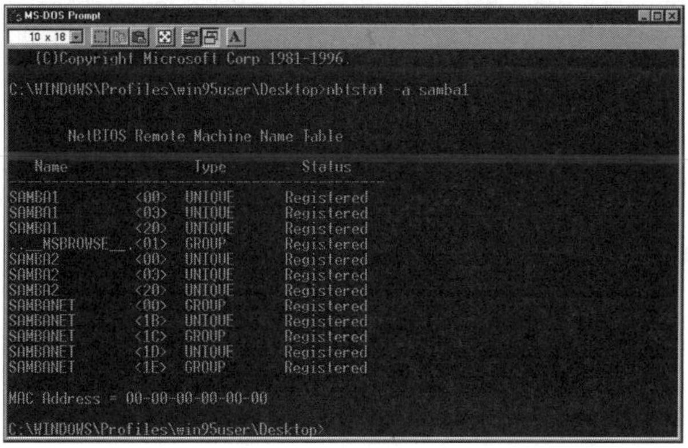

Figure 17.12
Using `nbtstat` from DOS.

- `nmblookup` under Linux/UNIX—This command is similar to the DOS `nbtstat` command and allows you to query NetBIOS names.

  Use `nmblookup -S` *nbname* to look up the status of *nbname*. An example appears in Listing 17.2.

> **LISTING 17.2 USING nmblookup FROM LINUX**
>
> ```
> [root@samba1 seus]# nmblookup -S sambanet
> querying sambanet on 10.0.0.255
> 10.0.0.1 sambanet<00>
> 10.0.0.150 sambanet<00>
> Looking up status of 10.0.0.1
> received 12 names
>     SAMBA1          <00> -          M <ACTIVE>
>     SAMBA1          <03> -          M <ACTIVE>
>     SAMBA1          <20> -          M <ACTIVE>
>     ..__MSBROWSE__. <01> - <GROUP>  M <ACTIVE>
>     SAMBA2          <00> -          M <ACTIVE>
>     SAMBA2          <03> -          M <ACTIVE>
>     SAMBA2          <20> -          M <ACTIVE>
>     SAMBANET        <00> - <GROUP>  M <ACTIVE>
>     SAMBANET        <1b> -          M <ACTIVE>
>     SAMBANET        <1c> - <GROUP>  M <ACTIVE>
>     SAMBANET        <1d> -          M <ACTIVE>
>     SAMBANET        <1e> - <GROUP>  M <ACTIVE>
> num_good_sends=0 num_good_receives=  0
> ```

COMMON PROBLEMS

Users encounter several common problems with browsing. We list some of them here.

UNABLE TO BROWSE THE NETWORK

You double-click on Network Neighborhood, and after a while, possibly after clicking on Entire Network, you see the dialog box shown in Figure 17.11, Unable to browse the network. There are several reasons why you might get this message:

- There is no master browser in your network, possibly because none has been configured, and your Windows 9X client is configured to never become a master browser.

  To rectify this problem, change local master to yes in your smb.conf and your Samba server will become a local master browser on next reboot.

- The broadcast address on your clients does not agree with the broadcast address on your server, so the server does not see requests from the clients. Again, your client will have to be configured not to become a master browser for this to occur.

  To rectify this problem, ensure that the broadcast addresses and netmasks agree on both systems.

- The guest account does not exist on the Samba server, or the guest account parameter is missing and the account nobody does not exist. This means that Samba cannot give the client access to the IPC$ share when it tries to browse.

  To rectify this problem, ensure that the guest account exists.

- nmbd or smbd is not running so the GetBackupList request goes unanswered, or the client cannot connect to the IPC$ share in order to perform a NetServerEnum2 request.

  To rectify this problem, that Samba is starting properly.

CAN'T SEE ANY SERVERS, OR CAN ONLY SEE YOUR OWN CLIENT

When you try to browse the network, you double-click on the Entire Network icon, and then on the icon for your workgroup or domain, but you see only your own client in the list. This problem can be caused by one of the following problems:

- Connectivity problems, such that the client is not seeing your Samba server's announcements, nor are GetBackupList requests getting to the server.

  To rectify this problem, use the troubleshooting procedure outlined in Chapter 5 to check these problems out.

- The server is in a different workgroup to your client.

  To rectify this problem, change the workgroup parameter in the smb.conf file on your Samba server and restart Samba.

CAN'T SEE REMOTE SERVERS IN BROWSE LISTS

You double-click on Network Neighborhood, and finally get a browse list, but you cannot see any of the servers that you know are in other subnets.

This problem is caused by not having a remote announce or remote browse sync parameter in your smb.conf file, or because you have not configured one of your Samba servers as a Domain Master Browser.

MORE INFORMATION

Check out these resources:

- http://technet.microsoft.com/cdonline/content/complete/windows/win95/technote/w95brows.htm
- BROWSING.txt in /usr/doc/samba-$version

FROM HERE...

You have reached the end of Part III. Part IV embarks on more advanced topics such as the following:

- Configuring Samba as a primary domain controller or a backup domain controller
- Configuring Samba to use LDAP for authentication and user accounts

PART **III**

CH **17**

- Obtaining the best performance from Samba
- Samba and other operating systems

Advanced Topics

## CHAPTER 18

SAMBA AND OTHER OPERATING SYSTEMS

In this chapter *by Richard Sharpe*

Samba runs predominantly on UNIX systems and the focus of this book is Samba on Linux; however, Samba has been ported to operating systems such as VMS, Coherant, AmigaOS, and others. In the same way that Samba makes an excellent tool for accessing files on Linux and UNIX systems from PCs, it can be used from these other operating systems to enable PC users to access their files on OpenVMS systems, MVS systems, and so on.

This chapter provides information about running Samba on the following operating systems:

- OpenVMS, including both VAX and Alpha processors
- MVS
- Stratus VOS

In each case, pointers to additional information are provided.

In most cases, the versions of Samba provided on these other operating systems lag behind the version that is current for Linux and UNIX. However, they still provide the basic functionality of file and print sharing.

> **Caution**
>
> Some of these versions are so out of date that you are not likely to find anyone who can help with them. The current documentation will be misleading because it will refer to parameters that do not exist for your version, and it will not document those parameters that have been removed.

SAMBA AND VMS

Although Compaq (formerly Digital) has had its own SMB server software for OpenVMS (formerly just VMS), ULTRIX, and Tru64 UNIX (formerly Digital UNIX), called PATHWORKS, for a considerable time, there are advantages to using Samba for file and print serving. This is especially so when Samba is already in use elsewhere in an organization.

Samba has been available for OpenVMS since 1995. The current version is Samba 2.0.3 for OpenVMS and is available in both source form and as binaries for OpenVMS Alpha and VAX. It was released in November 1999. The port was done and is maintained by Eckart Meyer, who says, "The Samba for VMS project started in 1995 with a 1.9.13 release, then there was a 1.9.16p11 and finally (end of 1998), a 1.9.17p4 release before the port was redone for Samba V2 [in late 1998]."

Samba for OpenVMS, like Samba for Linux, supports only NetBIOS over TCP/IP. This means that you will not be able to support clients that have only DECnet or NetBEUI, and you must convert your clients to TCP/IP. Samba for OpenVMS supports UCX (formerly The Ultrix Connection) for TCP/IP access to the network. It also supports UCX emulation as provided by the following packages:

- Multinet from Process Software (formerly TGV Multinet)

- TCPware from Process Software
- Pathway from Attachmate (formerly The Wollongong Group)

| Note | Unfortunately, because CMU/IP does not have UCX emulation, Samba for VMS does not support it. |

| Note | Pathway is no longer available as a product. |

The following general steps are involved in installing Samba for VMS:

1. Get the source and C Run Time Library from the Binary Packages area of one of the Samba mirrors. This step is actually optional because you do not need to rebuild from source. You can start at step 3 if you have no need for the source.
2. Compile the source, build executables, and skip to step 5.
3. Get the binary kit and C Run Time Library from the Binary Packages area of one of the mirrors.
4. Link the binaries to produce executables.
5. Install the executables in your preferred location.
6. Configure Samba to run on your system.

Each of these steps is discussed in turn.

GETTING THE SOURCE OR BINARY KITS FOR OPENVMS

To obtain the source or binary kits, point your browser at www.samba.org and select your local mirror. When you reach your local mirror, specify the path /samba/ftp/ Binary_Packages/vms/ in one of the following ways:

- http://au1.samba.org/samba/ftp/Binary_Packages/vms/ for Australia. Note that there are two mirrors for Australia: au1.samba.org and au2.samba.org.
- http://us1.samba.org/samba/ftp/Binary_Packages/vms for the United States. Note that there are three mirrors for the United States: us1.samba.org, us2.samba.org, and us3.samba.org.

When you have selected the correct location you will see a list of files like that shown in Figure 18.1. There are several files that you might want:

- samba-2_0_3-vms0-bin_alpha.zip—A ZIP file containing the binaries of Samba 2.0.3 for OpenVMS for Alpha.
- samba-2_0_3-vms0-bin_vax.zip—A ZIP file containing the binaries of Samba 2.0.3 for OpenVMS for VAX.

PART

IV

CH

18

- `samba-2_0_3-vms0.zip`—A ZIP file containing all the sources for Samba 2.0.3 for OpenVMS.

- `samba_crtl-020-bin_vax.zip`—A ZIP file containing the special C Run Time Library for Samba for the VAX architecture.

- `samba_crtl-021-bin_alpha.zip`—A ZIP file containing the special C Run Time Library for Samba for Alpha architecture.

- `unzipaxp.exe`—An unzip program for the Alpha architecture (formerly called Alpha AXP).

- `unzipvax.exe`—An unzip program for the VAX Architecture.

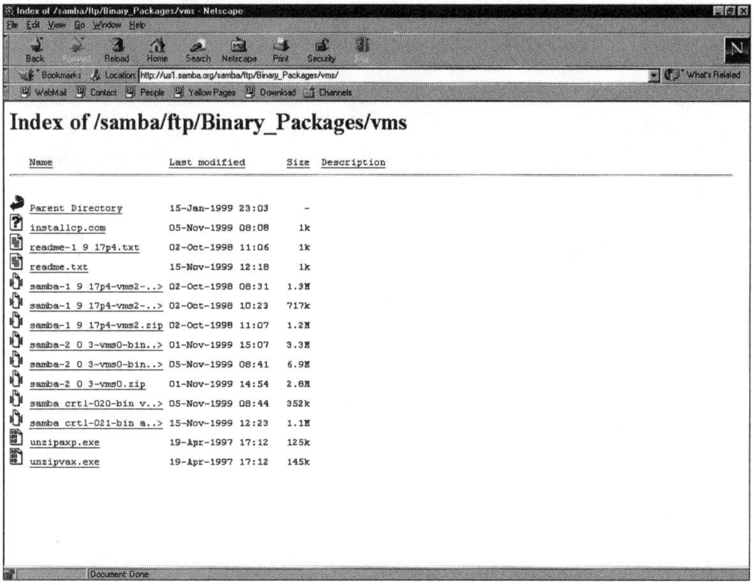

Figure 18.1
The files available for Samba for VMS.

The binary kits are not distributed as executable files; instead, they are distributed as object files that must be linked to be usable. In addition, this version of Samba for OpenVMS is distributed with its own C Run Time Library (RTL), which the Samba executables are linked against: They are not linked against the system C RTL shared image.

If you want to build from sources, you need the following files:

- `samba-2_0_3-vms0.zip`

- `samba_crtl-020-bin_vax.zip` if you have a VAX, or `samba_crtl-020-bin_alpha.zip` if you have an Alpha

- `unzipvax.exe` if you have a VAX, or `unzipaxp.exe` if you have an Alpha

If you want to start with a binary package and skip building from sources, you need the following files:

- `samba-2_0_3-vms0-bin_vax.zip` if you have a VAX, or
  `samba-2_0_3-vms0-bin_alpha.zip` if you have an Alpha

- `samba_crtl-020-bin_vax.zip` if you have a VAX, or `samba_crtl-020-bin_alpha.zip`
  if you have an Alpha

- `unzipvax.exe` if you have a VAX, or `unzipaxp.exe` if you have an Alpha

After you have downloaded the correct files, move on to the appropriate step.

BUILDING SAMBA FROM SOURCES

Before extracting source or object files from ZIP files, you must create a foreign command
called UNZIP. The following shows how to do this:

```
$UNZIP :== $<DEVICE>:[<DIRECTORY>]UNZIP.EXE
```

You will probably want to put this in your login command procedure
(SYS$LOGIN:LOGON.COM) for future use.

The first step in building Samba from sources is to extract the source. Follow these steps:

1. Change to a new directory or create a new directory:
    ```
    $ mkdir [.samba]
    $ cd [.samba]
    ```

2. Extract the source files:
    ```
    $ unzip [...]samba-2_0_3-vms0.zip
    ```

3. Extract the C RTL for your architecture:
    ```
    $ unzip [...]samba_crtl-020-bin_arch.zip
    ```

    where *arch* is replaced with vax or alpha depending on the architecture of your
    system.

4. Build the sources with
    ```
    $ @[.vms]build
    ```

You might be asked if you want to install Samba at this point. If you do, skip forward to the
"Installing Samba for OpenVMS" section. You should also read the file readme.vms that is
unpacked by the source distribution because it contains instructions on rebuilding Samba
using MMS or MMK. You use this procedure if you want to rebuild only part of the
distribution.

LINKING SAMBA FROM BINARIES FOR OPENVMS

If you have downloaded a binary kit, use the following instructions to produce executables
ready to run on your system:

1. Create a temporary directory and change to it:
    ```
    $ mkdir [.samba]
    $ cd [.samba]
    ```

2. Extract the binary distribution into it:

   ```
   $ unzip samba-2_0_3-vms0-bin_arch.zip
   ```

   where *arch* is replaced with vax or alpha depending on the architecture of your system.

3. Extract the C RTL for your architecture:

   ```
   $ unzip [...]samba_crtl-020-bin_arch.zip
   ```

   where *arch* is replaced with vax or alpha depending on the architecture of your system.

4. Link the objects and the RTL with the following command:

   ```
   $ @link
   ```

After you have linked Samba, the next step is to install it.

INSTALLING SAMBA FOR OPENVMS

To install Samba, tell the installation procedure where in the file system the Samba executables and other files should be installed. The installation script suggests SYS$SYSDEVICE:[SAMBA], but you can choose any location you like. A logical name called SAMBA_ROOT is created during the installation to allow you to access directories and files relating to Samba.

To install Samba under VMS, enter the following command, and then follow the prompts:

```
$ @install
```

Or, if you have built Samba from source, enter the following command:

```
$ @[.vms]install
```

When the installation procedure is complete, you can delete the source or binary tree.

CONFIGURING SAMBA FOR OPENVMS

After Samba is installed, you must configure it in the same way you would configure Samba under Linux or other versions of UNIX. That is, you edit the file SAMBA_ROOT:[LIB]SMB.CONF. You can edit this file with an ordinary text editor, such as edt.

> **Note**
>
> All directory and path specifications should be given using UNIX syntax. For example, use /dua0/my/directory/my.file rather than DUA0:[MY.DIRECTORY]MY.FILE.

You can use the same parameters as for Samba under Linux; however, some facilities are not implemented including encrypted password support and locking support.

RUNNING SAMBA FOR OPENVMS

When the Samba installation command procedure runs, it generates the Samba startup file SYS$STARTUP:SAMBA_STARTUP.COM. This command procedure is usually included in

SYS$MANAGER:SYSTARTUP_VMS.COM (or SYS$MANAGER:SYSTARTUP_V5.COM under older versions of VMS). This command procedure performs the following actions:

- Defines the logical name SAMBA_ROOT
- Starts the NMBD process
- Sets up SMBD as a UCX service
- Defines the logical name SAMBA_EXE to point to both the architecture-dependent directory and the common directory for Samba executables

Note

SMBD.EXE is linked against the system symbol table. If you ever upgrade your OpenVMS system, you should relink Samba. However, it is unlikely that the few symbols Samba uses will change.

You might want to define global symbols for the various commands that can be used, such as

```
$ SMBCL*IENT :== $SAMBA_EXE:SMBCLIENT
$ SMBST*ATUS :== $SAMBA_EXE:SMBSTATUS
$ NMBL*OOKUP :== $SAMBA_EXE:NMBLOOKUP
```

Table 18.1 shows several systemwide logical names that you can define to affect the behavior of Samba. These logical names should be defined in SYS$STARTUP:SAMBA_STARTUP.COM.

TABLE 18.1   LOGICAL NAMES CONTROLLING SMBD

Logical Name	Value and Definition
SAMBA_SWAP_FILE_TIMES	If defined, swap VMS Creation Time and VMS Modification Time when presenting them to the client.
SAMBA_ALTERNATE_DIRECTORY_PROTECTION	If present, ignore VMS directory protection policy and unconditionally use Samba-specific settings from SMB.CONF. This allows directories created with the Delete-bit set.
SAMBA_FILESPEC_ENCODE	Controls the encoding of filenames: 0 or CHECK—No encoding if EFS is present (ODS5) (not possible on VAX or VMS before V7.2; the default on Alpha) 1 or ALWAYS—Always use encoding (default on VAX) 2 or NEVER—Never use encoding (disks must be ODS5)
SAMBA_CASE_ENCODE	If present, case is encoded in the filespec so that it is preserved as seen by the client.
SAMBA_SMBD_OPTIONS	Options to any SMBD process (in UNIX format, so you must enclose them in double quotes).

RUNNING SAMBA FOR VMS WITH MULTINET

Samba for OpenVMS supports MultiNet V4.0 Rev A when operating in UCX emulation mode. To check for UCX emulation mode, use the following command:

```
$ SHOW LOGICAL/SYSTEM UCX$DEVICE
```

If this logical name is not defined, use the following steps to enable UCX emulation mode:

```
$ MULTINET CONFIGURE
NET-CONFIG> SET LOAD-UCX-DRIVER TRUE
NET-CONFIG> EXIT
```

Finally, reboot your system.

RUNNING SAMBA FOR VMS WITH TCPWARE

You must make no changes to run Samba for OpenVMS with TCPware because the various command procedures detect TCPware and make the appropriate configuration changes.

RUNNING SAMBA FOR VMS WITH PATHWAY

You must make no changes to run Samba for OpenVMS with Pathway because the various command procedures detect Pathway and make the appropriate configuration changes.

> **Note**
>
> Attachmate has discontinued Pathway.

SAMBA AND MVS

Samba has been ported to run on OS/390 UNIX System Services. This is an environment that runs under OS/390 that makes it possible to easily run UNIX applications under OS/390.

Mortice Kern Systems (www.mks.com) has ported several versions of Samba to OS/390, including 1.9.15plx and 1.9.18p1. The current version available is 1.9.18p1. The actual porting work was done by David J Fiander.

In the following sections we explore how to obtain Samba for MVS, how to install it, how to configure it, and how to run it.

OBTAINING SAMBA FOR MVS

Two ways to get Samba for MVS are

- Proceed to the FTP site ftp://ftp.mks.com/pub/s390/gnu/ and retrieve either the source or the binary distribution. Figure 18.2 shows the contents of the FTP site.

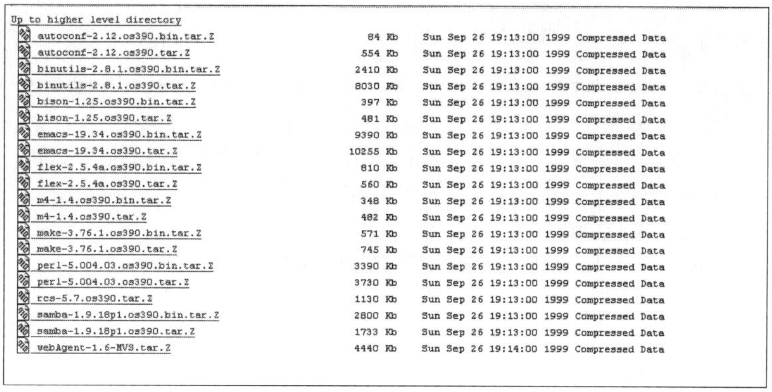

Figure 18.2
The MKS FTP site has both a binary and a source distribution of Samba for MVS.

```
Up to higher level directory
  autoconf-2.12.os390.bin.tar.Z              84 Kb   Sun Sep 26 19:13:00 1999 Compressed Data
  autoconf-2.12.os390.tar.Z                 554 Kb   Sun Sep 26 19:13:00 1999 Compressed Data
  binutils-2.8.1.os390.bin.tar.Z           2410 Kb   Sun Sep 26 19:13:00 1999 Compressed Data
  binutils-2.8.1.os390.tar.Z               8030 Kb   Sun Sep 26 19:13:00 1999 Compressed Data
  bison-1.25.os390.bin.tar.Z                397 Kb   Sun Sep 26 19:13:00 1999 Compressed Data
  bison-1.25.os390.tar.Z                    481 Kb   Sun Sep 26 19:13:00 1999 Compressed Data
  emacs-19.34.os390.bin.tar.Z              9390 Kb   Sun Sep 26 19:13:00 1999 Compressed Data
  emacs-19.34.os390.tar.Z                 10255 Kb   Sun Sep 26 19:13:00 1999 Compressed Data
  flex-2.5.4a.os390.bin.tar.Z               810 Kb   Sun Sep 26 19:13:00 1999 Compressed Data
  flex-2.5.4a.os390.tar.Z                   560 Kb   Sun Sep 26 19:13:00 1999 Compressed Data
  m4-1.4.os390.bin.tar.Z                    348 Kb   Sun Sep 26 19:13:00 1999 Compressed Data
  m4-1.4.os390.tar.Z                        482 Kb   Sun Sep 26 19:13:00 1999 Compressed Data
  make-3.76.1.os390.bin.tar.Z               571 Kb   Sun Sep 26 19:13:00 1999 Compressed Data
  make-3.76.1.os390.tar.Z                   745 Kb   Sun Sep 26 19:13:00 1999 Compressed Data
  perl-5.004.03.os390.bin.tar.Z            3390 Kb   Sun Sep 26 19:13:00 1999 Compressed Data
  perl-5.004.03.os390.tar.Z                3730 Kb   Sun Sep 26 19:13:00 1999 Compressed Data
  rcs-5.7.os390.tar.Z                      1130 Kb   Sun Sep 26 19:13:00 1999 Compressed Data
  samba-1.9.18p1.os390.bin.tar.Z           2800 Kb   Sun Sep 26 19:13:00 1999 Compressed Data
  samba-1.9.18p1.os390.tar.Z               1733 Kb   Sun Sep 26 19:13:00 1999 Compressed Data
  webAgent-1.6-MVS.tar.Z                   4440 Kb   Sun Sep 26 19:14:00 1999 Compressed Data
```

- Proceed to the MKS Download S390 OpenEdition GNU Utilities site and select the Samba link. You can go directly to http://www.mks.com/s390/gnu/register_samba.htm to fill out the download request form before downloading Samba for MVS.

In what follows, we will talk about the first method because it is the simpler method.

Two files at this FTP site are of interest to you:

- samba-1.9.18p1.os390.bin.tar.Z—The Samba for MVS binary kit, which contains the Samba binaries required for MVS.

- samba-1.9.18p1.os390.tar.Z—The Samba for MVS source kit, which contains the Samba sources for MVS.

Decide which file you want to retrieve, and download that file from the FTP site. The following might assist you in deciding which file to download:

1. If your main interest is simply to run Samba, then you are probably only interested in the binary kit: samba-1.9.18p1.os390.bin.tar.Z.

2. If you need to include support for features that are not in the binary kit or you want to fix bugs, then you will want to download the source kit and rebuild it.

Note

Much of the following material is excerpted from the README.OS390 that comes with Samba for MVS, or from Web sites that provide information on Samba for MVS. These Web sites are referenced in the "More Information" section at the end of this chapter.

BUILDING SAMBA FOR MVS

If you decide to download the source, you must build Samba before you can use it. Because Samba for MVS is based on Samba 1.9.18, it does not use configure scripts, which means you must edit the Makefile to build it for MVS.

The steps to take are as follows:

1. Change directory to the samba-1.9.18p1 directory and edit the file source/Makefile.

2. Make sure that the OS/390 section is uncommented, while sections for other operating systems are commented out. You should see the following in the Makefile (I have included some of the surrounding text so you can see where it fits in):

```
# see also README.jis
#####################################

# This is for OS/390
#
#
#
FLAGSM = -DOS390 -DFAST_SHARE_MODES
LIBSM =
AWK = awk
CC=c89

# This is for SUNOS 4. Use the SUNOS5 entry for Solaris 2.
# Note that you cannot use Suns "cc" compiler
# as it's not an Ansi-C compiler. Get gcc or acc.
# Note that if you have adjunct passwords you may need the GETPWANAM
```

> **Note**
>
> The only section that is uncommented is the OS390 section. This is important; otherwise, you will get errors during the compile.

3. Build Samba by issuing the following command:

```
make
```

If all has gone well in step 3, you will have a series of executable files that need installing. Consult the next section for information on installing Samba under OS/390.

> **Note**
>
> By default, Samba will be installed in the HFS directory /usr/local/samba. If you want to install it in another directory, change the BASEDIR variable in the Makefile and rebuild Samba.

INSTALLING SAMBA FOR MVS

The process of installing Samba for MVS will depend on whether you built Samba or downloaded the Samba for MVS binaries. If you built Samba from sources, enter the following command, which will copy all the required binaries to their final destination (usually the HFS directory /usr/local/samba):

```
make install
```

After you have installed Samba in this way, you will have to change the directory to the Samba library directory (`/usr/local/samba/lib` unless you have changed `BASEDIR`), and execute the following command:

```
mv codepages codepages.ASCII
```

If you downloaded the binary kit and want to install it, use the following instructions:

1. Ensure that the directory `/usr/local` exists, and create it if it doesn't.

2. Change the directory to `/usr/local` and extract the binary kit using

   ```
   uncompress samba-1.9.18p1.os390.bin.tar.Z
   cd /usr/local
   tar xvf /path/to/samba-bin/samba-1.9.18p1.os390.bin.tar
   ```

This code will extract the Samba binary directory into `/usr/local/samba`, and you should have the following directories available:

- `bin`—The Samba binaries are kept here.

- `docs`—The various documents that come with the source are put here. Note that this directory does not contain the full set of documents that is available with a Samba 2.0.x release.

- `lib`—Files such as `smb.conf` and `printcap` are kept here.

- `private`—Private files, such as the `smbpasswd` file, would be kept here.

- `var`—Log files and lock files are kept here.

You do not need to rename codepages if you installed from the binary kit because this file is restored as `codepages.ASCII`.

CONFIGURING SAMBA FOR MVS

Several steps must be performed before Samba for VMS can run. These include

1. Update `/etc/services` to include entries for the two ports that Samba uses. To do this, add the following to `/etc/services` (they can go at the end or in the correct numerical order):

   ```
   #
   # NetBIOS Services
   #
   netbios-ns    137/udp    # NetBIOS name service
   netbios-dg    138/udp    # NetBIOS datagram service
   netbios-ssn   139/tcp    # SMB file and print services
   ```

Note

We have added the `netbios-dg` service because you will need it in future versions of Samba if they ever are ported to MVS.

PART
IV

CH
18

2. Add a definition for localhost to the `/etc/hosts` file because the default distributed by IBM does not contain this definition. Add the following somewhere near the beginning of the file, but only if there is not already an entry for 127.0.0.1 in the hosts file:

    ```
    127.0.0.1    localhost
    ```

3. Ensure that the dataset `<DSN>.PROFILE.TCPIP` on your OS/390 system does not contain line numbers. It has been observed that when the dataset `PROFILE.TCPIP` contains line numbers, the `gethostname` routine returns names with trailing spaces in them.

4. Update `/etc/rc` to start up parts of Samba during system initialization. `nmbd` must be started up at system initialization time and `smbd` should be as well. Add the following to `/etc/rc` to start Samba:

    ```
    if [ -f /usr/local/samba/lib/smb.conf ]
    then
       _BPX_JOBNAME=NMBD /usr/local/samba/bin/nmbd -D
       _BPX_JOBNAME=SMBD /usr/local/samba/bin/smbd -D # optional
    fi
    ```

5. If you don't want to start `smbd` from `/etc/rc`, you must add the following line to `/etc/inetd.conf`:

    ```
    netbios-ssn stream tcp nowait BPXOINIT /usr/local/samba/bin/smbd smbd
    ```

6. If you have modified `/etc/inetd.conf`, you will need to restart `inetd`. You can do this in the following way:

    ```
    ps ef | grep inetd  # Look for the pid
    kill -HUP <PID>     # PID is the one found above
    ```

7. Your last step is to start the Samba daemons manually if you want to avoid an IPL of your OS/390 mainframe. Use the following commands to start Samba:

    ```
    /usr/local/samba/bin/nmbd -D
    /usr/local/samba/bin/smbd -D   # Optional ...
    ```

In addition, two new `smb.conf` parameters with Samba for MVS are

■ `translate map`—A global parameter that enables you to specify the type of certain files based on patterns on their names, for example:

```
translate map = *.o,binary
translate map = *.gz,binary
translate map = *.htm,text
```

Translate maps are checked in the order they are specified in the `smb.conf` file. They specify how files are to be treated; that is, that text conversions are to be applied to all files that match the format (for example, `*.htm` in the preceding example).

■ `text conv`—A per-share parameter that enables you to specify what sort of conversions should be performed. This parameter has the general format

```
text conv = [filetype,]{text|binary}
```

The default is binary, that is, no conversion is applied.

Running Samba for MVS

When running Samba under MVS, one important point to be aware of is that an `smbd` process will be created for each connected client PC. However, each process consumes an MVS address space, an expensive resource, and this `smbd` process will hang around for as long as the client remains connected, even if the client is doing nothing.

You can allow OS/390 to reclaim these idle address spaces by using the standard Samba parameter `dead time`. Implement this in the following way, which specifies that all clients that have been idle for nine hours should be disconnected:

```
[global]
...
   dead time = 540
```

This allows your system to reclaim idle address spaces overnight. You might use a smaller value if you want to reclaim idle address spaces quicker.

For more information about running Samba when RACF is in use on your OS/390 mainframe, see the `README.OS390` file that comes with the Samba distribution as well as the following URL: `http://www.s390.ibm.com/products/oe/bpxqa9.html`.

Samba for the Amiga

Several people have ported Samba to the Amiga. The current maintainer of Samba for the Amiga is Olaf Barthel. It works with several TCP/IP packages for the Amiga, including

- AmiTCP V4.x
- AmiTCP Genesis
- Miami and Miami Delux TCP products

Samba for the Amiga requires AmigaOS 2.04 or better and does not work with AmiTCP V3.x or INet-225.

The following sections explore how to obtain Samba for the Amiga, how to install Samba for the Amiga, how to configure Samba for the Amiga, and how to run Samba for the Amiga.

Obtaining Samba for the Amiga

You can obtain Samba for the Amiga from Aminet. Point your browser to `http://us.aminet.net/~aminet`, and then select Search tool for Aminet files. When the search page comes up, enter the word `Samba` into the keywords field and press Enter. This will result in a page that lists each file that matches your search. At the time of writing the file you want is `samba_2.0.6.lha`. You should download this file and extract the files from within it.

Note

When a new version of Samba is released, you will most likely find another version in the search results, `samba_2.0.7.lha`.

You can extract the files from the archive using the following commands (assuming that you downloaded the archive to `Work:samba_2.0.6.lha`):

```
MakeDir RAM:amiga_samba_2.0.6
CD RAM:amiga_samba_2.0.6
Lha x Work:samba_2.0.6.lha
```

Go on to the next step after you have extracted the archive.

> **Note**
>
> The Samba for Amiga archive that you downloaded contains instructions for installing Samba on the Amiga. These are kept in the file `install.amiga` that you will find in the directory just created.

INSTALLING SAMBA FOR THE AMIGA

The archive that you extracted in the previous step contains all the necessary binary files for Samba. To install them in the correct places, use the following commands:

```
MakeDir Work:Samba
Copy RAM:amiga_samba_2.0.0/install Work:Samba all clone
```

Next, you must modify your `S:User-Startup` file to ensure that the Samba binaries can be found on your system. You can do this by opening this file with Ed and adding the following two lines to the end of it:

```
Assign Samba: Work:Samba
Path Samba:bin add
```

Next, you must configure your TCP stack to know about Samba. If you use AmiTCP 4.x, the following instructions provide the information you need. If you use one of the other supported TCP stacks, you should consult the file `install.amiga` from the Samba for the Amiga archive for more information.

First, you must add four new services to the services file. You can do this by editing the file `AmiTCP:db/services` and adding the following lines to the end of that file:

```
netbios-ns 137/udp
netbios-dgm 138/udp
netbios-ssn 139/tcp
swat 901/tcp
```

Next, configure `inetd` to start up the appropriate programs when packets for Samba come in. You can do this by editing the file `AmiTCP:db/inetd.conf` and adding the following lines to the end of the file:

```
netbios-ssn stream tcp nowait root Samba:bin/smbd smbd
netbios-ns dgram udp wait root Samba:bin/nmbd nmbd
swat stream tcp nowait root Samba:bin/swat swat -a
```

Finally, you must add the pcguest account to the AmiTCP passwd file, `AmiTCP:db/passwd`. You can do this by editing the file `AmiTCP:db/passwd` and adding the following line to the end of the file:

```
pcguest||<ID>|100|PC Guest|SYS:|NewShell
```

In this case, `<ID>` should be a UID that does not already appear in the `passwd` file.

CONFIGURING SAMBA FOR THE AMIGA

After you have installed Samba for the Amiga, you must configure it. However, this uses the `smb.conf` file like any Samba installation and uses the same parameters as Samba for Linux does. To change your Samba configuration, simply edit `Work:Samba/lib/smb.conf` and modify the parameters as required. Parameters that you will probably want to change include

- `workgroup`
- `netbios name`
- `domain master`
- `local master`
- `os level`

The default `smb.conf` file is similar to that supplied with Samba for Linux but has been customized to work with Samba for the Amiga.

RUNNING SAMBA FOR THE AMIGA

There is nothing more to do except restart your Amiga. When you do that, the Samba daemons will start when the appropriate packets are received by your Amiga. In particular, `nmbd` will be started when the first UDP datagram on port 137 is received, and it will continue to run until you shut your Amiga down (or `nmbd` crashes). When requests come in for file accesses, `smbd` processes will start as required.

If you require `nmbd` to be started when your Amiga starts, you will need to make the following modifications:

1. Remove or comment out the entry for `nmbd` in the file `AmiTCP:db/inetd.conf`.
2. Make sure that your TCP/IP stack is being started up before you start `nmbd`. You will probably want to move the startup to the file `S:User-Startup`.
3. Add the following to your `S:User-Startup` file after the point where you start your TCP/IP stack:
   ```
   Run > NIL: Samba:bin/nmbd -D
   ```

SAMBA ON VOS

Samba is also available for Stratus' VOS operating system. Like the versions of Samba available for other non-UNIX operating systems, the VOS port is quite old, being a port of Samba 1.9.17p4. It is available in binary format for many versions of VOS at `ftp://ftp.stratus.com/pub/vos/network/`. See the documents `samba.txt` and `samba_p4a.txt` for more information.

MORE INFORMATION

For more information on Samba for VMS, see `http://ifn03.ifn.ing.tu-bs.de/ifn/sonst/samba-vms.html`.

For more information on OS/390 UNIX Services, see `http://www.s390.ibm.com/products/oe/`.

For more information on Samba on BeOS, see `http://www.beosbible.com/R4.5/experimental.html`

For more information on Samba on the Amiga, try the Amiga Samba mailing list at `rask-samba@kampsax.dtu.dk`. It also has a Web page at `http://www.kampsax.k-net.dk/~rask/Samba/mailinglist/`.

For more information on Samba on VOS, see `ftp://ftp.stratus.com/pub/vos/network/`.

FROM HERE...

In this chapter, we have looked at Samba on several different operating systems. The next few chapters look at substantially more important topics:

- Samba as a PDC and BDC, where you will learn about using Samba as a primary domain controller and a backup domain controller.

- Samba and LDAP, where you will learn about integrating Samba with LDAP.

- Samba and performance, where you will learn about some of the issues that affect Samba's performance.

- Samba and the enterprise, where you will learn about some of the issues of using Samba in the enterprise.

## CHAPTER 19

SAMBA AND WINDOWS NT DOMAINS

In this chapter

by Tim Potter

With the release of the Windows NT operating system, Microsoft introduced a new method of managing groups of workstations and servers by gathering them into groups called *domains*. Domains centralize authentication and administration of resources across a Windows NT network. Samba can participate in the domain security model either as a domain member or as a domain controller.

Domain controller support in Samba is currently considered experimental, and I do not recommend that you use it in mission-critical situations. However, this should not be seen as too discouraging because many people have reported success with using Samba in a domain controller role.

Caution

You can interrupt network operations on an existing Windows NT domain by misconfiguring Samba's domain controller capabilities. The authors accept no responsibility for any data loss or other damage that might be caused by this.

This chapter looks at the following topics about Samba and Windows NT domains:

- A brief introduction to the Microsoft Windows domain model with the roles and relationships between the different elements of domains.
- An overview of Samba's support for the Microsoft domain model, and how the different domain elements are implemented using Samba.
- Future directions for domain support in Samba.

THE MICROSOFT DOMAIN MODEL

Windows NT domains enable a Windows NT administrator to group workstations and servers under the authority of a domain controller. These groups of machines are typically ones that have some logical relation to each other, such as all the machines in a single office or all machines within a department that is part of a larger company.

Using domains to group related machines also allows them to be centrally administrated. An administrator can add, modify, and delete users and groups on one machine. Services on Windows NT machines can be administered and software installed remotely using domain administration tools. Domains are a definite improvement on using workgroups or peer-to-peer networking.

Security advantages to using domains instead of peer-to-peer networking for groups of Microsoft Windows machines are also evident. In the domain model, a central machine, the domain controller, performs all user logons and authentication. Typically, this machine is a Windows NT Server in a computer center or locked room that can be secured more easily than a group of workstations on users' desks.

Only a brief introduction to Microsoft Windows NT domains is given here. For more detailed information on administering Windows NT domains, consult the Microsoft training documentation for the Windows NT Server operating system.

DOMAIN STRUCTURES

The simplest way to implement a domain is to have all client machines under one domain with one domain controller. This structure is known as the *single domain structure* and appears in Figure 19.1. At present, this is the only domain structure supported by Samba.

Figure 19.1
A simple Microsoft Windows NT domain.

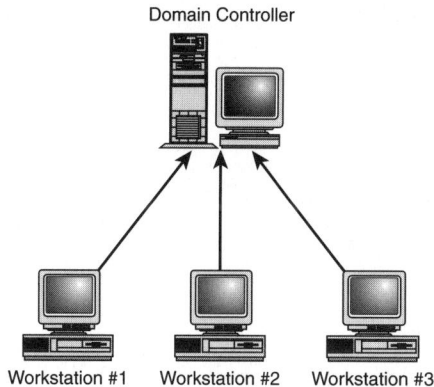

Domain Controller

Workstation #1   Workstation #2   Workstation #3

The disadvantage with arranging a domain in the single domain structure is one of scalability. As the number of domain members increases, the load on the domain controller increases, which can slow down user logins and file sharing over a busy network.

Microsoft recommends several other domain structures that can be used in an environment where there are many hundreds or thousands of machines under consideration. These structures are not particularly relevant to Samba but are included to complete the discussion on Windows NT domains:

- Single master domain—The single master domain structure consists of several single domains that all inherently "trust" a single other domain. Domain trust is a concept where two domains agree to consider users that have been validated in one domain to be valid in another.

- Multiple master domain—The multiple master domain structure differs from the single master domain structure in that there are multiple master domains that all trust each other.

- Complete trust—Under complete trust, all domains in an organization trust all other domains. This can lead to some interesting administrative situations because the number of interconnections between domains increases exponentially with the number of domains added.

The domain structures enumerated here cannot yet be created using Samba because Samba does not implement trust relationships between domains. Only the single domain model can be implemented with Samba.

DOMAIN ELEMENTS

So far in our discussion of domains, we have considered only two possible types of elements that construct a domain: domain members and domain controllers. These two types can be further subdivided into two other subtypes.

A computer participating in a Windows NT domain can have one of the following roles:

- Primary domain controller
- Backup domain controller
- Domain member
- Member server or standalone server

Each of these roles is described in detail next.

PRIMARY DOMAIN CONTROLLER

A *primary domain controller* (PDC) is typically a machine with the Microsoft Windows NT Server operating system installed. It is configured to act as the overseer of a domain and is responsible for several tasks within the domain. These include

- Authenticating user logons for users and workstations that are members of the domain.
- Replicating account information to backup domain controllers, described in more detail later, on the network. This replication process occurs at regular intervals, by default every three minutes.
- Acting as a centralized point for managing user account and group information for the domain. A user logged on as the domain administrator can add, remove, or modify account information on any machine that is part of the domain.

A PDC must be defined as such when Windows NT Server is installed and cannot be changed to a backup domain controller or standalone server without reinstalling the operating system. Only one PDC can be present for each domain.

Samba currently supports acting as a primary domain controller only in the development version. Limited PDC support exists in the Samba 2.0.x series of releases, and it has been put to use by a number of people. It is highly recommended that the Samba TNG version be used when PDC functionality is required. Chapter 24, "A Tour Through the Samba Source Code," contains instructions for obtaining the Samba TNG code.

Backup Domain Controller

A *backup domain controller* (BDC) is a Windows NT Server machine that can authenticate user logins in the event of the primary domain controller for the domain failing. If this event occurs, a backup domain controller machine will step in and authenticate user logins until the primary domain controller is restored. In a sensible network design, there is usually at least one BDC in each domain.

While the primary domain controller is down, no modifications can be made to the user account and group database. No user account or group information is lost except for changes that were not replicated from the PDC before it failed.

When the PDC for the domain comes up again, the BDC reverts from authenticating domain logons and hands this responsibility back to the PDC. If the PDC is unable to be restored, a BDC can be promoted to become the PDC for the domain.

Samba does not support backup domain controller functionality at this time, but this is slated for a future release. However, Samba TNG, an experimental version of Samba, contains this functionality. Chapter 24 contains instructions for obtaining the Samba TNG code.

Domain Member

A *domain member* is typically a machine with Windows NT Workstation installed and available for day-to-day use by users. Users on domain member machines can access network resources within the domain such as file and printer shares, as well as application servers. Domain members do not participate in authenticating user logins or replicating user account information.

The Samba 2.0.x series supports being a member of a domain.

Member Server and Standalone Servers

A member server is a Windows NT Server machine that is a member of the domain but is neither a primary domain controller nor a backup domain controller. A Windows NT Server that is not part of a domain is called a standalone server and is effectively a Windows NT Workstation.

Member servers can be used to offload functions such as file and printer sharing from the PDC. This reduces the load on the PDC and can improve login times for domain members. When members of the domain access shares on a member server, they are authenticated against a domain controller using pass-through authentication.

In Samba, no distinction is made between a domain member and a member server. Any server that is not part of a domain is a standalone server.

IMPLEMENTING A PDC WITH SAMBA

In this section, we will work through configuring Samba to act as a primary domain controller. Not all functions of a Windows NT Server primary domain controller are implemented, notably backup domain controller replication and remote administration functions. Samba will, however, process domain logons and manage roaming profiles, login scripts, and policies.

As an example, we will create a new domain called SAMBANET to which we will join a Windows NT Workstation machine called CLIENT2.

Note

PDC functionality requires a development version of Samba. All release versions, including version 2.0.6, support a Samba server acting as a PDC only in a very limited fashion. Chapter 24 contains information on how to obtain a development version of Samba.

CONFIGURING DOMAIN LOGINS

One feature of a primary domain controller is the capability to authenticate user logins from machines that are members of the domain. Setting the domain logons parameter to true and enabling logons for the Windows NT domain specified in the workgroup parameter, and setting a few other parameters does this.

Figure 19.2 contains a trace of a Windows NT Workstation logging on to the SAMBANET domain. The following steps occur when an NT Workstation logs on to a domain:

1. The NT Workstation broadcasts a NetLogon SAM LOGON request. This NetLogon request is sent to the NetBIOS name DOMAIN<1C>. This appears in frame 1 in Figure 19.2. If your domain uses WINS, your domain controllers will register the NetBIOS name DOMAIN<1C> with the WINS server as well, and a workstation will send a SAM LOGON request direct to the domain controllers as well.

2. The domain controller responds with the names of the servers that can support domain logons in the domain. This appears in frame 2 in Figure 19.2. Because there is only one domain controller in the SAMBANET domain, only the name \\SAMBA1 is returned.

3. The Windows NT Workstation then connects to the domain controller, if it does not already have a connection open, authenticates, and connects to the IPC$ share. Frames 3 and 4 in Figure 19.2 show this. Because the NT Workstation already has a connection in progress, we do not see any three-way handshake to create the connection.

4. The NT workstation then uses Microsoft's RPC functions over SMB to log on to the domain and retrieve profile information. This appears partially in frames 5 to 14. Because Ethereal does not presently understand MSRPCs, we cannot see the content of these in any meaningful way.

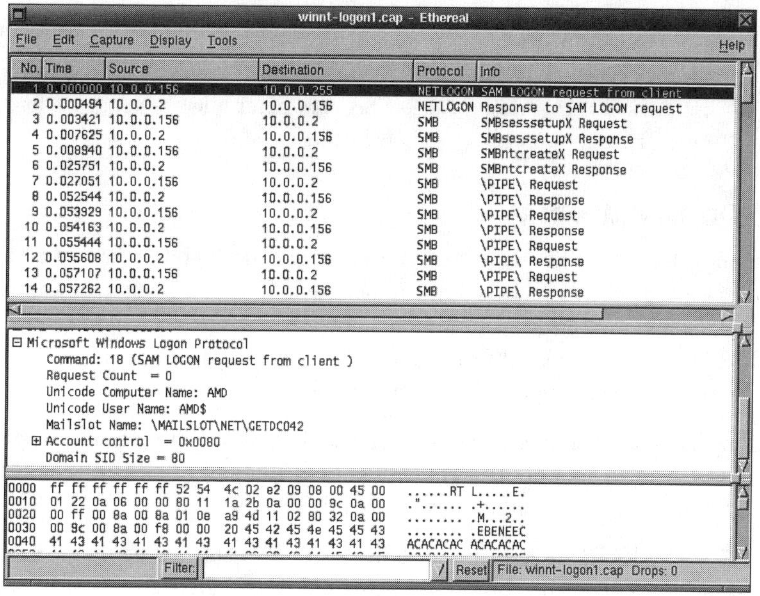

Figure 19.2
A Windows NT
Workstation
logs on to the
domain.

Listing 19.1 shows a sample smb.conf fragment that enables domain logons for the SAMBANET domain, as well as configuring some browsing parameters. These attempt to make the Samba server the local master browser as well as the domain master browser for the domain. Although this is not strictly necessary for correct operation of the Samba server, it will speed the collation of browse lists for the domain.

LISTING 19.1 smb.conf DIRECTIVES TO ENABLE DOMAIN LOGONS

```
[global]
        workgroup = SAMBANET
        domain logons = true
        encrypt passwords = true
        smb passwd file = /etc/smbpasswd
        domain master = true
        preferred master = true
        local master = true
```

→ For more information about Samba and browsing, **see** Chapter 17, "Samba and Browsing."

The following three parameters must be configured for Samba 2.0.x to function as a primary domain controller:

■   domain logons = true—This parameter must be set for Samba to function as a PDC. If this parameter is not set, Samba will not respond to the NetLogon requests, and workstations will not be able to log on to the domain.

- `encrypt passwords = true`—This parameter must be set for Samba to function as a PDC, because it will only use encrypted passwords in PDC mode.

- `smb passwd file = some-file`—This parameter must be set as well, to tell Samba where its encrypted passwords are kept.

ADDING DOMAIN MEMBERS

Having configured a Samba server to process domain logons, it would be useful to add some workstations to the domain as domain members. Users of the domain can log on to them and access resources in the domain. A domain member can be a Windows NT Server, a Windows NT Workstation, or a UNIX machine running Samba. Domains running on a heterogeneous network can have all types of domain members present.

Adding a domain member to a domain controlled by a Samba server is slightly different from adding a member to a domain controlled by a Windows NT Server. To add a domain member under Samba, three steps are required:

1. Add a UNIX user with the same NetBIOS name as the domain member but ending with a `$` character. For example, to add the machine called CLIENT1 to the domain, add a UNIX account named `client1$`. This account is known as a *workstation trust account* because the domain member machine uses it to authenticate itself to the PDC. The shell and home directory for the machine account can be set to `/bin/false` and `/dev/null`, respectively, because they are not actually used by Samba.

    For example, the `/etc/passwd` entry for the CLIENT1 machine would be

    `client1$:*:1234:5678:client1 trust account:/dev/null:/bin/false`

    Some versions of UNIX have an eight-character limit on the length of a username, so be careful naming client machines on these systems.

    Replace the user and group ID numbers, `1234` and `5678`, with values appropriate with any numbering scheme on your system. It is important that each workstation trust account has a unique user ID because Samba uses it to generate an NT security identifier for the machine.

Note

You can use the `useradd` command on many versions of UNIX and on Linux to add workstation trust accounts to the local password file. For example:

`useradd client$`

Note

User IDs for workstation trust accounts should not be reused when workstation trust accounts are added or deleted because the security identifier generated by Samba uses only the UNIX user ID to make it unique.

2. Add a machine entry to the smbpasswd file, which is usually located in the same directory as the smb.conf file. This file is the Samba equivalent of the UNIX /etc/ passwd file. To add a machine entry to the smbpasswd file, invoke the smbpasswd program as follows:

```
smbpasswd -a -m client1
```

Substitute the NetBIOS name of the machine to be added to the domain in the *client1* parameter. Note that the Samba daemons must be running for the smbpasswd program to execute properly.

Note

If the smbpasswd file does not exist, it must be created before machine or user accounts can be added using the smbpasswd program. This can be the case if Samba has been installed from source code rather than from a prepackaged binary distribution. To create an empty smbpasswd file, as root execute

```
touch /usr/local/samba/private/smbpasswd
```

assuming Samba has been installed in the /usr/local/samba directory.

If you are running Samba on a Linux distribution, you will want to use the following for most versions of Linux:

```
touch /etc/smbpasswd
```

3. Add the machine to the domain from the client side. Under Windows NT, this involves selecting the Network icon from the Control Panel and entering the name of the Samba domain as shown in Figure 19.3. The machine should now attempt to join the domain.

Figure 19.3
Adding a
Windows NT
machine as
a domain
member.

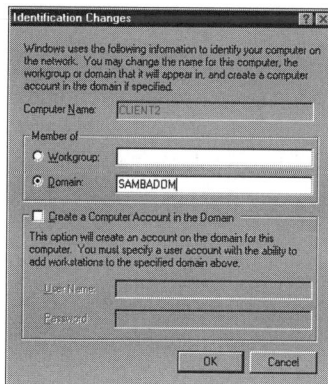

After clicking the OK button in the identification dialog, the Windows NT machine will join the domain and then will print out a message saying Welcome to the SAMBANET domain. The workstation must now be rebooted, and after it has been rebooted, will be able to log on to the domain. If your domain has a different name than SAMBANET, your domain name will appear in the welcome message.

> **Note**
>
> Note that when using a 2.0 version of Samba, the check box labeled Create a Computer Account in the Domain should not be checked because the machine account must be created using the `smbpasswd` program.

ADDING DOMAIN USERS

After Samba has been configured as a primary domain controller and workstations have been added to the domain as domain members, you must create some domain users. This step is necessary because initially there are no domain users on the Samba primary domain controller. Domain users must be created before users can log on to any Windows machines in the domain.

> **Note**
>
> Domain users are not the same as users on your NT Workstation, even though they might have the same name. A domain user account gives you rights to access services on the domain, whereas a local user account on your workstation only gives you the right to access services on your workstation.

To add domain users, follow these two steps. These are similar to the steps required to add a machine as a member of the domain.

1. Create a UNIX account on the Samba server with the name of the domain user to add. Like the machine accounts used in adding members to the domain, the home directory and shell are not used. Samba only requires a valid user and group ID number for each domain user.

2. Create an entry in the `smbpasswd` file using the `smbpasswd` program. This is done using the `-a` flag and the name of the user to add. Listing 19.2 shows the output from the `smbpasswd` program for a Samba administrator adding two domain users named alice and bob.

LISTING 19.2   ADDING DOMAIN USERS WITH THE `smbpasswd` PROGRAM

```
# smbpasswd -a alice
New SMB password:
Retype new SMB password:     .
Password changed for user alice
# smbpasswd -a bob
New SMB password:
Retype new SMB password:
Password changed for user bob
```

> **Note**
>
> The Samba daemons must be running for the `smbpasswd` program to add domain users successfully.

Users should now be able to log on from any Windows NT Workstation machines that have been added as domain members. You can now use the `smbclient` program to test domain logons for user accounts.

MAPPING UNIX USERS AND GROUPS

Samba has a few parameters that can be used in `smb.conf` to map UNIX users and groups on the Samba server to NT users and groups on client machines:

- `domain group map`—This enables a Samba administrator to map UNIX groups on the Samba PDC to NT domain groups on domain client machines.
- `domain user map`—Individual UNIX users can be mapped to NT domain users using this parameter.
- `local group map`—UNIX groups on the Samba PDC can be mapped to local NT groups with this parameter.

The format of the file references in the preceding configuration parameters are similar to the `username map` parameter used to map UNIX usernames to NT usernames described in Chapter 6, "File Sharing Under Samba."

- Lines starting with a # or a ; character are considered comments and are ignored.
- Each line specifies a UNIX group or username, and either a tab character or a = character, followed by an NT group or username.
- Domain names or NT group names containing space characters should be enclosed in double quotes.
- Groups from other domains can be specified by the remote domain name followed by a backslash and then the group name.

ADDING DOMAIN ADMINISTRATORS

Having added domain user accounts to the Samba controlled domain, it is useful to have accounts with domain and local administrator access. This is useful for performing system administration tasks on the client machines such as installing new software or starting and stopping services.

We can use the `domain group map` and `domain user map` parameters to give users domain Administrator access. But before this can occur, we need to tell Samba about our user and group mappings by adding some lines to the `[global]` section of the `smb.conf` file:

```
[global]
    domain user map = /usr/local/samba/lib/domainuser.map
    domain group map = /usr/local/samba/lib/domaingroup.map
```

These lines tell Samba to look in two files contained in the `/usr/local/samba/lib` directory to determine domain user and group mappings.

To map between the UNIX user root and the NT domain administrator, add the following line to the `domain user map` file:

```
root=Administrator
```

If we add the following line to the `domain group map` file, we can then have the members of the UNIX `adm` group appear to be members of the NT `Domain Admins` group:

```
adm="Domain Admins"
```

This technique is not limited to using Administrator accounts and groups but can be used to map any UNIX group to any NT group within the domain.

> **Note**
>
> If Samba is acting as a PDC for a Windows NT domain, the User Manager for Domains application cannot be used to add or modify account details on the PDC. This is a limitation of the current version of Samba.

CONFIGURING ROAMING PROFILES

Roaming profiles store user preferences, desktop settings, and any desktop files in a central location. This location is usually a file share on the primary domain controller, although it can be any SMB file server on the network. When a domain user logs on to a workstation in the domain, a copy of the user's profile is created and stored on the workstation. Upon logout, the profile is copied back to the server. This has the effect of the profile following the user around, or roaming, to all workstations the user logs on to.

Roaming profiles are enabled using the `logon path` parameter in the `smb.conf` file. Listing 19.3 gives a setting for `logon path` that points at a file share called `profiles` on the Samba server. All profile information will be saved under the directory named `/usr/local/samba/profiles`. This file share should be configured as per the listing to ensure that only that particular user can access his user profile.

LISTING 19.3 SAMPLE CONFIGURATION FOR ROAMING PROFILES

```
[global]
    logon path = \\%L\profiles\%U

[profiles]
    comment = Roaming profiles share
    path = /usr/local/samba/profiles
    read only = false
    create mask = 0600
    directory mask = 0700
    browseable = false
    guest ok = false
```

The roaming profiles directory, `/usr/local/samba/profiles` in Listing 19.3, must be writeable by all users in order for roaming profiles to be created. Ensure that this directory exists and is writeable by all users for profiles to operate correctly.

To disable roaming profiles for all users, set the logon path to be either an empty string or to point at the local `profiles` directory like this:

`logon path = %systemroot%\profiles\%U`

User profiles will now be stored on the local machine rather than be copied to the directory specified in the `logon path` parameter. Disabling roaming profiles is sometimes useful for slow network links or laptop machines.

> **Note**
>
> As discussed in Chapter 11, "Samba as a Logon and Profiles Server," `logon path` is used to specify the profile's location for Windows NT clients, whereas `logon home` is used for Windows 9x clients.
>
> In addition, although it is possible to place users' profiles in their home directories, Windows NT clients can get confused because they seem to maintain connections to the home share across multiple user logins.

CONFIGURING LOGIN SCRIPTS AND POLICIES

Windows NT provides user home directories and enables scripts to execute when users log in. This is usually configured using the User Manager for Domains application. It is often useful for these files to reside on a server machine such as the primary domain controller. Samba enables user home directories and login scripts to be set using the `logon home`, `logon drive`, and `logon script` parameters in the `smb.conf` file.

Listing 19.4 gives some configuration, which when added to the `smb.conf` file enables user home directories, logon scripts, and policies to be implemented by the Samba administrator.

LISTING 19.4 SAMPLE CONFIGURATION FOR USER LOGIN SCRIPTS AND HOME DIRECTORIES

```
[global]
    logon home = \\%L\%U
    logon drive = H:
    logon script = %U.bat

[netlogon]
    path = /usr/local/samba/netlogon
    writeable = false
    guest ok = false
    browseable = false
```

Note

In more complicated environments where NIS is in use, the use of %L in Listings 19.3 and 19.4 might not be appropriate. You can use %N in this case, which is the user's NIS home directory server.

HOME DIRECTORIES

A home directory for each user is specified using the logon home parameter. In Listing 19.4, logon home points to a file share on the Samba PDC with the same name as the user logging on. This corresponds to the UNIX home directory share created using the [homes] section of the smb.conf file.

If the client is a Windows NT machine, the logon home directory given by the logon home parameter will be automatically mapped to the drive given by logon drive.

LOGON SCRIPTS

The logon script parameter in Listing 19.4 specifies a logon script that executes when a user logs on. This points to an MS-DOS batch file that is called the same name as the user who is logging on.

Logon scripts are stored in a file share on the PDC called [netlogon]. The permissions on the [netlogon] share should prevent users from changing any file on it. It should also be secure from non-domain users connecting to it; hence, the settings of the writeable and guest ok parameters.

Any logon script that will be executed on a Windows machine must be in DOS text file format. That is, each line must be terminated by a carriage return followed by a linefeed character. Under UNIX, unless you are sure the text editor you use can save files in DOS text file format, it is often easier to create or edit login scripts using a Windows editor such as NOTEPAD.EXE.

POLICIES

The [netlogon] share also stores system policy information. *System policies* are a method of forcing desktop settings or configurations for Windows machines, users, and groups that are part of a Windows domain. Policies are a useful way to secure a machine that can be in a public access situation.

A large number of options can be set using policies for many different situations. Consult the Microsoft Windows training documentation for suggested implementation techniques and information on system policies.

You can create Windows NT policies using the System Policy Editor application. To implement policies for Windows NT client machines, save the policy created using the policy editor as a file called NTCONFIG.POL in the [netlogon] share. A Windows NT domain member client machine will access this file and use the information contained in it.

For Windows 95/98 machines, policies must be created using the POLEDIT.EXE application found on the Windows 95/98 installation CD-ROM. To implement policies on Windows 95/98 client machines, the policy should be saved as a file named CONFIG.POL on the [netlogon] share, and this will then be used by Windows 95/98 client machines on the domain.

> **Note**
>
> You must use the Microsoft tools to create policies because Samba does not understand how to create the NTCONFIG.POL and CONFIG.POL files.

CONFIGURATION PARAMETERS USED IN PDC SUPPORT

The following is an overview of the smb.conf parameters used to implement a primary domain controller under Samba.

> **Note**
>
> Samba administrators familiar with PDC support in previous versions of Samba might be aware of the domain admin group and domain admin users parameters. These parameters have been deprecated in more recent versions of Samba and should no longer be used.

Don't forget when using development versions of Samba to consult the documentation for that version. The installed manual pages and documentation can refer to the 2.0 release version of Samba, which might not describe domain controller parameters accurately.

All parameters are global parameters unless otherwise mentioned.

domain logons

Type: Boolean

Description: If Samba is acting as a primary domain controller, this parameter determines whether Samba authenticates logons for Windows NT clients. If domain controller support is not being used, domain logons determines whether Samba enables Windows 95/98 domain logons. These are not the same as Windows NT domain logons. See Chapter 12, "Accessing Samba from Windows for Workgroups and Windows 9x," for more discussion on this.

Default: false

time server

Type: String

Description: Windows client machines can synchronize their clocks from a Samba server if this parameter is enabled. Time can be updated by typing net time \\server /set /yes where *server* is the NetBIOS name of a Samba server. Primary domain controllers are typically also time servers for client machines in the domain.

Default: The default for this parameter is `false`. Samba will not advertise itself as a time server

logon path

Type: String

Description: The `logon path` points to the directory where roaming profiles for Windows 95/98 and Windows NT are stored. The default value for this parameter assumes a file share named `[profile]` is present on the Samba server, so this must be created for roaming profiles to operate correctly.

Default: The default is `\\%N\%U\profile`, where the `%N` expands to the NetBIOS name of the server, or name of the NIS directory server if NIS support is enabled. The `%U` macro expands to the username of the user connecting.

logon home

Type: String

Description: `logon home` specifies a home directory for the user when a Windows 95/98 user logs in or a Windows NT user logs in to a Samba PDC. This parameter is useful only if Samba is configured to serve domain logons using the `domain logons` parameter.

The home directory is used as the default location for opening or saving files in Windows applications, as well as being the default directory when running an MS-DOS command prompt.

Default: The default is `\\%N\%U`, which corresponds to a file share on the NIS or Samba server with the same name as the user connecting.

logon drive

Type: String

Description: The value of the home directory specified with `logon home` can be assigned a drive letter using this parameter. This drive is automatically mapped to point to the logon home directory when the user logs on. The value of the parameter should be in the format *drive:*, where *drive* is the drive letter to be mapped.

Default: An empty string; by default, no drive letter is mapped to the user's home directory.

logon script

Type: String

Description: The `logon script` specifies a batch (`.BAT`) or command (`.CMD`) file that is executed after a user logs in. The script is executed from a file share called `[netlogon]` on the Samba server, which must be explicitly created. This parameter is useful only if Samba is configured as a logon server using the `domain logons` parameter.

Note   Each line in the logon script must be terminated in DOS format with a carriage return followed by a linefeed.

Default: An empty string; no logon script is executed.

domain group map

Type: String

Description: The `domain group map` parameter points to a file that defines the mapping between UNIX group names and Windows NT group names. UNIX users that are members of the UNIX group appear as members of the Windows NT group. The domain group map file is in a similar format to the `username map` parameter described in Chapter 6.

All UNIX groups on the Samba server are exported as NT groups. There is currently no way to disable all these groups from being exported.

Default: Empty; no domain group mapping is performed.

domain user map

Type: String

Description: This parameter specifies a filename that defines mappings between UNIX users and NT domain users. The file has the same format as the `domain group map` file.

Default: By default, no domain user mapping is performed.

local group map

Type: String

Description: The file specified in this parameter enables UNIX group to NT local group mappings to be performed. The format of the file is the same as the `domain group map` and `domain user map` files.

Default: By default, no local group mapping is performed.

encrypt passwords

Type: Boolean

Description: This global parameter specifies whether SMB encrypted passwords are being used between your Samba server and its clients. It must be set to `true` or `yes` for PDC mode to work.

Default: By default, the value of this parameter is `false` or `no`.

PART

IV

CH

19

`smb passwd file`

Type: String

Description: This global parameter specifies the location of the NT password hashes that Samba uses when using encrypted passwords.

Default: The default for this parameter depends on how you have installed Samba. Under Linux it is usually `/etc/smbpasswd`, whereas under most versions of UNIX it is set to `/usr/local/samba/private/smbpasswd`.

IMPLEMENTING A BDC WITH SAMBA

One main feature of a backup domain controller is the replication of domain user account and group information from the primary domain controller. At the time of writing, this replication function is not supported using the current stable version of Samba but works in Samba TNG, an experimental version of Samba. Chapter 24 contains instructions for obtaining the Samba TNG code.

Backup domain controller support is planned for the 3.0.x releases of Samba.

IMPLEMENTING A DOMAIN MEMBER WITH SAMBA

We now look at making a Samba server a member of a Windows NT domain. In this example, the domain controller is a machine running Windows NT server, although it could quite easily be a machine running Samba as a PDC as described earlier in this chapter.

METHOD

You must take several steps to add a Samba server to a Windows NT domain:

1. A workstation trust account for the soon-to-be domain member must be created on the PDC machine.
2. The Samba server must run the `smbpasswd` program to join the domain.
3. The `smb.conf` file must be updated to reflect the server's new state as a domain member.

These steps are described in the following section. As an example, we will describe the Samba server CLIENT1 joining the Windows domain called NTDOM. A Windows NT Server called SERVER1 administers this domain.

CREATING A WORKSTATION TRUST ACCOUNT

The first step in becoming a domain member is to create a workstation trust account for the Samba server on the Windows NT server. This is done using the Server Manager application. Workstation trust accounts are sometimes referred to as machine accounts.

Start the Server Manager application by selecting it from the Administrative Tools (Common) menu on the Programs menu. This must be done as Administrator or a user that is a member of the Domain Administrators group. Add the Samba machine to the domain by selecting the Add to Domain option from the Computer menu. Enter the NetBIOS name of the Samba machine as a type of Windows NT Workstation or Server, click the Add button, and then click the Close button. This appears in Figure 19.4.

Note that during the time that this operation is performed, and when the client machine joins the domain, it is possible for a different client machine of the same name to join the domain. This is a known security risk in Windows NT.

Figure 19.4
Using Server
Manager to
add a machine
to the domain.

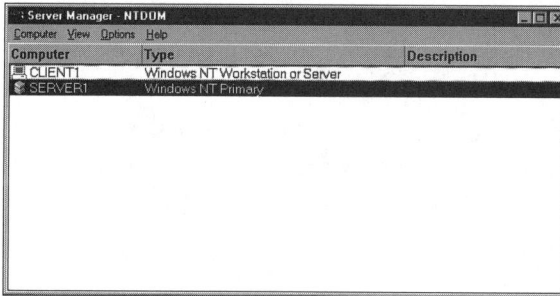

An entry for the Samba machine appears in the Server Manager window, but it will be grayed out because at this stage the machine has not joined the domain.

JOINING THE DOMAIN

The second step is to use the `smbpasswd` program to add the Samba server to the domain. To do this, ensure the Samba daemon programs `smbd` and `nmbd` are not running, and then execute the `smbpasswd` program in this form:

```
smbpasswd -j domain -r servername
```

The *domain* parameter should be replaced with the name of the domain the Samba server is to join. The *servername* parameter should contain the NetBIOS name of the PDC that controls the domain. Listing 19.5 shows the output produced when running `smbpasswd` for the CLIENT1 machine running Samba.

LISTING 19.5 JOINING AN NT DOMAIN USING THE smbpasswd PROGRAM

```
client1# smbpasswd -j NTDOM -r SERVER1
1999/11/26 20:42:53 : change_trust_account_password: Changed password
for domain NTDOM.
Joined domain NTDOM.
```

The message `smbpasswd: Joined domain NTDOM` indicates that the Samba machine joined the Windows NT domain successfully. The following are some error messages that can be produced if the `smbpasswd` operation was not successful:

- modify_trust_password: unable to set up the PDC credentials to machine *servername*. Error was: NT_STATUS_NO_TRUST_SAM_ACCOUNT—The machine account for the Samba server was not found. Check that the machine account was created properly with Server Manager application and that the domain name specified with the -j option was correct.

- modify_trust_password: Can't resolve address for *servername*—The PDC specified by the name *servername* could not be located. Check that it is spelled correctly and available on the network.

UPDATING smb.conf

Before the Samba daemons are restarted, the smb.conf file must be updated to reflect Samba's new role as a member of a Windows NT domain.

Add or modify the appropriate configuration parameters in the smb.conf file as shown in the following code. Note that the value of the security and encrypt passwords parameters are different from their defaults and most probably the existing values in smb.conf.

```
[global]
    workgroup = NTDOM
    security = domain
    password server = server1
    encrypt passwords = true
```

To finish the process, use the testparm program to check for errors in the smb.conf file, and restart the Samba daemon programs. The Samba server should now be a member of the Windows NT domain.

Having joined the domain, the Samba server is now fully visible in the Server Manager application. Double-click on the line containing the entry for the Samba server to browse the status of the machine. Some of the status buttons for the Samba server are available and return dummy information, and others produce an RPC error dialog box. These correspond to status functions that have not yet been implemented in Samba.

CONFIGURATION PARAMETERS

The following is an overview of the configuration parameters used to implement domain membership in Samba. All parameters are global parameters unless otherwise specified.

workgroup

Type: String

Description: When used in a domain member context, the workgroup parameter specifies the domain name of which the Samba server is a member.

Default: The default is the domain named WORKGROUP.

password server

Type: String

Description: This parameter defines the NetBIOS name of the machine with which to perform username authentication and validation. When the Samba server is acting as a domain member, the `password server` should point to the name of the PDC for the domain.

You can specify multiple names by separating them with commas. These servers are queried in turn to authenticate the user if the previous server does not reply.

Starting with Samba version 2.0.6, the password server can be the string *, which tells Samba to browse the network and determine the NetBIOS name of the PDC for the domain.

Default: An empty string; all password validation is done on the Samba server machine.

security

Type: String

Description: When using Samba in a domain member role, this parameter must be set to the string `domain`. Other settings for the `security` parameter appear in Chapter 5, "Configuring and Managing Samba."

Default: The default setting is `user`, as described in Chapter 5.

encrypt passwords

Type: Boolean

Description: The `encrypt passwords` parameter determines whether passwords used to authenticate users will be sent over the network encrypted. When Samba is acting as a domain controller or a domain member, encrypted passwords must be used.

Chapter 8, "Samba and Password Management," discusses the issues with encrypted and plain-text passwords.

Default: `false`; encrypted passwords are not used.

PART

IV

CH

19

IMPLEMENTING A MEMBER SERVER WITH SAMBA

Member servers are essentially machines running Windows NT Server that are members of a domain but are neither primary domain controllers nor backup domain controllers. Their function in a Windows NT network is to provide access to network resources such as printers or files without having the extra load of authenticating users for the domain.

Samba makes no distinction between a machine domain member and a member server because all machines running Samba can export file and printer shares if desired by the Samba administrator. Therefore, explicit member server support is not needed under Samba.

FUTURE DIRECTIONS

Domain controller-related functionality is constantly being added and improved in Samba. Future releases are likely to contain more features and make Samba more useful in a domain environment. At the time of writing, the following functionality is not implemented, or is currently being developed in a development version of Samba:

- Using the User Manager for Domains application to perform user maintenance tasks such as adding and removing users and groups.
- Backup domain controller support.
- Trust relationships between other domains.

Hopefully the Samba team will implement these functions sometime in the near future. Until then, Windows NT domains will remain only partially supported under Samba.

A mailing list exists to discuss issues related to Windows NT domain support under Samba. To subscribe to the `samba-ntdom` mailing list, send a message to `listproc@samba.org` with an empty subject and a message body of the following form:

`subscribe samba-ntdom Your Name`

Substitute your actual name for *Your Name*. Archives of the `samba-ntdom` mailing list are available at `http://us1.samba.org/listproc/samba-ntdom/`. Because this mailing list is primarily used by those who are using Samba TNG, it is a good place to find help on Samba TNG.

There is also a Web site devoted to providing information on Samba TNG: `http://www.kneschke.de/projekte/samba_tng/`.

FROM HERE...

This chapter has described the current capabilities of Samba as a Windows NT domain member and a Windows NT primary domain controller. The rest of this section of the book concentrates on other advanced topics using Samba:

- Integrating Samba with the Lightweight Directory Access Protocol (LDAP)
- Tuning and tweaking Samba for maximum performance
- High availability computing using Samba
- Troubleshooting Samba
- A tour of the Samba source code

## CHAPTER 20

SAMBA AND LDAP

In this chapter *by Jim Morris*

One of the major buzzes in the Information Technology (IT) industry over the past few years has concerned directory services. It seems lately that every trade journal has some article that mentions directory services.

Some network operating system (NOS) vendors have had working directory services available for years. Most other NOS vendors have announced that future products will include directory services. The free software movement even has several directory service offerings. Yet many IT professionals, especially those in small to medium businesses, might not know what a directory service is or what it can do for their businesses. This chapter provides a rudimentary introduction to directory services and specific information as to how Samba can utilize such services.

Just as is the case for many other network services, both proprietary and standards-based directory services exist. The most popular standardized protocol for accessing directory services currently available is known as the *Lightweight Directory Access Protocol (LDAP)*. LDAP provides a standard Internet protocol that enables any LDAP-compatible client application to communicate with any LDAP-compliant directory server.

In this chapter, we will examine in detail

- General information about what a directory service is
- Specific information on LDAP-compliant directory services
- An overview of popular LDAP servers
- Configuring Samba to perform user authentication using an LDAP server
- A sample LDAP schema for use with Samba

DIRECTORY SERVICES

To understand what a directory service is and how it can help the IT professional build a better network infrastructure, we will first examine directories in a historical perspective. We will then discuss the evolution of the directory service in the Information Age.

HISTORICAL DIRECTORY SERVICES

Since ancient times, organizations (especially governments!) have collected information. The problem has always been organizing that data into a format that makes it easily accessible. During the later half of the twentieth century, the amount of information accumulated by even the average business accelerated at a phenomenal rate. This was, in great part, because of the widespread proliferation of computers during the advent of the Information Age. It is likely that the Information Age is still in its infancy at this point in time.

A directory service, at its heart, is simply a mechanism for organizing data and making it easily accessible to the consumer of that data: the end user, if you will. Consider the most widely used directory service of the twentieth century: the traditional telephone book.

The common telephone book contains names, telephone numbers, and address information for people and companies served by the telephone company. To make all that data usable, it is ordered alphabetically by name. This makes it easy to find the telephone number and even the street address for a specific individual, business, or organization.

Some telephone books go even further in organizing the data presented by having separate sections such as the white pages, blue pages, and yellow pages. Each section typically contains a particular type of information: The white pages contain residential and business information organized alphabetically by name, the blue pages normally contain information for government offices, and the yellow pages contain a categorical listing of businesses and service offerings. These sections can be compared to a database on a computer with different search indexes or keys available for use. A business, for example, can be located either by name in the white pages or by a particular category in the yellow pages.

Other commonly used directories often follow the same format as the common phone book. For example, most companies maintain an employee phone list. This list will typically have all the employee telephone numbers organized by employee name and possibly by department. Many civic organizations maintain address and phone lists for their members, which follow the same familiar format.

DIRECTORY SERVICES IN THE INFORMATION AGE

Through the use of computers, electronic directory services can be created that are much easier to use and more powerful than their traditional paper counterparts. Modern computer technology enables vast quantities of information to be stored and rapidly accessed. Computers can provide powerful and flexible options for searching and organizing data—as opposed to having a fixed, unchangeable format. In other words, through searching and sorting techniques the user can see a customized version of the directory specific to her needs.

Note

Directories are often used not only for people, but also for other resources. Information that is more useful (and usable) when stored in a directory service can include company equipment and organizational information.

Computer-based directories often contain more information than that available in their traditional counterparts. For example, a public directory of individuals can include not only names, addresses, and telephone numbers, but also items such as email addresses, WWW home page URLs, and possibly even biographical information. A corporate directory of employees can contain a large amount of employee-specific information, including office location, supervisor name, pay grade, salary and benefits information, and computer passwords.

Obviously, you do not always want the users of the directory service to see all the information available. For example, in the case of an employee directory service within a company, sensitive information such as payroll and benefits information and passwords should not be accessible to just anyone. Limiting this access can be accomplished in several ways.

Most directory service providers (that is, directory servers) provide a security mechanism by which access to specific data or classes of data can be granted or denied to certain users. Another method of access control is often implemented in the directory client software itself. By this, an office administrator can be running a different directory client application from a network administrator, whereas an employee looking up a telephone number in the directory will run yet a third client application. The specific client application in each case would be designed to access just the data needed for that particular application. In all cases where sensitive data is available, it is important that the client software perform user authentication. This will help ensure that the wrong person does not gain access to important data.

DIRECTORY SERVICES VERSUS DATABASES

With the information presented so far, it might seem that a directory service does nothing more than a traditional relational database. Although it is true that a database server can be used to perform all the tasks of a directory service, important reasons exist for utilizing a directory service.

The chief advantage of a directory service over a more traditional database is that whereas databases ultimately utilize tables with fixed record structures, directory services are more generalized and can store much more unstructured real-world data. In other words, if a new type of data needs to be stored in a database, a record structure typically needs to be changed. With a directory service, storage of information is less structured. You can simply define a new attribute for a directory entry and add it to existing or new entries as the need arises.

A directory entry, although similar to a record in a database, is considered to be an *object*. Each object has attributes that describe it, along with a unique name. It is not necessary for two objects in the directory to have the same attributes, making the addition of new data to a directory much easier than to a traditional database.

Another important difference between directory services and databases is that directories are typically highly optimized for reading because the information is in most cases searched and read much more often than it is modified or added. Traditional databases must consider a balance between read and write performance, and typically incur much overhead in ensuring the integrity of the database during write operations.

ADVANTAGES OF COMPUTER-BASED DIRECTORY SERVICES

The advantages of computer-based directory services are numerous, but the most obvious advantage to a business is in the areas of data accuracy and centralization. Without a centralized directory service for employee information, each department—payroll, benefits, security, network services, and so on—maintains separate information on each employee. The possibility of inaccurate information greatly increases when the information is maintained in multiple databases and in multiple locations. If nothing else, maintaining information separately for each department is inefficient because of redundant data entry and storage. Figure 20.1 illustrates how data entry and storage might take place when no central directory service is utilized.

Figure 20.1
Data entry and storage without a directory service.

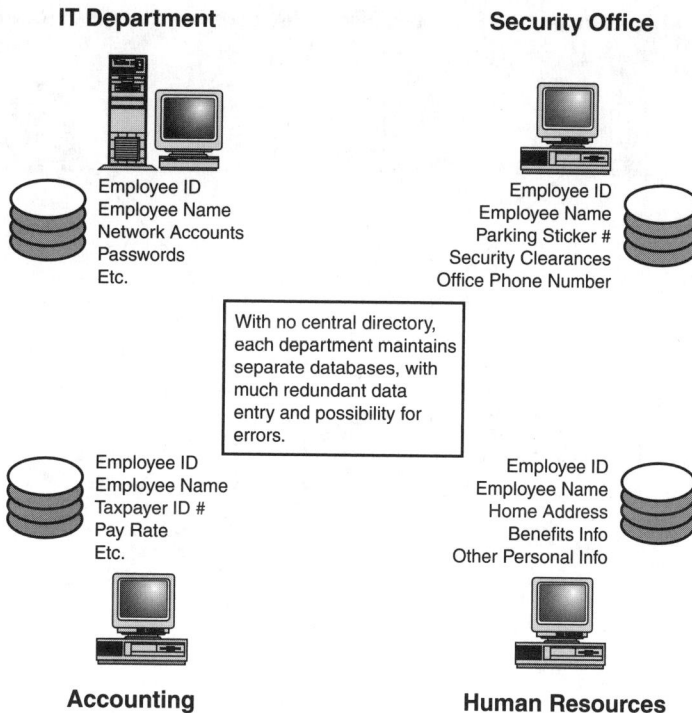

IT Department

Employee ID
Employee Name
Network Accounts
Passwords
Etc.

Security Office

Employee ID
Employee Name
Parking Sticker #
Security Clearances
Office Phone Number

With no central directory, each department maintains separate databases, with much redundant data entry and possibility for errors.

Employee ID
Employee Name
Taxpayer ID #
Pay Rate
Etc.

Employee ID
Employee Name
Home Address
Benefits Info
Other Personal Info

Accounting

Human Resources

By utilizing a directory service, all information for an employee or other resource is stored in a central location, using a directory entry for that employee, as shown in Figure 20.2. Each department edits the employee data that is specific to that department's function. For example, the network administrator can assign computer passwords and store them in the directory, whereas the payroll department can store pay scale and rate information for the employee. By using security mechanisms on the directory server in conjunction with custom client software, neither of these departments can access employee data that is not pertinent to its function.

ADVANTAGES OF STANDARDS

The historical directory service, the telephone book, follows a standard format. As you travel from city to city, or even country to country, the telephone book for most cities or regions uses the same format. This standardized interface enables you to pick up a telephone book anywhere you go and find the information you are looking for. The alternative (each phone book having its own unique format) would be unthinkable!

In a similar manner, it is to the advantage of the computer industry that a standardized mechanism for accessing a directory service be available. To this end, LDAP has been developed as the de facto Internet standard directory service protocol.

Figure 20.2
Data entry and
storage with a
central direc-
tory service.

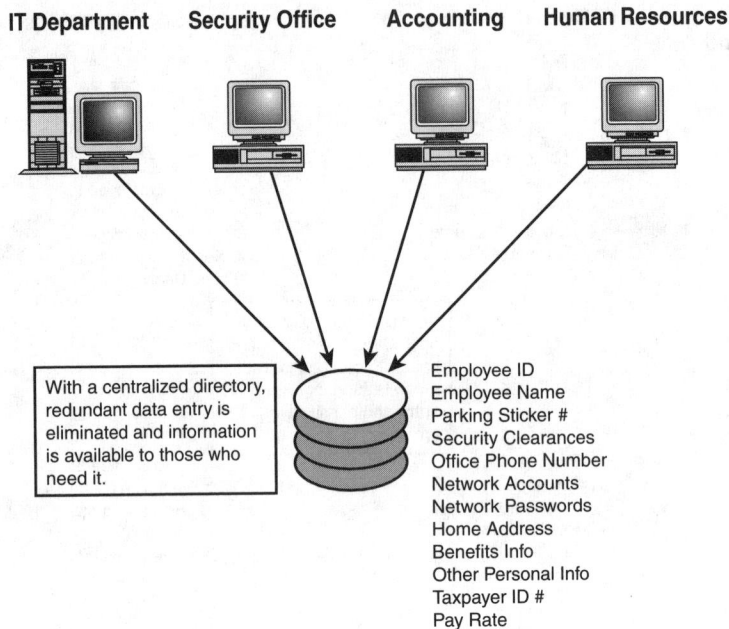

IT Department   Security Office   Accounting   Human Resources

With a centralized directory,
redundant data entry is
eliminated and information
is available to those who
need it.

Employee ID
Employee Name
Parking Sticker #
Security Clearances
Office Phone Number
Network Accounts
Network Passwords
Home Address
Benefits Info
Other Personal Info
Taxpayer ID #
Pay Rate

LDAP

LDAP is a protocol defining how a directory service *client* communicates with the directory service *server*. It is important to realize that LDAP is a protocol and does not define either a client or a server implementation. This means that it is entirely possible for an LDAP client application to be written in any programming language, by following the LDAP standard. And likewise, because the LDAP protocol does not specify the server implementation, LDAP servers can and have been implemented using a variety of technologies and a number of back-end databases for storing their data.

LDAP originated as a method for providing gateways to X.500 directory services. X.500 was the first standardized directory access protocol and has been in use for many years on large computer systems, typically mainframes. Unfortunately, X.500 historically has utilized the OSI communications protocol, and not the TCP/IP protocol popularized by the Internet. Because of the high resource requirements and protocol requirements, X.500 has never become very popular in the marketplace.

Because X.500 directory services never really gained popularity, developers at the University of Michigan, where LDAP originated, decided to take action. They added the capability to utilize a back-end database to the University of Michigan LDAP server, making LDAP essentially a directory service in itself (although it can also still act as an X.500 gateway).

An LDAP directory consists of several data objects stored in a hierarchical tree, often referred to as a *directory information tree*, as shown in Figure 20.3.

Figure 20.3
LDAP utilizes a hierarchical directory information tree.

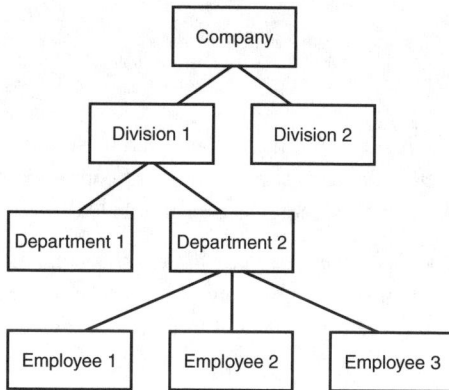

LDAP OBJECTS

The core data entity managed by LDAP is the object (also called an *entry*), as discussed earlier. An object is essentially a record in the directory. Each object in the LDAP directory has several attributes, but the most important of these is its *distinguished name (DN)*, which is a unique name that must be different from any other name in the LDAP directory. The DN is made of attributes of the directory entry that define it uniquely, in a manner similar to the domain name service (DNS) used to name servers on the Internet. In fact, the Internet DNS is a good example of a global directory service, used to locate specific computer systems using a human-readable name.

LDIF

LDAP Data Interchange Format (LDIF) defines a consistent method for working with LDAP data. LDIF is used to both enter data into an LDAP directory and to search and display data read from an LDAP directory, although the data can be parsed and presented in a more attractive format for the end user.

LDIF uses a combination of mnemonic attribute names to associate a textual value with that attribute for a specific LDAP object. The specific mnemonic attributes available can depend on the schema of the LDAP directory (a concept to be explained shortly). The following example gives you an idea of what LDIF data might look like for an entry in a corporate employee directory:

```
dn: uid=jmorris, ou=People, o=xyz.com
cn: Jim Morris
sn: Morris
givenname: Jim
objectclass: top
objectclass: person
objectclass: organizationalPerson
objectclass: inetOrgPerson
ou: Software Development
ou: People
l: Huntsville
uid: jmorris
```

```
mail: jmorris@xyz.com
telephonenumber: 123 456 7890
facsimiletelephonenumber: 123 456 7891
userpassword: xyzzy
```

The preceding LDIF entry defines an entry for an employee in a fictitious company, xyz.com. The first part of the entry is the DN (distinguished name) and consists of three comma-separated portions, which determine the object's place in the LDAP directory hierarchy.

The first part of the example entry's DN is its name, which is the same as the uid attribute, which is more likely to be unique than the user's name. The second portion of the DN defines which branch of the directory tree this entry falls under: a branch called People in this case. Finally, the entry is associated with a specific organization, xyx.com.

Tip from
Jim Morris

> Many LDAP servers provide utilities that allow input LDIF data files to be processed for the purposes of adding, modifying, and removing entries from the directory.

Note also that LDIF syntax comes into play when creating search queries for an LDAP server, using a programming language specific LDAP API.

ADVANCED LDAP TOPICS

Several LDAP-related topics are advanced and beyond the scope of this introductory material. However, in the interests of showing you the power of LDAP-based directory services, we will touch briefly on some of the more advanced features without going into too much detail.

REFERRALS

In many situations, it is not feasible for a single LDAP directory server to manage all the data in an organization's directory. In this case, certain portions of the LDAP hierarchy can be stored on one directory server, whereas other portions can be stored and managed by another server. Yet for simplicity, it is best that all end users be configured to access a single directory server for all information.

This can be accommodated through the use of *referrals*. If the LDAP server to which the end user submits a query does not have the requested information, but knows of another LDAP server that does, the LDAP server can return a referral result to the client. The client then has the option to either use the referral information to look up the desired information on another LDAP server or to ignore the referral, in which case the lookup fails.

For example, a central LDAP directory can manage certain employee information, while email address information is managed by an LDAP-compliant email server.

REPLICATION

Most LDAP server implementations provide a facility to perform replication of data between different servers. This can be useful for a variety of reasons. Replication can be used to ensure data integrity by keeping replicated data on a backup server, which can take over in the event of a primary server failure. Replication can be very useful for organizations that are distributed across a wide area network, where bandwidth constraints and cost can make it unfeasible for clients to use a single LDAP server that might be in a remote location. Instead, as shown in Figure 20.4, data can be placed on an LDAP server closer to the client system, with LDAP replication used to keep all LDAP server's directories in sync.

Figure 20.4
Distributed
LDAP servers,
with replica-
tion and refer-
rals.

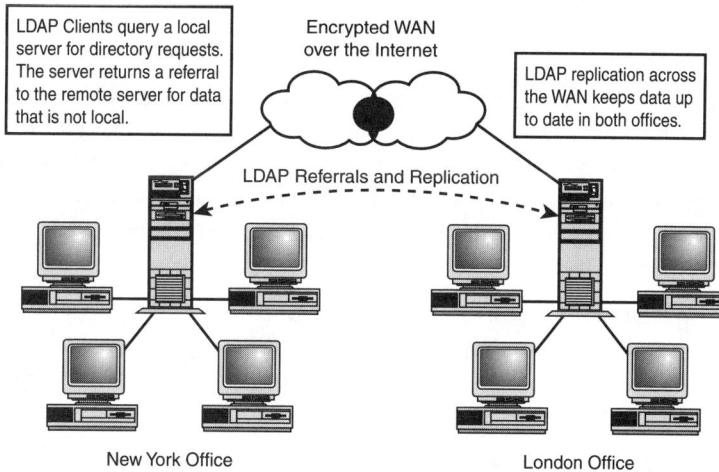

LDAP Clients query a local server for directory requests. The server returns a referral to the remote server for data that is not local.

Encrypted WAN over the Internet

LDAP replication across the WAN keeps data up to date in both offices.

LDAP Referrals and Replication

New York Office

London Office

SECURITY

As mentioned previously, a directory service must provide some security mechanism that determines to which objects or object attributes a directory user has access. LDAP servers use access control lists (ACLs) to accomplish this level of security. Additional security is provided by securing the actual connection to the LDAP server, through the use of encryption of some sort.

ACCESS CONTROL LISTS   ACLs control what a user can read, write, or view in the directory. For example, an administrative user, User A, can be given the ability to see and modify all attributes of any directory entry, whereas User B can have read-only access to view certain attributes and read-write access to certain other attributes. Other users can be restricted to a read-only view of only a subset of the data available for an entry.

ACLs can be assigned to specific users, or even groups of users. Unfortunately, although the LDIF syntax used to communicate with an LDAP server is standardized, ACL implementations are not yet standard between all LDAP servers. Because of this, you must refer to your specific LDAP server implementation for detailed information on setting up ACLs.

The following code shows an example of an ACL entry for the Netscape Directory Server in LDIF. This ACL enables members of an Administrators group to have full access to all entry attributes in the xyz.com LDAP tree used in earlier examples:

```
aci: (target = "ldap:///o=xyz.com") (targetattr = "*")
   (version 3.0; acl "allow all Admin group";
   allow (all) (groupdn = "ldap:///cn=Administrators, ou=Groups, o=xyz.com");)
```

Another ACL can be used to provide read-only access to names, locations, and email addresses to anonymous users:

```
aci: (target = "ldap:///o=xyz.com")
    (targetattr = "cn || sn || givenname || mail || l")
    (version 3.0; acl "Anonymous read-search access";
    allow (read, search, compare)  (userdn = "ldap:///anyone");)
```

SECURE ACCESS TO THE LDAP SERVER In many cases, especially when using an insecure external network such as the Internet, it is important to know that a secure connection exists between the LDAP server and the LDAP client. This is accomplished through user authentication and encryption of data after a connection is established. LDAP provides two methods to achieve these ends: Secure Socket Layer (SSL) and Simple Authentication and Security Layer (SASL).

SSL is implemented by most modern LDAP servers, most likely because of its popularity as a means of providing secure WWW connections. SSL is probably the best means of securing an LDAP server if you are in the process of creating a new directory service and have no existing authentication mechanism in place.

SASL provides a means to perform authentication using two defined methods: the Kerberos "ticket" system, and MD-5 hashing algorithms. Although the Kerberos system is very secure, it is also cumbersome to implement and manage. Because of these difficulties, Kerberos is not widely used. The MD-5 hashing algorithm is not really an encryption scheme, but more of a method of scrambling network passwords to make them harder to steal.

Because of the limitations of SASL, unless you are already using either Kerberos or MD-5–based systems, you will want to investigate the use of SSL to secure your LDAP server.

POPULAR LDAP SERVERS

As mentioned previously, several NOS vendors provide LDAP directory services. These services are provided in one of two ways: as a native LDAP server or as a proprietary directory server that has an LDAP interface. Table 20.1 lists currently available directory servers that are either native LDAP or LDAP-compatible.

TABLE 20.1 AVAILABLE LDAP SERVERS

Vendor	Server	Type	WWW Home Page
Novell	NetWare Directory Services (NDS)	Compatible	`http://www.novell.com/` `products/nds/index.html`
Sun Micro-systems	Sun Directory Services	Native	`http://www.sun.com/software/` `solaris/ds/ds-sds/index.html`
University of Michigan	U-Mich LDAP Server	Native	`http://www.umich.edu/` `~dirsvcs/ldap/ldap.html`
OpenLDAP	OpenLDAP Server	Native	`http://www.openldap.org`
Innosoft	Innosoft Directory Services	Native	`http://www3.innosoft.com/` `ids-products.html`

Netscape	Netscape Directory Server	Native	`http://www.iplanet.com/`
			`products/infrastructure/`
			`dir_security/dir_srvr/`
			`index.html`

Of the servers listed in Table 20.1, probably the most popular native LDAP servers at the moment are the Netscape Directory Server and the OpenLDAP server. OpenLDAP builds upon the strengths of the University of Michigan reference LDAP implementation, with the goal of providing a free, open source server and client API that is as rock solid as possible.

Note

Several other available products offer an LDAP-compliant interface but are not full-fledged LDAP directory servers. One such example is Microsoft's Exchange Server, which offers an LDAP interface to email address information.

Note

Only LDAP server products actually available and shipping as of January 2000 are included in Table 20.1.

PART
IV

CH
20

SCHEMAS

A central concept used by LDAP that has not yet been introduced in this chapter is that of *schemas*. Every LDAP server uses a schema, which defines every possible object class and attribute that can be stored by the LDAP server. The schema is somewhat comparable to the record structure in a database. The schema also to some measure defines the object hierarchy that can be created in the directory tree.

All LDAP servers ship with a default schema, which typically defines hundreds of object attributes and classes, which will normally meet the needs of most directory users. Sometimes, though, you might find that you need something not supported by the supplied schema. In this case, it is possible for you to extend the schema used by most LDAP servers while maintaining compatibility with LDAP clients that do not know about these extensions.

Because of differences in LDAP server implementations, you should consult the documentation for your specific LDAP server to find out how best to extend the schema.

Obtaining and Installing OpenLDAP

The sample Samba LDAP integration described later in this chapter assumes that you are running OpenLDAP on the Samba server system. You can obtain OpenLDAP from the source listed in Table 20.1. Compile and install OpenLDAP according to the instructions in the INSTALL and README files in the OpenLDAP source directory. The version of OpenLDAP used for this text, 1.2.9, can be installed on most systems by running the following commands:

```
tar xzvf openldap-1.2.9.tgz
cd openldap-1.2.9
./configure
make depend
make
cd test
make
```

If the tests pass successfully, you can install OpenLDAP by typing

```
cd ..
make install
```

The preceding steps should install the OpenLDAP distribution files in the directories shown in Table 20.2.

TABLE 20.2 OpenLDAP Installation Directories

Component	Location
Server programs (daemons and so forth)	/usr/local/libexec
User programs	/usr/local/bin
OpenLDAP development libraries	/usr/local/lib
OpenLDAP development headers	/usr/local/include
Configuration files	/usr/local/etc/openldap
LDAP databases	/usr/tmp

Note

The directory path for each LDAP directory you define can be changed using the `directory` keyword in OpenLDAP's `slapd.conf` file.

SETTING UP AN LDAP SCHEMA FOR SAMBA

Before installing Samba with LDAP support, it is a good idea to set up a schema for your LDAP server. Before doing this, you must define an LDAP directory for use with Samba, and then define the schema. With the OpenLDAP server, you define the schema using several configuration files.

OPENLDAP SERVER CONFIGURATION

The OpenLDAP standalone LDAP daemon, `slapd`, is configured using the file `slapd.conf`. Listing 20.1 shows an example of `slapd.conf`, which defines an LDAP directory for the domain `morris.net`. In this example, there is only one LDAP server, and no referrals or replication have been configured.

LISTING 20.1 `slapd.conf`

```
#
# See slapd.conf(5) for details on configuration options.
# This file should NOT be world readable.
#
include            /usr/local/etc/openldap/slapd.at.conf
include            /usr/local/etc/openldap/slapd.oc.conf
schemacheck        off

pidfile            /usr/local/var/slapd.pid
argsfile           /usr/local/var/slapd.args

#######################################################################
# ldbm database definitions
#######################################################################

database           ldbm
directory          /usr/local/etc/openldap/samba-ldap
suffix             "dc=morris, dc=net"
rootdn             "uid=root, dc=morris, dc=net"
rootpw             secret
#
index              cn
index              sn,uid,mail       pres,sub,eq
index              default           sub
#
defaultaccess      read
access    to dn=".*, dc=morris, dc=net"
          by self            write
          by *               search
```

If you want a user other than `root` to manage the LDAP directory, change the user ID listed on the `rootdn` line in Listing 20.1. You will probably also want to choose a root password other than `secret`!

The configuration in Listing 20.1 stores the Samba LDAP database in the directory `/usr/local/etc/openldap/samba-ldap`. You will need to create this directory and follow the steps given in the next section before starting `slapd`.

ADDING THE SAMBA SCHEMA

With OpenLDAP, the schema is defined in the file `slapd.oc.conf`. Listing 20.2 shows the entries that you need to add to this file to define the Samba schema. Use any standard text editor to add these entries to the end of `slapd.oc.conf`.

LISTING 20.2 `slapd.oc.conf` ADDITIONS (`samba-schema.txt`)

```
objectclass sambaAccount
        requires
                ObjectClass,
                uid,
                uidNumber,
                ntuid,
                rid
        allows
                gidNumber,
                grouprid,
                nickname,
                userpassword,
                ou,
                description,
                lmPassword,
                ntPassword,
                pwdLastSet,
                smbHome,
                homeDrive,
                script,
                profile,
                workstations,
                acctFlags,
                pwdCanChange,
                pwdMustChange

objectclass sambaGroup
        requires
                cn,
                rid
        allows
                ntuid,
                member,
                description

objectclass sambaBuiltin
        requires
                cn,
                sid
        allows
                ntuid,
                rid,
                member,
```

LISTING 20.2   CONTINUED

```
                    description

objectclass sambaConfig
        requires
                    id
        allows
                    nextrid
```

After you have added the schema entries, you can start the OpenLDAP server by typing

```
/usr/local/libexec/slapd
```

You will probably want to add this line to a system startup script, such as `/etc/rc.d/rc.local`. It is a good idea to have the LDAP server start before Samba when the system boots.

CREATING BASIC LDAP ENTRIES

Before populating the LDAP directory, we must first create the initial entries for the directory tree. Listing 20.3 shows an LDIF file that defines the initial entries for the `morris.net` domain in our example. If you use this as the basis for your own LDAP directory, be sure to edit the accounts, home directories, and so forth, as needed.

LISTING 20.3   INITIAL LDAP ENTRIES (`basic.ldif`)

```
dn: dc=morris, dc=net
dc: morris
o: MorriSoft
objectclass: organization
objectclass: dcObject

dn: uid=root, dc=morris, dc=net
uid: root
grouprid: 1
uidnumber: 0
gidnumber: 1
ntuid: Administrator
rid: 0
nickname: sadmin
ou: CTI
description: Admin
smbhome: \\vortex\root
homedrive: Z:
script: scripts\admin
profile: profiles\admin
acctflags: [DU          ]
objectclass: sambaAccount
```

To add the contents of the LDIF file to the LDAP database, use the `ldapadd` utility, a command-line client that comes with OpenLDAP. Add the contents of the LDIF file by running a command in the following format:

PART

IV

CH

20

```
ldapadd -D "uid=root, dc=morris, dc=net" -W < basic.ldif
```

You will be prompted for the root password, as configured by the `rootpw` entry in `slapd.conf`.

CREATING GROUP RECORDS

If you want to have various user groups in your LDAP directory, you can add the entries shown in Listing 20.4, using `ldapadd`. These entries are not mandatory for Samba operation with the LDAP server but can be useful for organizing your LDAP directory of users, and for assigning different rights to different users.

LISTING 20.4 GROUP LDAP ENTRIES (`groups.ldif`)

```
dn: cn=Domain Admins,   dc=morris, dc=net
member: Administrator,1f4,1
objectclass: sambaGroup
ntuid: Domain Admins
rid: 200
cn: Domain Admins

dn: cn=Domain Users,   dc=morris, dc=net
objectclass: sambaGroup
ntuid: Domain Users
rid: 201
cn: Domain Users

dn: cn=Domain Guests,   dc=morris, dc=net
objectclass: sambaGroup
ntuid: Domain Guests
rid: 202
cn: Domain Guests

dn: cn=Administrators, dc=morris, dc=net
description: Members can fully administer the computer/domain
sid: S-1-5-32-544
objectclass: sambaBuiltin
ntuid: Administrators
rid: 220
cn: Administrators

dn: cn=Users,   dc=morris, dc=net
sid: S-1-5-32-545
objectclass: sambaBuiltin
ntuid: Users
rid: 221
cn: Users

dn: cn=Guests,   dc=morris, dc=net
sid: S-1-5-32-546
objectclass: sambaBuiltin
ntuid: Guests
rid: 222
cn: Guests

dn: cn=Account Operators, dc=morris, dc=net
```

Listing 20.4   Continued

```
sid: S-1-5-32-548
objectclass: sambaBuiltin
ntuid: Account Operators
rid: 224
cn: Account Operators

dn: cn=Server Operators,   dc=morris, dc=net
sid: S-1-5-32-549
objectclass: sambaBuiltin
ntuid: Server Operators
rid: 225
cn: Server Operators

dn: cn=Print Operators,   dc=morris, dc=net
sid: S-1-5-32-550
objectclass: sambaBuiltin
ntuid: Print Operators
rid: 226
cn: Print Operators

dn: cn=Backup Operators,   dc=morris, dc=net
sid: S-1-5-32-551
objectclass: sambaBuiltin
ntuid: Backup Operators
rid: 227
cn: Backup Operators

dn: cn=Replicator,   dc=morris, dc=net
sid: S-1-5-32-552
objectclass: sambaBuiltin
ntuid: Replicator
rid: 228
cn: Replicator

dn: cn=Everyone,   dc=morris, dc=net
sid: S-1-1-0
objectclass: sambaBuiltin
ntuid: Everyone
cn: Everyone

dn: cn=Network,   dc=morris, dc=net
sid: S-1-5-2
objectclass: sambaBuiltin
ntuid: Network
cn: Network

dn: cn=Interactive,   dc=morris, dc=net
sid: S-1-5-4
objectclass: sambaBuiltin
ntuid: Interactive
cn: Interactive

dn: cn=Authenticated Users,   dc=morris, dc=net
sid: S-1-5-11
objectclass: sambaBuiltin
```

LISTING 20.4 CONTINUED

```
ntuid: Authenticated Users
cn: Authenticated Users
```

Add the contents of the LDIF file to the LDAP database, again using the `ldapadd` utility:

```
ldapadd -D "uid=root, dc=morris, dc=net" -W < groups.ldif
```

CONFIGURING SAMBA TO USE LDAP

At the time of this writing, the released version of Samba (2.0.6) did not include working LDAP support. However, several development versions of Samba included experimental support for the use of an LDAP server for user authentication. This LDAP support will be available in the next major production release of Samba, likely Samba 3.0.0. Keep that in mind as you read the following section on obtaining and installing Samba with LDAP support—it is highly likely that when Samba 3.0.0 is released, the steps to install the LDAP support could change.

OBTAINING AND INSTALLING SAMBA WITH LDAP SUPPORT

Before installing Samba for LDAP support, you must ensure that you first have a working LDAP server installed, along with LDAP development libraries and header files.

To get a copy of the development versions of Samba, you will need to utilize CVS (Concurrent Versioning System), a software development tool available for Linux, UNIX, Macintosh, and Windows systems. Instructions on using CVS to access the development versions of Samba are available at `http://www.samba.org/cvs.html`.

At the time of this writing, the two development branches with working LDAP support are the main branch of Samba and The Next Generation (TNG) branch. The TNG branch differs dramatically from Samba 2.0.x. For that reason, I chose to utilize the most stable development version on the main Samba branch, with known working LDAP support. This release is dated October 15, 1999. To obtain it, issue the following command, from the Linux prompt:

```
cvs -d :pserver:cvs@cvs.samba.org/cvsroot co -D "1999-10-15 00:00" samba
```

For your convenience, a copy of that version has been put up on the Web site for this book—`http://www.mcp.com/catalog/corp_bud.cfm?isbn=0789723190`—as a file named `samba-main-19991015.tar.gz`. To unpack this file, issue the command:

```
tar zxvf samba-main-19991015.tar.gz
```

After you check out this version of Samba using CVS or download and extract it as just discussed, you will end up with a directory containing the Samba source. To build Samba with LDAP support, do the following:

```
cd samba/source
./configure --with-ldap
make
make install
```

Note

Before performing the install of this experimental version of Samba, you should read the `source/README` file in detail to understand the installation details.

Other than the `--with-ldap` option passed to configure, the installation will proceed in the normal manner for installing Samba from source code. See Chapter 2, "Obtaining and Installing Samba," for more details on installing a Samba source distribution.

Note

When the development version of Samba is compiled with LDAP support, no other user authentication method will work. A working LDAP server and Samba schema must be set up before the Samba server will be available for use. I hope that a future released version of Samba with LDAP support will enable the LDAP authentication to be turned on and off using entries in `smb.conf`.

ADDING smb.conf PARAMETERS FOR LDAP SUPPORT

Several global options are used in the `smb.conf` file to configure the LDAP support in Samba. They appear in Listing 20.5.

LISTING 20.5 smb.conf GLOBAL OPTIONS FOR LDAP SUPPORT

```
[global]
ldap suffix = "dc=morris, dc=net"
ldap bind as = "uid=root, dc=morris, dc=net"
ldap passwd file = /usr/local/samba/private/ldappasswd
ldap server = localhost
ldap port = 389
```

The options in Listing 20.5 are described in detail in Table 20.3.

TABLE 20.3 SAMBA LDAP smb.conf OPTIONS

Option	Use
ldap suffix	Specifies the distinguished name (DN) suffix to use by default when searching the LDAP directory for a username.
ldap bind as	Specifies the DN that Samba will use when making connections to the LDAP server. This must be a DN with sufficient privileges to add new entries to the directory.
ldap passwd file	Used to give the name of a file that contains the password for the ldap bind as user. This file should contain the same password as the rootpw entry in slapd.conf.
ldap server	Specifies the name or IP address of the LDAP server. This could be the local host, if the LDAP server is running on the Samba server, or another host.
ldap port	Used to specify the TCP port number to be used for connections to the LDAP server. This should normally be port 389.

PART
IV

CH
20

> **Note**
>
> `ldap password file` contains a live password that is used to grant administrator access to the LDAP server. Serious care should be taken to ensure that this file is protected. For example, this file should be owned by root, with a group owner of root, and should not be world readable.

ADDING ACCOUNTS USING smbpasswd

To implement the changes you have made to the LDAP server and Samba, you need to restart the Samba server. After you do this, you can start using the Samba `smbpasswd` command to add Samba user and machine entries to the LDAP directory.

To add a machine-specific entry (needed for NT systems to access a Samba domain), use the `smbpasswd` command in the following manner:

```
smbpasswd -a -m <machine_name>
```

The very first time you use `smbpasswd` to add an entry to the LDAP directory, you might see a warning message about an object not found. You can safely ignore this warning because it will not happen again.

To add a user password entry in the LDAP directory, use

```
smbpasswd -a <user_name>
```

To change a password later on, use `smbpasswd` in the normal manner:

```
smbpasswd <username>
```

After you have added the necessary user and machine name entries to the LDAP directory, you should be ready to begin using the Samba server.

LDAP ENTRIES THAT AFFECT smb.conf OPTIONS

The `smbpasswd` command can only create and modify very basic information in the LDAP entries: the username and password. Several other attributes for each LDAP entry in the Samba schema that we have defined are of interest to you as the server administrator. These attributes are listed in Table 20.4. In each case, the value stored in the LDAP entry is equivalent to an `smb.conf` option, with some possible restrictions, noted in the table.

TABLE 20.4 SAMBA LDAP ENTRIES THAT REPLACE smb.conf OPTIONS

Attribute	smb.conf **Option**	**Comments**
smbHome	logon home	Home directory location used by Windows clients when doing a NET USE H: /HOME command. Example: \\vortex\jim

TABLE 20.4   CONTINUED

Attribute	`smb.conf` **Option**	Comments
`homeDrive`	`logon drive`	Local drive letter to connect home directory to, for NT Workstation logon processing. Example: `U:`
`script`	`logon script`	The logon script to be processed, relative to the `[netlogon]` share. Example: `logon.bat`
`profile`	`logon path`	Specifies the home directory for roving user profiles. Example: `\\vortex\profiles\jim`

Note

With the October 15, 1999, version of Samba, you cannot use substitution parameters in the LDAP directory entry. For example, when specifying the `profile` attribute, the text `\\vortex\profiles\jim` would be valid, whereas the text `\\%L\profiles\%U` would not. This restriction will hopefully be eliminated in a future Samba release with LDAP support.

Tip from
Jim Morris

The `smb.conf` options shown in Table 20.4 override the corresponding LDAP values. So, if you want to use the value stored in the LDAP directory, you will need to make sure you do not have the pertinent option in the `smb.conf` on your Samba server.

LDAP ENTRIES THAT AFFECT SAMBA CLIENTS

Some LDAP entry attributes in the Samba schema do not necessarily affect the operation of Samba but do get passed back to the client system. These values can be used to control the behavior of the client system and are listed in Table 20.5.

TABLE 20.5   SAMBA SCHEMA ATTRIBUTES THAT AFFECT CLIENTS

Attribute	Use
`pwdCanChange`	Determines whether users are allowed to change their own password. A good setting for this is `00000000`, which disables password setting from the client. If you are using an LDAP directory to maintain user information, you will normally want to use a custom LDAP client to perform password changes.
`pwdMustChange`	Specifies a password change interval in days. Because the password will likely be changed from a custom LDAP client, it is not desirable to have the client system try to set the password through another mechanism. To set the maximum interval, use the value `FFFFFFFF`.

MODIFYING SAMBA INFORMATION IN THE LDAP DIRECTORY

To modify the values of the LDAP entry for a particular user, you must use an LDAP client to make the changes. With the OpenLDAP `ldapmodify` client, you can submit changes by using an LDIF file as shown in Listing 20.6. This particular LDIF file is used to configure the LDAP data values from Table 20.4 for a specific user.

LISTING 20.6 LDIF FILE TO MODIFY SAMBA OPTIONS FOR A USER (changeuser.ldif)

```
dn: uid=jim, dc=morris, dc=net
changetype: modify
replace: profile
profile: \\vortex\profiles\jim
-
replace: script
script: jim.bat
-
replace: homeDrive
homeDrive: P:
-
replace: smbHome
smbHome: \\vortex\jim
-
```

Process the contents of the LDIF file by running a command in the following format:

```
ldapmodify -D "uid=root, dc=morris, dc=net" -W < morrisoft1.ldif
```

You will be prompted for the root password, as configured by the `rootpw` entry in `slapd.conf`.

ADDING USERS TO A GROUP

When we were creatingthe Samba schema, we added several Samba groups to the LDAP directory. To take advantage of those groups, we must modify the LDAP directory in two steps: We must add the user to the group, and then we must add an entry for the group to the user's entry in the directory.

To add the user to the group, we first must know the `rid` of the user because it is required for adding an entry to the group. Find out the `rid` for a user by typing

```
ldapsearch "uid=jim" "rid"
```

This will give us output somewhat like the following:

```
[root@vortex /root]# ldapsearch "uid=jim" "rid"
uid=jim, dc=morris, dc=net
rid=3eb
```

Now, we will use this information to add the user to the group `Domain Users`, using the LDIF file in Listing 20.7.

LISTING 20.7 LDIF FILE TO ADD USER TO GROUP (addusertogroup.ldif)

```
dn: cn=Domain Users, dc=morris, dc=net
changetype: modify
add: member
member: jim,3eb,1
-
```

After the user has been added to the group, the user's entry must be modified to add or replace the `grouprid` using the group `rid` we defined when we added this group (201), as shown in Listing 20.8. Note in this example the use of `replace`, which will modify the `grouprid` attribute if it exists or add it if it does not exist.

LISTING 20.8 LDIF FILE TO ADD GROUP TO USER ENTRY (addgrouptouser.ldif)

```
dn: uid=jim, dc=morris, dc=net
changetype: modify
replace: grouprid
grouprid: 201
-
```

CONCLUSION

We have covered a lot of ground in this chapter. We have learned the basics of what a directory service is and what it can do to reduce redundant data entry. We have learned about LDAP, one of the most popular and standardized directory services available today. We have also discussed how to install OpenLDAP and Samba and how to configure both of them using an LDAP schema for Samba.

It is important to remember that Samba can talk to any LDAP server. OpenLDAP was used for most of the examples in this chapter because it is readily available, open source, and free. But the main advantage of LDAP is that it is an open directory standard. From a user perspective, LDAP servers are interchangeable. One of the most popular LDAP servers is the commercial Netscape Directory Server, and Samba readily interfaces with it. With a commercial server, you are likely to receive more goodies such as graphical administration tools and client software—and technical support—if that is important to you.

Probably the most important thing to consider when contemplating the use of Samba with an LDAP directory is whether you really need to do so. Let me elaborate on that.

If you already have an LDAP directory in place, the obvious answer is to integrate Samba with that directory. You will probably just need to add the necessary Samba entries to your schema and add the appropriate new information to the user entries in the directory. Then Samba should be good to go.

However, consider the small business with just one or two servers and no LDAP directory already in place. In that case, the time and effort required to set up a directory service might not be worth it, especially if the LDAP directory is only going to be used by Samba.

PART
IV

CH
20

MORE INFORMATION

Many resources are available to learn more about LDAP and directory services in general. Several good books on the subject are available. The URLs listed in Table 20.1 should also help point you to some of that information. Also of use are the following resources:

- The samba, samba-ntdom, and samba-technical mailing lists. See `http://lists.samba.org` for information on subscribing.

- The file `docs/textdocs/LDAP.txt` in the Samba source distribution directory tree.

- The Samba-PDC LDAP Howto, available at `http://www.unav.es/cti/ldap-smb-howto.html`.

- `http://www.kneschke.de/projekte/samba_tng/`, which has lots of useful tips on installing and using the latest development versions of Samba, such as Samba TNG.

FROM HERE...

If you are setting up a Samba server in an environment that demands high performance, then the next chapter, "Samba and Performance," will be of interest to you. Also of interest if you are considering implementing enterprise features such as directory services will be Chapter 22, "Samba in the Enterprise."

CHAPTER **21**

SAMBA AND PERFORMANCE

In this chapter   *by Jim Morris*

Providing the highest level of network performance possible should be a primary goal of any network administrator. Just as users expect a certain level of performance from their local workstation, they expect to see a high degree of responsiveness from the network. It doesn't matter how much spare network bandwidth exists if the file and print server cannot sustain the client load. As far as the end user experience is concerned, the network server *is* the network for all intents and purposes.

In this chapter we will examine in detail

- Samba options that affect performance
- Tuning the operating system to improve server performance
- Network topology, as related to Samba performance
- File systems and their impact
- Memory sizing
- I/O subsystem selection

SAMBA OPTIONS THAT AFFECT PERFORMANCE

One of the great strengths of Samba is also one of its great weaknesses. Samba has an enormous number of configurable options, both at compile-time and at runtime. This is one of the reasons why Samba provides one of the best file and print server systems available today. However, knowing which options to change to improve performance (as well as which options to leave alone) can be a bewildering task, requiring you to wade through much documentation. Even after you find the option you think you need, a lot of trial and error can be involved in tuning its setting.

The next few pages present a concise list of some of the more important tuning options that are available for the Samba software package itself. Additionally, the default for each option and specific tuning tips will be made.

All options presented can be used in either the [global] section of your smb.conf or for a specific share, unless otherwise noted. To the extent possible, the various tuning options are listed in the order of impact on server performance.

TCP SOCKET OPTIONS

Because Samba implements the SMB protocol using TCP, any improvement you can make to the way your server handles TCP protocol connections will almost invariably improve the performance of Samba. You can set specific TCP socket options using Samba's socket options option. This option is put into the [global] section of the smb.conf file in the following format:

```
socket options = <socket options, separated by spaces>
```

Unfortunately, the socket options vary from system to system and are often not well documented. The socket options available under Linux might not be the same as those available under various commercial UNIX systems. On many systems, you can find out which socket options are available, along with their associated parameters (if any), by using the `man setsockopt` command to view the programming manual page for your system's `setsockopt()` C library function. You can also find some of the socket options listed in the `socket.h` include file for your system's C compiler.

The socket options in Table 21.1, available under Linux 2.2.x, are the options that would most commonly be used in performance tuning of your Samba server.

TABLE 21.1 TCP SOCKET OPTIONS FOR PERFORMANCE TUNING

Socket Option	Parameters	Use
TCP_NODELAY	None	Tells the TCP layer to send segments as soon as data is written by the application without trying to coalesce multiple writes from the application into one segment. This option has been reported to have a dramatic effect on most Samba servers, sometimes increasing the read performance for Samba clients as much as twofold. My benchmark testing shows a typical 50% performance gain from the use of TCP_NODELAY.
SO_KEEPALIVE	None	Sends periodic keepalive packets on the connection. If the remote end ever fails to respond, the smbd process for that connection can exit. Although this has no impact on performance, it does save server resources. If your system has this socket option, it is preferable to the use of the Samba keepalives option.
SO_SNDBUF	# of bytes	Sets the transmit buffer size. This option has an impact on performance. Values below 8192 can reduce throughput. Linux 2.0.x and 2.2.x default to 32768 for this option. The minimum you can set this to under Linux is 2048.
SO_RCVBUF	# of bytes	Sets the receive buffer size. This option has an impact on performance. Values below 8192 can reduce throughput. Linux 2.0.x and 2.2.x default to 32768 for this option. The minimum you can set this to under Linux is 256.
SO_SNDLOWAT	# of bytes	Sets the minimum number of free bytes that must be available in the socket send buffer before a select or poll call will return writable for the socket. This value has little impact on Samba performance, and Linux 2.2.x sets this value to 1, regardless of what the user requests.

PART

IV

CH

21

TABLE 21.1 CONTINUED

Socket Option	Parameters	Use
SO_RCVLOWAT	# of bytes	Sets the minimum number of bytes of data that must be available in the socket receive buffer before a select or poll call will return writable for the socket. This value has little impact on Samba performance, and Linux 2.2.x sets this value to 1, regardless of what the user requests.
IPTOS_LOWDELAY	None	Tunes the connection for low delays or latency. Typically used on LAN connections.
IPTOS_THROUGHPUT	None	Tunes the connection for maximum throughput. Typically used on WAN connections.

The socket option that makes the most impact on raw performance is the TCP_NODELAY option for a LAN environment. This is because the SMB protocol is a request-response protocol, and Samba typically assembles a whole response in memory and then writes it to the socket that was created for the client connection. If the TCP layer delays sending the data written by smbd in the hope that smbd will write some more, throughput can be drastically affected. A commonly used setting for the socket options would be

```
socket options = TCP_NODELAY SO_KEEPALIVE
```

For most local area networks, the other socket options do not have nearly as much impact as TCP_NODELAY, although the SNDBUF and RCVBUF sizes can have an impact. Those settings will likely need to be tuned for your specific operating system, network and applications.

> **Note**
>
> Many documents suggest setting socket options in the following way:
>
> ```
> Socket options = TCP_NODELAY SO_SNDBUF=8192 SO_RCVBUF=8192
> ```
>
> However, under Linux 2.0.x and 2.2.x, SO_SNDBUF and SO_RCVBUF default to 32768, so the previous setting might reduce performance.

FILE CACHING AND LOCKING OPTIONS

The file caching and locking options for Samba can have a definite impact on performance, as seen by a network client. Opportunistic locking in particular can lead to dramatic speed increases for Windows client systems, except for certain situations described in the following sections.

OPLOCKS

Opportunistic locking (*oplocks* for short) provides a mechanism by which SMB network clients get permission from the server to perform local caching of a network file. If the server grants the oplock, the client performs local caching of file data, potentially leading to greatly increased performance for the client. Of course, a client can only cache a file if no one else is accessing the file.

When a second network client requests a lock on a file that has oplocks on it, the server issues an `oplock break` request to the client that has an oplock on a file. The client then flushes any local modifications to the file and releases the oplock. This process obviously takes time and can potentially slow access to files that are in high demand for read/write access on a server. That said, the performance benefits of utilizing oplocks far outweigh the drawbacks, and in most cases, oplocks should be enabled on your Samba server.

Turn oplocks on or off on either a global basis or a share basis with this setting in your `smb.conf` file. The default setting in Samba 2.0.x is to enable oplocks:

```
oplocks = true
```

If you experience problems with the use of oplocks on certain shares, you might find that certain file types are to blame. Typically, you can see performance degradation in a file-based database on a Samba share when multiple clients access the database in Read/Write mode. You can disable oplocks on just certain files or file types by using the `veto oplocks` option, which takes one or more filename patterns as parameters. By placing the following into the definition of a specific share in the `smb.conf` file, you can disable oplocks on files with an extension of `.DBF` or `.MDX`:

```
veto oplock files = /*.dbf/*.DBF/*.mdx/*.MDX/
```

It is normally recommended that you disable oplocks only if you experience problems with their use.

As of Samba 2.0.5 and later, another option related to oplock processing is available: `level2 oplocks`. Level 2 oplocks are currently used only by Windows NT clients and enable a client to downgrade a read/write exclusive oplock to a read-only oplock. Multiple clients can hold `level2 oplocks` on a file that is open in read-only mode and perform local caching of that file. To control the setting for `level2 oplocks` on a global or share basis, put the following in your `smb.conf` file:

```
level2 oplocks = true
```

STRICT FILE LOCKING

File-level locking is required for many client applications to work. However, Samba can be configured as to whether file locking is strictly enforced or not. If strict locking is enabled, the Samba server will check for the existence of locks on each file read or write, which on some systems will impact performance. Strict locking is normally only required for network clients that do not explicitly check file lock status before reading or writing a file. Strict locking can be disabled on a share or global basis using

```
strict locking = false
```

Note that if network client software is ill behaved (that is, it doesn't check for file locks before modifying a file), it might be necessary to enable strict locking.

PART

IV

CH

21

SHARE MODES

DOS and Windows clients use share modes during file opens. Share modes enable a client to open a file with specific access rights and to gain exclusive or non-exclusive access to a file. For example, if a file is opened with an exclusive DOS share mode such as DENY ALL, the file is locked for that client. A DENY NONE share mode would allow use of the file by other network clients. The various DOS-specific share modes do not typically map directly to file modes on the Samba server, however, so they are simulated by Samba. Depending on how the Samba server was compiled, these share modes will be implemented using lock files, in a configured lock file directory, or using shared memory. Shared memory typically obtains the best performance and is enabled during the compilation of the Samba server on systems that support shared memory. On most Linux systems, the default compile options enable this option.

By disabling share modes, you can improve performance of the Samba server. However, by doing so, you can cause compatibility problems with DOS and Windows client software. Consider disabling share modes only if you are certain that one user will be using the share (possibly limited using the max connections option for a share). To control share modes, use the following for a specific share. (You typically do not want to set this on a global basis!)

```
share modes = <yes | no>
```

If the Samba server is using shared memory to implement share modes, it is possible that the shared memory could be used up if a large number of client systems are connected with open files. If this happens, network clients can have trouble when trying to save files to a Samba share, and your Samba server's log files can show memory allocation failures if the logging level is set high enough. In this case, you must increase the amount of RAM used for file share mode operations. This is adjusted with the shared mem size global option. The default setting is

```
shared mem size = 1048576
```

read size

The read size option is a global smb.conf setting. It is used only in the code that handles read prediction, and that code is turned off by default.

The default setting for this option in Samba 2.0.x is 16,384 bytes. My benchmark testing shows that doubling or halving this value has a small impact on performance, but typically by no more than a few percentage points.

Set this option in the smb.conf file using

```
read size = 16384
```

max xmit

The global max xmit option controls the maximum packet size that will be negotiated between a client system and the Samba server. The allowable range is 1–65,535 bytes, although going below 2,048 or so will likely cause severe performance degradation. The default is for Samba to negotiate a maximum packet size of up to 65,535 bytes with the connected client, which typically leads to the best performance, especially with large file transfers.

The main reason to use this option is to tune Samba for use with older SMB network clients such as Windows for Workgroups or various DOS SMB clients. These clients often have performance problems when using large packets. To tune the maximum transmit size for such clients, you could do the following in your `smb.conf` `[global]` section (preferably at the end of the `[global]` section):

```
[global]
include = /etc/smb-%R.conf
```

The `%R` is replaced by the negotiated client protocol, such as `LANMAN1`, `COREPLUS`, or `NT1`. In your `/etc` directory, you could have a file named `smb-LANMAN1.conf` with contents of

```
max xmit = 2048
```

Don't worry about supplying an include file for all protocols in this case. Just supply one for the exceptions to your default `smb.conf` settings. By including the file in `smb.conf` at the end of the `[global]` section, the settings in the include file override any previous settings for the same values in `smb.conf`.

LOGGING

Samba permits a great deal of log information to be captured. Although this can be a great aid in diagnosing network problems, it can have a negative impact on performance, especially if you use a logging level of 3 or higher. In this case, information is logged for every single network packet between the client and the Samba server. For normal network operations, I suggest that you run with a log level of 1, which will only log connects and disconnects from network shares. To do this, add the following line to the `[global]` section of your `smb.conf` file:

```
log level = 1
```

RAW READS AND WRITES

Some SMB clients support the use of raw read and write operations. If enabled, raw reads and writes allow up to 65,535 bytes to be transferred in a single packet. This can dramatically speed up the transfer of large files. These are controlled by the Samba `read raw` and `write raw` global options, both of which default to enabled in Samba 2.0.x. To set, use the following in your `smb.conf` file:

```
read raw = yes
write raw = yes
```

WIDE LINKS

The `wide links` Samba option controls whether the Samba server enables an SMB client to follow links in the underlying UNIX file system. If a subdirectory within a share is actually a link to an area outside that directory structure on the server, the client will have access to it if wide links are enabled. If they are disabled, access outside the top-level directory using a link will not be allowed. This option is enabled by default. However, if you disable wide links, possibly for security reasons, you should be aware that it will impact performance negatively. This is because the Samba server must check each file and directory access on the share to ensure that it does not involve a link outside the share.

To ensure that wide links are enabled, set the following on a global or share basis in your `smb.conf`:

```
wide links = yes
```

If wide links are disabled, you can lessen the performance impact by enabling the `getwd cache` option:

```
getwd cache = yes
```

In Samba 2.0.x, this option is defaulted to enabled.

TUNING THE OPERATING SYSTEM

To provide the maximum possible performance from your Samba server, you will need to tune all aspects of the system, and not just the Samba software package. You will need to consider general tuning of your operating system and hardware, as well as tuning to obtain optimum performance from your server's storage subsystem and network interfaces. Your tuning should also extend to considering your network topology, and evaluation of whether network topology changes are warranted for performance reasons.

GENERAL TUNING TIPS

In general, any tuning that can be done to enhance performance at the operating system level will also benefit Samba. Some specific things to look at when performing tuning at this level include the following.

FILE SYSTEM CACHING

The goal here is to devote the maximum amount of server RAM to performing file system caching and to keep the cached data in memory as long as possible. This ensures that the server is not bound by disk I/O speed when serving up commonly used files.

FILE AND INODE LIMITS

On many systems, limitations can exist on the maximum number of file handles that can be open at once. A limit can also exist on the number of inodes in the inode cache. If you have a Samba installation with large numbers of users and open files, you might find that you exceed the system defaults for these values and run out of file handles or inode cache entries.

Every time a client opens a file, `smbd` uses a file handle to access that file on behalf of the user. Also, every time a file is opened, its inode must be accessed to check permissions and find the on-disk blocks of the file.

If users find they cannot open files, you must examine the system log files and Samba log files on your server. If you see any messages indicating that an inode or file handle limit has been reached, you should increase the limits used by the system, if at all possible.

Of course, running out of open file handles will be fatal to a Samba daemon and will be noticed quickly. However, if your inode cache is not large enough, you will experience performance problems as your system must swap inodes between the cache and the disk.

We show you how to increase both of these later in this section.

NETWORK INTERFACE PERFORMANCE

Any tuning that can be done to the Ethernet interface and TCP/IP stack for the Samba server should be done. The extent of tuning that can be done will likely vary greatly from system to system.

LINUX-SPECIFIC TUNING

Because a large percentage of the readers of this book are likely to be working with Samba on the ever-popular Linux operating system, I would be remiss to not include as many Linux-specific tuning tips as possible. With that in mind, specific steps that can be taken under Linux are outlined in the following text.

LINUX KERNEL VERSION

The advent of the Linux 2.2.0 kernel brought many performance improvements to Linux, compared to the 2.0.x kernel series. Several of these improvements affect the performance of a Samba server. The following improvements should encourage you to upgrade any Samba server from Linux 2.0.x to the 2.2.x or later kernel version:

- Improved Symmetric Multiprocessor Support (SMP)—Linux 2.2.x greatly improves the scalability and performance of Linux on multiprocessor systems. I/O device access performance by multiple processors is also greatly improved.

- Improved Directory Caching (DCACHE)—This can dramatically improve Samba performance when the client accesses directories on the Samba server that contain a large number of files, especially many small files.

- Improved TCP/IP Stack—Later Linux kernel versions incorporate improvements into the TCP/IP protocol stack, including both performance and security fixes.

FILE SYSTEM CACHING

The default setting under Linux is normally such that most unused RAM (memory not allocated to a process) ends up being used as disk cache or buffers. However, using the `/proc` file system it is possible to tune the caching algorithm. This is all controlled using the special files in `/proc/sys/vm`.

DISK CACHE SIZES   The minimum and maximum sizes for the disk cache under Linux are controlled by the special file /proc/sys/vm/buffermem. The file contains three numeric values, outlined in Table 21.2.

TABLE 21.2   VALUES IN /proc/sys/vm/buffermem

Value	Default	Purpose
Min_percent	2	The minimum percentage of system memory that should be used for cache.
Borrow_percent	10	Determines the rate at which the system takes memory away from the cache when the system becomes short on memory.
Max_percent	60	The maximum percentage of system memory that should be used for cache.

> **Note**
>
> The preceding default values are for a system running the Linux 2.2.13 kernel. The defaults for other kernel versions can vary.

To find out your current cache size limits, try the following command line under Linux:

```
cat /proc/sys/vm/buffermem
```

You should see output similar to Listing 21.1.

LISTING 21.1   CHECKING THE BUFFER CACHE LIMITS UNDER LINUX

```
[root@speedy /root]# cat /proc/sys/vm/buffermem
2    10    60
[root@speedy /root]# echo "10 10 75" >/proc/sys/vm/buffermem
[root@speedy /root]# cat /proc/sys/vm/bdflush
40    500    64    256    15    3000    500    1884    2
[root@speedy /root]# echo "80 500 64 64 80 6000 6000 1884 2" \
   >/proc/sys/vm/buffermem
 [root@speedy /root]# cat /proc/sys/vm/buffermem
10    10    75
[root@speedy /root]# cat /proc/sys/vm/bdflush
80    500    64    64    80    6000    6000    1884    2
[root@speedy /root]#
```

If your system has a large amount of RAM, it might make sense to adjust the minimum and maximum cache size limits, although the borrow_percent setting should probably be left alone.

To adjust the minimum buffer to 10% of system memory and the maximum buffer to 75% of system memory, issue the following command. Issue this either at the command prompt or in a system startup file such as /etc/rc.d/rc.local on most Linux systems.

```
echo "10 10 75" >/proc/sys/vm/buffermem
```

DISK WRITE CACHING   After you've tuned the amount of memory that can be allocated to file system caching, the next area to look at is the handling of buffer cache writes. This is handled by the `bdflush` kernel daemon, which is tuned using parameters in the file `/proc/sys/vm/bdflush`. By tuning the `bdflush` daemon, it is possible to adjust how long written data is allowed to stay in the cache before being written (flushed) to disk and also how much data to write to disk at a time. Table 21.3 shows the values of the `bdflush` daemon.

TABLE 21.3 VALUES IN `/proc/sys/vm/bdflush`

Value	Default	Purpose
nfract	40	Maximum percentage of dirty buffers in the cache before activating `bdflush`. The higher the number, the longer writes can be delayed. The tradeoff is that many writes could potentially occur at once, when buffers need to be freed.
ndirty	500	Maximum number of buffers that can be written out at a time (per wakeup of `bdflush`).
nrefill	64	Number of buffers that the kernel will try to add to the free buffer list each time `refill_freelist()` is called.
nref_dirt	256	Number of dirty buffers found during a `refill_freelist()` operation that will cause `bdflush` to be activated.
interval	500	The interval in jiffies between kupdate flushes.
age_buffer	3000	Maximum number of jiffies (1/100 second) that the kernel waits before writing a dirty data block to disk.
age_super	500	Maximum number of jiffies (1/100 second) that the kernel waits before writing file system meta data such as superblocks.
Dummy2	1884	Unused.
Dummy3	2	Unused.

The following command line is an example of how you might tune these settings. You would put this in the `/etc/rc.d/rc.local` startup file on most Linux systems. This particular example tunes these parameters such that twice as much unwritten data can reside in cache at any one time, and dirty data is allowed to stay in the cache twice as long as the default.

```
echo "80 500 64 64 80 6000 6000 1884 2" >/proc/sys/vm/bdflush
```

FILE HANDLE AND INODE LIMITS

As previously discussed, if you are running a Samba server with a large number of users, it is possible to encounter a situation in which the system is running out of file handles or inode handlers. The maximum values for these kernel resources are controlled through different files under Linux 2.0.x and Linux 2.2.x, because of changes in the /proc file system. Under Linux 2.2.x, the default file handle limit is 4096 and the default inode limit is 8192.

> **Note**
>
> The rule of thumb is that the maximum number of inode handlers should be set to 2 to 3 times the maximum number of file handles.

To tune the file and inode limits under Linux 2.0.x, use the following commands:

```
echo "6000" >/proc/sys/kernel/file-max
echo "12000" >/proc/sys/kernel/inode-max
```

Under Linux 2.2.x, the following should be used:

```
echo "6000" >/proc/sys/fs/file-max
echo "12000" >/proc/sys/fs/inode-max
```

The previous commands would set the maximum number of file handles to 6000, and the inode handler limit to 12000.

PUTTING IT ALL TOGETHER

To put all the preceding tuning tips together, you could place the following lines into your rc.local or other Linux system startup file:

```
# Tune the Linux kernel to allow 6000 open files and up to
# 12000 inodes in memory.
echo "6000" >/proc/sys/fs/file-max
echo "12000" >/proc/sys/fs/inode-max
#
# Tune filesystem cache
echo "10 10 75" >/proc/sys/vm/buffermem
echo "80 500 64 64 80 6000 6000 1884 2" >/proc/sys/vm/bdflush
```

> **Note**
>
> The previous addition is for the Linux 2.2.x kernel. Adjust the file-max and inode-max tuning appropriately for the Linux 2.0.x kernel.

> **Note**
>
> Unless you have a very large amount of RAM (512MB perhaps) and know that you do not need RAM for other things, you might not want to tune the values in /proc/sys/vm/buffermem. If you set it at too high a percentage of system RAM, the system could spend excess time pruning the cache to regain system memory and causing some level of negative impact.

NETWORK TOPOLOGY AS RELATED TO SERVER PERFORMANCE

Probably one of the most critical factors in the end user experience when accessing your Samba server will be the network itself. It doesn't matter how speedy the server is if the physical network cannot move the data to the user fast enough. The raw bandwidth of the network, the physical topology, and the amount of traffic all factor into determining how quickly data can move from the server to the client system.

BANDWIDTH

The most obvious factor in determining network file system performance is the raw speed or bandwidth of the network itself. 10BaseT Ethernet running at 10Mbps has been used in the overwhelming majority of Ethernet installations since it achieved popularity in the mid 1980s. During the late 1990s 100BaseTX Ethernet became popular and affordable for small- to medium-sized businesses. Going forward, it appears that Gigabit Ethernet and its successors will come down in price even more quickly.

Your network bandwidth needs really depend on the type of applications for which the Samba server is used. If you use the server only for casual data file storage (documents, moderate size data files, and so forth), a 10Mbps network can be fine for years to come. You might want to consider moving to a faster medium such as 100BaseTX, however, if users intend to run applications from the Samba server, store and access multimedia video clips, or run other applications with large network-based files.

SEGMENTATION AND SWITCHES

An Ethernet network that is based on one Ethernet hub or even multiple hubs "uplinked" together consists of one physical *segment*. All network traffic on the wire is seen by all other systems on the network, because the network is in essence one big wire that the various systems take turns talking on, as shown in Figure 21.1. On a network with many high-bandwidth data transfers, and more than just a few systems, the number of network collisions will become significant, cutting the overall useable network bandwidth.

An Ethernet installation can be broken down into two or more segments with a device known as a *switch*. An Ethernet switch is in essence an intelligent network hub with a bridging function that examines the destination MAC address of Ethernet packets and switches them to the specific destination port that matches the destination address. Most switches learn the destination MAC address to switch port relationships dynamically and store the information in an internal switching table. Hubs with systems connected to the hub can be uplinked to a port on a switch as part of building or enhancing a network. Figure 21.2 shows the network of Figure 21.1, now segmented with a switch.

By switching the traffic to just the destination segment, a switch can dramatically decrease network traffic on other segments. Collisions are reduced as a result, and overall useable network bandwidth increases.

PART

IV

CH

21

An added bonus of using a switch is that most switches allow a directly connected Ethernet adapter to run in what is called *full duplex mode*. This means that the receive and transmit pairs of the connected Ethernet card are no longer sharing the same wire inside a hub. This allows simultaneous transmits and receives and a potential doubling of network bandwidth for the connected system; hence, the term *full duplex*.

Figure 21.1
Ethernet with a single segment. On a single network segment, packets from PC 1 destined to the server are echoed to every port on all network hubs on the segment.

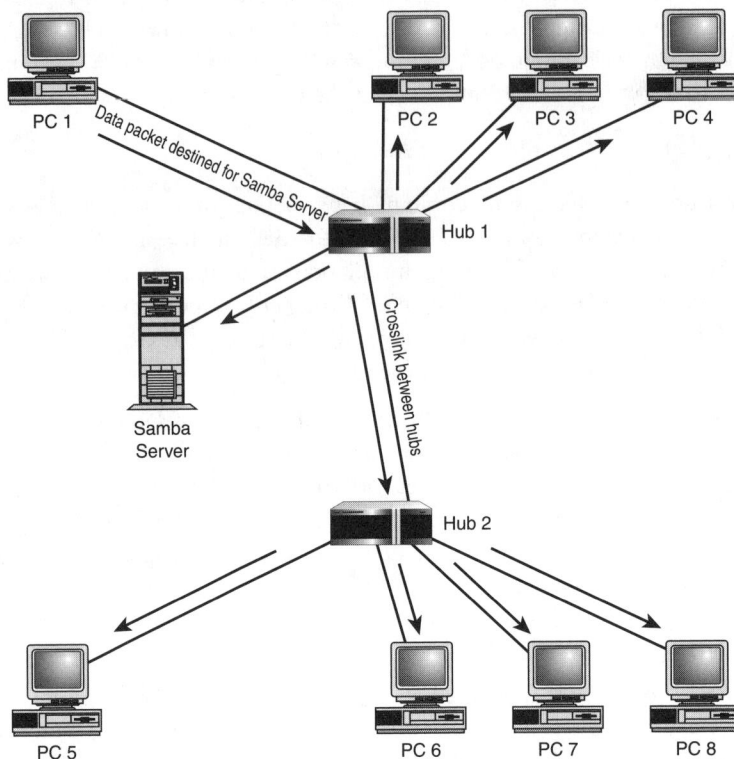

Typically, you should consider using a switch to break an Ethernet into multiple segments, or in lieu of a hub if your network is more than 50% utilized and has a large percentage of collisions. Most systems, including Linux, allow you to look at Ethernet statistics to determine the number of collisions. Figure 21.3 shows the output of the ifconfig command under Linux 2.2.x, giving the Ethernet statistics for a network interface. In this particular case, collisions have occurred only 0.29% of the time, based on the total transmitted and received packet counts. In this particular case, collisions are not a major problem. On a heavily loaded network, however, collisions can account for a significant portion of network bandwidth.

On a congested network with a single Samba server, you can improve performance by installing multiple Ethernet cards on the server. These Ethernet cards, with separate IP addresses, could then be put onto separate Ethernet segments (using a switch), to split the network load between the server and the clients. Note that some changes to the Samba server's smb.conf file might be necessary when using multiple interfaces.

Figure 21.2
Ethernet broken into segments using a switch. On a switched network segment, packets from PC 1 only reach the systems on the same hub and the Samba server.

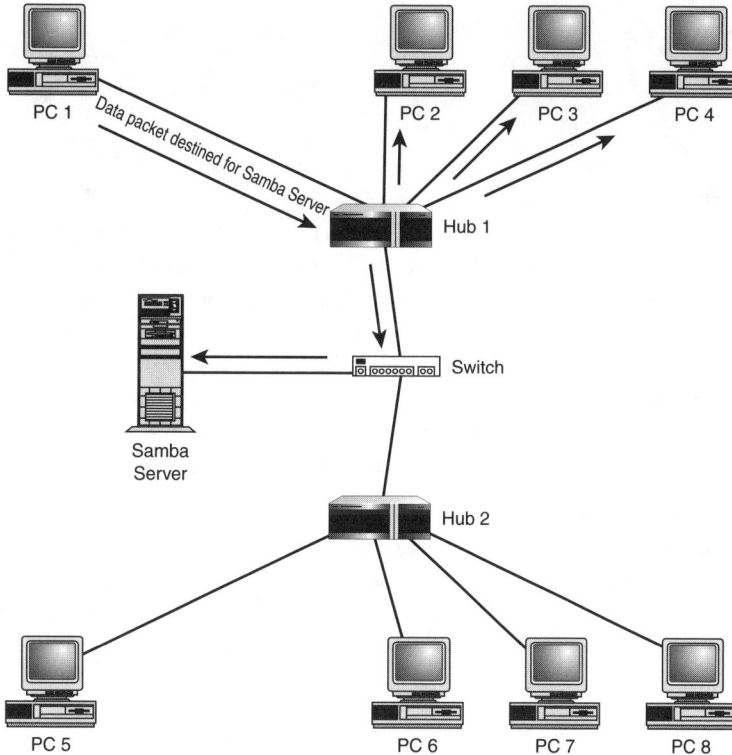

Figure 21.3
Using the Linux `ifconfig` command to check Ethernet statistics.

```
[jim@darkstar jim]$ /sbin/ifconfig eth0
eth0      Link encap:Ethernet  HWaddr 00:A0:CC:33:B3:38
          inet addr:192.168.0.1  Bcast:192.168.0.255  Mask:255.255.255.0
          UP BROADCAST RUNNING MULTICAST  MTU:1500  Metric:1
          RX packets:5493621 errors:2 dropped:0 overruns:0 frame:2
          TX packets:7899396 errors:0 dropped:0 overruns:0 carrier:0
          collisions:39168 txqueuelen:100
          Interrupt:17 Base address:0xa800

[jim@darkstar jim]$ ▮
```

What Do You Need?

Your network needs depend on both the intended use of the network and the number of users. In other words, for a small to medium business network, a single segment running at 10Mbps or 100Mbps can perform quite well for common business application and data storage. On the other hand, in a software development or graphic arts shop, where many potentially large files will be stored on the Samba server, a high-speed segmented network is necessary.

FILE SYSTEMS

Choosing the right file system for use on your Samba server is critical, as is appropriate sizing of the file system on which the Samba shares reside.

EXT2 FILE SYSTEM

Under Linux, the most obvious file system choice is the Extended 2 (Ext2) file system. This has been the dominant native file system for most Linux installations since the early '90s. The Ext2 file system has fairly high performance, with a configurable block and inode size at the time the file system is created. Ext2 is a fragmentation-resistant file system, meaning that the kernel file system driver attempts to store files contiguously on disk when possible. Ext2 also offers a fairly high degree of data protection because the file system is designed to limit the amount of data that can be lost after a crash. Several utilities are also available for working with the Ext2 file system as well to facilitate checking the file system and repairing damage.

The Ext2 file system has been around for several years and is starting to show its age, especially as hard drive capacities seem to increase in order of magnitude every year. The biggest factors to be aware of when choosing the Ext2 file system for use on a Linux-based Samba server are the file system limits. Under Linux 2.2.x, the Ext2 supports file systems of a terabyte in size but with a 2GB file size limit. To handle files larger than 2GB, special patches are available for the Ext2 drivers in the Linux 2.2.x kernel.

You should also be aware that after an abnormal system shutdown, the Ext2 file system can take quite a long time to check for errors. The bigger the drive, the longer it takes. It is not unusual to have an Ext2 file system check of a large 20 to 40GB drive take 10 to 20 minutes.

Because of the performance and size limitations of the Ext2 file system, it is highly recommended that you consider the use of a journaling file system when such file systems become stable and available under Linux.

JOURNALING FILE SYSTEMS

Most commercial UNIX systems offer what is called a *journaling file system*. Commonly used journaling file systems include the popular Veritas file system (VFS) used by several UNIX vendors, SGI's XFS journaling file system, and IBM's JFS file system. You should also note that Microsoft Windows NT's High Performance File System (HPFS) is a journaling file system.

A journaling file system uses journaling to control changes to the file system on disk. *Journaling* consists of taking disk change requests and logging them in a journal maintained by the file system. The actual modification of the file system does not occur until after the journal entry has been completely recorded. Several advantages to the journaling approach include the following:

- Filesystem Undo—The journal allows changes to the file system to be undone (for example, files can be undeleted).

- Better Crash Recovery—Data that was not completely written to disk at the time of a system crash can be easily recovered from the journal.

- Speedy File System Checks—Because a file system check after a system crash consists simply of ensuring that all entries in the journal have been posted to disk, file system checks are virtually nonexistent.

- Performance Improvements—Data can be written into the journal sequentially and written to disk later, when the system is not busy.

If you are running Samba on any commercial UNIX system, it makes sense to use a journaling file system if one is available.

At the time of this writing, the choices available to Linux system administrators were somewhat limited, with no production-quality journaling file system yet available. The journaling file systems at press time that are currently at some stage of development include the following:

- Ext3 Filesystem—This is intended to be a backward compatible enhancement to the Ext2 file system. It will add journaling to the underlying Ext2 file system, as well as overcoming some of the current limitations in the released Ext2 file system. For more information, see `ftp://ftp.linux.org.uk/pub/linux/sct/fs/jfs/`.

- XFS Filesystem—XFS is SGI's journaling file system for IRIX (SGI's version of UNIX for its MIPS-based workstations and servers). In 1999, SGI released the XFS file system code as open source to the Linux development community. See `http://oss.sgi.com/projects/xfs/` for more information.

- ReiserFS Filesystem—This is a GPL'ed journaling file system currently available for Intel-based Linux systems. It is primarily the work of a single individual, Hans Reiser. See `http://devlinux.com/projects/reiserfs/` for more information.

- IBM's Enterprise JFS—This is an IBM-sponsored port of the IBM journaled file system used on their high-end AIX servers to Linux. The project is being developed as open source. More information is available at `http://oss.software.ibm.com/developerworks/opensource/jfs/index.html`.

Of these four options, at the time of this writing, the farthest along in the development cycle is the ReiserFS, with SGI's XFS and IBM's JFS rapidly maturing. The Ext3 file system will probably be of the most interest to people running Linux systems with the current Ext2 file system, especially if it will be possible to upgrade to Ext3 without reformatting existing Ext2 drive partitions. Unfortunately, Ext3 is currently the farthest from completion of any of the three Linux journaling file systems.

NETWORK FILE SYSTEMS (NFS, CIFS, AND SMBFS)

Although not advisable from a performance standpoint, Samba makes it possible for network-mounted file systems on the Samba server to be exported to Windows systems using the SMB protocol. The primary reason one might choose to do this is to make available to Windows users a network share that might otherwise be inaccessible. For example, it is possible to mount an NFS share from a UNIX server and export it using Samba to Windows clients that do not have NFS client software installed.

When exporting a network file system using Samba, it is important to remember that network bandwidth requirements will be at least double what they would be for a local file system on the Samba server.

MEMORY SIZING

To achieve optimal performance from your Samba server, the system needs enough RAM to accommodate system operation without excessive use of disk swapping (virtual memory). Several factors contribute to the memory needs of a Samba server.

SAMBA PROCESSES

Samba can be run in one of two ways: in daemon mode or using the inetd "super server" available on some systems. Regardless of the method used to start Samba, there will be at least one instance of the smbd process for each client connection, along with some overhead for shared memory and, if in daemon mode, the initial smbd process.

It is important to note that one instance of smbd will be created for each connected client, not one instance per share. The per-user smbd process will handle access to all shares for a connected client. The amount of memory used for each smbd process varies from system to system and also depends on what each client is doing, because smbd allocates memory for internal data structures depending on client activity.

> **Note**
>
> If you are using virtual servers, there will be one smbd process for each client connection to each virtual server.

On a system with shared libraries, such as Linux, memory consumption can be as low as 250KB per process but can average at least 500KB per process. Some UNIX systems have been reported in Internet newsgroups to consume up to 2MB per smbd process. The only way to get a good idea of memory use per process on your system is to use the ps or equivalent command to examine the memory use for active smbd processes. Remember that if you have a system with shared libraries, the memory use shown for a process might or might not reflect shared code between running copies of a program.

> **Tip from**
> *Jim Morris*
>
> For a typical Linux-based Samba server, a good rule of thumb would be to allow at least 500KB per client connection for adequate performance. If you have compiled Samba without the -g flag, less memory will be required.

Operating System

When sizing RAM for your Samba server, consider the way the system will be running. How much RAM does the operating system itself take just to load the kernel and all required device drivers? This must be reflected in the total system RAM requirement. You might get a good idea of operating system memory use by checking memory use immediately after rebooting the system.

If the server will be booting to a text console, the memory overhead incurred by the operating system will obviously be less than if the system boots into a graphical shell such as X11.

Other Processes

What other uses will the Samba server be put to? Will it also act as a WWW server for Internet or intranet use? Will it be running a SQL server, sendmail, DNS, and so on? Will you be using a special print filtering software on spooled print jobs?

All these programs require some memory, and this must be considered in sizing RAM for your Samba server.

> **Note**
>
> From a security point of view, it is better not to use the machine for more than one function. In particular, a Samba server should not be used as a Web server that is accessible through the Internet.

File Cache Size

You should size the memory on your Samba server such that after all other memory consumption is taken into account, adequate RAM is left for performing file system caching. This is important to ensure optimum performance, by keeping every SMB network request from causing a physical disk access.

Calculating Total Server Memory Requirement

To pull all the memory requirements together, we will attempt to come up with some general guidelines for use in sizing memory needs for a Samba server.

Most Linux 2.0.x- and 2.2.x-based systems can perform quite well with limited amounts of RAM, especially when not running X11. If the server is really just a server and not a workstation, there is no reason to buy RAM for running X11 occasionally. The sizing in Table 21.4 takes this into account.

PART

IV

CH

21

TABLE 21.4 Server Memory Requirements

Element	Recommendation
Base operating system	16MB to 32MB for the typical Linux system.
Samba base smbd/nmbd processes	1MB, approximately.

TABLE 21.4   CONTINUED

Element	Recommendation
Shared memory for share modes	1MB, default.
Samba per-client smbd processes	0.5MB per client, approximately.
Other processes	Completely system-dependent. For a Linux system running in console mode, with DNS and email services, and limited WWW services, anywhere from 16MB to 64MB is sufficient.
File system cache	Buy as much RAM as you can afford to have left over for file system cache!

SAMPLE SERVER CONFIGURATION

As an example, consider a Linux-based Samba server in a medium-sized business with approximately 50 users. In addition to providing file and printer services using Samba, the server operates as a corporate email server, runs a SQL database server, and runs a CVS server for use by several software developers. To maintain responsive disk throughput, it might be desirable to maintain a minimum file system cache of 128MB.

Server RAM could be calculated as follows:

Linux-based system	= 16MB
Samba-based processes	= 1MB
Share-mode Shared Memory	= 1MB
Samba client connections (50 @ 0.5MB)	= 25MB
SQL Server (MySQL, mSQL, etc.)	= 32MB
CVS Server	= 16MB
sendmail, POP3, DNS	= 8MB
File System Cache	= 128MB
Total RAM Required	**= 227MB**

In this example, a system with 256MB would more than meet the memory requirements, with room for growth.

One important factor to remember is that not all users are actively accessing files on the Samba server all the time. If you use the smb.conf "dead time" parameter to disconnect inactive client connections, odds are that you would never have all 50 clients connected simultaneously in the previous example. Furthermore, things such as SQL queries, CVS commits, email services, and the like typically run intermittently. If you consider those factors, you will often find that you can serve many Samba clients with much less RAM than the previous example uses and still have excellent system performance. The numbers given previously should be considered a worst-case example, with 50 users concurrently accessing the Samba server, and so on for the other calculated items.

One of the strong points for both Linux and Samba is their combined efficiency. An older system, such as a 100MHz Pentium with 32–64MB RAM, can often provide quite adequate performance for a sizeable number of Samba clients, assuming only data file storage and printer services are required. This can be especially true if running a 10Mbps network, where the network speed cannot approach the disk I/O bandwidth of even a fairly slow server.

I/O Subsystem Sizing

When putting together a network file server, whether it is running Samba or not, the ultimate intent is to provide network-based file storage and possibly print services as well. It is important that the server have an I/O subsystem capable of meeting both the storage and performance needs of the network clients. At the same time, it is not necessary to spend more money than needed buying capabilities that will not be used.

In addition to storage space and performance considerations, the underlying technology is important in selecting an appropriate I/O subsystem for a server. For example, if the data on the file server is considered "mission critical," measures should be taken to protect the data through the use of redundancy (RAID) and some form of backup mechanism.

Storage Technology

A bewildering array of storage technologies is available today. You have multiple interface types to choose from (EIDE versus SCSI). You will also have to decide upon backup mechanisms and possibly even RAID storage arrays. The next few paragraphs will provide you with a brief education on the basic technologies available and why you might choose one over another.

EIDE Versus SCSI

Several storage technologies have become available over the years. Today, basically two predominant disk drive technologies are in use: EIDE and SCSI. Each technology has its advantages and disadvantages, and either one can be suitable for server use, depending on the server requirements.

Most desktop personal computers use EIDE hard disk drives. EIDE drives are popular because they are inexpensive and provide good single-user performance. With current EIDE drives achieving burst data transfer rates of up to 66Mbps using UDMA-66 technology, the performance of most modern EIDE drives is outstanding for many uses. There are several disadvantages to the use of EIDE drives in a server environment, however. Most systems can accommodate a maximum of four EIDE devices, with a CD-ROM drive often taking up one of these valuable slots. Probably the biggest disadvantage to the use of EIDE drives in a server is the fact that only one EIDE device on a channel can be active at once. There can be only one outstanding operation at a time for an EIDE device.

SCSI drive technology has been in use for many years and has seen many performance improvements. Whereas the SCSI-1 drives of the 1980s could only transfer data at a maximum of 5MBps, current LVD UltraSCSI2 drive technology achieves astounding data transfer rates of up to 160MBps. Wide SCSI interfaces allow up to 15 drives per interface, and narrow SCSI interfaces allow up to 7 drives per interface. The fact that most SCSI adapters allow multiple outstanding disk I/O requests to multiple target devices can give a crucial performance boost to a multiuser file server. Probably the only drawback to SCSI drive technology is that it can cost significantly more per megabyte of storage than a comparable amount of EIDE storage.

RAID

RAID stands for *Redundant Array of Inexpensive Disks* and is a mechanism by which multiple physical disks are combined into one array that acts as a single logical drive. This can be done using a special drive enclosure, controller card, or software drivers. Drives are typically combined into a RAID array for one of two reasons: to increase performance or to increase reliability (and sometimes both).

To increase performance, two or more drives can be *striped*. This means that the drives are combined to increase overall capacity and performance by distributing the data evenly across the disks in an interleaved fashion. This type of RAID is often classified as RAID-0. Performance for a striped array is often the performance of a single disk multiplied by the number of disks comprising the array. RAID-0 provides no measure of redundancy, and if a single drive is lost, the contents of the array will be lost (excluding backups). The only reason to use RAID-0 is to increase performance beyond that of a single drive.

Two mechanisms are used to achieve redundancy in a RAID array. The most basic is drive mirroring, usually termed RAID-1. In RAID-1, multiple drives are maintained as mirror images of each other that are maintained on a continual basis. If a drive in the array fails, the system can continue to operate seamlessly from the remaining drive. As long as one mirror drive continues to operate, the RAID-1 array is functional. Array capacity, however, will be the same as that of a single drive.

> **Note**
>
> In a RAID-1 array, read performance is often increased because reads are distributed across all drives. Writes, however, are often slightly slower than for a single drive because each write operation must be performed to multiple disks.

A third type of RAID is probably the most popular in large server installations: RAID-5. RAID-5 uses three or more disks to create a redundant array by distributing both data and checksum information across all drives in the array. Any one drive in the array can fail, and the array will continue to operate in a degraded mode. Overall array capacity is the total of the drives in the array, less one drive.

> **Note**
>
> RAID-5 is probably the most popular RAID configuration because unlike RAID-1, you only lose the capacity of one drive. With three drives, you have a useable capacity equal to the combination of two drives. Read performance can be enhanced because data is distributed across multiple devices. Writes can be somewhat slower than for RAID-1, though, because of the requirement to recalculate checksum information for each write.

SOFTWARE RAID Many operating systems, including Linux, offer the capability to create RAID drive arrays by using special software drivers. You can see several advantages to using software-based RAID. Probably the biggest advantage is cost. Software RAID comes with the operating system, so in essence, it costs nothing. In addition, software RAID can use any disk drives that the operating system supports, including EIDE or SCSI drives or even a mixture of drive technologies in a single array. On modern high-speed computer systems, software RAID can often perform as well or in some cases better than a true hardware RAID solution.

The use of software RAID comes with one major disadvantage: It is not transparent to the system and requires much initial setup and configuration at the operating system level. In addition, booting off a RAID array when using software RAID is not a trivial thing.

HARDWARE RAID You implement hardware RAID in two ways: by using a special RAID controller card, to which standard disk drives are attached, or by using an external RAID hardware solution.

Most RAID controller cards are essentially specialized SCSI controllers, typically of the Wide (16-bit) SCSI variety, and are available from a variety of manufacturers. These controller cards let you implement several RAID levels, with the most commonly supported options including RAID-0 (striping), RAID-1 (mirroring), RAID-0+1 (striping and mirroring), and RAID-5 (striped with checksum information).

Using a RAID controller is advantageous because you can use any SCSI drives that you want to in building the RAID array, including a combination of internal and external devices. The chief disadvantage to using a RAID controller card is that the card itself requires operating system driver support, so always check driver availability when considering any RAID controller. Furthermore, some RAID controllers are only that: They are not intended for use as general-purpose SCSI controllers, to which you can connect tape drives, CD-ROM drives, or other general purpose SCSI devices.

The most expensive RAID solutions typically consist of a *RAID box*, which looks like a single SCSI device to the system. The external RAID enclosure typically has its own controller, which controls the drives in the RAID array independently of the host system. This leads to the ultimate in system independence: You simply connect the RAID enclosure to any operating system-supported SCSI controller. The RAID enclosure typically has its own alarms to alert the system operator of failed drives, which can then be replaced at a convenient time. Often drives can even be hot-swapped without taking the system down. The RAID system will reconstruct the data on the replacement drive automatically as well.

PART

IV

CH

21

DETERMINING YOUR NEEDS

When choosing the I/O subsystem components for your Samba server, it is important to consider both the intended use of the system and other factors such as your network infrastructure and, of course, system cost.

CONSIDER NETWORK BANDWIDTH

If you run the Samba server on a 10BaseT Ethernet segment (or other network with comparable speed), the maximum data throughput the server can ever provide to a network client is approximately 1MBps. (This is 2MBps in full duplex mode using a switch). This is assuming the network is not busy and no collisions are occurring. You will find that even an inexpensive EIDE drive on an older Pentium system can sustain drive throughput of 3–4MBps. It makes no sense from a performance standpoint to create an Ultra2 Wide LVD striped RAID-0 drive array if the server's network I/O bandwidth will never exceed the bandwidth of a slower drive or disk array.

If your Samba server is running on a 100BaseTX network segment, network bandwidth can be as much as 200Mbps, or approximately 20MBps, using a switched, full duplex configuration. Although you will see both EIDE and SCSI drives advertised with data transfer rates well beyond 20MBps, reality is somewhat different. The advertised data transfer rate for most hard drives is a burst transfer rate, typically of data that is already in the drive's internal data buffer. Most high-performance drives cannot sustain a throughput anywhere close to 20MBps once head seeks, rotational latency, and other factors are considered.

So in the case of a 100BaseTX full-duplex network configuration, network I/O bandwidth can easily exceed the sustainable data bandwidth of any single drive in your server. You can address this fact in two ways: aggressive disk caching on the Samba server (for example, lots of system RAM and delayed writes) or through use of a RAID array to increase performance beyond that of a single drive.

CONSIDER THE NUMBER OF USERS

The number of concurrent users accessing the Samba server is important to consider when choosing an I/O subsystem. As mentioned earlier, SCSI technology permits multiple outstanding I/O requests to multiple devices. EIDE technology (even UDMA-66) permits only one device on a controller channel to be active at a time, with only one outstanding I/O request per device. The conclusion is obvious: SCSI drive subsystems tend to perform much better under a heavy user load than do EIDE drive subsystems.

CONSIDER EXPANDABILITY

No matter how much storage you provide initially, your users will use it up much more quickly than you expect them to! With this in mind, you should plan ahead and know how you intend to expand storage on your server at a future date. Keep in mind that while EIDE controllers permit a maximum of two devices per controller channel, SCSI (including RAID) controllers permit up to 7 devices for narrow (8-bit) channels and 15 devices for wide (16-bit) channels.

> Because of the performance limitations of EIDE drive interfaces, with only one active device allowed per controller channel, the consensus seems to be that you should only put one drive per controller on an EIDE-based network server. Otherwise, performance degradation can occur when accesses to two drives on the same controller occur.

CONSIDER RELIABILITY

The required reliability and acceptable downtime for the server should be an influencing factor in choosing an I/O subsystem. If the server is performing mission-critical functions and no downtime is acceptable in the event of a drive failure, I highly advise you to seek a RAID-1 or RAID-5 solution. On the other hand, if the Samba system will be a workgroup server and can be down for an entire day (while you install a new drive and reinstall all software), you can probably get by with a single SCSI or EIDE drive.

BACKUPS, BACKUPS, BACKUPS!

I cannot overemphasize the importance of implementing a routine backup schedule for your Samba server. In a business environment, the data stored on the server is often critical to the success of your company. As such, you should consider it a valuable commodity, and protect it.

It is important to understand that the intent of RAID is to safeguard against a disk drive failure. RAID gives no protection against a user accidentally deleting a file. In the event of an operating system or other glitch, if bad data is written to the RAID array, it is written to all disks in the array. The only way to safeguard the data itself on your Samba server is by using a backup solution on a regular schedule.

Most Linux and other UNIX systems include basic software capable of reading and writing to tape drives: programs such as `tar`, `cpio`, `dump`, `restore`, and so on. Find out what is available on your system, and set up a backup schedule. Buy a commercial backup application if the system utilities are insufficient. Popular commercial backup programs for Linux include BRU (`http://www.estinc.com`), arkeia (`http://www.knox-software.com`), and LONE-TAR (`http://www.lone-tar.com`). It can also be helpful to assign an individual who will be responsible for changing tapes on an assigned day and set up a tape rotation for them to cycle through.

Some commercial backup solutions for Linux include

- BRU from Enhanced Software Technologies
- Novanet 8 from NovaStore
- Arkeia from Knox Software

PART

IV

CH

21

> **Note**
>
> When choosing a backup device, it is important to consider the costs of blank media. A cheap device is not so cheap in the end if the blank tapes or cartridges cost twice as much as those for a slightly more expensive device.

> **Note**
>
> Optical devices such as CD-RW drives might seem to be the ideal backup solution. Unfortunately, their low capacity, slow speed, and requirement to use special CD mastering software make them bad choices as backup devices.

> **Note**
>
> The most popular backup devices for most UNIX systems are 4mm and 8mm tape drives or tape changers. These devices currently have the lowest media cost as well.

I/O SUBSYSTEM TUNING

If your operating system provides a mechanism to tune the operation of the drive I/O subsystem, you should take advantage of it. Although I cannot give advice on every system, here is some specific information related to tuning EIDE drives on a Linux system.

Linux provides a tool for use with EIDE drives called hdparm. This tool enables you to adjust several parameters that control the performance and operation of EIDE devices. hdparm also has the added benefit of giving you a rough estimate of the performance of your EIDE drive subsystem.

> **Caution**
>
> It is important that you read the man page and understand some of the more advanced options for hdparm before blindly using it. Also note that hdparm is strictly an EIDE performance adjustment tool and should not be used with SCSI or RAID devices.

It is critical that you query the capabilities of your drive before doing any tuning using hdparm. To do this, use the hdparm -i command as shown in Listing 21.2. This will show you the capabilities and current settings of the drive.

Check the following on an EIDE drive using hdparm:

- Is the drive's read-ahead feature enabled? (-A option)
- Is 32-bit I/O support enabled? (-c option)
- Is DMA mode enabled? (-d option)
- Is multi-sector I/O enabled on the drive? (-m option)
- Is the drive using the fastest possible PIO or DMA mode? (-p or -X options)

- Is interrupt unmasking enabled? (-u option)
- Is the drive's write caching feature enabled? (-W option)

LISTING 21.2 USING hdparm TO CHECK AND TUNE AN EIDE DRIVE

```
[root@speedy /root]# hdparm -i /dev/hda

/dev/hda:

 Model=IBM-DJNA-371800, FwRev=J78OA30K, SerialNo=GR0GRF82
 Config={ HardSect NotMFM HdSw>15uSec Fixed DTR>10Mbs }
 RawCHS=16383/16/63, TrkSize=0, SectSize=0, ECCbytes=34
 BuffType=3(DualPortCache), BuffSize=1966kB, MaxMultSect=16, MultSect=16
 DblWordIO=no, maxPIO=2(fast), DMA=yes, maxDMA=2(fast)
 CurCHS=16383/16/63, CurSects=-66060037, LBA=yes, LBAsects=35239680
 tDMA={min:120,rec:120}, DMA modes: mword0 mword1 mword2
 IORDY=on/off, tPIO={min:240,w/IORDY:120}, PIO modes: mode3 mode4
[root@speedy /root]# hdparm -A1 -d1 -c1 -m16 -W1 /dev/hda

/dev/hda:
 setting 32-bit I/O support flag to 1
 setting multcount to 16
 setting using_dma to 1 (on)
 setting drive read-lookahead to 1 (on)
 setting drive write-caching to 1 (on)
 multcount    = 16 (on)
 I/O support  =  1 (32-bit)
 using_dma    =  1 (on)
[root@speedy /root]# hdparm -Tt /dev/hda

/dev/hda:
 Timing buffer-cache reads:   64 MB in  0.69 seconds =92.75 MB/sec
 Timing buffered disk reads:  32 MB in  1.90 seconds =16.84 MB/sec
```

Some reasonable adjustments to tune a drive might be

```
hdparm -A1 -d1 -c1 -m16 -W1 /dev/hda
```

To test the performance of your drive, issue the following command:

```
hdparm -Tt /dev/hda
```

This should give you two numbers: a benchmark number for buffer-cache reads, which is for cached data access, and a number for actual buffered disk reads. This second number is the most important because it is an indicator of the drive's sustainable throughput.

I/O SUBSYSTEM RECOMMENDATIONS

Ultimately, the choice of an I/O subsystem for your Samba server comes down to a couple of deciding factors: The intended purpose of the server, and the amount you have budgeted to spend on the server.

If you are setting up a small departmental server where performance is not critical, you should consider using an inexpensive system with a single large EIDE drive and a tape backup

PART

IV

CH

21

solution. To cut costs even further, utilize a remote tape drive on another system (if available) to perform backups.

If you are setting up a high-performance server for a large number of demanding users (such as a software development team) or for a demanding application (such as streaming video), performance is the essential factor. You will want to consider using a SCSI-based RAID solution to increase the drive I/O performance beyond what a single drive can sustain. If performance is more important than reliability, set up a RAID-0 striped array to achieve the maximum performance possible. Remember to implement a good backup solution though, because a single drive failure will render an entire RAID-0 array useless. A combined RAID level such as RAID-0+1 can provide a better balance of performance and reliability, if cost is not a factor.

If the most important factor for your server is reliability, consider using RAID: either RAID-1 or RAID-5. External RAID solutions, although more expensive, are the easiest to maintain. Take a look at hot-swap carriers for the drives so that you can change a failed drive without even having to power down the system. Make sure that a good backup solution is in place, and change tapes on a regular basis.

MORE INFORMATION

For more information on various topics presented in this chapter, the following resources will be useful.

SAMBA PERFORMANCE TUNING

- The `smb.conf` manual page on your Samba server. Access by typing `man smb.conf`.
- The files `Speed.txt` and `Speed2.txt` in the `/usr/docs/samba-$version/docs/textdocs` directory on your Linux or UNIX system after you have installed Samba.
- The Samba WWW page and mailing list archives at `http://www.samba.org`.
- The Usenet newsgroup `comp.protocols.smb`.

LINUX KERNEL AND FILE SYSTEM TUNING

- The `/usr/src/linux/Documentation/proc.txt` file on your Linux system.

RAID UNDER LINUX

- The Linux Enterprise Computing page's RAID Solution information at `http://linas.org/linux/raid.html`.
- The Linux Documentation project's "Root RAID HOWTO" at `http://www.linuxdoc.org/HOWTO/Root-RAID-HOWTO.html`.
- The Linux Documentation project's "Software RAID HOWTO" at `http://www.linuxdoc.org/HOWTO/Software-RAID-HOWTO.html`.

- The latest Linux software RAID drivers, currently available from `http://www.kernel.org/pub/linux/daemons/raid/alpha/`.

- Various hardware manufacturers' sites, if using a RAID controller that has Linux support.

JOURNALING FILE SYSTEMS

- Ext3 Filesystem—For more information, see `ftp://ftp.linux.org.uk/pub/linux/sct/fs/jfs/`.

- XFS Filesystem—See `http://oss.sgi.com/projects/xfs/` for more information.

- ReiserFS Filesystem—For more information, go to `http://devlinux.com/projects/reiserfs/`.

- IBM JFS Filesystem—See `http://oss.software.ibm.com/developerworks/opensource/jfs/index.html` for more information.

FROM HERE...

If you are setting up a Samba server in an environment that demands high performance and high availability, you will definitely want to proceed to Chapter 22, "Samba in the Enterprise," before setting up your Samba server.

PART
IV

CH
21

CHAPTER 22

SAMBA IN THE ENTERPRISE

In this chapter

by Jim Morris

As more and more businesses choose to roll out Samba-based network servers, questions arise as to how to best handle and manage Samba at the enterprise level. When most Information Technology (IT) professionals discuss enterprise-class network services, the implication is that such services

- Are robust
- Are scalable
- Are highly available

In other words, an enterprise-class application can be used and trusted to run your entire business.

Samba has been used to provide field-proven file and print services for DOS, Windows, and OS/2 clients since 1993. In more recent years, Samba has been expanded to include enterprise-class features such as domain logons and advanced user authentication techniques.

Because a large majority of Samba server installations are running on the Linux operating system, the bulk of this chapter focuses on providing enterprise class services using Samba on Linux. In general, however, most of the discussion is applicable to commercial UNIX systems as well.

HIGH AVAILABILITY SYSTEMS

The most important aspect of enterprise network services is providing high availability (HA). It is possible to create highly reliable systems through the use of redundant hardware, RAID disk arrays, hot-swappable hardware, uninterruptable power supplies (UPS), and other means. Unfortunately, some single point of failure can still take your server down. Often it can be a network card, a system board, or some other critical system component.

HA systems are created by using special HA software solutions. A typical HA configuration consists of at least a primary server and a backup server, as shown in Figure 22.1. The backup server runs special *heartbeat* monitoring software that enables it to know when the primary server has failed. In the event of a failure, the backup server takes over the operations of the primary server. In a network environment, this typically means assuming the IP address of the primary server so that the switchover is transparent to end users. After the primary server is repaired, you can bring it back online either as the new secondary server or as the primary server again, after files are brought up-to-date.

As shown in Figure 22.1, some sort of file synchronization must be going on between these two servers if the data the user expects is to be present on the backup server. This can be done in several ways. A commonly used mechanism that is inexpensive to implement is to use a dedicated high-speed network connection (100BaseTX or 1000BaseTX) between the primary and backup servers. You can use file synchronization software to keep files up-to-date across this dedicated network connection without using bandwidth on the normal corporate network.

Figure 22.1
HA software enables switchover to a backup server when failure occurs.

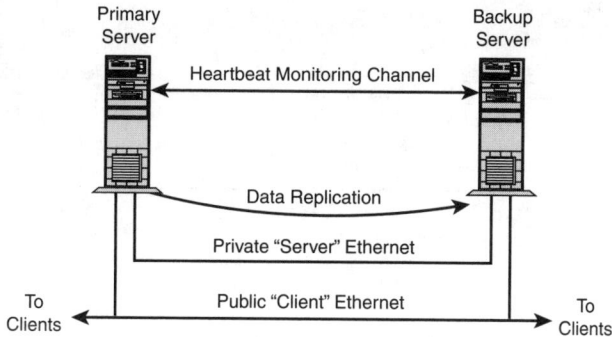

Note

Many commercial UNIX vendors have software or hardware options available specifically for the purpose of creating high availability enterprise class servers. If you are running a commercial UNIX system, especially on a non-Intel platform, you might want to investigate what your system vendor has to offer.

HIGH AVAILABILITY (HA) SOFTWARE FOR LINUX

As Linux has matured and has been deployed by more and more businesses, interest in providing HA solutions using inexpensive Linux-based systems has grown. Unfortunately, until the past year or two, no solutions existed to allow this to happen. Fortunately, this is one area in which Linux is rapidly maturing, and several HA software solutions are now available or under development.

Several HA software packages available for Linux at the time of publication are listed in Table 22.1.

TABLE 22.1   HA SOFTWARE PACKAGES FOR LINUX

Package	Source	Description
Heartbeat	http://www.linux-ha.org	Linux High Availability Project. Software that performs host monitoring and IP address takeover.
Heart	http://www.linux-ha.org	Software that does heartbeat monitoring only.
Fake	http://www.us.vergenet.net/linux/fake/	Software to perform redundant server switchover. Used in combination with Heart.
Mon	http://www.kernel.org/software/mon/	Host-monitoring software. Has the capability to take an action when a monitored server or subsystem fails.

TABLE 22.1   CONTINUED

Package	Source	Description
Linux Virtual Server Project	`http://www.LinuxVirtualServer.org/`	Uses the Heartbeat software from the High Availability Linux Project.
Piranha	`http://www.redhat.com/support/wpapers/piranha/`	Red Hat Software's clustering tool for Red Hat Linux 6.1. Based on the Linux Virtual Server, with some additional GUI tools.

The most notable HA software currently available for Linux is provided by the High Availability Linux Project, at `http://www.linux-ha.org`. The High Availability Linux Project is in a state of development but has reached a useful state before the time of this writing. Also worth taking a look at is the Linux Virtual Server project at `http://www.LinuxVirtualServer.org`.

Although discussion of all these packages is beyond the scope of this book, I will try to take you through the installation and configuration of the *Heartbeat* package, part of the High Availability Linux Project. In the next few sections, we'll walk through

- Configuring your hardware for HA monitoring
- Installing and configuring the Heartbeat HA software under Linux
- Setting up `rsync` to replicate Samba shares from the primary server to the backup server
- Configuring Samba's `smb.conf` file for use in an HA environment

CREATING A LINUX HIGH AVAILABILITY CLUSTER

The Heartbeat HA software for Linux enables you to configure two or more Linux systems to act as a *high availability cluster*. This HA cluster appears to the network as a virtual server at a fixed IP address that is not used by any of the servers composing the cluster. Figure 22.2 shows how two Linux systems appear as a third virtual server to network clients.

All clients access the virtual HA server for network services such as Samba. By using data replication, the amount of data lost to a primary server failure is kept to a minimum. If the primary server in the cluster fails, the backup server takes over operation of the HA cluster within seconds. This means that in most cases, network users will not even know that a server failure has occurred.

Setting up a Linux system to use the Heartbeat HA software requires several steps. Before installing the software, you must set up the required hardware. The steps to do so are outlined in the following sections.

Figure 22.2
Heartbeat HA Software allows creation of a high availability cluster.

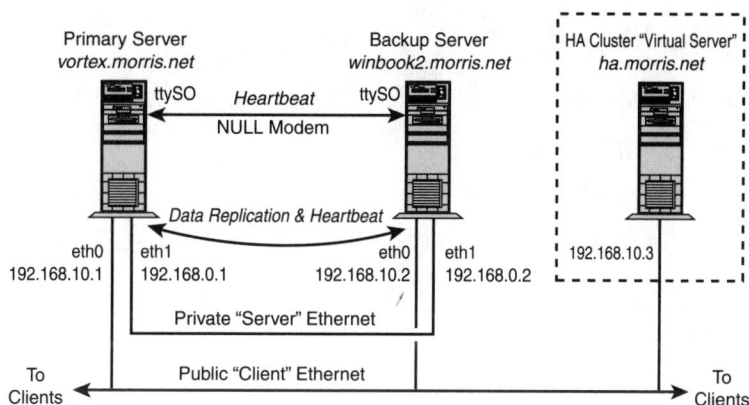

PREPARING THE HARDWARE

To use Heartbeat, the most obvious hardware requirement is that you have two PCs running Linux. The next decision to make is choosing the communications path used for system monitoring:

- Serial (RS-232C) using a NULL modem cable
- PPP over serial link
- Primary Ethernet (the one your client PCs talk to the servers on)
- Private Ethernet (dedicated Ethernet connection between servers)

Heartbeat can use one or more of these interface types. I highly recommend that you consider using multiple connections, such as a serial NULL modem and Ethernet. That way, if a connection goes down, an alternative communications channel still exists between the servers.

For our sample configuration, we will be using the setup shown in Figure 22.2. This setup has the following characteristics:

- An RS-232C NULL modem cable is used as a Heartbeat monitoring channel, connected to ttyS0 (COM1) on both Linux servers.
- The public Ethernet used to communicate with client PCs uses the eth0 device on both servers.
- A second Ethernet interface, eth1, is installed on both servers. This creates a private network for use by data replication and heartbeat monitoring software.

INSTALLING HEARTBEAT

The Heartbeat software is available as a source code package, which you can build on your system, or as an RPM package, which you can install on Red Hat and other Linux distributions. Both package formats are available through links on the book information Web site at URL http://www.mcp.com/catalog/corp_bud.cfm?isbn=0789723190. At the time of this writing, the filenames were

```
heartbeat-0.4.6-1.i386.rpm
heartbeat-0.4.6.tar.gz
```

The latest version can always be obtained from `http://www.linux-ha.org`.

To install the RPM package, type

```
rpm -i heartbeat-0.4.6-1.i386.rpm
```

If you are installing from source code, you can do so by issuing the following commands:

```
cd /usr/local/src
tar -xzf heartbeat-0.4.6.tar.gz
cd heartbeat-0.4.6
make
make install
```

Other than a few minor differences, the Heartbeat software should be installed in similar locations. If you installed from the RPM file, the documentation for Heartbeat is located under `/usr/doc/heartbeat`. If you installed from the source code package, the documentation is in the directory `/usr/local/src/heartbeat-0.4.6/doc`.

CONFIGURING HEARTBEAT

Several files must be created or modified to set up the Heartbeat HA software. We will go through these in order, presenting sample listings for the configuration shown in Figure 22.2.

CONFIGURING ha.cf

The first step in configuring Heartbeat is to create or edit the configuration file, `/etc/ha.d/ha.cf`. For the example setup, we will use the file shown in Listing 22.1.

LISTING 22.1 `/etc/ha.d/ha.cf`

```
#----------------------------------------------------------
# /etc/ha.d/ha.cf
#
# Configuration file for Heartbeat HA software for Linux.
#----------------------------------------------------------
#
#       keepalive: how many seconds between heartbeats
#
keepalive 2
#
#     deadtime: seconds-to-declare-host-dead
#
deadtime 10
#
#     serial     serialportname ...
serial /dev/ttyS0
#
#     Baud rate for both serial and ppp-udp ports...
#
baud 19200
#
```

LISTING 22.1   CONTINUED

```
#      What UDP port to use for udp or ppp-udp communication?
#
udpport 1001
#
#      What interfaces to heartbeat over?
#
udp eth1
#
#      Watchdog is the watchdog timer.  If our own heart doesn't beat for
#      a minute, then our machine will reboot.
#
watchdog /dev/watchdog
#
#      File to write debug messages to
debugfile /var/log/ha-debug
#
#
#       File to write other messages to
#
logfile /var/log/ha-log
#
#      Tell what machines are in the cluster
#      node      nodename ...  -- must match uname -n
node vortex.morris.net
node winbook2.morris.net
```

> **Note**
>
> The configuration files in this chapter are in the file `ha-scripts.tar.gz` on the Web site for this book:
>
> `http://www.mcp.com/catalog/corp_bud.cfm?isbn=0789723190`

> **Note**
>
> Most of the configuration files used in this chapter are identical on both servers that make up the high availability Samba system. If network interfaces or serial ports vary between your systems, you will want to edit the configuration files appropriately on your systems.

SETTING UP A WATCHDOG TIMER DEVICE

The watchdog option shown in Listing 22.1 requires the use of the Linux *watchdog timer* kernel driver. A watchdog timer is a mechanism used in high reliability systems to prevent failures due to system lockups. The watchdog consists of a countdown timer in either hardware or software, which software must reset periodically. If the watchdog timer ever expires, the system will be rebooted. The Linux kernel supports a variety of hardware-based watchdog timer devices, as well as a software-based watchdog timer implemented within the Linux kernel itself.

In the sample setup, we use the software watchdog timer, *softdog*. To load it, you must compile this module as part of your kernel by making the choices shown in Listing 22.2.

LISTING 22.2 KERNEL COMPILE-TIME OPTIONS FOR SOFTWARE WATCHDOG TIMER

```
Watchdog Timer Support (CONFIG_WATCHDOG) [Y/n/?] Y
*
* Watchdog Cards
*
    Disable watchdog shutdown on close (CONFIG_WATCHDOG_NOWAYOUT) [N/y/?] N
    WDT Watchdog timer (CONFIG_WDT) [N/y/m/?] N
    Software Watchdog (CONFIG_SOFT_WATCHDOG) [M/n/y/?] Y
    Berkshire Products PC Watchdog (CONFIG_PCWATCHDOG) [N/y/m/?] N
    Acquire SBC Watchdog Timer (CONFIG_ACQUIRE_WDT) [N/y/m/?] N
    Mixcom Watchdog (CONFIG_MIXCOMWD)  [N/y/m/?] N
```

Tip from
Jim Morris

The watchdog timer kernel options are found in the Character Devices section of the Linux kernel configuration.

Note

If you are already running another watchdog timer monitoring program, you should either disable it or disable the Heartbeat option to monitor the watchdog timer. This parameter is optional for use of the Heartbeat program.

Note

For more information on the Linux watchdog timer interfaces, see the file /usr/src/ linux/Documentation/watchdog.txt on your system.

On some systems, the software watchdog module might already be compiled as a loadable kernel module. To load it as a module, issue the following command:

`insmod softdog`

You can place this command at the bottom of the file /etc/rc.d/rc.sysinit to ensure that it is loaded at boot time, before loading of the HA software.

EDITING haresources

The next file to configure is the file /etc/ha.d/haresources. This file configures which IP address will be used for the HA cluster (the virtual server), as well as which services will be started and stopped on each system as the IP address control changes. Listing 22.3 shows a sample haresources file that configures WWW and Samba services to start and stop when the IP address moves from the primary to the backup server. The master node for the cluster is configured to be vortex.morris.net in the example.

LISTING 22.3 `/etc/ha.d/haresources`

```
#------------------------------------------------------------
# /etc/ha.d/haresources
#
# Configures the IP address and master server for the
# HA Cluster, and determines the services that will be
# stopped and started when the control of the HA
# cluster changes.
#------------------------------------------------------------
#
#        These resources in this file are either IP addresses, or the name
#        of scripts to run to "start" or "stop" the given resource.
#
#        The format is like this:
#
#node-name resource1 resource2 ... resourceN
#
#        If the resource name contains an :: in the middle of it, the
#        part after the :: is passed to the resource script as an argument.
#
vortex.morris.net IPaddr::192.168.10.3 httpd smb
```

> **Note**
>
> There should normally be only one entry in the `haresources` file.

The configuration line in Listing 22.3 does several things:

- It tells both systems that the primary server in the HA cluster is the system `vortex.morris.net`.

- It specifies the IP address to be used by the HA cluster, `192.168.10.3` in this case.

- It tells Heartbeat which services to start and stop when switching control of the HA cluster.

To start and stop services, the names given at the final parameters on the line in `haresources` should correspond with system service scripts in either `/etc/ha.d/resources.d` or `/etc/rc.d/init.d`. All scripts should be capable of taking a `start` or `stop` parameter to start or stop the specific service.

EDITING `authkeys`

The final file to configure for the Heartbeat HA software is `/etc/ha.d/authkeys`, which configures the authentication method used when the servers in the HA cluster communicate with each other. Use the contents of Listing 22.4 as your `authkeys` file.

LISTING 22.4 `/etc/ha.d/authkeys`

```
#
#        Authentication file.  Must be mode 600
#
```

```
LISTING 22.4    CONTINUED

#
#           Must have exactly one auth directive at the front.
#           auth    send authentication using this method-id
#
#           Then, list the method and key that go with that method-id
#
#           Available methods: crc sha1, md5.  Crc doesn't need/want a key.
#
#           You normally only have one authentication method-id listed in this
#           ➥file
#
#           Put more than one to make a smooth transition when changing auth
#           methods and/or keys.
#
#
#           sha1 is believed to be the "best", md5 next best.
#
#           crc adds no security, except from packet corruption.
#                   Use only on physically secure networks.
#
auth 1
1 crc
#2 sha1 HI!
#3 md5 Hello!
```

In Listing 22.4, we chose to utilize CRC authentication because all the HA cluster communication in the setup in Figure 22.2 occurs over either a secure NULL modem connection or over a private Ethernet connection.

As mentioned in the comments in Listing 22.3, the authkeys file should be readable and writeable only to the root user. To ensure this, issue the following command at the Linux prompt:

```
chmod 600 /etc/ha.d/authkeys
```

STARTING HEARTBEAT

If you installed Heartbeat from the RPM package, the appropriate files should have been installed into the /etc/rc.d directories on your system. If you installed from the source code (tar.gz file), you will need to create the appropriate files to start Heartbeat when your system starts.

Under Red Hat 6.x, Mandrake 6.x and 7.x, Caldera OpenLinux 2.2, and other Linux systems using System V initscripts, do the following:

```
cd /etc/rc.d/rc0.d ; ln -s ../init.d/heartbeat K40heartbeat
cd /etc/rc.d/rc1.d ; ln -s ../init.d/heartbeat K40heartbeat
cd /etc/rc.d/rc2.d ; ln -s ../init.d/heartbeat S40heartbeat
cd /etc/rc.d/rc3.d ; ln -s ../init.d/heartbeat S24heartbeat
cd /etc/rc.d/rc4.d ; ln -s ../init.d/heartbeat K40heartbeat
cd /etc/rc.d/rc5.d ; ln -s ../init.d/heartbeat S24heartbeat
cd /etc/rc.d/rc6.d ; ln -s ../init.d/heartbeat K40heartbeat
```

Note You do not need to issue all these commands if you installed from the RPM package.

If you installed from the RPM package, you will likely have files called `S24heartbeat` in the `/etc/rc.d/rc2.d` and `/etc/rc.d/rc4.d` subdirectories. I suggest that you delete these files and create the `K40heartbeat` links previously given. Do this by typing

```
cd /etc/rc.d/rc2.d
rm -f S24heartbeat ; ln -s ../init.d/heartbeat S40heartbeat
cd /etc/rc.d/rc4.d
rm -f S24heartbeat ; ln -s ../init.d/heartbeat S24heartbeat
```

The reason for changing these scripts is so that we have at least two runlevels, 2 and 4, which allow us to start the network without starting the Heartbeat HA software.

→ We will take advantage of this later to aid in error recovery. **See** "Recovering from a Server Failure," **p. 460**.

If you are running a Linux distribution such as Slackware that does not utilize this type of system startup file structure, you will want to invoke Heartbeat from the file `/etc/rc.d/rc.local` with the following line:

```
/etc/ha.d/heartbeat start
```

FILE SYNCHRONIZATION

At this point, you have configured all the software to create a Linux-based HA cluster. However, you must do one important thing to make the cluster truly useful. The data must be mirrored from the primary server to the backup server. Otherwise, if the backup server were to take over operation of the cluster, the Samba users would not see the expected data on network shares!

To set up mirroring, we will use the `rsync` program, available on all current Linux distributions. You can use `rsync` to mirror directory trees between systems. It is intelligent enough to delete files that are deleted on the source of the mirror operation and to copy only the changed data on each run.

In the sample setup we have been following from Figure 22.2, we want to mirror data from the primary server to the backup server. To do so, we will first set up each system to function as both an `rsync` server and an `rsync` client, with emphasis on maintaining a mirror of all public Samba shares.

Although you could only set the primary system as the `rsync` server, and the backup as a client, it is useful to have the server set up on both systems. That way, if you have to bring the primary back online after a failure has occurred, you can sync the files either manually or automatically to pick up changes that have occurred while the system was offline.

SETTING UP THE rsync SERVER

To set up rsync as a server, you first must ensure that you have the appropriate entries in several system files. In /etc/services, make sure you have the following entries:

```
rsync           873/tcp                 # rsync
rsync           873/udp                 # rsync
```

> **Note**   Red Hat 6.x, Mandrake 6.x and beyond, and some other systems already have entries for rsync in the /etc/services file.

In /etc/inetd.conf, add the following entry if it does not already exist:

```
rsync  stream tcp nowait root /usr/bin/rsync rsyncd -daemon
```

If your rsync application is in a location other than /usr/bin, you will need to adjust accordingly.

Next, we will need to create an rsync server configuration file, shown in Listing 22.5. In this case, we are configuring an rsync module definition for a set of Samba shares, all of which are beneath the /usr2/shared directory on the server.

LISTING 22.5   /etc/rsyncd.conf

```
#
# Example rsyncd.conf file
#
[samba-shares]
     comment = Samba Shares
     path = /usr2/shared
     auth users = syncuser
     secrets file = /etc/rsync.secrets
     hosts allow = vortex.morris.net, winbook2.morris.net
```

Notice the auth users and secrets file entries in Listing 22.5. These two lines enable us to utilize an authentication mechanism so that some level of security is provided. The user syncuser is not a real user account on either server but just an identifier that is passed when performing synchronization operations.

The contents of the file /etc/rsync.secrets appear in Listing 22.6.

LISTING 22.6   /etc/rsync.secrets

```
#
# rsync secrets file, /etc/rsync.secrets
#
# These username:password pairs do not have to be
# real users on the system.
#
syncuser:xyzzy
```

This file should be made accessible only to root on each system by typing this command at the Linux prompt:

```
chmod 600 /etc/rsync.secrets
```

SETTING UP THE rsync CLIENT

To use rsync on the client side (the backup server of our HA cluster in most cases), we must be able to supply the username and password listed in the last section. rsync enables us to do this using either environment variables or a file containing the username and password information.

We will invoke rsync in the following manner:

```
/usr/bin/rsync -av --delete --password-file=/root/syncpassword \
  vortex.morris.net:/usr2/shared/ /usr2/shared
```

This copies all files from the /usr2/shared directory on the primary server, vortex.morris.net, to the backup server, winbook2.morris.net. Obviously, you would change the hostname in the command to copy in the other direction.

The options specified retain all timestamp, ownership, and permissions for files. Files that do not exist on the source system will be deleted from the destination system, and the password for authentication will be taken out of the file /root/syncpassword, shown in Listing 22.7.

LISTING 22.7   root/syncpassword

```
syncuser:xyzzy
```

RUNNING rsync USING cron

To synchronize on a regular schedule, it is useful to create a scheduler entry to do so automatically. As root, edit the crontab file by typing

```
crontab -e
```

This puts you into a standard vi editor, with the root user's crontab entries loaded. To schedule rsync to run at five-minute intervals, add the following entry:

```
*/5 * * * * /usr/bin/rsync -av --delete --password-file=/root/syncpassword \
  vortex.morris.net:/usr2/shared/xfer/ /usr2/shared/xfer
```

Save the file by typing :x, and the scheduled job should now be run by the cron daemon.

SAMBA CONFIGURATION

For the HA cluster to provide seamless Samba services to network clients, you must ensure that both systems in the cluster have identical Samba setups. This includes forcing the NetBIOS machine name used by SMB networking to be the same for both systems. Don't worry that this will cause a conflict, because only one system should be running as a Samba server at any time at the cluster's IP address.

Listing 22.8 shows the `smb.conf` file used in the sample setup we have been talking about so far. It configures Samba to use a NetBIOS name of "HA" and also sets Samba to operate as a domain controller, with several shares.

LISTING 22.8   `smb.conf` FILE FOR SAMPLE HA SETUP

```
[global]
  workgroup = EMPIRE
  netbios name = HA
  server string = HA Linux Cluster / Samba %v
  encrypt passwords = Yes
  passwd program = /usr/bin/passwd
  passwd chat = *current*password* %o\n *ew*password* %n\n *ew*password* \
%n\n *updated*successfully*
  username map = /etc/smbusers
  UNIX password sync = Yes
  log file = /var/log/samba/log.%m
  max log size = 500
  time server = Yes
  deadtime = 15
  socket options = TCP_NODELAY SO_KEEPALIVE
  load printers = No
  domain admin users = jim
  logon script = %U.bat
  logon path = \\%L\profiles\%U
  domain logons = Yes
  os level = 65
  preferred master = Yes
  domain master = Yes
  dns proxy = No
  wins support = Yes
  message command = /bin/mail -s 'message from %f on %m' root < %s ; rm %s
  hosts allow = 192.168.10. 127.
  level2 oplocks = Yes
  strict locking = Yes
  dos filetime resolution = Yes

[homes]
  comment = Home Directories
  read only = No
  browseable = No

[netlogon]
  comment = Network Logon Service
  path = /usr2/shared/netlogon
  admin users = jim
  share modes = No
  root preexec = /usr2/shared/netlogon/genlogon.pl %U %G %L
  root postexec = rm -f /usr2/shared/netlogon/%U.bat

[profiles]
  comment = Roving Profile storage
  path = /usr2/shared/profiles
  read only = No
  root preexec = /usr/local/sbin/mkprofiledir.sh %U %G
```

LISTING 22.8   CONTINUED

```
[printers]
  comment = All Printers
  path = /var/spool/samba
  print ok = Yes
  browseable = No

 [xfer]
  comment = Temporary File Transfer Area
  path = /usr2/shared/xfer
  read only = No
  create mask = 0775
  directory mask = 0775
  map system = Yes
  map hidden = Yes

 [apps]
  comment = Applications
  path = /usr2/shared/apps
  read only = No
  force create mode = 0775
  force directory mode = 0775

 [data]
    comment = Data files
    path = /usr2/shared/data
    read only = No
    force create mode = 0775
    force directory mode = 0775
```

The important parameter in Listing 22.7 is the forcing of the hostname using the `netbios name` parameter. Also note that all Samba shares, with the possible exception of the user home directories, are stored in the `/usr2/shared` directory tree, making it easy to run `rsync` on the shares.

> **Note**
>
> The shares do not have to be located in the same location on both servers. If they are not, the `smb.conf` files will differ between the two machines, and the `rsync` command shown earlier can use different directory paths to replicate data.

> **Note**
>
> Samba 2.0.7 and beyond includes a new parameter that simplifies the process of configuring high availability Samba servers. This is the `source environment` parameter, which enables Samba to set environment variables from a file or script. Your `smb.conf` file can then pull in these environment variables via the `$(env)` macro as discussed in Chapter 9, "Samba Automation."

For Samba to work properly when services move from the primary to the backup server, you should ensure that all other support files are identical between the systems. These include files such as

- `/etc/smbpasswd` (possibly elsewhere on your system)
- `/etc/smbusers` (possibly elsewhere on your system)
- `/etc/passwd`
- `/etc/group`
- `/etc/printcap`
- User home directories in `/home`, and so forth

STARTING THE HA CLUSTER

At this point, you have hopefully done all the configuration necessary to create a high availability Linux cluster for use by Samba. To start operation, you can either reboot both servers or invoke the heartbeat program manually by typing

`/etc/rc.d/init.d/heartbeat start`

On a non-System V system such as Slackware, type

`/etc/ha.d/heartbeat start`

Tip from
Jim Morris   It is normally best to start the primary server before starting the backup server.

If all is well, you should be able to see output similar to that in Listing 22.9 in `/var/log/ha-log`.

LISTING 22.9   SUCCESSFUL STARTUP OF HA PRIMARY SERVER

```
16:16:17 info: Configuration validated. Starting heartbeat.
16:16:18 notice: Starting serial heartbeat on tty /dev/ttyS0
16:16:18 notice: UDP heartbeat started on port 1001 interface eth0
16:16:18 error: Cannot open /proc/ha/.control: No such file or directory
16:16:18 info: Requesting our resources.
16:16:19 INFO: Running /etc/ha.d/resource.d/IPaddr 192.168.10.3 status
16:16:19 INFO: Running /etc/ha.d/rc.d/ip-request ip-request
16:16:22 INFO: Running /etc/ha.d/rc.d/ip-request-resp ip-request-resp
16:16:22 received ip-request-resp IPaddr::192.168.10.3 OK
16:16:22 Acquiring resource group: vortex.morris.net \
IPaddr::192.168.10.3 httpd smb
16:16:22 INFO: Running /etc/rc.d/init.d/smb   start
16:16:25 INFO: Running /etc/rc.d/init.d/httpd   start
16:16:27 INFO: Running /etc/ha.d/resource.d/IPaddr 192.168.10.3 start
16:16:27 INFO: ifconfig eth0:0 192.168.10.3 netmask 255.255.255.0 \
broadcast 192.168.10.255
16:16:28 Sending Gratuitous Arp for 192.168.10.3 on eth0:0 [eth0]
```

The backup server should start up with messages similar to those shown in Listing 22.10 in its `/var/log/ha-log`.

LISTING 22.10 SUCCESSFUL STARTUP OF HA BACKUP SERVER

```
16:18:29 info: Configuration validated. Starting heartbeat.
16:18:30 notice: Starting serial heartbeat on tty /dev/ttyS0
16:18:30 notice: UDP heartbeat started on port 1001 interface eth0
16:18:30 error: Cannot open /proc/ha/.control: No such file or directory
16:18:30 info: Requesting our resources.
16:18:30 info: No local resources \
[/usr/lib/heartbeat/ResourceManager listkeys winbook2.morris.net]
16:18:30 INFO: Running /etc/ha.d/rc.d/ip-request ip-request
16:18:31 INFO: Running /etc/ha.d/resource.d/IPaddr 192.168.10.3 status
```

If you see output similar to that shown in listings 22.8 and 22.9, you are in business!

TESTING THE HA SETUP

To test the sample setup covered in this section, the following steps were performed in order. You could also do this with your setup to verify that things are working as expected.

1. Log on to the domain from a Windows 98 client PC, verifying that the Samba server HA was available and that all user shares connected as expected.

2. Delete a few files on a Samba share and copy a few new files over.

3. Monitor the backup server using a Telnet session, and verify that the file additions and deletions get mirrored from the primary cluster server.

4. Open a document on a network share from the client PC. Make a few changes, but do not save.

5. Shut down the primary cluster server. You can do this either by doing a system shutdown at the command prompt

   ```
   shutdown -h now
   ```

   or by shutting down the heartbeat HA software:

   ```
   /etc/rc.d/init.d/heartbeat stop
   ```

6. After giving the backup server a few seconds to take over the operation of the HA cluster, save the modified document from the client PC. If all is well, the document should be saved because the client should seamlessly handle the transfer of service.

When the backup server takes over the operations of the HA cluster, you should see some messages like those shown in Listing 22.11 in the backup server's /var/log/ha-log file.

LISTING 22.11 TAKEOVER OF HA CLUSTER BY BACKUP SERVER

```
15:49:14 warn: node vortex.morris.net: is dead
15:49:14 INFO: Running /etc/ha.d/rc.d/status status
15:49:14 Taking over resource group IPaddr::192.168.10.3
15:49:15 Acquiring resource group: vortex.morris.net \
IPaddr::192.168.10.3 httpd smb
15:49:15 INFO: Running /etc/rc.d/init.d/smb   start
15:49:16 INFO: Running /etc/rc.d/init.d/httpd   start
15:49:18 INFO: Running /etc/ha.d/resource.d/IPaddr 192.168.10.3 start
```

LISTING 22.11   CONTINUED

```
15:49:18 INFO: ifconfig eth0:0 192.168.10.3 netmask \
255.255.255.0 broadcast 192.168.10.255
15:49:18 Sending Gratuitous Arp for 192.168.10.3 on eth0:0 [eth0]
15:50:25 error: TTY write timeout on [/dev/ttyS0]   (no connection?)
```

When the primary server returns to service, the backup server will show messages like those in Listing 22.12 in its /var/log/ha-log file.

LISTING 22.12 BACKUP SERVER YIELDS CONTROL TO PRIMARY WHEN IT COMES BACK ONLINE

```
16:16:21 notice: node vortex.morris.net seq restart 1 vs 2514
16:16:21 info: node vortex.morris.net: status up
16:16:21 INFO: Running /etc/ha.d/rc.d/status status
16:16:22 INFO: Running /etc/ha.d/rc.d/ip-request ip-request
16:16:22 INFO: Running /etc/ha.d/resource.d/IPaddr 192.168.10.3 status
16:16:23 Releasing resource group: vortex.morris.net \
IPaddr::192.168.10.3 httpd smb
16:16:23 INFO: Running /etc/ha.d/resource.d/IPaddr 192.168.10.3 stop
16:16:23 IP Address 192.168.10.3 released
16:16:23 INFO: Running /etc/rc.d/init.d/httpd   stop
16:16:23 INFO: Running /etc/rc.d/init.d/smb   stop
```

RECOVERING FROM A SERVER FAILURE

After a failure has occurred, you will probably rectify the problem and then bring the failed server back online. The action required from you when bringing a failed server back online depends on whether it was the primary or backup server.

BRINGING THE PRIMARY SERVER BACK ONLINE

If the primary server failed, you will most likely want to initially bring it back up disconnected from the cluster or the network. Otherwise, it could attempt to take the cluster over before you have fixed the problem that caused the failure. If you are running a system with System V style initscripts (that is, you have the file /etc/rc.d/init.d/heartbeat), you should be able to bring the system up in single-user mode. To do this, if you are using the LILO boot loader, type

```
LILO: linux single
```

This is assuming that your kernel image is called "linux." If you are not sure what the kernel name is, press the Tab key at the LILO prompt to get a list of available kernels. The first one in the list normally is the default one that you have been using.

After the server is back up in single-user mode, correct the problem that caused the failure. After you have done so, you will want to restart network services, but do not start the Heartbeat HA package yet. To do this, we will go from single-user mode to either runlevel 2 or runlevel 4. This is the reason we changed the RPM-supplied initscripts in the section "Starting Heartbeat." To start in runlevel 4, from single-user mode, type

```
/sbin/telinit 4
```

After the system has started the network, you will want to use rsync to copy the most up-to-date data from the backup server, which has been serving Samba requests during the failure period. To do this in our sample setup, we would type

```
/usr/bin/rsync -av --delete --password-file=/root/syncpassword \
  winbook2.morris.net:/usr2/shared/ /usr2/shared
```

After all files are replicated, it is safe to bring the primary server back online as the controller of the HA cluster. To do so, go to your normal runlevel, either 3 (text mode) or 5 (GUI logon screen). Type

```
/sbin/telinit 3
```

BRINGING THE BACKUP SERVER BACK ONLINE

If the backup server failed, there is not much out of the ordinary to do. Simply bring the box back up and correct whatever problem has occurred. After the system is up and running normally with Heartbeat and data replication going, it should be ready to take the HA cluster in the event the primary server fails.

ADVANCED FILE SYNCHRONIZATION TECHNIQUES

There is a problem with the HA cluster setup we have developed in this chapter, shown in Figure 22.2. The problem is this: No matter how often file synchronization occurs, the backup server will never be quite up-to-date. This means that your network users could lose some data, depending on how recently the synchronization has occurred. To address the issue of maintaining up-to-date files between multiple servers in an HA cluster, several options exist:

- Shared drive(s)
- Distributed Shared File System (Coda)
- Network mirroring of drives using drdb

We will explore shared drives and the Coda file system further here. For more information on drdb, see http://www.complang.tuwien.ac.at/reisner/drbd/.

SHARED DRIVES

Figure 22.3 shows a hardware solution to the problem of file synchronization. Basically, all network storage is located in an external SCSI drive enclosure. Both servers are connected to this drive array with their SCSI controllers set to different addresses. During normal operations, only the primary server talks on this SCSI bus, controlling the disk array. However, in the event of a failure, the backup server takes over the drive array. This can require file systems to be checked, but if a journaling file system is in use, the time required to check the file system is minimal.

→ For a description of a journaling file system in use, **see** "Journaling File Systems," **p. 428**.

Figure 22.3
You can accomplish file synchronization using shared SCSI drive arrays.

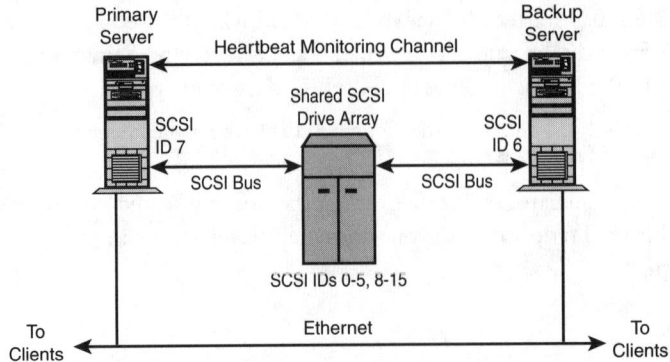

In most cases, the external SCSI disk array is configured using RAID-1 or RAID-5 to prevent the failure of a single disk drive from causing the entire HA setup to go down.

Setting up a dual-hosted SCSI disk array is an advanced topic, beyond the scope of this book. More information on the subject should be available from several SCSI system vendors, as well as the resources listed at the end of this chapter.

DISTRIBUTED SHARED FILE SYSTEM (CODA)

Another method of eliminating file synchronization issues is to use a network file system as the underlying file system that Samba shares with SMB client PCs. To eliminate potential network bandwidth issues, this shared network file system should reside on a separate network from the one on which Samba client requests are processed, as shown in Figure 22.4.

Figure 22.4
Using a Coda distributed file system to provide high availability.

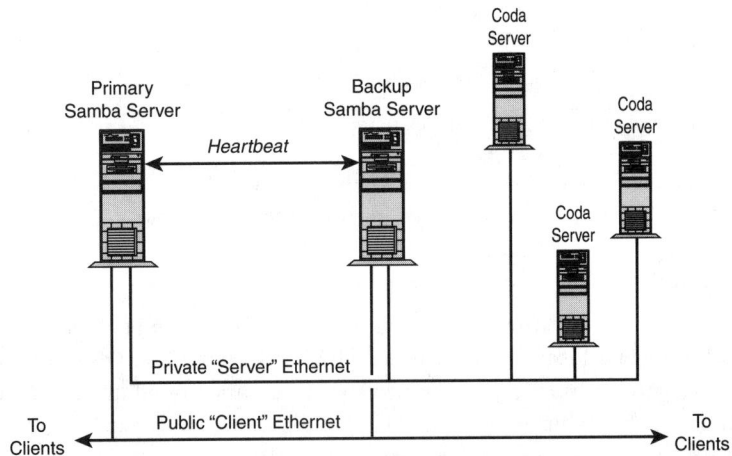

Note Information on the Coda file system is available from `http://www.coda.cs` `.cmu.edu.`

> **Note**   Linux 2.2 and later versions include support for the Coda file system.

Coda is a unique file system in that it provides many of the mechanisms needed for HA, including

- Disconnected client operation
- Server fail-over
- Server replication
- Automatic re-integration of offline changes

By combining Coda with a Linux-based HA cluster, you can achieve a very robust and reliable Samba server solution. Basically, with the Coda file system running across the same systems on which the HA cluster is running, the Samba server effectively "floats" around the cluster, depending on which system is currently in control of the HA cluster.

The only potential drawback is that I/O performance for Samba clients can be slower than for files residing locally to the machine the Samba server is running on. If high reliability is an absolute requirement, this slight performance hit might be acceptable.

SETTING UP SAMBA FOR HA

When we configured the HA cluster earlier in this chapter in Listing 22.7, we showed a sample `smb.conf` for Samba on that cluster. The only Samba configuration option we must pay special attention to on an HA configuration is the `netbios name` global option. Specifically, all systems in the cluster should be configured to use the same NetBIOS name so that client PCs connect seamlessly as control of the cluster moves from machine to machine.

→   For more details on the `netbios name` parameter, see "Samba Configuration," **p. 455**.

For the most part, all systems in the HA cluster should have identical `smb.conf` files, and all supporting files (such as user password files, user home directories, and shares) should also be available to each system.

One possible method of user authentication is to configure Samba to use an LDAP server, as documented in Chapter 20, "Samba and LDAP." By using an LDAP server that is also implemented using an HA solution, user authentication files will not have to be copied locally to each system in the Samba HA cluster.

SAMBA IN LARGE ORGANIZATIONS

Case studies have been conducted showing that a moderately powerful Samba server can service many hundreds of network clients while maintaining reasonable performance. One such study was conducted by the University of Brunel in the United Kingdom. This study is available on the Internet at `http://www.brunel.ac.uk/%7Epeter/samba/`.

Briefly, the study involved the real-world deployment of Samba services across a large university. Sun servers running Samba on the Solaris operating system are used at this site to provide file and print services for more than 20,000 users, running on more than 4,000 PCs.

During benchmark testing, as many as 450 Windows NT clients were actively connected to a low-end Sun server running Samba 1.9.18p10 on Solaris 2.5.1. The server in this case was running with 192MB of RAM and Fast (100Mbps) Ethernet. With that many clients, the system exhausted physical memory and began using more swap space. Even so, there was still at least 20% idle CPU time even under the heaviest loads measured. With increasing numbers of client connections, the time to load applications from a Samba share did not increase noticeably. Network login times remained consistent as well.

Based on their test results, the University of Brunel plans to support an average of 460 PCs using a single Sun Ultra server.

Although no special configuration is required when using Samba for a large network or domain, be careful not to overload your Samba server with too many users. The number of users that can be supported depends on many factors, including the available RAM and processor power on the Samba server, as well as network bandwidth.

NUMBER OF USERS PER SAMBA SERVER

The number of users that a single Samba server can support depends greatly on the amount of available RAM on the Samba server. As discussed in Chapter 21, "Samba and Performance," each Samba client connection consumes a certain amount of RAM on the server. You should tune the amount of server RAM to handle the maximum number of anticipated clients for that server.

→   For more information on tuning your Samba server's memory, **see** "Memory Sizing," **p. 430**.

→   Shared global memory, used to maintain file lock information between multiple Samba processes, can also become exhausted. To increase the shared global memory size, **see** "Share Modes," **p. 418**.

→   One other area of concern when implementing a Samba server for a large number of users is the number of available file and inode handles. To learn more, **see** "File and Inode Limits," **p. 420**, and "File Handle and Inode Limits," **p. 423**.

To a lesser extent, Samba performance depends on processor speed. If many active Samba processes (`smbd` and `nmbd`) are running, the amount of available processor time to service each client will be reduced. By monitoring server processor use, you can determine whether the system processor load is unacceptable. Several process-monitoring utilities are available for UNIX and Linux systems. Most Linux systems have the `top` program installed. Available for most UNIX and Linux systems is the `sar` program (System Activity Reporting), which gives very detailed reports of system resource use over time.

DISTRIBUTING USERS ACROSS MULTIPLE SERVERS

To reduce the load on a single server, you might want to distribute user connections to multiple Samba servers within a domain. You can do this while still using a single PDC to process domain logons. Simply maintain copies of commonly used shares on each server and use the domain logon script processing to decide which servers or shares to map for a particular user. You can still have shares that all users map to the primary Samba server for information that it might be hard to split across multiple servers.

Figure 22.5 shows an example of a setup where users in an accounting group have shares that are mapped to one Samba server, whereas users in a development group use other shares on another Samba server. All users in the example connect to the PDC for domain logon processing and for certain common shares.

Figure 22.5
Spread user connections across multiple Samba servers to reduce server load.

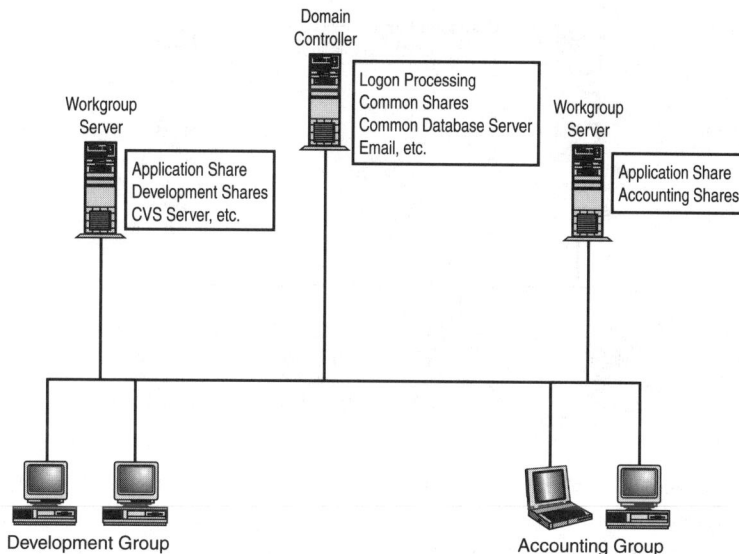

→ For more information on how you can set up logon script processing based on specific users or user groups, **see** "Logon Scripts," **p. 201**.

SAMBA VIRTUAL SERVERS

Often in a large organization, or even a small one, you can find the need to run more than one Samba server, but you do not have the machine resources to do so. One reason for running multiple servers might be that you need to use incompatible global smb.conf settings for different shares or users. Samba has configuration options that enable you to create *virtual Samba servers*, all existing on one machine. Each virtual Samba server can have its own unique settings.

The way we work this magic is by taking advantage of two features of Samba. The first is the capability to set not only the Samba server's primary NetBIOS network name but also a number of NetBIOS *aliases* as well. The second feature that enables us to create multiple virtual servers is the fact that Samba processes the smb.conf file each time a user connects. Part of the smb.conf processing involves the use of some special substitution parameters in the smb.conf. You can use these to do some neat things. The substitution parameter we are specifically interested in for our purposes is %L, which according to the smb.conf man page, will be replaced by the NetBIOS name of the server. By using the include directive in the smb.conf file, we can process different smb.conf options depending on which of the virtual servers the user is connecting to.

Figure 22.6 shows a real-world example of the way virtual Samba servers work, which we will describe in detail in the following text.

Figure 22.6
Samba allows the creation of virtual servers.

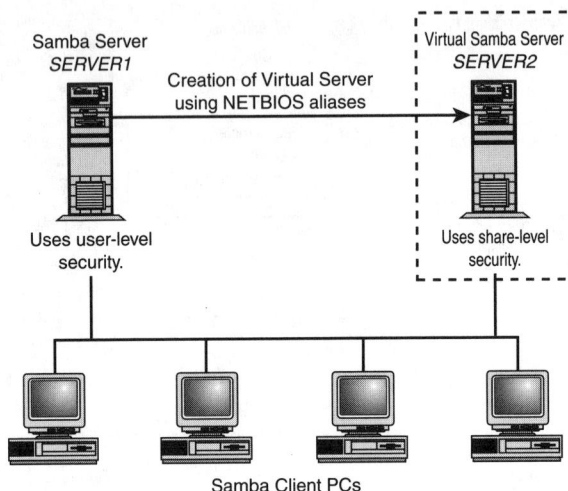

On a particular network, the need arose to have certain Samba shares that used share-level security rather than user-level security. But the desire was to have the Samba server itself, and the majority of network shares continue to use the user-level security model. The solution in this case was to create a second virtual server, which ran in share-level security mode.

To do this, the following modifications were made to the smb.conf file:

```
[global]
netbios name = SERVER1
netbios aliases = SERVER2
```

With this change, the primary name of the system continued to be SERVER1, which was its default based on the UNIX hostname. The system also showed up in browse lists under the NetBIOS name of SERVER2.

At the bottom of the [global] section, after all other common parameters for both servers, the following directive was placed:

```
include=%L.conf
```

And that was the end of the main smb.conf file.

Next, the rest of the original `smb.conf` file, from that point on, was placed into a file called `SERVER1.conf`, with the first Samba option in that file being the global option `security=user`, followed by the share definitions for SERVER1.

A new file called `SERVER2.conf` was created, with the first line `security=share`, followed by the share definitions for that virtual server.

After these changes, two servers were available to Windows client systems, each having their own set of shares and using different security modes.

→ For more information on virtual servers, **see** Chapter 9, "Samba Automation."

More Information

For more information on various topics presented in this chapter, the following resources will be useful:

- Linux High Availability HOWTO—This document was somewhat dated at the time of this writing but still has a lot of useful background information on high availability in general, as well as pointers on how to put it into practice. It is a good educational resource on the subject. It is available at
  `http://metalab.unc.edu/pub/Linux/ALPHA/linux-ha/High-Availability-HOWTO.html`

- High Availability Linux Project—Provides information on all the High Availability solutions for Linux. It can be reached at
  `http://www.linux-ha.org`

- Linux Enterprise Computing—Provides resources on Linux in the enterprise and links to other useful sites. It can be found at
  `http://linas.org/linux/`

From Here...

The remaining three chapters in this section are

- Troubleshooting Samba
- A Tour Through the Samba Source Code
- The Future of Samba

## CHAPTER 23

TROUBLESHOOTING SAMBA

In this chapter

by Richard Sharpe

One problem that users of Samba face is figuring out what the cause is when things go wrong. A couple of reasons for this are

- The complexity of the whole SMB protocol suite and Microsoft's extensions to it.
- Lack of information and knowledge about how the various components work.

In this book, we have provided you with enough background information so that you can understand what is going on when SMB clients are interacting with SMB servers. In this chapter, we provide a troubleshooting approach to resolving problems when they occur between SMB clients and Samba servers. With this knowledge and the troubleshooting approach, we think you will find it far easier to resolve problems with Samba.

The Troubleshooting Process

This usually involves an iterative approach taking the following form:

1. Determine the symptoms of the problem. Someone can tell you the symptoms, or you can observe the symptoms first-hand.

2. Because we are dealing with networked systems, you must form an opinion about whether the problem is local or remote. Often, the symptoms will help you form that opinion or will suggest tests you can perform to determine whether the problem is local or remote.

3. After you decide where you initially think the problem is, focus on that system with a standard set of tests to determine what the problem is or to rule out your initial diagnosis.

4. Perform a series of steps to track down and rectify the problem.

5. If you determine that your original decision was incorrect, select the other end of the network (the server) or the network, and go back to step 4.

6. Repeat steps 4 and 5 until you have resolved the problem.

The following sections provide suggestions on troubleshooting tools, procedures for isolating Samba problems, and examples of common problems with Samba.

Troubleshooting Tools

In any troubleshooting endeavor, the quality of your tools makes a big difference in your ability to solve your problems quickly. Many tools are available to help you diagnose problems between Samba and Windows clients. The following are some of these tools:

- `testparm`, to check that your `smb.conf` file does not contain any invalid parameters.
- `smbclient`, to check that you can reach your Samba server and that the shares you want are defined.

- Samba log files, to enable you to search for error messages relating to each Samba component. The location of the log files is specific to your system type. For Linux systems, they are usually in /var/log/samba. You can find more details in Chapter 5, "Configuring and Managing Samba."

- smbstatus, to check who has connections open to your Samba server and what shares they are accessing.

- nmblookup, to check what names have been registered on the network, which system is the Master Browser, and so on.

- DOS net view command, to check from a Windows system what shares are available on a server or what servers are visible on the network.

- DOS nbtstat command, to check on NetBIOS names, adapter status information, and so on.

- ping, to check that systems are reachable. You can use this command to ensure that name translation is working as well.

- tcpdump, to dump packets off the wire to check whether clients are talking to servers and vice versa. You can also use the tcpdump command to capture packets to a file for Ethereal to examine later.

- Ethereal, to analyze packets in detail and checking what is going wrong between a Windows client and Samba.

- Netmon, a program from Microsoft that is similar to Ethereal.

CLIENT PROBLEMS

If your problem is client based, the following approach usually yields a solution to the problem very quickly. A client-based problem is one where you have tried to use a client of some sort, such as smbclient, a DOS client command (net use), or a Windows client, to access a Samba server.

1. Because TCP/IP configuration problems cause all sorts of subtle and not-so-subtle problems, check this one out first.

   One of the simplest ways to check that your TCP/IP configuration is reasonable is with the ping command. This is available under both Windows and UNIX.

   Simply ping your Samba server from your client. However, ping will still work in some cases even if you have mistakes in your netmask or broadcast address. So you should also check that your netmask and broadcast addresses are correct because the Microsoft Windows browsing protocol is broadcast based.

   You should ping both by IP address and by name because this will help distinguish between datagram delivery problems and name translation problems (such as DNS lookup failures or WINS lookup failures). The following shows an example of pinging by IP address and then by name:

```
            C:\WINDOWS\DESKTOP>ping 10.0.0.2

Pinging 10.0.0.2 with 32 bytes of data:

Reply from 10.0.0.2: bytes=32 time=78ms TTL=255
Reply from 10.0.0.2: bytes=32 time=26ms TTL=255
Reply from 10.0.0.2: bytes=32 time=40ms TTL=255
Reply from 10.0.0.2: bytes=32 time=51ms TTL=255

C:\WINDOWS\DESKTOP>ping samba3
Bad IP address samba3.
```

The first `ping` succeeds and the second fails, which indicates that your server is reachable via IP but that name translation is not working, or that you have misspelled the name of your server. Name translation might fail because DNS is not working, WINS is not working, or both.

If `ping`ing the server fails, you will need to rectify that problem before proceeding. You might have a network infrastructure problem or a name translation problem. After you have fixed this problem, check to see whether you still have a problem.

Now, you might already have evidence that your TCP/IP configuration is working fine. This can be because you have managed to access shares on your Samba server.

If you have multiple network adapters, check that you have them all configured correctly.

2. Next, if TCP/IP is working and correctly configured, you should check your client configuration. That is, check that your client is in the correct workgroup/domain.

3. If your client's configuration is correct, your TCP/IP configuration is correct, and the network is working, start looking on the server.

   The first thing to check is that Samba is actually running. You can do this from a Linux/UNIX shell prompt with the following commands:

   `ps ax | grep mbd`

   You should see at least one copy of `nmbd(8)` and at least one copy of `smbd(8)`. If you find that one or another of these processes is not running, you should consult the Samba log files to find out why and rectify the problem. The log files are usually kept in `/var/log/samba` under Linux, but your `smb.conf` file will tell you where.

   If you are not getting sufficient logging information, increase the debug level and restart Samba. However, Samba will usually print error messages in its log files, regardless of the debug level.

4. If the Samba daemons are running, you need to figure out whether there is a configuration problem and what is going wrong in the interactions between the client and Samba. It is here that a good knowledge of the SMB protocol suite can be useful. It is also useful to be able to see what packets are being sent back and forth between SMB clients and servers.

Note

Check your Samba configuration thoroughly. Suggestions for solutions to common problems appear in the following text.

> Running `testparm` on your Samba server is very useful in finding configuration errors, but it cannot find the more subtle errors, like misspellings in the name of your workgroup or the names of directories supplied for the path of a share.

Because many users of Samba experience the same problems, the next section provides a list of common problems and suggestions on how to resolve them.

COMMON PROBLEMS WITH SAMBA

This section provides hints for diagnosing commonly observed problems.

BROWSING PROBLEMS

The following sections provide information on some common browsing problems. See Chapter 17, "Samba and Browsing," for more details.

YOU CAN'T BROWSE THE NETWORK

You double-click on Network Neighborhood, and after a while, possibly after clicking on Entire Network, you get the dialog box shown in Figure 23.1, Unable to browse the network.

Figure 23.1
Browsing the network gives you this error.

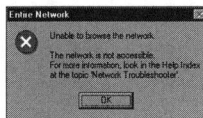

You might get this message for several reasons:

- No master browser is in your network, possibly because none has been configured and your Windows 9x client is configured to never become a master browser.

  To rectify this problem, change the `local master` and `preferred master` parameters to `yes` in your `smb.conf`, and your Samba server will become a local master browser when you restart `nmbd`. You do not need to set the `os level` parameter for Samba 2.0.6 because it defaults to 20. For earlier versions of Samba, however, you will need to set `os level` to a value such as 33, or Samba will not take part in browser elections.

Note

> From Samba 2.0.6 and beyond, the default values for the `local master` and `preferred master` parameters are `yes`. If you are experiencing browsing problems with Samba 2.0.6 and beyond, the problems are not likely to be configuration related.

- The broadcast address on your client does not agree with the broadcast address on your server, so the broadcast server does not see requests from the clients.

  To rectify this problem, ensure that the broadcast addresses agree on both systems.

- Your clients are configured to use WINS, but they cannot contact the WINS server to resolve names into addresses. This might be because the WINS server address is incorrect, packets are not reaching the WINS server, or `nmbd` is not running.

  To rectify this problem, ensure that your client is properly configured, the WINS server is reachable, and `nmbd` is running, if Samba is acting as your WINS server.

- The guest account does not exist on the Samba server, or the guest account parameter is missing and the account nobody does not exist. This means that Samba cannot give the client access to the `IPC$` share when it tries to browse.

  To rectify this problem, ensure that the guest account exists.

- `nmbd(8)` or `smbd(8)` is not running so the `GetBackupList` request goes unanswered, or the client cannot connect to the `IPC$` share to perform a `NetServerEnum2` request.

  To rectify this problem, ensure that Samba is starting properly.

You Can't See Any Servers or Can See Only Your Own Client

When you try to browse the network, you double-click on the Entire Network icon and then on the icon for your workgroup or domain, but see only your own client in the list. This problem can be caused by one of the following problems:

- Connectivity problems, such that the client is not seeing your Samba server's announcements and `GetBackupList` requests are not reaching the server.

  To rectify this problem, use standard tools like `ping` to ensure that packets can travel in both directions between the client and server.

- The server is in a different workgroup from your client.

  To rectify this problem, change the `workgroup` parameter in the `smb.conf` file on your Samba server and restart Samba.

You Can't See Remote Servers in Browse Lists

You double-click on Network Neighborhood and finally get a browse list, but you cannot see any of the servers that you know are in other subnets.

This problem is caused by not having a `remote announce` or `remote browse sync` parameter in your `smb.conf` file or because you have not configured one of your Samba servers as a Domain Master Browser.

You Can't Browse a Server

You are trying to browse a server that is in a browse list, but you keep getting the error message shown in Figure 23.2.

Figure 23.2
Windows says your server is not there.

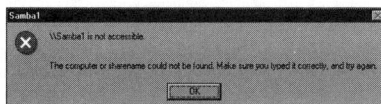

This problem occurs because the client can't talk to smbd(8) on your server. There are a few reasons you might get this message:

- The server you are trying to browse does not have smbd(8) running. Browsing a server requires that it respond to a NetShareEnum request on the IPC$ share; if smbd(8) is not running, you will get this message.

- The server you are trying to browse has not registered with the WINS server you use for NetBIOS name to IP address translation, or WINS is not working in your network. Browse lists are simply lists of NetBIOS names. To browse a server, your client must translate the server's NetBIOS name into an IP address, connect to the IPC$ share, and send aNetShareEnum API call to the server.

YOU NEED A PASSWORD TO BROWSE A SERVER

You are trying to browse a server to see a list of shares, and you are asked for a username and password before you can have access to the list of shares.

This problem occurs because the client cannot connect to the IPC$ share on the server to get a list of shares with the NetShareEnum API request. It is normally seen when Windows NT clients are trying to browse Samba servers because Windows NT clients often try to connect to the IPC$ share with a null username and password. Samba maps this to the guest account. If the guest account is not valid, you will be prompted for a username and password under Windows NT.

THE DEVICE DOES NOT EXIST ON THE NETWORK

This is a problem you can experience if your Samba server is at version 2.0.3 and you are on a Win9x client. You are trying to browse a server but it takes a long time to respond, and when it does, you get the message shown in Figure 23.3.

Figure 23.3
The device does not exist on the network.

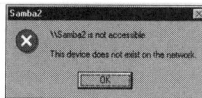

This problem is caused by a bug in Samba 2.0.3 and the fact that your password on that server is not the same as the password you used to log in to your Win9x client. This version of Samba fails to complete the SessionSetupAndX request, and the Win9x client gets no response back.

The solution is to upgrade your Samba server to the latest version, but a workaround is to make sure that your password is the same on all servers.

SHARE ACCESS PROBLEMS

The following sections provide some information on common share access problems. See Chapter 6, "File Sharing Under Samba," and Chapter 7, "Printer Sharing Under Samba," for more information on file and printer shares.

SHARE NAME NOT FOUND

This is a common problem. You have tried to access a share and get the message shown in Figure 23.4.

Figure 23.4
The share you asked for was not found.

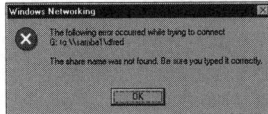

The most likely reason for this problem is that you have mistyped the name of the share to which you want to connect. Simply correct the name and resubmit the request.

NETWORK NAME NOT FOUND

This is a not-so-common problem that causes lots of problems until the solution is stumbled over. You have set up a share and are trying to access the share from a client. Each time you try, you get the window shown in Figure 23.5. You check the smb.conf and all looks fine, but you keep getting the error.

Figure 23.5
Windows complains that the network name was not found.

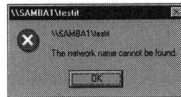

This can happen for a few different reasons:

- The path to the share does not exist. You have made a typo in the pathname or you forgot to create the shared directory.

    Simply fix the problem, and you will be able to access the share.

- The account you are logging in to does not have access to the directory that the share points to in its path parameter.

    Simply fix this problem, and you will be able to access the share.

THE DEVICE DOES NOT EXIST ON THE NETWORK

This is essentially the same problem as the previous browsing one. It occurs when you try to access a share on a Samba 2.0.3 server and your password on that server is not the same as the password with which you used to log in to your Win9x client. You will receive a message similar to the one shown in Figure 23.3.

You should upgrade your Samba server to the latest version. As a workaround, make sure that your password is the same on each server.

YOU MUST SUPPLY A PASSWORD TO MAKE THIS CONNECTION

You are trying to access a share, whether by browsing the share or through the Map Network Drive dialog box, and you keep getting a window similar to the one shown in Figure 23.6. If you are using an NT client, you will get a slightly different dialog box with space for a username as well.

Figure 23.6
Windows wants a password to access the service.

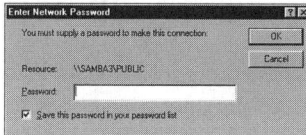

Several different things can cause this problem:

- Your password on the Samba server you are trying to access is different from the password you logged on to your Win9x client with.

   The solution here is to type your password for the remote server and make sure that your passwords are all the same on all servers, or make sure that all Samba servers use the one password source.

- You are using a Windows client that insists on using encrypted passwords, but your Samba server is not set up to use encrypted passwords. Versions of Windows that insist on using encrypted passwords include Windows 95 OSR2 and above, Windows 98, and Windows NT SP3 and above.

   The solution is to configure Samba to use encrypted passwords or switch off encrypted passwords in Windows. Samba comes with registry files that switch off encrypted passwords; they are kept in the Samba docs directory.

- You are using an early Windows client that insists on converting your password to uppercase before sending it to Samba. Windows for Workgroups and early versions of Windows 95 do this.

   When Samba receives a `SessionSetupAndX` request (sent the first time you try to access a share on a server), it tries the password as presented first. If that fails, it converts the password to all lowercase (because of what some versions of Windows do) and tries that. If you have a mixed-case password, neither of these will work.

   Samba still has one trick up its sleeve, however. If you set `password level = 4` (any number can be used, but larger numbers are more costly), Samba will try all combinations of up to four uppercase letters in the password after it has been converted to lowercase.

   The solution in this case is to insert the parameter `password server = 4` (or whatever number of uppercase letters you think people will use) into the `[global]` section of your `smb.conf` file and restart Samba.

THE NETWORK IS BUSY

You have tried to map a network drive but keep getting the error message shown in Figure 23.7.

Figure 23.7
The network is busy.

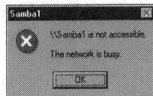

This probably occurs because your Samba server is configured to have a hosts deny for your workstation or your workstation has a hosts allow parameter that does not include your workstation.

A SPECIFIC FOLDER DOES NOT EXIST

You have tried to browse a folder and you get an error message like the one in Figure 23.8, but you can see that the folders exist, or at least ones very like them, except possibly for case differences.

Figure 23.8
Windows can't find a folder.

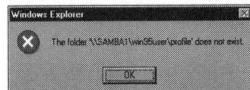

This problem is similar to a logon problem discussed next and is most likely caused by the case sensitive parameter being set to yes in the global section or for the share you are trying to access a folder in.

The solution is to remove the case sensitive parameter, restart Samba, and try again.

ACCESS IS DENIED

You have tried to access a folder or file from your Windows client but you get an error message similar to that shown in Figure 23.9.

Figure 23.9
Windows cannot provide access to the folder.

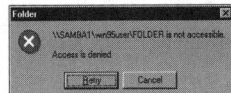

This is most likely due to a permission problem on your Samba server: You do not have permission at the UNIX level to access the requested folder or file. Check the permissions and ownership on the folder or file. When you have rectified them, try to access the folder or file again.

GUESTS PROMPTED FOR PASSWORDS

You have set up a share on your Samba server and have applied the guest ok = yes parameter to the share so that people who do not have accounts on your Samba server can access the share. Unfortunately, guests are prompted for a password before they can access the share.

This is most likely caused because you are using Samba 2.0.0 or greater. In these versions of Samba, the default `security` mode is user. To gain access to a resource, you must provide a username and password. You cannot simply put a single share into share-level security, and it is probably not a good idea to operate your Samba server in share-level security.

There are a few solutions to the problem:

- You can use the `map to guest` parameter in the [global] section, and set it to bad user. If this parameter is set to this value, when Samba encounters an unknown user trying to access a share, it maps it to the guest account and gives it access as guest. Of course, you also need `guest ok = yes` on the share.

- You can set up virtual servers as described in Chapter 9, "Samba Automation." One virtual server would be in share-level security and would contain the share you want to make available to everyone. The other server would be in user-level security and would contain all the other shares.

Users Cannot Write to a Share

You have set up a new share and your users have write access to the underlying files and directories for the share, but Windows will not let them write to the share. They can get messages such as `Unable to create folder ... Access is denied`.

This problem is most likely because the share is marked read-only or is not writable. By default, shares are read-only. In checking that a client can write to a share, Samba first checks that the share is writable. If it is not, access is denied at that point. Only after it has determined that the share is writable does it then check whether you can create the file or folder you want to create or whether you can write to the file you want to write to.

Logon Problems

The following sections provide more information on common logon problems. See Chapters 11–15 for more information on your specific client.

No Domain Server

You're at the domain logon prompt, and you typed in your correct username, password, and domain. However, every time you try to log in, you get a window similar to that shown in Figure 23.10.

Figure 23.10
Windows complains it cannot find a domain server.

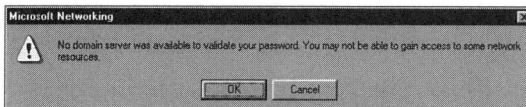

This problem occurs for several reasons:

- The netmask or broadcast address on your client does not match the one used by the Samba server. A client looking for a logon server tries to translate the name DOMAIN<1C>. If this name cannot be found, logons cannot proceed. If you are not using WINS, broadcasts are used to find the name.

  The solution in this case is to fix your netmast or broadcast address, whichever is incorrect.

- nmbd(8) is not running on your Samba server, so the client cannot perform the standard logon processing.

  The solution in this case is to find out why nmbd(8) is not running and rectify this problem.

DOMAIN PASSWORD IS NOT CORRECT

You are trying to log on to a Samba domain with a Windows 9x client, and on each occasion, you get a message similar to that shown in Figure 23.11.

Figure 23.11
Your domain password is not correct.

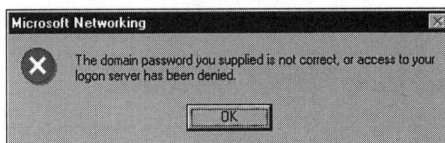

There are several reasons why you might get this message:

- Your password is incorrect. Simply supply the correct password and try again.

- Your client insists on using encrypted passwords but your Samba server is not configured for encrypted passwords. Versions of Windows that insist on using encrypted passwords include Windows 95 OSR2 and above, Windows 98, and Windows NT SP3 and above.

  The solution is to configure Samba to use encrypted passwords or switch off encrypted passwords in Windows. Samba comes with registry files that switch off encrypted passwords; they are kept in the Samba docs directory.

- You are using an early Windows client that insists on converting your password to uppercase before sending it to Samba. Windows for Workgroups and early versions of Windows 95 do this.

  When Samba receives a SessionSetupAndX request (which is sent the first time you try to access a share on a server), it tries the password as presented first. If that fails, it converts the password to all lowercase (because of what some versions of Windows do) and tries that. If you have a mixed-case password, neither of these will work.

  Samba still has one trick up its sleeve, however. If you set password level = 4 (any number can be used, but larger numbers are more costly), Samba will try all combinations of up to four uppercase letters in the password after it has been converted to lowercase.

The solution in this case is to insert the parameter `password server = 4` (or whatever number of uppercase letters you think people will use) into the `[global]` section of your `smb.conf` file and restart Samba.

■ The Samba server you are trying to log on to has a `hosts allow` or `hosts deny` parameter that does not allow you access to the server.

The solution is to check the `hosts allow` and `hosts deny` entries and ensure that your client is not in any `hosts deny` or is mentioned in the appropriate `hosts allow` parameters. You should then restart Samba and try again.

AN ERROR OCCURRED

You have just logged on to your Samba server with a Win9x client, your logon script flashes past very quickly, and you receive the message shown in Figure 23.12.

Figure 23.12
Windows could not create parts of your profile.

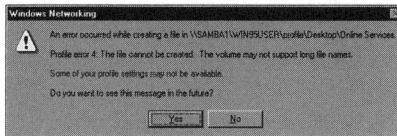

This problem is most likely because your Samba server has the parameter `case sensitive` set to `yes` in the `[global]` section or in the `[homes]` section. Windows is looking for files like `NETLOGON.BAT`, and folders like `DESKTOP`, but Samba is not matching the files that do exist because their case is not exactly the same (typically, they are all lowercase).

The solution is to remove the `case sensitive` parameter (as it defaults to `no`) or set it to `no`, restart Samba, and try again.

LOGON SCRIPT DOES NOT RUN

You have set up your Samba server as a logon server for Win9x clients and have created a `netlogon` script, but your `netlogon` script fails to run when users log on.

This is most likely caused by one of the following:

■ Your `netlogon` script does not exist. Check that you have created it and have moved it into the `netlogon` directory.

■ The `netlogon` share is not accessible to your users, or the `netlogon` script is not accessible to your users.

You should check that there are no `hosts deny` parameters on the `netlogon` share that prevent your clients from accessing it, and no other parameters, like `hosts allow`, `valid users`, and so on. Until you understand exactly how these parameters work, remove them so you can get logon scripts working.

You should also check the permissions of the logon script and ensure that it is accessible. It probably should permit everyone to read it. Executing the command `chmod u+r,g+r,o+r` on your logon script will make sure that everyone can read it.

- Your `netlogon` script has an erroneous command in it that is causing it to terminate prematurely. You should run the logon script in a DOS window on a Windows system to check that it works as you expect.

- Your `netlogon` script was constructed with a UNIX editor on your Samba server, and it does not have carriage returns as well as line feeds as end-of-line markers.

    One way to insert these characters is to use the `todos` command that is available on several Web sites. Instructions on how to construct a logon script properly appear in Chapter 11, "Samba as a Logon and Profiles Server."

PERFORMANCE PROBLEMS

Managing the performance of Samba is dealt with in Chapter 21, "Samba and Performance." However, there are occasions when performance becomes an issue.

Sometimes client bugs cause these issues. One such problem is listed in Microsoft Knowledge Base article Q236926. This article talks about bugs in the Windows 95 and Windows 98 TCP/IP stacks that lead them to retransmit packets too quickly when high delay links (like satellite links) are in use. This can lead to poor client performance when accessing NT servers or Samba servers.

For more information and a solution, please see the following:

```
http://support.microsoft.com/support/kb/articles/Q236/9/26.asp
```

PRINTING PROBLEMS

Most printing problems are caused by printer shares not being accessible, so they can be diagnosed as share problems. Thus, all the share accessibility problems discussed previously apply equally to printers. However, because Samba implements printing by running a program (for example, `lpr`) when print files are closed, additional problems can occur. These problems are usually caused when the program that Samba runs fails in some way. You should check the `print command` being used for any print queue that experiences problems. You can do this with the following command:

```
testparm | more
```

There are other things you can do to check that printing is working as well. For example, you could use a print command that creates a file in `/tmp` in the following way:

```
echo printing file %s >> /tmp/printing.log; lpr -s -P %p %s
```

DAEMON PROBLEMS

Several common problems prevent either `nmbd(8)` or `smbd(8)` from starting. These are explored in this section.

To check whether the daemons are running, you can use the following command:

```
ps ax | grep mbd
```

If this command does not list at least one running `smbd` process and at least one `nmbd` process, you should check the respective log files to find out what the problems are.

bind failed on port 139

You have configured Samba according to the documentation, but `smbd` will not start. Upon checking `log.smb` in the Samba log directory for your version of Linux or UNIX, you find the following message:

```
bind failed on port 139 socket_addr=0.0.0.0 (Address already in use)
```

This problem occurs when you have configured Samba to start up out of `/etc/inetd.conf`, and you then try to start Samba up manually or automatically during the system startup as well.

The problem here is that `inetd` is already listening on port 139. When you try to start up `smbd`, it also tries to listen on port 139, so it fails to start. You have two choices:

1. Start `smbd` and `nmbd` out of `/etc/inetd.conf`, and do not try to start Samba during a normal system startup. Simply remove the entry from the startup scripts for Samba. The instructions for doing this are specific to your version of Linux or UNIX.

   However, many versions of Linux use the SysV Init scripts, in which case you should simply remove the file called `Sxxsmb` from the run-level directory for the run level that you are in. This file will usually reside in `/etc/rc.d/rc3.d` if your system always boots up in run level 3.

2. Remove the two entries from `/etc/inetd.conf` that allow Samba to start up using `inetd`. These entries will begin with the strings `netbios-ssn` and `netbios-ns`. After you have done that and restarted `inetd` (which you can do on many UNIX systems with the command `killall -HUP inetd`), you can simply start Samba with the following command:

   ```
   /etc/rc.d/init.d/smb start
   ```

Note

Be careful to not use the `killall` command on non-Linux systems. For example, on Solaris, it kills all running processes, which is probably not what you want.

Get_Hostbyname: Unknown host

You have tried to start Samba, but on each occasion the daemons will not start. Upon checking the log files, you find the following message:

```
Get_Hostbyname: Unknown host blah
```

This occurs because your hostname is incorrect or it is not found in your `/etc/hosts` file or DNS. That is, `nmbd(8)` and `smbd(8)` could not translate your hostname into an IP address. You should correct your hostname and make sure that a valid address appears for it in `/etc/hosts` or in the DNS.

`Create_subnets: No local interfaces!`

You have tried to start Samba, but on each occasion the daemons will not start. Upon checking the `log.nmb` file, you find this message:

`Create_subnets: No local interfaces!`

This occurs because you do not have any broadcast devices configured. Broadcast devices include Ethernet and Token Ring. You should configure an Ethernet or other broadcast device on your system, and then try to start Samba.

MORE INFORMATION

Many resources are available when you are having problems with Samba:

- The Samba-Technical mailing list—You can use this mailing list to ask technical questions of the Samba community. This mailing list is archived on the Samba Web site.

- The Samba-NTdom mailing list—This mailing list is devoted to questions about Samba TNG, the version of Samba that has the most support for operating as a PDC and for integrating into NT domains. This mailing list is archived on the Samba Web site.

- The `comp.protocols.smb` newsgroup—People who ask and answer questions about problems with Samba frequent this newsgroup. There are even Samba team members who lurk on this list.

- The `linux.samba` newsgroup—People who ask and answer questions about Samba and Linux frequent this newsgroup.

- The Samba Web pages—These pages provide a wealth of information about Samba and contain searchable archives of the various Samba mailing lists. They are located at `www.samba.org`.

- `DIAGNOSIS.txt` from the Samba docs—This is usually in `/usr/doc/samba-$version/ docs/textdocs` under Linux. It will also be in your source directory under `docs/ textdocs`.

FROM HERE...

You have completed most of this book on Samba. The remaining two chapters deal with

- A tour through the Samba source, with information to help you get started with debugging Samba at the source code level.

- The future of Samba, with some insights to where the Samba team is taking Samba in the short and medium term.

Finally, Appendix A lists all the `smb.conf` parameters, along with a description of each and the versions of Samba in which they appeared.

## CHAPTER 24

A Tour Through the Samba Source Code

In this chapter   *by Richard Sharpe*

You have come this far, and we have talked about Samba functionality and how to configure Samba to take advantage of its features. However, how is all of this implemented? Have you ever had the urge to contribute to Samba or debug problems with Samba, but not known where to start, or could not figure out what all those files do?

If that is the case, this chapter is for you. In this chapter, we

- List the current versions of Samba in development
- Describe how to get the latest source for any version of Samba
- Show you how to keep up to date with the Samba source and commit changes if you have development access
- Describe the files and directories in the Samba tree
- Describe the function of most of the directories in the Samba source code along with information on what is implemented by individual files

VERSIONS OF SAMBA

Like many other open-source projects, Samba uses the Concurrent Version System (CVS) for source code management. The Samba source is kept in a central repository in Canberra, Australia.

At the time of writing, several versions, or branches, of Samba are under development:

- Samba 2.0.x, tagged with the string SAMBA_2.0. This is the branch in which the current production series of Samba is developed. Additionally, a branch SAMBA_2_0_RELEASE contains more thoroughly tested code; all releases are taken from that branch.
- Samba 3.0.0, the next major version of Samba to be released. This is the head branch of Samba, the branch that CVS serves by default.
- Samba UNICODE, where the project to convert Samba to using UNICODE internally is being conducted. This branch is tagged with the string SAMBA_UNICODE.
- Samba TNG, the next generation of Samba. This is tagged with the string SAMBA_TNG and is the area where Luke Leighton is heading the PDC and BDC development.

→ For more comments on these various branches of the Samba source code, **see** Chapter 25, "The Future of Samba."

When you download the Samba distribution from the Samba Web site (www.samba.org) you are not getting the latest source. You are getting the latest release of Samba. The source tree might have moved on from what you have. Similarly, when you install a vendor-supplied RPM, you are installing software that is behind the development tree.

Note

The latest development version can be very buggy, so when you pull down a copy of the latest source tree, you might have a lot of work to do.

Note

It is not advisable to use development software in production sites. Things change very quickly in the development trees.

GETTING THE LATEST SAMBA TREE

If you simply want to browse the latest source tree, you might be interested in CVSWEB, which enables you to browse a CVS source tree. To browse the Samba source via CVSWEB, access the location: `http://samba.org/cgi-bin/cvsweb/samba/`. You can elect to see only files from a particular branch if you want.

PART
IV
CH
24

However, if you are updating your Samba source on a regular basis, or if you want to become a developer, you will need regular CVS access to the source trees. Follow these instructions to gain access to the CVS source trees:

1. Install a recent copy of CVS. You can get a recent copy from most current Linux distributions or from `http://www.cyclic.com/cyclic-pages/howget.html`. You really only need the `cvs(1)` client program. You can get further documentation on CVS from `http://www.cyclic.com/cvs/doc-cederqvist.html`.

2. In the account that you are going to work on Samba, create a directory for the source:
   ```
   mkdir samba
   ```

3. Execute the following commands to log on to the CVS server:
   ```
   cd samba
   cvs -d :pserver:cvs@cvs.samba.org:/cvsroot login
   ```
   When asked for the password, enter `cvs`.

4. To check out the latest head branch, enter the following command:
   ```
   cvs -d :pserver:cvs@cvs.samba.org:/cvsroot co samba
   ```

5. This will check out (co) the head branch and create a directory called `samba` in your current directory containing the source code for the head branch. You might want to rename it according to the current version, for example:
   ```
   mv samba samba-2.0.x
   ```

If you want to check out one of the other versions of Samba that are available, you will need to use a slightly different command. The following shows you the appropriate checkout commands for a few versions:

- To check out the current Samba 2.0.x branch, use the following command:
  ```
  cvs -d :pserver:cvs@cvs.samba.org:/cvsroot co -r SAMBA_2_0 samba
  ```

- To check out the current Samba TNG branch, use the following command:

  ```
  cvs -d :pserver:cvs@cvs.samba.org:/cvsroot co -r SAMBA_TNG samba
  ```

- To check out the current Samba UNICODE branch, use the following command:

  ```
  cvs -d :pserver:cvs@cvs.samba.org:/cvsroot co -r SAMBA_UNICODE samba
  ```

Note
> Each of these commands creates the directory samba in the current directory and copies the requested branch into it. Perhaps you can see why I suggest that you change the directory name as soon as you have checked out the branch you want.

Note
> When you check out a branch, you get all the files associated with that branch, including the source. The structure of a Samba tree is discussed in the next section.

If you are planning to submit changes back to the CVS tree, you should join the Samba technical mailing list and discuss your ideas with others. To submit patches, read the instructions at http://www.samba.org/samba-patches/.

UPDATING YOUR SOURCE TREE

If you have already downloaded the Samba source once before and simply want to update your tree to include all the changes made by Samba team members, you can use the following instructions to update your tree:

```
cd samba/samba-3.0.x
cvs update -d -P
```

BUILDING SAMBA

Although instructions on building Samba are provided in Chapter 2, "Obtaining and Installing Samba," we provide a brief guide here. If you have built any other open-source UNIX-based software before, you will be familiar with the process.

In brief, here is the process:

1. If you have downloaded a `tar.gz` file, unpack the sources with the following command:

   ```
   tar zxvf samba-$version.tar.gz
   ```

   If you are not using GNU tar, you might need to use `gzip` to decompress the `tar.gz` file first.

2. Configure your source code for your OS:

   ```
   cd samba-$version
   ./configure
   ```

You can add various options to influence the build process and add optional code. For details, type `./configure --help`.

If `configure` failed, check out `config.log`, rectify the problem, and rerun `configure`.

3. Now, compile Samba:

   ```
   make
   ```

4. If you are not intending to build packages (for example, RPMs) of Samba, you can now install the software with

   ```
   make install
   ```

5. If you are on a system that is supported in the packaging directory, you can build source and binary RPMs with, for example,

   ```
   cd samba-$version/packaging/RedHat
   sh makerpms.sh
   ```

6. After you've built your source and binary RPMs, install them and test, test, test!

> **Note**
>
> When you are working on Samba, you might want to keep your development tree separate from the tree you downloaded. This will enable you to easily generate diff files as discussed next and submit them back to the Samba team.

Committing Changes from Your Source Tree

If you have made changes to your source tree and you feel that the changes should be submitted back to the Samba team, you will need to do the following:

1. Generate a unified diff(1) of the changes you have made. To generate a diff(1) of your changes, you will need the original unmodified files before you start. Therefore, you should get into the habit of backing up your files before you start changing them, or create a backup of the whole Samba directory.

> **Note**
>
> diff(1) is a tool that developers use to generate a file of differences between two, usually related, source files. A diff file generated from files A and B is essentially a set of instructions to a program like patch(1) to tell it how to convert file A into file B. Usually, diff files are much smaller that the source file B.

After you have made the changes you need and you feel they are working, you can generate a diff with

```
diff -U changed-file.bck changed-file > changed-file.diff
```

where `changed-file.bck` is the backup you made before you modified the file you changed. You can use the recursive option, `diff (-r)`, to diff entire directory trees.

2. Send the diff file to a Samba team member for review.

THE SAMBA SOURCE TREE

The Samba source tree consists of several files and directories. The purpose of these are described here:

- COPYING—Samba is distributed under the GNU Public License (GPL). This file contains a copy of the GPL and explains the terms and conditions under which you can modify Samba and when you can charge for providing Samba to other people.

- Manifest—This file contains a list of all the files and directories contained in the Samba tree, along with a short description of each item.

- README—This file contains information on the version of Samba that you have, as well as an answer to the question "What is SMB?"

- README-smbmount—This file contains information on the smbmount program and SMBFS.

- Read-Manifest-Now—This file is simply a reminder that you should read the manifest.

- Roadmap—This file sketches where the Samba team thinks Samba is going. (It is often out of date.)

- WHATSNEW.txt—This file tells you what is new in this version. It is up to date only when a version is released.

- docs—This directory contains all the available Samba docs, including man pages, HTML documents, text documents, and so on.

- examples—This directory contains examples that you might want to look at, including a sample smb.conf file, smbprint, and so on.

- packaging—This directory contains packaging information and files for different versions of Linux and UNIX.

- source—This directory contains the Samba source code.

- swat—This directory contains various support files for SWAT.

Each directory in the Samba tree is discussed in more detail in the following text.

> **Note**
>
> The Samba source tree is constantly changing, so you might find that the source tree you have downloaded contains more files or different files than this chapter outlines. This chapter is based on Samba pre-2.0.7.

docs

The docs directory contains the following files and directories:

- NT4-Locking.txt—This file contains registry entries to disable local caching (oplocks) on NT4.

- THANKS—This file thanks various people who have helped Andrew or other members of the Samba team over time. It is somewhat out of date, and more recent contributions are acknowledged in the CVS logs and on the Samba Web site.

- NT4_PlainPassword.reg, Win2000_PlainPassword.reg, Win95_PlainPassword.reg, Win98_PlainPassword.reg—These files contain the appropriate registry settings to switch off encrypted passwords from the respective clients. To apply a .reg file, simply copy it over to the Windows client and open it (double-click in most cases).

- Win9X-CacheHandling.reg—This file contains registry entries that allow Win9X systems to access files on shares where those files may also be in use from UNIX.

- WindowsTerminalServer.reg—This file contains registry entries that force Windows Terminal Server to use separate connections for each user, thus avoiding confusion between users.

- announce—This is an old announcement file for Samba 2.0.

- faq—This directory contains answers to various frequently asked questions about Samba.

- history—This file contains information about the history of Samba.

- htmldocs—This directory contains the various Samba docs formatted in HTML. Do not edit these files; they are generated from the files in yodldocs.

- manpages—This directory contains the various Samba man pages. Do not edit these files; they are generated from the files in yodldocs.

- textdocs—This directory contains the various Samba documents formatted as text documents. Do not edit these files; they are generated from the files in yodldocs.

- yodldocs—This directory contains the various Samba documents in yodl (Ye Olde Documentatione Language, or Yet oneOther Documentation Language) format. However, you must have YODL installed before you can rebuild the appropriate docs. The Makefile generated in the source directory will have a target for yodldocs, but it will fail if you do not have YODL installed.

packaging

This directory contains packaging instructions and files for many versions of UNIX and Linux. The following are the files and directories it contains:

- Caldera—This directory contains packaging instructions for Caldera OpenLinux. It contains the shell script makerpms.sh. Simply run this to create Samba RPMs (binary and source) for Caldera OpenLinux. Provided that the process works, your RPMs will end up in the normal place that RPMs are put under Caldera.

- Digital—This directory contains packaging instructions for TRU64 UNIX (formerly Digital UNIX).

- Example—This directory contains sample files for those who want to provide a packaging directory for other architectures.

- HPUX—This directory contains packaging instructions and files for HP/UX.
- PHT/TurboLinux—This directory contains packaging instructions and files for TurboLinux. Simply run the file makerpms.sh to build binary and source RPMs for TurboLinux.
- README—This file contains useful information but is somewhat out of date now.
- RedHat—This directory contains packaging instructions and files for Red Hat Linux. Simply run the makerpms.sh script to build binary and source RPMs.
- SGI—This directory contains packaging instructions and files for SGI's IRIX.
- Solaris—This directory contains packaging instructions and files in the pkg-specs directory.
- SuSE—This directory contains packaging instructions and files for SuSE 5.2 and 6.0. They consist of patch files and SPEC files. You can rebuild RPMs from these files, but they are specific to older versions of Samba and seem to require SMBFS 2.0.2 and 2.1.0.
- bin—This directory contains a script called update-pkginfo that is used when a new version of Samba is released. It updates the version number in all the SPEC files in the packaging directory.

Note

It is unfortunate, but many of the SPEC files in the packaging directory that are used to build RPMs for Linux are simply out of date and do not work, at least in my experience.

source

The source directory is where all the real action occurs. In this section we will discuss some of the many files you will encounter in the source directory.

Note

Samba is written in the C programming language.

Note

I have ignored one or two minor files, such as .cvsignore, which is used to indicate files in which CVS should ignore changes.

- Makefile—This is the master Makefile that you will use to build Samba. It is generated by the configure script that is discussed later.
- Makefile.in—This is the template Makefile that configure uses to build a real Makefile.

- `acconfig.h`—This file specifies to `autoconf` all the #defines that Samba can be built with. It is used by `autoconf` to build a new configure script.

- `aclocal.m4`—This file specifies Samba local tests for various options that the standard configure tests do not check for or are not good enough for. It is used by `autoconf` to build a new configure script.

- `architecture.doc`—This is a somewhat old document by Dan Shearer that has not been kept up to date.

- `change-log`—This is an obsolete file. The file `cvs-log` now contains information about changes to Samba.

- `client`—This directory contains the source code for the various clients, including `smbclient` and `smbmount`.

- `codepages`—This directory contains the source code for the various code pages supported by Samba.

- `config.cache`—This file caches the results of all the tests that `configure` makes. If you move this directory to another system, especially a different type of system, you will want to remove `config.cache`.

- `config.guess`—This file contains shell code to try to figure out your system type for `configure`.

- `config.log`—This file contains the results of the last configure run. If `configure` fails, you should look in this file to figure out why.

- `config.status`—This file can re-create the files that `configure` produces and saves you from running `configure` again if nothing has changed.

- `config.sub`—This file is part of `configure` and contains a routine that validates the configured type of the system.

- `configure`—This file is run to build your Makefile and produce the other configuration files needed by Samba. You need to run it only once. If you need to find out what flags it accepts, use

    `./configure --help.`

- `configure.developer`—Developers should use this configure script because it does other things that developers need. In particular, it forces `CFLAGS` to be set so that developers see many more error and warning messages and thus detect potential errors in their code.

- `configure.in`—This is the input file that `autoconf` uses to generate a configure script. You almost certainly do not have to touch this.

- `groupdb`—This directory contains routines for handling groups and authentication through NIS, LDAP, and local authentication files.

- `include`—This directory contains most of the include files that Samba needs, including `config.h`, which is generated by the configure script.

- `install-sh`—This shell script is used by Makefile to create installation directories. You do not need to touch the file under most circumstances.

- `internals.doc`—This is a somewhat out-of-date file that provides some information about Samba internals.

- `lib`—This directory contains several utility routines that the various parts of Samba require.

- `libsmb`—This directory contains several routines to handle sending and receiving SMBs, SMB error codes, and so on, that are needed by various parts of Samba.

- `locking`—This directory contains all the locking routines that Samba uses.

- `mem_man`—This directory contains a simple memory manager. This will be obsolete in future versions of Samba.

- `nmbd`—This directory contains the source code for `nmbd(8)`.

- `param`—This directory contains the routines that are used to handle parameters in the `smb.conf` file.

- `parsing.doc`—This file contains somewhat outdated information on how parameters from the `smb.conf` are parsed and how debug output is produced.

- `passdb`—This directory contains routines that provide access to various sources of passwords, including NIS, LDAP, and local system authentication files.

- `printing`—This directory contains routines that provide printing support for Samba, including CUPS support.

- `rpc_client`—This directory contains routines that implement the client side of several MSRPC API calls.

- `rpc_parse`—This directory contains routines that implement MSRPC parsing routines.

- `rpc_server`—This directory contains routines that implement the server side of MSRPC API calls.

- `rpcclient`—This directory contains routines that implement the `rpcclient` program, a program similar in interface to `smbclient`. It provides several useful commands to help administer Windows NT computers.

- `script`—This directory contains scripts that are used during the process of building and installing Samba.

- `smbadduser`—This is a shell script that simplifies the process of adding a user to the `smbpasswd` file.

- `smbd`—This directory contains the source code for `smbd(8)`.

- `smbwrapper`—This directory contains the source code for a preloadable shared library that provides services to non-SMB–aware applications.

- `tests`—This directory contains test programs used by `configure` to check what functionality is provided by the operating system on which it is being run. You should not need to touch these files.

- ■ ubiqx—This directory contains a library of routines to handle lists of all kinds. It is used by parts of Samba but may be replaced by TDB in future versions of Samba.

- ■ utils—This directory contains the source to various utility programs, including nmblookup and smbstatus.

- ■ web—This directory contains the source code to SWAT, the Samba Web Administration Tool.

The following sections provide more information on some of the directories just described. However, we describe them in a more natural order.

smbd

smbd(8) is the main component of Samba, in that it is the component that is responsible for file and print serving. Here, we describe each file in the smbd source directory. We have departed from alphabetic order so we can describe the most important files first.

It should be noted that an smbd(8) process is started by the master smbd(8), or is started by inetd(8), for each new client that connects to Samba. This gives Samba considerable robustness in the face of bugs because only the user who tickles a bug is penalized; other users will remain oblivious to the problem.

- ■ server.c—This file contains the main routine for smbd(8). It processes arguments, initializes various structures, and then sits in a loop processing SMBs as they come in from the client.

- ■ process.c—This file contains the code that processes SMBs. The processing starts in smbd_process and ends up in switch_message, which vectors through smb_messages, an array of function pointers and other information. The array smb_messages determines which routines are called for each SMB message type.

- ■ reply.c—This file is next most important because it contains many of the SMB reply routines. The routine reply_special handles NetBIOS session setup and other NetBIOS messages, while reply_tcon and reply_tcon_and_X handle requests to connect to shares. The routine reply_session_setup_and_X handles logons.

- ■ service.c—This file contains the routines that make connections to services. The routine make_connection finds the service required and makes sure the client has access. It also handles details like the [homes] and [printers] services, as well as special casing some IPC$ access requests. The routine find_service is responsible for finding a service in the smb.conf file (or the in-memory version of this file).

- ■ negprot.c—This file handles the negprot SMB (it implements the reply_negprot routine). The table supported_protocols contains the routines reply_corep, reply_coreplus, reply_nt1, reply_lanman1, and reply_lanman2. The appropriate routine is called according to the level of the protocol recognized by smbd(8).

- ■ blocking.c—This file contains the routines that handle all blocking lock requests by the client.

- `chgpasswd.c`—This file contains the routines that handle password changing for SMB clients.

- `close.c`—This file contains the routines that handle closing of files and directories.

- `conn.c`—This file contains the routines that manage connection structures for other routines.

- `connection.c`—This file contains the routines that handle claiming and yielding of connections. They are responsible for maintaining the information that needs to be saved about each connection.

- `dfree.c`—This file contains the routines to calculate free disk space.

- `dir.c`—This file contains the routines that handle directories, directory listings, and so on, for `smbd(8)`.

- `dosmode.c`—This file contains the routines that convert between DOS and UNIX modes on files.

- `error.c`—This file contains the routines that generate error SMB messages.

- `fileio.c`—This file contains the routines that read, write, seek, and sync files.

- `filename.c`—This file contains the routines that handle filenames for clients.

- `files.c`—This file contains the routines that manage file structures for `smbd(8)`.

- `groupname.c`—This file contains the routines that handle groupname maps for NT client access. Nothing in Samba 2.0.x uses this code as yet.

- `ipc.c`—This file contains the routines that handle IPC and named pipe communications. This includes print queue handling and `NetServerEnum` and `NetShareEnum` calls.

- `mangle.c`—This file contains the routines that handle filename mangling.

- `message.c`—This file contains the routines that handle message SMBs.

- `noquotas.c`—This file contains the routines that are used for quota handling if quotas are not in use.

- `nttrans.c`—This file contains the routines that handle "NT transaction" SMBs.

- `open.c`—This file contains the routines that handle file opening and sharing modes.

- `oplock.c`—This file contains the routines that handle opportunistic locks.

- `password.c`—This file contains the routines that handle passwords and authentication.

- `pipes.c`—This file contains the routines that handle pipe replies, including `reply_open_pipe_and_X`, as well as pipe writes, reads, and closes.

- `predict.c`—This file contains the routines that handle file read prediction.

- `quotas.c`—This file contains the routines that are used for quota handling if quotas are in use.

- `ssl.c`—This file contains the routines that handle SSL matters if SSL is compiled into Samba.

- trans2.c—This file contains the routines that handle SMB trans2 messages.
- uid.c—This file contains the routines that handle users, UIDs, groups, and GIDs, as well as the routines for becoming a user or group as needed.

> **Note**
> smbd(8) uses other routines when needed. This is only a general overview of the smbd(8) source.

nmbd

This directory contains the source to nmbd(8), the second most important part of Samba. nmbd(8) provides NetBIOS name lookup functions as well as many browsing functions.

> **Note**
> smbd(8) implements the NetServerEnum and NetShareEnum functions that are needed once a client has obtained a browse list. However, nmbd(8) handles browse lists and announcements.

> **Note**
> nmbd(8) is designed to run as a daemon only, and should not be started from inetd.

The following are the files in the nmbd directory, along with a brief description of each file:

- nmbd.c—This file contains the main routine for nmbd(8) and the routine process, which does most of the work, such as running elections, responding to name queries, and so on.
- asyncdns.c—This file contains the routines that handle DNS lookup of names for nmbd. If you have configured the source for asynchronous DNS (by removing the #define for SYNC_DNS), they fork a separate process to handle DNS queries.
- nmbd_become_dmb.c—This file contains the routines that implement the process of becoming a domain master browser on a network.
- nmbd_become_lmb.c—This file contains the routines that implement the process of becoming a local master browser on a network.
- nmbd_browserdb.c—This file contains routines for managing browse lists.
- nmbd_browsesync.c—This file contains routines to sync browse lists with domain and local master browsers.
- nmbd_elections.c—This file contains the routines for handling browser elections, including run_election.

- `nmbd_incomingdgrams.c`—This file contains routines that process incoming browsing-related datagrams, such as host announcements, workgroup announcements, and domain master browser announcements. It also handles requests for backup browse lists.

- `nmbd_incomingrequests.c`—This file contains the routines that handle incoming NetBIOS name management requests, such as name lookups, name registrations, and so on.

- `nmbd_lmhosts.c`—This file contains routines that handle the `lmhosts` file and NetBIOS names in the `lmhosts` file.

- `nmbd_logonnames.c`—This file contains routines that allow Samba to become a logon server by registering the NetBIOS name `WORKGROUP<1c>`.

- `nmbd_mynames.c`—This file contains routines that handle the process of adding the Samba server's own names and workgroups to the network.

- `nmbd_namelistdb.c`—This file contains routines for managing NetBIOS names for `nmbd`.

- `nmbd_namequery.c`—This file contains routines for performing NetBIOS name queries and dealing with the responses to name queries.

- `nmbd_nameregister.c`—This file contains routines for registering the Samba server's NetBIOS names.

- `nmbd_namerelease.c`—This file contains routines for releasing the Samba server's NetBIOS names.

- `nmbd_nodestatus.c`—This file contains routines for issuing node status requests against NetBIOS names.

- `nmbd_packets.c`—This file contains routines for sending NetBIOS packets for `nmbd(8)`.

- `nmbd_processlogon.c`—This file contains the routine `process_logon` for handling logon packets.

- `nmbd_responserecordsdb.c`—This file contains routines for managing the queue of response records to be sent to queries.

- `nmbd_sendannounce.c`—This file contains routines for sending browsing requests, including announcements, resets, announcement requests, and the like.

- `nmbd_serverlistdb.c`—This file contains routines to manage the `browse.dat` file and servers on the browse list.

- `nmbd_subnetdb.c`—This file contains routines for managing the subnets that Samba listens on and provides services in.

- `nmbd_synclists.c`—This file contains routines for synchronizing browse lists with other Samba servers.

- `nmbd_winsproxy.c`—This file contains routines for operating as a WINS proxy.

- `nmbd_winsserver.c`—This file contains routines for operating as a WINS server and maintaining the WINS database.

- `nmbd_workgroupdb.c`—This file contains routines for managing workgroups in the browse lists.

param

This directory contains the routines that handle reading the `smb.conf` file and all the parameters that Samba understands. It contains two files:

- `loadparm.c`—This file contains the definitions of all the parameters that Samba understands. The list of parameters is contained in the table `parm_table`.

- `params.c`—This file contains routines to parse the `smb.conf` file and initialize the globals structure and the share structures.

> **Note**
>
> When the `smb.conf` file is read, Samba squeezes spaces out of both the names in `parm_table` as well as the parameters in the `smb.conf` file. This means that "sec urity" in your `smb.conf` file matches the parameter name "security" in `parm_table`. You should not use obscure spellings like this, however.

client

This directory contains the code for the various clients, including the `smbclient` utility. This utility is used by several shell scripts, including `smbtar` and `smbprint`. It also contains the `smbmount`, `smbumount`, and `smbspool` utilities.

- `client.c`—This file contains the main routine for `smbclient` along with a lot of the support code. It also uses routines from `clitar.c` and `../libsmb/clientgen.c`.

- `clitar.c`—This file contains routines that implement the tar portion of `smbclient`.

- `smbmnt.c`—This file contains the code that does the actual mounting of SMB file systems. It is executed from `smbmount` in a forked process.

- `smbmount.c`—This file contains the code that is invoked to mount SMB file systems. It validates parameters and calls `smbmnt` to do the dirty work.

- `smbspool.c`—This file contains code that is the back end for CUPS, the Common Unix Printing System.

- `smbumount.c`—This file contains code that unmounts SMB file systems.

rpcclient

This directory contains the source code to the `rpcclient` program. The main file is `rpcclient.c`, which was copied pretty much from the `smbclient` code. The other files implement the MS RPC calls needed to access the appropriate functions on NT servers.

smblib

This directory contains a series of files that implement an SMB library for other parts of Samba to use. The smbclient code makes extensive use of smblib, as do other parts of Samba.

swat

This directory contains the graphics and static HTML associated with SWAT. It contains the following files and directories:

- README—This file contains instructions on installing and using SWAT.
- help—This directory contains the SWAT home page in English and Japanese.
- images—This directory contains the various images that SWAT uses.
- include—This directory contains the header and footer HTML for each of the Web pages generated by SWAT.

FROM HERE...

Well, only one more chapter to go, "The Future of Samba." Now that you have the lowdown on the Samba source code, we look forward to you helping out with the development of Samba!

## CHAPTER 25

THE FUTURE OF SAMBA

In this chapter   *by Richard Sharpe*

We have come to the end of this book about Samba, and it is time to say something about the future of Samba. There are lots of things for the Samba developers to do, but because there are only a small number of core developers, some priorities have been worked out and a vision has been developed around what will happen with Samba in the near future and the medium future. Over the longer term, it is harder to say what will happen with Samba.

In this chapter we will look at where the three main strands of Samba are going.

VERSIONS OF SAMBA

As you read in Chapter 24, "A Tour Through the Samba Source Code," four main source trees are in development for Samba:

- Samba 2.0.x
- Samba 3.0.x
- Samba UNICODE
- Samba TNG

Each of these is important in its own right, and we will look briefly at the future of each.

SAMBA 2.0

The Samba 2.0.x stream will see at least two more releases. These are 2.0.7 and 2.0.8. Version 2.0.7 will likely be released before publication of this book.

The following are the main focuses of these two versions.

SAMBA 2.0.7

This version of Samba will be mainly a bug-fix release, with as many of the known bugs as possible fixed.

In addition, some functionality from Samba 3.0.x will be implemented in Samba 2.0.7. The main piece of such code will be the TDB library from Samba 3.0.x, which will improve the performance of the various internal databases Samba uses.

SAMBA 2.0.8

This version of Samba will probably contain only one major new piece of functionality: the SPOOLSS code that has been working in what was the Samba 2.1.0 PreAlpha tree. Apart from that, Samba 2.0.8 will also be a bug-fix release.

SAMBA 3.0

Samba 3.0.0 will be the next major release of Samba. The current plan is that the following new features will be incorporated into Samba 3.0.0:

- TDB, the new internal database code—This code supports multiple simultaneous writers, persistent storage, and arbitrary keys and data. It is expected to replace many of the ad-hoc databases that have been used in Samba up to now.

  TDB is likely to be used in the following areas:
  - Internal locking
  - Connection tracking
  - Opportunistic lock tracking
  - The smbpasswd database
  - This new internal database code will be used as well in any other places that it seems relevant.

- UNICODE rewrite—Parts of Samba will be rewritten in 3.0.0 to use UNICODE from the ground up. This means that multi-byte character code problems will be found very quickly because all languages will be handled in UNICODE.

- Official PDC and BDC support—This will be based on the code in Samba TNG, but perhaps with fewer daemons than Samba TNG runs. There is no doubt that this code will be fairly well tested over the next few months. It will include SPOOLSS support, so NT printing will work properly.

- Virtual File System integration—This will allow Samba to dynamically replace the Posix file system. It was originally developed to integrate a large tape SILO system with Samba, and will see use in a subsystem that allows, for example, automatic CRLF translation.

- Samba Name Service Switch modules—These will allow NSS-aware hosts, such as Linux and Solaris, to provide better integration with Windows. For example, hostname resolution can be done via WINS, while authentication and username and group name enumeration could be done via an NT PDC.

- An SMB library, libsamba—An increasing number of applications use facilities from Samba. At present, there are many problems with doing this. To make it easier to use code already written for Samba, a library of such routines will be provided. Parts of Samba will also be rewritten to link against the same library.

- Full NT SPOOLSS printing support—The SPOOLSS implementation has been implemented as an experimental facility. It will be integrated into Samba 3.0 as a standard part of Samba. At that time, the current trick of falling back to Win9x style printing will be discontinued.

- New printing back end—This will remove some of the problems that exist in Samba today with printing. It will be based on TDB.

PART

IV

CH

25

- A new pool-based memory management package—This package will prevent problems that currently occur in some circumstances, and will allow all memory associated with a context to be freed with one call. It is expected to be used with the MSRPC code, as well as other sections.

- Auto diagnosis system—This will allow Samba to diagnose many of its own problems, and will assist administrators in setting up Samba and debugging problems.

Achieving these features will require a lot of work, so it is anticipated that Samba 3.0.0 will not be released before July 2000. In addition, some of this functionality might not make it into Samba 3.0.0 and might slip to later versions.

SAMBA UNICODE

This version of Samba is a developmental version that allows developers to provide UNICODE support in Samba from the ground up while not affecting the current production streams of Samba. When the UNICODE rewrite is complete, it will be back-integrated into Samba 3.0.0.

SAMBA TNG

This is the next generation of Samba. It is also an experimental release of Samba that has radically redesigned Samba around the concept of many daemons: one for each MSRPC service. Samba TNG has broken up Samba into pieces along the lines of Windows NT. This version of Samba is the most volatile, as total rewrites seem to occur overnight in this source tree. However, at some stage parts of it will be integrated back into Samba 3.0.0.

This version of Samba has attracted enormous interest from those parts of the Samba user base who want better integration with Windows NT.

MICROSOFT'S ACTIVE DIRECTORY SUPPORT

A whole new area of investigation is Microsoft's new Active Directory Services. These use LDAP to maintain information that is currently maintained in the SAM under NT 4. The Samba team has given little consideration to supporting Active Directory under Samba at this stage; this will probably have to wait until Samba 3.0.0 is in production.

MORE INFORMATION

To find out what the Samba team thinks will happen in the future, check out `http://au1.samba.org/samba/ftp/slides/`. This contains many presentations given by members of the Samba team.

FROM HERE...

Well, that is about it. You have reached the end of the book. We have tried to give you the tools to make you more productive with Samba and to try some of the more advanced things you might have heard about on mailing lists or on Web sites.

Thank you for staying with us, and we hope you have found the book useful.

APPENDIXES

ALL SAMBA PARAMETERS AND THEIR MEANINGS

Many people are still using older versions of Samba. For some people, the version they are using still works and they do not see a need to upgrade. Others are content with the version that ships with their Linux distribution. However, smb.conf parameters are added to new versions of Samba all the time, and parameters are removed as their function becomes obsolete. Keeping track of which parameters are relevant to your version of Samba can be a problem.

This appendix lists all available Samba parameters and their descriptions. The entries for each parameter provide information on what type of parameter it is, for example:

- Global—The parameter is set in the global section of smb.conf and applies across all shares
- Local—The parameter can be set on a per-share basis

A list of those versions of Samba to which the parameter is relevant is also included. You'll find information for versions of Samba back to 1.9.17 because some people still use old versions of Samba.

The material in this appendix is based on the man pages for all versions of Samba from 1.9.17 through to 2.0.7. Every attempt has been made to correct errors in the material, and formatting problems have been rectified.

> **Note**
>
> Permission has been given by Andrew Tridgell to use the man pages in this manner. The scripts that were used to generate the basic information will be donated to the Samba team for its use.

We trust you will find this information as useful as we think it is.

add user script

Type of parameter: Global

Supported in versions: **2.0.0 and above**

This is the full pathname to a script that will be run *as root* by smbd(8) under special circumstances described below.

Normally, a Samba server requires that UNIX users be created for all users accessing files on this server. For sites that use Windows NT account databases as their primary user database, creating these users and keeping the user list in sync with the Windows NT PDC is an onerous task. This parameter allows smbd(8) to create the required UNIX users on demand when a user accesses the Samba server.

To use this option, smbd(8) must be set to security=server or security=domain, and add user script must be set to a full pathname for a script that will create a UNIX user given one argument of %u, which expands into the UNIX username to create.

When the Windows user attempts to access the Samba server, at login (session setup in the SMB protocol) time, `smbd(8)` contacts the password server and attempts to authenticate the given user with the given password. If the authentication succeeds then `smbd(8)` attempts to find a UNIX user in the UNIX password database to map the Windows user into. If this lookup fails and `add user script` is set, `smbd(8)` calls the specified script as *as root*, expanding any `%u` argument to be the username to create.

If this script successfully creates the user, `smbd(8)` continues on as though the UNIX user already existed. In this way, UNIX users are dynamically created to match existing Windows NT accounts.

See also `security=server`, `security=domain`, `password server`, and `delete user script`.

Default: `add user script = empty string`

Example: `add user script = /usr/local/samba/bin/add_user %u`

admin users

Type of parameter: Local

Supported in versions: **1.9.17 and above**

This is a list of users who will be granted administrative privileges on the share. This means that they will do all file operations as the superuser (root).

Use this option very carefully because any user in this list will be able to do anything he or she likes on the share, irrespective of file permissions.

Default: `admin users = none`

Example: `admin users = win95user`

allow hosts

Type of parameter: Local

Supported in versions: **1.9.17 and above**

Synonym for `hosts allow`.

allow trusted domains

Type of parameter: Global

Supported in versions: **2.0.4 and above**

This parameter takes effect only when the security option is set to server or domain. If it is set to no, attempts to connect to a resource from a domain or workgroup other than the one in which `smbd(8)` is running will fail, even if that domain is trusted by the remote server doing the authentication.

This is useful if you want your Samba server to serve only resources to users in the domain of which it is a member. As an example, suppose that there are two domains: DOMA and DOMB. DOMB is trusted by DOMA, which contains the Samba server. Under normal circumstances, a user with an account in DOMB can then access the resources of a UNIX account with the same account name on the Samba server even if they do not have an account in DOMA. This can make implementing a security boundary difficult.

Default: allow trusted domains = Yes

Example: allow trusted domains = No

alternate permissions

Type of parameter: Local

Supported in versions: **1.9.17 and above**

This is a deprecated parameter. It no longer has any effect in Samba 2.0. In previous versions of Samba it affected the way the DOS read only attribute was mapped for a file. In Samba 2.0.x a file is marked read only if the UNIX file does not have the 'w' bit set for the owner of the file, regardless of whether the owner of the file is the currently logged on user or not.

announce as

Type of parameter: Global

Supported in versions: **1.9.17 and above**

This specifies what type of server nmbd announces itself as to a network neighborhood browse list. By default this is set to Windows NT. The valid options are

- NT—a synonym for NT Server
- NT Server—Windows NT Server
- NT Workstation—Windows NT Workstation
- Win95—Windows 95
- WfW—Windows for Workgroups

Do not change this parameter unless you have a specific need to stop Samba appearing as an NT server, because this might prevent Samba servers from participating as browser servers correctly.

> **Note**
>
> Windows 98 does not have a separate value because Win95 really translates into Win95 Plus in the code.

Default: announce as = NT Server

Example: announce as = Win95

announce version

Type of parameter: Global

Supported in versions: **1.9.17 and above**

This specifies the major and minor version numbers that nmbd(8) will use when announcing itself as a server. The default is 4.2. Do not change this parameter unless you have a specific need to set a Samba server to be a down-level server.

Default: announce version = 4.2

Example: announce version = 2.0

auto services

Type of parameter: Global

Supported in versions: **1.9.17 and above**

This is a list of services that you want automatically added to the browse lists. This is most useful for homes and printer services that would otherwise not be visible.

> **Note**
>
> If you just want all printers in your printcap file loaded, the load printers option is easier.

Default: no auto services

Example: auto services = fred lp colorlp

available

Type of parameter: Local

Supported in versions: **1.9.17 and above**

This parameter lets you turn off a service. If available = no, all attempts to connect to the service will fail. Such failures are logged.

Default: available = yes

Example: available = no

bind interfaces only

Type of parameter: Global

Supported in versions: **1.9.18 and above**

This global parameter allows the Samba admin to limit what interfaces on a machine will serve SMB requests. It affects file service smbd and name service nmbd in slightly different ways.

PART

V

APP

A

For name services it causes nmbd to bind to ports 137 and 138 on the interfaces listed in the interfaces parameter. nmbd also binds to the all addresses interface (0.0.0.0) on ports 137 and 138 for the purposes of reading broadcast messages. If this option is not set, nmbd services name requests on all of these sockets. If bind interfaces only is set, nmbd checks the source address of any packets coming in on the broadcast sockets and discards any that don't match the broadcast addresses of the interfaces in the interfaces parameter list. As unicast packets are received on the other sockets, it allows nmbd to refuse to serve names to machines that send packets that arrive through any interfaces not listed in the interfaces list. IP Source address spoofing does defeat this simple check, however, so it must not be used seriously as a security feature for nmbd.

For file services it causes smbd(8) to bind only to the interface list given in the interfaces parameter. This restricts the networks that smbd(8) serves to packets coming in those interfaces.

> **Note**
>
> Do not use this parameter for machines that are serving PPP or other intermittent or non-broadcast network interfaces because it will not cope with non-permanent interfaces.

If bind interfaces only is set, unless the network address 127.0.0.1 is added to the interfaces parameter list, smbpasswd and SWAT might not work as expected due to the following reasons.

To change a user's SMB password, the smbpasswd by default connects to the localhost - 127.0.0.1 address as an SMB client to issue the password change request. If bind interfaces only is set then, unless the network address 127.0.0.1 is added to the interfaces parameter list, smbpasswd will fail to connect in its default mode. smbpasswd can be forced to use the primary IP interface of the local host by using its -r remote machine parameter, with remote machine set to the IP name of the primary interface of the local host.

The SWAT status page tries to connect to smbd(8) and nmbd(8) at the address 127.0.0.1 to determine whether they are running. Not adding 127.0.0.1 causes smbd(8) and nmbd to always show not running even if they really are. This can prevent SWAT from starting, stopping, or restarting smbd(8) and nmbd(8).

Default: bind interfaces only = False

Example: bind interfaces only = True

blocking locks

Type of parameter: Local

Supported in versions: **2.0.0 and above**

This parameter controls the behavior of smbd(8) when given a request by a client to obtain a byte range lock on a region of an open file, and the request has a time limit associated with it.

If this parameter is set and the lock range requested cannot be immediately satisfied, Samba 2.0 internally queues the lock request and periodically attempts to obtain the lock until the timeout period expires.

If this parameter is set to `False`, Samba 2.0 behaves as previous versions of Samba would and fails the lock request immediately if the lock range cannot be obtained.

This parameter can be set per share.

Default: `blocking locks = True`

Example: `blocking locks = False`

browsable

Type of parameter: Local

Supported in versions: **1.9.17 and above**

Synonym for `browseable`.

browse list

Type of parameter: Global

Supported in versions: **1.9.17 and above**

This controls whether `smbd(8)` serves a browse list to a client doing a `NetServerEnum` call. Normally set to yes. You should never need to change this.

Default: `browse list = yes`

browseable

Type of parameter: Local

Supported in versions: **1.9.17 and above**

This controls whether this share is seen in the list of available shares in a net view and in the browse list.

See also `browsable`.

Default: `browseable = yes`

Example: `browseable = no`

case sensitive

Type of parameter: Local

Supported in versions: **1.9.17 and above**

Samba supports name mangling so that DOS and Windows clients can use files that don't conform to the 8.3 format. It also can be set to adjust the case of 8.3 format filenames. This parameter can take values of yes or no and controls whether filenames are case sensitive. If they aren't, Samba must do a filename search and match on passed names.

By default, Samba 2.0 has the same semantics as a Windows NT server, in that it is case preserving and not case sensitive.

Example: `case sensitive = yes`

Default: `case sensitive = no`

Casesignames

Type of parameter: Local

Supported in versions: **1.9.17 and above**

Synonym for `case sensitive`.

change notify timeout

Type of parameter: Global

Supported in versions: **2.0.0 and above**

One of the new NT SMB requests that Samba 2.0.x supports is the `ChangeNotify` request. This SMB allows a client to tell a server to watch a particular directory for any changes and reply to the SMB request only when a change has occurred. Such constant scanning of a directory is expensive under UNIX, hence an `smbd(8)` daemon performs only such a scan on each requested directory once every `change notify timeout` seconds.

`change notify timeout` is specified in units of seconds.

Default: `change notify timeout = 60`

Example: `change notify timeout = 300`

This example would change the scan time to every five minutes.

character set

Type of parameter: Global

Supported in versions: **1.9.17 and above**

This allows `smbd(8)` to map incoming filenames from a DOS Code page (see the `client code page` parameter) to several built-in UNIX character sets. The built-in code page translations are

- ISO8859-1—Western European UNIX character set. The parameter `client code page` must be set to code page 850 if the `character set` parameter is set to ISO8859-1 in order for the conversion to the UNIX character set to be done correctly.

- ISO8859-2—Eastern European UNIX character set. The parameter `client code page` must be set to code page 852 if the `character set` parameter is set to ISO8859-2 in order for the conversion to the UNIX character set to be done correctly.

- ISO8859-5—Russian Cyrillic UNIX character set. The parameter `client code page` must be set to code page 866 if the `character set` parameter is set to ISO8859-5 in order for the conversion to the UNIX character set to be done correctly.

- ISO8859-7—Greek UNIX character set. The parameter `client code page` must be set to code page 737 if the `character set` parameter is set to ISO8859-7 in order for the conversion to the UNIX character set to be done correctly.

- KOI8-R—Alternate mapping for Russian Cyrillic UNIX character set. The parameter `client code page` must be set to code page 866 if the `character set` parameter is set to KOI8-R in order for the conversion to the UNIX character set to be done correctly.

These MS-DOS code page to UNIX character set mappings are not currently dynamic, like the loading of MS-DOS code pages. This could change in the future.

See also `client code page`. Normally this parameter is not set, meaning no filename translation is done.

Default: `character set = empty string`

Example: `character set = ISO8859-1`

client code page

Type of parameter: Global

Supported in versions: **1.9.17 and above**

This parameter specifies the DOS code page that the clients accessing Samba will use. To determine what code page a Windows or DOS client is currently using, open a DOS command prompt and type the command `chcp`. This outputs the code page. The default for USA MS-DOS, Windows 95, and Windows NT releases is code page 437. The default for Western European releases of the preceding operating systems is code page 850.

This parameter tells `smbd(8)` which of the `codepage.XXX` files to dynamically load on startup. These files, described more fully in the manual page `make_smbcodepage(1)`, tell `smbd(8)` how to map lowercase to uppercase characters to provide the case insensitivity of filenames that Windows clients expect.

Samba currently ships with the following code page files:

- Code Page 437—MS-DOS Latin US
- Code Page 737—Windows 95 Greek
- Code Page 850—MS-DOS Latin 1
- Code Page 852—MS-DOS Latin 2
- Code Page 861—MS-DOS Icelandic

PART

V

APP

A

- Code Page 866—MS-DOS Cyrillic
- Code Page 932—MS-DOS Japanese SJIS
- Code Page 936—MS-DOS Simplified Chinese
- Code Page 949—MS-DOS Korean Hangul
- Code Page 950—MS-DOS Traditional Chinese

Thus, this parameter can have any of the values 437, 737, 850, 852, 861, 932, 936, 949, or 950. If you don't find the codepage you need, read the comments in one of the other codepage files and the make_smbcodepage(1) man page and write one. Please remember to donate it back to the Samba user community.

This parameter cooperates with the valid chars parameter in determining what characters are valid in filenames and how capitalization is done. If you set both this parameter and the valid chars parameter, the client code page parameter must be set before the valid chars parameter in the smb.conf file. The valid chars string then augments the character settings in the client code page parameter.

If not set, client code page defaults to 850.

See also valid chars.

Default: client code page = 850

Example: client code page = 936

coding system

Type of parameter: Global

Supported in versions: **1.9.17 and above**

This parameter determines how incoming Shift-JIS Japanese characters are mapped from the incoming client code page used by the client, into filenames in the UNIX file system. Only useful if client code page is set to 932 (Japanese Shift-JIS).

The options are

- SJIS, Shift-JIS—Does no conversion of the incoming filename.
- JIS8, J8BB, J8BH, J8@B, J8@J, J8@H—Converts from incoming Shift-JIS to eight-bit JIS code with different shift-in, shift-out codes.
- JIS7, J7BB, J7BH, J7@B, J7@J, J7@H—Converts from incoming Shift-JIS to seven-bit JIS code with different shift-in, shift-out codes.
- JUNET, JUBB, JUBH, JU@B, JU@J, JU@H—Converts from incoming Shift-JIS to JUNET code with different shift-in, shift-out codes.
- EUC—Converts an incoming Shift-JIS character to EUC code.

- **HEX**—Converts an incoming Shift-JIS character to a 3-byte hex representation, such as AB.

- **CAP**—Converts an incoming Shift-JIS character to the three-byte hex representation used by the Columbia AppleTalk Program (CAP), such as AB. This is used for compatibility between Samba and CAP.

comment

Type of parameter: Local

Supported in versions: **1.9.17 and above**

This is a text field that is seen next to a share when a client queries the server, either through the network neighborhood or through `net view` to list what shares are available. If you want to set the string that is displayed next to the machine name, see the `server string` command.

Default: No comment string

Example: `comment = Fred's Files`

config file

Type of parameter: Global

Supported in versions: **1.9.17 and above**

This allows you to override the config file to use, instead of the default (usually `smb.conf`). There is a chicken and egg problem here because this option is set in the config file! For this reason, if the name of the config file has changed when the parameters are loaded, it reloads them from the new config file.

This option takes the usual substitutions, which can be very useful.

If the config file doesn't exist, it won't be loaded (allowing you to special case the config files of just a few clients).

Default: `config file = defaults to /etc/smb.conf`

Example: `config file = /usr/local/samba/lib/smb.conf.%m`

copy

Type of parameter: Local

Supported in versions: **1.9.17 and above**

This parameter enables you to clone service entries. The specified service is simply duplicated under the current service's name. Any parameters specified in the current section override those in the section being copied. This feature enables you to set up a template service and create similar services easily.

PART

V

APP

A

> **Note**
>
> The service being copied must occur earlier in the configuration file than the service doing the copying.

Default: None

Example: `copy = otherservice`

create mask

Type of parameter: Local

Supported in versions: **1.9.17 and above**

A synonym for this parameter is `create mode`.

When a file is created, the necessary permissions are calculated according to the mapping from DOS modes to UNIX permissions, and the resulting UNIX mode is then bit-wise ANDed with this parameter. This parameter can be thought of as a bit-wise mask for the UNIX modes of a file. Any bit not set here is removed from the modes set on a file when it is created.

The default value of this parameter removes the group and other write and execute bits from the UNIX modes.

Following this, Samba will bit-wise OR the UNIX mode created from this parameter with the value of the `force create mode` parameter, which is set to 000 by default.

This parameter does not affect directory modes. See the parameter `directory mode` for details.

See the `force create mode` parameter for forcing particular mode bits to be set on created files. See also the `directory mode` parameter for masking mode bits on created directories. See also the `inherit permissions` parameter for inheriting permissions of parent directories.

Default: `create mask = 0744`

Example: `create mask = 0775`

create mode

Type of parameter: Local

Supported in versions: **1.9.17 and above**

This is a synonym for `create mask`.

deadtime

Type of parameter: Global

Supported in versions: **1.9.17 and above**

The value of the parameter (a decimal integer) represents the number of minutes of inactivity before a connection is considered dead and it is disconnected. The `deadtime` takes effect only if the number of open files is zero. This is useful to stop a server's resources from being exhausted by a large number of inactive connections.

Most clients have an auto-reconnect feature when a connection is broken, so in most cases this parameter should be transparent to users.

Using this parameter with a timeout of a few minutes is recommended for most systems.

A `deadtime` of zero indicates that no auto-disconnection should be performed.

Default: `deadtime = 0`

Example: `deadtime = 15`

debug hires timestamp

Type of parameter: Global

Supported in versions: **2.0.6 and above**

Sometimes the time stamps in the log messages are needed with a resolution of higher than seconds. This Boolean parameter adds microsecond resolution to the time stamp message header when turned on.

> **Note**   The parameter `debug timestamp` must be on for this to have an effect.

Default: `debug hires timestamp = No`

Example: `debug hires timestamp = Yes`

debug level

Type of parameter: Global

Supported in versions: **1.9.17 and above**

The value of the parameter (an integer) allows the debug level (logging level) to be specified in the `smb.conf` file. This is to give greater flexibility in the configuration of the system.

The default is the debug level specified on the command line or level zero if none was specified.

Example: `debug level = 3`

debug pid

Type of parameter: Global

Supported in versions: **2.0.6 and above**

When using only one log file for more then one forked `smbd(8)` process, which process outputs which message can be hard to follow. This Boolean parameter adds the process ID to the time stamp message headers in the logfile when turned on.

Note The parameter `debug timestamp` must be on for this to have an effect.

Default: `debug pid = No`

Example: `debug pid = Yes`

debug timestamp

Type of parameter: Global

Supported in versions: **2.0.0 and above**

Samba 2.0 debug log messages are time stamped by default. If you are running at a high debug level, these time stamps can be distracting. This Boolean parameter enables you to turn them off.

Default: `debug timestamp = Yes`

Example: `debug timestamp = No`

debug uid

Type of parameter: Global

Supported in versions: **2.0.6 and above**

Samba is sometimes run as root and sometime run as the connected user. This Boolean parameter inserts the current `euid`, `egid`, `uid`, and `gid` to the time stamp message headers in the log file if turned on.

Note The parameter `debug timestamp` must be on for this to have an effect.

Default: `debug uid = No`

Example: `debug uid = Yes`

default case

Type of parameter: Local

Supported in versions: **1.9.17 and above**

Samba supports name mangling so that DOS and Windows clients can use files that don't conform to the 8.3 format. It can also be set to adjust the case of 8.3 format filenames. This parameter, which can have the values `upper` or `lower`, controls the default case for new filenames.

Also see the `short preserve case` parameter.

Default: `default case = lower`

Example: `default case = upper`

default service

Type of parameter: Global

Supported in versions: **1.9.17 and above**

This parameter specifies the name of a service that will be connected to if the service actually requested cannot be found.

There is no default value for this parameter. If this parameter is not given, attempting to connect to a nonexistent service results in an error. Typically, the default service would be a guest ok, read-only service. Also, the apparent service name will be changed to equal that of the requested service. This is very useful because it allows you to use macros such as `%S` to make a wildcard service.

Any underscore (_) characters in the name of the service used in the default service are mapped to a slash.

Default: `default service = none`

Example: `default service = pub`

With the default service of `pub` and the following value for `pub`, any share name will work as long as a directory of that name exists.

```
[pub]
path = /%S
```

default

Type of parameter: Global

Supported in versions: **1.9.17 and above**

A synonym for `default service`.

delete readonly

Type of parameter: Local

Supported in versions: **1.9.17 and above**

This parameter allows read-only files to be deleted. This is not normal DOS semantics but is allowed by UNIX. This option can be useful for running applications such as rcs, where

PART

V

APP

A

UNIX file ownership prevents changing file permissions, and DOS semantics prevent deletion of a read-only file.

Default: `delete readonly = No`

Example: `delete readonly = Yes`

delete user script

Type of parameter: Global

Supported in versions: **2.0.0 and above**

This is the full pathname to a script that will be run as root by `smbd(8)` under the following special circumstances. Normally, a Samba server requires that UNIX users be created for all users accessing files on this server. For sites that use Windows NT account databases as their primary user database, creating these users and keeping the user list in sync with the Windows NT PDC is an onerous task. This option allows `smbd(8)` to delete the required UNIX users on demand when a user accesses the Samba server and the Windows NT user no longer exists.

To use this option, `smbd(8)` must be set to `security=domain`, and `delete user script` must be set to a full pathname for a script that deletes a UNIX user given one argument of `%u`, which expands into the UNIX user name to delete.

> **Note**
>
> This is different from the `add user script`, which works with the `security=server` option as well as `security=domain`. Only when Samba is a domain member does it get the information on an attempted user logon that a user no longer exists. In the `security=server` mode, a missing user is treated the same as an invalid password logon attempt. Deleting the user in this circumstance would not be a good idea.

When the Windows user attempts to access the Samba server, at login (session setup in the SMB protocol) time, `smbd(8)` contacts the password server and attempts to authenticate the given user with the given password. If the authentication fails with the specific domain error code, the user no longer exists, and `smbd(8)` attempts to find a UNIX user in the UNIX password database that matches the Windows user account. If this lookup succeeds and `delete user script` is set, `smbd(8)` calls the specified script as root, expanding any `%u` argument to be the username to delete.

This script should delete the given UNIX username. In this way, UNIX users are dynamically deleted to match existing Windows NT accounts.

See also `security=domain`, `password server`, `add user script`.

Default: `delete user script = empty string`

Example: `delete user script = /usr/local/samba/bin/del_user %u`

delete veto files

Type of parameter: Local

Supported in versions: **1.9.18 and above**

This option is used when Samba is attempting to delete a directory that contains one or more vetoed directories (see the `veto files` option). If this option is set to `False` (the default), and if a vetoed directory contains any non-vetoed files or directories, the directory delete fails. This is usually what you want.

If this option is set to `True`, Samba attempts to recursively delete any files and directories within the vetoed directory. This can be useful for integration with file-serving systems such as NetAtalk, which create metafiles within directories you might normally veto DOS and Windows users from seeing (for example, `.AppleDouble`).

Setting `delete veto files = True` allows these directories to be transparently deleted when the parent directory is deleted (as long as the user has permissions to do so).

See also the `veto files` parameter.

Default: `delete veto files = False`

Example: `delete veto files = True`

deny hosts

Type of parameter: Local

Supported in versions: **1.9.17 and above**

Synonym for `hosts deny`.

dfree command

Type of parameter: Global

Supported in versions: **1.9.17 and above**

The `dfree command` setting should be used only on systems where a problem occurs with the internal disk space calculations. This has been known to happen with Ultrix, but can occur with other operating systems. The symptom that was seen was an error of `Abort Retry Ignore` at the end of each directory listing.

This setting allows the replacement of the internal routines that calculate the total disk space and amount available with an external routine. The following example gives a possible script that might fulfill this function.

The external program is passed a single parameter indicating a directory in the file system being queried. This typically consists of the string `./`. The script should return two integers in ASCII. The first should be the total disk space in blocks, and the second should be the number of available blocks. An optional third return value can give the block size in bytes. The default block size is 1,024 bytes.

> **Note**
>
> Your script should *not* be setuid or setgid and should be owned by (and writeable only by) root!

Default: By default, internal routines for determining the disk capacity and remaining space will be used.

Example: dfree command = /usr/local/samba/bin/dfree

where the script dfree (which must be made executable) could be

```
#!/bin/sh
df $1 | tail -1 | awk '{print $2 $4}'
or perhaps (on Sys V based systems):
#!/bin/sh
/usr/bin/df -k $1 | tail -1 | awk '{print $3 $5}'
```

You might have to replace the command names with full pathnames on some systems.

directory mask

Type of parameter: Local

Supported in versions: **1.9.17 and above**

This parameter specifies the octal modes that are used when converting DOS modes to UNIX modes when creating UNIX directories.

When a directory is created, the necessary permissions are calculated according to the mapping from DOS modes to UNIX permissions, and the resulting UNIX mode is then bit-wise ANDed with this parameter. This parameter can be thought of as a bit-wise mask for the UNIX modes of a directory. Any bit *not* set here is removed from the modes set on a directory when it is created.

The default value of this parameter removes the group and other write bits from the UNIX mode, allowing only the user who owns the directory to modify it.

Following this, Samba will bit-wise OR the UNIX mode created from this parameter with the value of the force directory mode parameter. This parameter is set to 000 by default (that is, no extra mode bits are added).

See the force directory mode parameter to cause particular mode bits to always be set on created directories.

See also the create mode parameter for masking mode bits on created files, and the directory security mask parameter.

See also the `inherit permissions` parameter to inherit permissions from parent directories when creating files and directories.

Default: `directory mask = 0755`

Example: `directory mask = 0775`

directory mode

Type of parameter: Local

Supported in versions: **1.9.17 and above**

Synonym for `directory mask`.

directory security mask

Type of parameter: Local

Supported in versions: **2.0.5 and above**

This parameter controls what UNIX permission bits can be modified when a Windows NT client is manipulating the UNIX permission on a directory using the native NT security dialog box.

This parameter is applied as a mask (`ANDed` with) to the changed permission bits, thus preventing any bits not in this mask from being modified. Essentially, zero bits in this mask may be treated as a set of bits the user is not allowed to change.

If not set explicitly, this parameter is set to the same value as the directory mask parameter. To allow a user to modify all the `user/group/world` permissions on a directory, set this parameter to 0777.

Note

Users who can access the Samba server through other means can easily bypass this restriction, so it is primarily useful for standalone appliance systems. Administrators of most normal systems will probably want to set it to 0777.

See also the `force directory security mode`, `security mask`, and `force security mode` parameters.

Default: `directory security mask = `*`same as directory mask`*

Example: `directory security mask = 0777`

directory

Type of parameter: Local

Supported in versions: **1.9.17 and above**

This is a synonym for `path`.

PART

V

APP

A

dns proxy

Type of parameter: Global

Supported in versions: **1.9.17 and above**

Specifies that nmbd(8), when acting as a WINS server and finding that a NetBIOS name has not been registered, should treat the NetBIOS name word-for-word as a DNS name and do a lookup with the DNS server for that name on behalf of the name-querying client.

> **Note**
>
> The maximum length for a NetBIOS name is 15 characters, so the DNS name (or DNS alias) can likewise only be a maximum of 15 characters.

nmbd(8) spawns a second copy of itself to do the DNS name lookup requests because doing a name lookup is a blocking action.

See also the parameter wins support.

Default: dns proxy = yes

Example: dns proxy = no

domain admin group

Type of parameter: Global

Supported in versions: **2.0.0 and above**

This is an experimental parameter that is part of the unfinished Samba NT Domain Controller Code in the 2.0 release series. This parameter specifies a group that is mapped to the Domain Admins NT group. It has been made obsolete by the domain group map parameter in SAMBA_TNG.

domain admin users

Type of parameter: Global

Supported in versions: **1.9.18 and above**

This is an experimental parameter that is part of the unfinished Samba NT Domain Controller Code in the 2.0 release series. This parameter specifies users that will be given the special security identifier of the Administrator NT account. It has been made obsolete by the domain user map parameter in SAMBA_TNG.

domain controller

Type of parameter: Global

Supported in versions: **1.9.17-1.9.18p10**

This is a deprecated parameter. It is currently not used within the Samba source and should be removed from all current `smb.conf` files.

domain groups

Type of parameter: Global

Supported in versions: **1.9.18 and above**

This is an experimental parameter that is part of the unfinished Samba NT Domain Controller Code in the 2.0 release series. This parameter specifies UNIX groups that appear as NT groups. It has been made obsolete by the domain group map parameter in SAMBA_TNG.

domain guest group

Type of parameter: Global

Supported in versions: **2.0.0 and above**

This is an experimental parameter that is part of the unfinished Samba NT Domain Controller Code in the 2.0 release series. This parameter specifies a group that is mapped to the Domain Groups NT group. It has been made obsolete by the domain group map parameter in SAMBA_TNG.

domain guest users

Type of parameter: Global

Supported in versions: **1.9.18 and above**

This is an experimental parameter that is part of the unfinished Samba NT Domain Controller Code in the 2.0 release series. This parameter specifies users that are given the special security identifier of the Guest NT account. It has been made obsolete by the domain user map parameter in SAMBA_TNG.

domain logons

Type of parameter: Global

Supported in versions: **1.9.17 and above**

If set to `true`, the Samba server serves Windows 95/98 Domain logons for the workgroup it is in. For more details on setting up this feature, see Chapter 11, "Samba as a Logon and Profiles Server."

Also, this parameter must be set to `true` (or `yes`) if you are setting Samba up in PDC mode. This causes `nmbd(8)` to register the NetBIOS name DOMAIN<1C> and enables it to process NetLogon requests. NetLogon requests are used by Win9x clients to log on to a domain as well as by WinNT clients to find a domain controller.

PART

V

APP

A

Note

> Win95/98 Domain logons are not the same as Windows NT Domain logons. NT Domain logons require a primary domain controller (PDC) for the domain. The Samba 2.0.x series provide enough domain controller functionality that Windows NT Workstations can log on to the domain, but they have many deficiencies. See also the SAMBA_TNG code for more complete PDC support.

Note

> This parameter must not be enabled if there is an existing NT domain controller in the same domain as the Samba server because it will interfere with the NT domain controller's functionality.

Default: domain logons = no

Example: domain logons = yes

domain master

Type of parameter: Global

Supported in versions: **1.9.17 and above**

This parameter tells nmbd(1) to enable WAN-wide browse list collation. Setting this option causes nmbd to claim a special domain-specific NetBIOS name that identifies it as a domain master browser for its given workgroup. Local master browsers in the same workgroup on broadcast-isolated subnets give this nmbd their local browse lists, and then ask smbd(8) for a complete copy of the browse list for the whole wide area network. Browser clients then contact their local master browser and will receive the domain-wide browse list, instead of just the list for their broadcast-isolated subnet.

Note

> Windows NT primary domain controllers expect to claim this workgroup-specific special NetBIOS name that identifies them as domain master browsers for that workgroup by default (that is, there is no way to prevent a Windows NT PDC from attempting to do this). This means that if this parameter is set and nmbd(8) claims the special name for a workgroup before a Windows NT PDC can do so, cross-subnet browsing will behave strangely and might fail. Also, logon processing by your NT PDC might fail as well.

Default: domain master = no

Example: domain master = yes

dont descend

Type of parameter: Local

Supported in versions: **1.9.17 and above**

Certain directories on some systems (for example, the /proc tree under Linux) are either not of interest to clients or are infinitely deep (recursive). This parameter allows you to specify a comma-delimited list of directories that the server should always show as empty.

> **Note**
>
> Samba can be very fussy about the exact format of the dont descend entries. For example, you might need ./proc instead of just /proc. Experimentation is the best policy.

Default: none (that is, all directories are OK to descend)

Example: dont descend = /proc,/dev

dos filetime resolution

Type of parameter: Local

Supported in versions: **1.9.18p3 and above**

Under the DOS and Windows FAT file system, the finest granularity on time resolution is two seconds. Setting this parameter for a share causes Samba to round the reported time down to the nearest two-second boundary when a query call that requires one-second resolution is made to smbd(8).

This option is mainly used as a compatibility option for Visual C++ when used against Samba shares. If oplocks are enabled on a share, Visual C++ uses two different time reading calls to check whether a file has changed since it was last read. One of these calls uses a one-second granularity, the other uses a two-second granularity. Because the two-second call rounds any odd second down, if the file has a timestamp of an odd number of seconds, the two timestamps will not match, and Visual C++ will keep reporting the file has changed. Setting this option causes the two time stamps to match, and Visual C++ is happy.

Default: dos filetime resolution = False

Example: dos filetime resolution = True

dos filetimes

Type of parameter: Local

Supported in versions: **1.9.17p4 and above**

Under DOS and Windows, if users can write to a file, they can change the time stamp on it. Under POSIX semantics, only the owner of the file or root may change the time stamp. By default, Samba runs with POSIX semantics and refuses to change the time stamp on a file if

PART

V

APP

A

the user on whose behalf `smbd(8)` is acting is not the file owner. Setting this option to `True` allows DOS semantics, and `smbd(8)` will change the file time stamp as DOS requires.

Default: `dos filetimes = False`

Example: `dos filetimes = True`

encrypt passwords

Type of parameter: Global

Supported in versions: **1.9.17 and above**

This Boolean controls whether encrypted passwords are negotiated with the client.

> **Note**
>
> Windows NT 4.0 SP3 and above, Windows 95 OSR2 and above, and Windows 98 will, by default, expect encrypted passwords unless a registry entry is changed. To use encrypted passwords in Samba, see Chapter 8, "Samba and Password Management."

For encrypted passwords to work correctly, `smbd(8)` must have access to a local `smbpasswd(5)` file (see the `smbpasswd(8)` program for information on how to set up and maintain this file). Another approach is to set the `security` parameter to either `server` or `domain`, which causes `smbd(8)` to authenticate against another server.

exec

Type of parameter: Local

Supported in versions: **1.9.17 and above**

This is a synonym for `preexec`.

fake directory create times

Type of parameter: Local

Supported in versions: **1.9.18p4 and above**

NTFS and Windows VFAT file systems keep a create time for all files and directories. This is not the same as the `ctime` (status change time) that UNIX keeps, so Samba by default reports the earliest of the various times UNIX does keep. Setting this parameter for a share causes Samba to always report midnight 1-1-1980 as the create time for directories.

This option is mainly used as a compatibility option for Visual C++ when used against Samba shares. Visual C++-generated make files have the object directory as a dependency for each object file and a make rule to create the directory. Also, when NMAKE compares time stamps, it uses the creation time when examining a directory. Thus, the object directory will be created if it does not exist, but once it does exist, it will always have an earlier time stamp than the object files it contains.

However, UNIX time semantics mean that the create time reported by Samba will be updated whenever a file is created or deleted in the directory. NMAKE therefore finds that all object files in the object directory, except the last one built, are out of date compared to the directory and rebuilds these out-of-date object files. Enabling this option ensures directories always predate their contents and an NMAKE build will proceed as expected.

Default: `fake directory create times = False`

Example: `fake directory create times = True`

fake oplocks

Type of parameter: Local

Supported in versions: **1.9.17 and above**

Oplocks provide the way that SMB clients get permission from a server to cache file operations locally. If a server grants an oplock (opportunistic lock), the client is free to assume that it is the only one accessing the file, and it will aggressively cache file data. With some oplock types the client may even cache file open/close operations. This can give enormous performance benefits.

When you set `fake oplocks = yes`, `smbd(8)` will always grant oplock requests no matter how many clients are using the file.

It is generally much better to use the real oplocks support rather than this parameter.

If you enable this option on all read-only shares or shares that you know will only be accessed from one client at a time, such as physically read-only media like CD-ROMs, you will see a big performance improvement on many operations.

Caution

If you enable this option on shares where multiple clients might be accessing the files read-write at the same time, you can get data corruption.

This option is disabled by default.

follow symlinks

Type of parameter: Local

Supported in versions: **1.9.17 and above**

This parameter allows the Samba administrator to stop `smbd(8)` from following symbolic links in a particular share. Setting this parameter to `No` prevents any file or directory that is a symbolic link from being followed (the user receives an error). This option is very useful to stop users from adding a symbolic link to `/etc/passwd` in their home directory, for example. However, it will slow filename lookups down slightly.

This option is enabled (that is, `smbd(8)` will follow symbolic links) by default.

PART

V

APP

A

Default: `follow symlinks = yes`

Example: `follow symlinks = no`

force create mode

Type of parameter: Local

Supported in versions: **1.9.17 and above**

This parameter specifies a set of UNIX mode bit permissions that will always be set on a file created by Samba. This is done by bitwise ORing these bits onto the mode bits of a file that is being created. The default for this parameter is (in octal) 000. The modes in this parameter are bitwise ORed onto the file mode after the mask set in the `create mask` parameter is applied.

See also the parameter `create mask` for details on masking mode bits on created files. See also the `inherit permissions` parameter for details on inheriting permissions from the parent directory when files or directories are created.

Default: `force create mode = 000`

Example: `force create mode = 0755`

This example would force all created files to have read and execute permissions set for `group` and `other` as well as the read/write/execute bits set for the `user`.

force directory mode

Type of parameter: Local

Supported in versions: **1.9.17 and above**

This parameter specifies a set of UNIX mode bit permissions that will always be set on a directory created by Samba. This is done by bitwise ORing these bits onto the mode bits of a directory that is being created. The default for this parameter is (in octal) 0000, which will not add any extra permission bits to a created directory. This operation is done after the mode mask in the parameter `directory mask` is applied.

See also the parameter `directory mask` for details on masking mode bits on created directories. See also the `inherit permissions` parameter for details on inheriting permissions from the parent directory when files or directories are created.

Default: `force directory mode = 000`

Example: `force directory mode = 0755`

This example would force all created directories to have read and execute permissions set for `group` and `other` as well as the read/write/execute bits set for the `user`.

force directory security mode

Type of parameter: Local

Supported in versions: **2.0.5 and above**

This parameter controls what UNIX permission bits can be modified when a Windows NT client is manipulating the UNIX permission on a directory using the native NT security dialog box.

This parameter is applied as a mask (ORed with) to the changed permission bits, thus forcing any bits in this mask that the user might have modified to be on. Essentially, bits that are on in this mask can be treated as a set of bits that, when modifying security on a directory, the user has always set to be on.

If not set explicitly, this parameter is set to the same value as the force directory mode parameter. To allow a user to modify the entire user, group, and world permissions on a directory, with restrictions, set this parameter to 000.

> **Note**
>
> Users who can access the Samba server through other means can easily bypass this restriction, so it is primarily useful for standalone appliance systems. Administrators of most normal systems will probably want to set it to 0000.

See also the directory security mask, security mask, force security mode, and inherit permissions parameters.

Default: force directory security mode = *same as force directory mode*

Example: force directory security mode = 0

force group

Type of parameter: Local

Supported in versions: **1.9.17 and above**

This specifies a UNIX group name that will be assigned as the default primary group for all users connecting to this service. This is useful for sharing files by ensuring that all access to files on service will use the named group for their permissions checking. Thus, by using the UNIX chgrp command to change the group owner of files and directories within this service to the appropriate value, the Samba administrator can restrict or allow sharing of these files.

In Samba 2.0.5 and above, this parameter has extended functionality in the following way. If the group name listed here has a + character prepended to it, the current user accessing the share only has the primary group default assigned to this group if he is already assigned as a member of that group. This allows an administrator to decide that only users already in a particular group will create files with group ownership set to that group. This gives a finer granularity of ownership assignment. For example, the setting force group = +sys means that only users already in group sys will have their default primary group assigned to sys when accessing this Samba share. All other users will retain their ordinary primary group.

If the `force user` parameter is also set, the group specified in the force group overrides the primary group set in `force user`.

See also the `force user` and `inherit permissions` parameters.

Default: No forced group

Example: `force group = agroup`

force security mode

Type of parameter: Local

Supported in versions: **2.0.5 and above**

This parameter controls what UNIX permission bits can be modified when a Windows NT client is manipulating the UNIX permission on a file using the native NT security dialog box.

This parameter is applied as a mask (ORed with) to the changed permission bits, thus forcing any bits in this mask that the user might have modified to be on. Essentially, one bit in this mask may be treated as a set of bits that, when modifying security on a file, the user has always set to be on.

If not set explicitly, this parameter is set to the same value as the `force create mode` parameter. To allow a user to modify all of the user, group, and world permissions on a file, with no restrictions, set this parameter to 000.

Note

Users who can access the Samba server through other means can easily bypass this restriction, so it is primarily useful for standalone appliance systems. Administrators of most normal systems will probably want to set it to 0000.

See also the `force directory security mode`, `directory security mask`, `security mask`, and `inherit permissions` parameters.

Default: `force security mode = same as force create mode`

Example: `force security mode = 0`

force user

Type of parameter: Local

Supported in versions: **1.9.17 and above**

This specifies a UNIX username that is assigned as the default user for all users connecting to this service. This is useful for sharing files. Use it carefully because using it incorrectly can cause security problems.

This username is used only after a connection is established. Thus, clients still need to connect as a valid user and supply a valid password. When connected, all file operations will be performed as the forced user, no matter what username the client connected as.

In Samba 2.0.5 and above this parameter also causes the primary group of the forced user to be used as the primary group for all file activity. Before 2.0.5 the primary group was left as the primary group of the connecting user (this was a bug).

See also `force group`.

Default: No forced user

Example: `force user = auser`

fstype

Type of parameter: Local

Supported in versions: **2.0.0 and above**

This parameter allows the administrator to configure the string that specifies the type of file system a share is using that is reported by `smbd(8)` when a client queries the file system type for a share. The default type is `NTFS` for compatibility with Windows NT, but this can be changed to other strings such as `Samba` or `FAT` if required.

Default: `fstype = NTFS`

Example: `fstype = Samba`

getwd cache

Type of parameter: Global

Supported in versions: **1.9.17 and above**

This is a tuning option. When this is enabled, a caching algorithm will be used to reduce the time taken for `getwd(3)` calls. This can have a significant impact on performance, especially when the `widelinks` parameter is set to `False`.

Default: `getwd cache = No`

Example: `getwd cache = Yes`

group

Type of parameter: Local

Supported in versions: **1.9.17 and above**

Synonym for `force group`.

PART

V

APP

A

guest account

Type of parameter: Local

Supported in versions: **1.9.17 and above**

This is a username that is used for access to services that are specified as guest ok (see the following parameter). Whatever privileges this user has are available to any client connecting to the guest service. Typically this user exists in the password file but does not have a valid login. The user account ftp is often a good choice for this parameter. If a username is specified in a given service, the specified username overrides this one.

On some systems the default guest account nobody might not be able to print. Use another account in this case. You should test this by trying to log in as your guest user (perhaps by using the su - command) and trying to print using the system print command such as lpr(1) or lp(1).

Default: Specified at compile time, usually nobody

Example: guest account = ftp

guest ok

Type of parameter: Local

Supported in versions: **1.9.17 and above**

If this parameter is yes for a service, no password is required to connect to the service. Privileges will be those of the guest account.

See also the security parameter for more information about this option.

Default: guest ok = no

Example: guest ok = yes

guest only

Type of parameter: Local

Supported in versions: **1.9.17 and above**

If this parameter is yes for a service, only guest connections to the service are made. This parameter will have no effect if guest ok or public is not set for the service.

See also the security parameter for more information about this option.

Default: guest only = no

Example: guest only = yes

hide dot files

Type of parameter: Local

Supported in versions: **1.9.17 and above**

This is a Boolean parameter that controls whether files starting with a dot appear as hidden files.

Default: `hide dot files = yes`

Example: `hide dot files = no`

hide files

Type of parameter: Local

Supported in versions: **1.9.17 and above**

This is a list of files or directories that are not visible but are accessible. The DOS `hidden` attribute is applied to any files or directories that match. Each entry in the list must be separated by a slash (/), which allows spaces to be included in the entry. You can also use an asterisk (*) and question mark (?) to specify multiple files or directories as in DOS wildcards. Each entry must be a UNIX path, not a DOS path, and must not include the UNIX directory separator (/). The case sensitivity option is applicable to hiding files as well.

Setting this parameter affects the performance of Samba because Samba is forced to check all files and directories for a match as they are scanned during file listing and searching operations.

See also `hide dot files`, `veto files`, and `case sensitive`.

Default: No files or directories are hidden by this option by default (dot files are hidden by default because of the `hide dot files` option).

Example: `hide files = /.*/DesktopFolderDB/TrashFor%m/resource.frk/`

This example is based on files that the Macintosh SMB client (DAVE), available from Thursby, creates for internal use and also still hides all files beginning with a dot.

homedir map

Type of parameter: Global

Supported in versions: **1.9.17 and above**

If `nis homedir` is true and `smbd(8)` is also acting as a Win95/98 logon server, this parameter specifies the NIS (or YP) map from which the server for the user's home directory should be extracted. At present, only the Sun `auto.home` map format is understood. The form of the map is

`username server:/some/file/system`

and the program will extract the server name from before the first colon (:).

PART
V

APP
A

> **Note**
>
> A working NIS is required on the system for this option to work.

See also `nis homedir` and `domain logons`.

Default: `homedir map = auto.home`

Example: `homedir map = amd.homedir`

hosts allow

Type of parameter: Local

Supported in versions: **1.9.17 and above**

A synonym for this parameter is `allow hosts`.

This parameter is a comma-, space-, or tab-delimited set of hosts that are permitted to access a service.

If specified in the [global] section, it applies to all services, regardless of whether the individual service has a different setting.

You can specify the hosts by name or by IP number. For example, you could restrict access to only the hosts on a Class C subnet with something like `allow hosts = 150.203.5`. The full syntax of the list is described in the man page `hosts_access(5)`. Unfortunately, this man page might not be present on your system, so a brief description will be given here also.

> **Note**
>
> The localhost address 127.0.0.1 will always be allowed access unless specifically denied by a `hostsdeny` option.

You can also specify hosts by network/netmask pairs and by netgroup names if your system supports netgroups. The EXCEPT keyword can also be used to limit a wildcard list. The following examples may provide some help:

Example 1: Allow all IPs in 150.203.*.* except one

`hosts allow = 150.203. EXCEPT 150.203.6.66`

Example 2: Allow hosts that match the given network/netmask

`hosts allow = 150.203.15.0/255.255.255.0`

Example 3: Allow a couple of hosts

`hosts allow = lapland, arvidsjaur`

Example 4: Allow only hosts in NIS netgroup foonet, but deny access from one particular host

```
hosts allow = @foonet
hosts deny = pirate
```

Note that access still requires suitable user-level passwords. See `testparm (1)` for a way of testing your host access to see whether it does what you expect.

Default: None (that is, all hosts permitted access)

Example: `allow hosts = 150.203.5. myhost.mynet.edu.au`

hosts deny

Type of parameter: Local

Supported in versions: **1.9.17 and above**

The opposite of `hosts allow`. Hosts listed here are not permitted access to services unless the specific services have their own lists to override this one. The `allow` list takes precedence where the lists conflict.

Default: None (that is, no hosts specifically excluded)

Example: `hosts deny = 150.203.4. badhost.mynet.edu.au`

hosts equiv

Type of parameter: Global

Supported in versions: **1.9.17 and above**

If this global parameter is a non-null string, it specifies the name of a file to read for the names of hosts and users who will be allowed access without specifying a password.

This is not be confused with `hosts allow`, which is about hosts access to services and is more useful for guest services. `hosts equiv` may be useful for NT clients that will not supply passwords to Samba.

> **Note**
>
> The use of `hosts equiv` can be a major security hole because you trust the PC to supply the correct username. It is very easy to get a PC to supply a false username. I recommend that the `hosts equiv` option be used only if you really know what you are doing, or perhaps on a home network where you trust your spouse and kids...and only if you really trust them.

Default: No host equivalences

Example: `hosts equiv = /etc/hosts.equiv`

include

Type of parameter: Local

Supported in versions: **1.9.17 and above**

PART

V

APP

A

This allows you to include one config file inside another. The file is included literally, as though typed in place. It takes the standard substitutions, except %u, %P, and %S.

Default: No files are included by default.

Example: `include = /etc/smb.conf.%m`

inherit permissions

Type of parameter: Local

Supported in versions: **2.0.7 and above**

Permissions on new files and directories are normally governed by the `create mask`, `directory mask`, `force create mode`, and `force directory mode` parameters, but this Boolean parameter overrides them when set to `true` or `yes`. New directories inherit the mode of their parent directory, including bits such as `setgid`. New files inherit their read/write bits from the parent directory. Their execute bits continue to be determined by the `map archive`, `map hidden`, and `map system` parameters as usual.

Note that the `setuid` bit is *never* set using inheritance (the code explicitly prohibits this). This can be particularly useful on large systems with many users, to allow a single `[homes]` share to be used flexibly by each user.

See also the `create mask`, `directory mask`, `force create mode`, and `force directory mode` parameters.

Default: `inherit permissions = no`

Example: `inherit permissions = yes`

interfaces

Type of parameter: Global

Supported in versions: **1.9.17 and above**

This option enables you to override the default network interfaces list that Samba will use for browsing, name registration, and other NBT traffic. By default Samba queries the kernel for the list of all active interfaces and uses any interfaces except 127.0.0.1 that are broadcast capable.

The option takes a list of interface strings. Each string can be in any of the following forms:

- A network interface name (such as `eth0`)—This may include shell-like wildcards, so `eth*` will match any interface starting with the substring `eth`.
- An IP address—In this case the netmask is determined from the list of interfaces obtained from the kernel.
- An IP/mask pair.
- A broadcast/mask pair.

The mask parameters can either be a bit length (such as 24 for a C class network) or a full netmask in dotted decimal form. The IP parameters above can either be a full dotted decimal IP address or a hostname that will be looked up using the OS's normal hostname resolution mechanisms.

For example, the following line would configure three network interfaces corresponding to the eth0 device and IP addresses 192.168.2.10 and 192.168.3.10. The netmasks of the latter two interfaces would be set to 255.255.255.0.

```
interfaces = eth0 192.168.2.10/24 192.168.3.10/255.255.255.0
```

See also bind interfaces only.

Default: All broadcast-capable interfaces, except 127.0.0.1.

invalid users

Type of parameter: Local

Supported in versions: **1.9.17 and above**

This is a list of users that should not be allowed to log in to this service. This is really a paranoid check to absolutely ensure an improper setting does not breach your security.

A name starting with the at symbol (@) is interpreted as an NIS netgroup first (if your system supports NIS), and then as a UNIX group if the name was not found in the NIS netgroup database.

A name starting with the plus sign (+) is interpreted only by looking in the UNIX group database. A name starting with the ampersand (&) is interpreted only by looking in the NIS netgroup database (this requires NIS to be working on your system). The characters + and & may be used at the start of the name in either order, so the value +&group means check the UNIX group database, followed by the NIS netgroup database. The value &+group means check the NIS netgroup database, followed by the UNIX group database (the same as the @ prefix).

The current service name is substituted for %S. This is useful in the [homes] section.

See also valid users.

Default: No invalid users

Example: invalid users = root fred admin @wheel

keepalive

Type of parameter: Global

Supported in versions: **1.9.17 and above**

The value of the parameter (an integer) represents the number of seconds between keepalive packets. If this parameter is zero, no keepalive packets will be sent. Keepalive packets, if sent, allow the server to tell whether a client is still present and responding. In general, keepalives

PART

V

APP

A

should not be needed if the socket being used has the SO_KEEPALIVE attribute set on it (see socket options). Basically you should use this option only if you strike difficulties.

Default: keepalive = 0

Example: keepalive = 60

kernel oplocks

Type of parameter: Global

Supported in versions: **2.0.0 and above**

For flavors of UNIX that support kernel-based oplocks (currently only IRIX, but hopefully also Linux and FreeBSD soon), this parameter allows the use of them to be turned on or off.

Kernel oplocks support allows Samba oplocks to be broken whenever a local UNIX process or NFS operation accesses a file that smbd(8) has oplocked. This allows complete data consistency between SMB/CIFS, NFS, and local file access (and is a very cool feature).

This parameter defaults to on with systems that have the support, and off with systems that don't. You should never need to touch this parameter.

See also the oplocks and level2 oplocks parameters.

Default: kernel oplocks = off (for most systems)

kernel oplocks = on (for some IRIX systems)

Example: kernel oplocks = off

level2 oplocks

Type of parameter: Local

Supported in versions: **2.0.5 and above**

This parameter controls whether Samba supports level2 (read-only) oplocks on a share. In Samba 2.0.5 and 2.0.6 this parameter defaults to False, but in Samba 2.0.7 and above this parameter defaults to True.

Level2, or read-only oplocks, allows Windows NT clients that have an oplock on a file to downgrade from a read-write oplock to a read-only oplock when a second client opens the file (instead of releasing all oplocks on a second open, as in traditional, exclusive oplocks). This allows all openers of the file that support level2 oplocks to cache the file for read-ahead only (that is, they may not cache writes or lock requests) and increases performance for many accesses of files that are not commonly written (such as application .EXE files). When one of the clients that has a read-only oplock writes to the file, all clients are notified (no reply is needed or waited for) and told to break their oplocks to none and delete any read-ahead caches.

I recommend that this parameter be turned on to speed access to shared executables (and also to test the code).

For more discussions on level2 oplocks, see the CIFS spec.

Currently, if `kernel oplocks` are supported, level2 oplocks are not granted (even if this parameter is set to `true`).

> **Note**
>
> The `oplocks` parameter must be set to `true` on this share in order for this parameter to have any effect.

See also the `oplocks` and `kernel oplocks` parameters.

Default: `level2 oplocks = True` (This is the default as of Samba 2.0.7.)

Example: `level2 oplocks = False`

lm announce

Type of parameter: Global

Supported in versions: **1.9.18 and above**

This parameter determines whether `nmbd` produces Lanman announce broadcasts that are needed by OS/2 clients in order for them to see the Samba server in their browse list. This parameter can have three values: `true`, `false`, or `auto`. The default is `auto`. If set to `false`, Samba never produces these broadcasts. If set to `true`, Samba produces Lanman announce broadcasts at a frequency set by the parameter `lm interval`. If set to `auto`, Samba will not send Lanman announce broadcasts by default but will listen for them. If it hears such a broadcast on the wire, it will then start sending them at a frequency set by the parameter `lm interval`.

See also `lm interval`.

Default: `lm announce = auto`

Example: `lm announce = true`

lm interval

Type of parameter: Global

Supported in versions: **1.9.18 and above**

If Samba is set to produce Lanman announce broadcasts needed by OS/2 clients (see the `lm announce` parameter) then this parameter defines the frequency in seconds with which they will be made. If this is set to zero, no Lanman announcements will be made despite the setting of the `lm announce` parameter.

See also `lm announce`.

PART

V

APP

A

Default: lm interval = 60

Example: lm interval = 120

load printers

Type of parameter: Global

Supported in versions: **1.9.17 and above**

A Boolean variable that controls whether all printers in the printcap will be loaded for browsing by default. See the printers section for more details.

Default: load printers = yes

Example: load printers = no

local master

Type of parameter: Global

Supported in versions: **1.9.17 and above**

This option allows nmbd(8) to try to become a local master browser on a subnet. If set to False, nmbd will not attempt to become a local master browser on a subnet and will also lose in all browsing elections. By default this value is set to True. Setting this value to True doesn't mean that Samba will become the local master browser on a subnet, just that nmbd will participate in elections for local master browser.

Setting this value to False will cause nmbd(8) never to become a local master browser.

The default value of this parameter changed from Samba 2.0.6. Before Samba 2.0.6, the default value was no, which meant that by default a Samba server would not support browsing. From Samba 2.0.6 and above, the default is yes.

Default: local master = yes

lock dir

Type of parameter: Global

Supported in versions: **1.9.17 and above**

This is a synonym for lock directory.

lock directory

Type of parameter: Global

Supported in versions: **1.9.17 and above**

This option specifies the directory where lock files will be placed. The lock files are used to implement the max connections option.

Default: `lock directory = /tmp/samba`

Example: `lock directory = /usr/local/samba/var/locks`

locking

Type of parameter: Local

Supported in versions: **1.9.17 and above**

This controls whether locking is performed by the server in response to lock requests from the client.

If `locking = no`, all lock and unlock requests appear to succeed, and all lock queries indicate that the queried lock is clear.

If `locking = yes`, real locking will be performed by the server.

This option can be useful for read-only file systems that might not need locking (such as CD-ROM drives), although setting this parameter to `no` is not really recommended even in this case. Be careful about disabling locking either globally or in a specific service because lack of locking can result in data corruption. You should never need to set this parameter.

Default: `locking = yes`

Example: `locking = no`

log file

Type of parameter: Global

Supported in versions: **1.9.17 and above**

This parameter allows you to override the name of the Samba log file (also known as the debug file). This parameter takes the standard substitutions, allowing you to have separate log files for each user or machine.

Default: Compile-time setting, usually `/usr/local/samba/var/log.{smb,nmb}` or `/var/log/samba/log.{smb.nmb}`

Example: `log file = /usr/local/samba/var/log.%m`

log level

Type of parameter: Global

Supported in versions: **1.9.17 and above**

Synonym for `debug level`.

PART

V

APP

A

logon drive

Type of parameter: Global

Supported in versions: **1.9.18 and above**

This parameter specifies the local path to which the home directory will be connected (see logon home) and is used only by NT Workstations.

> **Note**
>
> This option is useful only if Samba is set up as a primary domain controller.

Example: logon drive = h:

logon home

Type of parameter: Global

Supported in versions: **1.9.18 and above**

This parameter specifies the home directory location when a Win95/98 or NT Workstation logs on to a Samba PDC. It allows you to do the following from a command prompt, for example:

NET USE H: /HOME

It is also used to specify the location of user's profiles for Win9x clients (contrary to what versions of the Samba man pages prior to 2.0.7 said). Because of a bug in the Win9x implementation of the NET USE /HOME command, it is possible to have a user's profiles in a subdirectory of the home directory, while still having the NET USE /HOME command work correctly as well. To achieve this, simply use the following:

logon home = \\%L\%U\.profiles

This option takes the standard substitutions, allowing you to have separate home directories for each user or machine.

> **Note**
>
> This option is useful only if Samba is set up as a logon server.

Default: logon home = \\%N\%U

Example: logon home = \\remote_smb_server\%U

logon path

Type of parameter: Global

Supported in versions: **1.9.17 and above**

This parameter specifies the home directory where roaming profiles (`NTUSER.DAT`/`NTUSER.MAN` files for Windows NT Workstations) are stored.

Contrary to what versions of the man pages say prior to Samba 2.0.7, this parameter cannot be used to set roaming profiles for Win9x clients. See the `logon home` parameter for more information on this subject. See also Chapter 19, "Samba and Windows NT Domains."

This option takes the standard substitutions, allowing you to have separate logon scripts for each user or machine. It also specifies the directory from which the desktop, start menu, network neighborhood, programs folders, and their contents, are loaded and displayed on your Windows 95/98 client.

The share and the path must be readable by the user for the preferences, and directories to be loaded onto the Windows NT Workstation client. The share must be writeable when the user logs in for the first time, so that the Windows NT client can create the `NTUSER.DAT` and other directories.

Thereafter, the directories and any of the contents can, if required, be made read-only. It is not advisable that the `NTUSER.DAT` file be made read-only; rename it to `NTUSER.MAN` to achieve the desired effect (a MANdatory profile).

Windows NT clients can sometimes maintain a connection to the `[homes]` share, even though no user is logged in. Therefore, it is vital that the logon path does not include a reference to the `[homes]` share. (Setting this parameter to `\\%N\HOMES\profile_path` will cause problems.)

This option takes the standard substitutions, allowing you to have separate logon scripts for each user or machine.

Note This option is useful only if Samba is set up as a primary domain controller.

Default: `logon path = \\%N\%U\profile`

Example: `logon path = \\PROFILESERVER\HOME_DIR\%U\PROFILE`

logon script

Type of parameter: Global

Supported in versions: **1.9.17 and above**

This parameter specifies the batch file (`.bat`) or NT command file (`.cmd`) to be downloaded and run on a machine when a user successfully logs on. The file must contain the DOS style cr/lf line endings. Using a DOS-style editor to create the file is recommended.

The script must be a path that is relative to the `[netlogon]` service. If the `[netlogon]` service specifies a path of `/usr/local/samba/netlogon`, and `logon script = STARTUP.BAT`, the file that will be downloaded is

`/usr/local/samba/netlogon/STARTUP.BAT`

The contents of the batch file are entirely your choice. A suggested command would be to add

```
NET TIME \\SERVER /SET /YES
```

to force every machine to synchronize clocks with the same time server. Another use would be to add

```
NET USE U: \\SERVER\UTILS
```

for commonly used utilities, or

```
NET USE Q: \\SERVER\ISO9001_QA
```

→ For more information on this parameter, **see** Chapter 11, "Samba as a Logon and Profiles Server."

Note

It is particularly important not to allow write access to the [netlogon] share or to grant users write permission on the batch files in a secure environment because this would allow the batch files to be arbitrarily modified and security to be breached.

This option takes the standard substitutions, allowing you to have separate logon scripts for each user or machine.

Note

This option is useful only if Samba is set up as a logon server.

Note

If you are using NET TIME \\SERVER /SET /YES on NT during logon, your users will need privileges to change the time on the workstation.

Example: `logon script = scripts\%U.bat`

lppause command

Type of parameter: Local

Supported in versions: **1.9.17 and above**

This parameter specifies the command to execute on the server host in order to pause printing or spooling of a specific print job. This command should be a program or script that takes a printer name and job number to pause the print job. One way to implement this is to use job priorities, where jobs having a too low priority won't be sent to the printer.

If a %p is given, the printer name is put in its place. A %j is replaced with the job number (an integer). On HPUX (see `printing=hpux`), if the `-p%p` option is added to the lpq command, the job will show up with the correct status. If the job priority is lower than the set fence priority it will have the PAUSED status, whereas if the priority is equal or higher it will have the SPOOLED or PRINTING status.

It is good practice to include the absolute path in the `lppause` command because the PATH might not be available to the server.

See also the `printing` parameter.

Default: Currently, no default value is given to this string unless the value of the printing parameter is SYSV, in which case the default is

`lp -i %p-%j -H hold`

If the value of the printing parameter is `softq`, then the default is

`qstat -s -j%j -h`

Example for HPUX: `lppause command = /usr/bin/lpalt %p-%j -p0`

lpq cache time

Type of parameter: Global

Supported in versions: **1.9.17 and above**

This controls how long lpq info will be cached for to prevent the `lpq` command being called too often. A separate cache is kept for each variation of the `lpq` command used by the system, so if you use different `lpq` commands for different users, they won't share cache information.

The cache files are stored in `/tmp/lpq.xxxx` where *xxxx* is a hash of the `lpq` command in use.

The default is 10 seconds, meaning that the cached results of a previous identical `lpq` command will be used if the cached data is less than 10 seconds old. A large value may be advisable if your `lpq` command is very slow. A value of 0 will disable caching completely.

See also the `printing` parameter.

Default: `lpq cache time = 10`

Example: `lpq cache time = 30`

lpq command

Type of parameter: Local

Supported in versions: **1.9.17 and above**

This parameter specifies the command to be executed on the server host in order to obtain lpq-style printer status information. This command should be a program or script that takes a printer name as its only parameter and outputs printer status information.

Currently, eight styles of printer status information are supported:

- BSD
- AIX

PART

V

APP

A

- LPRNG
- PLP
- SYSV
- HPUX
- QNX
- SOFTQ

This covers most UNIX systems. You control which type is expected using the `printing =` option.

Some clients (notably Windows for Workgroups) might not correctly send the connection number for the printer they are requesting status information about. To get around this, the server reports on the first printer service connected to by the client. This happens only if the connection number sent is invalid.

If a `%p` is given, the printer name is put in its place. Otherwise, it is placed at the end of the command.

Note

It is good practice to include the absolute path in the `lpq` command because the PATH might not be available to the server.

See also the `printing` parameter.

Default: Depends on the setting of the printing parameter

Example: `lpq command = /usr/bin/lpq %p`

lpresume command

Type of parameter: Local

Supported in versions: **1.9.17 and above**

This parameter specifies the command to be executed on the server host in order to restart or continue printing or spooling a specific print job. This command should be a program or script that takes a printer name and job number to resume the print job. See also the `lppause command` parameter.

If a `%p` is given, the printer name is put in its place. A `%j` is replaced with the job number (an integer).

Note

It is good practice to include the absolute path in the `lpresume` command because the PATH might not be available to the server.

See also the `printing` parameter.

Default: Currently, no default value is given to this string, unless the value of the `printing` parameter is SYSV, in which case the default is

`lp -i %p-%j -H resume`

or if the value of the printing parameter is `softq`, the default is

`qstat -s -j%j -r`

Example for HPUX: `lpresume command = /usr/bin/lpalt %p-%j -p2`

lprm command

Type of parameter: Local

Supported in versions: **1.9.17 and above**

This parameter specifies the command to be executed on the server host in order to delete a print job. This command should be a program or script that takes a printer name and job number and deletes the print job.

If a `%p` is given, the printer name is put in its place. A `%j` is replaced with the job number (an integer).

> **Note**
>
> It is good practice to include the absolute path in the `lprm` command because the PATH might not be available to the server.

See also the `printing` parameter.

Default: Depends on the setting of `printing =`

Example 1: `lprm command = /usr/bin/lprm -P%p %j`

Example 2: `lprm command = /usr/bin/cancel %p-%j`

machine password timeout

Type of parameter: Global

Supported in versions: **2.0.0 and above**

If a Samba server is a member of a Windows NT Domain (see the `security=domain` parameter), periodically a running `smbd(8)` process will try to change the machine account password stored in the file called *Domain.Machine*.mac where *Domain* is the name of the domain we are a member of, and *Machine* is the primary NetBIOS name of the machine on which `smbd(8)` is running. This parameter specifies how often this password will be changed, in seconds. The default is one week (expressed in seconds), the same as a Windows NT Domain member server.

See also `smbpasswd(8)` and the `security=domain` parameter.

Default: `machine password timeout = 604800`

PART
V

APP
A

magic output

Type of parameter: Local

Supported in versions: **1.9.17 and above**

This parameter specifies the name of a file that will contain output created by a magic script (see the `magic script` parameter, next).

> **Caution**
>
> If two clients use the same magic script in the same directory, the output file content is undefined.

Default: magic output = *magic script name*.out

Example: magic output = myfile.txt

magic script

Type of parameter: Local

Supported in versions: **1.9.17 and above**

This parameter specifies the name of a file that, if opened, the server will execute when the file is closed. This allows a UNIX script to be sent to the Samba host and executed on behalf of the connected user. Scripts executed in this way will be deleted upon completion, permissions permitting.

If the script generates output, output will be sent to the file specified by the `magic output` parameter (see the preceding section).

> **Note**
>
> Some shells cannot interpret scripts containing carriage-return-linefeed instead of linefeed as the end-of-line marker. Magic scripts must be executable as is on the host, which for some hosts and some shells requires filtering at the DOS end.

> **Note**
>
> Magic scripts are experimental and should not be relied upon.

Default: None. Magic scripts disabled.

Example: magic script = user.csh

mangle case

Type of parameter: Local

Supported in versions: **1.9.17 and above**

Samba supports name mangling so that DOS and Windows clients can use files that don't conform to the 8.3 format. It can also be set to adjust the case of 8.3 format filenames.

This parameter controls whether names with characters that aren't of the default case are mangled. For example, if this were yes, a name such as *Mail* would be mangled.

Default: `mangle case = no`

Example: `mangle case = yes`

mangle locks

Type of parameter: Local

Supported in versions: **2.0.4-2.0.5a**

This option was introduced with Samba 2.0.4 but has been removed in Samba 2.0.6 because Samba now dynamically configures such things on 32-bit systems.

It enabled Samba to work around bugs in Windows NT where Windows NT sent 64-bit locking operations to 32-bit systems like Linux, even though the Samba server had told NT that 64-bit operations were not supported.

mangled map

Type of parameter: Local

Supported in versions: **1.9.17 and above**

This is used to directly map UNIX filenames that cannot be represented on Windows/DOS. The mangling of names is not always what is needed. In particular, you can have documents with file extensions that differ between DOS and UNIX. For example, under UNIX, it is common to use `.html` for HTML files, whereas under Windows/DOS `.htm` is more commonly used.

Therefore, to map `html` to `htm` you would use

`mangled map = (*.html *.htm)`

One very useful case is to remove the annoying `;1` from the ends of filenames on some CD-ROMS (only visible under some UNIXs). To do this use a map of `(*;1 *)`.

Default: `no mangled map`

Example: `mangled map = (*;1 *)`

mangled names

Type of parameter: Local

Supported in versions: **1.9.17 and above**

This controls whether non-DOS names under UNIX should be mapped to DOS-compatible names (mangled) and made visible or whether non-DOS names should simply be ignored.

PART

V

APP

A

If mangling is used, the mangling algorithm is as follows:

1. The first (up to) five alphanumeric characters before the rightmost dot of the filename are preserved, forced to uppercase, and appear as the first (up to) five characters of the mangled name.

2. A tilde (~) is appended to the first part of the mangled name, followed by a two-character unique sequence, based on the original root name (that is, the original filename minus its final extension). The final extension is included in the hash calculation only if it contains any uppercase characters or is longer than three characters.

> **Note**
>
> The character to use may be specified using the `mangling char` option if you don't like tilde (~).

3. The first three alphanumeric characters of the final extension are preserved, forced to uppercase, and appear as the extension of the mangled name. The final extension is defined as that part of the original filename after the rightmost dot. If there are no dots in the filename, the mangled name will have no extension (except in the case of hidden files—see number 4).

4. Files with UNIX names that begin with a dot will be presented as DOS hidden files. The mangled name will be created as for other filenames, but with the leading dot removed and _ _ _ as its extension regardless of actual original extension (that's three underscores).

The two-digit hash value consists of uppercase alphanumeric characters.

This algorithm can cause name collisions only if files in a directory share the same first five alphanumeric characters. The probability of such a clash is 1/1,300.

Name mangling (if enabled) allows a file to be copied between UNIX directories from Windows/DOS while retaining the long UNIX filename. UNIX files can be renamed to a new extension from Windows/DOS and will retain the same base name. Mangled names do not change between sessions.

Default: `mangled names = yes`

Example: `mangled names = no`

mangled stack

Type of parameter: Global

Supported in versions: **1.9.17 and above**

This parameter controls the number of mangled names that should be cached in the Samba server `smbd(8)`.

This stack is a list of recently mangled base names (extensions are maintained only if they are longer than three characters or contain uppercase characters).

The larger this value, the more likely mangled names can be successfully converted to correct long UNIX names. However, large stack sizes will slow most directory access. Smaller stacks save memory in the server (each stack element costs 256 bytes).

It is not possible to absolutely guarantee correct long filenames, so be prepared for some surprises!

Default: `mangled stack = 50`

Example: `mangled stack = 100`

mangling char

Type of parameter: Local

Supported in versions: **1.9.17 and above**

This controls what character is used as the magic character in name mangling. The default is a tilde (~) but this might interfere with some software. Use this option to set it to whatever you prefer.

Default: `mangling char = ~`

Example: `mangling char = ^`

map archive

Type of parameter: Local

Supported in versions: **1.9.17 and above**

This parameter controls whether the DOS archive attribute should be mapped to the UNIX owner execute bit. The DOS archive bit is set when a file has been modified since its last backup. One motivation for this option is to keep Samba or your PC from making any file it touches executable under UNIX. This can be quite annoying for shared source code, documents, and so forth.

> **Note**
>
> `map.archive` requires the `create mask` parameter to be set such that the owner execute bit is not masked out (that is, it must include 100). See the parameter `create mask` for details.

Default: `map archive = yes`

Example: `map archive = no`

PART
V

APP
A

map hidden

Type of parameter: Local

Supported in versions: **1.9.17 and above**

This controls whether DOS-style hidden files should be mapped to the UNIX world execute bit.

> **Note**
>
> This requires the `create mask` to be set such that the world execute bit is not masked out (that is, it must include 001). See the parameter `create mask` for details.

Default: map hidden = no

Example: map hidden = yes

map system

Type of parameter: Local

Supported in versions: **1.9.17 and above**

This controls whether DOS-style system files should be mapped to the UNIX group execute bit.

> **Note**
>
> This requires the `create mask` to be set such that the group execute bit is not masked out (that is, it must include 010). See the parameter `create mask` for details.

Default: map system = no

Example: map system = yes

map to guest

Type of parameter: Global

Supported in versions: **2.0.0 and above**

This parameter is useful only in security modes other than `security=share`—for example, user, server, and domain.

This parameter can take three different values, which tell `smbd(8)` what to do with user login requests that don't match a valid UNIX user in some way.

The three settings are

- `Never`—User login requests with an invalid password are rejected. This is the default.

- **Bad User**—User logins with an invalid password are rejected unless the username does not exist, in which case it is treated as a guest login and mapped into the guest account.

- **Bad Password**—User logins with an invalid password are treated as a guest login and mapped into the guest account. This can cause problems because it means that any user incorrectly typing his password will be silently logged on as guest and will not know the reason he cannot access files he thinks he should. The user won't receive a message that he entered his password wrong. Help desk services will hate you if you set the map to guest parameter this way.

> **Note**
>
> This parameter is needed to set up Guest share services when using security modes other than share. In these modes the name of the resource being requested is not sent to the server until after the server has successfully authenticated the client, so the server cannot make authentication decisions at the correct time (connection to the share) for Guest shares.

For people familiar with the older Samba releases, this parameter maps to the old compile-time setting of the GUEST_SESSSETUP value in `local.h`.

Default: map to guest = Never

Example: map to guest = Bad User

max connections

Type of parameter: Local

Supported in versions: **1.9.17 and above**

This option allows the number of simultaneous connections to a service to be limited. If max connections is greater than zero, connections will be refused if this number of connections to the service are already open. A value of zero means an unlimited number of connections may be made.

Record lock files are used to implement this feature. The lock files will be stored in the directory specified by the `lock directory` option.

Default: max connections = 0

Example: max connections = 10

max disk size

Type of parameter: Global

Supported in versions: **1.9.17 and above**

PART
V

APP
A

This option allows you to put an upper limit on the apparent size of disks. If you set this option to 100, all shares will appear no larger than 100MB in size.

> **Note**
>
> This option does not limit the amount of data you can put on the disk. In the preceding case, you could still store much more than 100MB on the disk, but if a client ever asks for the amount of free disk space or the total disk size, the result will be bounded by the amount specified in `max disk size`.

This option is primarily useful to work around bugs in some pieces of software that can't handle very large disks, particularly disks over 1GB in size.

A `max disk size` of 0 means no limit.

Default: `max disk size = 0`

Example: `max disk size = 1000`

max log size

Type of parameter: Global

Supported in versions: **1.9.17 and above**

This option (an integer in kilobytes) specifies the max size the log file should grow to. Samba periodically checks the size and if it is exceeded will rename the file, adding an `.old` extension.

A size of 0 means no limit.

Default: `max log size = 5000`

Example: `max log size = 1000`

max mux

Type of parameter: Global

Supported in versions: **1.9.17 and above**

This option controls the maximum number of outstanding simultaneous SMB operations that Samba tells the client it will allow. You should never need to set this parameter.

Default: `max mux = 50`

max open files

Type of parameter: Global

Supported in versions: **2.0.0 and above**

This parameter limits the maximum number of open files that one `smbd(8)` file serving process can have open for a client at any one time. The default for this parameter is set very high (10,000) because Samba uses only one bit per unopened file.

The UNIX per-process file descriptor limit (rather than this parameter) usually sets the limit for the number of open files, so you should never need to touch this parameter.

Default: `max open files = 10000`

max packet

Type of parameter: Global

Supported in versions: **1.9.17 and above**

Synonym for `packet size`.

max ttl

Type of parameter: Global

Supported in versions: **1.9.17 and above**

This option tells `nmbd` what default "time to live" (that is, how long a name remains valid unless renewed) for NetBIOS names to use (in seconds) when `nmbd` requests a name using either a broadcast packet or from a WINS server. You should never need to change this parameter. The default is three days.

Default: `max ttl = 259200`

max wins ttl

Type of parameter: Global

Supported in versions: **1.9.18 and above**

This option tells `nmbd` when acting as a WINS server (`wins support =true`) the maximum "time to live" of NetBIOS names that `nmbd(8)` will grant (in seconds). You should never need to change this parameter. The default is six days (518,400 seconds).

See also the `min wins ttl` parameter.

Default: `max wins ttl = 518400`

max xmit

Type of parameter: Global

Supported in versions: **1.9.17 and above**

This option controls the maximum packet size that Samba will negotiate. The default is 65,535, which is the maximum. In some cases you may find you get better performance with a smaller value. A value below 2,048 is likely to cause problems.

PART

V

APP

A

Default: `max xmit = 65535`

Example: `max xmit = 8192`

message command

Type of parameter: Global

Supported in versions: **1.9.17 and above**

This specifies what command to run when the server receives a WinPopup style message. This would normally be a command that would deliver the message somehow. How this is to be done is up to your imagination.

The following is an example:

```
message command = csh -c 'xedit %s;rm %s' &
```

This delivers the message using `xedit`, and removes it afterward.

> **Note**
>
> *It is very important that this command return immediately.* That's why there is an ampersand (&) on the end. If it doesn't return immediately, your PCs may freeze when sending messages. (It should recover after 30 seconds, hopefully.)

All messages are delivered as the global guest user. The command takes the standard substitutions, although `%u` won't work (`%U` might be better in this case).

In addition to the standard substitutions, some additional ones apply. In particular:

- `%s`—The filename containing the message.
- `%t`—The destination that the message was sent to (probably the server name).
- `%f`—Who the message is from.

You could make this command send mail or whatever else tickles your fancy. Let us know of any interesting ideas you have.

Here's a way of sending the messages as mail to root:

```
message command = /bin/mail -s 'message from %f on %m' \
root < %s; rm %s
```

If you don't have a message command, the message won't be delivered, and Samba will tell the sender there was an error. Unfortunately WfWg totally ignores the error code and carries on regardless, saying that the message was delivered.

If you want to silently delete it, try this:

```
message command = rm %s.
```

Default: No message command

Example: `message command = csh -c 'xedit %s;rm %s' &`

min passwd length

Type of parameter: Global

Supported in versions: **2.0.3 and above**

This option sets the minimum length in characters of a plain-text password that `smbd(8)` will accept when performing UNIX password changing.

See also `unix password sync`, `passwd program`, and `passwd chat debug`.

Default: `min passwd length = 5`

Example: `min passwd length = 8`

min password length

Type of parameter: Global

Supported in versions: **2.0.3 and above**

Synonym for `min passwd length`.

min print space

Type of parameter: Local

Supported in versions: **1.9.17 and above**

This sets the minimum amount of free disk space that must be available before a user will be able to spool a print job. It is specified in kilobytes. The default is zero, which means a user can always spool a print job.

See also the `printing` parameter.

Default: `min print space = 0`

Example: `min print space = 2000`

min wins ttl

Type of parameter: Global

Supported in versions: **1.9.18 and above**

This option tells `nmbd(8)` when acting as a WINS server (`wins support = true`) the minimum "time to live" of NetBIOS names that `nmbd(8)` will grant (in seconds). You should never need to change this parameter. The default is six hours (21,600 seconds).

Default: `min wins ttl = 21600`

PART
V

APP
A

name resolve order

Type of parameter: Global

Supported in versions: **1.9.18p4 and above**

Programs in the Samba suite use this option to determine what naming services and in what order to resolve hostnames to IP addresses. The option takes a space-separated string of different name resolution options.

Here are the options and how they cause names to be resolved:

- lmhosts—Looks up an IP address in the Samba lmhosts file. If the line in lmhosts has no name type attached to the NetBIOS name (see the lmhosts(5) for details), any name type matches for lookup.

- host—Does a standard hostname to IP address resolution, using the system /etc/ hosts, NIS, or DNS lookups. This method of name resolution depends on the operating system; for example, on IRIX or Solaris. This may be controlled by the /etc/ nsswitch.conf file.

> **Note**
>
> This method is used only if the NetBIOS name type being queried is the 0x20 (server) name type; otherwise, it is ignored.

- wins—Queries a name with the IP address listed in the WINS server parameter. If no WINS server has been specified, this method is ignored.

- bcast—Does a broadcast on each of the known local interfaces listed in the interfaces parameter. This is the least reliable of the name resolution methods because it depends on the target host being on a locally connected subnet.

Default: name resolve order = lmhosts host wins bcast

Example: name resolve order = lmhosts bcast host

This will cause the local lmhosts file to be examined first, followed by a broadcast attempt, followed by a normal system hostname lookup.

netbios aliases

Type of parameter: Global

Supported in versions: **1.9.17 and above**

This is a list of NetBIOS names that nmbd will advertise as additional names by which the Samba server is known. This allows one machine to appear in browse lists under multiple names. If a machine is acting as a browse server or logon server, none of these names will be advertised as either a browse server or a logon server. Only the primary name of the machine will be advertised with these capabilities.

See also `netbios name`.

Default: Empty string (no additional names)

Example: `netbios aliases` = TEST TEST1 TEST2

netbios name

Type of parameter: Global

Supported in versions: **1.9.17 and above**

This sets the NetBIOS name by which a Samba server is known. By default it is the same as the first component of the host's DNS name. If a machine is a browse server or a logon server, this name (or the first component of the hosts DNS name) will be the name under which these services are advertised.

See also `netbios aliases`.

Default: Machine DNS name

Example: `netbios name` = MYNAME

nis homedir

Type of parameter: Global

Supported in versions: **1.9.17 and above**

This parameter gets the home share server from an NIS map. For UNIX systems that use an automounter, the user's home directory will often be mounted on a workstation on demand from a remote server.

When the Samba logon server is not the actual home directory server but is mounting the home directories through NFS, two network hops are required to access the users home directory. This is true if the logon server told the client to use itself as the SMB server for home directories (one over SMB and one over NFS), and can be very slow.

This option allows Samba to return the home share as being on a different server to the logon server, and as long as a Samba daemon is running on the home directory server, it will be mounted on the Samba client directly from the directory server. When Samba is returning the home share to the client, it will consult the NIS map specified in `homedir map` and return the server listed there.

> **Note**
>
> For this option to work, there must be a working NIS system, and the Samba server with this option must also be a logon server.

Default: `nis homedir` = false

Example: `nis homedir` = true

PART
V

APP
A

nt acl support

Type of parameter: Global

Supported in versions: **2.0.3 and above**

This Boolean parameter controls whether `smbd(8)` will attempt to map UNIX permissions into Windows NT access control lists.

Default: `nt acl support = yes`

Example: `nt acl support = no`

nt pipe support

Type of parameter: Global

Supported in versions: **2.0.0 and above**

This Boolean parameter controls whether `smbd(8)` will allow Windows NT clients to connect to the NT SMB-specific `IPC$` pipes. This is a developer debugging option and can be left alone.

Default: `nt pipe support = yes`

nt smb support

Type of parameter: Global

Supported in versions: **2.0.0 and above**

This Boolean parameter controls whether `smbd(8)` will negotiate NT-specific SMB support with Windows NT clients. Although this is a developer debugging option and should be left alone, benchmarking has discovered that Windows NT clients give faster performance with this option set to `no`. This is still being investigated. If this option is set to `no`, Samba offers exactly the same SMB calls that versions prior to Samba 2.0 offered. This information may be of use if any users are having problems with NT SMB support.

Default: `nt support = yes`

null passwords

Type of parameter: Global

Supported in versions: **1.9.17 and above**

Allow or disallow client access to accounts that have null passwords.

See also `smbpasswd(5)`.

Default: `null passwords = no`

Example: `null passwords = yes`

ole locking compatibility

Type of parameter: Global

Supported in versions: **1.9.18p10 and above**

This parameter allows an administrator to turn off the byte range lock manipulation that is done within Samba to give compatibility for OLE applications. Windows OLE applications use byte range locking as a form of inter-process communication, by locking ranges of bytes around the 2^{32} region of a file range. This can cause certain UNIX lock managers to crash or otherwise cause problems. Setting this parameter to no means you trust your UNIX lock manager to handle such cases correctly.

Default: `ole locking compatibility = yes`

Example: `ole locking compatibility = no`

only guest

Type of parameter: Local

Supported in versions: **1.9.17 and above**

A synonym for `guest only`.

only user

Type of parameter: Local

Supported in versions: **1.9.17 and above**

This is a Boolean option that controls whether connections with usernames not in the `user = list` will be allowed. By default this option is disabled so a client can supply a username to be used by the server.

> **Note**
>
> This also means Samba won't try to deduce usernames from the service name. This can be annoying for the `[homes]` section. To get around this, use `user = %S`, which means your user list will be just the service name, which for home directories is the name of the user.

See also the user parameter.

Default: `only user = False`

Example: `only user = True`

oplock break wait time

Type of parameter: Global

Supported in versions: **2.0.4 and above**

This is a tuning parameter added because of bugs in both Windows 9x and WinNT. If Samba responds to a client too quickly when that client issues an SMB that can cause an oplock break request, the client redirector can fail and not respond to the break request. This tuning parameter (which is set in milliseconds) is the amount of time Samba will wait before sending an oplock break request to such (broken) clients.

> **Caution**
>
> Do not change this parameter unless you have read and understood the Samba oplock code.

Default: `oplock break wait time = 10`

Example: `oplock break wait time = 20`

oplock contention limit

Type of parameter: Local

Supported in versions: **2.0.4 and above**

This is a very advanced `smbd(8)` tuning option to improve the efficiency of the granting of oplocks under multiple client contention for the same file. In brief it specifies a number, which causes `smbd(8)` not to grant an oplock even when requested if the approximate number of clients contending for an oplock on the same file goes over this limit. This causes `smbd(8)` to behave in a similar way to Windows NT.

> **Caution**
>
> Do not change this parameter unless you have read and understood the Samba oplock code.

Default: `oplock contention limit = 2`

Example: `oplock contention limit = 5`

oplocks

Type of parameter: Local

Supported in versions: **1.9.18 and above**

This Boolean option tells `smbd(8)` whether to issue oplocks (opportunistic locks) to file open requests on this share. The oplock code can dramatically (approximately 30 percent or more) improve the speed of access to files on Samba servers. It allows clients to aggressively cache files locally. You might want to disable this option for unreliable network environments. (It is turned on by default in Windows NT Servers.) For more information see the file `Speed.txt` in the `Samba docs/` directory.

Oplocks may be selectively turned off on certain files on a per-share basis. (See the veto oplock files parameter.) On some systems oplocks are recognized by the underlying operating system. This allows data synchronization between all access to oplocked files, whether it be through Samba or NFS or a local UNIX process. See the kernel oplocks parameter for details.

See also the kernel oplocks and level2 oplocks parameters.

Default: oplocks = True

Example: oplocks = False

os level

Type of parameter: Global

Supported in versions: **1.9.17 and above**

This integer value controls what level Samba advertises itself as for browse elections. The value of this parameter determines whether nmbd has a chance of becoming a local master browser for the workgroup in the local broadcast area. The default is zero, which means nmbd(8) will lose elections to Windows machines. See BROWSING.txt in the Samba docs/ directory for details.

> **Note**
>
> The default value of this parameter changed in Samba 2.0.6. Previously it was 0. From Samba 2.0.6 on, it is 20.

Default: os level = 20

Example: os level = 65. This will win against any NT Server.

PART
V
APP
A

packet size

Type of parameter: Global

Supported in versions: **1.9.17 and above**

This is a deprecated parameter that has no effect on the current Samba code. It is left in the parameter list to prevent breaking old smb.conf files.

panic action

Type of parameter: Global

Supported in versions: **2.0.0 and above**

This is a Samba developer option that allows a system command to be called when either smbd(8) or nmbd crashes. This is usually used to draw attention to the fact that a problem occurred.

Default: panic action = *empty string*

passwd chat debug

Type of parameter: Global

Supported in versions: **1.9.18p5 and above**

This Boolean specifies that the passwd chat script parameter should be run in debug mode. In this mode strings passed to and received from the passwd chat program are printed in the smbd(8) log with a debug level of 100. This is a dangerous option because it will allow plaintext passwords to be seen in the smbd(8) log. It is available to help Samba admins debug their passwd chat scripts when calling the passwd program and should be turned off after this has been done. This parameter is off by default.

See also passwd chat, passwd program.

Example: passwd chat debug = True

Default: passwd chat debug = False

passwd chat

Type of parameter: Global

Supported in versions: **1.9.17 and above**

This string controls the chat conversation that takes place between smbd(8) and the local password changing program to change the user's password. The string describes a sequence of response-receive pairs that smbd(8) uses to determine what to send to the passwd program and what to expect back. If the expected output is not received, the password is not changed.

This chat sequence is often quite site-specific, depending on what local methods are used for password control (such as NIS, and so forth).

The string can contain the macros %o and %n, which are substituted for the old and new passwords, respectively. It can also contain the standard macros \n, \r, \t, and \s to give linefeed, carriage-return, tab, and space.

The string can also contain an asterisk (*) that matches any sequence of characters. Double quotes can be used to collect strings with spaces into a single string.

If the send string in any part of the chat sequence is a fullstop (.), no string is sent. Similarly, if the expect string is a fullstop, no string is expected.

> **Note**
>
> If the unix password sync parameter is set to True, this sequence is called as root when the SMB password in the smbpasswd file is being changed, without access to the old password clear text. In this case the old password clear text is set to the empty string.

See also unix password sync, passwd program, and passwd chat debug.

Default: passwdchat=*old*password*%o\n*new*password*%n\n*new*password*%n\
n*changed*

Example: passwdchat=*EnterOLDpassword*%o\n*EnterNEWpassword*%n\
n*ReenterNEWpassword*%n\n*Passwordchanged*

passwd program

Type of parameter: Global

Supported in versions: **1.9.17 and above**

This is the name of a program you can use to set UNIX user passwords. Any occurrences of %u are replaced with the username. The username is checked for existence before calling the password-changing program.

> **Note**
> Many passwd programs insist on reasonable passwords, such as a minimum length or the inclusion of mixed case characters and digits. This poses a problem because some clients (such as Windows for Workgroups) uppercase the password before sending it.

> **Note**
> If the unix password sync parameter is set to True, this program is called as root before the SMB password in the smbpasswd file is changed. If this UNIX password change fails, smbd(8) will fail to change the SMB password also (this is by design).

If the unix password sync parameter is set, this parameter must use absolute paths for all programs called and must be examined for security implications.

> **Note**
> By default unix password sync is set to False.

PART
V

APP
A

See also unix password sync.

Default: passwd program = /bin/passwd

Example: passwd program = /sbin/passwd %u

password level

Type of parameter: Global

Supported in versions: **1.9.17 and above**

Some client/server combinations have difficulty with mixed-case passwords. One offending client is Windows for Workgroups, which for some reason forces passwords to uppercase when using the LANMAN1 protocol, but leaves them alone when using COREPLUS!

This parameter defines the maximum number of characters that may be uppercase in passwords. For example, if the password given were FRED and the password level were set to 1, the following combinations would be tried if FRED failed:

Fred
fred
fRed
frEd
freD

If password level were set to 2, the following combinations would also be tried:

FRed
FrEd
FreD
fREd
fReD
frED
and so on

The higher value this parameter is set to, the more likely it is that a mixed-case password will be matched against a single-case password. However, you should be aware that use of this parameter reduces security and increases the time taken to process a new connection.

A value of zero will cause only two attempts to be made: the password as is and the password all lowercase.

Default: `password level = 0`

Example: `password level = 4`

password server

Type of parameter: Global

Supported in versions: **1.9.17 and above**

By specifying the name of another SMB server (such as a WinNT box) with this option, and using `security = domain` or `security = server`, Samba can do all its username and password validation through a remote server.

This option sets the name of the password server to use. It must be a NetBIOS name, so if the machine's NetBIOS name is different from its Internet name, you might have to add its NetBIOS name to the `lmhosts` file, which is stored in the same directory as the `smb.conf` file.

The name of the password server is looked up using the parameter `name resolve order`. Thus, it may be resolved by any method and order described in that parameter.

The password server must be a machine capable of using the LM1.2X002 or the LM NT 0.12 protocol, and it must be in user-level security mode.

Caution

> Using a password server means your UNIX box (running Samba) is only as secure as your password server. *Do not choose a password server that you don't completely trust.*

Never point a Samba server at itself for password serving. This will cause a loop and could lock up your Samba server!

The name of the password server takes the standard substitutions, but probably the only useful one is %m, which means the Samba server will use the incoming client as the password server. If you use this, you must trust your clients, and you must restrict them with hosts allow!

If the security parameter is set to domain, the list of machines in this option must be a list of primary or backup domain controllers for the domain or the character asterisk (*). This is because the Samba server is cryptographically in that domain and will use cryptographically authenticated RPC calls to authenticate the user logging on. The advantage of using security = domain is that if you list several hosts in the password server option, smbd(8) will try each in turn until it finds one that responds. This is useful in case your primary server goes down.

If the password server option is set to the character asterisk (*), Samba will attempt to autolocate the primary or backup domain controllers to authenticate against by querying for the name WORKGROUP<1C> and then contacting each server returned in the list of IP addresses from the name resolution source.

If the security parameter is set to server, there are different restrictions that security = domain doesn't suffer from:

- You may list several password servers in the password server parameter, but if an smbd(8) makes a connection to a password server, and then the password server fails, no more users will be authenticated from this smbd(8). This is a restriction of the SMB/CIFS protocol when in security =server mode and cannot be fixed in Samba.

- If you are using a Windows NT server as your password server, you will have to ensure that your users are able to log on from the Samba server because when in security = server mode, the network logon will appear to come from there rather than from the user's workstation.

See also the security parameter.

Default: password server = *empty string*

Example: password server = NT-PDC, NT-BDC1, NT-BDC2

Example: password server = *

path

Type of parameter: Local

Supported in versions: **1.9.17 and above**

This parameter specifies a directory to which the user of the service is to be given access. In the case of printable services, this is where print data will spool before being submitted to the host for printing.

For a printable service offering guest access, the service should be read only and the path should be world-writeable and have the sticky bit set. This is not mandatory, of course, but you probably won't get the results you expect if you do otherwise.

Any occurrences of %u in the path will be replaced with the UNIX username that the client is using on this connection. Any occurrences of %m will be replaced by the NetBIOS name of the machine they are connecting from. These replacements are very useful for setting up pseudo home directories for users.

> **Note**
>
> This path will be based on `root dir` if one was specified.

Default: None

Example: `path = /home/fred`

postexec

Type of parameter: Local

Supported in versions: **1.9.17 and above**

This option specifies a command to run whenever the service is disconnected. It takes the usual substitutions. The command may run as the root on some systems.

An interesting example is to unmount server resources:

`postexec = /etc/umount /cdrom`

See also `preexec`.

Default: None (no command executed)

Example: `postexec = echo %u disconnected from %S from %m (%I) >> /tmp/log`

postscript

Type of parameter: Local

Supported in versions: **1.9.17 and above**

This parameter forces a printer to interpret the print files as postscript by adding `%!` to the start of print output. This is most useful when you have many PCs that persist in putting a Control+D at the start of print jobs, which then confuses your printer.

Default: `postscript = False`

Example: `postscript = True`

preexec close

Type of parameter: Local

Supported in versions: **2.0.6 and above**

This Boolean option controls whether a nonzero return code from `preexec` should close the service being connected to.

Default: `preexec close = no`

Example: `preexec close = yes`

preexec

Type of parameter: Local

Supported in versions: **1.9.17 and above**

This option specifies a command to run whenever the service is connected to. It takes the usual substitutions.

An interesting example is to send users a welcome message every time they log on, such as a message of the day. Here is an example:

```
preexec = csh -c 'echo \"Welcome to %S!\" | \ /usr/local/samba/bin/smbclient \
➥-M %m -I %I' &
```

Of course, this could get annoying after a while.

See also `preexec close` and `postexec`.

Default: None (no command executed)

Example: `preexec = echo \%u connected to %S from %m (%I)\ >> /tmp/log`

prefered master

Type of parameter: Global

Supported in versions: **1.9.17 and above**

Synonym for `preferred master` for people who cannot spell.

preferred master

Type of parameter: Global

Supported in versions: **1.9.17 and above**

This Boolean parameter controls whether nmbd(8) is a preferred master browser for its workgroup.

If this is set to true, on startup, nmbd will force an election, and it will have a slight advantage in winning the election. I recommend that you use this parameter in conjunction with domain master = yes so that nmbd can guarantee becoming a domain master.

> **Caution**
>
> Use this option with caution, because if there are several hosts (whether Samba servers, Windows 95, or NT) that are preferred master browsers on the same subnet, they will each periodically and continuously attempt to become the local master browser. This will result in unnecessary broadcast traffic and reduced browsing capabilities.

See also os level.

Default: preferred master = no

Example: preferred master = yes

preload

Type of parameter: Global

Supported in versions: **1.9.17 and above**

Synonym for auto services.

preserve case

Type of parameter: Local

Supported in versions: **1.9.17 and above**

This controls whether new filenames are created with the case that the client passes or whether they are forced to be the default case.

Default: preserve case = yes

See the section on mangled names for a fuller discussion.

print command

Type of parameter: Local

Supported in versions: **1.9.17 and above**

After a print job has finished spooling to a service, this command is used through a call to process the spool file. Typically, the command specified will submit the spool file to the host's printing subsystem, but there is no requirement that this be the case. The server will not remove the spool file, so whatever command you specify should remove it when it has been processed; otherwise, you will need to remove old spool files manually.

The print command is simply a text string. It is used verbatim, with two exceptions:

- All occurrences of %s and %f are replaced by the appropriate spool filename.
- All occurrences of %p are replaced by the appropriate printer name.

The server automatically generates the spool filename, and the printer name is discussed next.

The print command must contain at least one occurrence of %s or %f (the %p is optional). At the time a job is submitted, if no printer name is supplied, the %p will be silently removed from the printer command.

If specified in the [global] section, the print command given will be used for any printable service that does not have its own print command specified.

If there is neither a specified print command for a printable service nor a global print command, spool files will be created but not processed and (most importantly) not removed.

> **Note**
>
> Printing can fail on some versions of UNIX for the nobody account. If this happens, create an alternative guest account that can print, and set the guest account in the [global] section.

You can form quite complex print commands by realizing that they are just passed to a shell. For example, the following logs a print job, prints the file, and removes it.

> **Note**
>
> The semicolon (;) is the usual separator for commands in shell scripts.

```
print command = echo Printing %s >> /tmp/print.log; lpr -P \
%p %s; rm %s
```

You might have to vary this command considerably depending on how you normally print files on your system. The default for the parameter varies depending on the setting of the printing parameter.

Default: For printing = BSD, AIX, QNX, LPRNG, or PLP:

```
print command = lpr -r -P%p %s
```

For printing = SYS or HPUX:

```
print command = lp -c -d%p %s; rm %s
```

For printing = SOFTQ:

`print command = lp -d%p -s %s; rm %s`

Example: `print command = /usr/local/samba/bin/myprintscript %p %s`

print ok

Type of parameter: Local

Supported in versions: **1.9.17 and above**

Synonym for `printable`.

printable

Type of parameter: Local

Supported in versions: **1.9.17 and above**

If this parameter is yes, clients may open, write to, and submit spool files on the directory specified for the service.

> **Note**
>
> A printable service will always allow writing to the service path (user privileges permitting) through the spooling of print data. The `read only` parameter controls only non-printing access to the resource.

Default: `printable = no`

Example: `printable = yes`

printcap name

Type of parameter: Global

Supported in versions: **1.9.17 and above**

This parameter can be used to override the compiled-in default printcap name used by the server (usually `/etc/printcap`).

On System V systems that use `lpstat` to list available printers, you can use `printcap name = lpstat` to obtain lists of available printers automatically. This is the default for systems that define SYSV at configure time in Samba (this includes most System V-based systems). If `printcap name` is set to `lpstat` on these systems, Samba will launch `lpstat -v` and attempt to parse the output to obtain a printer list.

A minimal `printcap` file would look something like

```
print1|My Printer 1
print2|My Printer 2
print3|My Printer 3
print4|My Printer 4
print5|My Printer 5
```

where the | separates aliases of a printer. The fact that the second alias has a space in it hints to Samba that it's a comment.

> **Note**
>
> Under AIX the default printcap name is /etc/qconfig. Samba will assume the file is in AIX qconfig format if the string /qconfig appears in the printcap filename.

Default: printcap name = /etc/printcap

Example: printcap name = /etc/myprintcap

printcap

Type of parameter: Global

Supported in versions: **1.9.17 and above**

Synonym for printcap name.

printer driver file

Type of parameter: Global

Supported in versions: **1.9.18 and above**

This parameter tells Samba where the printer driver definition file (used when serving drivers to Windows 95 clients) is to be found. If this is not set, the default is

SAMBA_INSTALL_DIRECTORY/lib/printers.def

This file is created from Windows 95 msprint.def files found on the Windows 95 client system. For more details on setting up serving of printer drivers to Windows 95 clients, see the documentation file PRINTER_DRIVER.txt under the docs/ directory.

See also printer driver location.

Default: None (set in compile)

Example: printer driver file = /usr/local/samba/printers/drivers.def

printer driver location

Type of parameter: Local

Supported in versions: **1.9.18 and above**

This parameter tells clients of a particular printer share where to find the printer driver files for the automatic installation of drivers for Windows 95 machines. If Samba is set up to serve printer drivers to Windows 95 machines, this should be set to

\\MACHINE\PRINTER$

PART

V

APP

A

where *MACHINE* is the NetBIOS name of your Samba server, and *PRINTER$* is a share you set up for serving printer driver files. For more details on setting this up, see the documentation file `PRINTER_DRIVER.txt` under the `docs/` directory.

See also `printer driver file`.

Default: None

Example: `printer driver location = \\MACHINE\PRINTER$`

printer driver

Type of parameter: Local

Supported in versions: **1.9.17 and above**

This option allows you to control the string that clients receive when they ask the server for the printer driver associated with a printer. If you are using Windows 95 or Windows NT, you can use this to automate the setup of printers on your system.

Set this parameter to the exact string (case sensitive) that describes the appropriate printer driver for your system. If you don't know the exact string to use, you should first try with no `printer driver` option set, and the client will give you a list of printer drivers. The appropriate strings appear in a scroll box after you have chosen the printer manufacturer.

See also `printer driver file`.

Example: `printer driver = HP LaserJet 4L`

printer name

Type of parameter: Local

Supported in versions: **1.9.17 and above**

Synonym for `printer`.

printer

Type of parameter: Local

Supported in versions: **1.9.17 and above**

This parameter specifies the name of the printer to which print jobs spooled through a printable service will be sent. If specified in the `[global]` section, the printer name given will be used for any printable service that does not have its own printer name specified.

Default: None (but might be `lp` on many systems)

Example: `printer name = laserwriter`

printing

Type of parameter: Local

Supported in versions: **1.9.17 and above**

This parameter controls how printer status information is interpreted on your system, and also affects the default values for the `print command`, `lpq command`, `lppause command`, `lpresume command`, and `lprm command`.

Currently eight printing styles are supported:

```
printing = BSD
printing = AIX
printing = LPRNG
printing = PLP
printing = SYSV
printing = HPUX
printing = QNX
printing = SOFTQ
```

To see what the defaults are for the other print commands when using these three options, use the `testparm` program.

This option can be set on a per printer basis.

Default: Depends on the type of your system.

Example: `printing = bsd`

protocol

Type of parameter: Global

Supported in versions: **1.9.17 and above**

The value of the parameter (a string) is the highest protocol level that the server will support.

Possible values are

- `CORE`—Earliest version. No concept of usernames.
- `COREPLUS`—Slight improvements on `CORE` for efficiency.
- `LANMAN1`—First modern version of the protocol. Long filename support.
- `LANMAN2`—Updates to `LANMAN1` protocol.
- `NT1`—Current up-to-date version of the protocol. Used by Windows NT. Known as CIFS.

Normally, this option should not be set because the automatic negotiation phase in the SMB protocol chooses the appropriate protocol.

Default: `protocol = NT1`

Example: `protocol = LANMAN1`

public

Type of parameter: Local

Supported in versions: **1.9.17 and above**

Synonym for guest ok.

queuepause command

Type of parameter: Local

Supported in versions: **1.9.18p10 and above**

This parameter specifies the command to be executed on the server host in order to pause the printer queue. This command should be a program or script that takes a printer name as its only parameter and stops the printer queue, such that jobs are no longer submitted to the printer.

Windows for Workgroups does not support this command but it can be issued from the printer's window under Windows 95 and NT.

If a %p is given, the printer name is put in its place; otherwise, it is placed at the end of the command.

> **Note**
>
> It is good practice to include the absolute path in the command because the PATH might not be available to the server.

Default: Depends on the setting of the printing parameter

Example: queuepause command = disable %p

queueresume command

Type of parameter: Local

Supported in versions: **1.9.18p10 and above**

This parameter specifies the command to be executed on the server host in order to resume the printer queue. It is the command to undo the behavior caused by the previous parameter (queuepause command).

This command should be a program or script that takes a printer name as its only parameter and resumes the printer queue, such that queued jobs are resubmitted to the printer.

Windows for Workgroups does not support this command but it can be issued from the Printer's window under Windows 95 and NT.

If a %p is given, the printer name is put in its place; otherwise, it is placed at the end of the command.

Note

It is good practice to include the absolute path in the command as the PATH might not be available to the server.

Default: Depends on the setting of the printing parameter

Example: `queuepause command = enable %p`

read bmpx

Type of parameter: Global

Supported in versions: **1.9.17 and above**

This Boolean parameter controls whether `smbd(8)` will support the `Read Block Multiplex` SMB. This is now rarely used and defaults to off. You should never need to set this parameter.

Default: `read bmpx = No`

read list

Type of parameter: Local

Supported in versions: **1.9.17 and above**

This is a list of users that are given read-only access to a service. If the connecting user is in this list, that person will not be given write access, no matter what the `read only` option is set to. The list can include group names using the syntax described in the `invalid users` parameter.

See also the `write list` parameter and the `invalid users` parameter.

Default: `read list = empty string`

Example: `read list = mary, @students`

read only

Type of parameter: Local

Supported in versions: **1.9.17 and above**

This is an inverted synonym for `writeable` and `write ok`.

See also `writeable` and `write ok`.

read prediction

Type of parameter: Global

Supported in versions: **1.9.17 and above**

PART

V

APP

A

> **Note**
>
> This code is currently disabled in Samba 2.0 and may be removed at a later date. Hence, this parameter has no effect.

This option enables or disables the read prediction code used to speed up reads from the server. When enabled, the server will try to pre-read data from the last accessed file that was opened read-only while waiting for packets.

Default: `read prediction = False`

read raw

Type of parameter: Global

Supported in versions: **1.9.17 and above**

This parameter controls whether the server will support the raw read SMB requests when transferring data to clients. If enabled, raw reads allow reads of 65,535 bytes in one packet. This typically provides a major performance benefit. However, some clients either negotiate the allowable block size incorrectly or are incapable of supporting larger block sizes, and for these clients you might need to disable raw reads.

In general this parameter should be viewed as a system-tuning tool and left severely alone.

See also `write raw`.

Default: `read raw = yes`

read size

Type of parameter: Global

Supported in versions: **1.9.17 and above**

The option `read size` affects the overlap of disk reads and writes with network reads and writes. If the amount of data being transferred in several of the SMB commands (currently `SMBwrite`, `SMBwriteX`, and `SMBreadbraw`) is larger than this value, the server begins writing the data before it has received the whole packet from the network. In the case of `SMBreadbraw`, it begins writing to the network before all the data has been read from disk.

This overlapping works best when the speeds of disk and network access are similar, having very little effect when the speed of one is much greater than the other.

The default value is 16,384, but very little experimentation has been done yet to determine the optimal value, and it is likely that the best value will vary greatly between systems. A value over 65,536 is pointless and will cause you to allocate memory unnecessarily.

Default: `read size = 16384`

Example: `read size = 8192`

remote announce

Type of parameter: Global

Supported in versions: **1.9.17 and above**

This option allows you to set up `nmbd` to periodically announce itself to arbitrary IP addresses with an arbitrary workgroup name. This is useful if you want your Samba server to appear in a remote workgroup for which the normal browse propagation rules don't work. The remote workgroup can be anywhere that you can send IP packets.

For example, `remote announce = 192.168.2.255/SERVERS \ 192.168.4.255/STAFF` causes `nmbd(8)` to announce itself to the two given IP addresses using the given workgroup names. If you leave out the workgroup name, the one given in the `workgroup` parameter is used instead.

The IP addresses you choose would normally be the broadcast addresses of the remote networks, but can also be the IP addresses of known browse masters if your network config is that stable.

See the documentation file `BROWSING.txt` in the `docs/` directory.

Default: `remote announce = empty string`

Example: `remote announce = 192.168.2.255/SERVERS \ 192.168.4.255/STAFF`

remote browse sync

Type of parameter: Global

Supported in versions: **1.9.17p5 and above**

This option allows you to set up `nmbd(8)` to periodically request synchronization of browse lists with the master browser of a Samba server that is on a remote segment. This option allows you to gain browse lists for multiple workgroups across routed networks. This is done in a manner that does not work with any non-Samba servers.

This is useful if you want your Samba server and all local clients to appear in a remote workgroup for which the normal browse propagation rules don't work. The remote workgroup can be anywhere that you can send IP packets.

For example:

`remote browse sync = 192.168.2.255 192.168.4.255`

This line causes `nmbd(8)` to request the master browser on the specified subnets or addresses to synchronize their browse lists with the local server.

The IP addresses you choose would normally be the broadcast addresses of the remote networks but can also be the IP addresses of known browse masters if your network config is that stable. If a machine IP address is given, Samba makes no attempt to validate that the remote machine is available, is listening, or that it is in fact the browse master on its segment.

Default: `remote browse sync = empty string`

Example: `remote browse sync = 192.168.2.255 192.168.4.255`

PART
V

APP
A

restrict anonymous

Type of parameter: Global

Supported in versions: **2.0.4 and above**

This is a Boolean parameter. If it is true, anonymous access to the server will be restricted, namely in the case where the server is expecting the client to send a username, but doesn't. Setting it to true will force these anonymous connections to be denied, and the client will be required to always supply a username and password when connecting. Use of this parameter is only recommended for homogenous NT client environments.

This parameter makes the use of macro expansions that rely on the username (%U, %G, and so forth) consistent. NT 4.0 likes to use anonymous connections when refreshing the share list, and this is a way to work around that.

When restrict anonymous is true, all anonymous connections are denied no matter what they are for. This can affect the capability of a machine to access the Samba primary domain controller to revalidate its machine account after someone else has logged on the client interactively. The NT client will display a message saying that the machine's account in the domain doesn't exist or the password is bad. The best way to deal with this is to reboot NT client machines between interactive logons, using Shutdown and Restart, rather than Close all programs and log on as a different user.

Default: restrict anonymous = false

Example: restrict anonymous = true

revalidate

Type of parameter: Local

Supported in versions: **1.9.17 and above**

> **Note**
>
> This option only works with security = share and will be ignored if this is not the case.

This option controls whether Samba will allow a previously validated username/password pair to be used to attach to a share. Thus, if you connect to \\server\share1 and then to \\server\share2, it won't automatically allow the client to request connection to \\server\share2 with the same username as \\server\share1 without a password.

If revalidate is True, the client will be denied automatic access as the same username.

Default: revalidate = False

Example: revalidate = True

root dir

Type of parameter: Global

Supported in versions: **1.9.17 and above**

Synonym for root directory.

root directory

Type of parameter: Global

Supported in versions: **1.9.17 and above**

The server will chroot(1L) (that is, change its root directory) to this directory on startup. This is not strictly necessary for secure operation. Even without it, the server will deny access to files not in one of the service entries. It might also check for, and deny access to, soft links to other parts of the file system, or attempts to use .. (that is, the parent directory) in filenames to access other directories (depending on the setting of the wide links parameter).

Adding a root directory entry other than / adds an extra level of security, but at a price. It absolutely ensures that no access is given to files not in the subtree specified in the root directory option, including some files needed for complete operation of the server. To maintain full operability of the server, mirror some system files into the root directory tree. In particular you need to mirror /etc/passwd (or a subset of it) and any binaries or configuration files needed for printing (if required). The set of files that must be mirrored is operating system-dependent.

Default: root directory = /

Example: root directory = /homes/smb

root postexec

Type of parameter: Local

Supported in versions: **1.9.17 and above**

This is the same as the postexec parameter except that the command runs as root. This is useful for unmounting file systems (such as CD-ROMs) after a connection is closed.

See also postexec.

root preexec close

Type of parameter: Local

Supported in versions: **2.0.6 and above**

This is the same as the preexec close parameter except that the command is run as root.

See also preexec and preexec close.

root preexec

Type of parameter: Local

Supported in versions: **1.9.17 and above**

This is the same as the `preexec` parameter except that the command runs as root. This is useful for mounting file systems (such as CD-ROMs) before a connection is finalized.

See also `preexec` and `root preexec close`.

root

Type of parameter: Global

Supported in versions: **1.9.17 and above**

Synonym for `root directory`.

security mask

Type of parameter: Local

Supported in versions: **2.0.5 and above**

This parameter controls what UNIX permission bits can be modified when a Windows NT client is manipulating the UNIX permission on a file using the native NT security dialog box.

This parameter is applied as a mask (ANDed with) to the changed permission bits, preventing any bits not in this mask from being modified. Essentially, zero bits in this mask can be treated as a set of bits the user is not allowed to change.

If not set explicitly, this parameter is set to the same value as the `create mask` parameter. To allow a user to modify all the `user/group/world` permissions on a file, set this parameter to `0777`.

> **Note**
>
> Users who can access the Samba server through other means can easily bypass this restriction, so it is primarily useful for standalone appliance systems. Administrators of most normal systems will probably want to set it to `0777`.

See also the `force directory security mode`, `directory security mask`, and `force security mode` parameters.

Default: `security mask = same as create mask`

Example: `security mask = 0777`

security

Type of parameter: Global

Supported in versions: **1.9.17 and above**

This option affects how clients respond to Samba and is one of the most important settings in the `smb.conf` file. The option sets the security mode bit in replies to protocol negotiations with `smbd(8)` to turn share-level security on or off. Clients decide based on this bit whether (and how) to transfer user and password information to the server.

The default is `security = user`, because this is the most common setting needed when talking to Windows 98 and Windows NT.

The alternatives are `security = share`, `security = server`, or `security = domain`.

Note This default is different in Samba 2.0 from previous versions of Samba.

In previous versions of Samba the default was `security = share` mainly because that was the only option at one stage.

There is a bug in WfWg that has relevance to this setting. When in user- or server-level security, a WfWg client will totally ignore the password you type in the Connect Drive dialog box. This makes it very difficult (if not impossible) to connect to a Samba service as anyone except the user that you are logged into WfWg as.

If your PCs use usernames that are the same as their usernames on the UNIX machine, use `security = user`. If you mostly use usernames that don't exist on the UNIX box, use `security = share`.

You should also use `security = share` if you want to set up shares mainly without a password (guest shares). This is commonly used for a shared printer server. It is more difficult to set up guest shares with `security = user`. See the `map to guest` parameter for details.

It is possible to use `smbd(8)` in a hybrid mode where it offers both user- and share-level security under different NetBIOS aliases. See the NetBIOS aliases and the `include` parameters for more information.

This parameter can take the following values:

- `security = share`
- `security = user`
- `security = server`
- `security = domain`

`security = share`

When clients connect to a share-level security server, they need not log on to the server with a valid username and password before they attempt to connect to a shared resource. (Modern clients such as Windows 95/98 and Windows NT will send a logon request with a username but no password when talking to a `security = share` server.) Instead, the clients send authentication information (passwords) on a per-share basis at the time they attempt to connect to that share.

> **Note**
>
> `smbd(8)` always uses a valid UNIX user to act on behalf of the client, even in `security = share` level security.

Because clients are not required to send a username to the server in share-level security, `smbd(8)` uses several techniques to determine the correct UNIX user to use on behalf of the client.

A list of possible UNIX usernames to match with the given client password is constructed using the following methods:

- If the `guest only` parameter is set, all the other stages are skipped and only the guest account username is checked.

- If a username is sent with the share connection request, this username (after mapping—see `username map`) is added as a potential username.

- If the client did a previous logon request (the `SessionSetupandX` SMB call), the username sent in this SMB will be added as a potential username.

- The name of the service the client requested is added as a potential username.

- The NetBIOS name of the client is added to the list as a potential username.

- Any users on the user list are added as potential usernames.

If the `guest only` parameter is not set, this list is then tried with the supplied password. The first user for whom the password matches will be used as the UNIX user.

If the `guest only` parameter is set or no username can be determined and if the share is marked as available to the guest account, this guest user will be used; otherwise, access is denied.

> **Note**
>
> It can be very confusing in share-level security as to which UNIX username will eventually be used in granting access.

`security = user`

This is the default security setting in Samba 2.0. With user-level security, a client must first log on with a valid username and password (which can be mapped using the `username map` parameter). Encrypted passwords (see the `encrypted passwords` parameter) can also be used in this security mode.

Parameters such as `user` and `guest only`, if set, are then applied and may change the UNIX user for this connection, but only after the user has been successfully authenticated.

Note

> The name of the resource being requested is not sent to the server until after the server has successfully authenticated the client. This is why guest shares don't work in user-level security without allowing the server to map unknown users into the guest account automatically. See the `map to guest` parameter for details.

security = server

In this mode Samba will try to validate the username or password by passing it to another SMB server, such as an NT box. If this fails it will revert to `security = user`, but if encrypted passwords have been negotiated, Samba cannot revert back to checking the UNIX password file. It must have a valid `smbpasswd` file to check users against. See the documentation file `ENCRYPTION.txt` in the `docs/` directory for details on how to set this up.

Note

> From the client's point of view, `security = server` is the same as `security = user`. It only affects how the server deals with the authentication; it does not in any way affect what the client sees.

Note

> The name of the resource being requested is not sent to the server until after the server has successfully authenticated the client. This is why guest shares don't work in server-level security without allowing the server to automatically map unknown users into the guest account. See the `map to guest` parameter for details on doing this.

See also the `password server` parameter and the `encrypted passwords` parameter.

security = domain

This mode works correctly only if `smbpasswd` has been used to add this machine into a Windows NT domain. It expects the `encrypted passwords` parameter to be set to `true`. In this mode Samba will try to validate the username and password by passing it to a Windows NT primary or backup domain controller, in exactly the same way that a Windows NT Server would.

Note

> A valid UNIX user must still exist as well as the account on the domain controller to allow Samba to have a valid UNIX account to map file access to.

Note

> From a client's point of view, `security = domain` is the same as `security = user`. It only affects how the server deals with the authentication; it does not in any way affect what the client sees.

PART

V

APP

A

Note

The name of the resource being requested is not sent to the server until after the server has successfully authenticated the client. This is why guest shares don't work in domain-level security without allowing the server to automatically map unknown users into the guest account. See the `map to guest` parameter for details on doing this.

Caution

A bug is currently in the implementation of `security = domain` with respect to multibyte character set usernames. The communication with a domain controller must be done in UNICODE, and Samba currently does not widen multibyte usernames to UNICODE correctly. Thus, a multibyte username will not be recognized correctly at the domain controller. This issue will most likely be addressed in Samba 3.0.

See also the `password server` parameter and the `encrypted passwords` parameter.

Default: `security = USER`

Example: `security = DOMAIN`

server string

Type of parameter: Global

Supported in versions: **1.9.17 and above**

This controls what string appears in the printer comment box in print manager and next to the IPC connection in `net view`. It can be any string that you wish to show to your users. It also sets what appears in browse lists next to the machine name.

A `%v` will be replaced with the Samba version number.

A `%h` will be replaced with the hostname.

Default: `server string = Samba %v`

Example: `server string = University of GNUs Samba Server`

set directory

Type of parameter: Local

Supported in versions: **1.9.17 and above**

If `set directory = no`, users of the service may not use the `setdir` command to change directory.

The `setdir` command is only implemented in the Digital Pathworks client. See the Pathworks documentation for details.

Default: `set directory = no`

Example: `set directory = yes`

share modes

Type of parameter: Local

Supported in versions: **1.9.17 and above**

This enables or disables the honoring of the share modes during a file open. Clients use these modes to gain exclusive read or write access to a file.

UNIX does not directly support these open modes, so they are simulated using shared memory, or lock files if your UNIX doesn't support shared memory (almost all do).

The share modes that are enabled by this option are

```
DENY_DOS
DENY_ALL
DENY_READ
DENY_WRITE
DENY_NONE
DENY_FCB
```

This option gives full share compatibility and is enabled by default.

You should never turn this parameter off because many Windows applications will break if you do.

Default: `share modes = yes`

shared file entries

Type of parameter: Global

Supported in versions: **1.9.17-1.9.17p5**

This parameter is useful only when Samba has been compiled with `FAST_SHARE_MODES`. It specifies the number of hash bucket entries used for share file locking. You should never change this parameter unless you have studied the source and know what you are doing.

Default: `shared file entries = 113`

This parameter was retired with Samba 1.9.17p5 because it was handled automatically in Samba 1.9.18 and beyond.

shared mem size

Type of parameter: Global

Supported in versions: **1.9.17 and above**

PART

V

APP

A

It specifies the size of the shared memory (in bytes) to use between `smbd(8)` processes. This parameter defaults to 1MB of shared memory. If you have a large server with many files open simultaneously you might need to increase this parameter. Signs that this parameter is set too low are users reporting strange problems trying to save files (locking errors) and error messages in the `smbd(8)` log looking like `ERROR smb_shm_alloc : alloc of XX bytes failed`.

If your OS refuses the size that Samba asks for, Samba will try a smaller size, reducing by a factor of 0.8 until the OS accepts it.

Default: `shared mem size = 1048576`

Example: `shared mem size = 5242880`; set to 5MB for a large number of files.

short preserve case

Type of parameter: Local

Supported in versions: **1.9.17 and above**

This Boolean parameter controls whether new files that conform to 8.3 syntax are all in uppercase and of suitable length, are created in uppercase, or are forced to be the default case. This option can be used with `preserve case = yes` to permit long filenames to retain their case, while short names are converted to lowercase.

Default: `short preserve case = yes`

Example: `short preserve case = no`

smb passwd file

Type of parameter: Global

Supported in versions: **1.9.17 and above**

This option sets the path to the encrypted `smbpasswd` file. By default the path to the `smbpasswd` file is compiled into Samba.

Default: `smb passwd file= compiled default`

Example: `smb passwd file = /usr/samba/private/smbpasswd`

smbrun

Type of parameter: Global

Supported in versions: **1.9.17 and above**

This sets the full path to the `smbrun` binary. This defaults to the value in the make file. You must get this path correct for many services to work correctly.

You should not need to change this parameter as long as Samba is installed correctly.

Default: `smbrun = compiled default`

Example: `smbrun = /usr/local/samba/bin/smbrun`

socket address

Type of parameter: Global

Supported in versions: **1.9.17 and above**

This option allows you to control what address Samba will listen for connections on. This is used to support multiple virtual interfaces on the one server, each with a different configuration.

By default Samba will accept connections on any address.

Example: `socket address = 192.168.2.20`

socket options

Type of parameter: Global

Supported in versions: **1.9.17 and above**

This option allows you to set socket options to be used when talking with the client.

Socket options are controls on the networking layer of the operating systems that allow the connection to be tuned.

This option typically tunes your Samba server for optimal performance for your local network. Samba can in no way know the optimal parameters for your net, so you must experiment and choose them yourself. We strongly suggest you read the appropriate documentation for your operating system first (perhaps `man setsockopt` will help).

You might find that on some systems Samba will say `Unknown socket option` when you supply an option. This means you either incorrectly typed the option or you need to add an include file to `includes.h` for your OS. If the latter is the case, please send the patch to samba-bugs@samba.org.

Any of the supported socket options may be combined in any way you like, as long as your OS allows it.

This is the list of socket options currently settable using this option:

- SO_KEEPALIVE
- SO_REUSEADDR
- SO_BROADCAST
- TCP_NODELAY
- IPTOS_LOWDELAY
- IPTOS_THROUGHPUT
- SO_SNDBUF *
- SO_RCVBUF *

PART

V

APP

A

- SO_SNDLOWAT *
- SO_RCVLOWAT *

Those marked with an asterisk take an integer argument. The others can optionally take a 1 or 0 argument to enable or disable the option; by default they will be enabled if you don't specify 1 or 0.

To specify an argument use the syntax `SOME_OPTION=VALUE` (for example, `SO_SNDBUF=8192`).

Note You must not have any spaces before or after the equal (=) sign.

If you are on a local network, a sensible option might be

`socket options = IPTOS_LOWDELAY`

If you have a local network, you could try

`socket options = IPTOS_LOWDELAY TCP_NODELAY`

If you are on a wide area network, then perhaps try setting `IPTOS_THROUGHPUT`.

Caution Several of the options may cause your Samba server to fail completely. Use these options with caution!

Default: `socket options = TCP_NODELAY`

Example: `socket options = IPTOS_LOWDELAY`

source environment

Type of parameter: Global

Supported in versions: **2.0.7 and above**

This parameter causes Samba to set environment variables per the content of the file named. It is very useful in high availability environments and when you are trying to standardize your `smb.conf` file across multiple servers. In both cases you can use the same `smb.conf` file on all machines and customize them using environment variables on each server. The file must be owned by root and not world writable to be read (this is a security check).

If the value of this parameter starts with a "|" character, Samba will treat that value as a pipe command to open and will set the environment variables from the output of the pipe. This command must not be world writable and must reside in a directory that is not world writable.

The contents of the file or the output of the pipe should be formatted as the output of the standard UNIX env(1) command. This is of the form `SAMBA_NETBIOS_NAME=myhostname`.

Default: No default value

Examples: `source environment = | /etc/smb.conf.sh`, `source environment = /usr/local/ smb_env_vars`

ssl ca certdir

Type of parameter: Global

Supported in versions: **2.0.0 and above**

This variable is part of SSL-enabled Samba. This is available only if the SSL libraries have been compiled on your system and the configure option `--with-ssl` was given at configure time.

> **Note**
> For export control reasons this code is not enabled by default in any current binary version of Samba.

This variable defines where to look up the certification authorities (CA). The given directory should contain one file for each CA that Samba will trust. The filename must be the hash value over the distinguished name of the CA. How this directory is set up is explained in the file `SSLeay.txt` in the `docs/textdocs` directory of the source. All files within the directory that don't fit into this naming scheme are ignored. You don't need this variable if you don't verify client certificates.

Default: `ssl CA certDir = /usr/local/ssl/certs`

ssl ca certfile

Type of parameter: Global

Supported in versions: **2.0.0 and above**

This variable is part of SSL-enabled Samba. This is available only if the SSL libraries have been compiled on your system and the configure option `--with-ssl` was given at configure time.

> **Note**
> For export control reasons this code is not enabled by default in any current binary version of Samba.

This variable is a second way to define the trusted CAs. The certificates of the trusted CAs are collected in one large file, and this variable points to the file. You will probably use only one of the two ways to define your CAs. The first choice is preferable if you have many CAs or want to be flexible. The second is preferable if you have only one CA and want to keep things simple (you won't need to create the hashed filenames). You don't need this variable if you don't verify client certificates.

Default: `ssl CA certFile = /usr/local/ssl/certs/trustedCAs.pem`

PART

V

APP

A

ssl ciphers

Type of parameter: Global

Supported in versions: **2.0.0 and above**

This variable is part of SSL-enabled Samba. This is available only if the SSL libraries have been compiled on your system and the configure option --with-ssl was given at configure time.

> **Note**
>
> For export control reasons this code is not enabled by default in any current binary version of Samba.

This variable defines the ciphers that should be offered during SSL negotiation. You should not set this variable unless you know what you are doing.

ssl client cert

Type of parameter: Global

Supported in versions: **2.0.0 and above**

This variable is part of SSL-enabled Samba. This is available only if the SSL libraries have been compiled on your system and the configure option --with-ssl was given at configure time.

> **Note**
>
> For export control reasons this code is not enabled by default in any current binary version of Samba.

The certificate in this file is used by smbclient if it exists. It's needed if the server requires a client certificate.

Default: ssl client cert = /usr/local/ssl/certs/smbclient.pem

ssl client key

Type of parameter: Global

Supported in versions: **2.0.0 and above**

This variable is part of SSL-enabled Samba. This is available only if the SSL libraries have been compiled on your system and the configure option --with-ssl was given at configure time.

> **Note**
>
> For export control reasons this code is not enabled by default in any current binary version of Samba.

This is the private key for `smbclient`. It's needed only if the client should have a certificate.

Default: `ssl client key = /usr/local/ssl/private/smbclient.pem`

ssl compatibility

Type of parameter: Global

Supported in versions: **2.0.0 and above**

This variable is part of SSL-enabled Samba. This is available only if the SSL libraries have been compiled on your system and the configure option `--with-ssl` was given at configure time.

> **Note**
>
> For export control reasons this code is not enabled by default in any current binary version of Samba.

This variable defines whether SSLeay should be configured for bug compatibility with other SSL implementations. This is probably not desirable because currently no clients with SSL implementations other than SSLeay exist.

Default: `ssl compatibility = no`

ssl hosts resign

Type of parameter: Global

Supported in versions: **2.0.0 and above**

This variable is part of SSL-enabled Samba. This is available only if the SSL libraries have been compiled on your system and the configure option `--with-ssl` was given at configure time.

> **Note**
>
> For export control reasons this code is not enabled by default in any current binary version of Samba.

This parameter defines whether Samba will go into SSL mode. If neither the `ssl hosts` nor the `ssl hosts resign` parameter is defined, Samba will allow only SSL connections. If the `ssl hosts` parameter lists hosts (by IP address, IP-address range, net group, or name), only these hosts will be forced into SSL mode. If the `ssl hosts resign` variable lists hosts, only these hosts will not be forced into SSL mode. The syntax for these two variables is the same as for the `hosts allow` and `hosts deny` pair of variables; only the subject of the decision is different. It's not the access right but whether SSL is used. See the `allow hosts` parameter for details.

Default: `ssl hosts resign = empty string`

Example: `ssl hosts resign = 192.168`

This example requires SSL connections from all hosts outside the local net (which is 192.168.*.*).

ssl hosts

Type of parameter: Global

Supported in versions: **2.0.0 and above**

This parameter defines whether Samba will go into SSL mode. If neither the ssl hosts nor the ssl hosts resign parameter is defined, Samba will allow only SSL connections. If the ssl hosts parameter lists hosts (by IP address, IP-address range, net group, or name), only these hosts will be forced into SSL mode. If the ssl hosts resign variable lists hosts, only these hosts will not be forced into SSL mode. The syntax for these two variables is the same as for the hosts allow and hosts deny pair of variables; only the subject of the decision is different. It's not the access right but whether SSL is used. See the allow hosts parameter for details.

Default: ssl hosts = *empty string*

Example: ssl hosts = 192.168

ssl require clientcert

Type of parameter: Global

Supported in versions: **2.0.0 and above**

This variable is part of SSL-enabled Samba. This is available only if the SSL libraries have been compiled on your system and the configure option --with-ssl was given at configure time.

> **Note**
>
> For export control reasons this code is not enabled by default in any current binary version of Samba.

If this variable is set to yes, the server will not tolerate connections from clients that don't have a valid certificate. The directory or file given in ssl CA certDir and ssl CA certFile will be used to look up the CAs that issued the client's certificate. If the certificate can't be verified positively, the connection will be terminated. If this variable is set to no, clients don't need certificates. Contrary to Web applications, you really should require client certificates. In the Web environment the client's data is sensitive (credit card numbers) and the server must prove to be trustworthy. In a file server environment the server's data will be sensitive and the clients must prove to be trustworthy.

Default: ssl require clientcert = no

ssl require servercert

Type of parameter: Global

Supported in versions: **2.0.0 and above**

This variable is part of SSL-enabled Samba. This is available only if the SSL libraries have been compiled on your system and the configure option `--with-ssl` was given at configure time.

> **Note**
>
> For export control reasons this code is not enabled by default in any current binary version of Samba.

If this variable is set to `yes`, the `smbclient` will request a certificate from the server. This is the same as `ssl require clientcert` for the server.

Default: `ssl require servercert = no`

ssl server cert

Type of parameter: Global

Supported in versions: **2.0.0 and above**

This variable is part of SSL-enabled Samba. This is available only if the SSL libraries have been compiled on your system and the configure option `--with-ssl` was given at configure time.

> **Note**
>
> For export control reasons this code is not enabled by default in any current binary version of Samba.

This is the file containing the server's certificate. The server must have a certificate. The file may also contain the server's private key. See the document `SSLeay.txt` in the `docs/textdocs` directory of the source for how certificates and private keys are created.

Default: `ssl server cert = empty string`

ssl server key

Type of parameter: Global

Supported in versions: **2.0.0 and above**

This variable is part of SSL-enabled Samba. This is available only if the SSL libraries have been compiled on your system and the configure option `--with-ssl` was given at configure time.

> **Note**
>
> For export control reasons this code is not enabled by default in any current binary version of Samba.

PART

V

APP

A

This file contains the private key of the server. If this variable is not defined, the key is looked up in the certificate file (it might be appended to the certificate). The server must have a private key, and the certificate must match this private key.

Default: `ssl server key = empty string`

ssl version

Type of parameter: Global

Supported in versions: **2.0.0 and above**

This variable is part of SSL-enabled Samba. This is available only if the SSL libraries have been compiled on your system and the configure option `--with-ssl` was given at configure time.

> **Note**
>
> For export control reasons this code is not enabled by default in any current binary version of Samba.

This enumeration variable defines the versions of the SSL protocol that will be used. `ssl2or3` allows dynamic negotiation of SSL v2 or v3, `ssl2` results in SSL v2, `ssl3` results in SSL v3, and `tls1` results in TLS v1. TLS (Transport Layer Security) is the (proposed) new standard for SSL.

Default: `ssl version = ssl2or3`

ssl

Type of parameter: Global

Supported in versions: **2.0.0 and above**

This variable is part of SSL-enabled Samba. This is available only if the SSL libraries have been compiled on your system and the configure option `--with-ssl` was given at configure time.

> **Note**
>
> For export control reasons this code is not enabled by default in any current binary version of Samba.

This variable enables or disables the entire SSL mode. If it is set to `no`, the SSL enabled Samba behaves exactly like the non-SSL Samba. If set to `yes`, whether an SSL connection will be required depends on the variables `ssl hosts` and `ssl hosts resign`.

Default: `ssl=no`

Example: `ssl=yes`

stat cache size

Type of parameter: Global

Supported in versions: **2.0.0 and above**

This parameter determines the number of entries in the stat cache. You should never need to change this parameter.

Default: stat cache size = 50

stat cache

Type of parameter: Global

Supported in versions: **2.0.0 and above**

This parameter determines whether smbd(8) will use a cache to speed up name mappings that are not case sensitive. You should never need to change this parameter.

Default: stat cache = yes

Example: stat cache = no

status

Type of parameter: Local

Supported in versions: **1.9.17 and above**

This enables or disables logging of connections to a status file that smbstatus can read. With this disabled, smbstatus won't be able to tell you what connections are active. You should never need to change this parameter.

Default: status = yes

Example: status = no

strict locking

Type of parameter: Local

Supported in versions: **1.9.17 and above**

This is a Boolean that controls the handling of file locking in the server. When this is set to yes, the server will check every read and write access for file locks and deny access if locks exist. This can be slow on some systems. When strict locking is no the server does file lock checks only when the client explicitly asks for them.

Well-behaved clients always ask for lock checks when it is important, so in the vast majority of cases strict locking= no is preferable.

Default: strict locking = no

Example: strict locking = yes

PART

V

APP

A

strict sync

Type of parameter: Local

Supported in versions: **1.9.18p10 and above**

Many Windows applications (including the Windows 98 Explorer shell) seem to confuse flushing buffer contents to disk with doing a sync to disk. Under UNIX, a sync call forces the process to be suspended until the kernel has ensured that all outstanding data in kernel disk buffers has been safely stored onto stable storage. This is very slow and should only be done rarely. Setting this parameter to no (the default) means that smbd(8) ignores the Windows applications requests for a sync call. A possibility of losing data if the operating system itself that Samba is running on crashes exists, so there is little danger in this default setting. In addition, this fixes many performance problems that people have reported with the new Windows 98 Explorer shell file copies.

See also the sync always parameter.

Default: strict sync = no

Example: strict sync = yes

strip dot

Type of parameter: Global

Supported in versions: **1.9.17 and above**

This is a Boolean that controls whether to strip trailing dots off UNIX filenames. This helps with some CD-ROMs that have filenames ending in a single dot.

Default: strip dot = no

Example: strip dot = yes

sync always

Type of parameter: Local

Supported in versions: **1.9.17 and above**

This is a Boolean parameter that controls whether writes will always be written to stable storage before the write call returns. If this is false, the client's request guides the server in each write call (clients can set a bit indicating that a particular write should be synchronous). If this is true, every write will be followed by a fsync(2) call to ensure the data is written to disk.

Note
The strict sync parameter must be set to yes in order for this parameter to have any effect.

See also the strict sync parameter.

Default: sync always = no

Example: sync always = yes

syslog only

Type of parameter: Global

Supported in versions: **1.9.17 and above**

If this parameter is set, Samba debug messages are logged in to the system syslog only and not to the debug log files.

Default: syslog only = no

syslog

Type of parameter: Global

Supported in versions: **1.9.17 and above**

This parameter maps how Samba debug messages are logged on to the system syslog logging levels. Samba debug level zero maps onto syslog LOG_ERR, debug level one maps onto LOG_WARNING, debug level two maps onto LOG_NOTICE, debug level three maps onto LOG_INFO. All higher levels are mapped to LOG_DEBUG.

This parameter sets the threshold for sending messages to syslog. Only messages with debug level less than this value will be sent to syslog.

Default: syslog = 1

Example: syslog = 3

time offset

Type of parameter: Global

Supported in versions: **1.9.17 and above**

This parameter provides the value in minutes to add along with the normal GMT to local time conversion. This is useful if you are serving many PCs that have incorrect daylight saving time handling.

Default: time offset = 0

Example: time offset = 60

time server

Type of parameter: Global

Supported in versions: **1.9.17 and above**

PART
V

APP
A

This parameter determines whether nmbd advertises itself as a time server to Windows clients.

Default: time server = False

Example: time server = True

timestamp logs

Type of parameter: Global

Supported in versions: **2.0.0 and above**

Samba 2.0 time stamps to all log entries by default. This can be distracting if you are attempting to debug a problem. This parameter allows the time stamping to be turned off.

Default: timestamp logs = True

Example: timestamp logs = False

unix password sync

Type of parameter: Global

Supported in versions: **1.9.18p4 and above**

This Boolean parameter controls whether Samba attempts to synchronize the UNIX password with the SMB password when the encrypted SMB password in the smbpasswd file is changed. If this is set to True, the program specified in the passwd program parameter is called as root to allow the new UNIX password to be set without access to the old UNIX password. (The SMB password change code has no access to the old password clear text, only the new password clear text.)

See also passwd program and passwd chat.

Default: unix password sync = False

Example: unix password sync = True

unix realname

Type of parameter: Global

Supported in versions: **1.9.17 and above**

When set, this Boolean parameter causes Samba to supply the real name field from the UNIX password file to the client. This is useful for setting up mail clients and WWW browsers on systems used by more than one person.

Default: unix realname = no

Example: unix realname = yes

update encrypted

Type of parameter: Global

Supported in versions: **1.9.18p5 and above**

This Boolean parameter allows users logging on with a plain text password to have their encrypted (hashed) password in the smbpasswd file to be updated automatically as they log on. This option allows a site to migrate from plain-text password authentication (users authenticate with plain text password over the wire and are checked against a UNIX account database) to encrypted password authentication (the SMB challenge and response authentication mechanism). This is done without forcing all users to re-enter their passwords using smbpasswd at the time the change is made. This convenience option enables the changeover to encrypted passwords to be made over a longer period. When all users have encrypted representations of their passwords in the smbpasswd file, this parameter should be set to off.

For this parameter to work correctly, the encrypt passwords parameter must be set to no when this parameter is set to yes.

> **Note**
>
> Even when this parameter is set, users authenticating to smbd(8) must still enter valid passwords to connect correctly and to update their hashed (smbpasswd) passwords.

Default: update encrypted = no

Example: update encrypted = yes

use rhosts

Type of parameter: Global

Supported in versions: **1.9.17 and above**

If this global parameter is true, it specifies that the UNIX users .rhosts file in their home directory will be read to find the names of hosts and users who will be allowed access without specifying a password.

> **Note**
>
> The use of use rhosts can be a major security hole because you trust the PC to supply the correct username. It is very easy to get a PC to supply a false username. I recommend that the use rhosts option be used only if you really know what you are doing.

Default: use rhosts = no

Example: use rhosts = yes

PART

V

APP

A

user

Type of parameter: Local

Supported in versions: **1.9.17 and above**

Synonym for `username`.

username level

Type of parameter: Global

Supported in versions: **1.9.18 and above**

This option helps Samba to guess at the real UNIX username, as many DOS clients send an all-uppercase username. By default Samba tries all lowercase, followed by the username with the first letter capitalized, and fails if the username is not found on the UNIX machine.

If this parameter is set to nonzero, the behavior changes. This parameter is a number that specifies the number of uppercase combinations to try while trying to determine the UNIX username. The higher the number the more combinations will be tried, but the slower the discovery of usernames will be. Use this parameter when you have strange usernames on your UNIX machine, such as `AstrangeUser`.

Default: `username level = 0`

Example: `username level = 5`

username map

Type of parameter: Global

Supported in versions: **1.9.17 and above**

This option allows you to specify a file containing a mapping of usernames from the clients to the server. This can be used for several purposes. The most common is to map usernames that users use on DOS or Windows machines to those that the UNIX box uses. Another is to map multiple users to a single username so that they can more easily share files.

The map file is parsed line by line. Each line should be in the following format:

`root = admin administrator`

The list of usernames on the right can contain names of the form `@group`, in which case they will match any UNIX username in that group. The special client name asterisk (*) is a wildcard and matches any name. Each line of the map file may be up to 1023 characters long.

The file is processed on each line by taking the supplied username and comparing it with each username on the right side of the equal signs. If the supplied name matches any of the names on the right side, it is replaced with the name on the left. Processing then continues with the next line.

Any line beginning with a # or a ; is ignored.

If any line begins with an !, the processing will stop after that line if a mapping was done by the line. Otherwise, mapping continues with every line being processed. Using ! is most useful when you have a wildcard mapping line later in the file.

For example, to map from the name admin or administrator to the UNIX name root, you would use

```
root = admin administrator
```

Or, to map anyone in the UNIX group system to the UNIX name sys, you would use

```
sys = @system
```

You can have as many mappings as you like in a username map file.

If your system supports the NIS NETGROUP option, the netgroup database is checked before the /etc/group database for matching groups.

You can map Windows usernames that have spaces in them by using double quotes around the name. For example:

```
tridge = "Andrew Tridgell"
```

would map the windows username Andrew Tridgell to the UNIX username tridge.

The following example would map mary and fred to the UNIX user sys, and map the rest to guest. Note the use of the ! to tell Samba to stop processing if it gets a match on that line.

```
!sys = mary fred
guest = *
```

Note

The remapping is applied to all occurrences of usernames. Thus, if you connect to \\server\fred and fred is remapped to mary, you will actually be connecting to \\server\mary and will need to supply a password suitable for mary, not fred. The only exception to this is the username passed to the password server (if you have one). The password server will receive whatever username the client supplies without modification.

PART
V

APP
A

Also note that no reverse mapping is done. The main effect this has is with printing. Users who have been mapped might have trouble deleting print jobs because Print Manager under WfWg will think they don't own the print job.

Default: No username map

Example: username map = /usr/local/samba/lib/users.map

username

Type of parameter: Local

Supported in versions: **1.9.17 and above**

Multiple users may be specified in a comma-delimited list, in which case the supplied password will be tested against each username in turn (left to right).

The username line is needed only when the PC is unable to supply its own username. This is the case for the COREPLUS protocol or where your users have different WfWg usernames to UNIX usernames. In both these cases you might also be better using the \\server\ share%USER syntax instead.

The username= line is not a great solution in many cases because Samba will try to validate the supplied password against each of the usernames in the username= line, in turn. This is slow and is a bad idea for many users in case of duplicate passwords. You can get timeouts or security breaches using this parameter unwisely.

Samba relies on the underlying UNIX security. This parameter does not restrict who can log on; it just offers hints to the Samba server as to what usernames might correspond to the supplied password. Users can log on as whomever they please, and they will be able to do no more damage than if they started a telnet session. The daemon runs as the user that they log on as, so they cannot do anything that the user cannot do.

To restrict a service to a particular set of users you can use the valid users parameter.

If any username begins with a @, the name will be looked up first in the yp netgroups list (if Samba is compiled with netgroup support). This is followed by a lookup in the UNIX groups database and will expand to a list of all users in the group of that name.

If any of the usernames begin with a +, the name will be looked up only in the UNIX groups database and will expand to a list of all users in the group of that name.

If any of the usernames begin with a &, the name will be looked up only in the yp netgroups database (if Samba is compiled with netgroup support) and will expand to a list of all users in the netgroup group of that name.

Note that searching through a groups database can take quite some time, and some clients might time out during the search.

Default: The guest account if a guest service; otherwise, the name of the service.

Examples: username=fred

username=fred,mary,jack,jane,@users,@pcgroup

users

Type of parameter: Local

Supported in versions: **1.9.17 and above**

Synonym for username.

utmp

Type of parameter: Local

Supported in versions: **2.0.7 and above**

This Boolean parameter is available only if Samba has been configured and compiled with the option --with-utmp. If set to True then Samba will attempt to add utmp or utmpx records (depending on the UNIX system) whenever a connection is made to a Samba server. Sites can use this to record the user connecting to a Samba share for accounting purposes.

See also the utmp directory parameter.

Default: utmp = False

Example: utmp = True

utmp consolidate

Type of parameter: Global

Supported in versions: **2.0.7 and above**

This parameter is available only if Samba has been configured and compiled with the option --with-utmp. Normally, connecting to each share creates a utmp record, but if there are many TCP connections, each with many connections to and disconnections from the same share, it can be desirable to consolidate the shares down to one-per-connection.

Default: utmp consolidate = no

Example: utmp consolidate = yes

utmp directory

Type of parameter: Global

Supported in versions: **2.0.7 and above**

This parameter is available only if Samba has been configured and compiled with the option --with-utmp. It specifies a directory pathname that is used to store the utmp or utmpx files (depending on the UNIX system) that record user connections to a Samba server.

See also the utmp parameter. By default, this parameter is not set, resulting in Samba using whatever utmp file the native operating system is set to use (usually /var/run/utmp on Linux).

Default: No utmp directory

Example: utmp directory = /var/adm/

utmp hostname

Type of parameter: Global

Supported in versions: **2.0.7 and above**

This parameter is available only if Samba has been configured and compiled with the option `--with-utmp`. It specifies the `ut_host` field of the utmp and wtmp records. The default is the NetBIOS name (`%m`) of the Samba server, but a very useful alternative might be the Internet/DNS name (`%M`).

Default: `utmp hostname = %m`

Example: `utmp hostname = %M`

valid chars

Type of parameter: Global

Supported in versions: **1.9.17 and above**

This option allows you to specify additional characters that should be considered valid by the server in filenames. This is particularly useful for national character sets, such as adding u-umlaut or a-ring.

The option takes a list of characters in either integer or character form with spaces between them. If you give two characters with a colon between them, it will be taken as a *lowercase:uppercase* pair.

If you have an editor capable of entering the characters into the config file, it is probably easiest to use this method. Otherwise, you can specify the characters in octal, decimal, or hexadecimal form using the usual C notation.

For example, to add the single character Z to the charset (which is a pointless thing to do because it's already there) you could do one of the following:

```
valid chars = Z
valid chars = z:Z
valid chars = 0132:0172
```

The two previous examples actually add two characters and alter the uppercase and lowercase mappings appropriately.

> **Note**
> You must specify this parameter after the `client code page` parameter if you have both set. If `client code page` is set after the `valid chars` parameter, the `valid chars` settings will be overwritten.

See also the `client code page` parameter.

Default: Samba defaults to using a reasonable set of valid characters for English systems.

Example: `valid chars = 0345:0305 0366:0326 0344:0304`

The preceding example allows filenames to include the Swedish characters.

It is actually quite difficult to correctly produce a `valid chars` line for a particular system. To automate the process, `tino@augsburg.net` has written a package called `validchars` that automatically produces a complete `valid chars` line for a given client system. Look in the `examples/validchars/` subdirectory of your Samba source code distribution for this package.

valid users

Type of parameter: Local

Supported in versions: **1.9.17 and above**

This is a list of users that should be allowed to log on to this service. Names starting with @, +, and & are interpreted using the same rules as described in the `invalid users` parameter.

If this is empty (the default), any user can log on. If a username is in both this list and the `invalid users` list, access is denied for that user.

The current service name is substituted for %S. This is useful in the [homes] section.

See also `invalid users`.

Default: No valid users list (anyone can log on)

Example: `valid users = greg, @pcusers`

veto files

Type of parameter: Local

Supported in versions: **1.9.17 and above**

This is a list of files and directories that are neither visible nor accessible. Each entry in the list must be separated by a slash (/), which allows spaces to be included in the entry. The asterisk (*) and question mark (?) can be used to specify multiple files or directories, as in DOS wildcards.

Each entry must be a UNIX path, not a DOS path, and must not include the UNIX directory separator /.

The `case sensitive` option is applicable in vetoing files.

Be aware of this feature of the `veto files` parameter: If a directory is deleted that contains only files matching the `veto files` parameter (which means that Windows/DOS clients cannot see them), the veto files within that directory are automatically deleted along with it, provided that the user has UNIX permissions to do so.

Setting this parameter will affect the performance of Samba because it will be forced to check all files and directories for a match as they are scanned.

See also the `hide files` and `case sensitive` parameters.

Default: No files or directories are vetoed.

Example 1: Veto any files containing the word `Security`, any ending in `.tmp`, and any directory containing the word `root`.

```
veto files = /*Security*/*.tmp/*root*/
```

Example 2: Veto the Apple-specific files that a NetAtalk server creates.

```
veto files = /.AppleDouble/.bin/.AppleDesk-top/Network Trash Folder/
```

veto oplock files

Type of parameter: Local

Supported in versions: **1.9.18 and above**

This parameter is valid only when the `oplocks` parameter is turned on for a share. It allows the Samba administrator to selectively turn off the granting of oplocks on selected files that match a wildcard list, similar to the wildcard list used in the `veto files` parameter.

Default: No files are vetoed for oplock grants.

Examples: You might want to do this on files that you know will be heavily contended for by clients. A good example of this is in the `NetBench` SMB benchmark program, which causes heavy client contention for files ending with `.SEM`. To prevent Samba from granting oplocks on these files, use the line (either in the `[global]` section or in the section for the particular NetBench share):

```
veto oplock files = /*.SEM/
```

volume

Type of parameter: Local

Supported in versions: **1.9.17 and above**

This allows you to override the volume label returned for a share. Useful for CD-ROMs with installation programs that insist on a particular volume label.

The default is the name of the share.

wide links

Type of parameter: Local

Supported in versions: **1.9.17 and above**

This parameter controls whether the server may follow links in the UNIX file system. Links that point to areas within the directory tree exported by the server are always allowed. This parameter controls access only to areas that are outside the directory tree being exported.

> **Note**
>
> Setting this parameter can have a negative effect on your server performance because of the extra system calls that Samba must do to perform the link checks.

Default: `wide links = yes`

Example: `wide links = no`

wins hook

Type of parameter: Global

Supported in versions: **2.0.6 and above**

When Samba is running as a WINS server, this allows you to call an external program for all changes to the WINS database. This option primarily allows the dynamic update of external name resolution databases such as dynamic DNS.

The `wins hook` parameter specifies the name of a script or executable that will be called as follows:

```
wins_hook operation name nametype ttl IP_list
```

The first argument is the operation and is one of `add`, `delete`, or `refresh`. In most cases the operation can be ignored because the rest of the parameters provide sufficient information. Note that `refresh` may sometimes be called when the name has not previously been added. In that case it should be treated as an add.

The second argument is the NetBIOS name. If the name is not legal, `wins hook` is not called. Legal names contain only letters, digits, hyphens, underscores, and periods.

The third argument is the NetBIOS name type as a 2-digit hexadecimal number.

The fourth argument is the TTL (time to live) for the name in seconds.

The fifth and subsequent arguments are the IP addresses currently registered for that name. If this list is empty, the name should be deleted.

A sample script that calls the BIND dynamic DNS update program `nsupdate` is provided in the `examples` directory of the Samba source code.

wins proxy

Type of parameter: Global

Supported in versions: **1.9.17 and above**

PART

V

APP

A

This is a Boolean that controls whether nmbd will respond to broadcast name queries on behalf of other hosts. You might need to set this to yes for some older clients.

Default: wins proxy = no

wins server

Type of parameter: Global

Supported in versions: **1.9.17 and above**

This specifies the IP address (or DNS name: IP address for preference) of the WINS server that nmbd should register with. If you have a WINS server on your network, you should set this to the WINS server's IP.

You should point this at your WINS server if you have a multisubnetted network.

> **Note** Set up Samba to point to a WINS server if you have multiple subnets and want cross-subnet browsing to work correctly.

See the documentation file BROWSING.txt in the docs/ directory of your Samba source distribution.

Default: There is no default value for this parameter.

Example: wins server = 192.9.200.1

wins support

Type of parameter: Global

Supported in versions: **1.9.17 and above**

This Boolean controls whether the nmbd process in Samba will act as a WINS server. Do not set this to true unless you have a multisubnetted network and you want a particular nmbd to be your WINS server.

> **Note** Never set this to true on more than one machine in your network.

Default: wins support = no

workgroup

Type of parameter: Global

Supported in versions: **1.9.17 and above**

This controls what work group your server will appear to be in when queried by clients.

Note This parameter also controls the domain name used with the `security = domain` setting.

Default: Set at compile time to WORKGROUP

Example: workgroup = MYGROUP

writable

Type of parameter: Local

Supported in versions: **1.9.17 and above**

Synonym for writeable.

write cache size(s)

Type of parameter: Local

Supported in versions: **2.0.7 and above**

This integer parameter causes Samba to create an in-memory cache for each oplocked file if set to nonzero (it does not do this for non-oplocked files). All writes that the client does not request to be flushed directly to disk will be stored in this cache if possible. The cache is flushed to disk when a write comes in whose offset would not fit into the cache or when the file is closed by the client. Reads for the file are also served from this cache if the data is stored within it.

This cache allows Samba to batch client writes into a more efficient write size for RAID disks (that is, writes can be tuned to be the RAID stripe size) and can improve performance on systems where the disk subsystem is a bottleneck but there is free memory for user space programs.

This parameter specifies the size of the cache (per oplocked file) in bytes.

Default: write cache size = 0

Example: write cache size = 262144

The previous example sets a 256kB cache size per file.

write list

Type of parameter: Local

Supported in versions: **1.9.17 and above**

This is a list of users given read-write access to a service. If the connecting user is in this list, he will be given write access, no matter what the read-only option is set to. The list can include group names using the @group syntax.

PART

V

APP

A

Note that if a user is in both the read list and the write list, they will be given write access.

See also the read list option.

Default: write list = *empty string*

Example: write list = admin, root, @staff

write ok

Type of parameter: Local

Supported in versions: **1.9.17 and above**

Synonym for writeable.

write raw

Type of parameter: Global

Supported in versions: **1.9.17 and above**

This parameter controls whether the server supports raw writes SMBs when transferring data from clients. You should never need to change this parameter.

Default: write raw = yes

writeable

Type of parameter: Local

Supported in versions: **1.9.17 and above**

An inverted synonym is read only.

If this parameter is no, users of a service may not create or modify files in the service's directory.

> **Note**
>
> A printable service (printable = yes) will always allow writing to the directory (user privileges permitting), but only using spooling operations.

Default: writeable = no

Examples: readonly=no

```
writeable=yes
writeok=yes
```

GLOSSARY

access control lists (ACLs) A form of fine-grained control on who can access files and other objects managed by an operating system. They allow you to specify what access rights individual users do and don't have. Traditional systems require that you place users in groups, and then control access at the group level.

Windows NT supports ACLs, and many versions of UNIX have ACLs. However, Linux has only experimental ACL support at the moment. Samba does not currently support ACLs because different versions of UNIX have different ways of supporting ACLs. ACL support is under consideration for a future version of Samba.

authentication The process of verifying that someone is who he claims to be. This is usually achieved by accepting a username from him along with some sort of password or secret that only he should know. Under the SMB protocol, plain-text passwords can be used as a user's secret, but it can also use hashed passwords of some sort.

backup browser Maintains the browse list for a workgroup or domain by copying it from the master browser. Browse clients actually obtain the browse list from backup browsers rather than overloading the master browser.

backup domain controller (BDC) An SMB server in a domain that can authenticate users. A BDC does this by virtue of having a copy of the SAM databases that the PDC uses to authenticate users. *See primary domain controller.* A BDC is usually an NT server, but the Samba TNG code can also function as a BDC. A BDC keeps its copy of the SAM up-to-date by periodically retrieving the differences between its copy of the SAM and the current copy on the PDC.

broadcast address An address that causes all systems in a network to notice packets that contain such addresses in their destination field. For Ethernet, the broadcast address is an address of all ones (1); for example, FF:FF:FF:FF:FF:FF.

For TCP/IP, there are several different forms of broadcast address. The all ones address, for example, 255.255.255.255, is the limited broadcast address, and routers should not route packets carrying that address in the destination IP address field to other networks. Network and subnetwork broadcast addresses are also possible. For example, in the network 10.0.1.0/24, the subnetwork broadcast address would be 10.0.1.255 (that is, all ones in the host portion).

browse list The list of servers that a master browser builds up. The master browser builds up the browse list by listening to host announcements and workgroup announcements sent by servers in the network. When a client browses the network, it sends a `NetServerEnum` request to a backup browse server to obtain the browse list. This is performed over an anonymous connection to the `IPC$` share.

browse server A system in a network that maintains browse lists. A browse server can be either a master browser, in which case it collects the browse lists, or a backup browser, in which case it obtains the browse list from the master browser.

client A client system is any computer that accesses a server. Machines that you would normally think of as servers; for example, member servers in a domain, will act as clients at times (for example, when a user logs on to the server and must send an authentication request to a domain controller.

Common Internet File System (CIFS) The latest dialect of the SMB protocol.

domain A group of servers and clients that share a common security database. All users are authenticated against the central security database. A domain should be contrasted with a workgroup. Under Samba, there is very little difference between a domain and a workgroup. The `workgroup` parameter is used to set the domain and workgroup names.

domain controller A system in a domain that performs authentication for all other members of the domain. There must be a primary domain controller, and there can be several backup domain controllers. Samba can function as a domain controller. The Samba 2.0.x stream can function only as a PDC but not as a BDC. Samba TNG can function as both a PDC and a BDC.

domain master browser (DMB) Responsible for collating browse lists across multiple subnets. You need a DMB only if you have a domain that spans subnets. The DMB talks to the LMB in each subnet to collate browse lists across the whole network.

The DMB and LMB are usually the same machine, and if your PDC is a Windows NT server, this is necessarily the case. However, Samba allows the DMB and LMB functions to function on separate systems, with some slowdown in speed with which browse lists are updated.

domain name service (DNS) The worldwide collection of servers that manage translation of domain names to IP addresses and vice versa. Domain names are hierarchical names (for example, `www.samba.org`) that must be translated to IP addresses before computers can establish TCP/IP connections.

elections When a master browser goes down or a potential master browser comes up, an election can be initiated to determine which potential browser should become the local master browser (LMB). An election is carried out by broadcasting election requests and comparing the values sent out by other potential browsers with a server's own values.

file locking When more than one user (client) wants to read and write the same file, the file, or at least parts of the file, need to be locked to coordinate shared access. Samba provides the same file locking functions that Windows NT does, and thus allows multiple users to access the same file in coordinated ways.

GNU General Public License (GPL) Allows open-source software developers to share their work with people. It enables you to use the software and even modify the software but prevents you from selling your modifications in a proprietary fashion. Any modifications you make that you sell must be made available for all to use without charge. The full text of the GPL Version 2 of June 1991 is distributed with Samba as the file COPYING in the top level of the Samba source tree.

guest user A user who has not been authenticated by Samba. You can configure Samba to allow such users access to some shares and files on the Samba server as the guest user. The files the guest user can access are defined by a combination of the groups the guest user is a member of and of share-level parameters. The shares the guest user can access are defined by share-level parameters (such as `guest ok` or its synonym, `public`).

homes Users on a network usually require a home share so they can save files on the server. Often, for a Samba server, this will be the same as their home directory when they log in to the Samba server from UNIX or Linux.

Samba can arrange to have each user in the `/etc/passwd` file made available as a separate share without you having to create all those shares in the `smb.conf` file. You do this by having a `[homes]` share.

host announcement Each host on the network is required to send a host announcement periodically so that master browsers can build a browse list for the workgroup. When a host first comes up, it broadcasts these host announcements frequently, but after it has been operational for some time, it reduces its broadcast rate to once every 12 minutes. *See workgroup announcement.*

local master announcement A broadcast sent out by the local master browser to tell other browsers, especially the backup browsers, who the local master browser is.

local master browser (LMB) The master browser for the local subnet. The LMB is elected during browser elections. The LMB maintains the browse list for the local subnet and talks to the DMB to synchronize browse lists with other subnets through the DMB.

logon script A DOS batch script that is executed by Windows 9x and Windows NT clients when they log on to the network. A logon script enables administrators to set up all clients with a standard configuration.

logon server An SMB server that can authenticate users and implement the particular API calls that Windows 9x clients use to gain access to the network. This is not the same protocol used by Windows NT to join a domain or log on to a domain. To support NT logons, an SMB server must function as a domain controller, whereas to support Win9x logons, an SMB server does not need to support domain controller functions. Samba has been able to support Win9x logons for several versions.

master announcement An announcement sent by a local master browser to the domain master browser to inform the DMB of the presence of the LMB. As a result, the DMB will schedule a request to the LMB for its browse list so the DMB can synchronize browse lists between subnets.

master browser A potential browser that has won an election and become the master browser for its subnet. A master browser is responsible for collating the browse list for its subnet, and if it is part of a domain, it becomes the local master browser (LMB), where it is responsible for collating browse lists with the DMB.

MSRPC Microsoft's Remote Procedure Call implementation. MSRPC is based on DCE/RPC and is carried in SMB messages. It is used extensively for the Microsoft Windows Networking domain controller functionality.

NetBEUI The NetBIOS Extended User Interface specification. This is essentially NetBIOS over IEEE 802.3, and is sometimes referred to as NetBIOS Frame Format (NBF).

NetBIOS The Network Basic I/O System was designed by Sytek for IBM in the early 1980s. It provided for shipping file operations over the network to another server.

NetBIOS names and aliases Each Samba and Windows client and server have a NetBIOS name. NetBIOS names are 15 characters long, usually converted to uppercase for transmission over the wire. A sixteenth character is added to a NetBIOS name to indicate what type of name is being used. Samba allows you to give a server both a NetBIOS name and any number of NetBIOS aliases. This allows a Samba server to take on functions of other machines without changing client configuration.

NetBIOS-less SMB Windows 2000 and Windows NT SP6 have introduced a new version of SMB. Instead of implementing it over NetBIOS, SMBs are now carried directly over TCP connections. An unfortunate consequence of this is that virtual servers are no longer possible with NetBIOS-less SMB.

NetLogon request These are sent by Windows 9x and Windows NT clients when they want to log on to the network. They are broadcast as well as being unicast to a domain controller or logon server if WINS is configured in the network.

netmask A 32-bit mask that specifies which part of an IP address is the network/subnet number portion and which part is the host number portion. For example, a netmask of 255.255.255.0 indicates the first 24 bits of a local IP address are the network address, and the last 8 bits are the host number.

Open Source Software (OSS) Software that is developed using an open process. The source code of all such software is fully available for all to work on and use. Samba is an example of Open Source Software, as is Linux.

opportunistic locks (oplocks) Opportunistic locks, or oplocks, are not really locks at all. Instead, they are a mechanism and protocol for allowing clients to cache files that only they are operating on, or that are only being read by a group of users. Once a file is opened for writing by one client, and there are one or more readers of the file, it can no longer be cached. Evidence shows that oplocks provide performance improvements of 30 percent or more, depending on the type of access to the file.

passthrough authentication A technique where an SMB server can ask another server to authenticate incoming SMB requests. The SMB server receiving the authentication request from a client passes it on to an SMB server that has all the necessary authentication information. This can be an NT domain controller or a Samba server in PDC mode.

permissions Permissions specify who can access files under Linux and UNIX. All files have three sets of permission bits. They are Read, Write, and eXecute (RWX) bits for the User (or owner), the Group owner of the file, and all others. When a user requests access to a file, these permission bits are checked against the access the user has asked for, and access granted or denied depending on the access asked for and the permissions allowed.

policies A set of rules that specify what a client can do. They control what the logged-on user can do by affecting registry settings until that user logs out. A client gets the policy file from the `netlogon` share. A Windows 9x system looks for a file called `CONFIG.POL` and an NT client looks for a file called `NTCONFIG.POL`.

potential browser A system that can become a master browser depending on what other systems are in the network. All Windows NT Servers are potential browsers, as are Samba servers (as long as they are configured correctly). Windows NT Workstation systems and Windows 9x systems must be configured to become potential browsers.

primary domain controller (PDC) A domain controller that maintains the master copy of the Security Account Manager database in a domain. All other domain controllers, which must be BDCs, synchronize their SAMs with the PDC.

While BDCs can authenticate users using their copy of the SAM, they cannot update the SAM, so they cannot handle password changes. All these must be handled by the PDC, as must any adds, deletes, or changes to the SAM using User Manager for Domains. There can be only one PDC in a domain.

> **Note**
>
> It is possible to cripple a domain by bringing up a Samba server with incorrect settings such that the PDC stops functioning.

redirector A file system driver in Windows clients and servers that packages file operations into the corresponding SMB packets and sends them over the network to the appropriate server.

Remote Administration Protocol (RAP) A Microsoft-developed protocol for remotely administering some aspects of LanMan and NT servers. This protocol is sufficiently documented, so Samba servers can participate in browsing, among other things.

roaming profiles Roaming profiles allow a Win9x and NT user to log in to any client on the network and have her desktop preferences and other preferences follow her. Windows does this by merging files from the profiles area on the Server into the Registry on the client. Samba contains support for roaming profiles both for Win9x and Windows NT clients. There are differences between how these are implemented by Windows 9x clients and Windows NT clients.

Sam Bass beer The official beer of the Samba team.

Samba A freely available (under the GPL) SMB server for Linux, UNIX, OpenVMS, MVS, and several other operating systems.

server A computer that offers services to other computers, which are often regarded as clients.

Server Message Block (SMB) The Server Message Block (SMB) protocol was developed by IBM in 1984 to allow PCs to access servers. It has developed and grown since and is the basis of Microsoft Windows Networking.

share A directory in the file system, or a printer, that is packaged and made available under a single name for clients to access. A share can be a home share for a user, a printer share, or a public share.

Universal Naming Convention (UNC) A method of specifying a resource on the network. A UNC includes the server name, share, directory path, and filename. For example, `\\server\share\directory\path\file.txt`.

virtual servers A server running on Samba along with other servers running on the same machine. Samba implements virtual servers by taking note of the called NetBIOS name in a NetBIOS session request and making it available in the `%L` macro. A server can `include` different configuration files based on the `%L` macro. It is also possible to run multiple instances of Samba on one system by using separate `smb.conf` files and binding to different interfaces. These are not virtual servers; they would be regarded as separate instances of Samba.

Windows Internet Name Server (WINS) A name to IP address translation service for NetBIOS names. It is similar in concept to DNS but offers an essentially flat namespace. Because of the limitations of WINS, Microsoft is moving to DNS with Windows 2000.

workgroup announcement Similar to a host announcement. However, workgroup announcements are sent out by local master browsers and are destined for domain master browsers.

PART

V

APP

B

INDEX

J

K

T

X-Z

Special Edition
Using

The One Source for Comprehensive Solutions™

The one-stop shop for serious users, *Special Edition Using* offers readers a thorough understanding of software and technologies. Intermediate to advanced users get detailed coverage that is clearly presented and to the point.

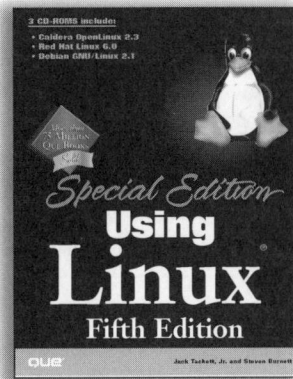

Linux, Fifth Edition
Jack Tackett, Jr., and Steven Burnett
ISBN: 0-7897-2180-5
$49.99 US/$74.95 CAN

Other *Special Edition Using* Titles

KDE
Nicholas Wells
ISBN: 0-7897-2214-3
$39.99 US/$59.95 CAN

UNIX, Third Edition
Peter Kuo
ISBN: 0-7897-1747-6
$39.99 US/$59.95 CAN

TCP/IP
John Ray
ISBN: 0-7897-1897-9
$29.99 US/$44.95 CAN

NetWare 5.0
Peter Kuo, John Pence, and Sally Specker
ISBN: 0-7897-2056-6
$39.99 US/$59.95 CAN

Microsoft SQL Server 7.0
Stephen Wynkoop
ISBN: 0-7897-1523-6
$39.99 US/$59.95 CAN

Lotus Notes and Domino R5
Randy Tamura
ISBN: 0-7897-1814-6
$49.99 US/$74.95 CAN

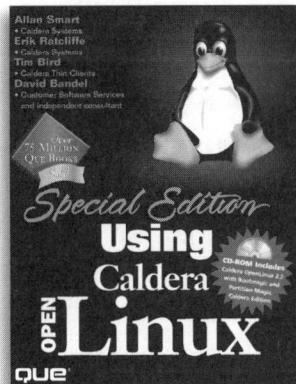

Caldera OpenLinux
Allan Smart, et al.
ISBN: 0-7897-2058-2
$39.99 US/$59.95 CAN

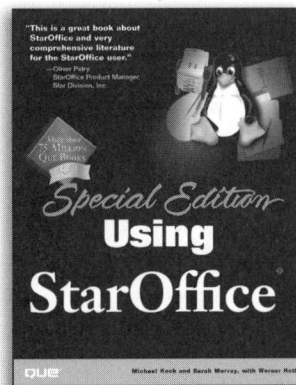

StarOffice
Michael Koch, et al.
ISBN: 0-7897-1993-2
$39.99 US/$59.95 CAN

QUE®

www.quepublishing.com

All prices are subject to change.

Other Related Titles

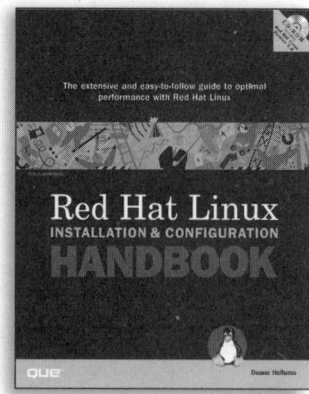

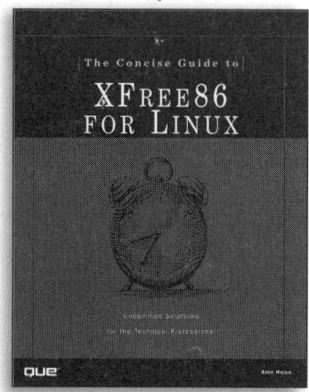